CHILD IN JERUSALEM

The author with her mother, 1913

CHILD IN Jerusalem

FELICITY ASHBEE

With a Foreword by H. V. F. Winstone

Syracuse University Press

For a listing of books published and distributed by Syracuse University
Press, visit our Web site at SyracuseUniversityPress.syr.edu

ISBN-13: 978-0-8156-0872-1
ISBN-10: 0-8156-0872-1

Library of Congress Cataloging-in-Publication Data

Ashbee, Felicity.
    Child in Jerusalem / Felicity Ashbee ; with a foreword by H.V.F.
Winstone.
        p. cm.
    ISBN 978-0-8156-0872-1 (hardcover : alk. paper) 1. Jerusalem—
Social life and customs—20th century. 2. Jerusalem—Description and
travel. 3. Ashbee, Felicity—Childhood and youth. 4. British—
Jerusalem—Biography. 5. Children—Jerusalem—Biography.
6. Children—Great Britain—Biography. I. Title.
DS109.93.A83 2008
956.94'4204092—dc22
[B]
2007040957

Manufactured in the United States of America

To
Cleota Reed, David Tatham,
and Alan Crawford without whom this book
would not have seen the light of day

FELICITY ASHBEE was born in Gloucestershire in 1913 and was educated at various schools in Jerusalem and England. From 1932 to 1936, she studied at the Byam Shaw School of Art in London, and she later exhibited at the Royal Academy. During World War II, she served in the Women's Auxiliary Air Force, where she was responsible for some memorable amateur theatricals. After the war, she worked briefly with her sister Helen in Manchester, designing textiles, and then settled in London. She was for many years a much loved teacher of art at various girls' schools. Her first book with Syracuse University Press was *Janet Ashbee: Love, Marriage, and the Arts and Crafts Movement*.

Contents

Illustrations

Foreword

FELICITY ASHBEE takes us back in these pages to the Jerusalem she witnessed through a child's eyes almost a century ago, and in doing so she brings a rare sense of timelessness to a tormented place. Jerusalem is both a city and an idea. It is Blake's synonym for an idealized England, Milton's vision of an Anglican paradise, the habitation of three disparate religions that came to dwell there in worship of the same God; a rambling city where the past once glorified and now oppresses the human spirit.

With the effortless innocence of childhood, Felicity, if I may be familiar in introducing the work of this redoubtable old lady, conveys a sense of fun—of concealing the wounds of political animosity and religious bigotry—in her delightfully naïve rendering of infant wonderment.

She tells her child's tale in the third person, so that the narrative has the poignancy of a *Little Women* story, disentangled as it were from the self who is its central character. In bridging the best part of a century, she takes us back to the immediate aftermath of the First World War, to the end of the Sanjuq of Al Quds after more than four centuries of Ottoman rule, to the beginning of a peace process founded on Woodrow Wilson's idealistic belief that if the lessons of the "war to end all wars" meant anything at all it was that every nation had an inalienable right of self-determination. Such matters were, of course, far from the child's thoughts at the time. She was six years old when she boarded ship with her sisters, their mother Janet, and their cousin Kathleen, "with her pale face and sad eyes, and her dark hair in its velvet band," and bringing up the rear "Nannie in her neat, velvet-trimmed

The author's father, C. R. Ashbee, in Jerusalem, 1919; reproduced by permission of King's College, Cambridge.

bonnet, carrying the baby Prudy, who was only eighteen months old and no use at all." The sharpness and detail of the infant memory are remarkable.

They arrived at Alexandria on a Dutch troopship before traveling on by train to savor the sights and sounds of British-mandated Palestine and its British-governed focal point, Jerusalem. Her distinguished father Charles Robert Ashbee—architect, designer, political activist (of the socialist-evolutionary rather than the revolutionary kind), disciple of William Morris, a founding spirit of the arts and crafts movement—had recently written a book called *Where the Great City Stands,* bringing to his architectural armory Walt Whitman's line from the poet's "Song of the Broad Axe"—

> Where the city of the healthiest fathers stands
> Where the city of the best-bodied mothers stands,
> There the great city stands.

Jerusalem, it seemed, was waiting for him. "CRA" had spent the early period of the war lecturing in America. As the conflict drew to its climactic end in 1917, he was appointed to a teaching job at the Sultania training college in Cairo. His wife Janet and their four daughters stayed behind at their English home in Chipping Campden, among the soft sandstone Cotswold villages whither he had moved fifteen years before from the East End of London, along with the Guild of Handicraft that he had founded in 1888 and with which his name will ever be associated.

Charles Ashbee himself, contrary to his passionate belief in progressive education, particularly in the application of hand skills to design processes and architecture, was seemingly indifferent to the education of his daughters. When girl followed girl and the chance of a boy vanished from his life, it was Felicity who found herself in the role of substitute son but without the advantage of the university education that almost certainly would have belonged to a male heir. Yet they were not, from Felicity's account of the critical years that led to puberty and adulthood, unhappy children. On the contrary, though formal education was largely denied them, they were inevitably surrounded by stimulating conversation. Their mother was an articulate and well-educated middle-class lady who was perfectly capable of putting her point of view in splendid letters and often heated exchanges with her husband and his friends. Words—controversial, creative, often didactic but seldom if ever censorious—were at the heart of their existence. The aesthetic movements that led during their father's lifetime from pre-Raphaelitism to art nouveau, cubism, and all the other *isms* of the age, were to them part of the language of everyday life. So, of course, was the example set by Morris in verse and an irrepressible array of visual disciplines and by Ruskin in the glorification of medieval craft; so too the battering rams of the Bauhaus and architectural Brutalism, and the advent of fascism and Soviet communism. For Felicity, an upbringing in rural England in the years immediately before the Great War was profoundly influential. She never married, and she remains a staunch atheist and radical socialist. In the early 1930s, she trained in painting and design at the Byam Shaw School of Art in London and became an inspirational teacher. Some of the posters she designed at the time of the Spanish Civil War are now in the Imperial War Museum in London. In World War II, she served in the Women's Auxiliary Air Force.

She remained through it all a person of enchanting manner, capable of much jollity and simple pleasure with her nephews and nieces, one of whom describes her as "a vivid, exciting person," as well as standing by deeply held convictions in circumstances that were often difficult and uncongenial. But this is not a biography. The life story of C. R. Ashbee has been told, along with that of his family, in magisterial fashion elsewhere,[1] and I must return to my own last.

The family was brought together by a chance event at the war's end. Sir Herbert Samuel was appointed high commissioner in Palestine in what came to be known to Arab and Jewish skeptics as the "Regime of Sweet Reason," a interregnum of calm when Zionists at the Paris peace negotiations set out their stall and the British military staff in Cairo, who had instigated the wartime Arab Revolt and in payment promised most of the Arab territories including Palestine to the sons of the Sharif of Mecca, tore itself apart on the jagged rocks of Zion and loyalty to the Arab cause. At the same time, Sir Ronald Storrs, aesthete and wit, erudite Oriental Secretary to the British high commissioner in Egypt, was appointed governor of Jerusalem, in "direct succession to Pontius Pilate." He had attended a lecture given by Ashbee at Charterhouse School and the two men developed a close rapport in Egypt, so as soon as his new job was confirmed, the governor asked his friend to take on the crucial appointment of civil administrator to the new military administration of the holy city. Jerusalem was badly in need of repair after centuries of Ottoman occupation in which there was neither the money nor the will to restore it. The perfect candidate was waiting in the wings.

Thus it was that in 1919, Janet Ashbee and her four daughters arrived at their new home in Jerusalem and Felicity began to make a mental note of her first impressions; "and when Felicity touched the peeling, rusty paint of the big iron gates, she had to draw back her hand quickly because it burned . . . They went on into the stone-floored hall of the house, cool and dark after the blinding sunlight, and their father, showing dimly in his white cotton coat, turned and said, 'Well, here we are.'" The reader has to remind him- or

---

1. Alan Crawford, *C. R. Ashbee: Architect, Designer and Romantic Socialist* (New Haven: Yale Univ. Press, 1985).

herself that the words consist of reported speech written almost a century after the event. Somehow, her recollections awaken a sense of the city before her father cleaned it up; before the mandates and the political settlements created new ghettoes, divided it into expedient spheres of religious and political influence, and changed it forever.

In February 1919, Ashbee had written an article in *The Times* in which he contrasted the Jerusalem of the imagination with the real city left us by the Turks, "a picturesque but filthy medieval town."[2] He was soon at work surveying the place assisted by two other architects and several draftsmen, turning

A section of the rampart walk,
Jerusalem, before restoration, 1919

Design by C. R. Ashbee for restoring and
replanting the rampart walk

2. Jill Hamilton, *God, Guns, and Israel* (Phoenix Mill, Gloucs.: Sutton, 2004).

*The Citadel, under
restoration in ca. 1921*

disused and abandoned sites into municipal gardens, libraries, and reading
rooms, oases of rest for pilgrims and residents, catering for all the languages
that brought priests and soothsayers of every denomination to the city's
gates. And not to be neglected in an Ashbee enterprise, there was the re-
newal of old knitting factories and hand-operated looms to be provided for,
the revival of defunct potteries and kilns where everyday pots and the mag-
nificently glazed and decorated tiles of the Al Aqsa mosque had once been
made.[3] His office was within the military governorate, and the military personnel knew him as "Civics." His elder daughters went briefly to the American School where they enjoyed the rare routine of an ordered educational
program. While their father took to the task with enthusiasm, it was his wife

3. Crawford, *C. R. Ashbee*, 181.

Janet who kept up the social presence expected of senior officials in occupied territories. She described with zest and a wonderful sense of the ridiculous the parties and conversations of the great and good who turned up in the city. Years later, Felicity would write her mother's story.[4]

The plan for the new Jerusalem was completed by the end of 1922, and Ashbee went off on another American lecture tour early in 1923. By then, the Jewish influx had begun, first as a trickle and eventually as a flood that would make Ashbee's Jerusalem largely irrelevant. That is another story, but it hovers in the subconscious and gives force and relevance to Felicity Ashbee's simple child's tale.

Finally, I must declare a personal interest. I knew the home of her childhood in the Cotswolds long before I knew the name Felicity Ashbee. I first visited it as a writer interested in the decorative arts in the 1950s. But I knew little of Ashbee or his family, other than what was revealed by their home and reputation as the domain of the Guild of Handicraft, until I began to research and write about the Middle East in the 1970s. Only then did I come upon Foreign Office files in the Public Record Office that related to the Jerusalem appointment. Only then did I begin to revive an interest in a place and a dynasty redolent of the English arts and crafts movement. It is a privilege to be associated with a name of the utmost importance to Britain's artistic heritage, through this introduction to Felicity Ashbee's story of Jerusalem in the 1920s.

H. V. F. Winstone, April 2007

4. Felicity Ashbee, *Janet Ashbee: Love, Marriage and the Arts and Crafts Movement* (Syracuse, N.Y.: Syracuse Univ. Press, 2002).

Preface

I HAVE REVISITED Jerusalem twice since that all-too-brief period when my family and I lived there between 1919 and 1923. My mother and I toured in Palestine in 1935, visiting many familiar sites and sights already etched into my memory. I visited again in 1980, at the invitation of the then mayor of Jerusalem, Teddy Kollek, in connection with the work that my father had undertaken and achieved just after the First World War in restoring many of the monuments of the Old City, not least the ramparts and the Dome of the Rock. It was this visit, rather than that in 1935 when I was a radical young woman in her early twenties, that stimulated me to write this memoir. Many recollections, by then overlaid deep in my memory by subsequent experiences, resurfaced through renewed contact with Jerusalem and its melting pot of races and religions. I realized that a child's-eye view of an English family's life in the Jerusalem of Mandate Palestine might throw light on some of the issues that arise in that great city in these more troubled times. But more, perhaps, I felt the need to record for myself and for my immediate family a period of my life during which I was immensely happy.

When writing this memoir some twenty-five years ago, I little thought that it would reach publication. At the time that I sent it round to a number of publishers, there seemed to be no appetite for this genre of book, nor perhaps sufficient interest in the historical context within which our life in Jerusalem was led. That it has been accepted for publication is of course a matter of great pleasure and satisfaction. But I am well aware that this could never have happened were it not for the enthusiasm with which my generous friends Cleota Reed and David Tatham have promoted the book as worthy of publication by Syracuse University Press. Equally important has been the warm welcome that it has received from the press's executive editor, Mary Selden Evans, who has been generous with her time and help.

The book was originally written on a portable typewriter with a rather worn ribbon. Legibility of the typescript was also affected by corrections and occasional handwritten additions. Increasingly sophisticated though they are, even today's scanners could not translate this patchy document into coherent text on disk. Cleota Reed undertook the task of retyping the entire manuscript onto disk, and for this tribute to our friendship I am deeply grateful. I also acknowledge the work done by my nephew Francis Ames-Lewis in editing Cleota's first draft and thus reducing the labor incurred by the press's copy editors. Francis has also made himself responsible for collecting the photographs. Many of these are reproduced from my father's Jerusalem records, which are extensively illustrated with photographs of monuments and sites in the Old City in around 1920. We are grateful to Gordon Bishop Associates for their help in undertaking the copy-photography: Gordon and his wife Nina welcomed the project with engaging excitement. Considerable help with gaining access to illustrations was provided also by Alan Crawford, by Patricia McGuire, the archivist at King's College, Cambridge, and by Mary Greensted of the Cheltenham Art Gallery and Museum. Finally, my thanks go to Caroline Marten for her devoted help and encouragement, and to her husband Michael for taking the photographs of the money boxes belonging to my sister Mary and me.

CHILD IN JERUSALEM

1

IT WAS RATHER FRIGHTENING and at the same time there was a thrill of excitement in looking down into the water through the little square holes of the steps. Felicity clutched the rail with a small nervous hand and set her feet firmly one after another over the transparencies.

She had never seen steps like these before, slung with ropes from the dark, towering side of the ship, and she didn't dare look up or down too much, because it would be so awful if it made her topple over and fall into the green harbor water below.

Mary, in sou'wester and burberry, was climbing steadily in front of her; her woollen-stockinged legs showed no hesitation, but then she was eight (which was two years older than Felicity) and very sensible.

Leading the way was their mother, her grey squirrel tippet round her neck, while close behind Felicity came Cousin Kathleen, with her pale face and sad eyes, and her dark hair in its velvet band. She held Helen tightly by the hand because Helen was only three, which was not a very useful age. Last of all came Nannie in her neat, velvet-trimmed bonnet, carrying the baby Prudy, who was only eighteen months old and no use at all. The harbor water got farther away, more impersonal and less frightening, and Felicity dared to look up properly and saw the deck of the ship. Three little girls were standing on the lowest rung of the railings with their arms hanging over the smooth wooden rail at the top. How delightful they looked, all three in scarlet jerseys, with halo-like straw hats on the backs of their heads. They looked unsmilingly down at the new arrivals, and Felicity looked back at them seriously, and wished she had a red jersey like theirs, and thought perhaps she could get to know them and play with them. Then she reached the top step and climbed onto the deck.

The first thing to do was to explore, and with so much that was strange and new to look at, there was hardly any time to realize that the ship didn't

The author with her mother and sisters, 1919

quite come up to the expectations suggested by her name. The *Princess Ju-liana* was a Dutch liner carrying troops to the Middle East, and when you came to look at her, there was nothing very princess-like about her.

If, however, you could stand on the bars of the deck rail without being noticed and told to get off because it was dangerous, you could look miles down to the strange shifting depths of the water. Or you could sit on the deck and stick your feet through the railings and collect used matches out of the little gutter that ran along the edge, and throw them down into the sea. Felicity found, though, that her eye could never follow them to the point where they reached the water, because the curve of the ship's side seemed to suck them in so that they vanished.

"Let's collect a store of matches," Mary said.

So they gathered a little heap of blackened trophies and settled down to the game in earnest. It was Cousin Kathleen's voice that finally disturbed them.

"Oh, that's where you are, children," she said rather crossly. "I've been hunting for you everywhere. Didn't you hear me calling? We have to go down to the lower deck now. Come along."

And she took them down the narrow steps bound with bright brass rims, and they smelled for the first time the special ship's odor of engine oil and varnished woodwork.

Down below, something seemed to have gone wrong. Their mother looked angry, and her face, under her wide-brimmed felt hat, was flushed and pink. In the subdued light of the corridor, the turquoise-studded silver brooch that pinned the band of grey squirrel round the hat's crown glowed dimly. She told the children that their cabin ("The place where we were going to sleep") had been taken by the officer in charge of the soldiers on board, and that he had stood astride in the entrance and refused to move out for them. "There's nothing for it but to sleep in the saloon, at any rate for tonight," she said, "or until something else is arranged."

The saloon! The word conjured up endless possibilities, and when the children were taken down to it, and saw its mysterious, dark tables, and the long curves of its crimson plush seats, they knew a thrill of expectation. Bedtime came, and when they realized they were to sleep on these crimson seats instead of in ordinary beds, they felt very experienced.

Felicity woke in the middle of the night to find the lights still on and dim wreaths of cigarette smoke resting motionless on the air. Among the dark tables, on which were many half-full and empty glasses, groups of men were standing about, still all dressed up, talking and smoking cigars. This was another world, a world of high adventure! She stroked the red plush lovingly and, with a sigh of contentment, snuggled back to sleep.

So, on that April afternoon of 1919, the great journey had begun—the journey that was to take the four children, with their mother and Nannie and cousin Kathleen, from the quiet of their grey stone Cotswold home to join their father in Jerusalem.

Felicity found him a little difficult to remember after all this time because he had been away such a lot. She knew he had often been on the sea during that strange something called "the War" that the grown-ups talked such a lot about because she had used those beautiful and sombre words about him in her prayers: "for those in peril on the sea." How dark and wide the sea seemed when she thought about it like that! Not like the bright waves at the place they had been to last summer: waves that broke over wet grey rocks with their hidden, strawberry-like sea anemones and the beautiful seaweed that was so bright and green when wet, and that shriveled into such dried-up, smelly brown lumps when she took it up from the beach in her bucket. Nor like the still harbor water of Liverpool as it had been yesterday, but blue-black and full of stormy waves with white spray whisking off them; and somewhere in the middle of it, in some ship she couldn't very well imagine, their father had been "in peril."

Of course he had been home in between, and Felicity remembered his lifting her up to peer over the muslin and pink-frilled edge of the cot to get her first glimpse of Helen soon after she was born. She could remember too the walks with him down through the rock garden to the little stream at the bottom, where the frog spawn gathered like great lumps of the hated tapioca, and the long, fascinating fairy stories he told that never came to an end. It was just a little difficult to remember exactly what he looked like. But now that they were going to Jerusalem-the-golden-with-milk-and-honey-blessed, she supposed it would soon come back to her.

The question of the cabin was settled the next morning. A friendly clergyman gave up his state cabin to Nannie and the two Little Ones, and another with four berths was found for the rest of the family. The state cabin was really much less exciting than it might have been, because it had an ordinary bed instead of the secret little bunks that the two bigger children slept in; but the joke was that Helen had to have a makeshift bed on the wide sill of the porthole, while the baby Prudy was squeezed into the wicker hamper (emptied for the purpose of all the baby things), which, being lined with spotted white muslin and blue bows, was padded and cushiony.

One bright morning there was a great commotion. Bells rang all over the ship, and everyone started shouting.

"Mines!" The voices echoed down the corridors. "Mines! They've got the otters down!"

The children were rushed into their cabin, asking excitedly, "What is it, Cousin Kathleen? What are otters? What are we going to do?"

"Cork-jacket drill," was the brief, unhelpful reply. And out of the shiny, red-brown cabin cupboards, with the little brass handles that clicked as you opened them, came the mysterious cork-jackets themselves.

They seemed to be made of a series of canvas pockets all fastened together, into which were stuffed great chunks of cork, and there were lots of tapes that crossed and tied all round you. They weren't at all comfortable when they were on, because whatever you did, they got in the way.

"But what are they for?" Felicity asked as, trussed up in hers and feeling rather foolish, she was pushed up the companion ladder again with her sister onto the deck.

"To keep you afloat in the water," Cousin Kathleen answered, which was not very reasonable, for the likelihood of their being in the water at all was very remote. After all, this could not be "peril-on-the-sea" because the sun was shining and there were no dark waves; and, anyway, the war had been over since before Christmas.

Up on the deck the people were standing about in crowds, all in their cork-jackets too, and looking most peculiar. The children's mother was wearing one, and even Nannie, who was carrying Prudy in her arms, had hers on over her uniform though her stiff white cap was still on her head; and Mary looked at Felicity, and they laughed at each other secretly.

But after all the fuss, nothing happened. When everyone had stood around for what seemed, to the children, an age, they were hot and fidgety, and Prudy had started whimpering. They all went down to their cabins again and the cumbrous jackets were taken off and stowed away in their lockers.

❧ The three attractive little girls in red jerseys turned out to be rather a disappointment. Whenever the children asked where they were, and couldn't they play with them, they were told they were being sick! It seemed rather a silly thing to be when the sun shone and there were so many fascinating wooden bars and iron knobs and shapes to jump over and play games among.

But there came a day when the *Princess Juliana* began to behave in a most unreckonable manner. When Felicity ran from one end of the deck to the other, the scrubbed, splintery boards rose up to meet her, and her knees bent when she didn't mean them to and she wasn't quite sure if her inside was where it usually was, well below the elastic of her green jersey knickers.

Finally, Cousin Kathleen, who looked even paler than usual with her dark eyes darker and more sad, said she thought it would be a good thing if the children came and lay down beside her on the deck and rolled themselves in rugs.

From the first moment Felicity knew instinctively that it was, on the contrary, a very bad idea. If she were standing up or running about, there was at least a reasonable chance of keeping her inside in the lower half of her, where it properly belonged. But once she lay down and could feel the slow, relentless movement of the ship, tipping first her feet up into the air and then her head, and giving her nothing to look at except the grey horizon, moving slowly up the bars of the deck rail till it showed over the top and then slowly down again, how could she stop her inside from doing the same thing?

Suddenly Cousin Kathleen pounced, and Felicity was ignominiously picked up and rushed down to the cabin. Before she knew what was happening, she was being horribly sick into the little round basin that so conveniently let itself down out of the wall for this purpose, while her mother's firm hand stroked the hair back from her forehead.

Afterward, she lay in her bunk in the half-dark, listening to the creaking of the ship and the throbbing of the engines and smelling the varnishy smell. And later, to her disgust, when she began to feel better and rather hungry, she was allowed only a sip of water and a very dull water biscuit, which flaked off and was prickly in the sheets, and stuck to the roof of her mouth. But by the next morning, she was quite all right again and came down to breakfast in the ordinary way with yesterday's disgrace almost forgotten.

Those meals on the ship kept their glamour to the last in spite of the tin of powdered milk that made a regular appearance. It was to be mixed with boiling water at the table. These cups of milk were a mockery of the blue and white cow peering over the gate on the tin's label. Even to the greatest milk-skin lover—and Helen was the only one of these in the family—the thick yellow crinkly film that gathered on the top before it was cool enough to drink was quite impossible, but the thrill of watching the table tilt with the ship's movement, and the jingle of the metal-handled knives as they jostled the spoons and forks across the cloth never palled.

⌘ One day, the ship's engines went silent, and the children clattered up the companion ladder and ran excitedly to the deck rails to see what was going to happen. After days of sea, green sea, heavy swelling grey sea, or deep white-frothed blue seas—like the Prussian blue that always got into every other color in your paint box—there was something else to look at.

Out of the water rose a great, misty island of a rock, yet not so much like a rock at all really, because rocks were wet and gray and shiny. It was more of an island mountain, Felicity thought, with tiny streets and houses climbing to the top, and little boats with shouting, sunburnt people rowing about between the ships in the harbor.

"Where are we? What is it?" the children clamored.

"The Rock of Gibraltar," their mother answered, as she leaned with them over the rail, watching.

There was a lot of coming and going on the *Princess Juliana*. Luggage kept coming up from the cabin and the hold, and the passengers dashed about trying to count their possessions to see that none was missing. The strange steps made out of holes suddenly appeared again and were slung over the ship's side and tied with ropes. People started going down them. Brown men with ragged clothes and flashing white teeth followed, balancing trunks and suitcases on their shoulders.

And there, among the crowds leaving the ship, went the three little girls in their red jerseys, and when they got to the bottom of the steps, they were lifted one by one into a little wobbling rowing boat piled with luggage, and rowed away. That was the last the children saw of them, three scarlet specks crowned with yellow straw hats, bobbing over the green water until they vanished into the shifting crowds of the harbor.

Then with a throb and a shudder the engines started again, and the ship turned slowly and nosed out into the sparkling blue of the open sea.

2

SO THIS WAS CAIRO.

Heat, and stickiness, and the grinding of trams, and the perpetual shouting of strange, hoarse voices outside the bedroom windows of the hotel.

Strange slatted shutters darkened the room, and when they were opened there was a glare of light stronger than the children had ever seen. The shutters themselves were painted green or had been once, with little metal hooks like fingers sticking out of the wall to hold them open. But now, the glare of the Egyptian sun had paled the paint to a dusty grey, flaking off here and there in protest.

Mary and Felicity lay in bed, and the bolster between them to keep them apart got hotter and heavier, and more in the way. It was always getting too far over to one side of the bed. The sheets grew damper and more wrinkly. The children were cross and miserable, and their stomachs ached. All they could do was to lie there and fidget, and look at the misty folds of the mosquito net gathered into its square, wooden canopy up in the ceiling, and sniff the musty smell of it, and listen to the rustling noise that it made (like dry grass being rumpled) when it was tucked under the mattress enclosing them in a half transparent tent.

"When are we going to Jerusalem?" they asked, irritably pushing damp fringes out of their eyes with restless hands. "In a day or two, when you're better," Nannie said, and so they just had to go on lying there, listening to the high-pitched hum of the mosquitoes trying to find a way to get in, and watching, fascinated, when they perched on the outside of the net on incredibly delicate legs and pushed their miniature elephant trunks through the net's tiny holes.

The children's father had come to meet the boat in Alexandria. When she saw him again, with his moustache, and the funny little soft tuft of beard in

8

The author's father at the Citadel, Jerusalem, 1920; reproduced by permission of King's College, Cambridge.

the middle of his chin, Felicity realized that she hadn't forgotten what he looked like at all. Several times in the Cairo hotel, he had tiptoed into their darkened bedroom, lifted the rustling folds of the mosquito net and sat down on the edge of the bed to talk them. "What is Jerusalem like, Daddy?" Mary had asked.

"A golden bowl filled with scorpions," he had answered. "But my two daughters shall ride on a donkey, and eat figs and honey. And when I have mended the walls that Suleiman the Magnificent built four hundred years before you were even thought of, you shall walk all round the city with me, and you shall see the footprint in the rock where the Prophet Mohammed went up into Heaven, and the Wailing Wall where the Jews still weep over the destruction of Jerusalem."

Scorpions in a golden bowl . . . a golden string wound into golden ball . . . Felicity thought of the chain their mother sometimes wore round her neck; an almost magic chain made out of silver filigree words, each one separated by a small, blood-red carnelian pierced with a silver pin. If only you could find the beginning, which was difficult because she wore the chain

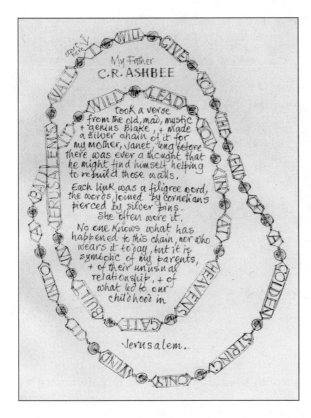

The author's drawing of her mother's silver and carnelian chain

looped twice, the words formed themselves into a verse that you could spell out, pulling the chain round gently so as not to hurt her as you read.

> I give you the end of a golden string
> Only wind it into a ball,
> It will lead you in at Heaven's gate
> Built in Jerusalem's wall.

If she were wearing that chain when she came up to hear your prayers, it was very difficult not to forget where you had got to in the middle of them, which would mean starting all over again.

As Felicity thought of the words now, the golden ball unwound itself before her, and rolled slowly out into hot darkness toward Jerusalem. It was night when they reached the Suez Canal, and there was a long wait in the

dark. Tall rickety poles dangled electric light bulbs at long distances from one another, which only seemed to make the darkness darker. After a while Mary and Felicity, bored with sitting still on the luggage and being good, strayed away a little distance to explore. The canal lay motionless, brown and smelly, except where there were pools of yellow from the lights.

"Let's poke around," said Mary; so they found themselves two sticks, and started turning over stones here and there, and whipping up the dust. Suddenly from under a small rock, there scuttled a strange little animal with eight legs and a twisted tail, which seemed to run sideways at them. Delighted, the children prodded it with their sticks. Then they heard their mother's voice saying, "Where have the two big ones got to?" And then, apparently to their father, "Oh, there they are. Just see what they are doing, would you?" and his slow strides came toward them. Suddenly he jumped, seized them each by a wrist, and dragged them away.

"Ow! Daddy, you're hurting!" Felicity cried out, scared by his quick movement.

"You must be careful what you play with," he warned. "Scorpions are dangerous; they sting." Then he called to their mother, "I'll take them for a little walk down by the canal," and with one on each side of him, held in a firm hand, he walked down to the edge of the muddy water. Something stirred at the water's edge, and a small sleek body slipped out into the stream.

"What was that?" the children asked.

"A water rat, I should think," their father said. "Now, if you'll listen carefully, I'll recite you a poem," and he launched out into,

> By the wide lake's margin I mark'd her lie—
> The wide, weird lake where the alders sigh—
> A fair young thing, with a soft, shy eye. . . .

No alders sighed by the canal's edge, but whenever Felicity heard that poem afterward, instead of "the dark, deep mere," the yellow lights and the hot brown banks of Suez rose before her eyes.

After that, it was a succession of slow uncomfortable trains with hard wooden seats, and nowhere to move to when you got fidgety and wanted to

walk about. Above the seats there were peculiar shelves held up by chains, with spare chains hanging from them that jangled with the train's lurching movement.

"What are the chains for, Mary?" Felicity had asked, and the wisdom of eight years answered a little scornfully. "To fasten prisoners to, of course." It was then that the Green Bag made its first appearance. It was a large green cotton shoe bag, which pulled together at the top with a string. In it was kept the children's potty, a most necessary piece of equipment on a long journey in a train without even a corridor, or any sanitary arrangements.

Then the train stopped at a station, the children were taken out onto the platform, or onto the sandy track beside the sleepers if it were only a halt, and one by one were sat upon the potty, which in time was put back again into its discreet green bag.

At the junction of Ludd, there was an agonizing moment when Felicity was sure the train was going to start while Helen still sat on the potty, smiling up at the crowds on the dusty platform, and batting her thick eyelashes at them coyly. And there stood their mother, her ringed fingers holding the green cotton bag and saying,

"Come along now, Heleny, quickly, there's a good girl."

And Felicity stood in the carriage with the door open, bouncing up and down in fear and suspense, in case the whistle blew and the train went off and left her mother and Helen on the platform.

They arrived in Jerusalem safely. No one had been left behind, and nothing had been lost.

It was a great moment when they walked up the path of their new home, the flagstones a glare of white that made the children screw up their eyes; and when Felicity touched the peeling, rusty paint of the big iron gates, she had to draw back her hand quickly because it burned.

They went on into the stone-floored hall of the house, cool and dark after the blinding sunlight, and their father, showing dimly in his white cotton coat, turned and said, "Well, here we are."

Then he clapped his hands, and two people came smiling and bowing into the hall; a plump, short woman with dark grizzly hair and an oily friendly face, her two eyes quite different colors (it wasn't until later that Fe-

Jerusalem from the ramparts

licity discovered the fascinating fact that one of them was made of glass, and could be taken out when she went to bed), and a dark-faced man in a long striped dress, with a wide yellow sash without ends, wound round his waist.

"This is our cook, Haani," said the children's father, and their mother put out her hand, smiling, and shook the plump, greasy hand of the woman, who bowed and giggled, and said a lot of things in some strange language. "And this is our man, Hassan," said their father; and the white teeth of the man in the sash flashed, as he took their mother's hand in his dark brown one and kissed it; then he touched his forehead with it bowing again and stepped back into the shadows. The final touch to their arrival was when their father said, "Well now, I think we'd better have something to eat," and turning to the smiling Haani, he grandly spoke to her in the same peculiar language that sounded so different from English. "That was Arabic, and it means we're going to have poached eggs," he said, looking down into Felicity's wide grey, wondering eyes, and he patted her upturned cheek.

3

THEIR FIRST YEAR in Jerusalem was spent in what the children knew as Canon Brown's house, though why he should have been called a canon when he was not a soldier, and had nothing to do with guns, they could never quite make out. Apparently he was some sort of a clergyman. Felicity imagined him as a busy little man in the long black habit and flat, wide-brimmed hat that so many of the clergymen she saw about the city seemed to wear.

The house was of stone in a large, wild garden. In the front was a round, gravel drive, with a big, dark bush of oleanders in the middle, whose pink flowers always seemed to be in bloom. Rough-trunked pine trees ringed the outer edge of the drive, and under them many years of shed pine needles made a springy, dry, brown carpet that smelled sweetly in the heat. The ant heaps were the only snag, because you could never be sure if the little, pointed mountains were disused ant castles or live ones until you suddenly found you were standing across an ants' thoroughfare, with an army of small, shiny-black or red-brown creatures busily careering over your sandaled feet.

The lower part of the house at the back was covered with a mauve-blue flower called cherry pie, though as it was neither the color of cherries, nor like any pies Felicity had ever seen, that didn't seem a very suitable name. But it smelled lovely, and looked pretty, and hummed with bees and insects in the hot sunlight. There was a little black-shadowed arbor too, where the children used to play house, and fig trees, whose smooth, grey branches grew close enough to the ground to be perfect climbing for a six-year-old.

A pepper tree with drooping feathery leaves and small scarlet berries, obviously made for dolls' food, grew against the wall enclosing the garden. This was a loose, stone wall that was apt to tumble down if you climbed onto it carelessly; into its dark crevices the bright-eyed lizards darted when you frightened them.

Janet Ashbee, with Prudence, Helen, Mary, and the author

It was to the little arbor that Hassan carried out a rug every day, and the three elder children would follow with their toys, and play interminable games of house, and school, and hospital in its dark, leafy shadows.

Between them they had quite a family of dolls. Mary's most beloved one was a baby doll with blue eyes that opened and shut, a smooth china head like a real baby's, and a painted down of hair that you could just feel rough under your fingers if you felt with your eyes closed. This doll had been brought from America by "Uncle" Frank, a friend of the children's father, who had also brought one for Felicity.

"You must be really careful of these dolls," their mother had said when Uncle Frank presented them in the timbered study of the old Cotswold house. "They are your most precious children." So they had at once been called Mary's Preshy and Fifi's Preshy (Fifi was the outcome of Helen's first stumbling attempt at her sister's name, and somehow it had stuck). Mary's Preshy, at least, had been loved and nursed with an intense devotion. Carefully packed in the depths of the big, black trunk, it had survived the journey

The author and her sister Mary with their mother, 1921

to Jerusalem and been embraced with passionate delight when unpacked at Canon Brown's.

To fill the gap made by the early end of Felicity's Preshy, who had died on the stone step of her mother's bedroom when Felicity had tripped and fallen headlong, her godmother had handed on two of her "children," complete with several changes of frilly, old-fashioned clothes. With them (and this was most prized of all) was a small lacquered box containing a miniature hairbrush, comb, and mirror, and even a fine-toothed scurf comb to make it quite complete.

Louisa (or Teddy-for-short) was the more attractive, because she had long, silken yellow hair with a fringe, which could really be brushed and combed without coming out, and a calm pink-and-white china face. Her body was covered in leather, but her arms were china from their jointed elbows down, and were finished off with elegant, tapering Victorian fingers. Her knees were jointed too, and there were several pairs of shoes and open-work silk socks to cover her shapely pink feet. She was a little inclined to fall over backward when she sat up, but that was something you overlooked because she was in every other way so desirable. Mabel, the other doll, had a soft stuffed body and legs; her china face was not quite so attractive, but her clothes, especially the crimson velvet frock with the low sash, easily made up for this.

Helen had one treasured doll with curling brown hair and eyes that opened and shut.

"What are you going to call her?" Mary had asked when Helen had unwrapped the exciting package on her birthday.

"I don't know yet," Helen had answered, and then, after prolonged thought, "Her name is Rosetta."

One day Mary forgot to bring Preshy in from the garden, and it was only when she was just going to bed that she remembered.

"Oh, Mummie, I've left my Preshy in the garden," she cried in an anxious voice. "I must get her in or the pariah dogs might hurt her in the night. Will somebody come with me?"

"We'll get Hassan to fetch her in for you, and anything else that may have been forgotten," her mother said, and she opened the hall door and called through to the kitchen. So Hassan went out into the gathering dusk, and a few minutes later came back carrying the rug bulging with forgotten playthings, the four corners of it gathered together in his hands, and, with a cheerful smile, dumped it on the floor of the hall. There was a sickening crack as it hit the stone floor, and Mary's hands flew to her face with an agonizing premonition.

"My Preshy!" she cried out in a voice not far from tears, and with frantic haste threw back the folds of the rug to find her treasure. When she saw the ruin of the baby head, its beautiful eyes an unsightly mechanism with a small lump of lead on a balancing prong of wire, lying nakedly among the fragments, the floodgates were loosed, and she wept uncontrollably.

Felicity stood by, horrified at the destruction and full of compassion at Mary's grief, trying to think of something helpful to say.

"Don't cry," she whispered, touching her sister's heaving shoulders timidly. But what was there to say? Surely, there was nothing, nothing to be done. It was one of those things that happened and that was so awful that you couldn't see past it to another day, or believe, in the first dreadful moment, that things could ever be the same again.

"Whatever is the matter?" their mother called out as she came into the hall from the study; but when she saw the magnitude of the disaster, she gathered the weeping Mary into her arms.

"There, there," she said. "Come along, pull yourself together, there's a brave girl." Then, after glancing at the size and number of the pieces where they lay jumbled up in the rug with sand and buckets and dusty dolls' clothes, she added comfortingly, "It's not as bad as all that; I think I might be able to stick her together again. I'll see what I can do after you're in bed tonight."

"But her eyes, Mummie, her eyes!" Mary's voice rose in a fresh crescendo as she caught sight of the glassy, dismembered eyeballs.

"Even her eyes we might be able to mend so that they work again. Now, here's a hanky. Give your noise a good blow, and don't think any more about it, and then both of you run along up to bed like good children. Nannie's waiting for you."

A gleam of hope dawned in Mary's hazel-brown eyes as she put up a wet face to be kissed; then, still shaken by huge, shuddering sobs, she took her sister's proffered hand, and they went upstairs together. "Don't cry any more, Mary," Felicity said. "Mummie will stick your Preshy together again, I'm sure she will, and make her quite like new." And in the morning, the un- believable had happened. There was Preshy all in one piece again. It was true, there were little seccotiny lines crossing her head and face, and it meant she had to be more carefully handled, and not left in the sun or washed in real water, but she didn't look very different. Most wonderful of all, as Mary lifted her up, and held her in sitting position, with a rattle and a click, her blue eyes opened.

ON SUNDAYS, the children's colored cotton frocks were changed for white ones, with bands of broderie anglaise at waist and cuff and neck. They were embellished with rows of narrow tucks, shiny and stiff with starch, which made a tearing sound when you forced them up from the folds into which they had been dressed. The cuffs were often stuck together when they were first put on after washing, and if you turned your head too sharply, you hurt your neck on the sharp, starched edge of the embroidery. Instead of sun helmets, the children wore frilly white muslin hats. Those hats were part of the burden of the hot walk to St. George's Cathedral. They were tickly and scratchy, and every time they were washed, the frills seemed to get scratchier and stiffer with starch, and the elastic tighter. Even if you sucked it a bit when no one was looking, it didn't make it very much more comfortable.

You trailed down the white road clutching a damp prayer book, and when a dust cloud caught up with you, you stood still, shutting your eyes tight till it swept past, while you felt the tingle of the hot dust pricking the backs of your bare legs. Felicity's prayer book was her special pride. It was covered in rich, pimply, maroon leather with her initials stamped in gold letters on the front. Its endpapers were of moiré silk, also maroon colored, like no other prayer book in the world. On the stiff, shiny flyleaf, in a neat slanting hand, were inscribed the words "To Felicity, on her fifth birthday, from her Uncle Nevill."

The pages, which were of a fascinating transparency, were both red and gilt at the edges, so that when you flicked them over they looked red, and yet when the book was shut tightly they were pure gold; and although the leather became damp and sticky with the clutch of a hot hand, the color never came off.

The author, her sisters, and their mother in their Sunday best, ca. 1921

By the time they arrived in church, the children's mouths were dry and gritty, but there was no chance of a drink; their mother was too afraid of the drinking water in a strange place, in case it had not been boiled. If their father took them, there was always a possibility that he might be worked upon, for he was more likely to take a risk.

One memorable Sunday, both Mary and Felicity pleaded so convincingly that their mouths would be too dry to sing, that after a slight hesitation he capitulated and took them into the vestry. There on the red plush table cloth stood a glass jug of water, with cloudy, yellowish sediment at the bottom, and the children could hardly wait till glasses were brought. They drank the warm, flat water greedily, with a feeling of slightly guilty excitement because they knew their mother wouldn't have approved; but the relief was so wonderful that they didn't really care. Then they tiptoed after their father into the coolness of the cathedral, trying not to clatter on the grating as they went up the aisle to their own row of chairs.

During the long service, Felicity had developed a special technique to make the time pass more quickly. The *Venite* was all right, because it started at the bottom of a page, and turning over in the middle made a break; the *Te Deum* was the real trial. So she would start off singing lustily, and then, after the first change in the tune, and the bit that went "Holy, Holy, Holy, Lord God of Sabaoth," which was rather nice and sad, she would let herself lag a phrase or two behind. She knew, of course, perfectly well really where the choir and the congregation had got to, but by singing softly to herself just those few phrases behind, she had a lovely surprise when she heard them racing into the climax well ahead of her.

There was also an element of excitement in finding her way in "Dearly beloved brethren, the Scripture moveth us in sundry places to acknowledge and confess our manifold sins and wickedness" (why should the Scripture want you to move anywhere?). As the meaningless but beautiful words rolled forth, a confused picture rose before Felicity's eyes. The manifold-sins-and-wickedness wrapped themselves round the kneeling figures behind the carved pew in dark folds, as a cloak "before the face of Almighty God." After this a large piece was left out, and it became a race to see if she could find the place again where he said "Therefore I pray and beseech you, as many as are here present" before he got to the end.

The Psalms were always much more difficult. In the first place she had to have help with the Roman numerals. Then, even when she had grasped the melody, it was a matter of pure guesswork as to how many words would be packed into one part of the tune and whether, when she had let herself soar up to the next phrase, she would find herself singing the same words as everyone else. The children's father liked the Psalms best, and would stand with his prayer book held well away from him, singing with dramatic assurance. A look of long-suffering boredom would come over his face, and he would heave his shoulders resignedly when it came to the hymns and the number on the board turned out to be "The Church's one Foundation" or "Jesu the very name of Thee."

But Felicity liked the hymns, especially rousing ones like "Stand Up, Stand Up for Jesus" (though this was rather too long) or "Onward Christian Soldiers." At least she could always be sure the words would fit neatly into the tune.

There was another advantage in going to church with their father, which was that he found the presence of two small daughters a very useful excuse for going out before the sermon. As the time drew near (and they knew roughly where it came in the service), they peered expectantly at each other round his legs. Relief swept over them if they saw him stoop to pick up his almost undented smooth grey hat, and his white narwhal stick with the ebony handle, and heard his whisper to come quietly, and not to trip over the hassocks or forget their prayer books. But if the tense moment passed, and the clergyman came down the steps and went up into the pulpit, they knew there was nothing for it but to settle themselves into the uncomfortable chairs that ran into their backs, and try to find something interesting to think about that would last the length of the sermon.

Of course there were the people to look at, especially the clergyman's own family who sat two or three rows in front on the other side of the aisle. The clergyman's wife always wore a shapeless, sponge-cloth dress that reminded Felicity of a bath towel, and the fidgeting of her little boy, who was about five years old, was always held up to the children as "how you should not behave in church." He was a pale child with fair hair and colorless eyes, whom the children's mother had nicknamed "The Sweet Pea" because he twined himself round his mother with tendril-like movements and had to be detached at intervals and set down again on his own chair.

One day, during a particularly long sermon, when even the best subjects for thinking about had been exhausted, Felicity stumbled upon the Table of Kindred and Affinity. She had no idea what it meant, but it made really interesting reading, whether she murmured it quietly inside her head, as a sort of incantation, or tried to work out the intricacies of the relationships. Who could her Husband's Mother's Brother be, whom she would not be allowed to marry, or her Sister's Daughter's Husband? After that first discovery, it was rather like a door into a secret garden, which could only be found if you had been really good; and sometimes, hunt as she might through the transparent, rustling pages, the Table of Affinity eluded her altogether, and she had to make do with the much duller Making of Deacons, or the Ordering of Priests.

Sometimes their father read one of the lessons, and it was always quite exciting when he stepped over her legs and walked in a stately way up to the lectern to find his place. There would be a dramatic pause as he stood behind the shining brass eagle whose spreading wings supported the Bible, waiting till the congregation had settled itself and stopped rustling. Then he cleared his throat and let the first sentences roll out.

One glorious Sunday Mary had a nosebleed. Before she could extract her handkerchief from her knickers' pocket, one, two drops of blood had splashed down onto the stone base of the black and white pillar where she knelt. It was a wonderful excuse for a hurried exit, and, of course, it wasn't worth while coming back again afterward, which meant a legitimate excuse for being back early from church, and a delightful extra hour playing in the garden before dinner.

Every Sunday after that the children's first thought as they went to their row of chairs was to look and see whether the Russian women who came down from the convent on the Mount of Olives to clean the cathedral had noticed the stains and scrubbed them off. But as the months passed, Mary's two drops of blood mellowed and darkened and became part of the pattern of Sunday, so that Felicity would have felt that something that "belonged" had been taken away if she had arrived one day and found them gone.

5

THE TWO ELDER CHILDREN did their lessons with Cousin Kathleen in the downstairs study and labored over their tables and dictation with pencils that got damper and stickier as the morning wore on. They read "Stumps," "Brownie in the Cherry Orchard," and the *Early Lessons* of Maria Edgeworth. For Felicity, Mrs. Edgeworth's priggish creations, Frank and Lucy, took their walks with Papa and Mama not through quiet English fields but along the sunbaked, dusty roads of Jerusalem; and Rosamund's coveted purple jar stood in the window of an American chemist just inside the Damascus gate.

"When can I have a prize?" Felicity asked one day.

"When she knows her seven-times table might be a good occasion," Cousin Kathleen put in quickly, before the children's mother had thought of an answer.

"And can I have a prize too?" Mary asked.

"You'll both have to earn them before you can have them," their mother said, "and I shall have to see if I have any prizes first."

But a day came at last when Felicity felt she really knew her seven-times, always an irregular and unfriendly table, and Mary had very conveniently achieved a dictation about Peter Pan, which miraculously had only one mistake. It was all quite fair, they both felt, and it was an added pleasure that both of them should be going to have prizes.

In the cool dimness of the study, Mary's dictation was ceremoniously handed to their mother. Then Felicity stood up, her hands clutched nervously behind her, and recited the awkward table. And it was all right, and none of it eluded her. Even when she was "jumped" once or twice with the worst ones like seven times six, she kept her head and didn't make a mistake.

Then came the breathless moment while their mother went to the cupboard to get out the prizes.

The suspense was terrifying and lovely, and Felicity's heart thumped, and she couldn't bear to wait, and yet the waiting made it even more desperately important. Their mother came back smiling, her hands holding the prizes still concealed behind her back. Then with a sudden movement, she brought them round and held them out in front of her.

And there, one in each hand, were two unbelievably enchanting little umbrellas. The children gasped, and swallowed, and with trembling fingers took them from her. They were both the same size and shape, with elegant pale brown wooden handles that curved round in a small hook into which four fingers just fitted comfortably. Mary's was white with little green sprigs all over it, and Felicity's was sprinkled with the most bewitching pink spots. When they were put up they curved like proper, grown-up umbrellas, but oh, so much more charmingly because they were small. They were light enough too, so that when you pressed the little spring that made the spokes fold down again, they didn't rush relentlessly onto your fingers and pinch them, as their father's large black one with the gold band did. Going to church the following Sunday was almost enjoyable, the children thought, as they set off, with the green-sprigged and the pink-dotted umbrellas bobbing proudly over their starched white hats.

In the afternoon when they got up from their rest, the children would go out on George. George was the first of a succession of donkeys. He was a quiet, flea-bitten animal, who was not too obstinate and did not need more than a normal amount of pushing and pulling to make him do as he was told. They took it in turns to ride, or sometimes rode one behind the other. When Felicity rode in front, she liked to feel the firm brushlike ridge of his shaven mane or rest her hands on the strange black mark that ran across his mousy brown shoulders.

"Why does he have that mark on him?" she had asked one day.

"All donkeys do," her father had answered. "Legend has it that it is a mark of honor ever since Christ entered Jerusalem on Palm Sunday riding upon an ass."

George responded willingly, if in his own time, to the prod of a small heel, and there was something friendly about the curve of his warm, round stomach, and the squeak of the saddle leather as you rode.

◈ Felicity went to bed a little before Mary because she was younger, and one evening, when she was washed and in her nightgown, and ready for someone to hear her prayers, her father came into the nursery and sat down on the side of the bed. He looked rather strange, she thought, and his eyes were red, almost as though he had been crying, only grown-ups didn't cry. The little hard knob in his throat above the loose collar of his shirt was moving in an odd way, and suddenly, for some unknown reason, she felt shy.

"Do you remember your Grannie?" he asked.

"Oh yes," Felicity had said, and saw again the small figure of Grannie as she stood on the platform waiting for the train to go at the start of their journey to Jerusalem. How small she had looked, and how white her hair under her little straw and velvet bonnet. She spoke in an odd way too, all in the back of her throat, which was because she came from Hamburg-in-Germany. That was the only time Felicity really remembered Grannie, standing there waving as their train slid slowly out of the station.

She remembered her other grandmother—the one who was her mother's mother—much more clearly. She liked the children to call her "Babooshka," because, she said, it was what the Russians called their grandmothers, and she had been born in Russia and lived there until she was grown up. Babooshka was large and soft, and always wore a high net collar on her black silk dress right up her neck to her ears. She had lots of chains and brooches, and little bits of black jet here and there, and a fringe of white curls, and rings on all her fingers.

Once, long ago, before they had left England, she had come to stay. At lunch one day some devil had entered into Mary, and she had put her silver napkin ring on her head like a crown when she came to say her grace at the end of the meal. As she lowered her head reverently, her eyes screwed up, her hands folded in front of her, the napkin ring had bounced off and hit the pie dish. "Gracious, child!" Babooshka had exclaimed, "Don't give me a fright like that! You'll be the death of me!" And she had closed her eyes and fluttered her ringed hands, and the children hadn't known whether to laugh or be serious.

"Grannie" with her granddaughter Mary, 1913

Now Felicity looked up at her father expectantly. "I'd like you to say your prayers to me to night," he said, "and I'll tell you a new bit to put in," and he took her onto his knees, and she started off rather quickly.

"God bless Mummie and Daddy, Mary, Helen and Baby, Babooshka and Uncle Nevill, and Grannie. . . ."

"And make Grannie look down on us from the stars," her father put in, in a strange, different-sounding voice.

"And make Grannie look down on us from the stars," she repeated after him and paused. "Why, Daddy?"

"Because Grannie has gone to Heaven, and we shan't see her on earth any more," he said. "I'd like you to remember her always. She was very fond of her grandchildren." He lifted Felicity off his knees, and as he bent and kissed her, she felt the funny little tuft of beard on his chin. Then, without looking back, he went quickly out of the room.

One night, after the children had been asleep for a long time, their mother came into the nursery carrying the lamp in her hand.

"Put on your socks, and your jerseys over your nightgowns," she said, putting the lamp down on the table, "and you shall see something beautiful."

Felicity was wide awake at once and struggled into the jersey her mother had laid inside the mosquito net, getting the buttons all mixed up and in the wrong buttonholes in her efforts to be quick. Whatever could be happening that made it all right to get out of bed in the middle of the night while it was still dark?

"Hurry, Mary, be quick!" she whispered, as she padded over to her sister's bed. And there was Mary, who never woke so easily, her eyes dazed with sleep, fumblingly pulling off the socks which she had just put on, and starting to lie down again.

"Don't go to sleep again, Mary, wake up!" Felicity said, dancing up and down in an agony in case they should be missing something. "Put your socks on, we're going to see something lovely!" Mary had barely found her way into the sleeves of her jersey when their mother came back into the room with their father behind her, and each took one of the children in their arms and carried them out and up onto the roof. And there was a sight that was more like magic than anything they had ever dreamed. Into the warm, velvet darkness, all mixed up with the stars, shot countless other stars that flashed green and red and a brilliant white. Some of them soared up with a whirr and a bang, to break into clusters that hung for a moment motionless, and then dropped slowly down over the sharp points of the cypresses and the white-domed roofs of the city. From the distant streets came the faint, continuous murmur of shouting crowds, a murmur that swelled louder each time another star-cluster rose into the dark. And all the bells of Jerusalem were ringing with a wild, jangling sound, peal tumbling out after peal, as though they couldn't get out fast enough the things they wanted to say.

Breathlessly, Mary, who was wide awake now, asked, "What is it, Daddy, what is it for?"

"It's for the signing of the peace," he answered, "and everybody is very happy. You must remember it always." The children nodded solemnly; they were not likely to forget. Then with eyes still dazzled by the lights of fairyland, they were carried down again into the bedroom and tucked up inside their mosquito nets.

6

THE FOLLOWING SPRING, Canon Brown wanted his house back, and the children's mother told them they were going to move into a new home.

"We've found another house in the Wadi el Jose," she said. "But it isn't quite ready yet. Daddy's going to do some alterations, and after that it has to be thoroughly cleaned. Then it will be whitewashed, and we shall move in. You'll be going to school then, too," she added.

"Going to school?" Mary and Felicity echoed her incredulously. "Aren't we going to have lessons with Cousin Kathleen any more?"

"No. Cousin Kathleen's not coming with us. She's going away. So you two Big Ones will be going to school at the American Colony."

How exciting it all sounded! The two children looked at each other with shining eyes. A new house and a real school, with lots of other children, instead of just lessons-in-the-study with Cousin Kathleen.

"Come on, Fifi," Mary said, "let's get Helen, and our dolls, and go out and play schools in the arbor. We'd better not play houses today anyway, because Helen might eat another doll's sand pudding like she did yesterday. And then Nannie would be cross again."

The workmen were still in the new house when they finally moved in, but the bedrooms gleamed a bluish white with their fresh coats of whitewash, and everywhere smelled cool and clean. The house was set in a large stretch of barren ground on the side of a steep hill overlooking the Wadi el Jose. Everything around it was brown and stony, and a loosely built wall divided the stones inside the garden from those in the valley outside. It was a white-domed, stone-built Arab house, tucked into the hillside, so that at the back there was only one floor, while in the front, where the land dropped steeply, there were two.

The house in the Wadi el Jose, 1920

No road led to it, and when the ploughing season came, the Arabs even ploughed up the narrow path across the field, which was the only way to get to it, and you had to spend a long time wearing a new path down. A steep and irregular flight of curved, stone steps led from the field down into the garden, and the children's father had had a little iron handrail put up as a precaution. It was painted with red lead, which soon changed to a poppy pink under the hot sun.

"Let's go discovering," Mary said as soon as they had found their way around the house, and with Felicity at her heels, she ran out to explore. At the top of the garden, in the curve of the steps, there was a nice easy fig tree, with low branches that even Helen could manage; it would have been quite perfect if it hadn't always had a stream of ants crawling over it. They were the small sort of ants that got into your sandals and up your knickers before you noticed them, but which managed to sting quite hard in spite of their size.

Below the fig tree the garden dropped sharply, and at the bottom was an olive tree, which the children quickly decided was *the* tree. It was very old, and had a hollow base, which made a perfect house for Helen and Prudy, who was now almost old enough to play sensibly. Farther up, the tree divided itself into two main branches, and near the tops of each of these, Mary and Felicity made their houses and settled themselves in. Their mother gave them rice and lentils and "smeed"—the name by which they knew semolina—and they kept these precious possessions in little pots and jars ranged in cardboard boxes fastened into the branches. Of course it was almost impossible to keep out the earwigs and the ants, but you got used to things like that, and it was a small inconvenience compared with the delight of sitting high up in the whispering, silver-grey leaves, looking out over the brown valley.

On the other side of the Wadi ran the white ribbon of the road, past the cemetery with the hundreds of little wooden crosses where all the dead soldiers lay buried, and on up, to the Mount of Olives itself, with the tall, ugly tower of Government House and the slender spire of the Russian convent near by. In the middle of the Wadi lay the Flat Rock, that most fascinating of all playgrounds, especially in the spring when every crevice held wild anemones, small brilliant blood-drops, and crowding purple and yellow irises.

Up four steps of the garden and across a small square space filled with chipped, white stones was a pepper tree, and under it the piece of ground that was given over to the two elder children for their own gardens. When you got tired of digging and raking, you could climb onto the stone wall and sit with your legs dangling over the steep drop below, and let the feathery leaves of the pepper ruffle your hair and tickle your shoulders, or reach up a hand and pick a cluster of berries to add to your store of "food."

At the other side of the house, by the kitchen window and the back door, was an almond tree; but it was very slender and not much use for climbing as the first branches were too high up to be reached from the ground. The children's father soon set to work to make something out of the garden. A large water butt was installed against the side of the house in an angle formed by the six steps leading up to the front door. In this butt was stored all the water that had been used for general household purposes during the day, and which was much too precious to throw away. Sometimes after a big wash, it would overflow, and then a fascinating stream of scummy, soap-sudsy water would well out and run down the hard, shallow earthen steps, and the children would rush at it with twigs and stones and try to direct it into the rows

Mary, Prudence, Helen, and the author with Nannie at the Wadi el Jose house,
ca. 1920

of wilting cosmos and hollyhocks on the other side of the path. But the real
watering was done in the evenings after the children were in bed. In the
mornings, all they could ever find were the frothy-edged circles around each
plant, already baked dry and cracked by the early sun.

Beyond the rows of flowers, the garden spread out into a steep, delightful wilderness whose slope soon became so slippery with wear that it made as
swift a toboggan run as could be found on any English snow field.

Hassan, who was part of Canon Brown's establishment, had stayed behind when the family moved, and a new handyman had taken his place
whose name was A-eed. He was a cheerful, ruddy-faced Christian Arab with
a wandering eye, who soon became a great friend of the children. A-eed
made them a simple toboggan out of an old soap box, and in this, sand-
wiched together, two at a time, they would spend happy hours shooting
down the earthen slope, and more often than not overturning with shouts of
laughter by the side of the stone wall at the bottom.

On the mornings when they were not at school, they would sit up in their houses in the olive tree, tipping out the unwanted earwigs and sending messages across to each other in a little basket which was hauled along on a string, while Helen and Prudy played at the foot of the tree. Then they would see Nannie coming out of the house in her brilliant white apron, and her straw hat draped in its dark blue georgette scarf, carrying the jug with the "elevenses." Over the jug was a piece of net to keep off the flies. As she walked, the little, bright blue beads around the net jingled against the china with a refreshing sound that called the children down from their hideouts. Sometimes it was just water, but more often it was lemonade, and occasionally, as a very special treat, it would be pure, squeezed grape juice, of which there was never enough.

As for the house, that too was full of surprises. When you went up the six stone steps and in at the front door, you came straight into a square courtyard open to the sky on the far side of which were Nannie's and the children's bedrooms, as well as the nursery. "That part of the house is where the Arab who lived here before us used to keep his womenfolk," the children's father said, "where no strange man could see them. A suitable place for me to keep my four daughters!" he added.

The drawing room with its plain whitewashed walls also led off the court. One wall was lined the whole length with books, and at the end stood the big piano. On the white stone of the floors glowed the weathered reds and blues of their father's collection of rugs; this he would add to every now and then, when he found some particularly lovely fragment down in the Old City.

A flight of stone stairs led from the court to the dining room and the kitchen below. And then there was the cistern. The lid of the cistern was in the floor of the courtyard, and the water supply for the whole house depended on how much rain could be stored in it during the three wet winter months. This would have been quite all right if the cistern had not been found to have a bad leak about two thirds of the way up. Once the water reached this level, either the dining room was flooded or the drain pipes that fed the cistern from the roof had to be deflected, so that the water rushed noisily across the courtyard and out of the front door.

Both alternatives were equally fascinating to the children. They asked

The drawing room of the Wadi el Jose house, 1920

politely after the cistern when they came down to breakfast on winter mornings, or if the damp patch on the dining room wall was already oozing, they
splashed cheerfully through the water in the courtyard on their way to the
stairs when the breakfast bell rang. This unfortunate leak meant, of course,
that the water never lasted out the summer months, and when the level became dangerously low it had to be supplemented by extra supplies from the
public tap. So by midsummer, the donkey started his daily trip to Herod's
Gate, with two large, battered petrol cans strapped onto his back.

The new donkey's name was Georgette, which had nothing whatever to
do with his sex. George had become too unwilling to respond to any cajol-
ery, and the children's mother had finally lost patience, and through a deal
with an Arab she had met one day in the Old City, she had acquired Georgette in part exchange.

"Can't he be George, too?" Felicity had asked. "George was so nice."

"No, he can't be George, because he isn't George," Mary had said.
"He's a different donkey, so he ought to have a different name."

"I know," Helen had said suddenly, "let him be 'Georgette' because that's the same . . . and it's different." So Georgette he became, and every morning at about eleven, when the heat was beginning to shimmer on the ripening corn, A-eed, with his white, cotton kaffiyeh fixed firmly on his head by the two black rings of his argal, would set off, stick in hand, goading the gentle Georgette up the steps and out into the field. Sometimes the children went with him, following single file along the narrow path through the corn, past the scattered olive trees to the road, a quarter of a mile away.

It was always an adventure going to Herod's Gate, because there were so many things that could happen. First of all, Abou Seleem's little shop might be open. If so, and they had remembered to ask beforehand, they might be able to buy one of the special boxes of Cadbury's chocolate biscuits.

As they rounded the corner, the first thing was to see if his awning was down, and if it was, they knew he would be there, concealed somewhere in the dark shadows inside. The chocolate biscuits were packed in seductive boxes covered with gold paper, and inside, each biscuit was wrapped either

Herod's Gate, Jerusalem, ca. 1920

in red, blue, or silver tinfoil. The first time they had gone to Abou Seleem's, their mother had been with them, and she had had a long conversation with the friendly old Arab while the children waited anxiously to see whether she would notice and buy one of the fascinating boxes of biscuits.

After the usual exchanges, Abou Seleem had asked, "And has the honorable lady any children?"

"But of course, you see them here," their mother had answered, "and I have two more little girls at home."

The old man had waved his hands deprecatingly. "Girl children are of no importance," he said. "I mean, have you any sons?"

And Felicity had felt the blush of mortification rising in her cheeks. Why couldn't she have been a boy? But she had known it was impossible ever since that sad November afternoon at Campden, years ago, when her hair had been cut short for the first time . . . and nothing happened: she was still a girl! She had been lifted onto the nursery table in her button boots, after the tea things had been cleared away, and in the fading light, lit by the flickering of the fire behind its tall wire guard, her straggling curls had been cut to a neat, boyish crop. Now, she would really turn into a boy! Tense with a secret expectation, she had gone down to the playroom clutching a comb wrapped round with tissue paper. This was to provide music to help the transformation. She had climbed onto the rocking horse, and, rocking herself dreamily to and fro to her favorite tune, "Where ha' ye been a' the day, Bonnie Laddie, Hieland laddie?" waited for the change to take place.

The memory of that first great disillusionment swept over her again now as she looked down at her dust-whitened sandals. Then she heard her mother's voice saying staunchly, "I don't want sons; I am very pleased to have four daughters," and her laugh rang as the old Arab shrugged his shoulders pityingly.

If Abou Seleem's was shut, or he had no biscuits, they went on, where the dusty road dipped down. Suddenly there opened out below them a wide flat stretch of ground, beyond which rose the castellated walls of the Old City and Herod's Gate. This open space was used as a resting place for camels on their way to the Mountains of Moab and the Dead Sea, and one of the excitements of going to fetch water with A-eed was to see if there were any camels there. You could tell, even before you reached the crest of the

road, by standing quite still and listening. If you heard an intermittent, muffled rumbling sound, it meant camels, and the thing was to see how many
there were.

"I wonder if it's hundreds and hundreds," Mary would say, and Felicity
would add, "It might even be thousands!" And they would run on ahead and
look down. And there they were! Hundreds of them, lying resting, with their
legs folded under them, while the few little donkeys, who each led six or seven
camels, hobbled with chains and weights to prevent their straying, tried to
find grazing on the barren, baked, brown earth. Sometimes Georgette would
break into an amble down the easy slope of the road, letting out a friendly
bray in greeting to the tethered donkeys below; and Mary and Felicity would
scamper laughingly after him, eager to get a nearer sight of the camels.

The resting camel drivers lounged in groups, their swarthy faces
wrapped round with red-edged, white kaffiyehs and their heavy, quilted
jackets grey with dust. How hot those jackets must be, Felicity thought, and
the long hair coats with no proper sleeves in which some of them were
rolled as they lay stretched out sleeping on the ground. And how hot the
camels must be too, with their great loads strapped on their backs. Each
camel had a load, either of straw or merchandise sewn into sacks, and on top
of some of these, wooden, cradle-like saddles were built for the drivers to sit
upon. Some of the halters were of old rope or frayed webbing, but sometimes there were really smart ones among them, stitched with bright blue
and yellow beads, while hanging down their foreheads would be the flat,
blue and white discs with the small black spot in the middle, to keep away
the Evil Eye.

"Don't they look scornful!" Mary said, as the two children stood and
watched the slow movement of the camels' heads on their long necks with
the loose folds of skin and the gentle, rhythmic chewing of their soft, velvet
lips. How those same velvet lips could envelope the spiky balls of the purple
thistle heads without being hurt was a perpetual mystery to the children.
With horrified fascination they would watch the camels' lips jut out, and
glimpse the slanting, yellow teeth as a purple ball, spikes and all, vanished inside and the slow chewing continued as before. And all the while, with
heavy-lidded, supercilious eyes, they stared the children out and slowly
turned their heads to watch them now as they moved on to Herod's Gate.

Camels at the Damascus Gate, Jerusalem, ca. 1920

And Felicity could feel those dark eyes, and the blue and white bead-eyes, and the Evil Eye itself, all boring into her back as she walked.

How difficult indeed it must be to reach the Kingdom of Heaven, if it were really easier for one of those camels, with their great loads and their humps, to pass through the eye of a needle! Even if it were like one of Nannie's largest darners, unless there were some magic they could use to make them grow smaller, like Alice did when she ate the bit of mushroom.

The tap of the public water supply was inside Herod's Gate itself, and A-eed and Georgette and the two children passed out of the blinding sun and into the black, echoing shadow of the great archway. A government official came at 11 o'clock each morning to unlock the tap for an hour, and a queue of people with petrol cans and earthen pots gathered to collect their day's supply of water.

While the children held Georgette, A-eed untied the tins and took his place among the peasant women in their brightly embroidered black dresses and their white veils and the Muslim women, all in black, whose faces even were completely hidden by black veils. What sort of faces did they have inside those mysterious veils? Or did they have faces at all, Felicity sometimes wondered. But she could only guess when a sudden wind flattened a veil against a face, molding it into a vague black nose and mouth and chin that looked hardly human.

Battered, clanking petrol cans were produced, and big brown earthenware pitchers with handles at either side. One by one they were filled and lifted onto the heads of the waiting women who then turned and went away with that wonderful, stately, gliding walk that looked so easy and was so hard to do as the children had discovered when they tried it with a book during their rest one afternoon. "Perhaps they practiced for hours and hours before breakfast when they were littler," Mary had suggested.

Then it was A-eed's turn, and the cans were filled and strapped on the donkey's back, and with heavings and shoutings and a few gentle blows with the stick, Georgette moved reluctantly under the dark archway of the gate and out into the sun again.

"Look, Mary! The camels are moving!" Felicity called suddenly. "A-eed, wait, wait, we want to watch them."

Slowly, unhurriedly, the camels were getting up. Perched on their high saddles, the drivers incredibly kept their balance while the camels, still kneeling on their front legs, untucked the hind ones, and straightened them out. A cloud of brown dust and powdered chaff rose round each one as it stood up, rumbling protestingly. Soon, roped together and ranged in lines, they moved off, one behind the other, with a little donkey proudly leading the way. Down the road they swung silently on their great, soft, padding feet, their heads high and scornful on their curved necks, and the children stood and watched them till they disappeared round the corner of the great wall, and only a dust cloud remained.

"Where are they going, A-eed?"

"To Salt, beyond the Mountains of Moab," he answered smiling. "Do you wish to go with them?"

Felicity screwed up her eyes, and shading them with her hand, looked far away to where the hazy mountain range merged into the hot sky. Perhaps one day she might ride with the camels into that magic distance, perched on a high saddle, with no fear of the Evil Eye, because of a flat glass bead clutched tightly in her hand. Then, as they started the hot trudge up the hill home, she turned to Mary and said, "What d'you think it'll be for dinner?"

7

AS SOON as they were well installed in Wadi el Jose, the two elder children began going to the American Colony school, and every morning they set off across the field on the start of the mile walk. After crossing the field above the house, the first thing they came to was the Muslim Slum, the name given by Mary and Felicity to a big, square barrack of a building standing by itself in a patch of stony ground. All its windows were barred, and on the bars were tied mysterious flapping rags of faded black cloth. The Slum seemed to house an incredible number of ragged Muslim women and their children.

When one of the big, leather-hooded carriages came by, with its Arab coachman whipping a bony pony, a hoard of barefooted children with matted hair would tumble out of the house and run, screaming, behind it to catch hold of the springs at the back and ride upon them, swinging.

Once, in a mood of wild daring, Felicity had tried it too, and for one thrilling moment, had gripped the dusty springs and swung with her legs tucked up as the carriage sped, bumping over the stony road. Mary had stood horrified and unbelieving, shouting, "Get off, Fifi! Get off! That's very naughty!" And always afterward, if Felicity were going to do something that was not allowed, or tell on Mary for something she had done, she was threatened with, "If you do, I'll tell about that time when you rode on the back of the carriage at the Muslim Slum."

After the Slum came the Wall. This was where the little Arab girl who had St. Vitus' dance used to sit. "That's what happens to little girls who fidget all the time," Nannie had warned. "They get St. Vitus' dance, and can never sit still any more." The little girl used to sit leaning her thin shoulders against the Wall, her head twitching, so that her tangled hair fell into her eyes and had perpetually to be swept aside with a thin brown jerking hand. Felicity tried hard not to stare at her too much because she knew it was rude, but an irresistible something drew her to look back over her shoulder after she had passed, and there were the little girl's sad, restless eyes watching her, and her small dusty bare legs jerking up and down.

Opposite the Wall was another wall, in which was set a large pair of iron gates. These were the gates of the Fourth Commandment, and, as Felicity went by, she always paused and peered between the rusty bars to see if she could catch a glimpse of the manservant, or the maidservant, or the "stranger-that-is-within-thy-gates."

At the end of the road was the Arab playground. This was a large, flat, arid space used as a football ground by the boys of an Arab school whose buildings were nearby. Crossing this playground was the worst part of the walk, and the children would hesitate and look at each other before they left the safety of the Wall. Would the boys be inside doing their lessons or out-side playing? If the playground was empty and silent as they ventured onto it, they breathed a sigh of relief and knew they could take their time, but if they heard the sounds of shouting and playing as they stood at the corner of the Wall listening, they had to steel themselves for the ordeal of crossing.

There was always a chance that they might not be noticed, and a wild, unreasonable hope that some cloak of invisibility might descend upon the two of them so that they could walk unseen through the midst of their ene-mies; but it never seemed to happen, and before they had got very far, the shouting and jeering started, and, if panic seized them and they ran, the boys began to throw stones. They were never very big stones and they didn't re-ally hurt, even if they pattered against the backs of your bare legs, but there was something very frightening about the gamble as to whether it would be possible to get across the seemingly endless stretch of hard brown earth without being noticed.

Every so often, after a particularly alarming passage, Mary would tell their mother, who would then make a raid on the schoolmaster and com-plain. After that, it would be all right for a bit; the boys would only look up from their marbles and the games they played with polished, whitened knuckle bones, and only laugh as the children passed and make remarks in Arabic, the jist of which was quite easy to understand.

Beyond the playground was Smelly Lane, a narrow alley between the blind side of a house and a high stone wall. Smelly Lane seemed to enclose in its short length all the sun of the day and all the strong smells of Jerusalem. The walls were so high and white and hot that the smells seemed to be trapped between them and could never get out. Once the children had found a dead black cat there, its stiff little body already collecting flies and ants, adding an extra pungency to the heavy air. Pariah dogs haunted Smelly Lane, and on days when the smells were particularly breathtaking, the children held their noses and ran.

The branches of a pepper tree and the pink blooms of an oleander showed over the top of the wall on the right, and Felicity was quite sure that inside was the garden of the old French song "Auprès de ma blonde" that their mother used to sing.

> Au jardin de mon père
> Les lilas sont fleuris,
> Au jardin de mon père
> Les lilas sont fleuris.
> Tous les oiseaux du monde
> Vont yfaire leurs nids;
> Auprès de ma blonde
> Qu'il fait bon, fait bon, fait bon,
> Auprès de ma blonde
> Qu'il fait bon dormir.

She couldn't see the lilacs, of course, nor all the birds of the world making their nests, but she could imagine them in their hundreds, circling round a little summer house in which *ma blonde,* with whom it was so good to be, lay like the sleeping beauty herself, her golden hair all around her.

It was in Smelly Lane (later on, after Helen had started going to school too) that Mary had her Great Adventure. Felicity had not been well and had been kept from school so that Mary and Helen walked home together. Nursery tea was already begun when they arrived late, Mary pale and strangely agitated, dragging a panting and slightly tearful Helen behind her. Breathlessly she told her story while Felicity listened wide-eyed and even Prudy sat still and didn't fidget.

When they were halfway through the lane, between the high stone walls, they met an Arab girl, not much bigger than Mary, who greeted them cheerfully and stopped to talk. Suddenly she caught sight of the safety pin in Helen's scarf. It was a bright new pin, keeping in place the white silk scarf that was crossed under Helen's chin and tucked inside her black-and-white-checked tweed coat.

"I think she wanted the safety pin, only I didn't know what she was saying at first," Mary said, "and then, *what* do you think she did?"

Felicity, speechless with suspense, shook her head.

"She picked up a huge, huge stone, and held it over her head, and she shouted at me that if I didn't give her the safety pin, she would *kill* me with the piece of rock!"

In the silence that followed this dramatic statement, Nannie's cup rattled into her saucer as she put it down hurriedly.

"Well, I never!" she said, and Felicity whispered, almost inaudibly, "Go on!"

Mary had undone the pin and held it out with frightened, fumbling fingers while Helen cowered behind, clutching the skirts of her sister's coat. The Arab child snatched it from her, and her mouth flashed into a smile. She dropped the rock and, her eyes shining, pinned the bright treasure into the front of her embroidered dress.

"I'll give you something in exchange," she said and, lifting up her long skirts, routed until she found in their folds a rusty safety pin, bent with age and use, which she laboriously fastened into Helen's scarf in place of the other.

"You must come to my house one day, and eat with me," she said, "and meet my old grandmother."

Then she shook Mary warmly by the hand and ran off across the fields. Going to school next day, Mary showed Felicity exactly where it had all happened. "And here's the actual rock she was going to kill me with," Mary said. "Isn't it, Helen?" And Helen, her hazel eyes big and dark, had nodded solemnly.

Leaving Smelly Lane behind and the oleanders of the hidden "*jardin de mon père*," the road stretched on, long and white, until at the end it turned a corner, and there were the pine and pepper trees, and the low stone wall that bounded the playground of the American Colony school. There were between thirty and forty children in the school, ranging in age from the babies who sat in the little red armchairs in the kindergarten to the very Big Ones in the top class, who were so dignified that they looked almost too big to go to school at all. Most of them were Swedish Americans, the children of the colony itself, but there were a few others, like Mary and Felicity, who came from outside. There was Eva, small and quiet and half-Egyptian, with her fringe of dark hair and her big, black eyes; and Meleky, a Muslim Arab, who, although she was twelve and soon going to be married, was not much bigger than Mary. The only other English child was a round, pink-faced eight-year-old called John.

The Americans used to tease the English children about the way they said "to*mah*toes" instead of "to*may*toes," and would chant after them with a mock-English accent: "Wouldn't you *lahf* to see a *cahf* run down the *pahth* in an hour and a *hahf* to have a *bahth?*" and Mary, Felicity, and John would retort with the same rhyme in exaggerated American.

All the teachers were members of the colony and were called Uncle or Aunt, Sister or Brother. Brother John, little and old and white-haired with a pink cherubic face, took Scripture, and Sister Hoolda, prim but friendly, whose behind stuck out when she walked, took reading, writing, and spelling. Then there was Brother Elijah, whom the children didn't see so much of, and who was very old too, with a yellow-brown skin and a smooth, bald head fringed with sparse white hair. Sister Tilly didn't do any teaching; the sewing room was her province and there she did the alterations to everybody's clothes. A long stone staircase led up outside the schoolhouse to her work room, which was over the classrooms. We would see her stout figure in its black skirt and stiff petersham belt going slowly up the stairs, her plump, pink face getting pinker and pinker under her white cork helmet as she neared the top.

But of all the teachers, Uncle Eena was the one who was really interesting. He was quite young and had very blue eyes and very blonde hair, and he took drill and gym in a stone-floored room with ropes and the swinging rings and the trapeze, and he always stood by the side of the piano when Anna Grace, one of the biggest girls, played the hymns at prayers.

The morning started with the whole school gathered together to sing hymns. They were not the sort of hymns you had in church, but were more like songs, with good, quick, rollicking tunes.

Count your blessings,
Count them one by one,
Then you will remember
What the Lord has done.

was one of Felicity's favorites, along with "Bringing Home the Sheaves." But
perhaps the most exciting of them was the one about Daniel:

Dare to be a Daniel
Dare to stand alone,
Dare to have a Purpose Firm,
And dare to make it known.

It was Helen who got the words mixed and always sang, "Dare to have a
Purple Sperm," but as nobody knew what a Purpose Firm was, a Purple
Sperm really seemed the more sensible version of the two and was at least
colorful. And so, as Felicity sang, there rose before her a vision of Daniel,
heavily draped in purple, daring everything and everybody, while the tawny
lions lay meekly at his feet.

The Purple Sperm acquired another meaning for the children too. Nannie had made their mother a small box for her dressing table with a text
embroidered on the inside of the lid in colored silks. This embroidery was
a speciality of Nannie's. It was done in cross-stitch on closely perforated
white card. The text in various colors was sometimes the sole decoration,
but when she wanted to make it particularly beautiful, she would stick
pressed wild flowers, gathered from the Wadi, round the embroidered
words.

The lid of their mother's box was too small to accommodate flowers but
the words were surrounded by a neat cross-stitched border in green silk. The
whole of the outside of the box was covered in a rich, purple satin, and in it
their mother kept her nail scissors and a button hook, a little wooden stick
with a white rubber hoof on one end for pushing down the skin round one's
nails, and her special pearl-handled nail cleaner. This box obviously *was* the
Purple Sperm, and Felicity found it hardly surprising that with something so
unique and so beautiful in his possession, Daniel should have been able to
dare so much.

Besides supervising gym and helping with the hymns, Uncle Eena taught French from a large picture of a farmyard that showed people and animals who must have been peculiar to France, for they were certainly never seen in Jerusalem. This picture unrolled like a map and was hung on the wall when the time came for the French lesson. As Uncle Eena pointed to each extraordinary object with a little wand and gave the French word for it, the children repeated it after him.

The playground, like every other playground, was flat and brown with plenty of loose stones which could be used for the "gold and silver" in "Tom Tiddler's Ground." The school played its own variant of "French and English" by turning it into Americans against English; but in this form, with Mary, Felicity, and John the only ones on the English side against a horde of twenty or more Americans, it never lasted long. It was a forlorn hope from the start, and Felicity's heart sank when it was suggested because she knew it meant a short, despairing effort to prevent the exultant Americans from grabbing all the treasure in the first minute, for even if you caught some of them and put them behind the lines, they were rescued again before you had time to turn around. The bigger boys sometimes made everybody play another less pleasant game. It was a sort of tag, but when you were caught, you were taken by two of them and, with your arms held firmly to your sides, were marched down to one of the cedar trees at the bottom of the playground to have your nose rubbed against the pink-brown bark.

Felicity had her own friends among the schoolchildren. There was Louisa, with her gold-brown hair and big blue eyes, who was almost her twin and who wore a little gold ring on her third finger that Felicity secretly coveted; and Louisa's brother Jock. Jock was two years older and only deigned to play with her if she could show she was worthy of it by daring to do all the things the big boys did. Neils, a quiet little half-Swedish boy with a pale face, followed Felicity about with silent devotion, but he never said very much. She found Spafford and David, two brothers who were cousins of Jock and Louisa's, more interesting. She liked Spafford the best of all because, although he too was two years older than she, he treated her as an equal and would take her climbing and show her secret hiding places.

Sometimes in the holidays Mary and Felicity would be invited to spend the whole day with Spafford and David, or with Jock and Louisa's family in their house with the big garden next door. Here there was an immensely high swing and beside it a high climbing pole up which Felicity would try to swarm like the big boys. But she could never get more than a quarter of the way up and nearly always got splinters in her knickers sliding down again.

One wonderful day they went for a picnic to Ain Karim.

"Can't I go too?" Helen had asked. "I go to school now."

"Not this time, Heleny," their mother answered. "This time it's for the Big Ones. You shall go when you're a little older."

"But I *am* four," Helen persisted.

"Four is much too little," Felicity said.

"Four," Helen persisted.

"Four is much too little," Felicity said. "You have to be seven *at least* before you can go on picnics to Ain Karim."

So Helen was consoled with a promise of tea under the olive tree with Nannie and Prudy while the two Big Ones went off on their picnic.

The children were all assembled at the American Colony, and then with the various Uncles, Aunts, Brothers, and Sisters who were going too. Laden with picnic baskets, they all piled into the large wagonette that was brought out for such occasions. It was a glorious and exciting expedition. When they arrived, they spent hours exploring, ranging among the olive trees and the rocks and in and out of dark hot shadow and burning, throbbing sunlight.

Spafford and Felicity roamed away together by themselves and after a long ramble sat down to rest on a big smooth boulder.

"It burns through my knickers," Felicity said, as she wriggled on the hot stone. "Doesn't it burn you too, Spafford?"

"I think my trousers are thicker than your knickers," Spafford answered, "but it's getting hot now!" The he jumped off and stood up.

"Let's roll it over and see if there's anything underneath it," he said, "We might find hidden treasure and then we'd be rich for ever and ever and live happily all the days of our life."

Felicity slithered to the ground at his side, and together they put their weight against the boulder and shoved. Suddenly, a yellow scorpion scuttled out from underneath it, almost over their feet, and shot away among the stones and the rustling pine needles.

"Oh, a scorpion, Spafford, it might have stung us!"

"Sister Hoolda was stung by a scorpion once," Spafford said solemnly. "She told us. It was in her hat only she didn't know. And when she put it on, it was like one of her great hatpins going *right* into her head!"

"One of her *huge* hatpins with the bead on the end?"

"Yes, like them."

"Did she die?" Felicity asked awestruck.

"No, of course not, silly! How could she die? She's alive now, isn't she? But she had to go to the doctor quickly and he cut a bit out of her head where the scorpion had bitten her so that the poison wouldn't go all over inside her."

Felicity shuddered as the awful picture rose before her eyes of Sister Hoolda battling with the scorpion in her hat, all mixed up with her hair and the hatpins. For a long time afterward, she looked carefully inside her sun helmet before she put it on.

They were already hungry when they heard voices calling them to dinner, and they raced each other to the shade of the pine trees where the rest of the party was collecting and where everything had been laid out on the warm, pine-smelling, dappled ground. What wonderful things there were to eat! Best of all (and these they could hardly wait till the end of the meal to enjoy) were the melons!—great big green melons with dark pink insides that you had to eat standing up and bending over so the juice didn't run down all over you.

In the middle of the afternoon, there was a dramatic moment when Eva swallowed a star-shaped yellow sweet whole, which stuck in her throat. With incredible boldness and presence of mind, Uncle Eena, who heard her choking, picked her up by the heels and held her upside down while he shook her. Horror-struck, Mary and Felicity watched Eva's protesting hands flapping wildly till at last the offending sweet dropped out of her mouth onto the pine needles and she was sat down, spluttering and tearful, but saved from a fearful fate. Only Uncle Eena would have dared to do that, Felicity thought, and he seemed more admirable than ever.

It was dark long before they arrived home. The stars were out in the warm indigo velvet of the sky when they were lifted sleepily out of the wagonette.

"Did you have a lovely time?" their mother asked.

"Oh, yes! And Eva got a sweet stuck in her throat and nearly choked!" Mary replied.

"But Uncle Eena turned her upside down and *shook* her and it fell out again," Felicity put in hurriedly.

"How very exciting!" her mother said, "and now, into bed, both of you, quickly." In the middle of the night Mary was very sick. "Too much melon," was Nannie's laconic comment.

8

"MY WORKMEN have finished repairing another stretch of the walls," the children's father said one morning at breakfast. "Who would like to come round with me?"

"Me! Me!" shouted Mary and Felicity together.

"All right, you shall both come. I shall be starting in about half an hour's time, so you had better run along and get yourselves ready; I don't want to be kept waiting."

Going round the walls was one of the things the children liked doing better than almost anything else, so it was hardly likely they would keep him waiting. In fact they were both hopping about on the steps by the front door for some minutes before he came out of the house in his white linen coat and pale corduroy riding breeches and strode before them up the steps and out into the field.

The rounds always started at the Jaffa Gate. Felicity's favorite gate was Herod's Gate, because it was quieter and more secret and somehow she felt that things which were almost magic might happen there. Her next best gate was the Damascus Gate with its busy crowds; and once through the archway, she liked to walk past the line of old men sitting on the ground puffing away at their hookahs. But although the Jaffa Gate took only third place in her affections it still had its points.

To begin with there was the melon market, which ran down near the Citadel, with its pile upon pile of stacked green melons and the thronging, shouting Arabs buying and selling. Then there was Mr. Ohan's shop, with carpets and embroideries hanging up, and brass and copper bowls and candlesticks, and old silvery looking plates and dishes. The children's father usually paid a call on Mr. Ohan, a smiling little Armenian, who would greet them, bowing and rubbing his hands together. He always offered his guests

The city walls, Jerusalem, ca. 1919

a special cup of black coffee and swept aside the rustling strings of the bead curtain that kept out the flies to usher them into the dark interior of his shop.

The coffee was served in tiny blue and white china cups without handles. Felicity had tried it once, but it was too syrupy and bitter; so while their father sat and sipped his coffee and discussed the price of carpets and amber and embroidery with Mr. Ohan, she and Mary poked around in the warm, dark, musty corners of the shop, whispering to each other as they looked at all the mysterious treasures that were Mr. Ohan's stock in trade.

At last their father drained his cup and said good-bye and then went out with his daughters through the rustling beads into the glare of the sunlight.

A stairway tucked behind the Jaffa Gate led directly up into the walls, and once on the level of the roofs, the real adventure began. The first thing to do was to look out through the castellations at the top of the wall into the streets and the busy crowds below. There were the familiar shops; there was the row of carriages waiting to be hired, some with one horse, and some,

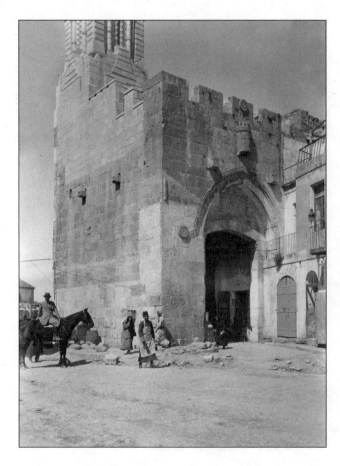

The Jaffa Gate, Jerusalem, with the author's father on horseback, 1920; reproduced by permission of King's College, Cambridge.

more expensive and faster, with two. (Surely that was Akhmed down there with his two white horses, which the children's father always tried to get if they were going on a long expedition.) The drivers dozed on their seats while the horses stood patiently, twitching their ears and whisking their tails to keep off the everlasting flies. How different it all looked from so high up, Felicity thought, and yet, how just the same.

"Come along," her father called, "We mustn't delay or we shan't have time to see the new bit."

So she tore herself away and followed him and Mary along the rampart. To begin with, the stone path they had to follow was quite wide. On her right was the wall itself, which was high, so she could only see out through the castellated parts, but on her left there was nothing. Sometimes there

The Citadel,
Jerusalem, ca. 1920

were houses right up against where they were walking, so close that she could almost have stepped onto their domed roofs, but there were also stretches of emptiness with nothing but a long drop into a distant street if she were to fall over. So she walked very carefully.

Suddenly the rampart path would narrow to a width of only a couple of feet, and here their father had had little iron handrails fixed into the wall and painted with red lead so that there was something to hold onto until the path grew wider again. Sometimes a fig tree growing in the courtyard of an Arab house below would stretch up its branches to the walls so that they had to step over its leaves as they passed, and sometimes the path stopped altogether and they had to climb up or down small irregular steps with more little iron handrails for support.

The author with her mother on the rampart walk, ca. 1920

"Look Fifi! We've got to Herod's Gate!" Mary called, and there they were, looking down from an Olympian height onto the water tap where A-eed brought Georgette to fill the petrol cans. And looking over the other side of the wall to the world outside the city was the camels' resting ground, empty and deserted today, except for a few children playing and the "hill which is called Golgotha."

"There is a green hill far away / Without a city wall . . ."

Felicity hummed the words to herself, but as usual, they just didn't seem to her to make sense. If that really was the hill where Jesus was crucified, it wasn't green at all, but brown like everything else; and it wasn't *without* a city wall, it was *with* one, the wall they were standing on now, and very close to it too, with only the narrow white road running in between. Perhaps whoever wrote the hymn had never been to Jerusalem and didn't really know what it looked like.

"There's the road that leads up home," Mary said, pointing. "And there goes the one the camels take when they're going to the Mountains of Moab. Oh, Daddy, do we have to turn back now? This is such a *nice* bit."

Their father looked down at them both and smiled as he saw their hot, eager faces. "No, this time we don't have to turn back," he said, "because now we're coming to the new bit we've just finished repairing. Now watch where you go, both of you—Fifi behind me and Mary last—we come to a very narrow bit in a few minutes."

So they started off again, with Felicity between her father and Mary. But only half her mind was on the narrowing rampart at her feet and her father's corduroys and shining brown gaiters in front of her; the rest of it strayed out over the wall to the exciting new views beyond. The rampart walk followed alongside the camel's road now for quite a distance so that she almost felt she was walking with them toward the mountains, and then, suddenly, it made a sharp turn to the right and she found herself looking out over the end of the wall where it dropped steeply to the valley below. And there was a sight of almost unimagined loveliness.

In the far, hazy distance, between the purple-bluish peaks of the mountains, lay the Dead Sea itself, a narrow strip of an indescribably lovely blue, softened by the heat and the miles between; and to the right, much nearer, the fairy-tale Russian church, its golden onion-shaped domes glowing as though they were on fire, grew out of the cypresses and the olives of the Garden of Gethsemane.

"Oh, Daddy, look!" both children exclaimed, as they rested their elbows on the hot stones of the wall and gazed out at the double wonder. "Our Golden Onions! Don't they look lovely?"

"And the Dead Sea too," Felicity added. "It isn't hidden from here; you can really see it."

Spafford had told her that the Dead Sea was so salty you could sit on the top of it like a cork, and even if you tried to sink, you couldn't. "If you dived

in," he had said, "your head would stay down at the bottom and your feet up in the air, and you'd soon be dead. That's why it's called the Dead Sea, see?"

But looking at the wonderful blue of it now, half haze, half brilliance, it was hard to believe that it could be anything but kind and beautiful, and as Felicity felt her father's hand on her shoulder, she let out a long, contented sigh.

9

IF THE CHILDREN'S FATHER were not going round the walls, he might be visiting Mr. Ohanessian and his pottery makers, and with a little persuasion, he might take them with him. To reach Mr. Ohanessian's, they had to thread their way through the narrow streets of the Old City, jostled by shouting Arabs who tried to force their loaded donkeys through the crowd. They were so narrow, those little streets, that there seemed only to be a small strip of brilliant sunlight running down the middle of the cobbles, and encroaching on either hand were the dark caves of the souks' mysterious shops. Chains hung down from their hidden ceilings to help the shopkeepers heave themselves over their counters if they wanted to get out into the street.

Holding each other by the hand so as not to get lost in the crowds, the two children followed their father's long strides. They passed the steps where the old Arab sat tinning copper saucepans and paused a moment to watch. He had just finished scrubbing one out with sand and water and had taken his little moving flame to melt the cake of tin and rub it over the saucepan's worn inside.

"It's a pity we didn't bring our big one with us that's used for the apricot jam," Mary said. "We could have done if we'd known we were coming this way. Mummie said it needed retinning."

"He does it so quickly, doesn't he!" Felicity said, as the molten silvery stuff covered the saucepan, which, a moment later, looked gleaming and new again. "Almost like magic!"

Reluctantly they moved on and into the souk where all the shops on one side sold the little oily sesame cakes. Like the bodies of flat, shortbread mice, they were laid out in rows on the great black metal baking tins, a faint dusting of flour-fine sugar all over them.

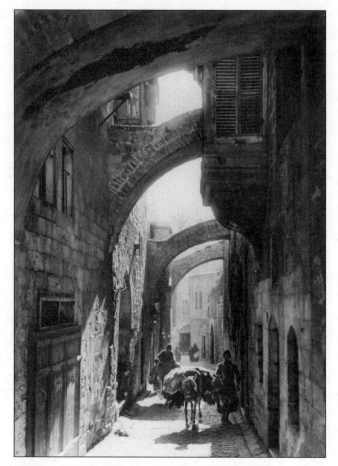

Street scene in the Old City, Jerusalem, ca. 1920

Somewhere toward the end of this souk was the shop where the big slabs of hell*a*wa stood, huge slabs of it, made of nuts or some unidentified ingredient—the children didn't know what. It looked like pale, oily concrete, and it oozed honey and sesame oil onto the black metal tin on which it was kept. It was sweet and mysterious and must have been eaten by the characters in the Arabian Nights as they told their tales. But it was no good asking their father if they might take some home with them for tea because he would only say, "No, *not* when you're with me. Ask your mother some time when you come down this way with her. I can't carry that gummy stuff about all morning."

"But, Daddy, *I'll* carry it," Mary would say, but it was no good, and he would just pretend he hadn't heard and stalk on ahead so that they had to run to catch up with him.

When they were with their mother and she stopped to buy some hell*a*wa, the Arab shopkeeper swept the flies aside with a bunch of leaves and eagerly chopped off a large square chunk, which he weighed in a brass scale hanging from a chain. Then he tossed it into a piece of rough brown paper and handed it to one of the children with a flashing smile. But however carefully you carried it, before you got home and could put it into its special pewter dish with the elegant filigree lid that rose into a sharp point like one of the minarets, the oil always seeped through the paper in dark patches.

Not very far beyond the hell*a*wa shop, they came to an even narrower side turning and went in at a doorway, cool with shadows. As soon as they got inside, they were met by the wonderful damp smell of potters' clay. And there sat Mr. Ohanessian's workmen, turning their wheels with bare skillful feet, while out of the lumps of wet clay on their little round spinning tables grew the most fascinating and unexpected shapes. As the children watched, a lump of glistening clay rose upward like a living thing. With a touch of the workman's wet brown hand, it narrowed from a round base to a slender neck and then flowered out again to a wider top. What was it going to be? One of those tall-necked vases like the painted blue and yellow one their mother used for flowers in the drawing room? Or a water pitcher, or a jug? It was too tall already for a bowl.

Suddenly the wheel stopped and the table slowed to a standstill. With a deft pressure of his finger and thumb, the potter squeezed the rim of the pot and, all of a sudden, it was a jug with a lip ready for pouring. Then he took a piece of wire, sliced the jug off the turntable, stood it outside to dry, and in a matter of seconds, there was another shapeless lump spinning and growing under his hands.

In the room next door, the painters sat at dusty trestle tables amid piles of plates and vases, bowls and jugs. With delicately poised brushes they transformed the dull, whitish-grey of the baked clay into glories of turquoise blue and yellow and black. The children stopped beside a man painting black Arabic letters—swirls and strokes and dots, onto the blue background of a big flat tile. When Mary asked what it was for, their father answered, "It's one of

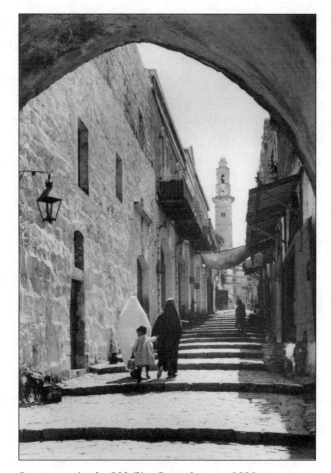

Street scene in the Old City, Jerusalem, ca. 1920

the tiles that go round the outside of the Dome of the Rock, and he is writing passages from the Koran, the book of the Prophet Mohammed. Now that you've seen them close, you'll know what they really look like when we see them presently, high up in the sunlight under the great dome."

Felicity thought of her paint box at home and wished she could keep her colors as brilliant as those of the Arab painter. But it was so difficult not to get them dirty, especially the yellow; the least little bit of some other color left in her brush when she thought she had really rinsed it clean, and everything became muddy, and she could never capture a clear, transparent yellow again.

Of course it didn't matter so much when it was something like the picture of the three witches from Macbeth that she had painted the other day, whose dark ragged clothes and pointed hats had gradually been submerged in a rising tide of smoke and darkness, over which she had rather lost control. But when it was a fairy, or an angel, or a star, it was heartbreaking if a golden wing or a shaft of heavenly light were suddenly tinged with cabbage. She made a firm resolution, there and then, to give her paint box a good wipe out before she used it again and to be even more careful about washing out her brushes.

"Well, and what is my Popatoos thinking about?" her father's voice broke in on her reflections. But it was too difficult to explain, so she just shook her head and said, "Nothing."

"I know what," he said suddenly. "Shall we ask Mr. Ohanessian whether one of his men could make each of you a money box, painted in turquoise, blue and black, with a little knob on the top, and a slit at the side to put the money in, and a fine glaze over it all? Would that suit you?"

"With our names on in Arabic?" Mary asked.

"With your names on in Arabic, if you like, certainly," he agreed.

"Can we watch him make them now?" Felicity asked eagerly.

But her father only laughed and pulled her ear and said, "Patience, patience!" and led them back through the clay-smelling passage to talk about it to Mr. Ohanessian, and to say good-bye before they went out into the street.

"Are we going to the Dome of the Rock now, Daddy?" Mary asked as soon as they were outside.

"And can we see the Wailing Wall on the way, too?" Felicity put in quickly.

"Yes, if we don't dawdle, I think we've just got time," their father said, and he set off ahead of them at a brisk pace.

The Wailing Wall had a peculiar fascination of its own that gripped the children as soon as they came round the corner at the end of it and heard the strange muttering, moaning sound of the Jews praying. It was different from anything else and it gave you a strange feeling, as though it was private somehow and you ought not to be watching. The blue sky shone down and the great white scarred stones of the Wall rose up to meet it, and yet you almost felt as though you were in church.

Money boxes belonging to the author and her sister Mary (front view, top, and back view with names in Arabic, bottom); photographs by Michael Marten.

The Wailing Wall, Jerusalem, ca. 1920

There stood the old Jews in their side curls and flat black hats or skull caps, some with prayer books and some just leaning against the wall praying. And there were women too, in dark dresses with shawls about their heads, who kissed the smooth, weathered stones as they prayed, or knocked their heads against them.

"Do you think they're *always* so sad?" Felicity whispered to her sister. "They must hurt themselves, bumping their heads like that."

"It's just their way of saying their prayers, I think," Mary whispered back, and then they saw their father beckoning them, and followed him out again into the cheerful, noisy shouting of the souks.

It didn't take long to get from the Wailing Wall to the Dome of the Rock. There, the spell descended on them as soon as they stepped into the silence of the Temple area. For Felicity there was a special magic about the great domed building, standing so independently in its white stone court. The sun seemed to collect itself and pour down onto the big square paving

The Dome of the Rock, Jerusalem, ca. 1920

The Dome of the Rock, detail, showing tiles by Ohanessian, ca. 1920

stones so that it came back and hit her with a glare of blinding whiteness and she could feel the heat coming up through the soles of her sandals. It throbbed on her shoulders and made a hot space inside the top of her hat so that the sweat began to trickle down inside the fringe of her hair.

And out of the whiteness grew the great Temple itself, with Mr. Ohanessian's turquoise tiles, looking quite tiny now, running like a ribbon round the top of the building; and crowning it all was the pure, magnificent shape of the faintly ribbed grey dome. [The Dome was regilded only at a much later date.]

Felicity drew a deep breath, and pushed her sun helmet back from her

The Dome of the Rock, interior, with the Sacred Rock,
ca. 1920

sticky forehead. Then they walked across the blinding silence into the mosque itself. They had to stand quite still when they got inside because the blackness was so intense that they couldn't see anything at all. Then a dim shape appeared, and someone gave them soft, flapping shoes to put on over their sandals. "Why?" she had asked the first time, and had been told, "Because it is holy ground."

Slowly the darkness took shape and Felicity began to see little red lights winking here and there. And there was a wonderful smell, too, like the Arabian Nights and Ali Baba and the sugar-dusty sesame cakes baking in the black ovens of the Old City, all rolled into one.

In the middle of the Temple, when she really began to be able to see, rose the somber shape of the Sacred Rock. If she climbed up on the stone rim at the foot of the low wall enclosing it, she could rest her chin on the top and just see over it. And right in the middle of the rock's dark uneven surface was the Prophet Mohammed's giant footprint, with even the marks of his toes showing.

The two children stared at it, fascinated.

"But, Daddy, did Mohammed *really* go up to Heaven from here? Really, *really?*"

And out of the darkness, their father answered softly, "That's how the story goes."

1 O

NOT VERY LONG after the family had moved to the house in the Wadi el Jose, Hezni arrived to help Nannie in the nursery part of the house and generally to make herself useful upstairs.

"Downstairs" was almost a separate establishment, with Jameelah, the stately Arab peasant girl, to wait at the table and Waardi, the old negress, in the kitchen. Jameelah had smooth black hair twisted into a knot at the back of her neck. She moved slowly and silently on her bare feet with the same perfect erectness as the women who carried their water pitchers on their heads from Herod's Gate. The children's father insisted that she wear the black, embroidered dress of the peasants, with a colored sash wound around her waist. She had a special jacket which she wore over the dress for Sundays and feast days that was made of velvet encrusted with embroidery. Felicity loved to see her wear this best jacket, because it looked rich and gorgeous, and the brilliant reds and yellows, greens and wicked pinks stood out like jewels from its heavy folds.

Haani, the plump cook with the glass eye who had been with the family at Canon Brown's, had gone, and Waardi had taken her place. She was coal black and had come from Kartoum, and it was impossible to tell from her big, ugly, friendly face what age she was. The children thought she must be very old indeed because she was so wrinkled and because her black hands, with their fascinating, coffee-colored palms, were so gnarled and rough. Waardi would do anything for them, and would always find a corner of the kitchen and a tub of soap and water when they wanted to wash their dolls' clothes.

But Hezni definitely belonged upstairs. She had gray eyes and a thick mane of red-brown hair that hung in a heavy pigtail down the back of her blue-and-white-checked frock. She always wore a white veil over her head,

The Ashbee family's servants, Waardi, Hezni, and A-eed, ca. 1920

but the solid shape of the pigtail showed through. She was a serious little thirteen-year-old Arab girl from one of the nearby villages, and she endeared herself to the two elder children soon after her arrival by her presence of mind in dealing with a terrifyingly big spider that suddenly appeared in the corner of their bedroom. It was one of those with hairy legs two inches long and a face so large that you could almost see its malevolent expression. "Hezni, Hezni! Come quick!" Mary screamed, while Felicity struggled to get the mosquito net untucked so as to jump up onto the bed with her legs well out of the way. Forewarned by the terror in Mary's voice, Hezni rushed in with a shovel in her hand and dealt with the spider quickly and efficiently, filling the children with admiration. She then scooped up the remains and tossed them out of the window.

Among her duties, Hezni had to help get the children into bed. There was no bath in the house, and in any case, water could not have been spared to fill it had there been one, so the children had their daily "bath" in a large tin *tisht*. This was the Arabic name for the six-inch-deep metal tub that

Hezni dragged in from the nursery and stood in the middle of their bed-room floor. She would stand by while they soaped themselves, lending a helping hand with the middles of their backs where it was so difficult to reach, and would then empty a big brass jug of water over them as they stood holding onto each other in the shallow tub.

Hezni had one failing, a tendency to disappear during the busiest part of the day when she was most needed, and that meant a hunt through house and garden till she was found in some quiet corner, usually playing happily with Mary's and Felicity's dolls.

Another favorite of the children was Ma'ssousah the milkwoman, who walked the eight miles from her village of Lifta every morning with the big pewter can of milk on her head. She never arrived later that a quarter past six so that the milk could be boiled and cooled in time for breakfast at seven. Ma'ssousah had a large family of her own and liked talking to the children, and if the milk looked a little blue and thin sometimes, it was only because she had added a drop or two of water to make up the quantity.

"Why have you put water in the milk, Ma'ssousah?" the children's mother asked one morning, looking sternly at the milkwoman's beaming, friendly face. "Ah, the lady must not be angry," Ma'ssousah said. "My nephew was thirsty and he put his lips to the can and drank. And I could not bear that your children—whom Allah bless, and give a long and happy life—should go short, so I added a little water. But, as Heaven is my witness," she added, looking fervently up at the ceiling, "it was no more than a drop."

One morning, just as the children had finished their breakfast, there was a ring at the front door bell. "Perhaps it's the Blot of Ink with our almond butter," Mary said, "Shall I go and see?"

"The Blot of Ink" was the label given by our mother Janet to the little wisp of a man, with a mournful face and side curls, who brought the daily supply of "almond butter," the deceptively beautiful name for margarine. He was so small and so nondescript in his half-Arab, half-Jewish costume, the incongruous red *ta-boosh* partly covering his wispy black hair, that the only thing he reminded you of was an inkblot that had got onto the margin of a copybook by mistake. He held the packet of almond butter already beginning to melt in his hands and hurriedly handed it over to Jameelah before a worse thing happened to it.

Ma'ssousah the milk woman, 1935

But when Mary opened the front door on this occasion, there was no Blot of Ink standing furtively on the step, with a limp packet of almond butter in a grubby palm, but one of the government inspectors. Mary came running down the stairs to fetch her mother. "It's not the Blot of Ink, Mummie, it's someone else; will you come, please?" So their mother went upstairs to see what was wanted, with Mary and Felicity close behind her.

"I believe you get your milk from Lifta, from Ma'ssousah the milk-woman," the inspector said, touching his cap politely, and referring to a little notebook in his hand.

"That's quite right," the children's mother said. "Why, is anything wrong?"

"I think it would be as well if you did not drink it today," he said. "One of her family, a young boy, has just been taken to hospital with typhoid."

"You're too late; the children have already had today's milk with their breakfast."

The inspector hastened to reassure her.

"I've no doubt it will be quite all right," he said. "I expect you always boil it. It was merely an added precaution. It would be as well to wait till we've had it all properly tested before you have any more." But the children's mother had turned to Jameelah who had joined the group and was standing behind her, listening. "Is Ma'ssousah still in the kitchen?" she asked. "If so, bring her here to me."

Shaken from her usual stately calm, Jameelah hurried downstairs while the children's mother called to Nannie to bring the jug containing the remains of the morning's milk, and in a minute she came out of the nursery into the courtyard carrying the jug in her hands.

"Is something awful going to happen, Mary?" Felicity whispered. "What's typhoid? What's Ma'ssousah done?" But Mary only said "Shh!" and then they heard Ma'ssousah's voice in rising expostulation as she came up with Jameelah from the kitchen. As the milkwoman reached the top step, the children's mother took the blue and white jug, and with a flourish, poured the milk out onto the stones of the courtyard at her feet.

"Why do you bring me poisoned milk?" she said dramatically. "Do you wish to kill my children?"

Ma'ssousah at once burst into loud lamentations.

"Bring me a knife!" she wailed, rocking herself to and fro. "I will cut off my right hand if ever I intended to bring poisoned milk to your innocent children. My nephew is ill, it is true; but he never touched the milk, may Allah strike me dead if I speak a word of anything but the truth."

There was a heavy pause. Thank goodness, no one had obeyed Ma'ssousah's frenzied demand for a knife! A-eed, out in the garden, and Waardi, in the depths of the kitchen, had probably neither of them heard what was going on, and Jameelah, her eyes larger and more lustrous than ever, seemed to be rooted to the spot. With the tears pouring down her lined brown face, Ma'ssousah seized the children's mother's hand and alternately pressed it to her forehead and covered it with kisses, beseeching her forgiveness and assuring her of her unending love and devotion.

The inspector coughed and prepared to take his departure. "Come along now, Ma'ssousah," he said, touching her on the shoulder. But she would not move till the children's mother spoke to her. "All right, Ma'ssousah, I believe you," she said at last. "Go in peace. And when the inspector tells me that your milk is clean again, you may return."

In a flash the tears were gone and the milkwoman's wet face was all smiles. Murmuring thanks and blessings, she seized first Mary's and then Felicity's hands, kissing them and pressing them to her forehead before she turned and went downstairs to the kitchen for a last cup of tea before her departure.

"She must have been speaking the truth," Felicity said as they went back to the nursery, "because Allah didn't strike her dead. I'm glad."

1 1

"I'VE A GREAT PIECE OF NEWS FOR YOU," the children's mother said to them one day at dinner. "A-eed is going to be married, and he's asked us all to come to the wedding."

"Are we *all* going, even Prudy?" Mary asked.

"No, I think Prudy is a bit too young," their mother said, "But Helen is quite old enough."

A-eed had come up to the drawing room that morning as their mother sat writing at her desk, and after kissing her hand and apologizing for interrupting her, said he had come to ask her a favor.

"My father has found me a wife," he said. "A good girl from my own village. He did not have to pay too much for her, and she can cook and sew. He told me to ask you to do us the honor of coming to the wedding."

"But of course, A-eed," she had answered, shaking him by the hand and congratulating him. "And may I bring some of my children?"

His father would be delighted to see the whole family, A-eed said. So the date was written down, and, beaming with pleasure, A-eed had gone back to the garden.

When the great day arrived, the children were dressed in their best white frocks and their straw hats with the big rosettes of cream-colored ribbon, sitting like small cabbages in the fronts of the brims. Helen was very excited as she walked between her parents in front of Mary and Felicity across the field path to the place where the carriage was waiting to take them to A-eed's village. It was their favorite carriage, and Akhmed, their favorite coachman, which added one more touch to the occasion. Akhmed went faster than all the others and his two white horses wore lovely little blue net ear caps with tassels on the ends. The tassels danced about as the horses tossed their heads to shake off the flies.

It was a long, hot drive, with Helen on the back seat under the hood between her father and mother, and Mary and Felicity facing them on the padded seat opposite. The shiny black leather was almost too hot to bear against the backs of their legs when they first sat down, and Felicity could feel the small black buttons burning through her cotton knickers. She had to sit very still, too, because the little, curling iron rails at the sides of the seat that were meant to keep you from falling out were too hot to hold.

It was the first wedding she had ever been to, and it was strange and exciting when they reached the village to see the crowds of shouting, cheerful villagers surging into the little church. It was quite small inside, too—not like the high, black-and-white gauntness of St. George's Cathedral, but warm and friendly. And there came A-eed and his bride, all dressed in white, walking up the aisle to stand before the priest and have the two gold rings put one on his finger and one on hers.

As they came out of the church afterward, A-eed, his smiling red face glistening with heat and excitement, suddenly seized Helen and lifted her onto his shoulders. Then he led the triumphant procession to the house where the reception was to be held, with his bride on his arm and Helen on his shoulders. She clutched his headdress firmly with both hands, flashing her hazel eyes regally at the delighted crowd.

On the threshold of the house the most exciting part of the ceremony took place. As they drew near, Felicity noticed a huge flat loaf of unleavened peasant bread nailed over the lintel of the door, and as the bride and bridegroom approached, the bride was handed a big knife. Fascinated, Felicity watched her reach up and struggle to cut a chunk out of the bread while her friends, laughing and shouting, hung onto her dress and caught at her arm to try to prevent her doing so. Only when a piece of bread had at last fallen from the loaf to the dust at their feet, were the couple allowed to go into the house and begin the serious business of eating and drinking.

"I *like* sitting on the floor and not having a chair or a table," Felicity whispered as she settled herself between her two sisters on a striped mattress on the floor of the rapidly filling room. "I like it too," Helen said. "And I like weddings. I wish there could be a wedding *every* day."

❧ It certainly was a feast. Peasant bread and small flat white goat cheeses and big plates of shortbreads and sesame cakes. There were huge heaps of golden apricots with their velvety skins, and green and black figs, and smudged, murky glasses of warm mulberry juice to wash it all down.

As they piled back into the carriage afterward and drove away, waved to by a happy crowd of villagers, Helen sighed contentedly. "It was a *nice* wedding, wasn't it, Mummie?" she said. "And I rode on A-eed's back, and I was taller than *anybody* else!"

A-eed's wedding was a sign that he would not be staying with the family much longer, and before many weeks had passed, a new boy, Eesa, set out with the donkey and the two children to fetch the water from the tap at Herod's Gate. Eesa was quite different from A-eed to look at as well as in other ways. He had light brown curly hair and large grey-green eyes set wide apart in a serious face. When extra guests came to dinner, he would put on his best dress with the shiny satin sash, give his hands an extra wash, and help Jameelah wait at the table.

It was Helen who, when she discovered what Eesa's name meant, came running to Prudy with a shocked look on her face. "Prudy," she said, "does he *know* is name is Jesus?" And Prudy looked up from her game under the fig tree with a slightly self-satisfied expression. "Yes, he does," she said. "I've already told him."

Eesa was very brave too. A pariah dog had found its way into the garden several nights running and had woken the children with its eerie howling, so Eesa lay in wait for it with an axe. In the early light of the morning, he had chased it up into the field, stunned it with a piece of rock, and finally killed it. When he came back, blood was dripping from the axe and he was smiling all over his almost saintly face. After that Felicity never minded quite so much when she lay in bed and heard the darkness echo with faint, distant howls. If the worst came to the worst, Eesa, who slept down by the kitchen, would rise from his bed and defend her with his axe.

The two elder children slept together in the room beyond the nursery, which had one window onto the garden and one that faced inward onto the court in the middle of the house. On hot summer nights, when Felicity couldn't sleep because the sheets had grown crumpled and sticky, and she was sure a mosquito was inside her net, she would lie awake listening. Were her mother and father alone downstairs? Or had they got guests, or a party even? When they had finished dinner, she would hear the dining room door open and then footsteps on the stone stairs coming up into the court. If it was just her parents, the footsteps were clear and distinguishable, and there might be a word or two, spoken softly. But she could tell if there were guests by their voices, laughing and talking as they came up the stairs into the court. Through the slats of the shutters, she could see the gleam of the lamp her mother carried as she led the way into the drawing room. Then the door shut, dimming the voices suddenly, and it would all be dark again.

Sometimes her mother would play the piano, and then Felicity would try very hard not to fall asleep in case she missed some of it. Or her parents would sing together to her mother's accompaniment, and through the soft dark would come the wistful strains of "Greensleeves" or "The Keys of Heaven."

> I will give you a coach and six,
> Six black horses as black as pitch.
> Madam, will you walk,
> Madam, will you talk,
> Madam, will you walk and talk with me?

That was better than any of the carriages at the Jaffa Gate! Better even than Akhmed, who had only two horses, though his *were* white ones. Then her mother's voice took up the melody.

> Though you give me a coach and six,
> Six black horses as black as pitch,
> Yet I will not walk,
> No I will not talk,
> No I will not walk nor talk with you.

And along the white road to the Mount of Olives, past the neat white crosses of the cemetery, pranced the six black horses as black as pitch, their necks arched proudly, picking their way elegantly on slender legs to a jingle of silver bells. But if her mother didn't play, there was nothing but the darkness of the bedroom, and in it, the little ticking, scratching noise of the beetles in the woodwork of the door.

It was funny how she never seemed to hear them in the daytime, not even in the quiet of the afternoon rest. Perhaps they did things the other way round, sleeping during the day and setting to work only at night. She found the little holes they bored and, sometimes, even the weeniest heaps of wood dust that came out of their tiny drillings, but she never managed to see one of them themselves. She just heard their persistent, rather creepy ticking as she lay awake in the dark. And outside the room in the bigger darkness, there was the distant bark of a pariah dog and the howling of the jackals and the hyenas in the deserted valley.

"Christian, dost thou see them, on the holy ground, / How the Hosts of Midian prowl and prowl around?"

Perhaps these were the Hosts of Midian, prowling round the still, brown, stony hills, padding over the Flat Rock, and gathering at the foot of the wall enclosing the garden, where the silver-grey olive leaves barely rustled under the starry sky. And then, before she realized she had even been to sleep, the morning suddenly came, and it would be bright, hard day, long before it was time to get up.

One such morning, Felicity woke with the first grasshoppers and could not bear to stay the long hours in bed until she heard Waardi stirring in the kitchen or Hezni coming to tell them to get dressed. So she untucked her mosquito net, climbed stealthily out of bed, and crossed the room to where Mary was still sleeping.

"Mary," she whispered. "Let's get up and go out and play in the garden. It's too nice to stay in bed."

Mary stirred and woke reluctantly, but, once awake, she too got up and they both dressed quickly and went to open the door. It was very difficult to open quietly because if you were too quick it rattled, and if you tried to open it slowly, it gave a low whining creak; then you stood still for a minute, your heart thumping, and waited to see if anyone had heard you. But it was all right. Nobody had, and the two children stole across the shutter-darkened nursery and opened the second door into the court. Outside it was already getting warm and the sky was a clear, brilliant blue above the line of the roof. It wasn't yet hot, though, and the cool of the night still lingered in the courtyard's shadowed corners, for the sun hadn't long been above the level of the hills.

In the hot weather Helen slept out in the court, and they had to pass her cot on their way to the front door. Felicity paused for a moment, resting a hand on the rail at the end of the cot, and peered through the misty folds of the mosquito net. Helen lay asleep, one small hand on the pillow, the fingers curled a little, the other tossed out, palm upward on the sheet. Felicity suddenly felt something well up inside her. She drew in her breath. This was a special moment, something she hadn't realized or seen before. Helen's little heart-shaped face on the pillow, and the curve of her thick, black lashes lying on her small, flushed cheek; this was, surely, Beauty.

"Oh, Mary, *look!*" she whispered. "Isn't she . . . doesn't she look . . ." she fumbled for a word, and not finding it, said, "Doesn't she look *pretty!*"

But how could she possibly explain what she meant, how to transmit that sudden awareness of the loveliness of things?

"Shh!" Mary said. "Come on, you'll wake her."

So the moment passed. They went softly across the court and out of the front door, and a moment later were in the garden. "Race you to the olive tree!" Mary called. "You go by the water butt and I'll go by the fig tree. Are you ready? *Go!*"

12

IN THE MIDDLE of the summer Prudy was ill. Doctors came and went, and the other children had to keep on remembering to be quiet, even during the day. When she was better it was decided that she needed sea air, and to get her away from the heat of Jerusalem she was sent with Nannie for a month to Jaffa. She came back again with an extra tan that showed off her yellow curls and trotted about the garden interfering with everyone else's games and talking incessantly of Jaffa. Mary and Felicity were thoroughly sick of the name of the place, and even their mother, when she heard Prudy launch out on a fresh narrative, would laugh and say, "The Jaffa record's being turned on again."

"In Jaffa," Prudy said, squatting on her heels beside Felicity, and poking a stick damagingly into her sister's mud pie, "all the people take their cats for walks on strings, and they eat *nothing* but marmalade!"

"Cats don't eat marmalade, silly!" Felicity said, scornfully.

"In Jaffa they do," Prudy said, settling herself down for a long talk. "*And* they fly to the moon. I flew to the moon, too," she added.

The really annoying thing was that, as none of the rest of them had ever been to Jaffa, they couldn't be *absolutely* sure she was making it up. Perhaps the Jaffa cats were different. Perhaps they *did* eat marmalade! But Felicity was quite, quite sure Prudy couldn't have flown to the moon. And yet when Nannie was asked if it were true, she only laughed.

"I met Mr. Rachel in Jaffa," Prudy went on, "and he gave me candy. *And* he had a Hind!"

"What's a Hind?" Helen asked, looking up from the doll's food of hollyhock petals and pepper berries she was preparing for her doll Rosetta.

"A Hind's a man that rides on a horse," Prudy answered promptly and convincingly. "Mr. Rachel lives in that house over there," she went on, pointing a small brown finger at the white house across the Wadi, on the distant road that led to the Mount of Olives. "He lives with Mrs. Rachel, who is *very* nice and who gives me candy too, and with the Hind, and with Mr. Quacky, who has no head and no arms and no legs."

"How can he have no head and no arms and no legs?" Mary said disbelievingly. "He'd be dead."

"Well, he just *hasn't* any, and he isn't dead," Prudy said firmly. "Oh, there goes Mr. Quacky now! I just saw him popping behind the fig tree. I must go and talk to him." And she trotted off. Felicity looked up quickly, but of course there wasn't anybody there; and she didn't believe that Mr. and Mrs. Rachel or Mr. Quacky were true at all. (How could you have no head and no arms and no legs? You'd be dead as Mary had said.) But she couldn't be absolutely sure because she hadn't been to Jaffa.

"Let's ask Nannie if we can go and play at the Flat Rock," she said to Mary. So they ran to find her and were told they could go if they were careful and didn't take off their hats and that she would follow later with her sewing and the two Little Ones.

The Flat Rock lent itself to every sort of game. You could play house on its shallow shelves and ledges or race across its flat brown surface, jumping over the tufts of vetch that grew in the crevices. In the spring there were sometimes a few shallow puddles of water to dabble in, or you could hunt for rare wild flowers for Nannie's collection. She kept these flowers pressed between the thin pages of her Bible and used them later as part of the decoration on her embroidered texts. Though they changed into something rather sad and colorless after pressing—thin ghosts of their former selves—they still had a certain charm when you came upon them suddenly as you turned the transparent, rustling pages.

Once, Felicity's hat had bounced off and bowled before her over the smooth rock. Laughing and shouting, she chased after it till at last it dropped over a ledge and came to rest beside a clump of scrub. When she reached it she found, neatly coiled up beside it, what appeared to be a bootlace.

"Mary! Look what I've found," she called out. "A yellow bootlace!" and put out a hand to grab it, only to see it uncoil itself and vanish silently into the rock. "Mary, it's gone!" she gasped, and as her sister came up panting and jumped down beside her, Felicity pointed with a rather unsteady finger to the place where her hat, with its large rosette of cream-colored ribbon, sat demurely.

"It wasn't a bootlace!" she said excitedly. "It was a *snake!*"

The next day when she told the story at school, Spafford asked, "Had it got black diamond-shaped spots on its back?"

Felicity wrinkled here forehead thoughtfully and sensing that it was an important moment, replied, "Yes, it had."

"Then it was the most dangerous of all snakes," Spafford said solemnly, and a little thrill of pleasure went through her as she realized the magnitude of her adventure.

Another favorite playground was the Arab and Jewish cemetery, but this was rather farther afield, and Nannie could only be persuaded to go there when she was feeling very energetic, which did not happen often. The Arab graves, which were shaped like cradles, were just high enough to climb into comfortably, and seemed to be specially designed for playing families. Mary would be the mother and Felicity the father while Helen would obligingly allow herself to be perpetually tucked up in imaginary sheets of the dry earth with which the graves were filled. If any Arabs came by, the children would jump out quickly and pretend to be doing something else, but if no one was about, Nannie went on with her sewing and didn't watch too closely what they were doing.

The Jewish graves were not nearly so interesting because they were just solid stone tombs with top-heavy Hebrew lettering cut into their smooth grey sides. "You almost think you could lift the lid and find spare blankets inside," Mary said the first time they went to play in the cemetery. "Like those big wooden chests we had at home in England."

13

MIDSUMMER BROUGHT THE APRICOT HARVEST, when the round rush baskets of golden, velvet-skinned "mish-mish" were carried into the house for the jam making. The Arab women who brought them sat in the court getting the kernels out of the crinkly brown stones of the fruit by smashing them open with pieces of rock.

How delicious those nutty white kernels were when once they were embedded in the jam! And how each of the children watched to see if they would be lucky enough to get one of them in their spoonful.

Then came the time when the first figs ripened on the fig trees in the garden, and down in the Old City the cave-like stalls in the fruit market were piled high with sticky green and blue-black figs, bruised and splitting with ripeness.

"What d'you think happened last night?" the children's mother asked one morning. "I heard a noise in the garden, so I got up and went out in my dressing gown to see what it was. And there, sitting up in the fig tree, picking *our* figs was a young Arab."

"What did you say to him?" Mary asked eagerly.

"I said, 'What are you doing stealing my figs?' and he looked at me with big sad eyes and said, 'I'm not stealing, gracious lady, I'm just borrowing a few of your figs for my poor old mother who is very ill.' "

The children laughed, and Felicity saw a picture of her mother standing out in the garden in her dark blue Arab silk *arbaya*, with the little bits of gold woven in lines down the middle of the back, and her hair floating over her shoulders. And she heard the rustling of the fig trees' leaves as the young Arab looked down at her mother with his mournful eyes and lied so glibly.

After the fruit, the olives ripened, and the crop had to be gathered. Once again the place was filled with women, their embroidered dresses tucked into their belts so that their brown legs showed, and carrying on their heads the big flat baskets in which to hold the olives. One day the children came back from school just in time to see a terrible thing happen.

As they jumped down the last of the stone steps into the garden, the branches of their special olive tree were swaying wildly to and fro, and as they ran to find out what was happening, they saw two of the Arab women high up in the leaves, shouting gaily to each other as they jumped up and down. And as they jumped, they shook the branches violently, so that the olives fell down like hail. And with the shower of small, dark green olives came tumbling the precious pots of lentils and rice and *ameed* from the children's store-cupboards up in the tree.

"Oh, Mummie, our food! Our food!" Mary wailed, as she watched their treasures scattered to the four winds.

"Never mind," their mother said. "They didn't realize quite what they were doing. And it's very hard to get the olives down any other way. I'll give you some new stores when they've finished. I have some dried beans for you that you haven't had before."

The children brightened at once.

"The little ones with the black stitch on their sides?"

"Yes, those are the ones, and you shall come with me tomorrow to get some macaroni. I can probably spare a little of that too."

The place where the macaroni was made was down in the Old City. Through a narrow doorway and along a dark passage, you came at last to a big room with a damp, dusty, floury smell. The light from a small window showed row upon row of thin wooden racks over which hung long strings of drying macaroni, like the swinging fringed bead curtain before Mr. Ohanessian's shop door. In the middle of the room, a peculiar machine was turning. It was worked by a patient, mangy little donkey with eyes blindfolded, who was yoked by a long wooden pole to some wheels in the middle of the machine. He plodded round and round, his small, unshod hooves making a thudding, shuffling noise on the hard earthen floor, and as he turned the wheels, long wormlike strings of macaroni came squeezing out.

It must have been in a place like this that Samson worked, Felicity thought, when he was "eyeless in Gaza" and the Philistines used him in the presses. Only Samson made wine instead of macaroni. "Poor little donkey, is

Street scene in the Old City, Jerusalem, ca. 1920

he blind too?" she had asked the first time they went there. "No, he only has his eyes bandaged," her mother had explained. "He doesn't mind so much that way because he doesn't realize he's going round and round." So Felicity comforted herself with the thought that perhaps the little donkey, in his blindness, imagined he was leading a string of camels down the winding, dusty road to Jericho.

By the time the olive crop was gathered, the corn had ripened, and the reapers with their sickles moved in to the field above the house and began harvesting. And after the reapers, their women followed, gleaning, with skirts tucked up, sweating cheerfully in their thick quilted jackets.

On their way home from school, the children would pause, fascinated, by the corner of the field (where always, afterward, for Felicity, Ruth "stood in tears amidst the alien corn") to watch the winnowing.

Sometimes a donkey would be trotting round and round on the thick carpet of yellow grain, its small hooves trampling the husks; and sometimes Arab children no bigger than Mary and Felicity would be helping by throwing the grain against a huge, square, propped-up sieve, so that the chaff went upward dustily and flew away with the wind. When they had finished, they would fill the sacks with the grain and bind the straw into bales. These they tied onto the donkeys' backs, who then trotted off, their small brown bodies almost hidden by the huge loads.

The field looked bare and unfamiliar after the harvesting. Instead of following the narrow pathway through the rustling corn, lightly stroking the bending ears with the palm of your hand, you could wander wherever you liked across the brown stony ground with the brittle, sun-whitened stubble crackling under your sandals.

In the autumn, the woodmen came. They moved into the corner of the field just above the house, with camels and donkeys laden with sacks of wood and huge iron scales for weighing. The children's mother had soon learned that it never paid to buy the wood sewn up in sacks. It was better to have them opened because the adding of a few small boulders to each sack to help the weight was just a part of the way business was done. So she and the children, who always came running out as soon as they heard that the woodmen had arrived, stood by and watched while the Arabs grumbled and protested. When they saw she would not relent, they shrugged their shoulders in resignation and cut open the mouths of the sacks; out tumbled half a dozen good-sized rocks to fall clanking onto the scales with the logs.

After the wood had been weighed and carried into the house and the woodmen had counted their money and packed up their scales and gone, Jameelah came, half-laughing, half-indignant to their mother and said, "I asked the woodmen why they sold you stones with the wood."

"And what did they say?"

"They said, 'Does the lady not expect to buy bones with her meat?' "

14

THAT WINTER there was a snowfall heavier than any Jerusalem had known for more than fifteen years. One morning the children woke to see an unfamiliar glare coming through the windows, and when they tried to open the nursery door to cross the court, it would only move a few reluctant inches where Eesa had shoveled a narrow path through the piled-up drifts. They hadn't seen snow since they had left England, and never anything quite as deep, nor snow walls as high as those banked up in the corners of the courtyard. The door to their father's bedroom was jammed by a drift, and not until later in the day could they get into the drawing room at all.

It was very exciting. Stories of Arab villages buried, and of rescue parties who went with food, walking about on the level of the white-domed roofs, which were almost indistinguishable in the drifts, made it seem even more of an event. But the cold spell hardly lasted at all, and in a disappointingly short time, the court was running with melted snow and the cistern's danger mark on the dining room wall was rapidly being reached.

Then came the rain, and everything was wet. The bedroom, nursery, and dining-room doors, which faced the court, ran with water, and the green tarpaulin, which in winter was slung across half of the open roof, flapped suddenly in the wind. Even though the tarpaulin protected them a little, the steps down into the dining room glistened darkly with the rain.

It was coming down these wet steps one day that catastrophe overtook Mary. The two elder children had their midday meal downstairs in the dining room with their mother, and their father when he was in; the two Little Ones had theirs upstairs in the nursery with Nannie. When everyone downstairs had been served, Jameelah carried the dishes up to the nursery, and if Mary and Felicity wanted a second helping, they took their plates upstairs for

Jerusalem in the blizzard of February 1920

Nannie to refill. It was a beefsteak pudding, a general favorite, enticingly wrapped with a white folded napkin, and Mary had soon finished hers and taken her plate up for more.

A few minutes later, her careful footsteps were heard again, coming down the steps. Suddenly there was a crash, the clatter of breaking china, and a scream, followed by a prolonged wail. The children's mother jumped up from the table and ran out to see what had happened, Felicity at her heels. The stone steps were littered with beefsteak pudding and broken plate, and there stood Mary, weeping noisily, with her hands pressed to a badly cut ear, while blood trickled alarmingly through her fingers and splashed down the front of her frock onto her feet.

Her mother's action was swift and efficient. Mary was swept upstairs, and the sound of her wails dwindled into a silence when the nursery door closed behind her. Felicity was left among the ruins. Feeling a little frightened, she went back into the dining room, but the sight of her unfinished dinner congealing on the plate only made her feel worse. She went over to the window and looked out at the garden and the leaves of the pepper tree rustling in the wind. Presently Jameelah hurried down the stairs, exclaiming as she passed the scene of the accident, but she went into the kitchen without noticing Felicity. A stream of conversation followed, interrupted every now and then by a sympathetic clucking from Waardi, in which Felicity distinctly heard the words "doctor" and "hospital" occurring.

What awful things were they going to do to Mary? She must find out. She went to the door of the dining room and steeled herself to step over the fragments of china and the horrible traces of Mary's blood. She mustn't step on that, whatever happened. There was no one about upstairs in the court-yard, and she hung around, not daring to go into the nursery and with no heart to go out alone into the garden.

She drifted into her mother's bedroom and over to the dressing table and lifted the lid of the Purple Sperm. The satin made a purring sound as she touched it, like Nannie's fingers did when she tied the ribbon under the chin of Prudy's bonnets. Felicity read the familiar cross-stitched text on the inside of the lid, aimlessly.

Suddenly there were footsteps in the garden and she ran over to the window to look out. A plump little man was coming down the steps from the field with an ominous black bag in his hand. A minute later the front door-bell clanged; someone crossed the court briskly and she heard her mother's voice as she opened the door to let him in. Then came his voice answering her in a peculiar, sing-song foreign accent. They went into the nursery and the door shut after them.

He must be the doctor Jameelah had spoken of, probably from the Italian Hospital where Nannie had gone that time when she was ill. Was he going to take Mary away with him? What could he be doing to her all this time? For it seemed an age of waiting before the nursery door opened again and her mother and the doctor came back across the court. She heard her saying good-bye to him and the front door being opened. As it closed on him and he was gone, Felicity ran out of the bedroom.

"Oh, there you are!" he mother said, turning round to meet her. "I was wondering where you had got to."

"Mary, what has he done to Mary?" the words tumbled out hurriedly.

"Mary's all right," her mother answered. "But he had to put some stitches in her ear because it was very badly cut."

Stitches! Felicity felt the prickles rising on her skin. Had he actually sewn up Mary's ear with a needle and cotton? A horrible picture flashed before her eyes of the doctor, stitching away laboriously, with pursed lips, as she herself did when, under Nannie's watchful eye, she struggled to master the intricacies of herringboning and buttonholing.

"Can I see her?" she asked, looking up at her mother anxiously.

"Yes, of course you can. But go quietly, because she's rather tired now. He couldn't help hurting her, you know, and she was very brave."

Felicity went quickly through the nursery and opened the bedroom door softly. The shutters were half closed, and Mary was lying propped up regally in bed, her head swathed in bandages, surrounded by her dolls. She lifted a languid hand in greeting.

"Did he really sew your ear? Really, *really?*" Felicity asked in an awestruck whisper, fingering a corner of the sheet as she stood by the side of the bed.

"Yes, he did. He did six stiches! And I didn't cry at all—at least, only a little. It was nearly *hanging off!*" Mary added proudly. "Jameelah told me. She saw it!"

How romantic, how exciting to have your ear nearly hanging off, and to have a doctor sew it on again, and now to be lying in bed, all bandaged up like a wounded hero! Felicity almost wished it could have happened to her, even if it *did* hurt. And she might have been brave too, perhaps ever braver than Mary. And then everybody would have been specially nice to her, and said, "What a brave little girl!" But it wasn't her, it was Mary, so now it was she who must be specially nice to her sister.

"Shall I fetch Louisa and Mabel and we could play hospitals? And you can comb Louisa's hair with her special teeny comb, if you like?" she added, which was the nicest thing she could possibly have suggested because no one but herself ever combed Louisa's hair. Mary nodded her head carefully, and the dolls were fetched and were soon undressed and spread out over the bedclothes, bandaged up with all sorts of incredible ailments.

Mary wore a bandage for several days afterward, which was then exchanged for an impressive crisscross of sticky plaster that the boys at school were always trying to pull off, so as to count the stitches in her ear.

❧ Not long after Mary's plaster was finally discarded (and perhaps in some subtle way to recompense her for her own, less interesting, unscarred ears), Felicity acquired her yellow boots. They had square toes with little round holes where the shoe cap was sewn onto the foot, and they were of a pure, shining, golden-yellow leather. Perhaps the most fascinating thing about them, though, were the eight little metal hooks (four on each side) looking at first sight almost like buttons, round which you twisted the laces before winding them round your ankles and tying them in a laborious bow. There was a sense of power and speed about flicking the laces round those hooks instead of fumbling to stick the tags through the holes, only to find when you got to the top that you had missed one so that the crosses were uneven, and had all to be undone again.

The boots had come from Schneller's Factory, the big stone building outside the German Colony where the blind people worked, and where the children's mother had taken Mary and Felicity on an expedition one day to see the baskets and brushes and boots being made. They had been met by a tall man in a dark cloth cap, who tapped his way about with a stick. He had steel-rimmed spectacles with dark green glass in them, and Felicity couldn't help wondering whether he was *really* blind, or had, perhaps, some secret way of seeing through the dark, mysterious surfaces. Even when he turned to lead the way to the brush-making room, and she could see the empty sockets with the small lids forever shut over the places where his eyes should have been, she had an uncomfortable feeling that he might have some extra eyes in his mind with which to read her thoughts.

They went all round the factory and saw the men and women, some wearing dark glasses, and some with pale unseeing eyeballs that had no centers to them, fitting brown and black bristles into white wood brushes and weaving baskets with sure, unhurried hands. The children stood fascinated and watched the unwavering fingers pick up a tool and use it, or fit a bunch of bristles into a hole, almost without feeling for it. It was hard to believe that they really couldn't see until you looked up again from their hands to their flat, empty faces.

It was in the boot department that the man with the cloth cap had left them for a moment, and when he came tapping his way back again, he was carrying the yellow boots in his other hand. "These are a very fine pair of children's boots," he said, "made to measure for a customer who afterward did not take them. The color was found not quite suitable," he added, as he held them out in the direction of the children's mother.

"What a funny color!" Mary said with a laugh. "Think of having yellow boots!"

But Felicity felt straight away that these were special boots. They had an "otherness" about them, with their square, yellow toes, and the little tabs at the back seam to pull them on by.

"Would you like to try them on?" her mother asked, looking down at her tense face with amusement.

Felicity nodded without speaking, and, sitting down quickly on the floor, pulled off her shoes and slipped her feet into the white cotton linings of the boots. And the full glory of them broke upon her as she was shown how to twirl the laces round the little metal hooks.

"Are they comfy!" her mother asked, and Felicity nodded again.

"No pinching anywhere? And not too big either?"

"They feel lovely," Felicity whispered, and stroked their shining toes. So they were paid for there and then, and she was allowed to keep them on, and went proudly away in them, carrying her shoes in her hand.

Even when her father greeted the boots' first appearance with "What ever has my Popatoos got on her feet?" and poked at them laughingly with the metal tip of his stick, and the boys at schooled chanted, "Yellow boots, yellow boots! Here come the yellow boots!" when she ran out onto the playground at break time, the spell was never lost. Felicity wore the boots stubbornly, deaf to taunts and laughter and secretly proud of the fact that nobody else had any that in the least resembled them.

15

"WHEN I HAVE MY BIRTHDAY, can I have a party, Mummie?" Felicity asked her mother as her eighth birthday began to draw near. "And can I have only boys?"

"Don't you want any little girl—Eva or Meleky?"

Felicity shook her head.

"Not even Louisa, your best friend?"

"I want only boys," she repeated firmly. Her relief was great when her mother consented: "All right, if that's what you would really like, tell me which boys you want to ask and I'll see if they would like to come." So a list was made out and the invitations sent and the great day finally arrived.

Waiting for her guests in the drawing room in her best frock, her nails specially cleaned with the pearl-handled nail cleaner that hurt so much, her short hair neatly parted and the fringe smoothed down, Felicity fidgeted about and kept running around the piano to the window to look out.

The piano was of a light, unstained brown oak, designed by the children's father and unlike any other piano in the world. Strictly speaking, it was a grand piano, but its shape was large and rectangular, supported by a forest of legs underneath. Hinged folding doors swung back to disclose the keys. Inside it was of silken, cream-colored wood with pictures painted all over it and a verse that told the story of the pictures. The doors of the keyboard and the lid were open now, to be ready for their mother to play for the party, and as Felicity waited, she read the verse again. It was irresistible; you always had to read it right round to the end once you had begun.

I dreamed that in a garden once I lay, she started off on the most left-hand of the folding doors, tracing the gilded letters with her finger and considering carefully each of the long, willowy ladies with their green and wine-colored and bluish dresses and their masses of hair. Each stood by herself

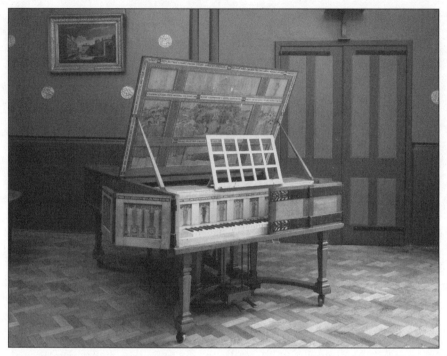

*The Broadwood semi-grand piano, encased to C. R. Ashbee's design ca. 1898; repro-
duced by permission of Cheltenham Art Gallery and Museum.*

in a small compartment, playing some strange musical instrument, and
around her bare feet were twined vine leaves and other unknown creepers.
Where three strange women garlanded with vine, rose, and woodbine—by this
time you had reached the compartments behind the keyboard—*on pipe, and
lute, and viol played to me.* After you had followed the verse onto the end of
the folding doors on the right, it switched to the inside of the lid, where it
was propped open by two slender oaken rods, and you had to follow it right
round the edge and then twice across. And in the middle of the piano's lid
was depicted the man who had written the poem and to whom all the elegant, slender-necked women were playing. He lay wrapped in a purple cloak,
and behind him a huge golden sun set among the cream-colored domes and
minarets of some city not unlike Jerusalem.

Felicity was so engrossed in trying once and for all to make up her mind
whether she liked the lady in the pale purple dress with the sort of double

The piano, detail "I dreamed that in a garden once I lay"; photograph by Michael Hall, reproduced by permission of Cheltenham Art Gallery and Museum.

The piano, detail "On pipe, and lute, and viol played to me"; photograph by Michael Hall, reproduced by permission of Cheltenham Art Gallery and Museum.

trumpet best, or the one in Hooker's green with a violin held a long way away from her chin, that she missed seeing her guests come down the stone steps into the garden and was startled into fresh excitement when the front door bell rang without warning. She could hear the door being opened to let them in, the shuffling of their feet, and the polite greetings as they were shown where to leave their coats.

There was a pause and some whispering outside. Felicity tingled all over and her heart thumped as the handle of the drawing room door turned slowly. Suddenly the door flew open, and in trooped the boys singing,

> Happy birthday to you,
> Happy birthday to you,
> Happy birthday, dear Fifi,
> Happy birthday to you.

They were led by Neils, his fair hair smoothed down across his pale forehead, his face even more solemn than usual, carrying on a silver cardboard plate the most wonderful, dreamlike, white-iced birthday cake that you could possibly imagine.

One after another they came in: David, Spafford, and Jack, getting bigger and bigger, till right at the back of the line, his blue eyes smiling, was Uncle Eena himself, strong and clean and elegant as ever. And suddenly shyness overcame Felicity and she felt her hands going damp and the color burning in her ears. So many boys, some of them as old as twelve and thirteen, and all had come to *her* birthday party! How had she dared to invite so august a gathering? But finally the sight of the cake, with its flawless, snowy surface, restored her confidence, and she shook hands boldly with them all.

The party was a huge success. They played postman's knock, and forfeits, and Poor Peter, and Russian scandal, and then a line of chairs was prepared and the children's mother sat down to the piano and, her hands poised above the keyboard, said, "Now, are you all ready for musical chairs?" There was a shout of "Yes!" and with a smile, she brought her hands down on the keys.

Out tumbled the melodies, one after another, joining themselves together, and weaving in and out—tunes you knew suddenly changing into melodies you had never heard before, and sad, haunting ones that made you want to linger and listen breaking suddenly into cheerful ones to hurry you on again. And just as you thought you were safe till the end of the phrase and would have time to get past the back of the next chair to the haven of the empty seat beyond it, the music stopped, and there was a wild, agonizing rush. But Felicity had reached the empty chair and she was safe for this time at least, though she almost hadn't got there in time, and the uncomfortable scratchiness of the chair's rush seat against the backs of her bare legs was a confirmation of her safeness.

The inside of the cake was even better than its snowy outside suggested, and she was allowed to cut the first slice by herself, without her mother even holding onto the handle of the knife. Uncle Eena was never at a loss for a game, and her admired Jock was on his best behavior. Altogether, everything was so successful that she could hardly believe it when the time came for them to go home.

"Don't forget to thank them all for the lovely cake," her mother whispered into her ear, as with a flushed, regretful face and shining eyes, Felicity stood at the door of the drawing room to say good-bye. One by one they shook hands and went out and behind them came Uncle Eena, and with him the expectation of one final pleasure. It was a secret thrill to Felicity that Uncle Eena used to pretend that he couldn't remember her name and often found fresh variants for it. She had been Fidelity and Facility, and once even, Velocity. Which of them would it be now? Or would he think of something new? She looked up at him expectantly as he took her hand in his . . . and he didn't let her down. With a serious face and only a betraying twinkle in his blue eyes, he shook her proffered hand firmly and said,

"It was a lovely party; thank you very much for asking me . . . Versatility!"

And as she laughed delightedly, the door closed behind him, and he was gone.

16

IN THE SUMMER following Felicity's eighth birthday, the children developed whooping cough, and the hot shade of the favorite olive tree echoed to paroxysms of coughing, interspersed every so often with a dramatic whoop. In the middle of it all, a telegram arrived from England. Babooshka was very ill, and their mother was being summoned back to see her.

Although neither Mary nor Felicity understood what lay behind it all, they felt a tenseness in the atmosphere and an unrest, as though something big might happen at any moment. And the very next day it did. The children's mother came to them and explained that she had to go back to England and that Sister Hannah and Sister Beulah from the American Colony were coming to help Nannie and their father look after the house and the two Little Ones while she was away.

"But to make it easier for them, so they won't have quite so much to do," she went on, "I am taking you two Big Ones with me."

"To England? Are we going to England, Mummie?" Mary asked, incredulously.

"In a boat?" Felicity added, her grey eyes wide with a dawning excitement.

"In a train first and then in a boat," their mother said. "Now run along and help Nannie get your things together. We must be all packed up before you go to bed tonight because we have to start very early in the morning. But *don't* talk to Helen and Prudy about it," she added, "because they would be disappointed at not coming too and I can't take you all."

"Can Teddy-for-short come with me?" Felicity asked. (This was her most beloved doll, a Victorian blonde.)

"No, I don't think there'll be room for her, as we don't want to take more luggage than we need. She'll be quite happy here till we get back again and there'll be so many things for you both to do and to look at that you would find no time for her at all."

The children hurried off to their bedroom to start assembling their things. "Can you remember England, Mary?" Felicity asked, as she turned the handle of the door.

"Of course I can, silly," Mary said. "There's lots of grass everywhere and it's very green and no stones. And the almond butter stays hard because it's not so hot as Jerusalem."

"I can't remember it very well; at least, only bits of it," Felicity said. "But I remember Babooshka," And then, as a sudden thought flashed on her, she added solemnly, "D'you think she's going to *die?*"

Mary stood still for a moment, thinking. "I don't know," she said slowly. "She's got white hair and she must be very old. Oh, well, perhaps God will wait till we get back anyway so that Mummie can see her." She added briskly and reassuringly. "Come on, we must help Nannie pack. No, *not* your yellow boots, Fifi; they're for winter and it'll be summer time, even in England, when we get there. They'll be much too hot."

Sister Hanna and Sister Beulah arrived that afternoon, in immaculate white frocks, their lined faces smiling out from under the shadows of their sun helmets. Each carried a small, neat, worn suitcase holding a few carefully packed belongings. Next morning, before the early coolness was gone and without saying a proper good-bye to Helen and Prudy, the children and their mother slipped quietly away and the journey began.

The first excitement was when the train ground slowly to a halt in the middle of a waste of desert, with no station in sight. Mary and Felicity craned their heads out of the window. The hard blue sky was cloudless, and the sun burned down on the shimmering metal rails that stretched across the unbroken ripples of white sand and disappeared into the haze of the horizon. People were beginning to collect round the engine, which the children could see if, at the risk of burning themselves on the outside of the carriage, they leaned out as far as they dared.

"I wonder what's the matter," Felicity said.

"Perhaps the engine's got too hot," Mary suggested. "They might be giving it some water."

The children's mother got up and went out of the compartment into the corridor. A minute later she came back again, closing the sliding door behind her.

"Look, children. I want you to listen to me for a moment," she said. They tore themselves away from the window and sat down dutifully on the sticky seats. "I think an inspector will be coming in here soon, and I have to sign some papers to say you are not suffering from any infectious disease." ("Whooping cough is an infectious disease," she added, in answer to their unspoken question.) "So, if you want to cough while he's in here, for goodness sake, hold your heads out of the window and try not to whoop."

Feeling very like conspirators, the children did as they were told, and when a little later the door slid open and an official came in they were leaning far out of the window again, whispering to each other delightedly. How almost wicked, and how exciting, to be a party to a secret like this! And to what, when you came to think of it, was sort of a lie. But as their mother was in it too, it couldn't be really bad.

"Are these your two children?" they heard the man ask as his fingers turned the stiff pages of her passport.

"Yes, that's right," their mother answered.

"Not suffering from any infectious disease?" he went on.

"You can see, they are both in perfect health," she said brazenly.

Felicity nudged Mary where they were squeezed together into the frame of the window. How boldly their mother spoke to the inspector, without a moment's hesitation! There was a rustling of papers and the squeak of her pen nib as she signed the forms.

Suddenly Felicity felt a cough rising up inside her. Somehow it must be swallowed down again. It would be too awful if, just at this crucial moment, she gave everything away by letting out an incriminating whoop. It was like one of those terror-laden moments of hide and seek, when in the dusty darkness under the bed or behind the curtain you got a tickle in your throat just as you heard the stealthy footsteps of the "he" coming cautiously into the room.

"I'm going to cough, Mary!" she whispered in an agony of apprehension.

"You can't cough now," Mary said fiercely. "Hold your breath, or swallow, or something!"

And then, just as she felt she was losing the battle, that she would burst unless she let out her breath, and that the cough could not possibly be kept down any longer, she was saved. There was a shrill whistle from the engine, and, with a jolt that sent the buffers clanking into each other all down the train, it started moving, and the first whoop was drowned by the noise of the grinding wheels.

"Thank you very much," the inspector said, raising his voice. "Port Said is another six hours," and the door of the compartment opened. As it shut behind him, both children burst into a paroxysm of coughing.

It was too late when they reached Port Said to do anything but go straight to the hotel and to bed. "What's the name of the boat we're going on?" Mary asked as her mother smoothed the sheets of the big bed the children were sharing and tucked in the mosquito net. "I don't know yet," she answered. "They couldn't give me a boat at the agency in Jerusalem; we shall have to go down to the dock first thing in the morning and see if anything has come in the night. Now try and go to sleep quickly, both of you, because you've had a long day, and I don't want you to be tired tomorrow. We shall have a lot to do." Then she went over to the window, pushed the shutters till they clicked back into their hooks against the wall, and went softly out of the room.

The roar and jangle of the trams and the clip-clop of horses' hooves rose up out of the hot dark, and a shifting pattern of light moved across the ceiling as some lighted vehicle passed in the street below. From the harbor came an occasional whistle or the muffled hoot of a ship. It seemed such a waste to have to go to sleep when everything was so new and so exciting! Felicity put out a cautious hand and felt over the sheet to where Mary lay in her half of the bed.

"Mary," she whispered, "d'you think our ship will have four funnels? I hope it does. What d'you think it'll be called?" and when there was no answer, she added, "Mary! You're not *asleep*, are you?" But there was no sound except Mary's quiet breathing. She turned over and stretched out her legs to try and find a cool part of the bed. They would all be asleep in Jerusalem now, Helen in her cot in the court, and Prudy in hers out on the narrow balcony over the dining room. The leaves of the fig tree would be rustling in the darkness of the garden and the Hosts of Midian gathering at the foot of the wall from the stony slopes of the Wadi el Jose. Tomorrow they would go down to the harbor and find a boat and then, like Sir Patrick Spens, they would sail "o'er the foam," only it would not be to Norroway but to England that the "trusty skipper" of the ship would set his course.

"To England, to England, to England o'er the foam": it didn't fit too badly . . . England. England, what would it be like? And trying to conjure up a clear picture of some place such as Mary had described, of green fields and no stones, and big pats of hard butter, Felicity at last fell asleep.

17

WHEN THEY LOOKED OUT of their bedroom window the next morning, there, lying quietly in the green harbor water was a beautiful big liner. "Mummie, look, look! A ship!" Felicity called out. "It's a big one with four funnels!" Their mother came over to the window, and when she saw it told the children to dress quickly.

"We'll go out to it as soon as we've had breakfast," she said, "and see if they have berths for us." The children hurried into their clothes and gave themselves a perfunctory wash, and an even more perfunctory brush to their hair. "No time for a parting this morning," Felicity said as she smoothed down her fringe with excited hands, and after breakfast, which was soon over, they were half walking, half running behind their mother as she strode quickly down to the dock.

There they stood on the glaring white stones of the quay while an Egyptian boatman rowed his little boat toward the steps and another, smiling eagerly, stood beside them and caught hold of it with a long hooked pole when it came within reach. With a strong and grubby hand, he helped Mary and Felicity to clamber in, and they sat down side by side on the flaking paint of the hot seats, their sandaled feet in the damp, salt-water-smelling bottom of the boat.

With warning shouts, the boatman swung out from the steps and started rowing across the deep green water. Transparent bluish jellyfish, like little soft umbrellas trailing floating strings, swam about in the water between the busy boats. Rowing boats like their own, full of passengers and luggage, and other boats piled high with green melons, miraculously threaded their way between the larger ships without bumping into them.

The liner they had seen from their bedroom window grew bigger and bigger as they neared her until she seemed to tower above them, a huge shape painted a creamy yellow-brown with row upon row of little round portholes. Oh quick, be quick, Felicity thought; how dreadful it would be if, just as they got close, the ship were to start moving slowly away! At last they reached her side, and the boatman fastened his hook into the long flight of steps slung from the deck to the water's level.

The boat bobbed up and down with the swell, and the children's mother chose her moment carefully before she caught hold of the steps and jumped onto them; after that she helped Mary up, and then it was Felicity's turn. For a terrifying moment, she felt she would never be able to get over that gap of sparkling water, that she would forever have to go backward and forward with the boatman and never be able to get out of his little boat while the big ship sailed away, carrying Mary and her mother to England o'er the foam.

Then with a "Whoa-oop" and a heave from the boatman, and her mother's hand pulling her, she had cheated the bright water and distant sea-weedy caverns of the kings of the jellyfish and was safe on the steps of the great liner, starting to walk up. There they were again, the same square holes that the steps seemed to be made of, only now they were more like wooden latticework over the windows of the Muslim houses to prevent strangers from seeing the women. Again, as she went up, her hand clutching the rail, the harbor water glittered up at her, beautiful and malevolent, through the small spaces, and she had to force herself to look up and not down between her feet.

When they reached the deck, it was far bigger than anything the children had seen before and stretched like a road on either side of where they stood. A white-coated steward came toward them and asked their mother what he could do for them. "I must see the captain immediately," she said. "I will see if he is disengaged now, Madam. Please follow me." They walked sedately behind him along the scrubbed empty deck and down the brass-rimmed stairs to the corridors of the deck below. After threading their way through what seemed to the children to be a maze of passages and turning innumerable corners, they arrived at a shiny paneled door. Here the steward asked them to wait a moment outside while he went in, closing the door behind him. A minute or two later, he reappeared, and with a "This way, please, and mind the step," he ushered them into the captain's cabin.

"In what way can I be of assistance to you?"

"Have you three berths on your ship for my two children and myself?" their mother asked, without wasting time on any preliminaries.

"Yes, I think we could probably find room for you," the captain answered, and then added, smilingly, "By the way, you haven't told me where is it you want to go."

"Oh, to England, of course."

His smile broadened. "Then I'm afraid we shouldn't be very much use to you," he said. "We're bound for Australia."

Australia! That was the pink country with a page all to itself in the atlas and that was right the other side of the world. Jock had once told Felicity that if she fell right through the playground at school, she would land in Australia where everybody walked on their heads. "They have to," he had added, "and everything's upside down there because of its being the other side of the world." But she hadn't quite believed him really.

"Australia!" she heard her mother's voice saying, just as she was trying to imagine what it would be like doing everything upside down (how difficult it would be to do up your buttons and brush your hair, or perhaps you didn't need to brush your hair if you walked about on your head.) "How stupid of me. I somehow never thought you would be going anywhere except England," and she laughed a little embarrassedly. "Well, that's that!" Then, putting out her hand, she added, "I'm so sorry to have taken up your time for nothing."

"Oh, not at all," the captain answered. "I'm only sorry I can't be of any use to you. Unless, that is, you'd like to change your mind and come to Australia instead!"

The children's mother laughed again.

"No, I'm afraid that's not possible just now. I expect we shall find another ship soon—I hope so." Then turning to the children, she said, "Well, come along. We'd better be off, or we may find ourselves in Australia whether we like it or not."

So the captain saw them out and found the steward to take them through the many corridors and up again onto the deck. Then they hailed another little rowing boat and were soon bobbing their way once more across the harbor to the quay.

"What a pity it wasn't going to England," Mary said as she trailed her hand over the boat's side, making the water run, ribbonlike, through her fingers. "It was such a *lovely* ship."

"*And* it had four funnels," Felicity said, regretfully. "But perhaps there'll be another one with four funnels that *will* be going to England . . . perhaps." But in the end they had to make do with two funnels, for when, the next day, the French liner *Marie-Louise* came in, bound for Marseilles, their mother decided they had better not wait any longer, and as soon as their passages were secured they went on board. In comparison with the shining Australia-bound liner, the *Marie-Louise* was a sad sight. Even to the children she didn't seem very big, and she was distinctly dirty.

"Lots of the other children seem to have whooping cough too," Mary remarked after they had come back from a first trip of exploration round the ship.

"What a good thing," their mother said. "Then you won't be able to give it to them," and she settled herself down in an easy chair in a corner where there was a little shade.

The children left her and ran over to the other side of the deck. "Oh, look, Mary," Felicity called suddenly as she climbed onto the railings. "There are boys in the water swimming!" Mary joined her quickly, and together they leaned over and watched, fascinated. Half a dozen brown-skinned Egyptian boys with sleek wet hair were swimming about among the jellyfish quite close to the ship's side. Their upturned faces were smiling and their white teeth flashed as they held out dripping hands, palms upward, and called, "Backsheesh! Backsheesh!"

One of the passengers threw a coin overboard, and as it touched the water and slipped, glinting, through the green depths, half a dozen brown bodies shot down after it, streaking through the greenish light of the water until a first hand reached out and grabbed the coin. Then in a misty cloud of tiny bubbles, the swimmers popped up to the surface and the cry came up again, cheerfully: "Backsheesh! Backsheesh! Backsheesh!"

"Where do you suppose they put all their money when they've got it?" Felicity asked. "They haven't any clothes with pockets they could put it in." "I think they must put it in their mouths," Mary replied, "though you'd think they might swallow it by mistake when they talk. Yes, look, look!" she pointed suddenly, "that one's cheek is quite bulgy; he must have caught a lot of pias-tres. Let's go and ask Mummie if we can have one or two to throw them."

➥ In spite of the smallness and grubbiness of the *Marie-Louise,* the voyage had all the proper thrills. There was the awful, irrevocable decision as to who was to have the top bunk with its enchanting little detachable ladder. And there was the peculiar smell and feel of a bath in salt water where the soap simply wouldn't make any lather at all and the whole level of the water kept shifting with the ship's movement. There was the throb of the engines and the creaking of the woodwork as you lay in your bunk at night listening to the swish of the waves outside the porthole. Who was riding those waves? Mermaids small enough to sit in the cockleshells, like the ones "my true love" wore round his hat in the song? Or the Sea King's henchmen, with their green hands, who tried to look in at the portholes as their wave horses swept them by?

Then there were the races round the deck with the French children and the funny little girl who wore a sailor suit. She had a huge bow of ribbon on her head almost completely concealing her hair, and she drank red wine with her dinner every day just like a grown-up. But perhaps the thing which gave the whole journey its most exciting flavor was the Diamond Star.

The Diamond Star was one of the most beautiful things the children had ever seen, and they certainly thought the most lovely in their mother's jewel box. It was a brooch about the size of a half-crown with eight points; the stones were quite tiny, but as they converged toward the center they got big-ger, until right in the middle there was one huge diamond. The children had only seen their mother wear it once. She had come into their bedroom in a black velvet evening frock to say good night, and on her breast had glittered the Diamond Star.

"Oh, Mummie, how *lovely!*" Felicity had exclaimed, "May I touch it?" and Mary had added, "Why don't you wear it more often?"

"I don't like it," their mother had answered. "It's an ugly setting. And anyway, it's too flashy."

"But diamonds should *flash!*" Mary had said. "I think it's beautiful!" Their mother had smiled and said, "Oh, well, one day it may come in useful. If we need some money, I shall sell it."

Now as the two children lay in their bunks that first night on the *Marie-Louise* and watched their mother undress, they noticed a mysterious little package stitched into the lining of her pink stays. She always wore boned stays with laces to do them up, and it was one of the special privileges that, when a pair of stays became too old and was discarded for a new one, the children were allowed to pull the bones out and play with them. You could have wonderful games bending the slender metal-tipped pieces of white whalebone between finger and thumb to send them pinging across the room.

"What's that little thing you've got sewn into your stays?" Mary asked, peering down over the edge of the top bunk. Their mother looked up, smiling. "You ought to be asleep," she said, then added, "It's the Diamond Star."

"Oh, Mummie, you're not going to *sell* it?" Felicity said in a shocked voice, raising herself on one elbow. "You *can't!*"

"Well, we shall have to see; perhaps I shan't need to. But I thought I'd better bring it along with me in case we got stranded somewhere. And this seems the safest place to keep it because I always have it on me. Now don't you dare tell anyone about it: it's a secret!"

A thrilling and awful secret! Something that almost made you feel you weren't just your ordinary self, Felicity thought, if she could have something as precious as the Diamond Star sewn into her vest (or her Liberty bodice in the winter!). It was a little like being a pirate, with gold pieces-of-eight sewn into the lining of his belt, only gold wasn't even half as exciting as the Diamond Star. She tried to put the thought of its possible sale out of her mind. It was just unthinkable that anyone else should be the possessor of so glorious a jewel.

For the rest of the voyage, she forced herself to keep awake each night until the moment when her mother came to bed and laid her folded stays at the end of her bunk. Then she would reassure herself that the secret package was still there—that the Star of Stars had at least not yet changed hands.

18

BUT, AFTER ALL, England turned out to be rather different; or rather, the England Felicity remembered was the grey stone Cotswold village of Campden and the converted Norman chapel where she had been born and lived her first years. In its rambling garden had stood an old, old apple tree, from whose gnarled branches Eve picked the first apple and, with Adam, hid ashamed among the ivy and the muscary nearby.

Under this same tree, Felicity could always see the names of the months of the year laid out on the grass in a neat circle; and because she always thought of them like that, it was very difficult to feel that June was the middle of the summer. June should really have been still in the spring, because with March, April, May, June, and July all being such short words they only reached about one third of the way round the year, and in what should have been midsummer there lay August, stretched out in the heat! After that, September and the other months with long names filled up the year till you got round to Christmas and January again. Beyond the Circle of the Months, there was the place where the angel stood with the flaming sword and, beyond that again, the wall where the old rat lived who finally married the Rat Princess. Then came the rock garden that led to the meadow and the stream. Here grew bushes covered with little white puffballs that Old Nannie had said the children mustn't touch because they were poisonous.

"If you put your fingers in your mouth after touching them, you might be very ill indeed," she had said.

But the corner of England where Babooshka lived was different. The house was a big red Victorian building matted with green and red creepers, with a steep roof of purple slates and windows that reminded the children of church. It had a wonderful porch, also roofed with purple slates, with stained glass windows where red and yellow birds nestled in cabbage-green leaves.

109

Halfway up the wide stairs there were more of these windows, which shed strange colored lights on the walls and banisters when the westerly sun shone through them. The banisters were the best thing about the house because they seemed to have been specially made for children who found walking downstairs dull. They were incredibly smooth and slippery and of a brilliant golden-syrup color. A stone pillar at their foot, adorned with a dark mark from the clutch of many small and grubby hands, stopped you from shooting into the hall.

Upstairs on the landing, the children had to be quiet because of Babooshka being ill in the big bedroom at the end, but out in the garden with its spacious lawns they could play as much as they liked. Curving paths bordered the smooth turf, damp and mossy where they wound their way under the copper beeches and the ilexes, and dry yellow gravel where they came out into the open. A gigantic clump of rhododendrons, so big that the children could walk about inside it, grew near the drawing room windows, but, although mysterious, it was too dark and spidery to be a really nice place to play. It was more fun seeing if they could jump into the big bush of pampas grass with its feathery plumes without cutting their hands and legs on the knifelike edges of its ribbony leaves.

But the longest and happiest hours of that summer month were spent on the seesaw that their mother had told them had been put there for her and their Uncle Nevill when they had been children. It was a large metal construction, painted a dark grayish-green, supported on a central pedestal, and it had a heavy, adjustable weight that could be moved from one end to the other by squeezing a lever on its top. Felicity, being the lighter of the two, always had the weight nearer her end so that Mary should not have an unfair advantage, and they invented a special version of Jack the Giant-killer where (as the seesaw could go round as well as up and down) an indefatigable giant pursued a jubilant Jack in never-ending circles.

When they first arrived and had passed by the stained glass windows of the porch into the lofty darkness of the hall, they were met by Nurse Parsons, their mother's childhood nurse. Mary remembered her (or said she did), but Felicity blushingly had to confess that she had forgotten. Nurse Parsons was small, precise, and ageless. She wore a long skirt, reaching nearly to the ground, and a wide belt of black petersham with a big beaten pewter buckle.

The author with doll at Godden Green, Kent, 1921

Her hair, which was neither mouse-colored nor grey, was carefully piled on her head so that it was impossible to find out how long it was or where the ends might be, and she always wore a high net collar with little tiny bones in it. When it was time for a meal, or when Babooshka had sent for them to visit her, Nurse Parsons would call the children in from the garden in a small voice that it was somehow impossible not to hear.

Besides Nurse Parsons, there were the two special nurses who looked after Babooshka, one for night and one for day. They were large and rather formidable, with stiff white collars and cuffs and white starched caps perched on their heads. When they were both awake together, they would sit by a fire in the little room next door playing cards.

When Nurse Parsons said, "Your grandmother would like to see you,"

The author and her sister
Mary with their mother at
Godden Green, Kent, 1921

the children would go softly up the stairs and tap a little timidly on the door of the nurses' room. "Oh, yes, your grandmother wants to see you," one of them would say as she opened the door. "You can go right in," and then you would open the other door and go into the big bedroom. Long glazed chintz curtains framed the big windows, and within these curtains hung others of a soft white stuff with frilled edges. Inside these again were biscuit-colored blinds, pulled half down by cords, each tipped with an ivory acorn.

A huge mirrored dressing table swathed in frilled white muslin stood near the window, and on it were arrayed a fascinating collection of tiny silver boxes, silver-topped bottles, and hand mirrors and brushes of polished yellowing ivory, inlaid with ebony initials.

The first time Felicity had gone to see Babooshka after they arrived, she had been struck straight away by the peculiar faint smell in the bedroom. It was an *old* smell, belonging somehow to something out of the past, and to Babooshka herself. And there she lay in the huge bed, her head with its white curls full of funny little leather curlers, propped up on countless pillows, her soft old hands, flecked with pale brown marks and covered with rings, straying querulously over the sheets.

"Good evening, Babooshka," Felicity said softly, standing a little shyly beside the bed. "Eh? Who's that? Oh, it's you children, is it?" she said, turning her head a little on the pillows. "Well, stand so that I can see you," and a ringed hand wandered over and caught hold of Felicity's small brown one with a soft, firm clutch.

Babooshka (Mrs. F. A. Forbes) with the author's mother and sister Mary, 1914

"So this is Felicity, is it? Well, if it isn't Dr. Carrick! Aren't you going to give your Babooshka a kiss?" And Felicity leaned over and kissed her grandmother's cheek, and the strange smell enveloped her as her face brushed against the pleats and frills of the voluminous flannel nightgown.

"Why does Babooshka call me Dr. Carrick?" Felicity asked her mother afterward. "Because she says you remind her of her brother, your great-uncle George. I remember him as a big, smiling giant of a man; he was a doctor at the court of the tsar in Saint Petersburg, where they were both born." Felicity felt rather proud, and, after that, whenever she went into the big bedroom with the view of the towering Wellingtonia out of the window and stood by her grandmother's bed, the visit was not compete unless Babooshka said, "Well, and how is Dr. Carrick today?"

The house had many other special attractions for the children, one of which was the bridge. This was a small gallery above the stained glass windows of the half-landing that led across to the bedroom of Nurse Parsons and the maids. The bridge was of dark varnished wood, elaborately carved, and through its design the light of three small windows shone, making it seem almost black. On a little bracket on the wall at the end of the bridge was a cuckoo clock, and the children would linger on the stairs going up or down in the hope of seeing its carved doors fly open and the hysterical cuckoo pop out to give its signal. As this was always prefaced by a preliminary whirring sound, there was usually time to dash up the last ten steps to get a better view.

It was great fun, too, to watch Nurse Parsons glide quietly across the bridge, silhouetted against the light, and to catch a glimpse as she opened the door of the canary in its cage that hung at the end of the green screen just inside. "Just the sort of place for a ghost to walk!" Mary said gruesomely, and afterward, Felicity always looked up at the bridge a little nervously if she had to come upstairs alone after dusk. There was only one lamp, fixed to the top of the banisters, and the dim light of its pale blue, harebell-shaped shade did not help to dispel the looming shadows.

Downstairs, the big dining room, with its paneled walls and tapestries, was connected to the passage that let to the servant's hall by the revolving, barrel-like cupboard of the buttery hatch into which the dishes were put at mealtimes. What a different world this was from the one in which barefooted Jameelah carried the dishes silently across the stone floor of the dining room in the Wadi el Jose, and what fun it was to spin the buttery hatch round and round, listening to its rumbling progress.

Once Felicity packed herself into it to have a ride. But the shelf dividing the upper from the lower half made the space too cramped to be comfortable, and being spun round in the dark, all screwed up like a ball, made her feel sick and suddenly afraid, and she screamed to Mary to stop it and let her out.

A green baize swinging door divided the servant's quarters from the rest of the house, and behind this door were the glories of Mrs. Broom and the dairy. Mrs. Broom was large and smiling, with a big bosom firmly encased in a white blouse that was tucked into a wide petersham belt like Nurse Parsons', though you couldn't see this, of course, when she had the top of her apron up. Her head was piled with pale marmalade-colored hair. If Felicity could persuade her that she wouldn't be a nuisance and that her hands were clean, she was sometimes allowed to help roll the butter balls with the criss-crossed wooden butter pats that were damp and sweet-smelling.

The dairy, with its red-tiled floor, was the coolest place in the world, cooler than anything ever was in Jerusalem, so that after a while the children wanted to run out again into the sunshine. But even the sun was a little disappointing, especially when it was so easily obscured by grey cloud, and in the middle of what was supposed to be summer they would hear Nurse Parsons' quiet carrying voice calling them to come in out of the rain. Rain belonged to the winter, they felt; they were used to the summer *being* summer.

But of all the attractions the house had to offer, perhaps the most alluring was the bath, and for Felicity, bathing in it almost made up for the fact of having to go to bed before anybody else. The bathroom was down six very steep stairs, and it had a fireplace and a large sash window looking out onto the cherry tree in the drive. The bath itself filled up one whole wall of the room. All around the inside of its smooth glazed china, blue-green mermaids and water babies disported themselves amid bubbles that never burst. To be able to slosh yourself, and "swim," in such fascinating company was a perpetual pleasure after the arid two inches of water in the tin *tisht* in Jerusalem.

"Your grandmother's waiting to say good-bye to you," Nurse Parsons said, as she called them from the terrace. "Run along quickly now, and don't make too much noise."

So they climbed the wide stairs and tapped for the last time on the door of Babooshka's room, and heard her querulous old voice say, "Come in!"

"So you've come to say good-bye to me, have you?" she said. "Well, come round here, I've something I want to give each of you." Her ringed fingers fumbled for a minute with the folds of the bedclothes, then flashed on the thing they sought.

"Here, Mary, come closer. This is for you. It's an icon. Look after it carefully," and she put a small flat object into Mary's hand, and closed her fingers round it. "Now give me a kiss." Mary bent dutifully over the flannel nightgown and the white curls, and did what she was told.

"Dr. Carrick? Where are you? Here's one for you," and Felicity felt the velvet back of the tiny picture as it was pressed into her palm. "Now kiss your old Babooshka good-bye." The soft fingers clutched her wrist and she was pulled down over the bed, and the strange smell swept over her again as her grandmother's lips brushed her cheek. Then, holding her new treasure carefully, she tiptoed after Mary out of the room.

Down in the hall, by the dim light of the churchlike windows, there were more good-byes. Hats and coats were put on, and after Mrs. Broom's ample embrace and the more restrained kiss of Nurse Parsons, the children found themselves sitting on the shiny black seats of the taxi with suitcases all around them.

"Next stop Venice!" their mother said, after they swept down the lime avenue and had waved a last good-bye through the little window at the back of the taxi to the group of figures standing round the porch. "Mary says that in Venice the streets are made of water and you have to go everywhere in a boat," Felicity said, a little incredulously. "Is it really true, Mummie?"

But all the answer she got was, "You'll have to wait and see."

19

IT WAS NIGHT when they arrived, and in the dark, the Venice railway station was like any other big terminus, with its shouting crowds, the shunting and grinding of heavy wheels, and sudden clouds of steam hissing up into the distant metal rafters of the roof. The children stood sleepily by the luggage while their mother hunted for a porter, and when she came back with a swarthy and grinning Italian, they struggled behind him to the exit.

Gradually, Felicity became aware of a change in the atmosphere, of a quietness growing where noise and clamor had been only a moment before. Then a new sound began slowly to fill her ears—the steady, peaceful lapping of water.

"Listen, Mary!" she said, touching her sister on the arm. "Water!" and then, suddenly, drew in her breath. "Oh, look! *Look!*" And there before them the magic of Venice spread itself. The twinkling lights, the painted mooring posts rising out of the dark water, the incredible palaces stretching on both sides into the distance, with a second, ghostly row of reflections at their feet.

Mary was the first to recover from her surprise. "There you are," she said. "I said the streets were made of water." And then pulling Felicity by the sleeve, she added, "Come on, we're going by boat. Look, Mummie's waiting to get in, and the luggage is in already. Wake *up!*"

From that moment, they were right inside the fairy tale. As the gondola left the landing stage and slid out into the middle of the canal, Felicity could only sit, clutching the little metal rail at the side of the cushioned seat and listening to the plock-plock of the water under the gunwale and the rhythmic swish of the gondolier's oar where he stood behind her on the high curving end of the boat. The children's mother laughed softly in the darkness as she heard their sigh of contentment. "Do you like it?" she asked. And they both answered together, "Oh, *yes!*"

When Felicity woke in the morning, her first thought was to run to the bedroom window and look out. Yes, there it was! Different in the bright sunlight after the dark, but it was all there; it wasn't a dream! There were the houses growing out of the water, some with stately steps going down to the spiral stripes of the mooring posts, and some whose front doors seemed to open right into the canal! No grinding and jangling of trams like Port Said and Marseilles, no roar of traffic like London; just the lapping of the water and the shout of a gondolier as, miraculously balanced on the high narrow stern of his boat, he leaned on his one long oar and swept under the hotel window out of sight round the bend of the canal.

The three days before they had to go on to catch their boat at Trieste seemed to fly by and vanish almost before they had begun. The days were too short to cram into them all the things that they simply had to do. Feeding the pigeons in the piazza of Saint Mark and, afterward, walking up the steps of the cathedral out of the blinding sun into the incense-smelling darkness.

"It reminds me of the Church of the Holy Sepulchre," Felicity whispered to her sister as they stood for a moment listening to the sound of distant chanting echoing thinly round the dusky columns. Only perhaps the Church of the Holy Sepulchre was even more mysterious because it was darker, and when you pushed open the black padded door and left the noisy street behind you, hundreds of winking candles glowed at you out of the heavy shadows and there was the drowsy smell of burning scented wax.

When they came out again, they chose a little hot round iron table with a striped umbrella swaying over it and laughed as they listened to their mother trying out her halting Italian as she ordered pale lemon water-ices in little fluted glass dishes. The children sat on the iron chairs with their legs dangling and let spoonful after spoonful of ice cream lie in the hollows of their tongues till it melted. They watched the smart Venetian women parading up and down the piazza, and the nurses, who proudly displayed their babies, sewn into beautifully hand-embroidered white linen pillows, on their arms.

Many happy hours were spent pressing their noses against the windows of the fascinating little shops in the side streets bordering the great square, although their mother would not let them buy anything until they had definitely made up their minds what they wanted. "And it must be something small," she said, "that won't make our luggage any heavier."

For Felicity, this involved the most fearful heart searching and indecision. Supposing when she made her choice she didn't *really* like it, or wished she had bought something else, or immediately afterward saw in the next shop the thing for which she had been waiting all her life. On the last day, her choice finally fell on a green glass rabbit, about half an inch high, with a little metal collar circling its absurd neck, on which hung a tiny bead. Mary chose one like it, only hers was an almost transparent white.

It was after they had bought these treasures and had received them, carefully wrapped in the finest tissue paper, that they saw and instantly fell in love with the two minute dolls in celluloid baths. They were still and pink and sexless and much too small to have proper faces, and Felicity's heart sank as she realized that in her hand she held the enchanting green glass rabbit, and yet this inch-long naked baby was what she had really always wanted.

It was all happening just as she had feared. But it was Mary who had the courage to say, "Oh, Mummie, *look! Can* we have them too? They're so weeny they wouldn't be a bit heavy for our luggage." Their mother looked down at their faces and relented. "Yes, I think you can each have one if you like," she said, "as they're so very small. But this must really be the last."

"Mine's going to be Haroun al Rashid," Mary said as she took the tiny package in her hand.

"Oh, but I wanted Haroun for mine!" Felicity said.

"Well, you should have thought of it first," said Mary, quite firmly. "Yours can be Fatima. It's a very nice name and they *were* in love with each other."

So Fatima it had to be, and she was nonetheless enchanting for having a second-best name, Felicity decided, as she clutched her two new treasures tightly in a hot hand.

On their way back to the hotel, their mother paused for a moment outside the window of a jeweler. "Look at that lovely pearl necklace!" she said. Both children flattened their noses against the glass and followed her pointing finger. It was a short rope of pearls, each one varying slightly in size, with enough irregularity of shape to make every bead glow with its own milky warmth.

"Shall I buy it—as a present to myself?" she said, looking down at the children. "You've each got your own presents and I think I'd like one too!" They were not quite sure if she was being serious or not and looked up at her questioningly.

"Isn't it awfully expensive?" Mary asked.

"£200."

"Ooh, *Mummie!*" they both gasped, and Felicity added, "Have you *got* all that money? Then they saw the twinkle in her eyes and laughed. "You're joking, aren't you?"

"Yes, of course, I'm joking," she said, laughing too. "But is a lovely necklace, isn't it? Look how each pearl shines with a different light. It must have taken a long time for the oysters to make such beautiful ones, and a long time to collect them, too. Well, never mind. I'll get myself a present another time! Come along!"

It had been on their second day in Venice that the affair with the spaghetti happened. The children and their mother had taken their places for lunch at the little square table in the hotel dining room, and their mother had picked up the menu card to choose what they were going to have. "I think we can't leave Italy without having real Italian spaghetti at least once," she said, and the waiter hovering behind her with his napkin under his arm bowed and vanished.

A few minutes later he reappeared with a large covered tureen, which he set down on the table. Dexterously and with both spoon and fork held in some mysterious way in his right hand, he put a large portion of spaghetti onto each plate while Felicity watched with admiration. She had never seen such long spaghetti before; it seemed to go on and on, and it was obvious from the first moment that it was going to be very difficult to eat. To make it more complicated, the waiter then added a lot of tomato sauce and a sprinkling of grated cheese, bowed again, and disappeared.

"I think I should tuck your napkin under your chin," her mother suggested, "everyone does here." So Felicity stuffed the corner of the white linen firmly into the collar of her frock and, after a furtive look at the other diners to see how they approached the matter, took up her fork and went into the attack. It was certainly not easy. The long strings slipped between the prongs of the fork, and if she tried twizzling them over and over, while some wound themselves obediently around, others unwound themselves and slithered back into the plate.

Then she discovered that, by bending rather closer to it, she could push a few of the ends into her mouth with the fork and suck; the spaghetti rushed up with a whistling sound, quite satisfactorily, while the surplus juice trickled down her chin and dripped back to join the rest. It was messy but it worked, and the taste was certainly delicious. She was so busily employed in what was turning out to be rather an amusing method of eating that she hardly noticed a small plump man get up from his seat at a table opposite and come toward them. Then she heard a thick guttural foreign voice say, "Excuse me, please. May I make a picture of this little lady?" Felicity looked up with half a dozen strings of spaghetti hanging from her mouth to see him standing there in front of her with a camera in his hand. His head was round and bald and shining and his bespectacled face was one broad smile.

But before anything could happen, her mother had leapt to her feet, her face flaming. "Certainly not," she said, her voice coming quick with anger. "If you please, I'll have no such thing. How can you make fun of the child when you can see she's having difficulties! Take your camera away!"

Suddenly Felicity realized that it was herself who was the center of attraction, and embarrassment overcame her as she saw the other guests turn in their chairs to watch with amusement what was happening at her table. The last ends of the spaghetti rushed into her mouth so quickly that she almost choked, and she saw Mary—who was somehow managing much more tidily—giggling at her over the top of the tureen. She felt the color sweep up into her face and burn her ears, and the collar of her frock where the napkin was tucked in began to feel damp and tight. How *could* you eat it any other way? And why did they all have to look at her? She felt the tears pricking at the back of her eyes, but she swallowed them down angrily with the tomato sauce and manfully jabbed at another bunch of the offending spaghetti.

Meanwhile, her mother stood like a lioness protecting her cubs till the little man had reluctantly shut up his camera and gone back to his half-finished dinner. Then she sat down, muttering angrily, "Never heard of such a thing!

Why, it might have been in all the German papers. Officious little man!" Then she turned on Felicity and said crossly, "Here, for goodness sake, take a spoon and finish the rest of the spaghetti decently!"

But it was the middle of their last night, just to make sure they could not possibly forget, that Venice really showed the children her magic. They had gone to bed while it was still half light and had lain wakeful in the hot, stuffy bedroom while the smells from the canal wafted up through the open window in the deepening dusk. At last the lapping of the water sent them to sleep, and it was quite dark when Felicity suddenly found herself wide awake again and listening, she didn't at first know for what. Then she saw flickering patterns of light moving across the ceiling and realized that what had wakened her was the sound of singing coming up from the water below. She turned over in the bed and shook her sister gently by the shoulder.

"Mary, wake up! Listen! They're singing!" she whispered, and then without waiting for an answer, she threw back the sheet, scrambled out of bed, and padded quickly across to the window. As she leaned out over the sill, which was still warm from the day's sun, and looked down into the canal, she drew in her breath with a little gasp of excitement. "Oh, Mary! Come quick, quick!" she called back over her shoulder, and as she heard her sister's bare feet coming toward her, she made room for her at the window and they both looked out together.

And it was a sight to make you believe you were not awake at all, or had stepped right into one of the stories in the gilt-edged colored fairy-tale books or the Arabian Nights. Gliding slowly along the dark velvet water of the canal was a procession of gondolas, each one lighted with swinging colored lanterns and decked with flowers. Some were open boats with padded cushion seats, and others had little canopies over them out of which the men and women leaned, with their arms twined round each others' shoulders.

The soft warm lights of the lanterns flickered over their faces and made their teeth flash, and the faint splash of the oars could only be heard every now and then between the laughter and the singing. The gondoliers on their high perches were singing too, and the fringes of their long colored sashes swung slowly to the rhythm of the rowing.

Someone tossed a pink rose up to one of them and he let his oar trail for a moment as he caught it, laughing, and tucked it behind his ear. Spellbound, the children watched, and they were so intent that they did not realize their mother had joined them till they felt her hands rest lightly on their shoulders.

"I thought this was where I should find you!" she said, and they knew she was smiling, though they couldn't see in the dark. "Isn't it lovely?"

"It's like—like magic!" Felicity said, hardly above a whisper; it didn't seem safe to speak too loud in case their voices broke the spell and everything vanished.

Somewhere hidden in one of the boats, a mandolin started playing, and as its gentle throbbing swelled and joined the voices, Felicity felt the prickles rising on her skin; it was so sad, and so beautiful, and so exciting. Slowly the boats slid by, their prows like birds' beaks nosing each other as one overtook another, or dropped almost imperceptibly behind. And as they passed, their quivering reflections made an inverted image of lights, and pink roses, and dim shapes, silently moving through the watery stars.

The end of the procession came at last, and the singing dwindled to a faint echo as the stern of the last gondola, with its white-shirted, swaying oarsman and his shimmering double, slipped round the bend of the canal. Darkness took over again, and the warm quiet and the lapping water. Both children slowly let out a long, pent-up breath.

"Wasn't that lovely," their mother said. "All specially for us on our last night."

"I wish we could stay here for always," Felicity said, impetuously.

"What, and never go back to Jerusalem, and Helen and Prudy and Daddy?" Mary said.

"Oh, no, not that. I just wish . . ."

"You'd better wish yourself to sleep, I think," their mother said. "Come along. We leave for Trieste tomorrow to catch our boat and we have to get up very early."

So they kissed, already a little sleepily, and let themselves be shepherded over to the big bed; and there, to the sound of distant singing, already half-merged in dreams, they were soon asleep.

20

THE LAST GANGWAYS had been heaved aboard, and the last ropes tossed to the waiting sailors. The sections of the deck rail had been slipped back into their slots, the smooth wooden parts at the top fitting so closely together that you hardly noticed the joins as you passed your hand over them. Slowly, so slowly that at first you didn't believe it was moving, the *Vienna* slid from the stone side of the quay, and the gap of water with its floating bits of harbor refuse—a melon rind, a sodden crust of bread—widened, and grew big and dark and green.

The crowd on the quayside who had come to see off their friends and relatives waved fluttering white handkerchiefs and shouted their last messages, their voices growing smaller and fainter as the distance increased until the churning of the propellers and the swish of the water obliterated them altogether.

Mary and Felicity hung over the rail, chattering to each other and pointing first to one thing and then to another as the big liner swung slowly round and began to make her way across the harbor. They had left Venice the day before, and their going had been marked by one final excitement. They had been standing on the crowded platform of the station after the gondola had taken them for the last time along the Grand Canal, and they had left it regretfully when their mother said suddenly, "I'm going to get those pearls! Wait here by the luggage, both of you!" And she disappeared in the shifting throng.

"Oh, *Mary!*" Felicity had said, "D'you suppose she's really going? D'you think she'll have *time?*"

"I don't know," Mary said a little doubtfully. "It's miles and miles to the shop."

"But supposing the *train* comes!" Felicity said, a sudden fear sweeping over her. This business of getting separated could be so frightening, and it always seemed to happen in connection with trains. Either you weren't going to get there in time, or else you would be in the train and the others on the platform. There had been a terrifying moment in Milan when Mary, protesting noisily, was grabbed by the hair and heaved up the steep steps into the corridor as the train started with a sudden jolt. Or, worst of all, everyone else would be in and you would be the last and you couldn't feel safe until the door had been shut firmly behind you and you were leaning out of the window, protected by the frame and the safety catch and the long comforting leather strap inside.

And then, just as she felt an unreasonable, humiliating lump rising in her throat and she was quite sure she heard the train rumbling in the distance, there was her mother standing in front of them again. "You didn't really think I was going, did you?" she said, and as Felicity nodded, trying hard to prevent the tears of relief from coming into her eyes, her mother added, laughing, "Silly-billy! Of course I was only joking! Here, take a case, each of you. Here comes our train."

Their stay in Trieste had been short but memorable. They had had breakfast in the cool of the early morning on the veranda of the hotel overlooking the harbor and had been served with little curly shavings of butter floating in iced water. To their mother's disgust, the eggs were bad! There had been a set-to with the headwaiter in which, with her halting Italian interspersed with French, she definitely had the worst of the battle; and then, when they had gone up the red-carpeted stairs to their bedroom to finish their packing, her dressing gown was nowhere to be seen. It was of pale turquoise Arab silk that folded into a small square. It was her very best one, not the dark blue one she wore for ordinary occasions at home. "Did you pack it without noticing?" Mary suggested helpfully.

No, she was quite sure she hadn't; it had been lying on the bed by her nightgown when they had gone down to breakfast. To make quite sure it was nowhere around, they hurriedly searched through all the cases, but there was no sign of it anywhere. There was nothing for it but to go down to the manager and have a scene; she was not going to let her best dressing gown go without putting up *some* sort of a fight! But in the end, after a long and heated dispute in which the porter and the two chambermaids all repeatedly and dramatically protested that they had never seen a garment such as the one described, they had had to go without it; their mother paid the bill and they all climbed into the waiting carriage. "Well, we shall never go *there* again!" she said, as they drove off down to the harbor. "I knew it was going to be a horrid hotel as soon as I saw those miserable little shavings of butter!"

❧ The *Vienna* had moved quite far from the quay now and was beginning to gather speed. The little figures left behind at the harbor's edge had stopped waving and were beginning to disperse. They looked hardly any bigger than the children's Rashid and Fatima, who were snugly packed away, each in its celluloid bath. That was the worst part about journeys, Felicity thought as she watched from her vantage point on the railings, this business of saying good-bye. Wherever you went, you nearly always had to leave someone behind, and that meant that you were sorry about them not coming with you or sorry that you could not stay with them. It took something away from the enjoyment of the start of the journey itself. The excitement of the early breakfasts that you never really wanted to eat, the shutting of the last cases, the whole thrilling, agitating business of tickets and trains and ships was tinged with sadness because of having to say good-bye.

But on the last part of this journey, at least, they had not had to leave anyone behind, and there was something satisfying and complete about the fact that they were all three of them on the *Vienna* and that none of the tiny waving figures on the quay belonged to them or were sad because they were going.

"Let's go down to the end of the deck and see what those children there are doing," Mary suggested when the harbor was too far away to be interesting any more. So they climbed down from the railings and sauntered along, and looked on for a bit, pretending not to be too interested. Presently, one of the group, a fair-haired little girl of about their age, came and joined them and leaned against the railings beside them.

"Where are you going?" she asked.

"Jerusalem," Mary answered. "That's where we live; we've just been staying in England because our grandmother was ill."

"We live in Jerusalem too," the little girl said. "What is your name?"

The children told her, then Felicity asked, "What's yours?"

"Cenus."

"*Cenus?*" Mary said, wrinkling up her forehead. "Are you sure you don't mean Venus?"

"No, of course I don't," was the rather scornful answer. "Cenus is a Jewish name."

A very peculiar name, Felicity thought. Her own was not a very ordinary one, and she was secretly very proud of the fact that people never seemed to understand what it was when she first told them, and nearly always asked her to spell it. That made it somehow more especially hers.

"Those are my two brothers over there," Cenus added. "They're called Moses and Aaron."

Felicity looked round quickly almost expecting to see someone in a crimson bath towel with a long beard, like the picture in the big Bible that showed Moses and Aaron holding up the tablets on Mount Sinai. Surely *ordinary* people weren't called names like that? But when Cenus called out shrilly, "Moses! Aaron! Come here!" two very ordinary little boys with dark hair and pink faces came up and joined them.

They shook hands solemnly with Mary and Felicity, and then no one quite knew what to do next. It was Aaron finally who had the bright idea that sealed a friendship to last the whole voyage. "Race you round the deck!" he said suddenly; and off they all went, laughing and shouting. They dodged around elderly couples taking stately promenades and jumped over the legs of prone forms in deck chairs till, one by one, they reached "home" again, panting and disheveled, their hair all tangled with the salt wind of the Adriatic, and the light of the setting sun in their eyes.

21

IN THE EARLY AUTUMN, after the children's return from England, things began happening that, it was obvious, would alter the whole pattern of their lives in Jerusalem. The first of these was the drainage scheme and the second, Mary's teeth.

There had been a good deal of talk about the drainage scheme for some time previously, but it was grown-up talk and not very interesting to either Mary or Felicity; when their father began speaking about it, they usually stopped listening or started a discreet conversation of their own. All they knew was that some sort of excavations were taking place in the Wadi el Jose, and that when the hot weather started, and the wind blew in a certain direction, a peculiar and unpleasant smell crept into the garden and even pervaded the house.

"I think drainage is bathrooms with taps and lavatory plugs that pull, like at Babooshka's," Mary said, when Felicity asked her one day was it was all about.

"But why do they have to dig up the earth in the Wadi el Jose?"

"Well, I think they have to have pipes for it to run away into when you pull the plug," Mary said.

Felicity was not very sure whether that made matters any clearer, but she supposed it must be right. It was difficult, though, to see how pipes right down in the valley were going to help very much.

The really unfortunate part about it was that they were no longer allowed to go and play on the Flat Rock; and as the late August heat continued, the unpleasant smell grew stronger and was noticeable much more often. Even the Little Ones knew all about it, and Helen would come in from a game under the olive tree with her small nose wrinkled up in disgust, saying, "Poof! Drainage is smelling again today!"

"If it gets much worse, we shall have to do something about it," the children heard their mother saying to their father one day. "I'm sure it's most unhealthy and I don't want the children getting ill. We've had enough trouble with the whooping cough this year as it is."

Their father snorted impatiently. "Well, I did my best to dissuade them," he said. "I told them often enough 'You can't have drainage without adequate water,' and if there is one thing the Wadi is short of it *is* water!"

"Can't you ask them to find us another house?"

"My dear, it isn't as simple as that," their father answered her.

"Are we going to go away from here, Mummie?" Felicity asked, after their father had gone out. (You could always tell he was a bit annoyed if he called their mother "my dear" in that sort of voice.) But she only said, "I don't know," and obviously wasn't really listening, so it was no good asking any more questions just then.

Mary's teeth were much more interesting. The middle ones were all right, and nice and straight, but those on either side, mysteriously called eye-teeth, were sticking out in a most unfortunate way. (Why they should have such an odd name Felicity could never understand—unless it were something to do with "an eye for an eye and a tooth for a tooth," but even then, the connection wasn't very clear.)

There had been a good deal of talk about Mary's teeth ever since they had started sticking out so badly. "Just like a rabbit's teeth they look!" Jock had said once, and Mary hadn't known whether to laugh or to be cross. So she had been taken to see a London dentist while they were in England. "He said it would be a 'long job,'" Mary had told her sister afterward, "and that I might have to go and see a dentist *every* day, and wear a band on them."

"What's a band?"

"Well, I think it's a bit of wire fixed on somehow, so as to make them come straight."

Now after their return, the whole question was being discussed again.

"I wonder who you'll go to," Felicity said thoughtfully.

She didn't somehow think Mr. Beaumont did things like that; he just did ordinary stoppings. Mr. Beaumont was the only member of the American Colony who was called "Mr.," and the children supposed it was because he had such an elegant chair in his small surgery, which he would tilt back suddenly when you least expected it. He was very nice and would let you try and pick up the fascinating and elusive beads of quicksilver from the palm of his hand before he mashed them up into the grey stuff he used for the fillings. But try as you might, the quicksilver never let itself be caught but divided itself up into even smaller beads that slid away from your fingers.

"Oh, I don't know," Mary said, and then added airily, "I might go away altogether."

"Go *away?* Oh, Mary, where *to?*"

"Well, I *heard* Mummie and Nannie talking together and saying something about Cairo," Mary said in an important and secret way, "and Helen might be coming with me," she added. As she spoke, Felicity felt a faint chill come into the air, the first uneasy breath of change. She put down the spade she had been digging with and sat back on her heels, repeating blankly, "Oh, Mary!" as she tried to sort out in her mind what this would really mean.

No Mary to whisper to at night before she went to sleep, till the back of her throat ached with trying to make herself heard; no Mary to send messages to through the rustling leaves of the olive tree; no Mary to help make the long walk back from school seem shorter by racing her through Smelly Lane or across the last field; no Mary to help enliven the dull readings of *Mrs. Markham's History for Children.*

It was their father's idea to read Mrs. Markham. "They must have some history," he had said. "History is what matters, never mind about the other things."

So every day, after they had had their tea and before Felicity's bedtime, they would settle down with him in the drawing room and have a chapter from the thick brown book with its solid paragraphs and close type. It was not a very interesting book, and Felicity found it hard to keep her mind from wandering onto other things. There were a lot of long words she didn't understand, and she couldn't keep asking what they meant because her father didn't like being interrupted in the middle of a sentence.

The children sat on either side of him and followed his smooth white ivory paper knife moving along the lines as he read, and saw with relief when the page turned over the end of the chapter approaching. It was at the ends of the chapters that the greatest interest lay, for then Mrs. Markham's children asked questions which she herself answered.

Mary and Felicity chose which children they wanted to be and their father read the answers where it said "Mrs. M." Felicity had an uncomfortable feeling that Richard and George and little Mary Markham had been listening with much more attention than she and her sister, because they always seemed to ask such grown-up and complicated questions; but it was fun taking turns with Mary in reading the bits out loud, and it made up for the dullness of the rest of the chapter.

But what should she do now if Mary was really going to Cairo? She couldn't be *all* the Markham children herself, or you would never know who was asking what! And the sing-songs! How could they have sing-songs if both Mary *and* Helen were going away? Half the thrill was seeing if she could race Mary in finding the page of the next song. This was not easy, because the songbook (a collection made by the children's parents, and printed at their father's press years ago) was arranged in a complicated way with two sets of numerals, Roman and ordinary.

On winter evenings after tea, their mother would sit down at the piano and swing back the folding doors of the keyboard while the children settled down around their father in front of the stove. The smell of smokily burning chunks of olive wood filled the air, and the one lamp cast big shadows in the corners of the room.

"I know what my choice is going to be!" Mary would say, a glint in her dark eyes.

Felicity looked at her apprehensively, trying to read her thoughts. Don't let it be "Come, Davie, I'll Tell Ye a Secret," she besought some unspecified deity, nor "A Golden Comb for Golden Hair." It was so dreadful if someone else picked the one you wanted for your choice; you quickly had to think of another. As the final notes of the first song died away, Mary was ready with her number: "Two, two!" she said triumphantly.

Two was one of the easiest of the Roman numbers, and then two again. Felicity turned the rough-edged pages hurriedly. She was saved! It was "The Golden Vanity," and she could sing the sad story of the little cabin boy and the perfidious skipper with unspoiled enjoyment, knowing her turn was next and that no one could now steal her favorite.

At last it was her choice.

"What number, Popatoos?"

"Two, eight."

There was a fluttering of pages and then a click as her mother's ringed fingers touched the notes for the first chord.

> Oh a golden comb for golden hair,
> And milk-white pearls for a neck as fair,
> And coral and amber all for me
> The day my ship comes home from sea.

Oh lingering, lovely tune, and her mother's voice at the piano rising with the others to the top note, and then dropping slowly and sadly down again.

> Oh never will that ship come home,
> Wherever she be sailing from;
> I warmed my hands beneath the stars
> By a fire made of her broken spars.

> With coral and amber I weighted him,
> And still he was light enough to swim,
> With silver chains I bound him down,
> There was never a corpse so hard to drown.

> His black hair lines an eagle's nest
> On a sea-girt rock in the lonesome west;
> Now jet for coral there must be,
> And instead of amber, ebony.

Sad, sad were the grey waves; and sad the spray dashing up against the wet rocks. A bleak wind ruffled the eagle's feathers as she sat on her eggs in the nest with its lining of black hair, and there was a glimmer of silver chains in the depths of the dark waters.

And then from a great distance Helen's small eager voice broke in. " 'The Silly Old Man,' I want 'The Silly Old Man,' " she said. And Felicity dragged herself back from the "lonesome west" to the warm lamplight and the glow of the stove on the flagstones, and the idiotic adventures of the Silly Old Man.

How could there be proper sing-songs if Mary and Helen went to Cairo? The only thing to do was to put the whole matter out of her mind and try not to think about it at all.

And then, suddenly, everything started happening at once. In the late autumn days when the olives had been harvested, and the corn cut and threshed and carried away, and the bare stubble fields were waiting to be ploughed up for the winter crop, Mary was packed off to Cairo—"It's not *really* Cairo, it's Heliopolis, just outside of Cairo," she said—with Nannie and Helen as well.

"Helen needs a change," their mother had said when Felicity asked why she was going too. "She hasn't been very well ever since she had whooping cough, and she got very thin and peaky while we were in England this summer. A few months with Nannie and Mary in Cairo will just put her right."

So Akhmed and his carriage with the two white horses came and fetched them away, with their luggage piled on the box beside the driver and Nannie in her neat velvet-trimmed bonnet holding onto Mary and Helen as they leaned round the side waving a last farewell.

Felicity had hardly had time to get used to the idea of what it was going to be like on her own (because Prudy at three years old didn't count as a playmate) when the second bombshell fell. It *was* decided that they must leave the house in the Wadi el Jose.

"Leave the *house!* Oh, Mummie, but where shall we go? Where shall we live?" Felicity asked, looking up at her mother a little anxiously. Leave the garden and their house in the olive tree? Leave their own little garden patches under the pepper's feathery branches where Mary had once so boldly chopped up a scorpion with her spade when it had scuttled out at them from a crack in the wall? (After the excitement was over, they had shoveled up the scorpion's remains and tossed them into the Wadi.) Leave the cistern and the charm of its capricious winter ways, and the slippery tobogganing slope beyond the cosmos and the hollyhocks?

"Why do we have to leave? Is it because of the drainage scheme?" she asked. Her mother said it was and that the smell was really getting too bad. "I don't think it's good for any of us," she said, "so Daddy and I decided it was better to leave now before it gets any worse. We're going to Mr. Richmond's house on the other side of the American Colony, so you won't have such a long way to walk to school now that you have to go without Mary."

"Where are the Richmonds going to live, and is Waardi coming with us?" Felicity asked, and a thousand other questions came crowding into her mind, all clamoring to be answered.

"Yes, Waardi *is* coming with us, and the Richmonds are going away for three months; by that time I expect we'll have found another place to live," her mother said. "Now run along out and play, like a good girl. I've got a great many things to sort out and a lot of packing to do."

Felicity wandered out into the garden. It was a bright October day with the sun shining. They were ploughing up the field above the house, and the stones showed whiter than ever where they lay on the darkness of the newly turned earth. The path across the field had half disappeared already and there would be no Mary to help her tread down the new one. Perhaps it was better they were going to another house; it would have taken her a long time to tread it down alone.

She went down the shallow earthen steps by the water butt and crossed the little square of white chipped stones to the three rock steps leading down to the olive trees. The autumn wind was rustling the leaves as she climbed its rough bark to her own perch. It seemed lonely and deserted, and she flicked a couple of lazy earwigs out of the pot of lentils as she settled herself into the crook of the branches and dangled her legs over the side. If she moved her right foot up a little, she could blot out the German kaiser's tower on the Mount of Olives, and if she let it fall, the whole of the tower showed. She could even see the little bits of sky peeping through at the top where the bells hung, before the tower rose on up to its pointed tip.

Perhaps it was a good thing to be leaving all the favorite places, because none of them would be quite the same if there was no Mary to enjoy them with her and everything had to be done alone. Perhaps it would be nice at the Richmonds' house anyway. She couldn't remember the house, though, of course, she remembered Mr. Richmond himself very well. He was a friend of her father's, and the thing that made him different from anyone else, and somehow a little more exciting, was his stiff leg. Nannie had warned them from the first time he had come to the house to tea not to "pass a remark" about it, but as he always had to put his leg up on a footstool or a chair, you couldn't help noticing, though of course you never said anything or, at least, not while he was there.

The other thing about Mr. Richmond that made him different was the look in his ice-blue eyes. Uncle Eena's eyes were very blue, but they hadn't the penetrating fiery quality of Mr. Richmond's. If it were true, as it said in the fairy tales sometimes, that eyes could be cold as ice and at the same time burn like a blue flame, then his eyes did, and it made you feel a little uncomfortable. You were never quite sure when he fixed them on you whether the look they gave you was a friendly one or not.

They had once been on a great expedition to Nebi Samuel, Mr. Richmond and Mary and Felicity and their father. The two grown-ups had ridden mules (Mr. Richmond managing very skillfully, in spite of his stiff leg), and the children, donkeys. They had taken a picnic lunch with them, wrapped up and squeezed into a large, pale blue linen shoe bag that was tied onto their father's saddle. Both children had been very proud of being thought old enough to manage their donkeys by themselves while their father and Mr. Richmond rode on ahead, talking together and paying no attention to them at all. It was a long hot ride over the stony brown hills, but they finally found a picnic place near the summit where they could lean their backs against a stone wall enclosing a vineyard.

After everything in the blue shoe bag had been eaten, Mary and Felicity left their father and Mr. Richmond propped somnolently against the wall, their hats tilted over their eyes, and went to forage for grapes. "This looks like a good place," Mary said as she disappeared between two rows of vines. Felicity could see her dark head bobbing up at intervals where a gap in the interlacing branches gave a glimpse of the row beyond.

The bunches of sun-warm grapes hung half-hidden among the leaves. They were small and golden brown, and were covered with a dusty bloom. How sticky they were when they burst between your fingers as you wrestled with the wiry stalks and tried to twist them loose from the parent branch! And how syrupy-sweet they tasted as your teeth broke through the dusty skins into the juicy insides!

When they came back with their booty and Mr. Richmond saw how many bunches of grapes they had each picked, he looked at them with his burning blue eyes and laughed. "Greedy guts!" he said. The children had looked at each other and at the grapes in their sticky hands a little shamefacedly. Did he *really* disapprove? They couldn't be sure.

Felicity shifted herself in the crook of the olive tree and looked out over the Flat Rock. Perhaps today she would really see Goliath in his golden armor, swaggering down the Wadi, and David standing on one of the flat ledges, stooping to find the right-sized pebble for his sling. It was a pity they couldn't play there any more: it had been such a very special playing place. But the valley looked rather sad and derelict now, littered with trenches for the drainage scheme and the pipes that were waiting to be laid in them. It was no longer the wide brown thoroughfare that their father's horse had so alarmingly bolted down one day, with herself perched up behind, frenziedly clutching the belt of his corduroy breeches.

"Hold on tight, Popatoos!" he had shouted at her over his shoulder. But she had only one hand to hold with because in the other was the same blue shoe bag with her and Mary's "elevenses." The horse had bucked and reared as soon as her father had lifted her up behind him (it had been "in hospital with boils," he had explained afterward), and Mary, whose turn was to have come afterward, let out a little gasp of fear. Then it had settled its teeth on the bit and charged off down the valley, with Felicity bumping up and down at the back, and Mary running frantically along behind in a vain effort to keep up.

At last her father had got the animal under control, and when it slithered to a halt, its neck lathered with soapy foam, a rather shaken Felicity was lifted down to the ground. "I didn't fall off," she said proudly as her sister joined her, panting. "And I didn't drop the 'elevenses' either!" But a bolting horse would have a hard job negotiating the trenches and the drain pipes now.

Perhaps she would find new favorite places in the Richmonds' garden that could be shown to Mary when she came back from Cairo; and anyway, it would be winter soon and there would be Christmas to start looking forward to, and after that her birthday.

She heard her mother's voice calling her in to tea, and as she slid down the trunk of the olive tree and jumped from the last low fork to the ground, the prospect of the move to the new house began to be almost exciting. Lots of things could happen when you had to pack up all the furniture and everything and move it in a lorry from one house to another. She had better go through Louisa's and Mabel's things after tea, and pack them, and make sure nothing was left behind. Yes, after all, perhaps it was going to be quite fun. She called out, "Com-ing!" and ran briskly across the garden and up the stone steps into the house.

2 2

THE MOVE TOOK SEVERAL DAYS. It was accomplished with the assistance of an army lorry, procured somehow with the help of the American Colony. As no one was moving into the house they were leaving in the Wadi el Jose, there was no particular hurry, and if something was forgotten, a special trip could be made to collect it the next day.

"It's rather like Robinson Crusoe always going back to the wreck of his ship for something else useful that he had forgotten!" the children's mother said, and Felicity agreed with a laugh. After that, the deserted house in the Wadi was always alluded to as "The Wreck."

The new house was much less interesting, for it was single-storied and had no stairs. All the rooms opened onto a central hall, but there was no courtyard. It had a rough wild patch of garden, full of stones, with a fig tree in one corner and a loose, tumbledown wall enclosing it.

Felicity soon slipped into the new pattern of things without her sisters, and even began to find that Prudy could be useful for playing some sorts of games. But they had not been long in the new house before there was an addition to the family to help in the absence of Nannie.

"Do you remember Miss Hands?" her mother asked her one day. "She used to give you and Mary lessons in Campden before we came to Jerusalem? She's coming out here from England to help us and to look after Prudy." Felicity nodded. She remembered Miss Hands dimly as a rather gaunt tall person with marmalade-colored, wispy hair swept up from the back of her neck and pale green eyes. She used to come to the house in Campden every morning and give lessons to Mary and herself and Barbara and Alistair, two other children who joined them. Alistair was a serious, black-haired little boy of Felicity's age who wore mittens, and Barbara had long fair sausage curls and sometimes came in a purple velvet frock that Felicity found most beautiful and desirable.

In Campden, if Barbara and Alistair arrived in good time, the four children played a game of which they never tired. It was to hide from Miss Hands and see how long it took her to unearth them after her arrival. The quickest thing to do if there was not much time left was to roll themselves up in the folds of the heavy William Morris curtains that hung by the step dividing the higher level of the big room from the lower. These curtains were of red-brown woolen tapestry, patterned with bushy-tailed squirrels that climbed in pairs forever through thick forests. The curtains were hot and tickly when you wrapped yourself up in them, and it was almost impossible to keep absolutely still and not give yourself away by fidgeting. Somehow, Miss Hands always seemed to find them very quickly when they chose the curtains to hide in.

Another good place had been the carved oak cupboard at the far end of the room. It had an upper compartment with two little latticed doors which were inside the big doors. This compartment made the lower half rather cramped, but the four children had just been able to fit in with their legs carefully tucked under them. The heavy carved doors had a spring lock, so they were always very careful not to let them shut completely but to leave a little crack open, which Miss Hands would certainly never notice.

One day they had decided to hide in the cupboard only at the very last moment, and there had been a wild rush to squeeze in. Mary pulled the doors behind them and there was an ominous click. The spring lock had shut fast! Instantly, Felicity felt the darkness inside grow menacing and stifling. It closed in on her and became more frightening as she began to scream. Supposing no one heard them! Supposing Miss Hands didn't come that day— she might be ill! Supposing they were there, shut up in the dark for ever-and-ever-amen! The others were screaming too now, and the noise had become so frantic that the sound of footsteps hurrying across the floor toward the cupboard was almost inaudible.

At last there was a double click; the big old key turned in the lock and, as four small frenzied pairs of hands pushed, the doors burst open. And there stood Miss Hands, half-laughing, half-scolding, surrounded by the bright comforting light of day, the light that Felicity had almost thought she might never see again! For a second she felt again now a sense of wild relief. Yes, she remembered Miss Hands.

A few days later Miss Hands arrived in Jerusalem, and as Felicity presented a cheek to be kissed, she noticed the same yellowish tortoiseshell combs stuck precariously in the same wispy hair, and she decided that Miss Hands had not altered at all.

One of the big compensations for her sister's absence was that her father now began to read aloud to Felicity whereas before the honor had been reserved for Mary because she was the eldest. Throughout the previous spring, and until their visit to England, Felicity had been consumed with jealously at the thought of all the stories that her sister alone was hearing. Mary and her father had worked their way right through the Arabian Nights, and then Odysseus, fragments of whose exciting adventures Mary would sometimes relate in the darkness of their bedroom after she, too, had come to bed.

Once, after much and persistent badgering, Felicity had persuaded her father to read something just for her alone, and he had chosen the ballad of Kate Barlass who had barred the door to the king's enemies with her own arm. Spellbound, Felicity had drunk in every word and the next day could not resist flaunting her secret to Mary when she and Nannie and the two Little Ones were sitting in the shade outside the front door.

"Daddy read to me *specially* yesterday," she said, as causally as she could. "A much nicer story than yours."

"It wasn't a nicer story than Odysseus, *I* know," Mary answered. "What was it anyway?"

"It was a long, long poem."

"A poem isn't a story, silly," Mary said, scornfully.

"This was. It was a story *and* a poem, all together," Felicity said firmly, and then added rashly, "I'll fetch it and read it to you, if you like."

As she said it, she knew she was tempting Providence, but it was done now, and the challenge was quickly taken up. So she went into the drawing room and started, with her courage already failing, to hunt through the many books on the shelves. She had no idea of the name of the book, but she

FOREWORD

The prominent role played by military establishments and groups in the less developed countries of the world has raised important practical questions for the United States in the field of foreign affairs, and has stimulated scholarly interest in causes and consequences, including relationships to other aspects of the dynamics of the societies concerned. In the case of the former colonial areas of Asia and Africa, revolutionary armed forces contributed to the disintegration of the colonial order after World War II and in many instances played directly the dominant role in bringing new nations into being. After having made this contribution to the changing political order, the military often did not fade, as some expected, from the political stage as civil authority became established. When civilian government did emerge, it was in some cases only to be followed by the reappearance of the military as a contender for power, or by the parallel emergence of the military as an interest group with substantial clout.

In Latin America analogous revolutionary armed forces brought independence to most of the Central and South American region more than a century before the wave of decolonization in Africa and Asia took place following World War II. In spite of the great lapse in time, military establishments are still playing a dominant role in many countries of Latin America, a circumstance which has evoked much special attention and concern in discussions of contemporary Latin America. Moreover, in recent years the number of governments in which the military have taken power from civilian regimes has increased after a period when a trend seemed to be away from military intervention in civil government. In a number of countries—Argentina, Bolivia, Brazil, Panama, Peru, and Ecuador—the military now exercises direct political control. In others—Guatemala, Nicaragua, El Salvador, Honduras and the Dominican Republic, for example—the military has exerted unusual influence in affairs of state. In only a very few—notably Chile, Colombia and Uruguay—is the influence of the military substantially limited to the circumscribed domain of defense affairs.

Three categories of what might be termed "comparative" studies of the military as an institution in society have developed. The role of the military as a *general phenomenon* has received attention since the 1930's in a large and growing literature, including a number of extensive theoretical studies.[1]

---

[1]The more definitive studies include, for example, Samuel P. Huntington's *The Soldier and the State* (1959); Morris Janowitz's *The Professional Soldier* (1960); and Samuel Finer's *The Man on Horseback* (1964).

The role of the military in a new nation has also received extensive attention, especially in the last decade.[2] With respect to the Americas there is a much longer interest in the subject. Indeed it has been impossible to consider the past century and a half of Latin American political-social history without a major concern with the military—with *caudillos, golpes* and military juntas. The older scholarship on Latin America concerned with the role of the military primarily in an historical perspective has been complemented by a new scholarship more behavioral and environmental in its orientation and conceptually related to the other two categories of military studies. For reasons which will be briefly discussed below, the literature on the military in Latin America has been more controversial than that of the other two categories mentioned above.

At the University of Miami, the Center for Advanced International Studies has had underway for several years a number of research projects devoted to the military in Latin America. And beginning with this monograph on the institutional nature and role of the military establishments in two key countries, Bolivia and Argentina, we have scheduled several publications on the subject.[3]

In common with others who are aware of the wide variety and complexity of military institutions and roles in Latin America, we have long been uneasy about the overabundant generalizations that underlie much of US thinking and many US policies toward military establishments in Latin America. Particularly disturbing has been the predilection to view "the military" as a highly homogeneous group with perceived interests of remarkable similarity throughout the area. "The military" has been pictured variously as retarding political development, providing minimum order for evolutionary political processes, siphoning off resources needed for economic development, acting as modernizing agents in development, etc., etc. But few studies have taken into account the deep differences *within* the military

---

[2]The more extensive studies include, for example, *The Role of the Military in Underdeveloped Countries* (1962), edited by John J. Johnson; Morris Janowitz's *The Military in the Political Development of New Nations* (1964); and H. Daalder's *The Role of the Military in Emerging Countries* (1962). See also *The Politics of Developing Areas*, by Gabriel Almond and James S. Coleman (1960).

[3]Among other of the Center's efforts, a major study of the political and socioeconomic role of the military in Latin America sponsored by the Directorate of Doctrine, Concepts and Objectives of Headquarters, United States Air Force, has been completed under the direction of Dr. Clyde C. Wooten, Associate Director of the Center. This study included case studies of 12 Latin American countries. A book reflecting the results of this and subsequent research is under preparation by Dr. Wooten and Colonel Charles D. Corbett, a research associate of the Center and the author of the present study.

officer corps and the effects of these divisions on the sociopolitical policies advanced by what is a rather unique regional political elite. As the author of this monograph observes, the Latin American military is an old and complex institution in old and complex societies. Because of its traditional structural location in each of the societies of which it forms such a prominent part, the military has been no more immune to the stresses of the twentieth century than has the society at large. Its reaction and response to those stresses, however, is the product of unique historical experiences; it varies, and will continue to do so, among countries.

Another and perhaps more serious matter that has troubled us is the persistence with which many North Americans have projected their own perceptions and political prejudices onto the picture they have drawn of the Latin American military and have then allowed these to shape their thinking about how the military fits into the present and future of Latin America. For a long period, of course, it was a case of simply continuing with the early stereotypes of the fat, mustachioed *jefe*, crisscrossed with bandoliers and wearing a whopping sombrero, which were based largely upon our contacts with and knowledge of Mexican revolutionary forces and our tutelage relationships with the constabulary of the small countries of Central America and Hispanola. More recent has been the influence of the models we have structured of what Latin American societies should be like according to standards of *our* choosing and arbitrary judgments of how military establishments do or do not fit into these models. And giving a special fillip to this exercise in big-brotherness have been domestic differences and debate over US policies toward Latin America.

Of central importance has been the direct issue of US military aid programs and interrelations between the objectives and results of these programs and other US aid efforts. President Truman's introduction of an Inter-American Military Cooperation bill in 1947 revealed early differences over the military assistance issue and the underlying theme of the military's role in Latin American societies. Under Secretary of State Dean Acheson opposed the bill on the grounds that it would encourage the Latins to spend money for arms that should go for developing industry and raising living standards.[2] It is significant that in its first public airing after World War II, the question of military assistance for Latin America turned not on issues of security but on those of politics and development. The Congress showed

---

[2]The text of Acheson's letter to the Defense Department opposing the bill appears in an April 1947 supplement to *Human Events*.

scant interest in the bill, and it was not until after the start of the Korean War that military assistance to Latin America was authorized in Title IV of the omnibus Mutual Security Act of 1951.

The events of the fifties, in the new context of the military assistance agreements effected under the Mutual Security Act, attracted the serious attention of opinion-forming elements to the Latin American military and especially to their political role. Milton Eisenhower's widely publicized trips to the region in 1953 and 1955, the advent of military governments in Venezuela and Colombia, and the overthrow of Perón in Argentina brought the domestic politics of South America to the attention of a US increasingly convinced that it could not ignore such political upheavals in any part of the world. Events in the northern tier were particularly impelling after Vice President Nixon's discomfiting visit to Venezuela in 1958. And, of course, Castro's 1959 victory in Cuba was followed by a spate of revolutionary and counterrevolutionary alarms in Central America and the Caribbean.

Twelve Latin American countries had signed military assistance agreements with the US by 1958, and some form of military supply was being provided to seven others. The aid was justified in cold-war terms—strong Latin American forces would relieve US troops of the burden of defending the hemisphere in the event of war and insure the future availability of strategic resources.[3]

Congressional concern over the civil-military issue developed slowly, and in the war environment of the early fifties the Administration's military assistance requests for the hemisphere were met with little demurrer. Opposition intensified, however, as the decade came to a close. Senator Wayne Morse, convinced that US aid was weighing heavily against democratic elements in domestic power struggles, led a successful move to limit grant military aid to $55 million in the revised Mutual Security Act of 1959, and, in a classic example of an idea doomed by events already underway, wrote in a provision that "internal security requirements should not, unless the

---

[3]See US 82nd Congress, 1st Session, House Foreign Affairs Committee, *Hearings on MSA for 1951*, Washington, 1951, pp. 1080-1082, and Senate Foreign Relations Committee, *Hearings on MSA for 1951*, Washington, 1951, p. 38. *Department of State Bulletin*, March 30, 1954, pp. 463-464, posited the following fundamental assumptions for US hemispheric security policy: 1) that the hemisphere was threatened by communist agression both from within and without; 2) that the security of strategic areas of the hemisphere and of inter-American lines of communication were vital to the security of every American country; 3) that the protection of these strategic areas and communications was a common responsibility.

President determines otherwise, be the basis of military assistance programs to American Republics."[4]

The unspoken assumption, of course, was that Latin American military establishments could not always be counted upon to use their arms in the best interests of their societies and, by extension, in ways conducive to the furtherance of US interests in the region. This concept of a predatory group acting upon rather than within its society has proved persistent.

The first important analytical rationale for such a blanket black legend of the military's role in Latin America appeared in a 1959 study prepared for the Senate Foreign Relations Committee by the University of New Mexico. Professor Edwin Lieuwen, in a major contribution to this study, posited the idea of social revolution as the overwhelming problem for Latin America in the postwar years and pictured the military as a major obstacle to this revolutionary process. Lieuwen attacked the underlying assumptions of hemispheric security policy and concluded that military assistance was counterproductive in that it promoted artificial stability and frequently put the US in the position of supporting unpopular governments. The study recommended that the US gradually reduce its military aid with a view to eliminating it within a few years.[5]

Lieuwen's analysis became widely influential after its incorporation into his book, *Arms and Politics in Latin America*, published in 1961, and helped to establish as something of a US doctrine the emerging image of the Latin American military as a dysfunctional element obstructing social reform. However, events in Cuba and the reading in the US of communist pronouncements relative to wars of national liberation conditioned the hemispheric security policies of the Democratic administrations of the sixties and kept Latin American armed forces on the military assistance lists despite increasing manifestations of Congressional misgivings about their political role. An early review of policy assumptions by Defense Secretary McNamara moved the emphasis from continental defense to domestic counterinsurgency and civic action, except for some possible assistance by Latin countries in anti-submarine warfare. Civic action gave the military a respectable role, accepted for the time being by even the most liberal critics, in the evolutionary process envisioned by the Alliance for progress.

---

[4]*The Mutual Security Act of 1959*, section 105(b)(4). See also US 86th Congress, 1st Session, Senate Foreign Relations Committee, *Report on Hearings, the Mutual Security Act of 1959*, Washington, 1959, pp. 73-74.

[5]See US 86th Congress, 2nd Session, Senate Foreign Relations Committee, *United States-Latin American Relations*, Washington, 1960, pp. 10-51.

The question of civil military relations would not fade away, however. Military dictatorships in Korea, Pakistan, and Turkey caused Congressmen to grumble again about the deleterious effects of military assistance on "the struggle for democracy" in considering the Foreign Assistance Act of 1962,[6] and a widely publicized photograph of a US tank battering down the gates of the presidential palace in Lima, Peru, during a coup in July 1962 caused a flurry of outrage.[7]

The anomalies in a policy that sought urgent social renovation *and* a large measure of stability in societies dominated in varying degrees by what were pictured as conservative—if not reactionary—military establishments proved a challenge to US political and social scientists, who confronted the issues in respectable numbers for the first time during the sixties. They found a very limited data base upon which to build, and in the Latin American military establishments themselves, secretive, closed, clannish corporations little given to leaving trails in the public record. Nevertheless, a torrent of analysis followed, much of it cast in terms of how US military assistance affected civil-military relations and the goals of the Alliance for Progress. Government-sponsored research units joined universities and the traditional policy-oriented organizations in examining one or another facet of the military's role in the region. Professor Lyle McAlister surveyed the literature and some of the technical apparatus in 1967:

> The more scholarly literature exhibits several distinct patterns and trends. In terms of scope and focus, the bulk of it deals in broad theories and generalization. . . . Intensive analyses of particular aspects, causal factors, or situations are relatively rare . . . . In terms of approach and conceptualization, recent literature, while still retaining a normative flavor and a preoccupation with intervention, has accepted the military as an integral component of Latin American society interacting with other elements rather than acting against them. . . . In terms of content and substance the most noticeable feature . . . is . . . the absence of firm data and of empirical support for conclusions offered. What has really come out of it is a set of propositions and counter-propositions about the role of the Latin American military—which are theoretically testable—and about what their role ought to be—which are not.[8]

---

[6]See US Congress, 1st Session, Senate Foreign Relations Committee, *Hearings on International Development and Security*, Washington, 1961.

[7]Professor Lieuwen later posited a cause-and-effect relationship between the actions of the leader of the unit that stormed the palace and his US-inspired training in counterinsurgency. "Neo-Militarism in Latin America: the Kennedy Administration's Inadequate Response," *Inter-American Economic Affairs*, Spring 1963, p. 15.

[8]L. N. McAlister, "Recent Research and Writings on the Role of the Military in Latin America," *Latin American Research Review*, Vol. II, No. 1 (Fall 1967), pp. 28-29.

However, not all, or even most, of the literature that influenced American perceptions of the Latin military during the sixties was of the scholarly type. Distortions and arbitrary generalizations were characteristic of the articles and editorials in the media that treated military assistance and its effects on civil-military relations. Latin American officers were most often pictured as simple-minded seekers after unneeded sophisticated toys who capriciously upset governments for their own selfish ends. Latin American spokesmen for the "democratic left" encouraged that image. A widely paraphrased statement by Juan Bosch after his ouster from the presidency of the Dominican Republic tended to confirm this view in the minds of many:

> In the majority of Latin American countries the military chiefs represent the proverbial gun in the hands of a child. . . . The . . . oligarchies would not represent a mortal danger for democracy . . . if they did not have at their disposal armed forces supplied by irresponsible military chieftains who have no political education.[9]

Simon G. Hanson, who was harshly critical of US military assistance in his periodic evaluations of the Alliance for Progress, summed up the US liberal view in 1967 when he demanded that the Latin American military demonstrate: "1) Respect for constitutional government and 2) a willingness to adjust military expenditures to the country's needs."[10]

In the Congress, the Administration made an attempt to convince increasingly skeptical lawnmakers that the military assistance program had important intangible benefits in that "the professional influence and attitudes of the US military are beginning to be reflected in Latin American armies, in spite of the 400-year history of authoritarian military government in that part of the world."[11] But this approach backfired immediately when long lists of US-trained Latin American officers holding key jobs in military governments were produced by the critics. Senator Wayne Morse delivered a blast at the idea in hearings held in 1967:

> military coups . . . fed by our military aid . . . are destroying the objectives of the Alliance. . . . The whole rationale that our military aid tends to teach civilian control of the military and to interest them in civic action has been totally refuted by events.[12]

The argument was consequently largely abandoned in Washington, although it continued in use frequently by spokesmen for the US Southern Command in

---

[9]*The New Leader*, October 14, 1963.

[10]*Five Years of the Alliance for Progress: An Appraisal*, Inter-American Affairs Press, Washington, 1967, p. 155.

[11]US Congress, 1st Session, House Appropriations Committee, *Hearings on Foreign Operations Appropriation for 1965*, Part I, pp. 399-400.

[12]Quoted in Hanson, *op. cit.*, p. 158.

Panama. The fact that it was offered at all gave unwarranted credence to a simplistic cause-and-effect relationship between US assistance and political activism, or the absence thereof, on the part of Latin American officers. It tended to confirm in the minds of many Congressmen and the interested public the distorted image of the Latin American military as a whole which was being presented from so many sides.

The "moderating influence" rationale was the last attempt the Democratic Administration made to justify in political terms the supply of major military items to hemispheric forces. Secretary McNamara spelled out the death knell for what Lieuwen had ridiculed as the "myth of collective defense" in a security policy statement in 1967:

> With respect to Latin America we have, over the past seven years, thoroughly reoriented our military policy to bring it into line with the nature and scope of the real threat. Our policies now recognize explicitly the low probability of conventional attack on any American state from outside the hemisphere. As a result, we see no requirement for Latin American countries to support large conventional military forces, particularly those involving expensive, sophisticated military equipment, ships and aircraft. We view expenditures for such forces as an unwarranted diversion of resources from the more urgent and important tasks of economic and social development.[13]

This rather imperious judgment, coming at a time when the larger countries were turning to Europe for jet airplanes, ships and tanks, could only confirm the popular perception of Latin American officers as anachronistic Quixotes pointing with alarm to cold-war villains—now revealed as windmills to the enlightened—for the selfish purpose of equipping themselves with the twentieth century trinkets of war. And despite the drumbeating for the civilizing effects of civic action and positive contributions to economic development, that is generally the image that Americans brought into the seventies.

Thus our perceptions have come to have two dominant and somewhat contradictory components that greatly condition US policies toward the Latin American military: 1) that the primary interest of the armed forces is domestic politics and 2) that they conjure up nonexistent external security threats to justify demands for the expensive, sophisticated equipment required for modern war.

The critical missing link in such perceptions is an adequate appreciation of the nature and importance of *professionalism* in Latin American military establishments. As Colonel Corbett develops in his analyses below, profes-

---

[13]Quoted in *Inter-American Economic Affairs*, Vol. 21, No. 4 (Spring 1968), p. 84.

sionalism is perhaps the most distinguishing feature of the military in most Latin American countries. Certainly it cannot be said with accuracy, as Professor Lieuwen has said, that "the notion that the armed forces are primarily a military institution" is "a myth."[14] Even less can it be said that "the dominant role of all military establishments is perforce political, and the sole target for the use of violence is the suppression of internal dissidence."[15]

This is not to say that the Latin American military are apolitical in the same sense as is generally believed for the US and most West European countries. Quite the contrary: with a very few exceptions politics have been and probably will long remain a principal order of business for the military. However, quite clearly professionalism and politics are not mutually exclusive in the Latin American setting. It can be well argued, in fact, that it is because of professionalism, rather than the reverse, that the armed forces do engage so heavily in politics. Often, and again as Colonel Corbett's studies demonstrate, intervention in politics is for the purpose of protecting or promoting the interests of the military establishment as a professional institution. Beyond this the elaborate system of continuing education that has characterized the professionalization process enhances the effectiveness of the officer corps as a political interest group and its status as an elite. The war colleges that have achieved prominence since World War II have greatly broadened the military's intellectual horizons and capabilities and have served as an institutional base for the study of developmental problems. This combination of traditional power, continuing education, and concern for broad national issues is unique to the military as a political grouping in Latin America.

Interestingly, and perhaps quite significantly for the future, Soviet commentators have taken special note of the role of professionalism in influencing the attitudes and courses of the military in Latin America and of the possibility that this can be turned to advantage in the "anti-imperialist" (anti-US) struggle there. Perceiving Latin America as currently undergoing a rapid "intensification of the revolutionary process" and as subject to the "objective and subjective conditions" necessary for the "flowering of Lenin's theory of the transition of a democratic agrarian revolution into a socialist

---

[14]See *The West Point Conference on Latin America Problems*, US Military Academy, Final Report, 1964, p. 56.

[15]George I. Blanksten, "Political Groups in Latin America," in John H. Kautsky, ed., *Political Change in Undeveloped Countries* (New York: John Wiley and Sons, 1962), p. 142.

revolution,"[16] the Soviet leadership is calling for closest attention to the "recent experiences of the revolutionaries on the Latin American continent ... truly a 'continent in upheaval' " which is "becoming a hot bed of anti-imperialist struggle."[17] Among other of the factors which Moscow sees as contributing to the revolutionary process in Latin America is, according to Secretary of the Central Committee of the CPSU Boris Ponomarev, "a new phenomenon" whereby "new state forms may appear, characterized by the participation of the armed forces in progressive developments."[18]

> The social nature and reasons for this phenomenon require a thorough study on the part of the science of Marxism-Leninism. This becomes even more important when we bear in mind that the form of revolutionary development, as has been confirmed by the entire historical experience, largely depends on the position adopted by the armed forces.[19]

One of the main points stressed in the studies which Ponomarev called for is the interrelationship of "professionalism and politization" within the armed forces of Latin American countries. Arguing that the armed forces "are experiencing directly all of the growing influences of the institutional crisis" in Latin America, a recent authoritative article characterized "the problem of professionalism in the army" as "one of the more profound expressions of this crisis." Military professionalism, the article asserted, is threatened on the one side by the reactionaries who attempt to transform the army into instruments of dictatorship and the officer corps into "bureaucratic clients," and, on the other, by the populist left which wants to replace the professional army with a "workers' militia." The threat has also "become increasingly evident from the imperialist side," and particularly through US efforts "to foist on" the Latin American military a counterinsurgency and civic action posture.

> ... Objectively such a military policy on the part of the US has come increasingly into conflict with the professional interests of the armed forces on the continent, which are interested in acquiring modern weapons of various types, in the development of their own armaments industry, in the creation of a network of military schools of a broad type, etc. In the over-all these conflicts are a part of the growing contradictions between the desire of Latin American

---

[16]A. F. Shul'govskii, "Urgent Problems of Latin American Studies," *Vestnik Akademii Nauk (Herald of the Academy of Sciences)*, No. 8, August 1970, p. 108.

[17]B. Ponomarev, "Topical Problems in the Theory of the Revolutionary Process," *Kommunist*, No. 17, October 1971, p. 59.

[18]*Ibid.*

[19]*Ibid.*, p. 74.

countries for independence and the neo-colonalist policy of imperialism.

The professionalization and modernization of the armed forces, the article continued, has brought an increasing involvement of the military in social and economic life.

> ... Such an expansion of the professional activities of the armed forces has prepared a significant group of the military for carrying out "civilian" administrative tasks, created cadres which could take into their own hands the direction of state offices. This process has had a considerable psychological influence on the army. . . . Professionalism and politization are not two mutually exclusive concepts, but two inseparable components in the process which is taking place in the armed forces.[20]

While acknowledging that it would be "incorrect to assume that politization goes only in the direction of the growth of progessive attitudes among the military,"[21] the Soviets still insist that the "leftward trend" is becoming more and more pervasive. "The further one goes the more the army in Latin America becomes 'socialized' " since its outlook and attitude are developing "against the general background of the growing anti-imperialist, democratic and liberationist struggle in all countries of the Third World [and since] this struggle has reached a particularly broad scope precisely in the countries of this region."[22] In any event, the Soviet Union clearly sees the military in Latin America as an important target for influence, either directly or through the communist parties.

One approach is to reassure the military concerning communist views on the desirability of maintaining regular armed forces. It is said that the anti-communist ideologists cite the liquidation of the Cuban army, when Castro came to power, as a way of frightening the military and intensifying their opposition to the communists.[23] It is insisted, however, that Marxism-Leninism favors the maintenance of regular armed forces and that far from being anti-military, communists defend the professional interests and welfare of the forces.

> In struggling against simplistic anti-militarism, the communists of the countries of the continent pay special attention to the defense of the professional interests of the military, and demand improve-

---

[20]A. F. Shul'govskii, "Latin America: The Army and Politics," *Latinskaia Amerika*, No. 4, 1971, pp. 8-13.

[21]*Ibid.*, p. 13.

[22]Kh. Kobo and G. I. Mirskii, "Concerning Some Peculiarities of the Evolution of the Armies of the Latin American Continent," *Latinskaia Amerika*, No. 4, 1971, p. 52.

[23],A. F. Shul'govskii, "Latin America: The Army and Politics," *op. cit.*, pp. 34-36.

ments in their material conditions, which acquire great significance in the condition where the reactionary seek to place the military in opposition to the working class and other strata of the toilers.[24]

As a specific example, the Communist Party of Honduras is cited for translating and publishing an abridged version of Marshal V. D. Sokolovskii's book, *Military Strategy*, for distribution to the armed forces. The introduction to the book states that the publication

... is an attempt to bring about our rapprochement through discussions and consideration of critical current questions of military theory with officers of goodwill who like us think about the future of our country and who seek in the study of Marxist-Leninist doctrine, theories, concepts and methods, with the help of which it will be possible to solve difficult economic, social, cultural and political problems of the Honduran people.[25]

The communist strategy is admittedly based on the idea that it is "extremely important to radicalize the attitudes in the military ranks in order to deepen the liberating anti-imperialist process."[26]

Another approach that is open to Moscow is to supply military assistance to such of the Latin American countries as may become willing to accept it. So far, outside of Cuba, the Soviet Union has made only a few tentative attempts to sell arms to Latin American countries. However, it should be noted that posture-wise the leadership appears prepared to go in this direction. The Soviets make a special point of their willingness to assist the armed forces of any Third World country in order to further its independence from and resistance to western interests. And in point of fact the Soviet Union has become a major supplier of military aid to those countires, to a total of almost $8 billion by 1971.[27] As explained in a recent Soviet commentary:

No longer do the imperialists enjoy a monopoly in the sale of arms, which makes the political positions of the new national states that much stronger. During the lifetime of Mohammed V of Morocco, France offered to supply airplanes to that country provided it abandoned its policy of non-alignment. The King refused to accept that condition and approached the Soviet Union, which duly furnished the Moroccan army the required planes with no strings attached.[28]

---

[24]*Ibid.*, p. 39.

[25]*Ibid.*

[26]*Ibid.*, p. 40.

[27]US Department of State, *Communist States and Developing Countries*, Research Study RECS-3, May 15, 1971, p. iii.

[28]*The Third World – Problems and Prospects* (Moscow: Progress Publishers, 1970). p. 27.

One specific observation of Soviet analysts on the Latin American military merits pondering: "The stronger the political power of the army now becomes, the less are the chances of the establishment of a personalized military dictatorship."[29] In the present study Colonel Corbett reaches much the same conclusion.

There can be little doubt, Colonel Corbett believes, that the officer corps will continue as powerful political elites in the years ahead. Indeed, their power and influence will probably grow under pressures of developmental demands and within the aegis of expanded national security doctrines related to these demands. But the diversity of the officer corps—particularly the divisions over policies of national development and generational differences—limits the potential of the actual use of power. Nowhere is this better illustrated than in the experiences of the military *qua* government in Argentina and Bolivia.

Thus the mode of civil-military relations—the style and content of military participation in the political process—will vary widely and will continue to preclude sweeping generalizations. The most one can say with assurance along these lines is that the recognition of a nexus of economic (or national) development and national security will be a primary element in conditioning civil-military relations.

In the area of policy, it is apparent that neither the models of pure professionalism nor the models designed to explain military intervention in politics in terms of sheer wantonness fit current realities in Latin America. It is equally apparent that traditional perceptions of the officer corps as stabilizing and conservative forces—perceptions of some comfort during the past 20 years to policymakers concerned with the cold war and Vietnam—are no longer generally valid, if indeed they ever were. As Colonel Corbett observes, probably in no other region of the world are military establishments undergoing the degree of institutional self-examination as are the armed forces of Latin America today. The importance of the establishments in the political arena will make the results of that self-analysis of great concern to both the Latins and the US, and the variety of experiments emerging from it will no doubt perplex US policymakers. The propensity for "packaging" policies for such a diverse region will need more than ever to be resisted. It has not proved effective in the past and the intrusion of extra-hemispheric influences and ideologies—with their varying appeals—will make such an

---

[29]Kobo and Mirskii, "Concerning Some Peculiarities of the Evolution of the Armies of the Latin American Continent," *op. cit.*, p. 47.

approach still less productive, and even dangerous, to US interests in the future.

The present monograph is the product of what we believe to be a very forward looking program on the part of the United States Army. That program allows officers with a primary interest in international affairs the opportunity to substitute a year of independent research and study for the regular course at the Army War College. Colonel Charles D. Corbett availed himself of this option to spend the academic year 1971-1972 with the Center for Advanced International Studies at the University of Miami. This monograph represents a part of his research effort while at the Center. It also reflects, as Colonel Corbett notes in the preface that follows, personal research done earlier, as well as a broad knowledge and background developed over many years of professional interest in Latin America and living and traveling in the area.

> Mose L. Harvey
> Director, Center for Advanced International
>   Studies
> University of Miami

PREFACE

The case studies presented here are the product of a long-standing interest in the institutional nature of the military establishments in Latin America, and of their place in the societies of which they form such a prominent part.

The manuscript was prepared during the academic year (1971-1972) which the author spent at the Center for Advanced International Studies of the University of Miami as a US Army Research Associate. Most of the research for the Argentine study was done earlier, although the author did visit Buenos Aires in January-February of 1972 to update it. The Bolivian study relies heavily upon the *Revista Militar* and Bolivian newspapers as documentary sources. (The former is a remarkable military house organ which has been published, with some interruptions, since 1885. It contains social items, promotion lists, biographical sketches, and occasional exhortations from the high command to the officer corps, in addition to the usual professional articles of any military journal.) Most of the research was done in the summer and fall of 1971 using, in addition to materials available at the Center, the files in the Library of Congress, the US Army Library in the Pentagon, the collection at the library of the US Army School of the Americas in the Panama Canal Zone, and many particularly informative copies of the *Revista* provided by Bolivian friends.

The author is fortunate to count as friends a large number of Bolivian and Argentine officers of all ranks, and has "shared their bread and salt" many times under many conditions in the course of official duties. Although these associations are reflected here, the studies are the result of primary research unconnected with the author's official responsibilities.

The advice and assistance of Dr. Clyde Wooten, Associate Director of the Center, were invaluable in the formative stages of the Bolivian study. The suggestions of Dr. Jaime Suchlicki, Associate Director of the Latin American Institute at the Center, and Colonel Thomas W. Flatley of the US Army War College faculty, were also very helpful. The Argentine study was read in parts by numerous colleagues over the years, and in an earlier version benefited greatly from suggestions by Dr. John Finan, Professor of Latin American History at The American University. I am also grateful for the encouragement of Dr. Mose Harvey, Director of the Center, and for preparation of the Foreword which introduces this study.

Charles D. Corbett

University of Miami
Coral Gables, Florida
June 1, 1972

TABLE OF CONTENTS

PART ONE: AN OVERVIEW

PART TWO: BOLIVIA AS A CASE STUDY

PART THREE: ARGENTINA AS A CASE STUDY

PART ONE

AN INTRODUCTORY OVERVIEW

I
INTRODUCTION

Serious study of the Latin American military as a complex institution within complex societies is a recent phenomenon. Despite a continuing interest in civil-military relations in the region, neither US policy nor scholarship has remained abreast of the changing institutional nature of military establishments or of their structural location in developing societies.[1] Perceptions have frequently been distorted by normative concepts—based on US and European patterns—of what the military role *ought* to be. Much attention has been devoted to shifts in what is viewed as a struggle for dominance between the foces of *civilismo* and the forces of *militarismo*, with the tenets of political liberalism serving as the guideposts against which gains of one side or the other are measured.[2]

The events of the fifties generated considerable optimism that military influence was on the decline. Scholars and journalists deduced a "twilight for tyrants" from the downfall of Perón in Argentina, Perez Jimenez in Venezuela, Rojas Pinilla in Colombia and Trujillo in the Dominican Republic.[3] Yet a decade later a national news magazine decried the fact that three out of four citizens of the South American subcontinent were living under some kind of military regime.[4] At this writing five South American countries (Argentina, Brazil, Peru, Bolivia, and Ecuador) have military governments.

The assessments of the fifties are understandable when viewed against perceptions which prevailed at that time. It was generally believed that

---

[1]Recent scholarly works have begun to redress the balance somewhat. Among them: Alfred Stepan, *The Military in Politics: Changing Patterns in Brazil* (Princeton, N.J.: Princeton University Press, 1971); Jose Nun, *Latin America: The Hegemonic Crisis and the Military Coup*, Institute of International Studies Monograph (Berkeley: University of California Press, 1969); Luigi R. Einaudi and Alfred C. Stepan, *Latin American Institutional Development: Changing Military Perspectives in Peru and Brazil* (Santa Monica, Calif.: RAND Corporation, 1971); Lyle McAlister, et al., *The Military in Latin American Sociopolitical Evolution: Four Case Studies* (Washington, Center for Research in Social Systems, the American University, 1970). Robert Potash's *The Army and Politics in Argentina, 1928-1945* (Stanford, Calif.: Stanford University Press, 1969), provides an excellent in-depth analysis of an earlier period which will be extended in a new work. Einaudi is preparing a book-length work on Peru.

[2]For example, see Edwin Lieuwen, *Arms and Politics in Latin America* (New York, Praeger, 1961).

[3]*Ibid.* For the journalistic view see Tad Szulc, *Twilight of the Tyrants* (New York, Holt, 1959).

[4]*Time*, December 27, 1968. p. 23.

militarism would fade with the disappearance of the *caudillo* tradition and the charismatic military strongman. The process was to be speeded by the emergence of strong middle sectors and increasing professionalization of the military.

The predictions were partly correct. The *caudillo* has largely disappeared. Few North Americans can name the officers who have come and gone in positions of top power in the military governments of Brazil (since 1964), Argentina (since 1966), or Bolivia (since 1969). (A surprising number of Latin Americans cannot name them either.) A President Velasco in Peru makes fewer headlines than the minister-generals who form his cabinet. The *caudillo* and his coterie, with their frequently narrow and predictable interests, have in large measure been supplanted by institutional representatives whose military constituencies embrace broad and far-reaching interests.

II
MILITARISM VS. PROFESSIONALISM

The concept of militarism versus professionalism is central to US perceptions of the Latin American military. The persistence of militarism, and the failure of recognized gains in professionalism to stem it, have puzzled academicians and policymakers.

The classic examples of militarism reside in the historical alliances in many European countries between the officer corps—comprised of the second sons of the aristocracy who frequently practiced the profession of arms as an honorific occupation—and the traditional ruling classes. Because of their status, they formed what seemed to be an exemplary constabulary for support of the existing system. The classic maneuver to break up this alliance and remove the military from the political equation—or at least drastically to limit its influence—was "professionalization." Officership was made a full-time, paid profession, requiring long years of specialized preparation for advancement through a rigidly bureaucratized system. A durable tradition of civil control further shaped the position of the military within society and defined its role as an apolitical one.

Even a cursory examination of classic definitions of militarism points up how poorly they fit the Latin American situation. Three of the most widely-accepted definitions are:

1) a domination of the military man over the civilian; an undue preponderance of military demands; an emphasis on military considerations, spirit, ideals, and scales of value;[5]

2) exaltation of military ways as supreme and the infusion of large sections of the population with a supportive ideology; representatives of armed forces, usually with the connivance of highly placed civilians, are able to exercise great influence on all phases of social and political life;[6]

3) an attitude toward public affairs that conceives of war and the preparation for war as the chief instruments of foreign policy and the highest forms of public service.[7]

Except for brief periods in El Salvador and Paraguay, no Latin American country has ever approached any of the conditions described above. Civil wars were endemic following independence and numerous border clashes,

---

[5]Alfred Vagts, *A History of Militarism* (New York: W. W. Norton & Co., 1937), p. 11.

[6]Kurt Lang, *Military Sociology* (London: Basil Blackwell, 1965), p. 18.

[7]*Encyclopedia of the Social Sciences*, Vol. I (New York: McMillan Co., 1933), p. 446.

leading in four instances to major wars, have occurred in both the 19th and 20th centuries. Nevertheless, Latin America as a whole has been characterized by its generally peaceful international relations.[8] Recent research tends to undermine the image of a region-wide nineteenth century alliance between the oligarchy and the military, and certainly in this century the various officer corps have been largely middle class in composition. (Indeed, the intensive socialization process of the career system, described later, brings into question the weight assigned in the past to class analysis as a technique in studying military institutional change.) The primary manifestation of classic militarism has been the officer corps' frequent use of military power to dominate domestic processes. Viewing this phenomenon against "western" traditions, US analysts have most often conceptualized a predatory group acting upon rather than within its society, positing the choice for US policymakers between support for "high-handed military dictatorship and struggling civilian democracy."[9]

Latin American militarism, then, must be viewed in this narrower context of domestic politics, and in this context there is a close relationship between the concepts of militarism and professionalism.

Because they are based on "western" experiences, Huntington's distinguishing characteristics of the military professional—expertise, responsibility, and corporateness—are helpful but not sufficient to define professionalism in the Latin American context. With respect to the first characteristic, the controlled application of violence is singled out as the peculiar skill of the officer; that its application be utilized only for socially approved purposes is the imperative of the second; and the bureaucratized, hierarchical, and socially delimited nature of the military institution contributes to the last.[10]

An astute analyst of civil-military relations in Latin America has posited a different set of requirements for a professional army: (1) recognition of the specific duty to act as guarantor of the state's security against foreign aggression; (2) inculcation of strict patterns of authority with emphasis on the necessity of discipline and obedience within a hierarchically organized command system; (3) formal training for officership; and (4) institutionalization of a military career with a regular salary and a clearly defined pattern of

---

[8]See Peter Calvert, *Latin America: Internal Conflict and International Peace* (New York: St. Martins Press, 1969).

[9]The phrase is from Edwin Lieuwen, Senate Foreign Relations Committee, *United States-Latin American Relations*, 86th Congress, 2nd Session, 1960, p. 51.

[10]Samuel P. Huntington, *The Soldier and the State* (Cambridge, Mass.: Belknap Press, 1957). pp. 7-18.

promotion and advancement within the organization based on the univer-
salistic criteria of ability and achievement.[11]

Both sets of requirements presuppose a narrow, functional area of
expertise for the officer and sharply limit the military institution's role in
society to the primary socially acceptable use of violence, i.e., security against
overt aggression.[12]

General Benjamín Rattenbach, an Argentine military sociologist, differ-
entiates between "organic" and "vocational" aspects of professionalism.
Organic professionalism signifies placing the military career on a stable basis
through the satisfaction of two conditions: (1) education of career officers in
a formal school system; and (2) promulgation of laws that assure regularized
and fair promotions, assignments, retirements, and administrative action.
Vocational professionalism requires that the officer devote full time to his
profession. General Rattenbach agress that *apoliticismo* has not followed
from professionalization, but argues that the phenomena are independent in
the Latin American context and likely to remain so:

> The old European professionalism could create a theory of
> conduct appropriate to its ends—*apoliticismo*—that worked well for
> its environment of developed political culture. Among us it did not
> work, and we now know why. Consequently we must create a new
> theory more appropriate to our environment that takes into account
> the logical and very real relations between politics and the armed
> forces so that they cease being constant factors of perturbation and
> assist the country to achieve development and greatness. In other
> words we have to define anew the role of these forces in the breast of
> society, differentiating it from the European or North American
> *schema* and molding it to the reality of nations under development.
> Thus, for example, one could say that they have for a current
> mission in such countries not only exterior defense and internal
> security, but also contributing to the development of the nation in
> the economic and social aspects as well as the cultural and political.
> They are not indifferent to any of these aspects, feeling as they do
> that they are integral components of the society.[13]

That the armed forces not only are "not indifferent" to these aspects but
increasingly seek to play an institutional role in national development in its
broadest terms is indicated by the nature of military regimes that came to

[11]Liisa North, *Civil-Military Relations in Argentina, Chile and Peru* (Politics of
Modernization Series, No. 2, Institute of International Studies, Berkeley: University of
California, 1966), p. 14.

[12]For a critical analysis of Huntington's model from a US military point of view, see Lt.
Col. Zeb Bradford and Maj. James Murphy, "A New Look at the Military Profession,"
Army, Vol. 19 (February 1969), pp. 58-64.

[13]"El Profesionalismo Militar en el Ejercito Argentino," *Temas Militares*, Vol. I, No. 3
(March-April 1967). pp. 9-16.

power during the sixties. The expansion of institutional concerns to the socio-economic area has been most noticeable in South America. The style, content, and manifestations of the new concerns vary by country, but characteristically grow out of expanded concepts of national security that see economic development and increased social integration (nation building) as *sine qua nons* for the internal and external security of the state.

Such expansion in roles and missions generates inevitable tensions and strains in rigid, hierarchical institutions where tradition is a major force for cohesiveness. Despite differences of great importance, it is possible to identify some common characteristics and phenomena in modern South American armies.

III
THE CAREER SYSTEM
AND FORMATION OF POLITICAL ELITES

What comprises the "armed forces?" Do they include all of the institutions that society arms for its order and security? In Panama or Nicaragua, where one "national guard" provides police services as well as guaranteeing territorial integrity and defense against external aggression, the entity is easily defineable. In Argentina and Brazil, these functions are differentiated in complex structures. Specially designed organizations are charged with customs and border patrol duties, provincial and federal police jurisdictions are carefully defined, and the *internal* defense roles of *military* forces are quite amorphous, whereas their classic mission of defense against external threats is clear and universally accepted. If we accept the "armed forces" as comprising all of society's armed institutions, and the "military forces" as being those concerned primarily with external defense, there are still gray areas in the definitions. The air force most closely fits the "military" definition, but the coast guard functions of the navies and the territorial defense missions of all armies distort the distinctions for those forces.

Obviously there is no single voice of the "armed forces" in those countries where the coercive forces of the state are complexly organized. However, there is little practical difficulty—whatever might be the theoretical problem—in delimiting that sector of the "armed forces" in the larger South American countries that has been directly involved in national politics since World War II.

First, one can say that the armies predominate in political activity. Only a handful of officers from the navies have held important political posts, and since the air forces became separate after World War II, only Bolivia has had a chief executive from that service. Secondly, only the officer corps participates actively in the political game. Enlisted men have not achieved important political influence, and although there have been attempts (e.g., in Venezuela and Brazil) by politicians to manipulate them, the rank and file generally have followed the orders of their officers in political fights. Thirdly, only field grade officers of the line, of the "combat arms," play important political roles. Junior line officers, lawyers, doctors, veterinarians, finance officers, quartermasters and maintenance officers do not figure in the political councils. And in rather a marked change from the past, retired officers are

7

generally out of the picture unless they maintain strong contacts within the active establishment.

Usually a very small group within the larger body of command corps officers makes the decision on whether the army will play a role in any given situation. Exercise of the coup option requires only the ability to mobilize the support necessary for a temporary power advantage. The hierarchical nature of the institution and the pattern of loyalty established by the annual reshuffling of general officers will normally give the command group that power. Ensuing decisions are infinitely more complex and participation in the deliberative process much more broadly based. Coups may in some cases still be personalistic (e.g., Bolivia in 1964 and 1969) but the consequences are institutional concerns. The capability to move the government apparatus, and through it the society, in a desired direction depends on the accrual of broad support from the field grade command corps officers. The mobilization and maintenance of this support calls for widespread contacts on the part of the leaders and the careful manipulation of many control mechanisms in a highly sensitive and rank-conscious organization. As will be demonstrated, the officer corps have become increasingly heterogeneous in viewpoints, and failure in this intra-institutional political task leads to a counter-coup by a group that more nearly reflects institutional sentiments.

The mobilization, by a military junta, of institutional support for political programs is complicated not only by the variety of views within the officer corps, but by the nature of the career system. Popular perceptions notwithstanding, that system is geared to the production of military professionals who, in their formative years, certainly do not conceive of the presidency or a ministerial post as the capstone of a military career.

All members of the command corps are graduates of the military academy in South American armies. There are no career line officers from any other source. Branches (cavalry, infantry, artillery, etc.) are chosen early, usually during the first year of the four-year course, and form the basis for life-line association. Technical officers (quartermaster [*intendencia*] and ordnance [*material de guerra*]) also attend the academies, but their training is differentiated from that of the line cadets after the first year and the associations are not nearly as close. Academy life is rigorous, with every aspect of the daily routine carefully structured and controlled. Only the cream of the officer corps is selected to command and administer the academies, and great attention is devoted to the top priority task of character formation. All academies have a mixture of civilian and military *profesores*;

some of the former are tenured professors, others are part-time instructors from national or private universities. Tradition is carefully nurtured.[14]

The *subteniente* receives his ceremonial saber, usually from the president, at elaborate graduation ceremonies, and goes off to join a regiment. Officers with a high class standing get a choice of the more desirable units, but all are committed to several years of duty with troop units after commissioning. Discipline is rigid within the officer complement, the colonel's whim is absolute law, and in isolated areas the society approaches that of a "total institution."[15] Near the cities life is less confining, but the colonel will still take an interest in the social life and overall behavior of the *subteniente*, who must also have the permission of higher authority to marry. After about four years he is promoted to *teniente*, and sometime during the ensuing few years will attend a 6-8 month course at an *Escuela de Aplicación* to sharpen his talents in his combat specialty and broaden his capabilities as a company officer. Promotion to captain will come at about the eighth year, and he will probably return to an advanced course at his branch school.

The overriding imperative at this point is to get into the command and general staff course and gain the coveted title of *diplomado de estado mayor* (general staff officer) which opens the road to positions in the higher headquarters and eventual promotion to colonel. Attendance may be by application or selection, but in either case it involves months of intensive preparation for the qualifying examinations, which cover a dismayingly broad range of academic and military subjects. Once accepted, he faces one to three years of intensely competitive study, with under-achievers being dropped from the course at the end of each year.[16] In addition to military organization, administration and tactics—generally keyed to the division

---

[14]One Brazilian writer on military affairs says the academies produce a man with a singular kind of image of the national reality, "very subjective and very romantic . . . the nation is an idolized and venerated woman, a kind of fragile mother figure that demands all from her sons. Patriotism is characterized as a manifestation of pious virtue. The nation is perceived as an abstract quality that claims blind and eternal dedication." Vicente Barreto, "La Presencia Militarista," in *Temas Militares*, Vol. I, No. 3 (March-April 1967), pp. 35-39. Although similar beliefs are quite common among Latin American intellectuals, the author's familiarity with several academies and association with cadets from seven countries at the US Army School of the Americas, leads him to believe that Señor Barreto's formulation is overstated, although it might not have been twenty years ago.

[15]A place of residence and work where a large number of like-situated individuals, cut off from the wider society for an appreciable period of time, together lead an enclosed, formally administered life. Erving Coffman, *Asylums* (Garden City, New York, 1961) p. 13.

[16]The full course is three years in Argentina, Brazil, Bolivia, and Chile, two years in Ecuador, Paraguay, Peru, and Uruguay, one year in Colombia and Venezuela.

level—he will study theories of revolutionary warfare, psychology, sociology, economics, and political theory, along with massive doses of military history.

Here he will also hear the views of the army's "intellectuals," those senior officers who by reason of their positions or reputations have come to be looked upon as spokesmen for the institution. He will also hear a variety of civilian speakers, and the "academic" side of his education will be in the hands of civilian professors. The course will include tours of his country's strategically important locations, and a trip abroad which frequently includes a tour of the United States.

Those officers who survive the full course and become general staff officers find new opportunities open to them as planning or action officers on the general staff of the army or in important territorial headquarters, as instructors or directors in the school system, and as commanders of battalions and groups.

Most of those selected for promotion to colonel, after about 20 years' service, will attend a one-year Higher Military Studies course devoted to national problems and goals at the broadest level which considers all the dynamic forces of the society—military, political, economic, sociological, and psychological. The product of this course of study is usually a national strategy paper that includes general plans and guidelines for reaching the goals agreed upon in seminar sessions. The small student body includes important civilians from government and the professions, and lecturers from government, industry, and the academic community address the students. The graduates fill key staff and command positions and form probably the most influential element of the military-political constituency. These are the officers whose support is essential to the stability and success of any military government.

The point at which significant liaisons are established between officers and important civilian elements varies by country and is always changing. The war-college-level schools obviously are important in this cross-fertilization process. Alfred Stepan has identified, by profession or occupational grouping, civilian students at the Brazilian *Escola Superior de Guerra* over a number of years, and the range is surprising. By 1966 some 599 officer graduates had been complemented by 224 students from private industry and commerce, 297 from high levels of government, 39 congressmen, 23 judges, and 107 from the professions.[17] Luigi Einaudi says that civilian attendance at the Peruvian Center of Higher Military Studies became routine in the sixties, and

---

[17]Einaudi and Stepan, *Latin American Institutional Development, op. cit.*, p. 81.

that 16 of the 43 students in the 1971 course were civilians.[18] In Bolivia the course is normally comprised of about half officers and half civilians; through 1967 ninety three officers and 58 civilians had graduated.[19] In 1970, the National War School class in Paraguay counted a senator and a congressman among its 14 students.

The Argentine Army War College (*Escuela de Altos Estudios*) does not admit civilian students, but they are traditionally in a majority at the National War College. The 1971 class counted 27 students from ministries and state enterprises, 8 from private industry, 4 from police and paramilitary units, one university professor, and 11 officers. Venezuela's new war college (*Instituto de Altos Estudios de la Defensa Nacional*) counted 11 civilians from government ministries and state enterprises among the 31 students in its first class, which got underway in January 1972. The "colonels' courses" in Colombia and Chile are designed primarily to qualify officers for promotion to general, although some government functionaries do attend them.

Other links are established by territorial commanders and their staffs with local political leaders, and the common practice of appointing military governors, mayors and police chiefs (*interventors*) in times of crisis and civil strife acquaints a wide number of officers with political figures from the civilian side. The large military household staffs that surround most Latin American presidents (the *casa militar*) provide many rising officers an opportunity to get to know key political figures. Traditional family alignments and associations undoubtedly play an important role but are very difficult to establish.[20]

Graduation from the General Staff course marks a kind of watershed in the officer's orientation. Up to this point, and for a few years thereafter, he has seen himself first and foremost as a military professional, schooled intensively in the military arts and sciences. He takes his profession seriously, assiduously follows developments in organization, tactics and weaponry in other parts of the world, and in many cases writes and publishes on military-related topics. He chafes at the obsolescence of his equipment and the lack of money for maneuvers, and compensates with intellectual activity and meticulous, detailed planning for any conceivable contingency.

---

[18]*Ibid.*, p. 25.

[19]These data and those immediately following were gathered by the author in visits to various military schools of the region in 1970 and 1972.

[20]There is, however, some work on the subject. See, for example, Rogelio García Lupo, "Los Alsogaray: Una dinastia militar" in *Política*, Vol. VII, No. 71-72 (March-April 1968), pp. 29-39. The article traces the long affiliation of the Alsogaray family, traditionally respected in the Argentine Army, with "liberal" political factions.

The core of his curriculum in the Command and General Staff course is directly related to improving traditional military skills in the management of violence on a large scale and over great distances.[21] If he is sent to a US school during these years, as many are annually, his course will concentrate almost entirely on military techniques and will stress the personal satisfaction to be gained from becoming proficient at them.[22]

There is a distinct "professional" air about any gathering of South American officers at the *jefe* level (majors and lieutenant colonels), and they feel not in the least intimidated in any professional conversation with a US counterpart by the latter's combat experience in two or perhaps even three wars. Among officers from Argentina, Brazil, Chile, and Peru there is a noticeable air of superiority in another sense. Their training, and the high degree of institutional socialization involved, cause them to look upon the military officer as a superior being. In the officer's view, his calling and its high purpose set him aside from other men, and lend to his actions an unselfish aura which is uncharacteristic of his social environment, where opportunism is the norm among politicians, lawyers, businessmen, and other professionals.

---

[21] All general staff schools in Latin America routinely use division and even corps-sized operations as teaching vehicles, many drawn directly from World War II European battles. There has been a recent tendency to make staff college exercises conform more closely to actual capabilities in terms of the size of units employed in map maneuvers (i.e., regiments and brigades instead of divisions and corps) but little inclination to limit employment of highly sophisticated forces (i.e., armor and helicopter units) that are not likely to be in Latin American inventories for some years. As one school commandant explained to the author, he had waited over 10 years after learning armor tactics at Fort Knox to see the first armored infantry unit formed in his army, but when that time had come there were officers who knew how to employ and maintain it.

[22] Some 765 Latin American officers had attended Command and General Staff courses in the United States through 1969, according to data gathered by Ernest W. Lefever of the Brookings Institution and made available to the author. Through 1971, another 246 had graduated from the course at the US Army School of the Americas in Panama, which is essentially the 40-week course from the Command and General Staff College at Fort Leavenworth translated into Spanish.

IV
EXPANDED SECURITY DOCTRINES

Once the officer's professional or military-oriented education is terminated with graduation from the general staff course and he gets involved in larger issues, he becomes concerned about the anomalies of his profession in a region that has had a minimum of international conflict. In the absence of a serious, short-range external threat, he frequently universalizes the communist threat to the "western, Christian" world and posits a role for his country in countering it. Military interpretations of the local manifestations of that threat, and considerations of the nature of the military response, have led in recent years to a redefinition and expansion of the concept of national security. The salient characteristic is a nexus of security and economic development which frequently transcends the definitions of national security policy generally ascribed to by other western countries.[23]

Two issues raised by the expanded national security concept predominate in military institutional debates: (1) the politics of development and (2) the military role in the process. There is almost unanimous agreement on the existence of a nexus of economic development and national security, but there are deep divisions within the various officer corps over specific policies and goals. Two important schools of thought can be identified. Both have nationalist overtones and elitist proclivities, and demarcations are not always sharply defined; in any given country it might be difficult to classify General A or General B into either category. However, the differences are real and will probably intensify during the decade, and an attempt at defining them even in a general manner is worthwhile. Rubrics and labels are misleading but necessary. For lack of better terms we could call one school "liberal-internationalist" and the other "authoritarian-nationalist."[24]

Officers identified with the first have a commitment to democratic forms but are not averse to a period of tutelary rule by the military. Mobilization politics is seen as ruinous. The role of the armed forces during the tutelary period is complex, but emphasis remains strong on classic "territorial

---

[23]See, for example, Huntington, *The Soldier and the State, op. cit.*, p. 1. The two primary components of national security policy are military security policy (the external threat) and internal security policy (the threat of subversion). Huntington's formulation of "situational security policy" is particularly attractive to Argentine theorists. Situational security policy "is concerned with the threat of erosion resulting from long-term changes in social, economic, demographic, and political conditions tending to reduce the relative power of the state."

[24]Alfred Stepan uses these classification in his excellent study of the Brazilian military. The author has generalized them somewhat for the purposes here.

security" concerns, force modernization, and increased professionalism. Interest in industrialization centers on its importance to national mobilization and its contributions to the attainment of true sovereignty through strong, autosufficient security forces. There is a strong concern for "situational" security policy in the regional context for the short term and in the world context for the longer view. The primary security threat is seen as internal subversion, aided and abetted by the world communist movement, and close ties with the US and other western countries are seen as a necessary component of the response. There is no deep objection to state enterprises and state control of certain sectors, but private enterprise remains the driving force of the economy and foreign investment is viewed as essential.

The "authoritarian nationalists" hold that development means much more than the old liberal goal of economic growth. Important elements believe that sweeping structural revisions of existing socio-economic patterns are required. The old liberal political philosophy, with its concern for abstractions such as liberty and democracy, has proved unable to put together and sustain a development program. An alternative to a Cuban-style revolution must be found in each country, and it must fit that country's unique and particular traditions and imperatives. The internal enemy is frequently pictured as that sector of society allied with foreign and international markets. The continuation of 19th century integration of domestic economies with the international economic and monetary systems is viewed as detrimental to the development process, and arguments for free trade and the international division of labor as specious ploys to permit continuation of what is seen as a steadily declining relationship between he industrialized center and the raw-material-producing periphery. The external enemy is identified as economic imperialism. Its steady penetration and influence undermine national sovereignty in the political sphere as well as the economic, (e.g., when attempts are made to subordinate national decisions to global objectives of great-power strategy, such as sanctions against Cuba, the Latin American nuclear-free zone, the Inter-American Peace Force.) Insurgency and subversion are seen as the effects of underdevelopment; national security demands development and it is therefore an implied mission of the armed forces. The latter are truly national institutions, in touch with all sectors of society and represented in the furtherest reaches of the national territory. They are able to coordinate conflicting interests and to distribute the inevitable sacrifices of the development process equitably, since they are above narrow sectoral interests. An indeterminate period of military rule is seen as being necessary for the transformation of society. Old liberal distinctions between civil and military government are no longer relevant; the

14

distinctions now are between sectors of the society who support national development and those who would maintain the status quo.[25]

The three military governments that have dominated Brazil since 1964 have demonstrated varying degrees of conformance to the two descriptions given above, according to Stepan's study. After deposing Goulart in 1964, the first regime under Marshal Castelo Branco, dominated by officers with strong links to the *Escola Superior de Guerra*, was characterized by these policies: (1) an active, anti-communist foreign policy based on the interdependence of the free world; (2) a preference for a semi-free-enterprise economic system supported and guided by strong central government; (3) a dislike and distrust of "irrational nationalism" and an emphasis on technical solutions; and (4) an intellectual commitment to democracy.[26]

Castelo Branco's "liberal" doctrine of austerity and internationalism was opposed by a more "humanitarian and nationalist" sector of the officer corps, which was against even a limited revival of political party and congressional activity (the *linha dura*). These officers achieved greater representation with Marshal Costa e Silva in 1967, and many of the earlier economic and political policies were reversed or vitiated. When Costa e Silva became incapacitated in 1969, there was another succession crisis within the military turning largely on the same issues. General Medici's selection as president probably represented a partial victory for the "nationalist" sector.

Peru's revolutionary military government has been in power just over three years at this writing, and to date offers the most clear-cut example of the transfer of "nationalist" war college security doctrines to the executive offices of government. Shortly after assuming power the military junta nationalized the International Petroleum Company's holdings, expelled the U.S. military missions, and undertook a vast and far-reaching program of social reforms that included the most drastic Latin American agrarian reform since the Mexican revolution.

---

[25]For representative formulations that include some or most of these concepts, see Francisco Arias Pellerano, "La participación política de las fuerzas armadas," *Estrategia*, No. 2 (July-August 1969), Pp. 23-39; General Juan E. Guglialmelli, "Las fuerzas armadas y su missión general prioritaria: desarrollo integral del potencial nacional," *Circumil*, No. 691 (January-March 1970). pp. 123-144; General Osiris G. Villegas, *Políticas y Estratégias op. cit.*; General Lyra Tavares, "El ejército brasileño y la actual coyuntura nacional," *Estratégia*, No. 2 (July-August 1969), pp. 43-56; Gen. Edgardo Mercado Jarrín, "Política y Estrategia Militar en la Guerra Anti-Subversiva," *Revista Militar del Peru* (November-December 1967), pp. 4-33; General Alfredo Ovando Candia, "Carta-Mensaje Del Gral. Ovando a Los JJ. y OO. de las FF.AA.," *Revista Militar* (Bolivia) (April-June 1969), pp. 151-154.

[26]Stepan, *The Military in Politics, op. cit.*

15

The military's concern with socio-economic reform was manifested following a 1962 coup, when the governing junta undertook Peru's first significant land distribution program. The outbreak of guerrilla warfare in the Andes in 1965 prompted a swift and effective suppression campaign, but the experience deepened military sentiments that had been signaled by the land reform project, and the episode was dissected and analyzed within the heart of the institutional structure in succeeding years.

The lessons the officers were deriving from their analysis were clearly spelled out by General Edgardo Mercado Jarrín (who was to become foreign minister and chief theoretician of the revolutionary government) in a series of speeches he made during a visit to US military installations in 1967:

> In general, the process of the ideological capture of the masses in Latin America is being carried out on the basis of the delay or postponement in the carrying out of promised reforms. Castro-communist activists and agitators are giving wide publicity to what they call 'the lack of capacity of the governments to carry them out' and are impressing upon the working and peasant masses that only through 'violent revolution' can they achieve the order and justice they seek; in this way they rapidly succeed in having large sectors of the population lose their confidence in the governments. . .
>
> We must point out that the process of development which Latin America has undertaken in the decade of the sixties, although slow, is the primary arm that is holding back the intensification of subversive action . . . There exists an evident direct relationship between development and subversion. The battle against subversion has come to illustrate the intimate relationship that exists between development policy and security policy. Without development there is no security and vice versa.[27]

On the subject of the military's role, General Mercado had this to say:

> The armed forces of the hemisphere have a full appreciation of the communist danger, and will not tolerate its implantation on the continent. But the anti-communism of the armed forces will not be sufficient to guarantee and preserve our liberty if the policies of the nations are not directed to economic development, without privileges to groups, and to structural changes that bring about an effective social justice that permits the elimination of existing contradictions.

The military intervention against the government of Fernando Belaunde in October 1968 must be viewed in the context of its achievements against this standard, although other factors also were at play. The apparent spark for the coup was the highly unpopular contract with the International Petroleum Company, a subsidiary of Standard Oil, which was announced in September.

---

[27]From a copy of the speech in the author's possession. General Mercado was named army commander in January 1972.

16

In the pre-dawn hours of October 3, a well-planned coup placed a military junta headed by General Juan Velasco Alvarado into office, and the officers embarked upon a far-reaching program of reforms. Significantly, 13 of the 19 members of the first cabinet were graduates of the Center for Higher Military Studies.

Important institutional strains have not yet surfaced in the Peruvian experience although there are increasing indications of differences.[28] In his perceptive essay, Einaudi concluded:

> The internal political diversity of the armed forces . . . over the long run may inhibit the adoption of consistent development policies. The very bureaucratic complexity of the military allows the development of some diversity. But it also acts as an internal self-regulating mechanism inhibiting policies whose effects . . . might threaten to increase internal diversity to the point of endangering the viability of the military institutions themselves. Should the military officer corps produce individual leaders whose personal vision of the struggle for development exceeds institutionally established limits, such men will have to resign (or) be replaced. . . .[29]

The officer corps of Bolivia and Argentina have proved much less adaptable in reaching agreement on the forms and direction that national development should take and the military's role in the process. Institutional factors have precluded a concerted effort at reform politics and have at times threatened to rend the military corporate structure in both countries and lead rival factions and their civilian allies into civil war.

After a stormy and chaotic political history that saw 179 military coups in 126 years of its existence as an independent state, Bolivia underwent a sweeping social revolution in 1952, and for the next 12 years was dominated by the *Movimiento Nacionalista Revolucionario* (MNR).

The overthrow of the MNR regime in 1964 plunged the Bolivian military back into politics after 12 years of civilian government. After a period of junta rule, legal process was re-established in 1966 with the election to the presidency of General René Barrientos Ortuño, who had led the 1964 coup. Barrientos' regime has most frequently been characterized as laissez-faire. Military support, or at least political neutrality on the part of the army, was critical to the survival of his regime. The military institution did not assume the full weight of responsibility for the direction of national policy, however, until Barrientos' death in a helicopter crash in April 1969. That event

---

[28]See, for example, President Velasco's 1971 Army Day speech attacking elements seeking "to undermine the unity of the armed forces" in *La Prensa* (Lima), December 11, 1971.

[29]*Latin American Institutional Development, op. cit.*, p. 61.

unleashed a two-year political crisis which produced three successful coups and a kaleidoscopic shift in national orientations. During one phase private US interests were nationalized, the Peace Corps was expelled, diplomatic relations were established with the Soviet Union, and a "popular assembly" advocating Cuban-style reforms came into being—all this under military aegis. At this writing a "restorative" military government is in power.

Effective power in Argentina, from the time of its "national organization" in the mid-nineteenth century—following a decade of civil war—until 1930, was in the hands of strong executives whose power base was generally independent of the military. The military coup of 1930 brought to the political stage the most professional officer corps in Latin America, and since that time it has been unable either to refrain from politics or to unite sufficiently to implement any coherent program. The 1966 coup was intended to bring about a vast transformation of the society, with the united military as the motive force of the "revolution." After six years, three officer-presidents, and two more coups growing out of institutional differences over policies of national development, the armed forces are as divided as the factionalized society, and the dominant group within the officer corps has announced plans to hold elections and turn the problems of national integration back to civilian leadership.

The two case studies that follow attempt to explain the institutional dynamics that have limited the potential power of the officer corps as "engines of change" in Bolivia and Argentina. A certain asymmetry of treatment is inevitable; the two countries are vastly different on any scale of comparison—size, economy, culture, racial homogeneity, etc. In institutional terms Bolivia's modern army might be said to be a poor quality and reduced-scale image of that of her larger neighbor, but even here the differences make questionable the value of direct comparison.

The two cases have common interest primarily as examples of the complexities faced by tradition-bound Latin American military institutions—with an unquestioned potential for exercising great power—in reconciling established standards of professionalism with new imperatives of socio-political reform. They illustrate the fact that probably in no other region of the world are military establishments undergoing the degree of institutional self-examination as are the armed forces in Latin America. Previously acceptable political roles—as moderators in crisis situations or guarantors of national traditions—are being challenged while classic military missions are re-examined. Geopolitical considerations in the regional context, and technological-cost factors in the wider arena militate against adoption of a completely threat-oriented *Weltanschauung* similar to that which governs

18

military missions in countries faced with a clear and present danger to their national integrity. Classic military concerns (i.e., territorial security and relative power) continue, however, to play a much greater part in the formation of military men and military thought than has been realized or acknowledged heretofore in US analyses and tend to balance the proclivity for "Nasserist" solutions to national development. The common inability of the officer corps in these two quite different South American countries to agree upon ends and means and to take advantage of their undisputed potential poses some interesting problems in institutional dynamics and political interaction and raises some questions about the long-term ability of the military to play a leading—as opposed to a moderating—role in the process of national development.

PART TWO:
BOLIVIA AS A CASE STUDY

I
FOUNDATIONS FOR A PROFESSIONAL ARMY

Early History

The military forces of Simón Bolívar, led by Marshal Antonio José de Sucre, won independence for Upper Peru in 1825. Bolívar, dictator of Peru at that time, wanted the area to join Peru, but Sucre pressed for independence, and in 1826 became the first President. Two years later he resigned in the face of internal disorder and military mutiny and left the new country to a native Bolivian who had been his lieutenant.

General Andrés Santa Cruz ruled for a decade.

In 1835 Santa Cruz invaded Peru, then in a state of anarchy, and formed a short-lived confederation of the two states. Chile opposed the confederation and in a brief campaign defeated its forces. Santa Cruz fled, and the confederation collapsed. Two other military men held the presidency for comparatively short periods, followed by General José Ballivian, an enlightened autocrat who served for six years. Civil strife and dictatorial regimes marked the following decades. Three *caudillos* characterize the period.

Manuel Isidro Belzú (1848-1855) gave a new word to the Bolivian vernacular: *Belcismo* in Bolivia describes blatant demagogy and venal opportunism. Mariano Melgarejo (1864-1871), was a grotesque tyrant, an habitual drunkard, who governed by terror until an armed revolt drove him out of the country. Hilarión Daza (1876-1879), despite his military weakness, provoked a war with Chile over the exploitation of nitrate deposits in the Bolivian coastal province of Antofagasta.

In the War of the Pacific (1879-1881) Chile easily defeated Bolivia and her ally, Peru, annexed Antofagasta, and cut Bolivia off from the Pacific.[1]

Bolivia lost another huge slice of territory along its northern border to Brazil in 1903, but the small-scale fighting involved was carried out largely by the private army of a local rubber baron.

Of the period following the Pacific War, Osborne observed:

> ... In 1880 Bolivia entered on an era of more responsible government. The revised Constitution, promulgated in 1880, lasted until 1931, lawless dictatorship came to seem like a nightmare from the past and by the twenties of the present century comparative political tranquillity and evidences of increased material prosperity

---

[1]Descriptions of the battles of this era, with maps and troop lists, are included in Col. M. Fernando Wilde Cavero, *Historia Militar de Bolivia* (La Paz, n.p., 1963).

had won for Bolivia the reputation of being one of the more stable and reliable of the Latin American republics.[2]

The army was completely demoralized as a result of the War of the Pacific, and the various governments took some measures to rebuild it in the ensuing years. A military academy was formally opened in Sucre in 1891, under the direction of a Bolivian officer who had graduated from the French *Ecole de Guerre*. After graduating its first class of 11 *subtentientes*, the academy was moved to Oruro, and then finally to La Paz in 1899. A French mission headed by General Jacques Sever accepted a contract in 1905 to assist in the reorganization of the army. The mission stayed four years, and left a rudimentary general staff on the European model as its only lasting legacy. A German mission under Major Hans Kundt, which arrived in 1911, was more influential. Kundt was named chief of the general staff, and Major Friedrich Muther became director of the military academy during the mission's first contract, which terminated when the officers returned home at the outbreak of World War I. Kundt returned to La Paz in 1921, and so pleased the government with the parades he produced on national holidays that he was named Minister of Defense in 1925. He was again chief of the general staff in 1931 when his meddling in internal politics caused his dismissal.[3]

The Chaco War and Its Aftermath

Fifty years of relative peace were shattered in the thirties by the Chaco War. The Chaco is a lowland region that includes a large part of Paraguay's northwestern border, the eastern plains of Bolivia, and north-central Argentina. No clear line of demarcation between Paraguay and Bolivia had existed since Bolivia became an independent nation, and following numerous frontier incidents, the dispute flared into open warfare in 1932. The Paraguayans were better led, and had more accessible lines of communication and the advantage of the low altitude which disabled Bolivia's *altiplano* Indian troops. The Bolivian army did not acquit itself well, and was gradually pushed back, with Paraguay occupying most of the contested area. By 1935 the conflict was stalemated. In 1938 a peace agreement gave the greater part

---

[2]Harold Osborne, *Bolivia: A Land Divided* (3rd ed., rev., London, Oxford University Press, 1964), p. 64.

[3]Information on the academy (*Colegio Militar*) and its history appears from time to time in the *Revista Militar* (hereafter referred to as *RM*) but data must be cross-checked. A fairly accurate historical article appears in the issue of July-September 1958, pp. 73-77. For information on the foreign missions, see Julio Diaz, *Historia del Ejército de Bolivia 1825-1932* (La Paz, Imprenta Central del Ejército, 1940), pp. 760-775.

of the region under contention to Paraguay, and, with the loss of her outlet to the Atlantic via the Paraguay River, Bolivia became completely landlocked.

The war and its consequences were too cataclysmic not to have had an effect on the nineteenth century society that still existed in Bolivia. Casualties were heavy (some 60,000 soldiers were lost), and the war drained the nation's economy. Young intellectuals among the veterans began to question the legitimacy of the mining and landowning oligarchy that controlled the nation.

The political effervescence that followed reached also into the ranks of younger officers who felt that civilian leadership had been negligent in the war effort and was incompetent to carry out the social and economic reforms demanded by veteran groups. In 1936, a military coup deposed the traditionalist government of President José Luis Tejada Sórzano and installed Colonel David Toro in the presidency. Toro embarked on a program resembling the national-socialism of European Fascism. He was overthrown in 1937 by Lt. Colonel Germán Busch, who continued the drift toward a version of the corporate state. His regime came to an end with his suicide in 1939, and the oligarchy reasserted its power with the help of older officers. Two generals, Carlos Quintanilla and Enrique Peñaranda, served as presidents from 1939 to 1943.

The general staff had badly bungled the management of resources during the Chaco War, and a Superior War School was established in 1938 to train officers in general staff procedures and techniques. An Italian military mission was brought to Cochabamba to organize the school. The school has been in continuous operation since its founding, although the name was changed to Command and General Staff School (ECEM) in 1950. With the inauguration of the ECEM, the Bolivian army adopted the European system of distinguishing general staff officers (*diplomados de estado mayor*) from line officers. Once qualified by graduation from the School and successful completion of other requirements, an officer was allowed to use the coveted initials DEM following his title, and became eligible for assignment to certain key positions reserved by law to general staff officers.[4] A School of Arms, to give branch professional training to junior officers of the infantry, cavalry, and artillery, was opened in Cochabamba the same year (1938) and has operated since that time.

Although numerous young officers were involved in politics in the years immediately following the Chaco War, the officer corps as a body did not

---

[4]A brief history of the Command and General Staff School appeared in *RM* (October-December 1969), pp. 63-70.

play a prominent part until 1943, when a secret "lodge" called *Razon de Patria* (RADEPA) joined forces with the newly-created MNR in a successful coup. RADEPA had been formed by junior officers in Paraguayan prison camps during the war; it turned its attention to politics after Toro and Busch showed the way. Major Gualberto Villarroel was selected by RADEPA as liaison between itself and the MNR, and became president after the surprisingly easy overthrow of the junta.[5] Victor Paz Estenssoro, finance minister in the new government, and other MNR ideologues had early identified the mining component of the oligarchy as the primary enemy and pushed for radical measures to increase the extractive industry's contribution to national revenues. The commercial and mining establishment (called *La Rosca* by Bolivians) fought back, and when exchange controls were imposed on the heretofore practically sovereign enterprises, an all-out effort against the government was mounted. There are indications that troop commanders and even some members of RADEPA were bribed. During one of the frequent mob riots that La Paz suffered, in July 1946, the army failed to protect the government buildings, the presidential palace (*Palacio Quemado*) was sacked, and Villarroel and his close aids were killed and strung up.

The 1952 Revolution

An alliance of conservative factions regained control of the government through its control of the limited electorate—no more than 200,000 or so of the population of almost three million. For the first time, at least in the twentieth century, large-scale retribution was taken against officers who had been closely associated with the previous government. Military disciplinary archives include the case files of more than a hundred field grade and junior officers who were tried by military courts in 1946 for political activities. Many were finally convicted of violating military law by joining secret lodges and "participating in political activities," and were discharged from the service.[6] Some officers went into exile with Paz and the MNR nucleus, while other sympathizers, active and discharged, planned and participated in the MNR coup attempt of 1949, which assumed some aspects of a civil war. An Argentine border police officer told the author that as a young agent in

---

[5]An eyewitness account of the 1943 coup by a German advisor to the Bolivian Army may be found in Col. Kurt Conrad Arnade, "The Technique of Coup D'Etat in Latin America," *United Nations World* (February 1950), pp. 21-25. The MNR side is explained in José Fellman Velarde, *Victor Paz Estenssoro, el hombre y la revolución* (La Paz, E. Burrillo, 1955), pp. 117-133.

[6]Colonel Carlos Manuel Silva, "La Justicia Militar y Los Guerrillas," *RM* (January-March 1968), pp. 81-82.

August 1949 in the Argentine border town of La Quiaca, he was with a party that apprehended Victor Paz Estenssoro and "about a dozen" followers who planned to capture the village of Villazon on the Bolivian side. Included were "a few" professional officers, among whom he identified Major Clemente Inofuentes, who later held high positions in the post-revolutionary army. A Bolivian officer told the author some years later that Inofuentes was in fact Paz's military adviser during his exile. There is no doubt that many officers were involved. General Froilan Calleja led the revolt in Santa Cruz, and, after the MNR victory in 1952, became the first minister of defense.

The 1949 insurrection failed, and again there was a sizeable purge of army officers who found themselves on the wrong side. One authority says "almost a thousand" persons were tried by military courts following the uprising, but that a general amnesty[7] suspended action before sentencing. Other authorities estimated the number of officers tried and exiled at between 250 and 300.[8]

The MNR sought power again, this time legally, in the elections of 1951, but when it was barred by a military junta from taking office on what it considered a technicality, the party returned to the insurrectionary path. In three days of fighting, April 9-11, 1952, party militias defeated the troops of the La Paz garrison and gained power. General Antonio Seleme, a member of the junta, abetted the rebel victory by collusion, but developed doubts about the outcome midway through the struggle and sought diplomatic asylum in the Chilean embassy in La Paz. Thus, the MNR nucleus gained power with no debt to the standing army.

The poor showing of the army is probably attributable to institutional perturbations and personal animosities growing out of the 1946 and 1949 trials and purges, and to General Seleme's confusing role in the insurrection. That the army was badly divided and demoralized in the months preceding the coup is indicated by a message the Minister of Defense addressed to the officer corps in early 1952 in which he expressed his despair at the political factionalism and lack of professionalism and pleaded for institutional unity in a time of crisis.[9] Two officers who were captains at the time told the author

---

[7]*Ibid.*, p. 82.

[8]Nazario Pardo Valle, in his pro-MNR *Calendario Histórico de La Revolución* (La Paz, E. Burrillo, 1957), says that by mid-1950 over 260 MNR militants and officers had been tried by military courts for their part in the 1949 uprising, and notes that 53 discharged officers were reincorporated by the government after the MNR victory of 1952. Velarde, in *Victor Paz*, says that the army lost over 300 field grade officers to exile or discharge between 1946 and 1949, and that most of them joined the MNR.

[9]His letter was published in *RM* (March 1952) p. 1.

that officers of their interior garrison believed that General Seleme was the leader of yet another change of the palace guard and that no vital army interests were at stake. This could well have been true at other garrisons. The roles played by individual officers and units in La Paz during the momentous three days remains a subject of considerable discretion. The *Colegio Militar* and the presidential guard battalion fought hard and valiantly to defend the government, and punitive action was taken against both afterward. Estimates concerning the number of casualties in the capital vary from several hundred to two or three thousand.

II
THE IMPACT AND AFTERMATH OF THE 1952 REVOLUTION

The First Years

A central problem of any social revolution is the disposition of the regular military establishment once the new governing groups have control of the state apparatus. Many factors condition the solution: the army's stand in the revolutionary struggle, its cohesiveness during the consolidation phase, the presence of other armed groups, the country's international relations and particularly the security of borders, the ideology of the victorious faction, etc.

Bolivia's only Latin American example in 1952 was Mexico, and the circumstances were vastly different. Mexico's revolution involved about two years of civil war and scattered rebellion, during which the old army was destroyed and a revolutionary force formed from loosely disciplined bands loyal to regional leaders. This revolutionary army was subsequently brought under the effective control of the political apparatus with a series of "taming" maneuvers which included bureaucratizing its structure, reducing its size, professionalizing the officer corps, and for a time incorporating it as a recognized "sector" of the dominant revolutionary party.

The Bolivian army numbered about 18,000-20,000 at the time of the 1952 Revolution. Probably some 1200-1300 of that number were officers, based on prevailing officer/soldier ratios. Most of the remainder were one-year Indian conscripts. Although early historians of the period maintain that 80 percent of the officers were discharged or exiled, subsequent research would indicate that this figure is too high.[10] About two-thirds of the conscripts were sent home but the revolutionary tribunals probably discharged or exiled no more than 300 officers (most of them after the abortive counter-coup of January 1953). General Alfredo Ovando Candia, armed forces chief in later years, estimated that between 100 and 250 officers were dismissed between April 1952 and January 1953, and the armed forces cut from 20,000 to 5,000 during the same period.[11]

There was, however, a general housecleaning of senior officers. Only two of the 26 officers who were promoted to brigadier general or colonel in the

---

[10]Alberto Ostría Gutiérrez, The Tragedy of Bolivia (New York, Devin-Adair Co., 1956), among others hold that about 80 percent of the officer corps was discharged or exiled.

[11]In an interview with William H. Brill. See Brill, Military Civic Action in Bolivia (unpublished Ph.D. dissertation, University of Michigan, 1966), pp. 81-83.

annual promotions of 1949 played any role in the post-1952 army.[12] The party and miner militias, provided with army weapons during the fighting, were allowed to flourish, and control of the army was vested in officers of proven loyalty to Paz and the MNR. The first Minister of Defense was General Froilan Calleja, who had held Santa Cruz for the MNR during the abortive coup of 1949. General Miguel Ayllon, who had served in the Villarroel cabinet, became army commander. Colonel Gualberto Olmos, who had been wounded in the 1949 insurrection, was placed in command of the new presidential guard regiment "formed of officers and soldiers who have fought six long years for the MNR."[13]

Paz himself announced in late 1952:

We have returned dignity and a true function to the armed forces, eliminating from its ranks all those who used their arms against the people. At the same time, those officers who had been dismissed due to their loyal cooperation with the popular regime of Villarroel have been reincorporated into the military institution.[14]

Major Inofuentes, who had been at Paz's side in 1949, was promoted to colonel and given the key job of coordinator of the army's development activities in support of the revolution's goals. His interpretations of MNR doctrine on the military's "productive" role in society provided the rationale for its first feeble efforts at road building and well digging, but also, more importantly, laid the foundation that allowed the army to capitalize on US "civic action" proposals in the sixties. His official title was Director of Planning of the General Staff of the National Revolutionary Army. (His articles appeared regularly in the 1953 editions of the *Revista Militar*.)

After purging the leadership and insuring that MNR stalwarts were effectively in control, Paz generally ignored the army. The irregular militias provided an effective counterweight to the impoverished regular forces. General Ovando in later years wrote bitterly of these dark days in the army's history, when officers were refused admittance to arsenals and magazines by militia guards, when the few army vehicles had to be parked downhill so they could be restarted because there were no batteries, when officers had to live "in rented garages" and share their rations with the entire family, when official mail had to be posted in envelopes used on both sides for lack of office supplies.[15] The military budget declined precipitously. Prior to 1952

---

[12]The list appeared in *RM* (January-March 1949).

[13]From an Olmos speech published in *RM* (April-May 1953), p. 186.

[14]*Discursos y Mensajes* (Buenos Aires, Ed. Meridiano, 1953) p. 8.

[15]*RM* (April-June 1968), pp. 151-152. Other officers have given the author similar accounts.

over 20 percent of the federal budget had customarily been allocated to defense expenditures. This was halved shortly after the MNR took power, and had dropped to a low of 6.7 percent by 1957.[16]

The MNR hierarchy seriously considered the complete elimination of the army, a proposal vigorously advocated by miner leader Juan Lechín and the more radical wing of the party. It was only with difficulty that Paz prevailed in his view that the military could be tamed and integrated into the revolutionary plan. Given its complete demoralization, the breakdown of the never-efficient logistics and communication system, and the presence of the heavily armed irregular militias, there is little doubt that the army could have been effectively destroyed with a concerted effort in 1952-53.

Paz chose instead to leave the old structure essentially intact after the January 1953 purges, keeping it on a starvation diet and closely controlling the leadership. A widely publicized reorganization took place for the record, but the major innovation was a change in name from Bolivian Army to Army of the National Revolution. In his first message to the "reorganized" force, Paz promised support for its developmental activities, including heavy engineering equipment.[17] One of his first moves was the establishment of an army engineering school. To placate the left, there was some talk of transforming the class structure of the officer corps, and when the military academy was reopened in October 1953 (under the command of the completely dependable Colonel Olmos) apparently the cadets were required to take a party oath.

This first, and only, class of "MNR cadets" graduated in August 1954 after ten months of training. Paz delivered the graduation address. He denied that the army had been destroyed after April 1952, as claimed by his opponents; he said it had been reorganized on sounder bases. Paz pointed out that the new cadet corps was made up not only of the common people (*hijos del pueblo*) but included also those of the "*burguesia y clase media.*" He said the new army was an institution of production and a builder of schools and roads, in addition to being the defender of the nation.[18]

---

[16]For budget information, see Joseph E. Loftus, *Latin American Defense Expenditures: 1938-1965* (Santa Monica, Calif., Rand Corp., January 1968), p. 37, and James W. Wilkie, *The Bolivian Revolution and US Aid Since 1952* (Los Angeles, University of California Press, 1969), pp. 60-61. Charles W. Anderson, *Politics and Economic Change in Latin America* (Princeton, N.J., D. Van Nostrand Co., 1967), using Bolivian Central Bank statistics, indicates that 24 percent of the public budget was devoted to defense in 1951, 14 percent in 1952, and 7 percent in 1957 (pp. 330-331).

[17]Paz's first message and reorganization plans were published in *RM* (January 1953).

[18]*RM* (August-September 1954), pp. 131-135.

Although rhetoric about integrating the lower classes into the officer corps persisted for a long while among the politicians of the MNR, little was said on the subject within the army. In a graduation speech at the academy in 1955, in the presence of Paz and party dignitaries, Colonel Hugo Suarez Guzmán, the Director of Studies, charged the new officers to serve the national revolution "like sons of the middle class, to which we all belong."[19]

There is no doubt that Paz succeeded completely in dominating the army during his first term. Commanders grumbled incessantly about their lack of resources—even uniforms and shoes were frequently lacking for the annual crop of conscripts—but they grumbled within military channels and their complaints were absorbed by the thoroughly loyal top leadership. MNR stalwarts moved up the hierarchical ladder smoothly, sharing the defense ministry and the army command and general staff positions. They exhorted the army to accept willingly its role as an instrument of the revolution, to become self-sufficient in food, and to teach not only the ignorant conscripts but the *campesinos* (peasants) surrounding their garrisons.[20] They appeared in full braid at practically all ceremonial functions with the president and other party functionaries, completing the picture of a complaisant and integrated military.

Great institutional tenacity was evidenced by the more traditionally oriented middle echelons of the army during these lean years, with its most tangible manifestations in the career school system. All the army schools were kept open, although the students devoted much of their time to repairing the facilities and scrounging materials. The School of Arms and the Command and General Staff School were located in Cochabamba, and there were seldom funds to pay for the movement of officers, to say nothing of their families, from outlying units to the schools. Classes were made up largely of officers from nearby units, but some of the more ambitious officers left their families in La Paz or distant garrisons to live with relatives or friends in order to gain the coveted diplomas.[21]

---

[19]*RM* (January-April 1956), p. 68.

[20]See the speech by Minister of Defense Col. Armando Prudencio in *La Nación*, April 1, 1954. Col. Olmos became Minister of Defense in 1955, while Colonels Luis F. Rodriguez Bidegain, René Gonzalez Torres, Armando Fortún Sanjinés, and a few other Paz favorites dominated the army high command during the MNR's first term.

[21]The School of Arms had about 20 graduates from its ten-month advanced course in 1955, the Command and General Staff School ten from its two-year course. The widow of ex-president Villarroel spoke at the graduation ceremonies of the latter. *RM* (January-April 1956), p. 38.

Some money was even found for study abroad, mostly at the United States Army School of the Americas in Panama. Seven officers attended in 1954, and the number steadily increased thereafter.[22]

Improving Fortunes

Army fortunes improved somewhat under the MNR's second administration from 1956-1960. President Siles Zuazo's regime is seen as a Jacobin phase in the revolution by most observers,[23] and he was less doctrinaire about the military's role, placing greater emphasis on the army's traditional image as a symbol of national sovereignty and defender of the nation's interests. His first message to the army implied this view:

> The structure of the state will remain incomplete and the image of the fatherland will lack vigorous expression unless we give attention to the necessities of the new revolutionary army. . . . It is one of my intentions to make it possible for the army to participate fully (*posibilitar la saludable concurrencia del* ejército) in the effort to raise the civic and patriotic spirit of the revolutionary people of Bolivia.[24]

The President undertook to reduce the raging inflation and to impose some discipline on the labor sector that had been Paz's chief support. The strength of the army was increased only slightly during the period, but its prestige and importance rose enormously with the new functions it was given

---

[22]Officers who studied in Panama or the US during these years received five US dollars before leaving Bolivia, and normally were completely dependent thereafter on the small per diem paid by the US Government. Among the trainees of those years was the current president, then Captain Hugo Banzer Suarez, who stood number one in his motor transportation officer course in Panama in 1956.

[23]James M. Malloy, *Bolivia, The Uncompleted Revolution* (Pittsburgh, University of Pittsburgh Press, 1970), pp. 216-280, sees the politics of the 1952-1964 period of the revolution as primarily a battle over alternative models of development, with the ideological struggle raging principally around two models: a "democratic bourgeois society" and a "government of workers and peasants." The former was projected as a state-capitalist model dominated by a progressive middle class elite, the latter as a state-socialist model run by a mixed elite with preponderant working class representation. He indentifies three phases of the struggle, roughly coinciding with presidential terms, during the 12-year period of MNR control of the revolution. From 1952 to 1956 Paz and the party elite established a state-socialist system based on a center-left coalition that attempted to satisfy their development aims (accumulation for investment) and the aims of the party's worker-urban middle-class supporters (consumption). The result was wild inflation and eventually an intolerable burden on the urban middle sectors. During President Siles Zuazo's term from 1956 to 1960, a center-right coalition was formed which shifted the burden of social costs to worker groups. Since these included the armed militias of the economically important mines, internal violence and economic stagnation resulted. in the last phase of MNR control, Paz formed a new center-right coalition, this time on a "state-capitalist" model, supported economically by the US under the Alliance for Progress.

[24]*RM* (May-August 1956), p. 31.

33

after 1957. Siles' reforms were largely at the expense of labor, and he lost the support of the miner militia. Guillermo Bedregal, a leading MNR figure, dates the political resurgence of the army from 1957:

The breakdown in the revolutionary front that occurred in 1957, during the unsuccessful general strike of the Bolivian Workers' Central, produced the determining initiative for the reinforcement of the power of the armed forces. The government, deeply involved in the anti-inflationary fight . . . at the mercy of the unchecked rush of politically inspired and anarchic strikes, fomented by the labor leadership, had recourse to the simple expedient of strengthening the armed forces as a counterbalance, seeking by this artificial and risky path the maintenance of order within the revolution.[25]

Siles also sought to divide the armed peasant bands which appeared in the east. In the ensuing struggle he found it necessary to establish a military zone in the Cochabamba Valley and became considerably dependent upon the army for the maintenance of peace there. Bedregal says this move let the army into the party's decision-making councils for the first time, and that its influence began to grow at the expense of the other sectors.[26]

Siles was hesitant about total dependence upon the army, however, and on at least one occasion used a peasant militia from Cochabamba to put down a rebellion in the mines rather than calling upon the regular forces. The army was not strong enough to disarm the peasant bands, and depended largely on negotiation to maintain peace. The task became more difficult as the 1960 elections approached and the varying factions of the MNR sought support from the peasant chieftains and other irregular armed elements.[27]

Although it was not aligned with any factions, the officer corps was politically sensitive as the MNR sought a way out of the economic and political immobilism of the fifties. There were no important attempts to influence the elections by army officers. Some officers had attachments to the Bolivian Socialist Falange, but the death of its long-time leader in a 1959 coup attempt (quashed by the army) had left the party disorganized, and in general the military appeared content to let the MNR work out its internal squabbles and attack the country's problems. The victory went to Paz

[25]Guillermo Bedregal, "El Problema Militar en Bolivia," *Politica*, (Vol. V, No. 54, October 1966, n.p.).

[26]*Ibid.* For an excellent analysis of Siles' political and economic program, and of the pressures bearing upon him, see Malloy, *Bolivia,* pp. 235-280.

[27]The MNR also armed "commando" squads in the population centers. Guillermo Lora, an unsympathetic historian, describes these bands, which he claims were often mercenaries paid with whiskey and cash, in *La Revolucion Boliviana* (La Paz, n.p., 1964).

Estenssoro again, and despite the fact that he had to accept miner leader Juan Lechín as his vice president to maintain some semblance of unity with the left, he opted for the state-capitalist model of development, with the support of the Alliance for Progress. That decision, and the changes in the US hemispheric security policy instituted by the Kennedy Administration in response to the Cuban experience, brought a change in prospects for the army.

New Horizons

The Kennedy Administration's hemispheric security policy had far-reaching effects on the Bolivian army. The military civic action doctrine was completely compatible with the "productive" role the army had been assigned by the MNR, and counterinsurgency was an acceptable mission that brought with it the kind of equipment the army wanted and could most easily absorb. The increase in United States military aid to Bolivia is indicated by the following table:

US Net Financial Commitments (Disbursements)[28]
(millions of dollars)

1958	.1
1959	.3
1960	--
1961	.4
1962	2.2
1963	2.4
1964	3.2

Training in US facilities also showed a sharp rise, from about 25 officers per year during the fifties to an average of 160 during the early sixties. According to one study, by the end of 1963 Bolivia had more graduates from the US Army Special Warfare School at Fort Bragg than any other Latin American country.[29]

---

[28]Adapted from tables in Wilkie, *The Bolivian Revolution*, pp. 60-61. The Agency for International Development *Economic Data Book* (1968 edition), p. 10, lists total military assistance for the 1946-1967 period as 18.7 million dollars, but yearly totals are given only for 1966 (2.4 million) and 1967 (2.9 million).

[29]Willard F. Barber and C. Neale Ronning, *Internal Security and Military Power: Counterinsurgency and Civic Action in Latin America* (Ohio State University Press, 1966), p. 149.

There was also a steady rise in Bolivian Government defense expenditures during the period, although they remained quite low in absolute terms.[30]

Army strength, meanwhile, had risen to about 12,000 men, if computed immediately after conscription early in the year. Conscripts seldom served their full 12-month term because of monetary limitations, and army strength frequency was halved by October.

General Alfredo Ovando Candia became Chief of Staff of the army in 1957, Army Commander in 1960, and three years later moved up to the most powerful post in the military structure, Armed Forces Commander in Chief. Bolivia's political and military fortunes were to be greatly influenced by this enigmatic officer during an entire decade.

Military interest and leverage in political matters were expanded by a steady broadening of the definition of national security during the early sixties, and by the army's almost sovereign administration of the military zones established in Cochabamba and Santa Cruz to keep a lid on the endemic violence there.

Following the 1952 insurrection, *campesinos* had occupied the rich farmlands of western Santa Cruz province and the Cliza and Ucureña valleys in Cochabamba. The MNR's agrarian reform program of August 1953 was essentially *de jure* recognition of his situation. *Campesino syndicatos* were formed to resist any attempts to force surrender of the lands, and the leaders came to be regional *caudillos* with considerable political clout. José Rojas, the full-blooded Indian boss of the Ucureña valley, was named Minister of Rural Affairs for a time in 1959. The peasants had obtained large quantities of arms during the 1949 "civil war" when MNR supporters in the local army garrisons opened arsenals to them. They added to their equipment again in 1952 in raids on government arsenals in the general dissolution of centralized control and discipline that followed the revolutionary coup.

Rojas' arch rival for power in Cochabamba was Miguel Veizaga, *caudillo* of the Cliza valley. Their feud was frequently aggravated by political leaders who sought their support, and by government use of their private armies from time to time against the miner militias. In the 1960 MNR in-fighting for the presidential nomination, Rojas supported Paz while Veizaga backed Walter Guevara Arze. Veizaga's men captured Paz on one of his campaign trips to

---

[30]Most sources indicate a rise in the percentage of government expenditures devoted to the military from about seven percent in 1957 to between 12 and 13 percent in 1963. Wilkie, *The Bolivian Revolution*, gives 12.6 for 1962, 12.4 for 1963 (pp. 60-61). Loftus, *Latin American Defense Expenditures*, shows a rise in absolute terms from 2.4 million (1960 US) dollars in 1958 to 6 million in 1963 (pp. 11). Colonel Julio Sanchez, Ambassador to Washington, is quoted in Brill, *Military Civic Action*, as saying that the army got $7.5 million, or about 13 percent of the national budget in 1963 (p. 83).

Cliza and Guevara had to intervene to get him freed. The bloody rivalry brought martial law to the entire province in March 1960. A military commission finally arranged a shaky truce, but it was repeatedly broken and the province was later put under army control.

The rivalries in Santa Cruz were more complex because of the presence of strong party militia units formed by the MNR, the long-time history of smuggling, strong *falangist* sentiment, and latent interest among some sectors in affiliation with Brazil. Luís Sandovál Morón was for years the most powerful *caudillo* of the province and a political figure courted by all factions. His chief rival was Reubin Julio Castro. Bloody fighting between their followers resulted in Santa Cruz being declared a "military zone" in August 1960 and placed under military control. General Barrientos was the first military prefect (*interventor*).[31]

A succession of officers went to the two areas over the years as perfects or on pacifying commissions, and the commanders of the Seventh Division at Cochabamba and the Eighth at Santa Cruz came to be regarded as the principal central government representatives in the areas, even in interludes of relative peace when civil government was re-established. The congress became increasingly uneasy about these virtually autonomous military zones, as is indicated by sharp interpellations of the Minister of Defense in 1961 and 1962.[32] In the latter year there was an attempt by the deputies to declare null and void the enabling decrees that established the zones.

The establishment of a School of Higher Military Studies in 1960 and the Supreme Council for National Defense in 1961 institutionalized the broader concerns of national defense policy. The former was inaugurated during Siles' term to educate "the high-level civilian and military hierarchy on problems of a strategic nature that concern or affect Bolivia."[33] The latter body was formalized in a presidential decree of December, 1961 as the "highest advisory body charged with problems of national defense", and had as its members the President, Vice-President, Minister of Defense, all cabinet members, the chairmen of the congressional committees on foreign relations and defense, the Commander in Chief of the Armed Forces and each of the service commanders.[34]

---

[31]Richard Patch has written extensively on *campesino* affairs. For an account of the early years of peasant league organization, see his essay "Bolivia and US Assistance" in *Social Change in Latin America Today* (New York, Vintage Books, 1960), pp. 119-142.

[32]*Actuaciones parlamentarias del Ministro de Defensa Nacional, Sr. Juan Luís Gutiérrez Grainer, en los años 1961 and 1962* (La Paz, 1963).

[33]Supreme Decree No. 05441, March 21, 1960.

[34]Supreme Decree No. 0741-65, April 1961.

An army general has always served as permanent secretary of the Supreme Council. The charter gave the Council responsibility to direct, orient, and resolve matters dealing with international defense policy, economic and financial planning that affected defense, mobilization, and coordination of the participation in national defense matters of other elements of the government. Under the emerging broad definitions of national defense, the Council structure gave the military, through the permanent secretariat, a legal national forum for presentation of the army viewpoint on almost any question.

General Ovando reminisced about these years in a remarkable "open letter" to the officers of the armed forces in 1968.[35] He traced the evolution of the army from colonial days, and underlined the importance of the Chaco War and its aftermath in awakening a social consciousness among officers. He credited Busch, Villarroel, and the 1943-46 MNR with having "opened the road for the national revolution" by "weakening the walls of reaction" with their economic and social reforms. He indicated that after its return to power in 1952, the MNR turned its back on the military institution, making it a simple cell in the party structure, and entrusting the coercive power of the state to an armed rabble. Ovando said that "the resistance" formed among members of the general staff, and that improvements in the army were carried out "behind the back of the president and of the MNR generals." He ridiculed the MNR claim that it created the prestigious Center of Instruction for Special Troops (CITE), insisting that it was formed without a cent being allocated in the budget by the sweat of the army and the assistance of "comrades in arms who in secret gave us parachutes and invaluable technical assistance."[36] Ovando went on to claim that he "single-handedly" procured vehicles abroad to motorize a battalion, and delivered them by air to the La Paz airport "before the astonishment and surprise of the then Secretary of Defense." He also attacked the MNR claim that it had organized the River and Lake Force in 1963, saying that officers who formed it had to study abroad surreptitiously to make it possible. He said that "it was necessary to offer its command to an MNR general in order to get the signature on the decree legalizing its creation."[37]

---

[35] *RM* (April-June 1968).

[36] CITE was formed in 1963 with officers trained by an Argentine advisory group, according to an anniversary article appearing in *RM* (July-August 1968), p. 222. The acronym came to refer to both the training center and its operational parachute battalion.

[37] Ronant Monje Roca, an MNR militant from his junior officer days, was the first commander. Monje was prominent in the "military cell" of the MNR and used the

Ovando's bitter remarks in 1968 about the MNR were probably motivated by events of that year. His description of his own role in the rebuilding of the army is consistent with that offered in many prior conversations, however. Although it is hard to imagine that he could unilaterally negotiate foreign assistance of the scale mentioned without the knowledge of the president, he is given almost universal credit within the officer corps for having modernized the army in the face of indifference, if not opposition.

An enigmatic, taciturn man, Ovando had few close confidants. Most interviewers who talked with him came away with the impression of a sincere and dedicated professional soldier committed to an almost obsessive drive to professionalize the army and insulate it from political squabbles. There were, however, occasional references to Kemal Ataturk in his conversations, and in the "open letter" mentioned above he prescribed for Bolivia "governmental action, or revolution, as remoralizing (*moralizadora*) as that of José María Linares and as constructive and nationalistic as that of Kemal Ataturk in Turkey."[38] And nobody doubted who was to play Ataturk.

The 1964 Coup

Victor Paz Estenssoro's decision in 1963 to seek the presidency for a second consecutive term split the MNR, and its squabbling factions sought support wherever it was to be found. The prize was the vice presidency and a share of control in top party councils, since Paz was unbeatable. The military cell of the MNR, apparently dominated by the old "party generals," proposed General René Barrientos for the vice presidency. Barrientos had gained considerable peasant support in the eastern lowlands on various pacification missions to the warring leagues. He had been named *interventor* in Santa Cruz in 1961 when that department was declared a military zone, and in 1963, with Colonel Eduardo Rivas, had settled at least temporarily some long-standing feuds among peasant bands in Cochabamba. *Barrientistas* were able to get Rivas named to the executive secretariat of the MNR before the 1964 convention, and a vigorous campaign for Barrientos was launched. Despite their best efforts, Paz selected a party wheelhorse, but after an assassination

---

Revista de la Fuerza Fluvial y Lacustre (River and Lake Force Magazine) to push the party line. After the ouster of Paz in 1964, Ovando replaced Monje and his entire staff, who had adopted naval titles, with army colonels. The River and Lake Force was subsequently rechristened the Bolivian Navy, and the officers once again use naval titles.

[38]Linares, Bolivian president from 1857 to 1861, is described by Osborne, *Bolivia*, as "a capable and upright administrator who carried autocracy to the point of fanaticism and suppressed every stirring of opposition with no less ruthless ferocity than his predecessors" (p. 57).

attempt on Barrientos added to his already widespread popularity, Paz changed his mind and accepted the ambitious officer as his running mate.

Ovando's principal concern during this period appeared to be that of preventing a split in the army over the election issue. He apparently had never taken an active part in the "military cell" of the party, and certainly never gave warm support to Barrientos' candidacy. Taking advantage of nationwide student and teacher strikes, the complete disarray in the MNR, and a general feeling that Paz's violation of the tradition of no self-succession cast a shadow of illegitimacy on his election, both men apparently began separately to plot Paz's overthrow almost immediately after his inauguration in August.[39]

Ovando's loyalty was critical to Paz. Having alienated the left wing of the party, and with it the still-potent miner militia, his principal strength lay with the armed forces. Barrientos also recognized that fact, and his actions after August appeared to be aimed at moving Ovando off center by intensifying areas of military dissatisfaction with the government while championing the causes of dissenters of any hue. He breathed new life into the now mythologized concept that social concern had been introduced into Bolivian history by the military "martyrs" Busch and Villarroel. He was a peripatetic figure, whose political office and military status gave him a forum on any subject and *entrée* into any garrison. His long association with Cochabamba earned him allies among the peasant leagues there, and support in the key Seventh Division with its CITE unit and schools command. It was from there on November 3, after the Seventh Division declared itself in rebellion, that Barrientos called for Paz's resignation.

Despite the fact that he had allowed coup planning in the general staff, the weight of the circumstancial evidence would indicate that Ovando had given no commitment of support to Barrientos before his *pronunciamiento*. There was a noticeable lack of coordination among army units after the Cochabamba garrison pronounced itself against the government, and Ovando himself issued no public proclamations. He closeted himself with the army general staff in the Miraflores headquarters on the 3rd, and emerged the following day to escort Paz to the airport on his journey into exile. The Miraflores complex houses the military communications center, and no doubt key commanders were polled during the momentous interval. Apparently a compromise was reached with the commander of the presidential guard battalion also, since subsequent press accounts cite no military in-fighting.

---

[39]Interviews to this effect with Barrientos and two colonels from Ovando's staff appear in William H. Brill, *Military Intervention in Bolivia: The Overthrow of Paz Estenssoro and the MNR* (Washington, Institute for the Comparative Study of Political Systems, 1967), pp. 23-29.

Most of the important provincial garrisons had declared for Barrientos by the afternoon of November 4, and on the next day, having reached an accord, Ovando and Barrientos announced that they would serve as co-presidents. Ovando, however, was subjected to a cacaphony of cat-calls and jeers when the two appeared together on the balcony of the *Palacio Quemado*, and he withdrew as co-president.

To seek in the nature and character of the military institution the underlying motivations for a resurgence of military rule—after 12 years of revolutionary civilian government—is to encounter frustration. There was no threat to the corporate structure or interests of the military in 1964; it was in better shape than it had been in years, and had every reason to expect that the trend would continue. Neither communism nor other radical doctrines were involved: Paz had broken relations with Cuba in August, and was embarked upon an economic program that was in consonance with Alliance for Progress policies which were enthusiastically accepted by the junta that succeeded him. There was no hint of reversing "revolutionary" gains. Barrientos told army leaders in a January 1965 speech that his government would make "a revolution within the revolution," and that the "grand social conquests," including universal suffrage, agrarian and educational reform, and nationalized mines, would be maintained.[40]

A rationalization offered by some Bolivian officers is that the army withdrew support from Paz because it was reluctant to continue its coercive role against the miners on behalf of the MNR or any other political party. Army occupation of the mining centers in December 1963, when some foreign technicians were held hostage at the Catavi mine, promised trouble for the future as the government continued its efforts to rationalize the operations of the mining commission and cut costs, and indeed bloody clashes were to occur in 1965 and again in 1967. Ovando's expressed sentiments and actions of later years give some credence to this thesis. It would be safe to say that the 1964 coup was probably pushed more by pressures internal to the military than pulled by political factors external to the institution, although the latter were present.

As has occurred so frequently in Bolivia, events turned principally on the driving ambitions of strong men. One, Paz, insisted on holding on to power in the face of a tradition that prohibited consecutive second terms, splitting his machine, alienating powerful supporters, and putting himself temporarily at a power disadvantage; the other two had at hand the power to seize control, and were able to reach an accord on how to apportion it. Neither felt loyalty

---

[40]*RM* (February-March 1965), pp. 7-11.

to the party of the revolution and both were willing to divide power to prevent damage to the military establishment (*la Institucion*). The enormous prestige of Ovando, and the early commitment to elections, were sufficient to keep opposition elements in the military neutral. These elements, however, were to play a much more active role in succeeding events.

Ovando did not remain long in the shadows. Barrientos exiled leftist miner boss Juan Lechín and ex-president Siles and sent the army into the mines in May 1965 to break strikes. Several days of open warfare ensued. There were dozens of deaths and numerous exiles. Ovando, as armed forces chief, negotiated a truce with the new mine leaders, and the following month was again named co-president. This time there were no complaints.

Barrientos resigned in January 1966, as required by the constitution, to campaign for the elections announced for July. It would appear that he was taking a decided risk in doing so, but perhaps he was a shrewd judge of the character of his chief competitor. Ovando controlled the army, but Barrientos enjoyed great popular support and had an enthusiastic following among the younger officers of the army and air force. A move against him would have doubtless revived the simmering peasant league feuds in Cochabamba, and those leagues allied with Barrientos were stronger during this period. It was too risky for an innately cautious man. Almost certainly a deal was made before Barrientos stepped down to campaign that pledged his support for Ovando in the subsequent election.

III
THE INSTITUTIONAL STRUCTURE

The Bolivian army that underpinned the Barrientos-Ovando regime was a far cry from the ragtag bands that kept the nineteenth-century *caudillos* in power, or even from the parade ground forces that marched off to the Chaco. The quality of the conscripts had not greatly changed, but they were less important in what was (and is) essentially a cadre force of career and noncommissioned officers. Building on the European heritage of Kundt and the Italians, and isolated from day-to-day politics by the MNR, the officer corps centered its corporate identity in its school system during the early fifties. With the assistance of US and Argentine advisors after 1956, and with new blood in the form of Bolivian graduates of foreign staff colleges, organizational concepts that continue to prevail came out of ECEM during the decade. Formal professional education became a mania, and although the schools are inferior to those of larger neighbors, the structure is probably the most elaborate of any in less-developed countries of equal size in the world. Table I shows the importance of school attendance in the idealized career pattern.

The great majority of Bolivian line officers are graduates of the military academy, a fact of considerable importance. Most officers given field commissions during the Chaco War have retired, and the few officers commissioned directly for political reasons in 1952-53 never reached positions of prominence. Only specialists from the civilian professions— medical, veterinary, legal—are commissioned from other sources and are classed as "*officiales asimilados*." Between 100 and 150 *novatos* (plebes) are selected from the 800-1000 applicants for the military academy each January. Attrition rates reach 25 per cent in the early months, and in recent years about 100 survive the first year, of whom 75 to 85 go on to graduate. Applicants must be between 18 and 19 and are supposed to be secondary school graduates. The latter requirement may be waived if the candidate can pass the written examination with a high score. Applicants must produce certificates of good moral character from both the national police and those of their locality, a recommendation from a "responsible sponsor," and a health certificate.[41] Appointments to the *Colegio* are eagerly sought by middle-class parents, and some plan the secondary education of their children with the entrance examination in mind. The army sponsors a type of ROTC

---

[41]A good article on the *Colegio*, which includes a description of the admission process, curriculum and organization, appears in *RM* (July-September 1969).

BOLIVIAN ARMY SCHOOL SYSTEM
(Officers)

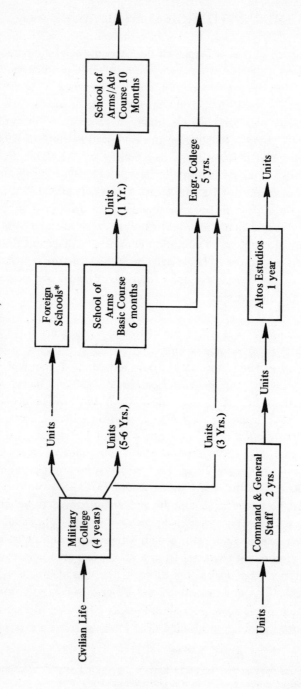

Civilian Life → Military College (4 years)

Units → Foreign Schools*

Units (5-6 Yrs.) → School of Arms Basic Course 6 months

Units (1 Yr.) → School of Arms/Adv Course 10 Months

Units (3 Yrs.) → Engr. College 5 yrs.

Units → Command & General Staff 2 yrs. → Units → Altos Estudios 1 year → Units

*Foreign School — Students receive equivalent credit of Bolivian school upon completion.

training in secondary schools of La Paz that allows the graduates to enter the *Colegio's* second year. Boys in the latter program are distinguished by khaki uniforms and red berets, and are seen in great numbers on the streets of La Paz.

The *Colegio* is located in the La Paz suburb of Irpavi in a spectacular setting, with the bleak and precipitous mountains in the background complementing the flat parade grounds. Low gray stone and stucco buildings and neatly trimmed flower gardens contribute to the controlled military atmosphere. The panelled office of the commandant, filled with athletic and riding trophies, opens on to a second story balcony from which he addresses the corps of cadets on occasion. Classroom buildings, the laboratory, and the library are tidy and well kept, the dining area clean and cool, living areas spartan but adequate. The cadets' academic day runs from eight-thirty to four o'clock, with an hour-and-a-half for lunch.

The first two years are divided about equally between academic subjects (history, geography, chemistry, physics, algebra, and geometry) and military training. The third year heavily emphasizes the military side, and at mid-year the cadets choose a branch of service: infantry, artillery, cavalry, engineer, or signal. The last year is almost completely devoted to branch training. Graduation is in December, and the President invariably presents the traditional saber to the new *subteniente.* Class standing influences the choice of first assignment. Cavalry is the top branch choice, and assignments to one of the units around La Paz are eagerly sought. The cities of Cochabamba and Santa Cruz are second choices. Frontier postings, or the isolated garrisons in the Beni, Pando, or Oriente are the fate of most graduates, and almost none escape them during the first five years. The mining areas are unpopular because of the antipathy toward the army that pervades the region.

The faculty normally includes five or six civilian professors with university credentials who teach most of the academic subjects, and a dozen or more army officers who teach military subjects and staff the organization of the cadet corps. The Argentine and US military missions have provided instructors in the past, and Bolivian officers stationed in the area often teach in their areas of specialty. The commandant enjoys a great degree of autonomy over all aspects of *Colegio* operations, including curriculum content, and new commandants have frequently made drastic changes. A general consensus among informed observers is that the program is equivalent to about two years of university training.[42]

---

[42]The author visited the *Colegio* in July 1970, and also enjoyed a close association with Bolivian cadets at the US Army School of the Americas. Much of the "subjective" content of this section derives from that association. He also benefited from a questionnaire kindly completed by the *Colegio* staff in 1971.

The new officer incurs a service obligation of eight years. If he voluntarily resigns during this period he is obligated to repay the costs of his academy education. He can expect a promotion to lieutenant after four years, and another to captain at the end of eight. After the first promotion, he can marry with the permission of the high command.

Frontier service is dreaded and avoided where possible. It is boring, uncomfortable, and frequently lonely. Facilities seldom permit families to accompany the officer. Minimum periods of frontier service are required in each grade for further promotion, however, and few escape it. It is somewhat sweetened by counting double for retirement.

Life is better in the *altiplano* and around Santa Cruz. Government-provided housing is sometimes available for married officers. A typical three- or four-room adobe house constructed with troop labor for a captain is not nearly as pretentious as the homes of professional men in the surrounding community, but considerably better than those of the working class. Free medical care and a low-cost prescription service are available to the officer and his family—which can extend to parents and blood relatives. Emoluments vary widely by size of family, location of service, availability of government housing, technical qualifications, etc. The basic salary for a junior officer was estimated at about the equivalent of $40 in the early sixties, but that could be tripled by allowances.

Twice during his first ten years the officer will attend the School of Arms (*Escuela de Aplicación de Armas*) in Cochabamba. His first stay will be for the six-month basic course that runs from June to December. Here about one-quarter of his classroom time is devoted to "general subjects"—including international law, sociology, military law, military history, and cultural history—with the remainder devoted to small unit tactics and techniques. In the ten-month advance course he devotes about 20 percent of his hours to general subjects (military geography, military history, leadership and psychology), and the remainder to battalion-level tactics and techniques. The curriculum for both courses includes time for maneuvers and exercises on the ground, but in fact they are seldom held because of resource shortages. Average attendance is 25-27 per course, and the faculty includes four to five civilian and three to five military instructors as a norm. Facilities are adequate but instructional supplies are always scarce. The authorized curriculum is violated routinely, and courses are sometimes abbreviated or cancelled altogether because of national crises or fund limitations. However, attendance at the School of Arms is obligatory for promotion and most officers will suffer great personal hardship to attend.

The Military Engineering School in La Paz was founded by President Paz Estenssoro in the early days of the revolution to provide technicians for his *ejército productora* (productive army). It initially turned out graduates on the level of construction foremen after a one-year course, but has evolved into a full-fledged five-year engineering school whose graduates are entered on the professional register of civilian engineers. Officers may enroll after three years of service if they can pass a tough entrance examination. About 25 to 27 young officers enter every year, but only five to seven graduate as geodetic or construction engineers. The faculty is made up of alumni and engineering professors from the University of San Andres.

Graduation from the Command and General Staff School in Cochabamba is critical to the career of an officer. The coveted diploma and status as a *Diplomado de Estado Mayor*, or general staff officer, are required by the Organic Law of the Armed Forces for command of tactical units or service on the army general staff. *Diplomados* and graduates of the engineering school also are considered for promotion one year earlier than nongraduates with equal time in grade. Officers who receive the top rating (*muy bueno*) from the School of Arms, who have served at least two years as captains and not more than two years as majors, and who have good efficiency and conduct ratings, may apply for enrollment in the two-year course, which starts in February. Twenty to 25 are selected annually, and 12 to 15 finish the entire course, which includes writing a thesis that must be submitted for approval within one year of graduation. Academic subjects again occupy a considerable portion of the classroom hours. In 1967 the curriculum required 41 hours of sociology, 40 hours of international law, 40 hours of "political economics," and a 250-hour block on "revolutionary war" that included studies of political theories and development philosophies. Division-level tactics and general staff techniques form the core of the military instruction, but considerable time is devoted to operations at corps-, field army- and theater-level. Three to four civilians and four to five military instructors comprise the faculty, with occasional assistance from senior officers stationed in the vicinity. The school is chronically underfunded and understaffed, and educational materials are always in short supply, but it remains a "must" for the ambitious officer.

In common with other senior tactical schools in Latin America, the Bolivian Command and General Staff School teaches tactical employment and logistical support of military aggregations (i.e., field armies) that far exceed the requirements of national strategy and the possibilities of even total mobilization. There is a deeply held belief among senior officers that knowledge of military management at this strategic level is a necessary part of the professional baggage of any general staff officer. It is yet another manifestion of the "universalist" view of the profession of arms that prevails throughout Latin America. Reinforcing the practice is the fact that the Bolivian school is not a developer of doctrine; its program is an eclectic amalgam of doctrines taught in the general staff schools that most influence it—those of the US, Argentina, Brazil, and Peru. Graduates of these schools are frequently assigned as instructors or in administrative positions that allow them to influence the curriculum, and there is a continuing debate about which of the big four offers the best professional education. Graduates of foreign general staff schools are granted the coveted *Diplomado*, but only after passing their "qualifications," which include submission of a thesis and usually a year's successful service at the general staff level.

The School of Higher Military Studies (*Escuela de Altos Estudios Militares*) is a nine-month series of morning lectures and seminars conducted for selected army, navy, and air force colonels in La Paz and distinguished civilians with an interest in national security affairs. The course usually consists of 25 to 30 students, evenly divided between officers and civilians, with lawyers and university professors counting heavily among the latter. The class also takes organized tours of the mining and petroleum producing areas of the country, and to strategic frontier points. Military graduates are awarded the title *Diplomado de Altos Estudios Militares*, and the initials DAEM replace the general staff designation DEM as a part of their official title. Graduation from the course is a prerequisite for promotion to general officer under the Organic Law, and in fact few promotions to colonel go to nongraduates.

All of the officer schools except Higher Studies look to the Director of Military Institutes on the Army General Staff for educational guidance and direction, and for assistance in the budgeting wrangles. The Director is a colonel, and his staff seldom exceeds three officers and a clerk, so that school commandants are left largely on their own. He has an influential voice in who attends the command and staff school, prepares and grades promotion examinations, and grades the theses submitted by prospective *Diplomados de Estado Mayor*, so the job is a key one in the career system. The Director also supervises the apportionment of the coveted assignments to study abroad (*becas*); however, the army commander himself routinely intervenes in the distribution of officer *becas*. Bolivia sends officers every year to military schools in Argentina, Brazil, and Peru in addition to the United States and to US schools in the Canal Zone.[43]

---

*See Footnote 43 on page 49.

Except for the Engineering School, all of these institutions operate on completely inadequate budgets with understrength and at times under-qualified faculties. The system, however, provides a continuing, progressive education of fairly broad scope which reinforces the elitist status of a group in a backward country with few competing elites. It is an extremely efficient instrument of institutional socialization which probably smoothes out any class motivations or prejudices before officers reach influential ranks, and which certainly generates an intense loyalty to *la Institucion*. Officers are reunited with *Colegio* classmates at various stages in their carrers, and the hierachy is afforded an opportunity to reinforce or modify the institutional line, and to get feedback from the corps. It provides an equitable means of eliminating substandard officers as the career pyramid narrows, and for identifying the elite for top command (an important function in an army that does not fight wars). In the Bolivian context, it undoubtedly also provided the institutional core and soul that allowed the army to wait out the early years of the revolution and to reflourish when the opportunities allowed. One can speculate as to the success the MNR might have enjoyed had it possessed the fixed doctrine and evangelistic sophistication to make use of the school system for politicizing the army. The possibilities for an ideological group possessed of these attributes are obvious.

Internal Structure

Promotions and new assignments are announced annually at year's end. Promotion from *subteniente* to *teniente*, and from *teniente* to *capitan*, are made almost automatically after four years in each grade, barring disciplinary incidents or completely substandard performance. Thereafter, selection is influenced greatly by completion of schooling, types of assignments, and performance ratings. Command of a unit is a requirement, along with frontier service and seniority (five years in each grade for promotion to major, lieutenant colonel, and colonel). The Organic Law provides for a Senate veto over promotions to colonel or general. Two general ranks (*general de brigada* and *general de división*) are in use. The higher is traditionally reserved for the armed forces commander and the Minister of Defense when he is a military man, but may also be held by the army commander and the president of the Supreme Tribunal of Military Justice. Active major generals have also filled the Inter-American Defense Board position, the army inspector general post,

---

[43] Articles on the schools appear regularly in the *RM*, usually in conjunction with the celebration of graduations or anniversaries. Data are frequently inconsistent between issues and one must review a large number of articles spanning several years to compile a coherent and complete picture. This description results from such an effort.

and commanded the School of Higher Military Studies. The divisions may be commanded by either colonels or one-star generals, and the chiefs of staff of the armed forces and the army are usually one-star generals.

The Bolivian army is not an operational force, and, despite sporadic employment of a few units against guerrilla groups and organized violence in the mining areas, it has never developed an operational "mystique." Emphasis has been, rather, on supporting an army presence throughout the national territory, maintaining frontier garrisons and protecting the central government apparatus, and the army is organized accordingly. There are ten divisions, with headquarters in Viacha, Oruro, Villa Montes, Camiri, Roboré, Riberalta, Cochabamba, Santa Cruz, Trinidad, and Potosí. There is an Engineer Command with five battalions scattered around the interior, and several specialized units of artillery, rangers, etc. Schools, arsenals, maintenance centers and depots complete the organization, all directed from the headquarters at the walled and guarded Miraflores compound in La Paz.[44]

Each of the divisions except the first at Viacha occupies a military region, corresponding to the administrative departments, and is further subdivided into circumscriptions and districts, the latter two mainly for administration of the universal military service law. Division strengths and organization vary by area but manpower seldom exceeds 1,000, even in the population centers of Santa Cruz, Oruro, and Cochabamba. The Seventh Division, in the latter city, is a key unit in a number of respects and its commander is always chosen with great care. He has command jurisdiction over the officer school complex there, the Sargento Paredes Noncommissioned Officer School (*Escuela de Clases*) and the elite Center of Instruction for Special Troops (CITE) with its parachute battalion. The CITE provides the only mobile, operationally ready and uncommitted force available to the high command. The motorized regiment at Viacha, just outside La Paz, is usually held in reserve in times of crisis in the eventuality of trouble in the always volatile mines, and the guards units in La Paz are seldom employed elsewhere for obvious reasons. The NCO School, which graduates 60-70 corporals annually after a three-year course, provides a provisional battalion of hardy and disciplined troops for crisis situations, and they have occasionally been employed to check the peasant militia in and around Cochabamba.

---

[44]Promotion criteria, territorial organization, and legal norms governing the army are spelled out in minute detail in the *Ley Orgánica del Ejército*. The basic law dates from 1927, with major revisions in 1953, 1966, and 1969. Major reorganizations are treated frequently in the *Revista Militar*. For example, the issue of July-September 1969 includes a detailed and quite complete description of the divisional organization and functions, headquarters locations, etc.

IV
THE MILITARY IN POWER

The Barrientos Years

When the military took power in 1964 an elite nucleus of officers trained in the career school system was approaching positions of institutional power. Having graduated from the *Colegio Militar* between 1941 and 1944, they were too young to participate in any important way in the Villarroel regime, and were still junior officers when the revolution of 1952 brought the MNR to power. With few exceptions they escaped the army purge that followed, and devoted themselves to institutional concerns and educational development in the lean years of MNR rule. To a remarkable degree they provided the governmental and armed forces leadership at operational levels after 1964. Nineteen of the most successful comprised the unusually large promotion lists to brigadier general of 1967 and 1968:[45]

The educational background of this group is impressive. Three were at the top of their *Colegio Militar* class. All completed the career schools of the army, and all but three are graduates of the Higher Military Studies course. (Two of the nongraduates are engineers; the other is a rehabilitated officer who was cashiered for political reasons in 1952.) Thirteen studied abroad at mid-career and higher level military schools: seven in the US, the others in France, Germany, Argentina, Peru, and Brazil.

Between 1964 and 1971 twelve of these officers occupied cabinet posts in the government, six on two or more occasions (not including the ministry of defense, a traditional military post; interestingly, only one occupied that post during the period). The group also provided four ambassadors. They dominated the army institutional structure below the high command level, serving as commanders or operations chiefs of the ten divisions and the Engineer Command, as commandants or directors of studies in the military academy and career schools, and as principal officers of the army general

---

[45]Promotion lists are published in the La Paz newspapers and in *Los Tiempos* of Cochabamba. Fairly complete biographical data, particularly on career patterns, appeared in the *RM* of January-March 1968 for the officers on the list of that year. Other information in this section comes from interviews with the principals or acquaintances. The officers involved are Generals Hugo Ortiz Mattos, Remberto Iriarte Paz, Alberto Guzmán Soriano, Eduardo Méndez Pereyra, Efrain Guachalla Ibañez, Cesar Ruiz Veladre, Juan Lechín Suárez, Marcos Vasquez Sempértegui, Jesús Via Solis, David La Fuente Soto, Sigfredo Montero Velasco, Luis A. Reque Teran, Gonzalo Guzmán Agudo, Hector Fuentes Ibañez, Eufronio Padilla Caero, Jaime Flores Becerra, Jaime Paz Galarza, Rogelio Miranda, and J. Zenteno Anaya.

51

staff. The traditional practice of reassigning top officers annually gave them opportunities for a variety of jobs.[46]

Events connected with the repression of the Che Guevara guerrilla band in 1967 proved beneficial to most of this group. Two directed the counter-guerrilla operation as division commanders, and two others gained wide notice as judge and prosecutor in the trial of French revolutionary theoretician Regis Debray, who was captured in the operation zone. Others won acclaim in planning and logistics jobs connected with the training of new units and the administration of outside military assistance which increased considerably during the emergency. Following that crisis, members of this group moved for the first time into the High Command. General Marcos Vasquez Sempértegui, top graduate in his *Colegio* class of 1942, became army Chief of Staff in 1968, and General Ruiz Velarde was named Chief of Staff of the Armed Forces under Ovando.

The increasingly divergent views between Ovando and the professional elite had much to do with shaping the events of the next few years. The differences fell into two main areas; the politics of development, and the role of the military in a developing society. There is no evidence that Ovando had expressed himself in a substantive fashion on the former before 1968, and there is every indication that the elite group, and most foreign observers, believed him to favor a relatively apolitical, traditionally-organized force in the second area.

There are few clues to the development of Ovando's political philosophy. One acquaintance holds that his unpopularity following the 1964 coup, in contrast with the acclaim afforded Barrientos, convinced him that an espousal of popular causes was necessary to political success. The same source believes that circumstances surrounding the Guevara incursion awakened Ovando to an "anti-imperialist," nationalist sentiment with deep roots in Bolivia that could be exploited politically.

The first public airing of his political beliefs appeared in early 1968 in the long and completely uncharacteristic "open letter" previously cited, which he sent to senior officers in all three services before it was published.

In the letter, he lists these "principles" that guided his political thought:
... in order that the country be ours, the basic industries must belong to the state (*deben ser estatales*). The highest priority must go to metalurgy, without which we can never break the barriers of

---

[46]One exception was Juan Lechín Suarez, who served for four years as chief of the Bolivian Mining Commission (COMIBOL) during its most productive period, from 1964 to 1968. He graduated second in his 1942 *Colegio* class, and is a graduate of the US Army Artillery School and the Command and General Staff College at Fort Leavenworth, Kansas.

backwardness and integrate ourselves economically into the reality of a continent undergoing change. There cannot be a strong army without the complement of a strong heavy industry. Natural resources, and the terms of their exploitation, also constitute an inseparable part of national sovereignty. The country must move toward the control of their full exploitation through its own resources and entities.

He sketched a role for private enterprise in the derivative industries, a vast plan for state assistance to agricultural development, and a rationalization of university education to support the grand scheme, and came down hard on foreign oil companies:

There are other aspects that I would like to emphasize strictly and concretely. With reference to petroleum, the Davenport Code must be annulled as soon as possible, and tax established that reaches 50 percent of gross production; special regulations for gas must be established; and control for the state obtained over its refining, transport, marketing and industrialization through *YPEB*.[47]

He stressed the importance of in-country smelters, and hinted that the Barrientos government had failed to follow the intent of the military junta in its dealings with mining concessions. Ovando was extremely sensitive to nationalist criticism that the Barrientos government was dealing with the "economic imperialists" and that his position made him at least a tacit supporter of these policies.

On the military's role, Ovando said the military institution is not and must never be an armed political party, but:

in the full use of its constitutional rights and under the most expansive interpretation of the principles that govern its existence, it must insure that the decisions of the people are respected and complied with and preserve the national patrimony and the resources that it contains. The best committee for the defense of the natural resources and the most legitimate is that constituted by the people and their armed expression, the national army.

When these opinions were made public in mid-1968 the political situation was more muddled than usual. The Cuban-supported guerrilla band had been eliminated, but the incident left great domestic turmoil in its aftermath. Conflicting stories on the circumstances of Che Guevara's death damaged the credibility of army spokesmen, and an attempt by the high command to sell exclusive publication rights to his diary precipitated

---

[47]The acronym refers to the state oil monopoly. There is a similarity here to the programs and speeches of Peru's President Velasco, but Ovando's article preceded the Peruvian coup of October 3, 1968 by some months. He was, however, familiar with developmental philosophies being taught in the Peruvian Army's Center for Higher Military Studies. For an analysis of the latter, see Luigi Einaudi's essay in Einaudi and Alfred Stepan, *Latin American Institutional Development*.

suspicions of private gain in high places. Debray's trial brought in an influx of foreign reporters and some diplomatic pressure from France, where his family was prominent. There were sensational charges of CIA infiltration at the highest levels in the government, and a major scandal developed around the delivery of a copy of Guevara's diary to Fidel Castro by the Interior Minister.[48] Rumors of new guerrilla bands, forming or in action, were rampant, and government announcements gave credence to some of them.

The government suffered chronic budget deficits, and violence and strikes in the mines reversed the annual growth rate of about seven percent that sector had enjoyed between 1961 and 1966. Oil had become an important source of foreign exchange for the first time in 1966 with the development of the Santa Cruz fields and completion of a pipeline to the Chilean coast in 1967, but nationalist opposition to rumored processing plants on the coast made the issue a source of great dissension. The cost of the anti-guerrilla war, and US refusal of a $12 million "stability loan," precipitated a sharp financial crisis in early 1968.

Barrientos responded by appointing an all-military cabinet in July 1968, provoking an open quarrel with Ovando, who maintained that the armed forces could not spare top officers from their duties to serve in the cabinet.

The feud between the two leaders and the scandals rocking the government were highly disturbing to the army general staff, and when Ovando began openly to campaign for the presidency among the peasant leagues in the east, General Vasquez joined with spokesmen of the MNR and the Socialist Falange (FSB) in urging him to resign his post.[49] Ovando responded by firing Vasquez as the Chief of the Army General Staff on August 10. General Juan José Torres, chief of the armed forces general staff, was dismissed at the same time for reasons that are not clear, although it may have been at Barrientos' insistence in retribution for Torres' vehement public opposition to any processing of Bolivian petroleum on Chilean territory. On August 20 Vasquez failed in a coup attempt that had the support of important elements of the MNR and the FSB. Vasquez had been the top graduate in his 1942 *Colegio* class, and was probably the most respected

---

[48]The Interior Minister, Antonio Arguedas, fled Bolivia after admitting that he had sent the diary to Castro, and later charged that he had been forced to act as a CIA agent for over four years. He returned voluntarily to face a military trial. See the analysis by Malcom Browne in the *New York Times* of September 17, 1968 and November 8, 1968. The trial records by some fluke fell into the public domain, and the La Paz newspaper *Presencia* published a series on the whole affair during the first week of April 1969 that revealed publicly for the first time how severely the scandals had shaken the government.

[49]See *Presencia*, May 24, 1968, and the Ronant Monje Roca letter in *Los Tiempos* of July 2, 1968.

member of the elite nucleus. He explained his actions in a message addressed to the armed forces from exile and printed in *Los Tiempos* of Cochabamba on May 8, 1969:

> There is nothing more pernicious and corrosive for an institution like ours than to allow it to be dragged into political turbulence and to be asked to employ weapons in defense of certain persons. I unsheathed my sword so that the armed forces of the nation could return to their barracks with honor and dignity . . . I shall devote my every effort and also my life, if necessary, to prevent their use against the people once again, or to prevent their being used as a pawn by anyone whose ambition is to climb to power and whose only qualification is the fact that he wears a uniform and whose only right is military might.

This justification for the August 1968 coup attempt was written one month after Barrientos' April 1969 death in a helicopter crash. Vasquez had been stripped of his rank and separated from the army, and his bitterness no doubt influenced the attack on Ovando. His coup attempt had been aimed at displacing both Barrientos and Ovando, however. Before the former's death he had publicly attacked the president's "voracious ambition" as scandalous and detrimental to Bolivia's development. Privately he had frequently maintained that Barrientos' ambitions and desire for great wealth had overridden his concerns for the country. The coup attempt had the support of some old-line MNR politicians and inactive officers, including the same Admiral Monje Roca whom Ovando had fired as chief of the River and Lake Force in 1964. It apparently was hastily conceived, and appeared to have been confined largely to the capital area.

The 1969 Coup

Ovando was out of the country when Barrientos was killed in April 1969. General Ruiz Velarde, acting armed forces chief, acquiesced in the accession of Vice President Siles. Siles' cabinet included only two military men: General Eduardo Gallardo Ballesteros was kept on as defense minister, and Colonel Eufronio Padilla Caero was appointed Minister of Interior. General Torres was appointed by Ovando to the largely honorary post of president of the Supreme Tribunal of Military Justice.

Ovando, looking to the 1970 elections, moved to gain the support of the peasant leagues which had backed Barrientos, and to a large degree inherited it by default. His main opposition came from retired General Armando Escobar Uria, the popular mayor of La Paz and a famous Chaco War hero, but Ovando was able to restrict the latter's campaign activities outside La Paz through control of the military prefects and mayors appointed by Colonel Padilla.

Siles' attempts to replace these officers with civilians, Escobar's growing popularity in La Paz, and the return from exile of many old-line party leaders probably contributed greatly to Ovando's decision to depose the president rather than take a chance in the June elections. The activities of General Vasquez, whom Siles had allowed to return, were particularly worrisome; he continued to enjoy great favor within the army elite and spoke out strongly in support of Siles and for a nonpolitical stance on the part of the army. The fear of losing control of the army in the eight months remaining before the election was probably the determining factor. Ovando had Siles arrested and flown to Chile while the latter was touring in Santa Cruz on September 26. There was no bloodshed.

Ovando announced that he had taken power to avoid the dangers of "anarchy, capitulation, and disorder." He pledged to secure national sovereignty over the means of production, inprove the mining sector, promote heavy industry, enhance the rights of workers, and establish a nationalist economic policy.[50]

Within the next few weeks the government announced that it would establish relations with communist nations, including Cuba. Relations were formalized with Rumania in October, and the first Bolivian ambassador to Moscow was dispatched in December.

Corporate Concerns

Ovando appointed a mixed civilian-military cabinet and proceeded to implement the program he had outlined in 1968, nullifying the petroleum code and a few months later nationalizing the Gulf Oil operations. These moves, and the inflammatory "revolutionary" rhetoric of some of his cabinet ministers, met resistance among the professional elite of the army. General Torres had been brought back into the high command as armed forces commander replacing Ovando, but all the other positions had gone to members of the elite.

Early opposition to the nationalization plans apparently caused the ambassadorial "exile" to Great Britain of General Juan Lechín Suarez. Later diplomatic exiles included Generals Remberto Iriarte Paz and Joaquin Zenteno Anaya, ambassadors to Argentina and Peru respectively.

Institutional concerns, however, prompted the first countermoves. In a remarkable interview with a reporter friend from the leftist magazine *Marcha* of Montevideo in December of 1969, Ovando indicated that the future role of the army would be almost entirely that of an instrument of production and

---

[50]*New York Times*, September 27, 1969.

development, with dependence on a "guerrilla strategy" for the external defense mission. He answered affirmatively when the reporter asked whether Bolivia should pull out of the Inter-American Defense Board, cancel its arms agreements with the United States, and cease training its people abroad.[51]

This interview raised a great alarm among the "professionalist" officers, coming as it did hard on the heels of an attack by General Torres on the "professional" mystique of the elite before the visiting Inter-American Defense Board in November 1969. Torres told the visitors that the armed forces of Bolivia had begun to consider the problems of defense in terms of economic and social development tasks that could no longer be postponed.

> The armed forces do not have to be . . . typecast as organizations exclusively dedicated to checking the political phenomenon of international communism, but fundamentally as co-participants and efficient agents of the battle against . . . economic underdevelopment from which follow the elements that later go to make up the political setting that has set off the subversive struggle in the continent . . . The arch conservatives see in the armed forces an exceedingly efficient instrument to return to the night of the past while they remain allied with the foreign monopolies. For their part, the popular classes look at the armed forces as the truest instrument of redemption since they (the armed forces) will no longer accept the role of simple wardens in an unjust order.[52]

Torres went on in the same discourse to attack the conventional view of the historical process in Bolivia. He said the debate over military or civilian control of the government was artificial and irrelevant, because the real problem

> consisted in deciding whether the aristocracy or the bourgoisie was going to control the armed forces. What is truly important is to know what interests the armed forces are protecting, or alternatively, what interests are affected by the actions of the armed forces.[53]

He scandalized the army hierarchy by openly criticizing the Inter-American Defense Board, implying that it was anachronistic because of its exaggerated stress on the communist threat to the hemisphere, and telling the members that the Board had lost respect in many quarters.

Another threat to *la Institucion* surfaced with the word that there was to be a reduction in army strength. Around a million dollars normally devoted

---

[51]*Marcha*, December 19, 1969. The interview also appears in *Christianismo y Revolucion*, April 23, 1970.

[52]The speech was partially reproduced in *Estrategia* (Buenos Aires, No. 4, November-December 1969), pp. 22-24.

[53]Einaudi, *Latin American Institutional Development*, quotes a strikingly similar formulation made by a sociologist advisor to the military regime in Peru in 1971 (p. 62).

to the annual conscription program was to be applied instead to a national literacy campaign, and the army was to bear the brunt of the campaign as well as suffer the costs.[54]

Another point of difference developed out of the visit of the Rockefeller presidential mission in early 1969. The general staff reacted favorably to what it interpreted as sympathy for continued military assistance, but Ovando told Rockefeller that water drilling rigs, tractors and agricultural machinery, and roadbuilding equipment were more appropriate items of US aid to Latin America than arms.[55] In a published government response to President Nixon's major policy speech on Latin America on October 31, 1969, the government criticized the military recommendations of the Rockefeller Report, accusing Rockefeller of "waving the bloody threat of imminent communist takeover," and declaring that the government "can take care of itself and if the US wishes to give effective aid, plows would be better than bayonets."[56]

Influential members of the professional elite saw these policies as a challenge to their perception of the security threat and of the armed forces' mission, and they intensified their opposition. They did not feel strong enough to challenge Ovando directly at the time, but they induced him in July 1970 to abolish Torres' position and replace it with a Superior Council of the Armed Forces, the chairmanship of which was to be rotated among the army, navy, and air forces commanders.

The position of Commander in Chief of the Armed Forces had always been an organizational anomaly, representing in effect a second army high command, given the overwhelming preponderance of that service. The political effect of the second headquarters was to divide or dilute army influence. Establishment of the Superior Council represented an attempt to consolidate army influence and simultaneously to remove Torres from the leadership of a radical faction of younger officers. It was a setback for Ovando, but in his search for popular bases of support he continued to resist army demands for stronger action against the warring student factions which had made a battleground of the downtown San Andres University, and for a concerted attack against a band of guerrillas, which included students, and which had attacked a US-financed mining operation at Teoponte in the

---

[54]*El Diario*, La Paz, December 16, 1969.

[55]Richard W. Patch, *American Universities Field Staff Reports*, West Coast South America Series, XVII, No. 1, December, 1969.

[56]*Ibid.*

northwest. The antagonism between Ovando and General Rogelio Miranda, army commander and president of the Superior Council, was an open secret in the last half of 1970.

Ovando's selection of Miranda as army commander had temporarily neutralized more popular officers with large personal followings like General Zenteno and Lechín, and had divided his opposition among the elite. Miranda's inability to rally a majority of key officers behind his coup plans did not save Ovando in the end, but it did open the path for Torres to pre-empt the movement.

The 1970 Coup

A move against Ovando was almost certainly planned for July, but the death of his son in an airplane crash that month led to a nationwide expression of sympathy for the family. Torres meanwhile, with no legal base, found his situation precarious as sides were formed, and had to seek refuge in Ovando's house when Minister of Interior Colonel Juan Ayoroa aligned with the Miranda faction and dispatched the political police to arrest him.

Miranda made his move in early October, calling upon Ovando to resign and turn his powers over to a triumvirate of the three service chiefs. Apparently there was considerable private negotiation with Ovando before the situation became public knowledge, and it is not certain that General Sattori of the air force and Admiral Alberracin of the navy were fully committed to Miranda's plans. The latter barricaded himself in the Miraflores compound with the loyal Ingavi regiment and operated from there during most of the critical week after October 1. Some officers in the La Paz garrisons rallied to Ovando's defense, and others sought a compromise by urging both Ovando and Miranda to resign in favor of an officer the army could agree upon. Ovando did resign on October 5, but all indications are that he threw his support to the forces Torres was now mobilizing, and neutralized the junta by persuading General Satorri to announce publicly his withdrawal. Miranda, having access to the military communications center at Miraflores, decided that he lacked sufficient personal support and resigned the following day, relinquishing the headquarters to General Guachalla, the armed forces chief of staff. The junta had tried to form an all-military cabinet by naming, without their knowledge in some cases, several popular officers from the elite and, in an obvious bid for support, most of the key unit commanders. In its only published bulletin, the junta promised elections within two years and a return of the armed forces to the barracks. It also reappointed, as mayor of

La Paz, the popular General Escobar, who had been sacked by Ovando as one of his first acts after taking power.[57]

Access to the bowl where La Paz nestles is by a narrow and precipitous road that crosses the *altiplano* rim at El Alto, site of the international airport and an air force garrison. If reinforcements—whether regular forces or irregular bands—can be blocked there, the fate of the government palace lies in the hands of the units stationed in the city. This strategic location, rather than the 1940-vintage Mustang or two it can employ, probably constitutes the major chip the air force can play in power struggles centered on La Paz. Torres mustered his forces there, and called upon the entrenched Ingavi regiment to surrender and avoid a fratricidal bloodbath. Miranda's departure undermined the resolve of many of the junior officers, despite announced support from the *Colegio Militar*, and when the presidential guard unit (*Colorados*) adopted a neutral stand the garrison found itself isolated.

General Torres was in possession of the *Palacio Quemado* by October 9, and with a few exceptions the key unit commanders pledged support to the new Torres-appointed army commander.

The confusion and indecision that reigned when Miranda finally made his move in October can probably best be understood in the light of the great authority that Ovando continued to enjoy throughout the military institution. He had become army chief of staff in 1957, army commander in 1960, armed forces chief in 1963, and had actively encouraged an almost mythical image of himself as the rebuilder of an institution destroyed and degraded by the 1952 revolution. He had in fact been, for almost a decade, the dispenser of promotions and choice assignments. Practically all of the colonels and many of the generals were in his debt, and to the more junior officers he was a revered, if distant, father figure. Many were genuinely disturbed by the move against him, and the issues, outside of a small circle, were not clear.

Torres had to have army support or neutrality to remain in power, and benefited largely from the latter. A few officers shared his radical convictions, and they were placed quickly in key, if second echelon, positions in La Paz units and in the government. There were many officers who were personally loyal to Ovando and who accepted Torres as his heir when Ovando failed to make a fight of it. And there was the majority of career-minded officers who did not want to risk their futures in the confused high command in-fighting. A mixture of the two latter motives probably prompted General Reque Teran, Comptroller in Ovando's cabinet and one of the army's most respected

---

[57]Copy in the hands of the author. The *New York Times* carried a running account of the coup in the editions of October 5-9, 1970.

officers, to accept the army commander's post. General David La Fuente was carried over temporarily as Minister of Defense in the new cabinet, helping to maintain the impression of uninterrupted transfer of authority at the top.

Torres pledged "a popular, nationalist government resting on four pillars—the peasant farmers, the workers, the students, and the armed forces." The level of "revolutionary" rhetoric increased perceptibly and contacts with the Soviet Union and East European countries multiplied. Anti-US sentiment showed a marked upswing, culminating in expulsion of the Peace Corps from Bolivia. Torres acquiesced in the convocation of a "popular assembly" in La Paz that sparked an intensified reaction from middle class groups and the military. The latter were also disturbed by indications that officers close to Torres were attempting to establish cells of support among enlisted men and noncommissioned officers after manifestoes allegedly emanating from a *Vanguardia de Suboficiales* appeared. Torres incorporated the army sergeant major into the general staff amid great fanfare, and Torres' wife and the wives of his closest supporters became active in charitable activities associated with the families of NCO's.[58]

Despite a shift of units and commanders, Torres was not able to gain control of the army. He appointed as army chief of staff a young officer who had not graduated from the Higher Military Studies course, and in the installation ceremony General Reque Teran identified him as "one of those . . . young officers of the new generation" and spoke of the "inquietudes" of the young officers.[59] But the officers who backed Torres' radical programs were apparently too few in number and too low in rank to allow him to control those positions of great weight in the "political order of battle" that had formed since 1964. He threatened occasionally to rearm the irregular peasant and miner militias, but knew from his own long years of service that even sympathetic officers would not stand for it. He resurrected a noncontroversial pre-1952 general to head the defense ministry, and tried to concentrate control of the Superior Council in the latter's hands—all to no avail. He weathered several coup attempts, the most serious coming in January 1971 when Colonel Hugo Banzer Suarez, Military Academy commander, apparently planned to kidnap him at the graduation ceremonies. Torres had been tipped off and failed to appear. Banzer is a military intellectual and one of the most respected young colonels in the army. He is a graduate of the US Army Armor School and was for a time military attache in Washington. He had been kept on after the 1970 coup despite complicity

---

[58]*RM* (October-December 1970), p. 125.
[59]*Ibid.*, p. 16.

with the Miranda group. probably at the insistence of the three service commanders. Following the January plot, however, he and several other officers were discharged from the army and exiled.[60]

The 1971 Coup[61]

Banzer's second move against Torres was a well-planned campaign that reflected a thorough knowledge of military sentiment within the institution and an appreciation for broader political considerations. He fashioned an unlikely political alliance with fellow exiles in Argentina representing the old MNR and their blood enemies of yore, the Bolivian Socialist Flange (FSB). He chose as the focal point of his movement the eastern lowlands province of Santa Cruz, where the economy had been drastically crippled by Gulf Oil's nationalization and by state takeover of private sugar mills. This region has long been an FSB stronghold, and the commanders of the two divisions in the province apparently were in on the plans from the beginning. The tough ranger regiment of Colonel Andres Selich provided the muscle to overcome the limited opposition. (Selich was named Minister of Interior in the new government.) Within two days after the rangers took control of the seat of the provincial government in Santa Cruz on August 19, every important garrison in the country had announced for the rebels and most had made overt moves to take control of key facilities in their respective areas. The key Cochabamba garrison was controlled by the commander of the Seventh Division, General Florentino Mendieta, who became Defense Minister in the new government. In La Paz the military academy, the Castrillo regiment, which Torres had brought in to replace the banished Ingavi, and the motorized battalion at nearby Viacha, declared for the rebels. Only the presidential guard unit, the Colorados, remained loyal to Torres, and when the air force joined the bandwagon his last hope was gone and he sought diplomatic asylum.

Banzer consolidated his position with dispatch. He made no glowing promises and warned of considerable austerity. With the exception of the two military men mentioned above, his first cabinet was made up of MNR and FSB civilians. The professional elite was called home from diplomatic and punitive exile, or resurrected from relative obscurity. General Miranda became head of the mining commission (COMIBOL). General Iriarte Paz, former ambassador to Argentina, was first named armed forces commander,

---

[60]*New York Times*, January 11, 1971.

[61]This account comes largely from US newspaper articles read carefully between the lines, and some educated conjecture. The *New York Times* carried a running account of the coup in the editions of August 20-25, 1971.

but, in a dispute that bodes ill for future military unity, was replaced in October by General Zenteno Anaya, who was recalled from an ambassadorship in Peru. General Vasquez was reinstated with rank and seniority. The new service commanders and their staffs are from Colonel Banzer's age group, with academic and professional credentials similar to those described for older members of the professional elite.

At the end of his first term in 1922 he was able to select his successor, Marcelo T. Alvear, a wealthy and cultured *porteño*. However, he became increasingly embittered at Alvear's subsequent indifference toward his advice. Alvear's term from 1922 to 1928 was one of great prosperity in Argentina, and the government is chiefly distinguished for its failure to influence this era in any way. Alvear was not distasteful to the old Conservatives, counting as friends many among the "liberal" wing of that party, and probably represented a president acceptable to the middle classes.

Alvear reinstituted the practice of appointing senior officers as ministers of war, and his selection of General Agustín Justo represented a victory for a small "professionalist" army clique that sought a crackdown on officer-politicians and a return to institutional autonomy for the army. This "lodge" was formed within the Círculo Militar, a social club for officers organized in Buenos Aires in 1889, which has played an important role in military-political decisions ever since.

The Ministry of War and Navy had been divided into separate ministries in 1912, and the navy was to come into its own in the next two decades. Tonnage and capabilities grew to exceed the combined capabilities of the Chilean and Peruvian navies, and British training aided in the formation of a competent and impressive force.

In the political arena, an intra-party reaction to the mysticism and egoism of Irigoyen set in during these years. Alvear came to head the "anti-personalist" faction of the UCR, which by now counted some influential members. However, the old magic of Don Hipólito prevailed, and he was reelected in 1928 with almost 900,000 popular votes and two-thirds of the electoral votes.

The old man, now some 78 years old, assumed his office in October of 1928 and went into such deep seclusion that a contemporary writer said "for quite a while his very existence was placed in doubt, as there were very few people who had actually seen him in the flesh and no photographs of him were to be found." Continuing his insistence on supervising even minute details of the government, he succeeded in bringing administration almost to a standstill. His aides enriched themselves by selling admittance to his office, and the system led to widespread corruption throughout the government. Irigoyen resolutely set out to remove non-Radicals from provincial governments, and interventions resumed.

Economic Strains and
Military Reaction

The depression struck Argentina in 1929. In that year exports declined by 229 million pesos although imports continued to increase. The trade balance equaled only one-half of the country's requirements for remittances abroad to cover profit on foreign capital and services on the foreign debt. In 1930 the passage of the Smoot-Hawley tariff in the United States, together with a severe crop failure in Argentina, caused exports to drop by 772 million pesos in relation to the previous year, resulting in an unfavorable trade balance of 284 million pesos. In an economy tied to the world market these imbalances spelled domestic disaster, and no sector of the economy escaped the effects. Old charges were revived that Irigoyen was undermining the economy by drawing on the national bank and private banks without the passage of appropriations by the Congress. The public payroll was even more grossly inflated. Irigoyen said nothing and did little in his almost total isolation. The *Buenos Aires Herald* of September 2, 1930 editorialized:

> The government has . . . filled the civil service with thousands of incompetents. . . . The president has attempted to operate every office, and aspired to the fatherhood of his people by appointing all properly humble supplicants to government offices.

Irigoyen resumed his tinkering with the military establishment, which had regained a large measure of autonomy. Favorites were promoted without regard to seniority or given choice assignments, and the chain of command was routinely violated. The general log jam in public administration had a drastic effect on military construction and material purchase plans, bringing them almost to a complete halt. Despite all this, Irigoyen himself and the party in general retained great support in the military. He allowed a slight rise in strength and approved the first pay raises since his initial term, and leaders frequently made laudatory remarks about the armed forces. The opposition's tentative soundings about possible army collaboration in plans to prevent his election in 1928 found no important takers.

Because of his reforms as Alvear's Minister of War, General Justo had become a popular figure with the military, rivaling that of another charismatic leader, General José F. Uriburu, a Prussianized officer who had come to personify the ideal type of the "new army." Discontented officers began to look to Justo or to Uriburu for leadership, precipitating a split in the militant anti-Irigoyen minority into *Justista* and *Uriburista* factions. The Justo faction joined forces with the conservative oligarchy, and the Uriburu faction became an ultra-nationalist pro-fascist group supported by many provincial intellectuals, while most of the middle-class officer corps remained pro-Radical.

Both groups began to plot Irigoyen's ouster separately, while the intensifying effects of the depression spread a feeling of helplessness and frustration among the majority of the officer corps who never participated in the coup planning, further eroding the government's support. Both Uriburu and Justo sought adherents among the officers stationed in the capital, and both enjoyed support from important civilian elements. The general alignments anticipated divisions that reappeared frequently in later years. Justo initially planned a short period of junta rule or a face-saving legal succession by a government functionary, to be followed in short order by elections. Cooperation of the non-Irigoyenista parties was to be sought from the start; the target was Irigoyen. Uriburu favored action solely by the military, whose absence of political debts would allow an elitist government to modify basic institutions, probably in the corporatist mold of Italy and Spain, for which he had expressed admiration. He had support from important conservative-nationalist sectors of the old regime.[12]

Following the resignation of his Minister of War, Irigoyen apparently recognized the fact that he had no support, and on Setpember 5, 1930, he resigned in favor of Vice President Enrique Martínez. The stratagem failed and Uriburu's faction seized control with little resistance.

---

[12]The best account of the pre-coup alignments and maneuvers is in José María Sarobe, *Memórias sobre la revolución del 6 de septiembre de 1930: Al servicio de la democracia* (Buenos Aires, 1957).

V
MILITARY INSTITUTIONAL DISAGREEMENTS
AND RESTORATION OF OLIGARCHICAL RULE

Uriburu's government was characterized by the presence of many experienced politicians and professional men from the old conservative groups. There was little direct involvement in day-to-day matters by officers except for his close aides. Irigoyen's followers were systematically removed from all national and provincial offices, and older officers closely connected with the Radicals were discharged or exiled. The government with some success wrestled with the continuing economic problems of the depression, but found little support for its programs of institutional change. Justo refused to participate in the administration, and his insistence on a return to elections was probably a decisive factor in coalescing opposition to Uriburu's plans for drastic constitutional changes. The two factions compromised on elections under rules that would effectively neutralize the *Irigoyenista* Radicals and prevent their return to office. A coalition of the Conservative, Anti-Personalist Radical, and Independent Socialist parties, later to be labeled the *Concordancia*, elected Justo to the presidency in November 1931 in an openly fraudulent election. The Radicals boycotted the elections after their most popular candidates were barred and most top party leaders exiled.

The coup of 1930 is universally recognized as a turning point for civil-military relations in Argentina, and justifiably so. Between the period of national consolidation in the 1860's and 1930, military contributions to national development had been almost wholly in purely military areas. A successful foreign war was fought, the Indians were annihilated and the area of national control vastly extended, exploration and mapping expeditions reached the farthest corners of Patagonia and the Chaco, and the last of the regional *caudillos* were brought to heel. Strong civilian governments and strong ministers of war rationalized military administration and organization and brought a high degree of professionalism to the officer corps. The military institution prospered under oligarchical control and popularly elected governments. It helped to socialize the immigrant and offered a path of upward mobility to practically all levels of the society. But in 1930 it tasted the forbidden fruit of total power, and established new patterns of civil-military relationships that have haunted the institution and the nation since.

Justo's efforts to deal with the effects in Argentina of the international economic crisis of the period were sympathetically viewed by the military, and his prestige enabled him generally to sideline the military as a political force. Opposition to a trade alliance with Great Britain was widespread in the armed forces, as it was among the public in general, but potential disaffection on this issue was counterbalanced by Justo's support for professionalization of the armed forces. The military gave him negative support through the absence of opposition, although many among the officers were repelled by the manipulation of elections and by the restoration of upper-class political domination.

Industrial Growth

Light industry enjoyed a slow but steady growth in the thirties, supplying the domestic market with many consumer goods that could no longer be imported due to depression-caused shortages of foreign exchange. Some 463,000 persons were employed in industry in 1935, almost half of whom were in food processing and textiles. This figure had grown to 680,000 in 1939, and had passed the 800,000 mark at the end of the decade. Local industry was providing some 77 percent of domestic consumption in 1940. It is interesting to note that the percentage of the work force employed in the food processing and textile industries remained almost constant. A great majority of the industries were very small. Less than one-tenth of one percent of the industries operating in 1941 employed more than 1,000 workers; two percent employed 100 or more, and 23 percent had only one artisan.[13]

Direct military involvement in industry dates from the Radical era. General Mosconi was instrumental in the development of the state oil monopoly in the 1920's, while General Manuel N. Savio became the father of Argentine heavy industry. Savio was largely responsible for laws establishing an infant iron and steel industry at San Nicolás and a complex of military industries formalized by law in 1941 as the Dirección General de Fabricaciones Militares.

Labor

Union growth during the thirties was sluggish, and the established unions tended to moderation and cooperation with the Conservative government. The temper of the latter may be derived from the action of President Justo in breaking a bricklayers' strike by deporting the Italian immigrant leaders. Apparently there was a great deal of bureaucratization in the union hierarchy, and the fervor of the earlier days was lost. This is reflected in a drop of 70 percent in meeting attendance between 1935 and 1940. However, there is

[13]United Nations, *Statistical Abstract of Argentina*, 1948, p. 9.

also a possibility that police restrictions on union gatherings had some effect. Membership grew from around 370,000 in 1936 to 472,828 in 1940. The CGT accounted for over half of this membership throughout the period. Unions fomented 109 strikes costing one and one-third million work days in 1936 and 82 strikes costing one and one half million work days in 1937. There was a sharp decrease in strike action in 1939, with only 49 strikes; and again in 1940 only 53 were called, with a loss of 224,151 work days.[14]

In spite of all their administrative apparatus and some superficially impressive collective bargaining agreements, the unions had achieved little for the Argentine worker in the decade 1930-40. Official figures from the Department of Labor, which was a minor agency of the Ministry of Interior, indicated that there actually was a decline in the workers' living standard of some 20 percent between 1929 and 1937. The minimum monthly wage necessary to maintain the basic living standard in 1935, again officially computed, was 164 pesos, while the average monthly wage in Buenos Aires was 127 pesos. By 1940 the minimum monthly standard was 168 while the average wage remained at about 130.[15] Agricultural workers and those in industry in the provinces were even worse off.

The first tenancy reform law was passed in 1921 under Socialist party sponsorship, but intransigence on the part of landholders vitiated it. A new law passed in 1932 had more teeth, but the depression in world grain prices in the thirties made enforcement difficult. However, together with the price support legislation of 1942, it represented a start in agrarian reform. Nothing was done for the some 800,000 peons who helped run the large manager-operated farms. Conditions for these laborers varied widely. In the sugar cane districts of the northwest they lived in hovels made of cane stalks. In Patagonia on the sheep *estancias* the men lived without their families in military-like barracks. In the cattle and grain belt living conditions were generally fair. Progression up the economic ladder for these people and most of the smaller tenants meant migration to urban areas, since the social value of land kept it off the market, not to mention the problem of credit.

---

[14]Pan American Union, *Labor Trends and Social Welfare in Latin America*, 1943, p. 1; and *Monthly Labor Review*, V. 52, pp. 1123-1125 (May 1941).

[15]*Monthly Labor Review*, V. 52, (May 1941), p. 1124.

VI
THE PERON ERA

Old Tensions and New: The World War and Social Change

The major socio-political problem as Argentina entered the decade of the forties was the integration of the new urban proletariat. The government appeared blissfully ignorant of the significance of this unfamiliar element, and the small labor movement was not nearly equipped to aid effectively in integrating it. This was to be the task of Perón.

The terms of Justo's two presidential successors were complicated by the tensions arising out of the developments in Europe leading to World War II. Civilians and the military alike were divided over the struggle between the Allies and the Axis. Many officers, particularly those resentful of what they saw as an exploitive economic relationship developed with Britain by Justo, were pro-Axis. Many Argentines, on the other hand, remembering the prosperity the country had experienced during World War I, received with sympathy the declaration of neutrality proclaimed by President Roberto M. Ortiz in 1939.

Vice President Ramón S. Castillo stepped into the presidency in 1940 when Ortiz resigned because of ill health, continuing the *Concordancia* domination. As the end of the presidential term approached, the government selected a wealthy pro-British sugar planter, Robustiano Patrón Costas, as the presidential candidate and began the usual "arrangements" to assure his election. There was considerable opposition and Castillo openly sought military support to guarantee the outcome.

The military had again recouped much of its institutional autonomy, and there were many professionalist officers who resented Castillo's efforts to drag them back into the political arena. The concept of "politics" that had developed and been propagated in the Superior War School was tawdry, and there was a disinclination to allow the institution to be placed in the position of supporting manipulation and fraud. There was still considerable Radical sentiment in the officer corps, and important leaders of that party, in keeping with traditional Radical foreign policy, urged the officers to prevent Argentine involvement in the war even if it meant denying office to Patrón Costas. And there was the ever-present conservative strain that feared the new urban masses, the labor movement, and international communism. Many officers had visited Germany, Italy, and Spain during the preceding decade and admired the authoritarian order and efficiency they saw.

A small group of officers stationed in Buenos Aires formed a "lodge" in now traditional fashion to coordinate military response, taking advantage of

97

all the disparate opposition currents. They gained adherents in key positions, although the group's membership probably never reached a hundred, and were successful after much difficulty in persuading a general officer, Arturo Rawson, to lead a bloodless coup on June 4, 1943, which ousted President Castillo.

Two days after General Rawson became provisional President, he was forced by his military associates to resign because of policy disputes. General Pedro Ramírez followed Rawson in the presidency. His distinctly authoritarian government established firm control over political parties, the press, and labor unions, and alienated liberal elements in all sectors of society. Colonel Juan Domingo Perón, *eminence gris* of the military lodge, took advantage of the widespread dissatisfaction to organize a successful opposition, and in 1944 forced Ramírez out in favor of Perón's choice, General Edelmiro Farrell. Perón became the key figure in the government as War Minister and Labor Secretary, and between 1943 and 1946 he extended his political power by boldly courting labor support.

The Emergence of Perón

In a relatively short period of time Peron gained broad popular backing without directly challenging the leadership. When it became clear that his ambitions extended to the presidency, the military leadership in October 1945 moved to expel him from the government and undermine his political base of power. A popular front consisting of labor supporters, Radical politicians, allies among the police and others enabled him to face down the removal attempt and emerge as President in a decisive victory at the polls four months later.

If social revolution in Latin America can be defined as the bringing of urban labor and the peasants into the effective political life of a nation, the Perón era in Argentina must be viewed as having fulfilled the first half of the requirement. Urban labor and a not overly enthusiastic military became the main props of his regime, and the changes both underwent have greatly affected Argentine life since 1955. The labor movement achieved remarkable unity, for Argentina, under the carrot-and-stick policies of Perón. The central labor organization, *Confederación General de Trabajo*, had a membership between four and six million before the end of the regime and remained until the end its main political support. In exchange Argentine labor received long-awaited rights and benefits which added up to one of the most liberal social and job security systems in the region. An unexpected concomitant was a marked decline in productivity after about 1951, and a calamitous rise in featherbedding practices.

The industrialization program flowered under the hothouse economic conditions generated by the war, and was an integral part of the nationalist aims of *Justicialismo*, Peron's political movement. It grew in part at the expense of agriculture, being financed by exchange differentials administered by the *Instituto Argentina para el Producción e Intercambio* (IAPI). The disinvestment that occurred in agriculture as a result has been not a small part of the troubles of succeeding governments. The forced-feeding of industry also led to neglect of the transportation and utilities systems, purchased from foreign owners by Perón in furtherance of nationalistic aims. The new national enterprises absorbed many more workers than had been employed in the past, as did the vast bureaucracy that grew with statism.

Political changes included a new constitution in 1949, which added the concepts of *Justicialismo* to the federal structure of 1853; abrogation of the no-reelection rule; purging of the courts; crippling of established political parties; and establishment of the Peronista party. Internal control was tightened by organization of an 18,000-man federal police force. The concept of *desacato* (criticism of public officials) was carried to extremes that made hazardous any criticism of the regime.

Justicialismo is without doubt the most significant and far-reaching legacy of Peron. Its motto, "political sovereignty, economic independence, social justice," reflects nothing new in Argentine political thought; the innovation consisted of Peron's serious attempt to implement the latter two aims.

The search for economic independence led to industrialization and development schemes that have had to be continued, whether rational or not, in the face of a rabid nationalism. The search for social justice came to mean almost exclusively benefits to urban labor.

Trade union membership skyrocketed under Perón. (The extent of growth is not clear. Perón claimed that there were six million members in the CGT, but the post-Perón Ministry of Labor estimated something over two million.) The old Department of Labor, a minor agency of the Department of Interior, became the Secretariat of Labor and Social Welfare, with ministerial prestige in fact if not in name. Social security institutes were established, covering virtually all the country's workers. A low-cost housing program with an initial appropriation of half a billion pesos was started. Mandatory vacation programs for all persons working for hire were legislated, and largely under pressure from the Secretariat, average daily wages increased greatly, almost doubling between 1942 and 1945. Belated concern for the working classes, for the first time enjoying the protection of governmental power, was evident everywhere.

Under the benevolent umbrella of the new Secretariat, labor organization was extended to industries where physical violence and assassination had frequently squelched it in the past. The first and most dramatic success was achieved in the industry that had brought modern management techniques to Argentina over sixty years previously, the packinghouses (*frigorificos*) which processed the pampa beef destined for European markets. A general strike was called at all the plants around Buenos Aires in September 1943, and despite violent opposition from management, the government's influence was decisive in bringing about the signing of the first collective bargaining contract in the history of the industry. Later the *Federación de la Indústria de la Carne y Afines*, one of the most important trade unions in Argentina, was to grow from this success. A complex and decentralized system of labor courts was established to interpret and enforce labor legislation and collective bargaining agreements.[16]

Opposing Forces

Perón's re-election in 1951 was followed by increasing polarization between supporters and opposition. Factionalism within the military was exacerbated by Perón's purge of those opposing or thought to oppose him and by his promotion and preferential assignment of supporters. A result was the forging of political alliances between military officers and parties of the right and center to oppose Perón. The Catholic Church, after a long period of cordial relations with Perón, was drawn into the political struggle when he accused a group of priests in 1954 of agitating against his government and took an increasingly anti-clerical attitude. His personal peccadillos with women alienated the straight-laced military hierarchy as much as they did the Church. A contract executed by the government with a subsidiary of an American petroleum company for oil exploration in Patagonia was interpreted by nationalist officers as a sell-out, and his rapprochement with the United States after his earlier ultra-nationalist and anti-American pose cost him support.

In 1951 Perón successfully put down a revolt led by a number of generals and subsequently forced into retirement some officers of all three military

---

[16]For a discussion of labor relations during the period, see Robert J. Alexander, *Labor Relations in Argentina, Brazil, and Chile* (Chicago, 1962). Also Moises Poblete Troncoso and Ben B. Burnett, *The Rise of the Latin American Labor Movement* (New York, 1960).

services. In June 1955, dissident elements of the navy launched a rebellion in Buenos Aires, but the army remained loyal and the uprising was crushed.

A successful revolt was planned and directed from the provinces in the following September. Tensions increased during the weeks following the navy uprising as factions within the government and the military, hoping to exploit the widespread unrest engendered by the abortive revolt and the increasing rift with the Church, maneuvered for position. Finally, on September 16, 1955, insurgent factions in all three branches of the armed forces staged a coordinated rebellion. After three days of a virtual civil war, Perón, fearing naval bombardment of Buenos Aires, resigned and took refuge on a Paraguayan ship in Buenos Aires harbor.

VII
THE MILITARY IN POWER: A DECADE OF FRUSTRATION
IN THE SEARCH FOR NATIONAL INTEGRATION

Military Factions

The Army dominated the provisional governments that followed Perón's downfall. General Eduardo Lonardi, a career soldier who had been retired after participating in the revolt of 1951, headed the first of these, which lasted until November 13. Lonardi was replaced as provisional president by General Pedro E. Aramburu. Much available evidence points to an early alignment between Lonardi, some of the older army generals, and important civilian rightist elements, including Catholic nationalists, who sought an all-military cabinet and a stronger ruling hand. Aramburu removed from office many officers associated with this group in May 1956. Some were exiled to diplomatic posts while a few of the more intransigent were jailed in Patagonia. Among these was General Leon Justo Bengoa, around whom this "*Golpista*" faction later rallied.[17]

Purging the military of peronists continued to occupy Aramburu throughout the year, and the inevitable attempt at a counter-coup came in June. The Army Mechanics' School in Buenos Aires revolted, as did elements at Santa Rosa and La Plata, led by dismissed Generals Tanco and Valle. Martial law was declared and at least 48 persons, including 31 civilians, were killed in putting down the revolt, some by execution following military trials. This was the last major uprising definitely ascribable to peronist military leadership. However, dissension over government response to the prevalent anarchy between Aramburu and his vice president, Admiral Isaac Rojas, led to a sharpening of the lines between the *Golpistas* and the backers of Aramburu's plans for a mixed civilian-military government with early elections. *Golpista* pressure, particularly from the air force, forced Aramburu to grant that faction additonal recognition in the government in May, including appointment of General Toranzo Montero as Army Inspector General. In exchange he obtained reluctant acquiescence in plans for election of a national assembly in July, reinstatement of the constitution of 1853, and national elections in February 1958.

---

[17] An analysis of the immediate post-Perón period is contained in Fritz L. Hoffman, "Perón and After," *Hispanic American Historical Review* (November 1956), pp. 510-527.

Political Factions

The July constitutional assembly elections brought to light the chaotic conditions in the political parties and groups. Fifteen national and 26 provincial parties participated in the elections. The Radical party, long beset with internal differences, had openly split in 1956. The *Unión Cívica Radical Instransigente* followed Arturo Frondizi, and Ricardo Balbín headed the *Unión Cívica Radical del Pueblo*. Both claimed to be perpetuating the principles of Hipólito Irigoyen, but had that worthy been alive he would have had difficulty in recognizing either faction as his heir. At this time Balbín's wing was probably closer to the traditional radical-liberal philosophy than was that of Frondizi, who was accused of trying to "out-Perón Perón." (The positions were to be reversed after the national elections of 1958.) The UCRP won 118 seats and the UCRI 76 in the assembly. The real winners were not present. The peronists, prohibited from competing as a party, cast 2,146,946 blank votes, according to *La Nacion* (August 11), more than any lawful party received. After much acrimonious debate and several walkouts by major factions, the constitution of 1853, with Article 14 expanded to recognize twentieth century social and economic aspirations, was reinstated.

Labor did not escape the pervasive factionalism of the period. The seemingly monolithic CGT split under the pressure of government *interventors* and the promises of liberal elements in the governments; 62 unions remained subject to peronist leadership while 32 repulsed it. This split weakened labor's efforts to influence the government, despite many nuisance strikes, and the CGT's attempt at a major general strike October 22-25, 1957, was a failure.

The handwriting on the wall had been exceedingly clear after the votes were counted in the constitutional assembly election, and in the period following the assembly the parties feverishly sought coalitions that would capture the peronist vote in the national elections. Frondizi and the UCRI emerged victorious, winning a plurality in all the provinces and in the capital, control of the congress, and all the governorships at stake. Frondizi steadfastly denied any deal, but some observers claim he had agreed, through his intermediary, Rogelio Frigerio, to return the CGT to peronist control, legalize the movement, free the peronist leaders in jail, and allow the eventual return of Perón himself. He did reinstate many peronist leaders in the CGT shortly after assuming office and he freed many political prisoners.

Solicitations of peronist support by Frigerio and R. Damonte Taborda, a publisher and Frondizi aide, angered the military; using the fall labor strike as justification, the military, led by Vice President Gomez, pressed for strong action against the peronists. Frondizi acquiesced on November 12, declaring a state of seige and suspending constitutional rights. Over 700 *peronistas* and "nationalist" agitators were arrested. Frondizi forced the resignation of Gomez several days later, but this surrender to the military demands had set a pattern that was to be repeated frequently during the ensuing three years.[18]

The military now became his primary prop. Troops broke the January 1959 strikes that occurred during Frondizi's trip to the United States, and the general strike of April 4 called by the "62" peronist unions. The army supervised the provincial elections in San Luis in March. The June 23 resignation of all the civilian members of the cabinet did not give the military pause. In July the navy compelled Frondizi's Secretary of the Navy to resign; in September General Toranzo Montero refused to accept dismissal as army Chief of Staff and in the ensuing feud succeeded in having the Secretary of the Army fired. As the congressional by-elections of March 1960 approached, the military insisted on putting the nation on an "internal war" footing, and martial law was declared. (Frondizi's UCRI retained 106 of 192 congressional seats in the elections, the UCRP won 80, and about one million blank ballots were cast.) General Toranzo Montero insisted on the intervention of Cordoba province after the elections, and in October again forced the resignation of the Secretary of the Army for opposing his policies.

The reduction by half of blank ballots cast and the subsequent successes of the UCRI in several muncipal elections apparently emboldened Frondizi to attempt a broadening of his base of support. As 1960 closed, he named Dr. Acuña Anzorena, who was acceptable to the CGT, Minister of Labor and Social Security. On January 2, 1961 he pledged restoration of labor control to the CGT and softened his stand toward peronist participation in future elections. By March he felt strong enough to ease General Toranzo Montero out of his job as army Chief of Staff, but the latter left with ominous threats of future action if tougher measures were not taken against the peronists, and the *New York Times* of April 3, 1961 reported a majority of the military leaders were in sympathy with Toranzo. An imprudent August meeting with the Cuban revolutionary Che Guevara almost undid Frondizi's patient work, but was smoothed over with the resignation of the minister who arranged the meeting. The year ended with Frondizi looking forward, apparently with confidence, to the important congressional elections of March 19, 1962.

---

[18]Exhaustive accounts of these events, and those described later, appear in the excellent Buenos Aires dailies. The weekly column "La Semana Política" in *La Nación* is particularly valuable to the researcher. Buenos Aires also counts several good weekly news magazines. *Confirmado* appears to be the best in terms of accuracy of basic information.

Those elections were disastrous for Frondizi and the UCRI. They lost their majority in the Chamber of Deputies, retaining only 76 seats. The peronist forces won 43 seats and 6 key provincial governorships, including Buenos Aires. The reaction was instantaneous. Frondizi tried desperately to maintain his position. He fired Interior Minister Vítolo (the classic Latin American gesture following a failure at the polls), outlawed further *peronista* activities, promised to purge the executive branch of *peronista* influence (meaning Sr. Frigerio) and ordered military *interventors* into the 6 key provinces won by the *peronistas*. It was all to no avail. A last-minute attempt at reconciliation with the UCRP of Ricardo Balbín failed, and the military took over. José María Guido, former president of the senate and vice president by virtue of the forced resignation of Gomez, took up the baton as front man for the military regime. Frondizi was exiled to Martín García island to contemplate the vagaries of the political arts in a factious and fragmented nation.

Frondizi had made a creditable showing in the economic sphere, freeing the peso, abolishing many exchange controls, settling the claims of the foreign utility companies (this going far toward restoring the national credit), and fostering a quite spectacular economic growth under the laissez faire policies of Economics Minister Álvaro Alsogaray. In the area of foreign policy Frondizi discovered that rampant nationalism has many faces, and the Cuban issue most clearly posed them for him. United States insistence at Punta del Este on condemnation of Cuba posed what one writer called an "indissoluble problem" for Frondizi. The Right, particularly the *Golpista* military faction, demanded the condemnation while the Left would not have it.[19] The Right prevailed when in February 1962 Frondizi cut diplomatic ties with Cuba; this action might go far to explain the drastic loss of leftist support he suffered in the following month's elections. This contributed, of course, to his final, fatal failure as a political leader: he was not able to form a firm base of support and he failed to win his most important election.

Azules and Colorados

The military united only long enough to depose Frondizi and reiterate its consensus of oppositon to *peronismo* in any form. Its deep and lingering divisions of opinion over the form the government should take and its own role in it immediately generated forces that began to pull and push the figurehead president. In the first flush of unity Guido and his military backers

[19] For a discussion of armed forces' attitudes toward communism at this time, see Mario Orsolini, *La crisis del ejército* (Buenos Aires, 1964), pp. 51-53, and Carlos Florit, *Las fuerzas armadas y la guerra psicológica* (Buenos Aires, 1963), pp. 62-63.

annulled the provincial election results and appointed *interventors*, recessed the congress indefinitely by decree, and in June nullified the congressional elections of March 18 in order permanently to bar the peronist deputies. (A federal court ruled this last move unconstitutional, but was overruled by the appeals court on a government motion.)

The crucial battle, however, was raging within the officer corps of the three services, and in the absence of the moral authority of a traditonally strong president, the struggle was fierce and its outcome portentous. The high command that managed Frondizi's overthrow was composed largely of officers with an authoritarian bent. The *Golpistas*, with General Carlos Severo Toranzo Montero as their spokesman, continued to favor an outright military government for an indefinite period. They were opposed by a larger, less-rigid faction—later called Colorados—which sought a solution more in keeping with tradition. The Colorados retained a commitment to constitutionalism and apparently would have been satisfied with "safe" elections that precluded peronist participation and an arrangement that assured a strong military voice in the government. Admiral Isaac Rojas was the spokesman for this group. Both groups were determined to root out peronism from all sectors of the society. For six months following Frondizi's ouster these factions quarrelled over the top military posts and their future role.

When new election laws and voting rules generally satisfactory to the Colorados were announced in July, Toranzo Montero and his brother, also an army general, attempted a counter-coup, which failed when the air force and navy remained neutral. They did succeed in forcing some cabinet changes, but the revolt alienated many of their supporters among the Colorados, and precipitated the coalescence of an opposition clique of army officers with its nucleus in the cavalry corps. Their leader was 48-year-old Brigadier General Juan Carlos Ongañia, whose primary motivations appeared to have been based upon a desire to get the army out of politics and back to its "specific" role. Elections were the means to that end, so the *legalistas*, or Azules as they came to be called, became champions of early elections, "return to normalcy," and cessation of the scandalous spectacles caused by military officers in the *Casa Rosada* who were holding the entire military institution up to ridicule.

Ongañia turned from words to action on September 19. Having gained the allegiance of major troop commanders at Campo de Mayo and other garrisons in Buenos Aires province, and with some air force support, he pushed tank columns into the capital in a lightning thrust that left two dead and some 37 wounded among the Colorado forces which attempted to check them. The navy split over the question of which side to support. Although the prevailing sentiment was with the Colorados, the suddenness of the move foreclosed any immediate reaction, and the Azules took control of the center of Buenos Aires. The immediate end was control of the army, and Onganía placed confidants in the war ministry and the general staff, and installed tank men as commanders of the four army corps. The effect, of course, was control of the government. After some early hesitation, Guido acquiesced in the new arrangement and remained as president. All 14 active service admirals requested retirement within a few days. Some 250 Colorado officers were arrested, 110 of whom later drew light sentences while the others generally got off with forced retirement.

The new high command issued Army Communique 150, which declared that the armed forces would not govern and that the nation would return to constitutionalism as soon as elections could be arranged. There was an implied commitment to prevent a peronist victory. In the succeeding weeks elections were announced for the following July, and a new statute was issued governing political activities and election procedures. The new laws included provisions that effectively disqualified a peronist party by that name (as well as communist parties) and introduced a proportional representation system to preclude peronists under any label from achieving legislative majorities in the national or provincial legislatures.

There was considerable opposition to early elections, not only among the hard-line Colorados remaining in the officer corps, but among important conservative elements of the civilian society. The Colorados, with encouragement from some civilians, rallied behind Admiral Isaac Rojas on April 2, 1963 in a last-gasp effort to regain control of the government. Army, navy, and air force elements joined the Rojas forces, and several small but intense fights ensued over the next four days before Onganía's tankers and infantry prevailed. Several hundred officers were brought before military courts in April and May for their part in the "rebellion," and as many as 400 were probably separated from the service. Senior officers with known Colorado sentiments were rounded up from outlying garrisons, confined on ships or on Martín García island, and later separated. The *Escuela Superior de Guerra* had to suspend classes for a year so that loyal student officers there could replace the ousted Colorados. Many deep animosities among service families remain from that period, and there is still bad blood between the army and air force as a result of casualties from a strafing attack on a halted tank column near Buenos Aires.[20] The navy paid for its role in the revolt by a sharp reduction in its marine component.

---

[20] The author was in Argentina from 1963 to 1965 during which time he was acquainted with a large number of officers of all ranks from both factions. Much of the discussion of army attitudes and divisions comes from personal knowledge.

Ongañia never wavered in his determination to hold elections, and after a frantic period of political activity they came off peacefully on July 7, 1963. The *Unión Cívica Radical del Pueblo* (UCRP), heirs to Irigoyen as the more orthodox wing of Radicalism, led the field in all contests–the presidency, congress, and provincial governorships. The vote was split among a large array of parties and coalitions, however, and Dr. Arturo Illia, UCRP leader, became a minority president with only a quarter of the popular vote. *Peronistas* cast blank ballots accounting for about 19 percent of the popular vote in the presidential contest.

The only military candidate, retired General Pedro Aramburu, running at the head of a centrist coalition, won about 14 percent of the popular vote.

Radicalism Revived

Illia's personalistic and doctrinaire Radical approach to governing had remarkable similarities to Irigoyen's. His only concrete pledges had been drawn from old Radical nationalist sentiments: i.e., to annul foreign oil contracts and concessions, withdraw from the International Monetary Fund, and "restore the integrity of the Argentine Government." Despite the fact that his election had depended on the votes of other parties in the electoral college, he did not seek their collaboration. His cabinet was undistinguished and he met with it only twice, preferring to run the government with the help of a small coterie in the *Casa Rosada.* With a typical Radical belief in solutions through politics alone, he tinkered with the provincial electoral machinery in an attempt to increase Radical control at the expense of the peronists and other parties. (Despite his efforts, the peronists won 44 of the 99 contested seats for the national chamber of deputies in the March 1965 elections.)

Illia's vascillations in the economic area were more damaging to his survival possibilities. He inherited a huge foreign debt which haunted him throughout his 32-month administration, as well as a bevy of overstaffed and inefficient state enterprises. Any improvement in the latter situation would have required a confrontation with the heavily-peronist labor unions, and the administration simply did not have that kind of strength. Inflationary borrowing and the steady issuance of paper currency led to giant jumps in the cost of living, routine devaluations, and a thriving gray market in foreign exchange. The government fell behind on public payrolls, including military salaries, on several occasions. Half-hearted attempts at price and wage controls and meatless days produced nationwide grumbling and open violations of the complicated laws.

Again with perfect Radical logic, Illia believed he could control the armed forces through his selectees for the ministries and by reincorporating and rewarding Colorado officers whose nationalist sentiments were akin to his own. He actively pursued the latter plan through his Defense Minister, Leopoldo Suarez. However, the scheme, called *Plan Cojines*, finally had to be abandoned in the face of open and outraged opposition on the part of the Azules.[21] The military was also disturbed by Illia's refusal to allow Argentina to participate in the Inter-American Peace Force in the Dominican Republic intervention of May 1965. Ongañia in particular believed in the necessity for concerted hemispheric action against the threat of international communism. Illia violated a long-standing tradition that had allowed the army commander to have a decisive voice in the selection of the secretary of war, and named Brigadier General Castro Sanchez to that post in November 1965, against Ongañia's expressed opposition. Ongañia resigned immediately. General Pascual Pistarini replaced him, and coup plotting apparently began immediately thereafter.

---

[21] Ties between the UCRP and the Colorados were notorious and well known. See Philip B. Springer, "Disunity and Disorder: Factional Politics in the Argentine Military," in *The Military Intervenes: Case Studies in Political Development*, Henry Bienen, ed. (Hartford, Conn., 1968), pp. 146-168. Also *La Nación*, November 2, 1964.

VIII
THE 1966 COUP: A MILITARY FORMULA FOR RENOVATION OF THE ARGENTINE SOCIETY

The 1966 coup was not the work of a secret society or a cabal of officers. It was planned in the war ministry with all the resources of the general staff, although not all contributors were aware of the nature of the end product, and coordinated between the services like a military contingency plan. Representatives of powerful civilian elements also participated in the elaboration of programs to be implemented by a new government. Only the date was left open. General Onganía must have been aware of the general outlines of the planning, but there is no evidence that he actively participated. There is similarly no evidence that any other leader was ever seriously considered for the successor government. That a coup was coming, indeed foreordained, appeared to have been accepted by informed elements of the capital throughout the early months of 1966. The subject was widely discussed in newspapers, on the radio, and in every *confiteria.*

In a perceptive analysis written shortly after the coup, James W. Rowe, who was living in Buenos Aires, had this to say:

> Whatever the justification of the June *golpe*, it was no ephemeral matter, and was linked to a long-maturing crisis of values and authority which has been under way for many years. The 'revolutionary' ferment prior to the *golpe* went far beyond mere concern over the alleged impotence of the Illia government . . . or even the specter of Peronist success in the elections scheduled for next March . . . and was importantly related to the anxious—sometimes desperate—concern of heterogeneous groups of younger officers, middle management, professionals, and others, to break the political and institutional impasse of the last decade.[22]

The proximate cause for the June 28 *golpe* was a dispute between War Minister Castro Sanchez and Army Commander Pistarini over the latter's precipitate firing of a corps commander. Pistarini "withdrew" army recognition of Castro Sanchez, and when the president backed his minister and attempted to dismiss Pistarini, troops occupied strategic positions in Buenos Aires and deposed Illia. The maneuver came off without a hitch. No shots were fired, there was no real resistance, there were no exiles or political prisoners. As subsequent events were to make clear, the *golpe* was not aimed at persons but at the system.

---

[22]James W. Rowe, "Onganía's Argentina: The First Four Months," *American Universities Field Staff Reports,* East Coast South America Series, V. XIII, No. 7, November 1966.

A military junta comprised of the three service commanders took control, and during the next 24 hours dissolved the national congress and all provincial legislatures, replaced the elected governors and all members of the supreme court, and dissolved political parties (party records, funds, and office equipment were later impounded).

Diagnosis and Prescriptions

Following a long, legalist tradition that puts great stress on form and style, the coup was legitimated in an "Act of the Argentine Revolution." Following general staff procedures, this basic document was accompanied by implementing annexes. The "Act" and the annexes were signed by the three service commanders. The basic document, the "Act," was in effect the agreement between the three service commanders to effect the coup and take certain immediate steps. Its prologue explains that the three commanders decided to take their drastic step after a final, exhaustive analysis of the general condition of the country. The analysis made clear, the document states, that the lamentable conduct of public administration by the Illia government, coming as the culmination of many other errors committed by previous governments, of structural faults in the society and failures to apply adequate systems and techniques to contemporary realities, had provoked the rupture of the spiritual unity of the Argentine people, causing them to fall into skepticism and apathy. The chronic deterioration of economic-financial matters, the breakdown of authority and general absence of order and discipline, had led to deep social unrest, allowing a subtle and aggressive Marxist penetration into all sectors of national life, and encouraging extremist movements that brought with them the danger of collectivist totalitarianism. The three commanders resolved to "assume political and military power," carry out the steps mentioned above, promulgate a revolutionary statute, offer the presidency to General Onganía, and once he had been sworn, dissolve the junta. The "Act" was not made public immediately.

Annex 1, entitled "Message of the Revolutionary Junta to the Argentine People," was released to the press on June 28. It did not mention the dangers of Marxist penetration. Great emphasis was placed on economic stagnation, inflation, and the "fallacy of a formal and sterile legality," which in the name of liberty and electoral freedom had fostered a "vote-seeking system" that divided the country and mocked true democracy. The fundamental cause of the disintegration of the country was "the division of all Argentina into different sectors, and the existence of a rigid political structure, coupled with anachronistic political and economic measures. . . ." The object of the revolution was said to be the transformation and modernization of this

112

structure. The announcement went on to outline the initial political steps mentioned above, and concluded with exhortations to unity.

The Statute of the Revolution, Annex 2, was read at the installation of General Ongañia on June 29. He swore to observe faithfully the ends (*fines*) of the revolution, the Statute of the Revolution, and the constitution of the Argentine nation. The Statute has a short prologue and 14 articles. It grants legislative powers to the president, provides for stability in the judiciary after the initial wholesale replacement of federal and provincial magistrates, promises respect for all international obligations, and provides that the service chiefs will designate a successor in the event of the death or incapacitation of the president. Annex three, which was not publicized at the time, is entitled "Political Objectives—Revolutionary Ends." It includes a vaguely-worded prologue of "general objectives," and six short sections of specific objectives under foreign policy, internal policy, economic policy, labor policy, welfare policy, and security policy. The first states a determination to "participate in the defense of the free, western, Christian world." The second promises to restore unity, authority and a respect for law under a "republic regime," and to promote a national culture based on the country's unique traditions without abandoning universal norms common to the civilized, Christian western world.

Economic policy would promote development and assure access to its fruits to "all those disposed to realize a sustained effort to obtain it." Labor objectives aim at an equilibrium between the interests of labor and management, keeping the organizations of each "within the specific frame of its own function." The last two sections promise social welfare programs and the achievement of security capabilities that will assure that the other objectives can be reached.[23]

The general vagueness of these statements represents a compromise between long-standing views represented on the army general staff and articulated by civilian intellectuals associated with individual officers, and the old Azul and Colorado factions. Officers of the former alignment were in most key positions—as they had been since 1962—and the generally authoritarian tone of the documents represents a significant shift in their political orientation over the intervening four years. There is no mention of a return to civilian government by these former champions of constitutionalism. There is apparent unanimity between the factions that the

---

[23]The Revolutionary Act, with its annexes, is reproduced in Osiris G. Villegas, *Politicas y Estrategias Para el Desarrollo y la Seguridad Nacional* (Buenos Aires, 1969), pp. 309-321.

institutional structure of the government has proved inadequate to the tasks of the mid-twentieth century. There is, however, no agreement on what forms should replace it. That search would shape Argentine politics in the succeeding years.

New Disputes

General Onganía gave little public recognition to the revolutionary acts. He made it abundantly clear that he would not accept military interference in the day-to-day conduct of government, but he did acquiesce in the institutionalization of a military voice by including the three service commanders along with the five principal cabinet ministers in a new National Security Council. A Military Committee, comprised of the Defense Minister and the service chiefs, was also added to the organizational chart, with direct access to the president. His cool and distant relations with the committee were to cause him subsequent problems, as its uniformed members sought to use it as the vehicle for overseeing compliance with their revolutionary goals.

Onganía's most controversial early move was university reform, including a general purge of "subversive" faculty members and professional students. Some brutality occurred at the huge University of Buenos Aires, and a considerable number of intellectuals left the country rather than comply with the new Organic Law of National Universities. Onganía's prudish attempts to enforce conservative dress, abolish "suggestive" scenes from the theater and motion pictures, and dictate public morals in general were applauded by the conservative Catholics who were present in great numbers in the government, but drew only scorn and ridicule from the sophisticated *porteños*. Conservative Catholic influence appeared to wane after the spate of bad publicity following the university interventions.

Onganía opened discussions with the labor movement, but was quick to crack down on those violating the new regulations appearing daily. He moved early against the corrupt port unions, whose thievery and featherbedding had made Buenos Aires one of the world's most expensive ports. The state enterprises proved a tougher nut. An army engineer general was appointed to straighten out the railroads, the most overstaffed and deficit-ridden of all (around $1 million per day), but there was little noticeable progress against the strongest unions in Argentina.

Overall economic conditions actually worsened during the first six months of the new regime. Inflationary pressures increased, budget deficits mounted, and inept and sometimes contradictory monetary policies confused businessmen. There were grumblings inside the armed forces that Onganía was completely ignoring the service chiefs. When General Pistarini sought a greater voice in government councils in November, Onganía fired him out of hand and to the surprise of many observors easily made it stick. He apparently had learned some hard political lessons, however. He reshuffled his cabinet and dismissed some of the "political Catholics" from top posts and brought in recognized technicians, but maintained a balance between "liberal" and "nationalist" elements. Adalberto Krieger Vasena, the new economy minister, was a liberal with an excellent international reputation who undertook a successful overhauling of economic and monetary policies. Guillermo Borda, a nationalist ex-*Peronista*, was appointed Minister of Interior, and undertook a long and unsuccessful fight against proponents of early elections and a return to party government. General Julio Alsogaray was named army commander and his brother Álvaro, a laissez-faire economist frequently accused of having a 19th century liberal position on economics and politics, was sent to Washington as ambassador.

Krieger Vasena's orthodox policies began to revive the economy, but results were hard to see before 1968. In that year the GNP increased by about 4.5 percent. The peso was convertible, and over 100 million dollars worth of government securities were sold abroad. Petroleum output rose and there was a drop of 42 percent in the deficits of state enterprises, largely in the railroads. Industry expanded by about 8 percent.[24]

Onganía had visualized the revolutionary renovation in three stages: economic, social, and political.

He had devoted his attention to the first, and was fighting a holding action on the other two during his first two years in office. It was a neat, military-like plan, but pressures were building for some evidence of his intentions in the social and political areas. He had taken no action to build a political base, yet autocratically refused to give his one source of support—the armed forces—a voice in policymaking councils. The Military Committee was never consulted, and the National Security Council's plans and projects were ignored.

The liberal military leadership, heirs to the Azul traditions, grew increasingly to fear that Onganía was coming under the dominance of a "nationalist" coterie around him that advocated a corporate form of government. Led by General Alsogaray, they began in 1968 to put increasing pressure on Onganía to set an election date and clarify his political plans.

The *Ateneo*, a rather exclusive clique of Catholic activists, elaborated many of the *nacionalista* sentiments in its debates and discussions during the

---

[24]Agency for International Development, *Latin America–Economic Growth Trends*, E/CN. 12/825, Washington (December 1968), pp. 11-88, 11-101.

Illia administration, and allusions to plans for implementation of the doctrine appeared in books and articles by some of the more prominent members. Some of the plans had unmistakable elements of the corporate structure espoused by Mussolini in Italy and Vargas in Brazil during the thirties. General Onganía was a frequent participant in religious retreats attended by *Ateneo* members, and they were among his earliest and closest advisors.

At the core of nationalist political philosophy was a conviction that the appalling factionalism of Argentine society could not be cured by a return to the fractious party system of the past. Its adherents believed that a different form of participation in national life could heal the deep antagonisms, and that the loss of political democracy was not too high a price to pay for what they called "social democracy." Early in the Onganía government, they offered a solution to the nagging problems of what to do with the peronists by advocating their absorption into broader economic interest groups that would be represented in an ascending hierarchy of economic and social councils.

Onganía tried to walk a middle road. His economic policies were generally liberal, at home and internationally. Some of his bluenosed attempts to dictate public morals were clearly from the other camp. But it was Onganía's silence on the question of politics and the future structure of the state—specifically his failure to set a date for elections—that most alarmed the liberals.

General Alsogaray and his mentor-brother, Álvaro, apparently were convinced that the politically innocent Onganía had been seduced by the *nacionalistas.*

Their *bête noire* and that of the liberals was nationalist Minister of Interior Guillermo Borda, whose past peronist associations and continuing courtship of the movement infuriated officers who were jailed by Perón and who had maneuvered since 1955 to bar the peronist bloc from the levers of power. His pronouncements on future political developments said little of elections or of an end to the irregular regime, and to the liberals had a definite corporatist tinge.

Onganía's Mandate Challenged

When General Alsogaray continued to complain that Onganía was not being faithful to the original intent of the revolution, and tried to achieve a greater voice for the military committee, Onganía peremptorily fired him in August 1968 and named General Alejandro Lanusse as the new army commander. The other service chiefs, declining Onganía's request to stay on for the few weeks remaining before annual reassignments were ordinarily

116

announced, were replaced also. Alsogaray complained in a subsequent press conference that Onga̅nia was grasping total and absolute personal power in violation of the revolutionary statutes and warned that "recent events . . . reveal an inclination toward systems and especially toward people not precisely linked with the democratic spirit and foundations of the revolution." The Buenos Aires press interpreted his firing as a consequence of his opposition to Borda. The latter made a point of addressing the School of Higher Military Studies shortly afterward, assuring the officers there that the political objectives of the revolution had not changed, and that it sought a representative democracy "incorporating certain new forms," which were not specified.

Onga̅nia's great personal prestige and a rather surprising talent for balancing off opposing forces within the military, coupled with Lanusse's determination to preclude an open split in the army, restored a semblance of harmony for a while, although the arguments continued to rage under the surface. Paradoxically, some of the military reforms instituted by Onga̅nia contributed to undermining one of his objectives: the withdrawal of the army from active politics. Following the Azul victory in 1962, Ongania had set out to professionalize the army. In addition to a reorganization and streamlining of troop units, there had been an upgrading of the elaborate school system for officers, which absorbs the energies of up to 25 percent of the officer corps as students, instructors, or administrators.

The schools at the apex of the structure—the Superior War School, the Superior Technical School, and the Higher Studies School—revamped their curricula and teaching methods to broaden the scope of instruction, to bring in greater numbers of outside speakers, and to include individual research and seminar techniques. All three were centralized in 1968 under a single Institute for Higher Instruction. Major General Juan E. Guglialmelli, who had headed the school system during the mid-sixties, developed and propagated a "developmentalist" doctrine in the schools which established a nexus between national security and economic development that had a profound influence upon the officer corps. He posited economic development, in its broadest terms, as the essence of national security, and gave only secondary consideration to traditional military capabilities, since "economic aggression has been the most characteristic form of external aggression in Latin America."[25] The *desarrollistas* within the military characteristically found

[25]The quote is from an August 1969 speech Guglialmelli gave at the Círculo Militar, reproduced in *Circumil* (January-March 1970), pp. 130-131. His views on the military role in the national development process appeared regularly in the *Revista de la Escuela Superior de Guerra* when he was director. See, for example, the issue of March-April 1965, p. 8.

many civilian allies, largely among the Catholic-nationalist sectors, and intellectuals from this grouping added political dimensions to the argument. Typical is the scholarly justification for a "redemptive" role for the military in an article written in 1969 for the magazine *Estrategia* by Dr. Francisco Arias Pellerano, Director of the Political Science Departments of the University of Buenos Aires and the Catholic University. Dr. Arias holds that the old liberal philosophy is dead, and its institutions of little utility to developing countries. Marxism likewise is exhausted and in a process of decline. A new philosophy is required. The old liberal, civilian elite has not made the transition; they are bogged down in ancient abstractions of "liberty, democracy and election." They have proved unable to devise a development program that enjoys majority support, that mobilizes capital and canalizes it to the basic sectors of production and the infrastructure. They content themselves with preaching about an abstract liberty and democracy. Argentina has suffered a total default of civilian leadership. Past military interventions, for whatever circumstantial reasons undertaken, have been failures. Power has been returned to traditional parties and the cycle resumed. Past revolutions failed because: (1) they were brought off at the request of civilian groups; (2) they were limited to mere declarations with only vague programs; (3) they lacked an ideological apparatus; and (4) they always ended with a return of power to the traditional politicians who had caused the revolution in the first place, thus planting the seeds for yet another insurrection.

As custodians of sovereignty, says Dr. Arias, the armed forces have to redefine it periodically. Forms of external domination, he argues, are more subtle today, particularly "economic imperialism." The main task is development of basic industry to break the "tutelary" relationship with the developed world. To accomplish this, some social sectors must suffer temporarily, but all must participate. The role of the armed forces is to distribute the sacrifice objectively and to coordinate the various interests involved, since only they are above the particular sectoral interests.[26]

There is great support in Argentina for these political views, even from traditional advocates of economic liberalism such as the great Buenos Aires newspaper *La Prensa*; they part ways with the developmentalists over the latter's proclivities for strong protectionism and rigid controls over foreign participation in the developmental process.

Within the armed forces, there is a broad middle level of officers who have little faith in democratic, representative systems. To them, politics is an

[26]Francisco Arias Pellerano, "La participación política de las fuerzas armadas," *Estrategia*, No. 2 (July-August 1969), pp. 28-39.

opprobrius term. Many were involved as *interventors* at various levels of provincial and municipal government after the coup of 1962, and were appalled by the corruption and incompetence they found in the courthouse gangs and city hall crowds. Some were able to effect what they saw as fundamental reforms in tax assessment and collections, disbursing procedures, police protection, etc. in the eight to ten months they were in control, and speak with despair of the return to "politics as usual" that followed the elections of 1963. The ruthless academic pruning that substitutes for war in the career process of elimination has produced a highly educated, technically-minded meritocracy with little appreciation for the reconciliatory arts of politics. And finally, they see little hope of a solution to the problem of what to do with the peronists within the traditional political system.

Officers who hold some or most of these sentiments may be a majority in the major-lieutenant colonel ranks (*jefes*), but they probably are not a majority among the *oficiales superiores* who dictate army policy. Molded during the ferment of the forties, these officers maintain a belief in the trappings of constitutionalism, however thin the facade, and appear to believe sincerely that truly representative government can some day be made to work. They tend to think that other problems will resolve themselves if the "peronist question" can be settled, and put less emphasis on economics than do the nationalist *desarrollistas*. They share with their brethren a conviction, growing out of the intensive socialization process of the military educational system, that the officer is a superior being. His calling and its high purpose set him apart from other men, and lend to his actions an unselfish aura that is uncharacteristic of his environment, where opportunism is the norm among politicians, lawyers, businessmen, and other professionals. Unlike the nationalists, who would give this elite the dominant voice in running the country, the more traditional leadership fears that the officer corps will be sullied and irretrievably tarnished by its continued sole responsibility for governing, and seeks a withdrawal to a more manageable "moderator" role in the political process.

The more traditional faction, led by General Lanusse, became increasingly alarmed at the growing signs of popular discontent in 1969 and 1970. Terrorism rose dramatically and violent strikes became commonplace, particularly in the industrial center of Cordoba. The old parties strengthened their insistence that some announcement of political plans be made, and the military committee began pressing Onganía on that score. The kidnapping in May 1970 of ex-President Aramburu and the government's seeming impotence in finding him or his kidnappers caused a nationwide stir. On June 8 General Lanusse's office issued a communique explaining that, in view of the

119

President's refusal to consider a political plan developed by the National Security Council (CONASE), it had been decided to propose changes in the revolutionary statutes which would insure a greater participation by the army commander in "basic decisions of the government." Onganía responded by firing Lanusse for stating views "which go beyond his specific area of competence," but found himself without sufficient support to make his action stick in his only real base—the military. In a series of communiques that followed, the "Junta of the Commanders in Chief of the Argentine Armed Forces" announced its decision to "reassume the political power of the republic, with Lt. General Juan Carlos Onganía ceasing to serve in the post of President of the Argentine Nation," made certain personnel changes in the federal police and the cabinet, and promised to name a new president within ten days. The junta explained that the armed forces, by their action in 1966, had assumed full responsibility for the revolution, and could not fully delegate that responsibility to anyone. "The disagreements between the unanimous opinion of the armed forces and General Onganía on essential points of the revolution have imposed upon the Junta of Commanders in Chief the necessity of reassuming the leadership of the nation to prevent deviations that are alien to our democratic formation."

The Junta and Reinterpretation of Revolutionary Goals

The junta issued its new policies on June 21 in a long, normative document of 160 articles, many with numerous subheadings. In the political area, it called for "efficient and stable democracy founded on a political system, which with the effective participation of the community and under a representative, republican and federal type of government will insure the freedom of man and the full exercise of his fundamental rights." The political goal was to be achieved by modifying and reforming the bases of Argentine political organizations; maintaining political pluralism, backed by active participation by the population and legitimate, genuine representation in the Congress by political parties; and strengthening an authentically representative legislative power.[27] The program was very similar to the one described by the CONASE director, General Osiris Villegas, in a book published in 1969.[28]

The weekly newsmagazine *Confirmado* saw the move as an integrative one, rather than as representing a split between divergent schools. "All tendencies being present in the higher ranks of the armed forces, a solution

[27]The text appeared in *La Prensa* of June 21, 1970.
[28]See note 23.

120

was sought by bringing together all the sectors of intellectual value in the country . . . the liberal line assumes the leadership of the political process, the nationalist camp will attend to the functioning of the public infrastructure." The magazine also remarked on the fact that the new Foreign Minister and Economics Minister had both been professors at the Advanced Naval War School.[29]

There was an immediate flurry of speculation that the military was seeking a political way out of its problems (*la salida politica*) and old party leaders announced reorganization plans. *Confirmado* noted a "new spirit of tolerance" in Buenos Aires as political jokes reapppeared in theaters and on television; one of the junta members, Brigadier Rey of the air force, confirmed that the service chiefs had appointed a board of three senior officers to represent them in planning for a return to political activity, adding that the junta desired that the "solution be structured through consultations with all qualified men in the country."[30]

For reasons that are still somewhat obscure, Lanusse did not assume the presidential office. In a rather bizarre and unprecedented action, the three service chiefs decided to bring in a relatively unknown officer who was completely outside of the hierarchy and chain of command. Brigadier General Roberto Marcelo Levingston was serving as military attache in Washington and Argentine delegate to the Inter-American Defense Board when he was named President of the Argentine Republic. Levingston was a career intelligence officer, chosen perhaps precisely because he had no personal following in the command corps, nor history of active participation in politics.

The Nationalist Challenge

Levingston's selection proved to be a grievous error from the standpoint of the junta. He not only refused to play the figurehead's role, but upset the delicate balance that had been meticulously maintained between "liberals" and "nationalists." Following a brief settling-in period during which he was occupied with the aftermath of the Aramburu kidnapping and murder, Levingston came out strongly on the nationalist side, and electrified the country with an October announcement that elections would not be held for four or five years. He demanded the resignation of the liberal economics minister, a protégé of Kreiger Vasena, and replaced him with a left-of-center

---

[29]*Confirmado*, June 24-30, 1970, pp. 12-16.
[30]*Ibid.*

protectionist, meanwhile exhorting the nation to reduce its dependence on foreign technology and capital. General Guglialmelli was brought out of retirement to head an economic planning agency, and in December the president outlined a five-year plan providing for the "Argentinization" of the economy and drastically restricting the role of foreign capital.[31]

Opposition solidified from all sectors. The peronists and the Radicals bitterly attacked the postponement of elections, and in November provoked a 36-hour general strike that had more political than economic overtones. The violence that had been endemic since 1969 in the industrial city of Cordoba erupted into bloody riots in March of 1971, and there were confrontations between the federal police and the army that reflected political loyalties and tensions. On March 20, Levingston fired General Ezequiel Martinez, Chairman of the Joint Staff and top military planner for political reorganization, and again insisted that the "second stage" of the revolution would require another four years before elections could be considered. In an elaborate ruse, Levingston tried to oust Lanusse as army commander by separately convincing the other two members of the junta that his counterpart had acquiesced in the move.[32] The move backfired and on March 23 he himself was ousted. The junta announced that it would assume political power "until the Argentine revolution has been completed." Lanusse became president, and on July 9 announced a "moderate nationalist" economic program calling for a high degree of state intervention, but with guarantees for foreign and domestic private investment in specified areas. He also promised early elections within the new economic framework, and on July 28 Interior Minister Mor Roig announced that elections would be held by May 1973. Lanusse subsequently set the date at March 25, 1973.

---

[31]See the description of the five-year plan in the *New York Times* of December 25, 1970 and Levingston's address to the Special Meeting of the Board of Governors of the Inter-American Development Bank in Buenos Aires on March 1, 1971; reproduced in *Proceedings* of the IDB, pp. 15-18.

[32]This strange attempt was described to the author—during a visit to Buenos Aires in January-February 1972—as a "typical cloak and dagger maneuver by a career intelligence officer." The speaker was a high-ranking army officer who had been close to the events. The international air mail edition of *La Nación* gave considerable coverage to Levingston's intrigues following his ouster.

IV
ARGENTINE *CIVILISMO* AND *MILITARISMO*
IN PERSPECTIVE

The weakness of other political institutions in Argentina is the single most important factor contributing to the military's strong role. Political parties, the labor movement, business groups, and the university community are all factionalized and historically have been unable to find overlapping areas of common interest. The military is also factionalized, but its strong sense of hierarchy and elaborate socialization process have allowed one sector or another to dominate sufficiently at any one time to make it the strongest of several divided institutions.

True representative government has never been given much of a test in Argentina, due in part to the overwhelming power of the executive and to his constitutional authority to intervene at all levels of government. From the "national organization" of the mid-19th century, real power has resided in the hands of the president and his collaborators or appointees at the head of provincial governments. The army became important in the equation after the 1930 coup, but had played surprisingly little part in politics before that time. The German-monitored professionalization process, regularized by stringent organic laws after 1900, sharply differentiated the twentieth century military institution from its predecessors and held the promise of a European-style evolution in civil-military relations, in a society increasingly "Europeanized" by vast waves of immigration. The Radical movement, which was to be thwarted so frequently by military intervention in later years, deliberately politicized the officer corps in its attempts to gain and hold absolute power during the vast shifts in socioeconomic forces early in the century. Irigoyen's failure as an executive, the world depression, and a predilection for fascism brought the officer corps openly into the political arena in 1930, never to absent itself thereafter. Perón's opportunistic manipulation of the social revolution that the Radicals had failed to comprehend or lead posed the central problem of civil-military relations until 1966.

The 1966 revolution differed in its basis and scope from earlier military takeovers. As explained by Dr. Mor Roig, Lanusse's Minister of Interior:

> It is my understanding that, fundamentally, the movement of June 28, 1966 was not undertaken in order to bring down a president who was not honest, as ascetic as Dr. Illia is. Furthermore it was not undertaken because (individual) liberties were suppressed. Likewise it was not undertaken because the social tranquility of the Republic had been compromised, since except for some marginal agitation the country lived in social normality. The crisis was to be found in the

institutional political system. Consequently, in my judgment, the transcendent basis that the Revolution could have had and that could justify it . . . was institutional reform.[33]

Except for a residual fear of retribution if the peronists should gain additional power—and a reluctance to see ousted Colorado officers reinstated—no fundamental corporate interests were under threat. Personnel strength was not an issue.[34] Promotions through lieutenant colonel had been handled on the basis of merit, as a general rule, for many years, and the services enjoyed almost complete autonomy in setting standards. Even higher promotions have been remarkably free of political influence.[35] There was no fundamental disagreement on modernization or equipment acquisition plans: The Radicals have always supported strong forces, and General Onganía instituted his sweeping reorganization and modernization program (the Plan Europa) with the full approval of the Illia government. Pay is generally in accord with civilian scales for technicians and professionals of similar education and responsibilities.

The 1966 intervention was pushed more by internal institutional developments than pulled by external political or economic factors. As has been demonstrated, between 1962 and 1966 a previously persistent but not altogether reputable desire for a military-controlled authoritarian, elitest government was provided with a respectable rationale, and gained intellectual adherents heretofore missing. Economic nationalists, Catholic conservatives, and revisionist historians agreed with military *desarrollistas* that the old liberal political philosophy had proved itself incapable of moving Argentina toward her rightful place in the sun, and that sweeping structural revisions were required in the society. The nexus of national security and economic development was posited as the rationale that justified military leadership of the redemptive process, while simultaneously providing an intellectual solution to the ancient dilemma posed by the conspicuous political role of highly professionalized officers.

General Benjamín Rattenbach argues that political interventions may be explained by the absence of legal, systematized channels for the military to

---

[33]*La Nacion*, April 5, 1971.

[34]In 1930 the personnel of the armed forces numbered about 50,000. By 1943, on the eve of the coup that opened the path to power for Perón, that figure had doubled. When he was overthrown in 1955 the forces had grown to about 200,000. Strength decreased somewhat after 1955, and in 1967 total armed forces manpower was about 137,000.

[35]For example, the 50 or so brigadier generals on active duty in the army meet annually to draw up the order of merit list for lieutenant colonels. After review and approval by the army commander, the list becomes the basis for promotions within grade allocations to colonel, and is seldom if ever modified by other authorities.

make inputs except in the area of its specific expertise—national defense.[36] The state planning structure that evolved with the 1966 "revolution" was an attempt to correct this situation. The three service chiefs and the defense minister sat on the National Security Council and formed the Military Committee, both at the very top level of government, with direct access to the President. The Defense Minister also sat on the National Development Council, and in the words of one of the principal architects of this *schema:*

> the National Development Council and the National Security Council do not constitute special and distinct institutions, but are the national government itself, at its highest level. In its breast, all the individual policies and strategies are coordinated in their two vital aspects, development and security.[37]

This organization would appear to satisfy General Rattenbach's admonition that the peculiar conditions of Argentine tradition and society demand inclusion of the officer corps within the framework of state institutions in such a way that their interests in the broader development of the country can be expressed. However, the proposition assumes that the military will be able to arrive at a consensus and speak with a reasonably united voice. As has been demonstrated, such is not the case. Not only does the officer corps reflect the basic disagreements over national policy found in the polity, but there are also bitter differences between the military as an institution and the military as government. Thus the political fruits of professionalization have been bitter indeed. The establishment of a professionalized, middle class military has produced yet another pressure group that can neither refrain from politics nor unite sufficiently to carry out a program conceived by the institution.

At this writing the Liberals are again in the ascendancy, and in the classic manner have apparently opted to return the major responsibility to civilian politicians through elections in 1973, resuming the political role of guardians of the constitution and moderators of crisis situations. The true strength of the nationalist *desarrollistas*, within and without the ranks, will be reflected by the success of these plans.

---

[36]General Benjamín Rattenbach, "El Professionalismo Militar en el Ejército Argentino," *Temas MIlitares*, Vol. 1, No. 3 (August 1967), pp. 9-16.

[37]Villegas, *Politicas y Estrategias*, p. 72.

BIBLIOGRAPHY–BOLIVIA

Abadie-Aicardi, Raul F. *Economía y sociedad de Bolivia en el Siglo XX; el antiguo régimen.* Montevideo: Ediciones del Rio de la Plata, 1966.

Alexander, Robert J. *The Bolivian National Revolution.* New Brunswick, New Jersey: Rutgers University Press, 1958.

————. "Bolivia: The Government and Politics of the National Revolution." *Political Systems of Latin America,* ed. by Martin Needler. Princeton: Van Nostrand, 1964.

Arnade, Charles W. *The Emergence of the Republic of Bolivia.* Gainesville: University of Florida Press, 1957.

Ayala Mercado, Ernesto. *Que es la Revolución Boliviana.* La Paz: n.p., 1956.

Baker, Ross K. *A Study of Military Status and Status Deprivation in Three Latin American Countries.* Washington: Center for Research in Social Systems, 1967.

Barber, William F., and Ronning, C. Neal. *International Security and Military Power, Counterinsurgency and Civic Action in Latin America.* Columbus: Ohio State University Press, 1966.

Barrientos Ortuño, René. *Meditación para los bolivianos.* La Paz: n.p., 1967.

Barton, Robert. *A Short History of the Republic of Bolivia.* La Paz: Los Amigos del Libro, 1968.

Bedregal, Guillermo. "El Problema Militar en Bolivia." *Política,* Vol. V, No. 54 (October, 1966), pages unnumbered.

Brill, William H. *Military Intervention in Bolivia: The Overthrow of Paz Estenssoro and the MNR.* Washington: Institute for the Comparative Study of Political Systems, 1967.

————. *Military Civic Action in Bolivia.* Unpublished Ph.D. dissertation, University of Pennsylvania, 1965.

Cleven, Nels Andrew Nelson. *The Political Organization of Bolivia.* Washington: Carnegie Institution of Washington, 1940.

Díaz, Julio. *Historia del Ejército de Bolivia 1825-1932.* La Paz: Imprenta Central del Ejército, 1940.

Díez de Medina, Fernando. *Bolivia y su Destino.* La Paz: Editorial E. Burrillo, 1962.

Finót, Enrique. *Nueva Historia de Bolivia.* La Paz: Editorial Gisbert, 1954.

Fronda, Esteban. "El militarismo en Bolivia." *Espartaco* (La Paz), No. 5 (April, 1964).

Greene, David G. "Revolution and the Rationalization of Reform in Bolivia." *Inter-American Economic Affairs,* Vol. 19 (Winter, 1965), 3-25.

Gutiérrez, Alberto Ostria. *The Tragedy of Bolivia–A People Crucified.* New York: Devin-Adair, 1958.

Klein, Herbert S. *Parties and Political Change in Bolivia, 1880-1952.* New York: Cambridge University Press, 1969.

————. "David Toro and the Establishment of Military Socialism in Bolivia." *Hispanic American Historical Review,* Vol. 65, No. 1 (1965), 25-52.

————. "German Busch and the Era of Military Socialism." *Hispanic American Historical Review,* Vol. 67, No. 2 (May, 1967), 166-184.

La'berman, Jacobo. *Bolivia: 10 años de revolución 1952-1962.* La Paz: Dirección Nacional de Información, 1962.

Lora, Guillermo. *La Revolución Boliviana.* La Paz: n.p., 1964.

Malloy, James M. *Bolivia, The Uncompleted Revolution.* Pittsburgh: University of Pittsburgh Press, 1970.

Martin, Lois Deicke. *Bolivia in 1956: Analysis of Political and Economic Events.* Stanford: Stanford University Hispanic American Studies, 1958.

Osborne, Harold. *Bolivia, A Land Divided.* London: Oxford University Press, 1964.

Pardo Valle, Nazario. *Calendario Histórico de la Revolución.* La Paz: n.p., 1957.

Patch, Richard W. "Bolivia: The Restrained Revolution." *The Annals*, CCCXXIV (March, 1961).

————. "Bolivia: US Assistance in a Revolutionary Setting." *Social Change in Latin America Today*, ed. by Richard N. Adams. New York: Vintage Books, 1960.

————. "The Bolivian Falange: A letter from Richard Patch." *American Universities Field Staff Reports*, West Coast South America Series, May 1959.

Paz Estenssoro, Victor. *Discursos y Mensajes.* Buenos Aires: Ediciones Meridiano, 1953.

Peñaloza, Luis. *Historia del Movimiento Nacionalista Revolucionario: 1941-1952.* La Paz: Libreria Editorial Juventud, 1962.

Revista de la Fuerza Fluvial y Lacustre (La Paz). 1963-1965.

Revista Militar (La Paz). 1944-1969.

Revista Naval de Bolivia (La Paz). 1967-1969.

United States Army. *Area Handbook for Bolivia.* Washington: The American University, 1963.

Velarde, José Fellman. *Victor Paz Estenssoro, El Hombre y la Revolución.* La Paz: n.p., 1955.

Walinsky, Louis J. *Walinsky Report—Economic and Policy Implications of Bolivia's Ten Year Development Plan.* Washington: US Government Printing Office, 1962.

Wilde Cavero, Manuel Fernando. *Historia Militar de Bolivia.* La Paz: n.p., 1963.

Wilkie, James Wallace. *The Bolivian Revolution and US Aid Since 1952.* Los Angeles: University of California Latin American Center, 1969.

Wood, David. *Armed Forces in Central and South America.* London: Institute for Strategic Studies, 1967.

Zavaleta Mercado, René. *La revolución boliviana y la cuestión del poder.* La Paz: Direccion Nacional de Informacion, 1964.

Zondag, Cornelius H. *The Bolivian Economy 1952-65: The Revolution and its Aftermath.* New York: Praeger, 1966.

Zook, David. *The Conduct of the Chaco War.* New York: Bookman, 1960.

BIBLIOGRAPHY—ARGENTINA

Academia Nacional de Historia. *Historia Argentina Contemporanea, 1862-1930.* Buenos Aires, El Ateneo, 1963.

Argentina. Secretaría de Guerra. *Revista de la Escuela Superior de Guerra.* Buenos Aires, 1964-1969.

Balestra, Juan. *El Noventa.* 3d. ed. Buenos Aires: Farina, 1959.

Beltran, V. R. "The Army and Structural Changes in 20th Century Argentina: An Initial Approach." *Armed Forces and Society.* Edited by J. Van Doorn. The Hague: Mouton, 1968.

Bielsa, Rafael. *Caracteres jurídicos y políticos del ejército, su mision especial.* 3rd ed. Santa Fe: Universidad Nacional del Litoral, 1956.

Bienen, Henry, ed. *The Military Intervenes; Case Studies in Political Development.* Hartford, Conn.: Russel Sage, 1968.

Blanksten, George I. *Perón's Argentina.* New York: Russell & Russell, 1967.

Cáracano, Ramon J. *Guerra del Paraguay.* Buenos Aires: Domingo Viau j Cia, 1939.

Chilcote, Ronald H. *Military Intervention and developmental tendencies: preliminary analysis for study and research of Argentine experience.* Field Report Series 1. Riverside, Calif.: Latin American Research Program, University of California, 1966.

Ciria, Alberto. *Partidos y poder en la Argentina moderna.* Buenos Aires: Jorge Alvarez, 1964.

Del Mazo, Gabriel. *El Radicalismo.* Buenos Aires, 1957.

Fernández, Júlio A. "The Nationalism Syndrome in Argentina," *Journal of Inter-American Studies* (October, 1966).

Ferns, H.S. *Britain and Argentine in the Nineteenth Century.* Oxford: Clarenden Press, 1960.

Ferrer, Aldo. *The Argentine Economy.* Translated by Marjorie M. Urquidi. Berkeley and Los Angeles: University of California Press, 1967.

Florit, Carlos A. *Las fuerzas armadas y la guerra psicológica.* Buenos Aires: Editorial Arayu, 1963.

Galvez, Manuel. *Vida de Hipólito Irigoyen.* Buenos Aires, 1939.

Garcia Lupo, Rogelio. *La rebelión de los generales.* Buenos Aires: Editorial Jamcana, 1963.

Germani, Gino. *Política y sociedad en una época de transición.* Buenos Aires: Editorial Paidos, 1962.

Germani, Gino and K. H. Silvert, *Estructura social e intervención militar en America Latina.* Buenos Aires: Editorial Eudeba, 1965.

Goldwert, Marvin. "Dichotomies of Militarism in Argentina." *Orbis* (Fall, 1966).

————. "The Rise of Modern Militarism in Argentina." *The Hispanic American Historical Review* (May 1969).

Gonzales Calderon, Juan A. *El General Urquiza y la Organización Nacional.* Buenos Aires: Kraft, 1940.

Grondona, Mariano C. "La estructura civico-militar del neuvo estado argentino." *Aportes* (Paris), VI (October, 1967).

Horowitz, Irving Louis. "Militarism in Argentina." *New Society*, II. (June, 1963.)

Imaz, José Luis de. *Los que mandan.* Buenos Aires: Editorial Universitaria, 1964.

Johnson, Kenneth F. *Argentina's Mosaic of Discord 1966-1968.* Political Studies Series No. 6. Washington, D.C.: Institute for the Comparative Study of Political Systems, 1969.

————. *El espectro de la ideologia politica argentina.* Buenos Aires: Universidad Catolica Argentina, 1967.

Kane, Joseph P. ed. *Argentina Election Factbook, July 7, 1963*. Washington, D.C.: Institute for the Comparative Study of Political Systems, 1963.

Kennedy, John J. *Catholicism, Nationalism and Democracy in Argentina*. Notre Dame, Ind.: Notre Dame University Press, 1958.

Martinez Estrada, Miguel. *Radiografia de la Pampa*. 5th ed., Buenos Aires, 1961.

Maligne, Augusto A. *Historia militar de la Republica Argentina durante el siglo 1810 a 1910*. Buenos Aires: La Nacion, 1910.

Marks, Gilbert W. "The Gordian Knot: Political Conflict in Post-Perón Argentina." Albuquerque, University of New Mexico, October 1968 (Mimeographed).

McGann, Thomas F. *Argentina, the Divided Land*. Princeton, New Jersey: D. Van Nostrand, 1966.

North, Liisa. *Civil-Military Relations in Argentina, Chile and Peru*. Berkeley: Institute of International Studies of the University of California, 1966.

Ochoa de Eguileor, J. and V. R. Beltran. *Las Fuerzas Armadas Hablan*. Buenos Aires: Editorial Paidos, 1968.

Organizacion de Estados Americanos. Comite Interamericano de la Alianza para el Progreso. *El esfuerzo interno y las necesidades de financiamiento externo para el desarrollo de la Argentina*. Washington, D.C.: Union Panamericana, 1969.

Orsolini, Mario. *La crisis del ejercito*. Buenos Aires, 1964.

―――――. *Ejercito argentino y crecimiento nacional*. Buenos Aires, 1965.

Pendle, George. *Argentina*. 3rd. ed. London: Oxford University Press, 1965.

Perón, Juan Domingo. *Tres revoluciones*. Buenos Aires: Excorpion, 1963.

Poblete Troncoso, Moises & Ben Burnett. *The Rise of the Latin American Labor Movement*. New York, 1960.

Potash, Robert A. *The Army and Politics in Argentina, 1928-1945: Irigoyen to Perón*. Stanford, Calif.: Stanford, Stanford University Press, 1969.

―――――. "Argentina." *The Military in Latin American Sociopolitical Evolution: Four Case Studies*. Lyle McAlister, ed., Washington, D.C., American University, 1970.

Ramos, Jorge Abelardo. *Historia politica del ejército Argentino*. Buenos Aires: A. Pena Lillo, 1959.

―――――. *Revolución y Contrarevolución el la Argentina*. Buenos Aires: A. Pena Lillo, 1961.

Ramicone, Luis. *La organización gremial obrera en la actualidad*. Buenos Aires: Bases, 1963.

Ranis, Peter. "Background to the 1965 Argentine Elections." *The World Today*, XXI (May, 1965).

Rennie, Ysabel. *The Argentine Republic*. New York: McMillan, 1945.

Rodriguez, Coronel Augusto G. *Reseña historica de ejército argentino (1862-1930)*. Buenos Aires: Dirección de Estudios Historicos de la Secretaria de Guerra, 1964.

Romero, José Luis. *A History of Argentine Political Thought*. Introduction and translation (of the third edition) by Thomas F. McGann. Stanford, Cal.: Stanford University Press, 1968.

Rowe, Leo S. *The Federal System of the Argentine Republic*, Washington, D.C., 1921.

Rowe, James W. "Argentina: An Election Retrospect." *American Universities Field Staff Service Reports*. East Coast South America Series, V. XI, No. 1, February 1964.

―――――. "Argentina's Durable Peronists. A Twentieth Anniversary Note." *American Universities Field Service Reports*. East Coast South America Series, V. XII, No. 2, April 1966.

―――――. "Argentina's Restless Military." *American Universities Field Staff Service Reports*. East Coast South America Series, V. XI, No. 2, May 1964.

130

_____. *The Argentine Elections of 1963: An Analysis.* Washington, D.C.: Institute for the Comparative Study of Political Systems, 1963.

_____. "Ongaňia's Argentina: The First Four Months." *American Universities Field Staff Service Reports.* East Coast South America Series, V. XIII, No. 7. November 1966.

Saldias, Adolfo. *Historia de la Confederación Argentina.* Buenos Aires: El Ateneo, 1951.

Sanchez, Viamonte, Carlos. *El Ultimo Caudillo.* Buenos Aires, 1930.

Saravia, Jose Manuel. *Argentina 1959: un estudio sociológico.* Buenos Aires: Ediciones del Atlantico, 1959.

Sarobe, Jose Maria. *Memorias sobre la revolución del 6 de Septiembre de 1930: Al servicio de la democracia.* S. R. L. Buenos Aires, Ediciones Gures, 1957.

Scobie, James R. *Argentina: A City and a Nation.* New York: Oxford University Press, 1964.

Sierra, Vicente D. *Historia de la Argentina.* Buenos Aires: Garriaga, 1962.

Silvert, K. H. "The Costs of Anti-Nationalism in Argentina." *Expectant Peoples: Nationalism and Development.* Edited by K. H. Silvert, New York: Random House, 1963.

Sommi, Luis V. *La Revolución del 90.* Buenos Aires: Pueblo de America, 2d. ed., 1957.

Springer, P. B. "Disunity and Disorder: Factional Politics in the Argentine Military." *The Military Intervenes: Case Studies in Political Development.* Edited by H. Bienen. New York: Russell Sage, 1968.

Sueldo, Horacio. *Fuerzas Armadas: Argentina,* 1930-1960. Buenos Aires: Editorial Sur. 1961.

Van Doorn, Jacques, ed., *Military Professions and Military Regimes.* The Hague: Mouton, 1967.

Villegas, Osiris. *Politicas y Estratégias Para el Desarrollo y la Seguridad Nacional.* Buenos Aires: Circulo Militar, 1969.

Whitaker, Arthur P. *Argentine Upheaval.* New York: Praeger, 1956.

_____. "Left and Right Extremism in Argentina." *Current History,* XI-IV, (February, 1963).

FOOTNOTES

FOREWORD

[1]The more definitive studies include, for example, Samuel P. Huntington's *The Soldier and the State* (1959); Morris Janowitz's *The Professional Soldier* (1960); and Samuel Finer's *The Man on Horseback* (1964).

[2]The more extensive studies include, for example, *The Role of the Military in Underdeveloped Countries* (1962), edited by John J. Johnson; Morris Janowitz's *The Military in the Political Development of New Nations* (1964); and H. Daalder's *The Role of the Military in Emerging Countries* (1962). See also *The Politics of Developing Areas*, by Gabriel Almond and James S. Coleman (1960).

[3]Among other of the Center's efforts, a major study of the political and socioeconomic role of the military in Latin America sponsored by the Directorate of Doctrine, Concepts and Objectives of Headquarters, United States Air Force, has been completed under the direction of Dr. Clyde C. Wooten, Associate Director of the Center. This study included case studies of 12 Latin American countries. A book reflecting the results of this and subsequent research is under preparation by Dr. Wooten and Colonel Charles D. Corbett, a research associate of the Center and the author of the present study.

[2]The text of Acheson's letter to the Defense Department opposing the bill appears in an April 1947 supplement to *Human Events*.

[3]See US 82nd Congress, 1st Session, House Foreign Affairs Committee, *Hearings on MSA for 1951*, Washington, 1951, pp. 1080-1082, and Senate Foreign Relations Committee, *Hearings on MSA for 1951*, Washington, 1951, p. 38. *Department of State Bulletin*, March 30, 1954, pp. 463-464, posited the following fundamental assumptions for US hemispheric security policy: 1) that the hemisphere was threatened by communist agression both from within and without; 2) that the security of strategic areas of the hemisphere and of inter-American lines of communication were vital to the security of every American country; 3) that the protection of these strategic areas and communications was a common responsibility.

[4]*The Mutual Security Act of 1959*, section 105(b)(4). See also US 86th Congress, 1st Session, Senate Foreign Relations Committee, *Report on Hearings, the Mutual Security Act of 1959*, Washington, 1959, pp. 73-74.

[5]See US 86th Congress, 2nd Session, Senate Foreign Relations Committee, *United States-Latin American Relations*, Washington, 1960, pp. 10-51.

[6]See US Congress, 1st Session, Senate Foreign Relations Committee, *Hearings on International Development and Security*, Washington, 1961.

[7]Professor Lieuwen later posited a cause-and-effect relationship between the actions of the leader of the unit that stormed the palace and his US-inspired training in counterinsurgency. "Neo-Militarism in Latin America: the Kennedy Administration's Inadequate Response," *Inter-American Economic Affairs*, Spring 1963, p. 15.

[8]L. N. McAlister, "Recent Research and Writings on the Role of the Military in Latin America," *Latin American Research Review*, Vol. II, No. 1 (Fall 1967), pp. 28-29.

[9]*The New Leader*, October 14, 1963.

[10]*Five Years of the Alliance for Progress: An Appraisal*, Inter-American Affairs Press, Washington, 1967, p. 155.

[11]US Congress, 1st Session, House Appropriations Committee, *Hearings on Foreign Operations Appropriation for 1965*, Part I, pp. 399-400.

[12]Quoted in Hanson, *op. cit.*, p. 158.

[13]Quoted in *Inter-American Economic Affairs*, Vol. 21, No. 4 (Spring 1968), p. 84.

[14]See *The West Point Conference on Latin America Problems*, US Military Academy, Final Report, 1964, p. 56.

[15]George I. Blanksten, "Political Groups in Latin America," in John H. Kautsky, ed., *Political Change in Undeveloped Countries* (New York: John Wiley and Sons, 1962), p. 142.

[16]A. F. Shul'govskii, "Urgent Problems of Latin American Studies," *Vestnik Akademii Nauk (Herald of the Academy of Sciences)*, No. 8, August 1970, p. 108.

[17]B. Ponomarev, "Topical Problems in the Theory of the Revolutionary Process," *Kommunist*, No. 17, October 1971, p. 59.

[18]*Ibid.*

[19]*Ibid.*, p. 74.

[20]A. F. Shul'govskii, "Latin America: The Army and Politics," *Latinskaia Amerika*, No. 4, 1971, pp. 8-13.

[21]*Ibid.*, p. 13.

[22]Kh. Kobo and G. I. Mirskii, "Concerning Some Peculiarities of the Evolution of the Armies of the Latin American Continent," *Latinskaia Amerika*, No. 4, 1971, p. 52.

[23]A. F. Shul'govskii, "Latin America: The Army and Politics," *op. cit.*, pp. 34-36.

[24]*Ibid.*, p. 39.

[25]*Ibid.*

[26]*Ibid.*, p. 40.

[27]US Department of State, *Communist States and Developing Countries*, Research Study RECS-3, May 15, 1971, p. iii.

[28]*The Third World – Problems and Prospects* (Moscow: Progress Publishers, 1970). p. 27.

[29]Kobo and Mirskii, "Concerning Some Peculiarities of the Evolution of the Armies of the Latin American Continent," *op. cit.*, p. 47.

AN INTRODUCTORY OVERVIEW

[1]Recent scholarly works have begun to redress the balance somewhat. Among them: Alfred Stepan, *The Military in Politics: Changing Patterns in Brazil* (Princeton, N.J.: Princeton University Press, 1971); Jose Nun, *Latin America: The Hegemonic Crisis and the Military Coup*, Institute of International Studies Monograph (Berkeley: University of California Press, 1969); Luigi R. Einaudi and Alfred C. Stepan, *Latin American Institutional Development: Changing Military Perspectives in Peru and Brazil* (Santa Monica, Calif.: RAND Corporation, 1971); Lyle McAlister, et al., *The Military in Latin American Sociopolitical Evolution: Four Case Studies* (Washington, Center for Research in Social Systems, the American University, 1970). Robert Potash's *The Army and Politics in Argentina, 1928-1945* (Stanford, Calif.: Stanford University Press, 1969), provides an excellent in-depth analysis of an earlier period which will be extended in a new work. Einaudi is preparing a book-length work on Peru.

[2]For example, see Edwin Lieuwen, *Arms and Politics in Latin America* (New York, Praeger, 1961).

[3]*Ibid.* For the journalistic view see Tad Szulc, *Twilight of the Tyrants* (New York, Holt, 1959).

[4]*Time*, December 27, 1968. p. 23.

133

[5]Alfred Vagts, *A History of Militarism* (New York: W. W. Norton & Co., 1937), p. 11.

[6]Kurt Lang, *Military Sociology* (London: Basil Blackwell, 1965), p. 18.

[7]*Encyclopedia of the Social Sciences*, Vol. I (New York: McMillan Co., 1933), p. 446.

[8]See Peter Calvert, *Latin America: Internal Conflict and International Peace* (New York: St. Martins Press, 1969).

[9]The phrase is from Edwin Lieuwen, Senate Foreign Relations Committee, *United States–Latin American Relations*, 86th Congress, 2nd Session, 1960, p. 51.

[10]Samuel P. Huntington, *The Soldier and the State* (Cambridge, Mass.: Belknap Press, 1957). pp. 7-18.

[11]Liisa North, *Civil-Military Relations in Argentina, Chile and Peru* (Politics of Modernization Series, No. 2, Institute of International Studies, Berkeley: University of California, 1966), p. 14.

[12]For a critical analysis of Huntington's model from a US military point of view, see Lt. Col. Zeb Bradford and Maj. James Murphy, "A New Look at the Military Profession," *Army*, Vol. 19 (February 1969), pp. 58-64.

[13]"El Profesionalismo Militar en el Ejército Argentino," *Temas Militares*, Vol. I, No. 3 (March-April 1967). pp. 9-16.

[14]One Brazilian writer on military affairs says the academies produce a man with a singular kind of image of the national reality, "very subjective and very romantic . . . the nation is an idolized and venerated woman, a kind of fragile mother figure that demands all from her sons. Patriotism is characterized as a manifestation of pious virtue. The nation is perceived as an abstract quality that claims blind and eternal dedication." Vicente Barreto, "La Presencia Militarista," in *Temas Militares*, Vol. I, No. 3 (March-April 1967), pp. 35-39. Although similar beliefs are quite common among Latin American intellectuals, the author's familiarity with several academies and association with cadets from seven countries at the U.S. Army School of the Americas, leads him to believe that Señor Barreto's formulation is overstated, although it might not have been twenty years ago.

[15]A place of residence and work where a large number of like-situated individuals, cut off from the wider society for an appreciable period of time, together lead an enclosed, formally administered life. Erving Coffman, *Asylums* (Garden City, New York, 1961) p. 13.

[16]The full course is three years in Argentina, Brazil, Bolivia, and Chile, two years in Ecuador, Paraguay, Peru, and Uruguay, one year in Colombia and Venezuela.

[17]Einaudi and Stepan, *Latin American Institutional Development, op. cit.,* p. 81.

[18]*Ibid.,* p. 25.

[19]These data and those immediately following were gathered by the author in visits to various military schools of the region in 1970 and 1972.

[20]There is, however, some work on the subject. See, for example, Rogelio García Lupo, "Los Alsogaray: Una dinastia militar" in *Politica*, Vol. VII, No. 71-72 (March-April 1968), pp. 29-39. The article traces the long affiliation of the Alsogaray family, traditionally respected in the Argentine Army, with "liberal" political factions.

[21]All general staff schools in Latin America routinely use division and even corps-sized operations as teaching vehicles, many drawn directly from World War II European battles. There has been a recent tendency to make staff college exercises conform more closely to actual capabilities in terms of the size of units employed in map maneuvers (i.e., regiments and brigades instead of divisions and corps) but little inclination to limit employment of highly sophisticated forces (i.e., armor and helicopter units) that are not likely to be in Latin American inventories for some years. As one school commandant explained to the author, he had waited over 10 years after learning armor tactics at Fort Knox to see the first armored infantry unit formed in his army, but when that time had come there were officers who knew how to employ and maintain it.

[22]Some 765 Latin American officers had attended Command and General Staff courses in the United States through 1969, according to data gathered by Ernest W. Lefever of the Brookings Institution and made available to the author. Through 1971, another 246 had graduated from the course at the U.S. Army School of the Americas in Panama, which is essentially the 40-week course from the Command and General Staff College at Fort Leavenworth translated into Spanish.

[23]See, for example, Huntington, *The Soldier and the State, op. cit.*, p. 1. The two primary components of national security policy are military security policy (the external threat) and internal security policy (the threat of subversion). Huntington's formulation of "situational security policy" is particularly attractive to Argentine theorists. Situational security policy "is concerned with the threat of erosion resulting from long-term changes in social, economic, demographic, and political conditions tending to reduce the relative power of the state."

[24]Alfred Stepan uses these classifications in his excellent study of the Brazilian military. The author has generalized them somewhat for the purposes here.

[25]For representative formulations that include some or most of these concepts, see Francisco Arias Pellerano, "La participacion politica de las fuerzas armadas," *Estrategia*, No. 2 (July-August 1969), pp. 23-39; General Juan E. Gugliamelli, "Las fuerzas armadas y su mission general prioritaria: desarrollo integral del potencial nacional," *Circumil*, No. 691 (January-March 1970). pp. 123-144; General Osiris G. Villegas, *Politicas y Estratégias, op. cit.*; General Lyra Tavares, "El ejército brasileño y la actual coyuntura nacional," *Estrategia*, No. 2 (July-August 1969), pp. 43-56; Gen. Edgardo Mercado Jarrin, "Politica y Estratégia Militar en la Guerra Anti-Subversiva," *Revista Militar del Peru* (November-December 1967), pp. 4-33; General Alfredo Ovando Candia, "Carta-Mensaje Del Gral. Ovando a Los JJ. y OO. de las FF.AA.," *Revista* Militar (Bolivia) (April-June 1969), pp. 151-154.

[26]Stepan, *The Military in Politics, op. cit.*

[27]From a copy of the speech in the author's possession. General Mercado was named army commander in January 1972.

[28]See, for example, President Velasco's 1971 Army Day speech attacking elements seeking "to undermine the unity of the armed forces" in *La Prensa* (Lima), December 11, 1971.

[29]*Latin American Institutional Development, op. cit.*, p. 61.

BOLIVIA AS A CASE STUDY

[1]Descriptions of the battles of this era, with maps and troop lists, are included in Col. M. Fernando Wilde Cavero, *Historia Militar de Bolivia* (La Paz, n.p., 1963).

[2]Harold Osborne, *Bolivia: A Land Divided* (3rd ed., rev., London, Oxford University Press, 1964), p. 64.

[3]Information on the academy (*Colegio Militar*) and its history appears from time to time in the *Revista Militar* (hereafter referred to as *RM*) but data must be cross-checked. A fairly accurate historical article appears in the issue of July-September 1958, pp. 73-77. For information on the foreign missions, see Julio Diaz, *Historia del Ejército de Bolivia 1825-1932* (La Paz, Imprenta Central del Ejército, 1940), pp. 760-775.

[4]A brief history of the Command and General Staff School appeared in *RM* (October-December 1969), pp. 63-70.

[5]An eyewitness account of the 1943 coup by a German advisor to the Bolivian Army may be found in Col. Kurt Conrad Arnade, "The Technique of Coup d'Etat in Latin America," *United Nations World* (February 1950), pp. 21-25. The MNR side is explained

in José Fellman Velarde, *Victor Paz Estenssoro, el hombre y la revolución* (La Paz, E. Burrillo, 1955), pp. 117-133.

[6]Colonel Carlos Manuel Silva, "La Justicia Militar y Los Guerrillas," *RM* (January-March 1968), pp. 81-82.

[7]*Ibid.*, p. 82.

[8]Nazario Pardo Valle, in his pro-MNR *Calendario Histórico de La Revolución* (La Paz, E. Burrillo, 1957), says that by mid-1950 over 260 MNR militants and officers had been tried by military courts for their part in the 1949 uprising, and notes that 53 discharged officers were reincorporated by the government after the MNR victory of 1952. Velarde, in *Victor Paz*, says that the army lost over 300 field grade officers to exile or discharge between 1946 and 1949, and that most of them joined the MNR.

[9]His letter was published in *RM* (March 1952) p. 1.

[10]Alberto Ostria Gutierréz, *The Tragedy of Bolivia* (New York, Devin-Adair Co., 1956), among others holds that about 80 percent of the officer corps was discharged or exiled.

[11]In an interview with William H. Brill. See Brill, *Military Civic Action in Bolivia* (unpublished Ph.D. dissertation, University of Michigan, 1966), pp. 81-83.

[12]The list appeared in *RM* (January-March 1949).

[13]From an Olmos speech published in *RM* (April-May 1953), p. 186.

[14]*Discursos y Mensajes* (Buenos Aires, Ed. Meridiano, 1953) p. 8.

[15]*RM* (April-June 1968), pp. 151-152. Other officers have given the author similar accounts.

[16]For budget information, see Joseph E. Loftus, *Latin American Defense Expenditures: 1938-1965* (Santa Monica, Calif., Rand Corp., January 1968), p. 37, and James W. Wilkie, *The Bolivian Revolution and US Aid Since 1952* (Los Angeles, University of California Press, 1969), pp. 60-61. Charles W. Anderson, *Politics and Economic Change in Latin America* (Princeton, N.J., D. Van Nostrand Co., 1967), using Bolivian Central Bank statistics, indicates that 24 percent of the public budget was devoted to defense in 1951, 14 percent in 1952, and 7 percent in 1957 (pp. 330-331).

[17]Paz' first message and reorganization plans were published in *RM* (January 1953).

[18]*RM* (August-September 1954), pp. 131-135.

[19]*RM* (January-April 1956), p. 68.

[20]See the speech by Minister of Defense Col. Armando Prudencio in *La Nación*, April 1, 1954. Col. Olmos became Minister of Defense in 1955, while Colonels Luis F. Rodriguez Bidegain, Rene Gonzalez Torres, Armando Fortún Sanjinés, and a few other Paz favorites dominated the army high command during the MNR's first term.

[21]The School of Arms had about 20 graduates from its ten-month advanced course in 1955, the Command and General Staff School ten from its two-year course. The widow of ex-president Villarroel spoke at the graduation ceremonies of the latter. *RM* (January-April 1956), p. 38.

[22]Officers who studied in Panama or the US during these years received five US dollars before leaving Bolivia, and normally were completely dependent thereafter on the small per diem paid by the US Government. Among the trainees of those years was the current president, then Captain Hugo Banzer Suarez, who stood number one in his motor transportation officer course in Panama in 1956.

[23]James M. Malloy, *Bolivia, The Uncompleted Revolution* (Pittsburgh, University of Pittsburgh Press, 1970), pp. 216-280, sees the politics of the 1952-1964 period of the revolution as primarily a battle over alternative models of development, with the ideological struggle raging principally around two models: a "democratic bourgeois society" and a "government of workers and peasants." The former was projected as a state-capitalist model dominated by a progressive middle class elite, the latter as a state-socialist model run by a mixed elite with preponderant working class representa-

tion. He identifies three phases of the struggle, roughly coinciding with presidential terms, during the 12-year period of MNR control of the revolution. From 1952 to 1956 Paz and the party elite established a state-socialist system based on a center-left coalition that attempted to satisfy their development aims (accumulation for investment) and the aims of the party's worker-urban middle-class supporters (consumption). The result was wild inflation and eventually an intolerable burden on the urban middle sectors. During President Siles Zuazo's term from 1956 to 1960, a center-right coalition was formed which shifted the burden of social costs to worker groups. Since these included the armed militias of the economically important mines, internal violence and economic stagnation resulted. In the last phase of MNR control, Paz formed a new center-right coalition, this time on a "state-capitalist" model, supported economically by the US under the Alliance for Progress.

[24]*RM* (May-August 1956), p. 31.

[25]Guillermo Bedregal, "El Problema Militar en Bolivia," *Politica*, (Vol. V, No. 54, October 1966, n.p.).

[26]*Ibid.* For an excellent analysis of Siles' political and economic program, and of the pressures bearing upon him, see Malloy, *Bolivia,* pp. 235-280.

[27]The MNR also armed "commando" squads in the population centers. Guillermo Lora, an unsympathetic historian, describes these bands, which he claims were often mercenaries paid with whiskey and cash, in *La Revolucion Boliviana* (La Paz, n.p., 1964).

[28]Adapted from tables in Wilkie, *The Bolivian Revolution,* pp. 60-61. The Agency for International Development *Economic Data Book* (1968 edition), p. 10, lists total military assistance for the 1946-1967 period as 18.7 million dollars, but yearly totals are given only for 1966 (2.4 million) and 1967 (2.9 million).

[29]Willard F. Barber and C. Neale Ronning, *Internal Security and Military Power: Counterinsurgency and Civic Action in Latin America* (Ohio State University Press, 1966), p. 149.

[30]Most sources indicate a rise in the percentage of government expenditures devoted to the military from about seven percent in 1957 to between 12 and 13 percent in 1963. Wilkie, *The Bolivian Revolution,* gives 12.6 for 1962, 12.4 for 1963 (pp. 60-61). Loftus, *Latin American Defense Expenditures,* shows a rise in absolute terms from 2.4 million (1960 US) dollars in 1958 to 6 million in 1963 (p. 11). Colonel Julio Sanchez, Ambassador to Washington, is quoted in Brill, *Military Civic Action,* as saying that the army got $7.5 million, or about 13 percent of the national budget in 1963 (p. 83).

[31]Richard Patch has written extensively on *campesino* affairs. For an account of the early years of peasant league organization, see his essay "Bolivia and US Assistance" in *Social Change in Latin America Today* (New York, Vintage Books, 1960), pp. 119-142.

[32]*Actuaciones parlamentarias del Ministro de Defensa Nacional, Sr. Juan Luis Gutiérrez Grainer, en los años 1961 and 1962* (La Paz, 1963).

[33]Supreme Decree No. 05441, March 21, 1960.

[34]Supreme Decree No. 0741-65, April 1961.

[35]*RM* (April-June 1968).

[36]CITE was formed in 1963 with officers trained by an Argentine advisory group, according to an anniversary article appearing in *RM* (July-August 1968), p. 222. The acronym came to refer to both the training center and its operational parachute battalion.

[37]Ronant Monje Roca, an MNR militant from his junior officer days, was the first commander. Monje was prominent in the "military cell" of the MNR and used the *Revista de la Fuerza Fluvial y Lacustre* (River and Lake Force Magazine) to push the party line. After the ouster of Paz in 1964, Ovando replaced Monje and his entire staff, who had adopted naval titles, with army colonels. The River and Lake Force was

subsequently rechristened the Bolivian Navy, and the officers once again use naval titles.

[38]Linares, Bolivian president from 1857 to 1861, is described by Osborne, *Bolivia*, as "a capable and upright administrator who carried autocracy to the point of fanaticism and suppressed every stirring of opposition with no less ruthless ferocity than his predecessors" (p. 57).

[39]Interviews to this effect with Barrientos and two colonels from Ovando's staff appear in William H. Brill, *Military Intervention in Bolivia: The Overthrow of Paz Estenssoro and the MNR* (Washington, Institute for the Comparative Study of Political Systems, 1967), pp. 23-29.

[40]*RM* (February-March 1965), pp. 7-11.

[41]A good article on the *Colegio*, which includes a description of the admission process, curriculum and organization, appears in *RM* (July-September 1969).

[42]The author visited the *Colegio* in July 1970, and also enjoyed a close association with Bolivian cadets at the US Army School of the Americas. Much of the "subjective" content of this section derives from that association. He also benefited from a questionnaire kindly completed by the *Colegio* staff in 1971.

[43]Articles on the schools appear regularly in the *RM*, usually in conjunction with the celebration of graduations or anniversaries. Data are frequently inconsistent between issues and one must review a large number of articles spanning several years to compile a coherent and complete picture. This description results from such an effort.

[44]Promotion criteria, territorial organization, and legal norms governing the army are spelled out in minute detail in the *Ley Orgánica del Ejército*. The basic law dates from 1927, with major revisions in 1953, 1966, and 1969. Major reorganizations are treated frequently in the *Revista Militar*. For example, the issue of July-September 1969 includes a detailed and quite complete description of the divisional organization and functions, headquarters locations, etc.

[45]Promotion lists are published in the La Paz newspapers and in *Los Tiempos* of Cochabamba. Fairly complete biographical data, particularly on career patterns, appeared in the *RM* of January-March 1968 for the officers on the list of that year. Other information in this section comes from interviews with the principals or acquaintances. The officers involved are Generals Hugo Ortiz Mattos, Remberto Iriarte Paz, Alberto Guzmán Soriano, Eduardo Méndez Pereyra, Efrain Guachalla Ibañez, Cesar Ruiz Veladre, Juan Lechin Suárez, Marcos Vasquez Sempértegui, Jesús Via Solis, David La Fuente Soto, Sigfredo Montero Velasco, Luis A. Reque Teran, Gonzalo Guzmán Agudo, Hector Fuentes Ibañez, Eufronio Padilla Caero, Jaime Flores Becerra, Jaime Paz Galarza, Rogelio Miranda, and J. Zenteno Anaya.

[46]One exception was Juan Lechin Suarez, who served for four years as chief of the Bolivian Mining Commission (COMIBOL) during its most productive period, from 1964 to 1968. He graduated second in his 1942 *Colegio* class, and is a graduate of the US Army Artillery School and the Command and General Staff College at Fort Leavenworth, Kansas.

[47]The acronym refers to the state oil monopoly. There is a similarity here to the programs and speeches of Peru's President Velasco, but Ovando's article preceded the Peruvian coup of October 3, 1968 by some months. He was, however, familiar with developmental philosophies being taught in the Peruvian Army's Center for Higher Military Studies. For an analysis of the latter, see Luigi Einaudi's essay in Einaudi and Alfred Stepan, *Latin American Institutional Development*.

[48]The Interior Minister, Antonio Arguedas, fled Bolivia after admitting that he had sent the diary to Castro, and later charged that he had been forced to act as a CIA agent for over four years. He returned voluntarily to face a military trial. See the analysis by Malcom Browne in the *New York Times* of September 17, 1968 and November 8, 1968. The trial records by some fluke fell into the public domain, and the La Paz newspaper *Presencia* published a series on the whole affair during the first week of April 1969 that revealed publicly for the first time how severely the scandals had shaken the government.

[49]See *Presencia*, May 24, 1968, and the Ronant Monje Roca letter in *Los Tiempos* of July 2, 1968.

[50]*New York Times*, September 27, 1969.

[51]*Marcha*, December 19, 1969. The interview also appears in *Christianismo y Revolucion*, April 23, 1970.

[52]The speech was partially reproduced in *Estrategia* (Buenos Aires, No. 4, November-December 1969), pp. 22-24.

[53]Einaudi, *Latin American Institutional Development*, quotes a strikingly similar formulation made by a sociologist advisor to the military regime in Peru in 1971 (p. 62).

[54]*El Diario*, La Paz, December 16, 1969.

[55]Richard W. Patch, *American Universities Field Staff Reports*, West Coast South America Series, XVII, No. 1, December, 1969.

[56]*Ibid.*

[57]Copy in the hands of the author. The *New York Times* carried a running account of the coup in the editions of October 5-9, 1970.

[58]*RM* (October-December 1970), p. 125.

[59]*Ibid.*, p. 16.

[60]*New York Times*, January 11, 1971.

[61]This account comes largely from US newspaper articles read carefully between the lines, and some educated conjecture. The *New York Times* carried a running account of the coup in the editions of August 20-25, 1971.

[62]"Subjective" control is achieved by causing military officers to identify with the political group in control of the state; "objective" control is achieved by turning the military inward to its specific duties and competence. *The Soldier and the State* (New York, Vintage Books, 1964), pp. 80-85.

[63]This formulation is from José Nun. Nun points out that structural factors generate a chronic tendency toward instability, while circumstantial factors are accidental, operate at short term, and tend to stem from structural factors. *Latin America: The Hegemonic Crisis and the Military Coup.*

[64]Over half the population is under 20; only 19 percent is over 40. Agency for International Development, *Economic Data Book: Latin America* (Washington, US Government Printing Office, December 1968), p. 8.

ARGENTINA AS A CASE STUDY

[1]For a sketch of Alsina's career, see *Diccionario de la República Argentina* (Buenos Aires, 1950), p. 38.

[2]Col. Augusto G. Rodríguez, *Reseña histórica del ejército argentino* (1862-1930) (Buenos Aires, 1930), pp. 72-85.

[3]See, for example, Gen. Roca's speech to the London Board of Trade in 1887, welcoming British capital and interest in Argentina. Quoted in José Luis Romero, *Las Ideas Políticas en Argentina* (Mexico, 1946), p. 193.

[4]For a general discussion of the economic background of the period, see Ysabel F. Rennie, *The Argentine Republic* (New York, 1945), pp. 172-178. Also John J. Johnson, *Political Change in Latin America* (Stanford, California, 1958), pp. 95-97.

[5]For background on church-state relations at this time, see J. Lloyd Mecham, *Church and State in Latin America* (Chapel Hill, North Carolina, 1934), esp. pp. 294-302. Also

Jorge Abelardo Ramos, *Revolución y Contra Revolución en la Argentina* (Buenos Aires, 1961), p. 198.

[6]Quoted in Romero, *Las Ideas,* p. 211.

[7]This revolt is discussed in Gabriel del Mazo, *El Radicalismo* (Buenos Aires, 1957), p. 606.

[8]This sketch is taken principally from the following works: Manuel Galvez, *Vida de Hipólito Irigoyen* (Buenos Aires, 1939; Carlos Sanches Viamonte, *El Último Caudillo* (Buenos Aires, 1930); Del Mazo, *El Radicalismo*; Harold E. Davis, *Latin American Leaders* (New York, 1949); Hipolito Irigoyen, *Mi vida y mi doctrina* (Buenos Aires, 1957); Carlos J. Rodriguez, *Irigoyen, su revolución politica y social* (Buenos Aires, 1943).

[9]An excellent discussion of the 1905 revolution and the military reforms that followed it may be found in Dario Canton, "Military Interventions in Argentina," a paper presented at the London Conference on Armed Forces and Society in September 1967. The paper was later published in Jacques van Doorn, ed., *Military Professions and Military Regimes* (The Hague, 1967).

[10]Galvez, *Vida*, p. 119.

[11] Ministerio del Interior, Departmento Nacional de Trabajo, *Investigaciones Sociales Serie A.*, No. 5, 1914; see also Ministerio de Hacienda, Direccion General de Estadistica de la Nación, *Boletin* 229, 1914; and United Nations Department of Economic Affairs, *Economic Survey of Latin America, 1949.*

[12]The best account of the pre-coup alignments and maneuvers is in José María Sarobe, *Memórias sobre la revolución del 6 de septiembre de 1930: Al servicio de la democracia* (Buenos Aires, 1957).

[13]United Nations, *Statistical Abstract of Argentina*, 1948, p. 9.

[14]Pan American Union, *Labor Trends and Social Welfare in Latin America*, 1943, p. 1; and *Monthly Labor Review*, V. 52, pp. 1123-1125 (May 1941).

[15]*Monthly Labor Review*, V. 52, (May 1941), p. 1124.

[16]For a discussion of labor relations during the period, see Robert J. Alexander, *Labor Relations in Argentina, Brazil, and Chile* (Chicago, 1962). Also Moises Poblete Troncoso and Ben B. Burnett, *The Rise of the Latin American Labor Movement* (New York, 1960).

[17]An analysis of the immediate post-Perón period is contained in Fritz L. Hoffman, "Perón and After," *Hispanic American Historical Review* (November 1956), pp. 510-527.

[18]Exhaustive accounts of these events, and those described later, appear in the excellent Buenos Aires dailies. The weekly column "La Semana Politica" in *La Nación* is particularly valuable to the researcher. Buenos Aires also counts several good weekly news magazines. *Confirmado* appears to be the best in terms of accuracy of basic information.

[19]For a discussion of armed forces' attitudes toward communism at this time, see Mario Orsolini, *La crisis del ejército* (Buenos Aires, 1964), pp. 51-53, and Carlos Florit, *Las fuerzas armadas y la guerra psicológica* (Buenos Aires, 1963), pp. 62-63.

[20]The author was in Argentina from 1963 to 1965 during which time he was acquainted with a large number of officers of all ranks from both factions. Much of the discussion of army attitudes and divisions comes from personal knowledge.

[21]Ties between the UCRP and the Colorados were notorious and well known. See Philip B. Springer, "Disunity and Disorder: Factional Politics in the Argentine Military," in *The Military Intervenes: Case Studies in Political Development*, Henry Bienen, ed. (Hartford, Conn., 1968), pp. 146-168. Also *La Nación*, November 2, 1964.

[22]James W. Rowe, "Ongañia's Argentina: The First Four Months," *American Univer-*

sities Field Staff Reports, East Coast South America Series, V. XIII, No. 7, November 1966.

[23]The Revolutionary Act, with its annexes, is reproduced in Osiris G. Villegas, *Politicas y Estrategias Para el Desarrollo y la Seguridad Nacional* (Buenos Aires, 1969), pp. 309-321.

[24]Agency for International Development, *Latin America–Economic Growth Trends*, E/CN. 12/825, Washington (December 1968), pp. 11-88, 11-101.

[25]The quote is from an August 1969 speech Guglialmelli gave at the Círculo Militar, reproduced in *Circumil* (January-March 1970), pp. 130-131. His views on the military role in the national development process appeared regularly in the *Revista de la Escuela Superior de Guerra* when he was director. See, for example, the issue of March-April 1965, p. 8.

[26]Francisco Arias Pellerano, "La participación política de las fuerzas armadas," *Estrategia*, No. 2 (July-August 1969), pp. 28-39.

[27]The text appeared in *La Prensa* of June 21, 1970.

[28]See note 23.

[29]*Confirmado*, June 24-30, 1970, pp. 12-16.

[30]*Ibid.*

[31]See the description of the five-year plan in the *New York Times* of December 25, 1970 and Levingstone's address to the Special Meeting of the Board of Governors of the Inter-American Development Bank in Buenos Aires on March 1, 1971; reproduced in *Proceedings* of the ICB, pp. 15-18.

[32]This strange attempt was described to the author–during a visit to Buenos Aires in January-February 1972–as a "typical cloak and dagger maneuver by a career intelligence officer." The speaker was a high-ranking army officer who had been close to the events. The international air mail edition of *La Nación* gave considerable coverage to Levingstone's intrigues following his ouster.

[33]*La Nación*, April 5, 1971.

[34]In 1930 the personnel of the armed forces numbered about 50,000. By 1943, on the eve of the coup that opened the path to power for Perón, that figure had doubled. When he was overthrown in 1955 the forces had grown to about 200,000. Strength decreased somewhat after 1955, and in 1967 total armed forces manpower was about 137,000.

[35]For example, the 50 or so brigadier generals on active duty in the army meet annually to draw up the order of merit list for lieutenant colonels. After review and approval by the army commander, the list becomes the basis for promotions within grade allocations to colonel, and is seldom if ever modified by other authorities.

[36]General Benjamín Rattenbach, "El Professionalismo Militar en el Ejército Argentino," *Temas Militares,* Vol. 1, No. 3 (August 1967), pp. 9-16.

[37]Villegas, *Politicas y Estrategias*, p. 72.

INDEX

SELECTED 1972 MONOGRAPHS IN INTERNATIONAL AFFAIRS

SOVIET CIVIL DEFENSE 1969-1970, Leon Goure ($1.75).

Describes developments in the Soviet civil defense program and related activities at the turn of the decade. Deals with current Soviet views on nuclear war and the role of civil defense in ensuring victory and the survival of the Soviet state, and recent Soviet efforts to improve their long-standing program for the protection of the population and economy from attacks with nuclear, chemical and bacteriological weapons, and for maintaining critical production and popular morale.

THE LATIN AMERICAN MILITARY AS A SOCIO-POLITICAL FORCE: CASE STUDIES OF BOLIVIA AND ARGENTINA, Charles D. Corbett with a Foreword by Mose L. Harvey ($3.95, $4.95 hardcover).

A unique attempt to study the Latin American military as a complex institution within complex and widely differing societies, but one which, regardless of differences as between countries, has long represented a powerful political elite throughout the region and one which under the pressures of developmental demands promises to become of ever greater importance in the years ahead. The study gives special attention to the effects of the professionalization process and other institutional developments, including especially the development of programs for advanced study, on the military's socio-political propensities and capabilities, and then subjects generalized assessments to a detailed consideration of particular conditions in Bolivia and Argentina. Throughout the study, as the Foreword emphasizes, is implicit evidence that US concepts and attitudes with respect to the role of the Latin American military are ill founded, leading to possibly serious errors in US policy determinations.

SCIENCE AND TECHNOLOGY AS AN INSTRUMENT OF SOVIET POLICY, Mose L. Harvey, Leon Goure, and Vladimir Prokofieff with a Foreword by Ambassador Foy D. Kohler ($4.95, $5.95 hardcover).

Provides a documentary and analytical accounting of the Soviet strategy for science and technology under contemporary conditions, and of current Soviet efforts to attain supremacy in "this main arena in the competition between socialism and capitalism," including "competition for military superiority." Examines the concern of the leadership over obstacles hindering these efforts; measures being taken to overcome obstacles, including measures to utilize more effectively foreign accomplishments; the mounting allocation of resources to scientific-technological progress; the special attention Moscow is giving to Western concepts regarding science and technology as a unifying force. The study is based upon an exhaustive examination of Soviet sources and includes extensive selections of documentary materials bearing upon key problem areas.

SOVIET STRATEGY FOR THE SEVENTIES: FROM COLD WAR TO PEACEFUL COEXISTENCE, Foy D. Kohler, Mose L. Harvey, Leon Goure, and Richard Soll ($4.95, $5.95 hardcover).

Fundamental to an understanding of the current Soviet world outlook under "conditions of the new correlation of world forces," this study surveys and analyzes Soviet purposes and expectations within the context of peaceful coexistence between states with different social systems and provides selections of authoritative documentary materials for each of the main areas of Soviet strategic thinking and planning under the peaceful coexistence doctrine.

THE LATIN AMERICAN SCENE OF THE SEVENTIES: A BASIC FACT BOOK, Irving
B. Reed, Jaime Suchlicki, and Dodd L. Harvey.

Provides in ready reference form current descriptive and statistical information for each
of the twenty-four Latin American and Caribbean countries, with emphasis on situations
and developments regarding the economy, social structures, and politics reflecting the
rapid state of change both domestically and in external relationships. Includes an analytical introduction for the Latin American region as a whole highlighting current major
problems and trends, particularly as these bear upon relations with the US and upon the
place of Latin America in the changing international scene. The study will be revised and
reissued at two-year intervals.

SOVIET PENETRATION OF LATIN AMERICA, Leon Goure, Mose L. Harvey, and
Jaime Suchlicki ($3.95, $4.95 hardcover).

An examination and analysis of the mounting interest and attention of the USSR toward
Latin America. In contrast to an apparent acceptance prior to the 1960's of the "geo-
graphic fatalism" of US dominance of Latin America, the Soviets now see opportunities
to score important gains in what they call "this strategic rear of the United States." The
study explores the strategic framework in which Moscow is developing its current
policies for Latin America, changing Soviet perceptions of the region and the opportunities it offers, the increasing scale and expanding scope of Soviet activities in the region,
the growing vulnerabilities of the region to Soviet influence, and the implications for US
national interests.

THE MILITARIZATION OF SOVIET YOUTH, Leon Goure ($4.95, $5.95 hardcover).

Explores and analyzes current Soviet efforts to instill in the youth nationalism, militarism and a readiness for war on a scale unprecedented in peace time, even in the Soviet
Union, and which are leading to an increasing militarization of the entire Soviet educational system. Suggests that the military-patriotic indoctrination program should be
viewed not only as an important and far-reaching development in Soviet education, but
also as likely to have significant influence on future Soviet relations with the rest of the
world and on the evolution of the Soviet system.

US-SOVIET COOPERATION IN SPACE: A DOCUMENTARY ACCOUNTING, Mose L.
Harvey, Dodd L. Harvey, and Linda C. Ciccoritti with an introductory overview by
Ambassador Foy D. Kohler ($4.95; $5.95 hardcover).

Examines and analyzes recent developments and current trends and prospects for US-
Soviet space cooperation against the background of a comprehensive accounting of
previous efforts at cooperation extending back to the International Geophysical Year and
continuing through the Eisenhower, Kennedy, Johnson, and early Nixon Administrations. Interrelates space policies of both nations with their basic foreign policies and
objectives and with their efforts to advance science and technology, and to use science
and technology as instruments of policy. Extensive documentary materials are included.

SOURCES OF INSTABILITY IN LATIN AMERICA, Jaime Suchlicki, Jan Peter Wogart,
and Donald R. Morris, ($3.95; $4.95 hardcover).

Concentrates on those features of the Latin American scene which are making for
changes in orientations of Latin American societies, especially as regards continuation of
the "American system" as it has traditionally existed in both domestic affairs and in
foreign relations of the countries of the area. Deals particularly with situations and
trends with respect to the youth and intellectuals; the nationalism-anti-Americanism
syndrome; the search for new economic orientation; the changing attitudes and roles of
the military, the clergy, and the technological-managerial elite; the persistence of obstacles
to moderinization; and the dynamics of social mobility and population movements and
stresses.

The
MONSTER
of
FLORENCE

BY DOUGLAS PRESTON

Blasphemy
Dolci Colline di Sangue (with Mario Spezi)
Tyrannosaur Canyon
The Codex
Ribbons of Time
The Royal Road
Talking to the Ground
Jennie
Cities of Gold
Dinosaurs in the Attic

BY DOUGLAS PRESTON AND LINCOLN CHILD

The Wheel of Darkness★
The Book of the Dead★
Dance of Death★
Brimstone★
Still Life with Crows★
The Cabinet of Curiosities★
The Ice Limit★
Thunderhead★
Riptide★
Reliquary
Mount Dragon
Relic

BY MARIO SPEZI

Inviato in Galera
Dolci Colline di Sangue (with Douglas Preston)
Le Sette di Satana
Il Passo dell'Orco
Toscana Nera
Il Violinista Verde
Il Mostro di Firenze

★Available from Grand Central Publishing

The
MONSTER
of
FLORENCE

DOUGLAS PRESTON
with MARIO SPEZI

GRAND CENTRAL
PUBLISHING

Grand Central Publishing

Hachette Book Group USA

237 Park Avenue

New York, NY 10017

Visit our website at www.HachetteBookGroupUSA.com.

Printed in the United States of America

First Edition: June 2008

10 9 8 7 6 5 4 3 2 1

Parts of this book first appeared in *Dolci Colline di Sangue* (Sonzogno, 2006) as well as in the *Atlantic Monthly* and *The New Yorker*.

Grand Central Publishing is a division of Hachette Book Group USA, Inc. The Grand Central Publishing name and logo is a trademark of Hachette Book Group USA, Inc.

Library of Congress Cataloging-in-Publication Data

Preston, Douglas J.

    The monster of Florence / Douglas Preston, with Mario Spezi.

      p. cm.

    ISBN-13: 978-0-446-58119-6 (regular edition)

    ISBN-13: 978-0-446-50534-5 (large print edition)

    ISBN-10: 0-446-58119-4 (regular edition)

    ISBN-10: 0-446-50534-X (large print edition) 1. Serial murders—Italy—Florence—Case studies. I. Spezi, Mario II. Title.

    HV6535.I83F5666 2008

    363.152'3—dc22   2008000771

Book design by Giorgetta Bell McRee

To my partners in our Italian adventure: my wife, Christine, and my children Aletheia and Isaac. And to my daughter Selene, who wisely kept her feet planted firmly in America.
—Douglas Preston

A mia moglie Myriam e a mia figlia Eleonora, che hanno scusato la mia ossessione.
—Mario Spezi

The
MONSTER
of
FLORENCE

TIMELINE

1951   Pietro Pacciani murders his fiancée's seducer

1961   January 14. Salvatore Vinci's wife, Barbarina, found dead

1968   August 21. Barbara Locci and Antonio Lo Bianco murdered

1974   September 14. Borgo San Lorenzo killings

1981   June 6. Via dell'Arrigo killings
       October 22. Bartoline Fields killings

1982   June 19. Montespertoli killings
       August 17. Francesco Vinci arrested for being the Monster

1983   September 10. Giogoli killings
       September 19. Antonio Vinci arrested for illegal possession
          of firearms

1984   January 24. Piero Mucciarini and Giovanni Mele arrested
          for being the Monster
       July 29. Vicchio killings
       August 19. Prince Roberto Corsini murdered
       September 22. Mucciarini and Mele released from prison
       November 10. Francesco Vinci released from prison

1985   September 7. Scopeti killings
       October 8. Francesco Narducci drowns in Lake Trasimeno

1986   June 11. Salvatore Vinci arrested for the murder of his wife,
          Barbarina, in 1961

1988   April 12. Trial of Salvatore Vinci begins
       April 19. Salvatore Vinci acquitted, disappears

1989   August 2. Date of FBI psychological profile of the Monster
          of Florence

1992 April 27–May 8. Search of Pacciani's house and grounds

1993 January 16. Pacciani arrested as the Monster of Florence

1994 April 14. Pacciani's trial begins
November 1. Pacciani convicted

1995 October. Chief Inspector Michele Giuttari takes over the
Monster investigation

1996 February 12. Pacciani acquitted on appeal
February 13. Vanni arrested for being Pacciani's
accomplice

1997 May 20. Trial begins for Lotti and Vanni, accused as the
Monster's accomplices

1998 March 24. Lotti and Vanni convicted

2000 August 1. Douglas Preston arrives in Florence

2002 April 6. Narducci's body exhumed

2004 May 14. *Chi L'ha Visto?* program aired on Italian television
June 25. Preston leaves Florence
November 18. Spezi's home searched by police

2005 January 24. Second police search of Spezi's home

2006 February 22. Interrogation of Preston
April 7. Spezi arrested
April 19. Publication date of *Dolci Colline di Sangue*
April 29. Spezi released from prison
September/October. Preston returns to Italy with
Dateline NBC

2007 June 20. *Dateline NBC* program on the Monster of Florence
September 27. Trial of Francesco Calamandrei as the
Monster of Florence begins

2008 January 16. First hearing in trial of Giuttari and Mignini
for abuse of office

CAST OF SECONDARY CHARACTERS,

IN APPROXIMATE ORDER OF APPEARANCE

Chief Inspector Maurizio Cimmino, head of the Florentine police's mobile squad.

Chief Inspector Sandro Federico, police homicide detective.

Adolfo Izzo, prosecutor.

Carmela De Nuccio and **Giovanni Foggi**, killed on Via dell'Arrigo, June 6, 1981.

Dr. Mauro Maurri, chief medical examiner.

Fosco, his assistant.

Stefania Pettini and **Pasquale Gentilcore**, killed near Borgo San Lorenzo, September 13, 1974.

Enzo Spalletti, Peeping Tom arrested as the Monster, released when the Monster struck again while he was in jail.

Fabbri, another Peeping Tom questioned in the case.

Stefano Baldi and **Susanna Cambi**, killed in the Bartoline Fields, October 22, 1981.

Prof. Garimeta Gentile, gynecologist rumored to be the Monster.

"Dr." Carlo Santangelo, phony medical examiner who haunted cemeteries at night.

Brother Galileo Babbini, Franciscan monk and psychoanalyst who helped Spezi deal with the horror of the case.

Antonella Migliorini and **Paolo Mainardi**, killed in Montespertoli near Poppiano Castle on June 19, 1982.

Silvia Della Monica, prosecutor in the case, who received in the mail a piece of the Monster's last victim.

Stefano Mele, immigrant from Sardinia, who confessed to murdering his wife and her lover on August 21, 1968, and was sentenced to fourteen years in prison.

Barbara Locci, wife of Stefano Mele, murdered near Signa with her lover on August 21, 1968.

Antonio Lo Bianco, Sicilian bricklayer, murdered with Barbara Locci.

Natalino Mele, son of Stefano Mele and Barbara Locci, who was sleeping in the backseat of the car and who witnessed his mother's murder at age six.

Barbarina Vinci, wife of Salvatore Vinci back in Sardinia, probably murdered by him on January 14, 1961.

Giovanni Vinci, one of the Vinci brothers, who raped his sister back in Sardinia, and was a lover of Barbara Locci.

Salvatore Vinci, the ringleader of the 1968 double homicide, lover of Barbara Locci, who probably owned the Monster's gun and bullets, which may have been stolen from him in 1974, four months before the Monster's murders began. Arrested for being the Monster.

Francesco Vinci, youngest of the Vinci clan, lover of Barbara Locci, uncle of Antonio Vinci. Arrested for being the Monster.

Antonio Vinci, son of Salvatore Vinci, nephew of Francesco Vinci, arrested for illegal possession of firearms after the Monster's killings in Giogoli.

Cinzia Torrini, filmmaker who produced a film on the Monster of Florence case.

Horst Meyer and **Uwe Rüsch**, both twenty-four years old, killed in Giogoli, September 10, 1983.

Piero Luigi Vigna, lead prosecutor in the Monster case in the 1980s, responsible for the arrest of Pacciani. Vigna went on to head Italy's powerful antimafia unit.

Mario Rotella, examining magistrate in the Monster case in the

1980s, who was convinced the Monster was a member of a clan of Sardinians—the so-called "Sardinian Trail" leg of the investigation.

Giovanni Mele and **Piero Mucciarini**, the brother and brother-in-law of Stefano Mele, arrested for being the two Monsters of Florence.

Paolo Canessa, prosecutor in the Monster case in the 1980s, who is today the public minister (equivalent to a U.S. attorney) of Florence.

Pia Rontini and **Claudio Stefanacci**, killed at La Boschetta, near Vicchio, July 29, 1984.

Prince Roberto Corsini, murdered on his estate by a poacher, August 19, 1984, the subject of rumors that he was the Monster.

Nadine Mauriot, thirty-six years old, and **Jean-Michel Kraveichvili**, twenty-five years old, killed by the Monster in the Scopeti clearing, Saturday, September 7, 1985.

Sabrina Carmignani, who came across the Scopeti clearing on Sunday, September 8, 1985, the day of her nineteenth birthday, and encountered the aftermath of the murder of the French tourists.

Ruggero Perugini, the chief inspector who took over the Squadra Anti-Mostro and prosecuted Pietro Pacciani. He was the model for **Rinaldo Pazzi**, the fictional chief inspector in Thomas Harris's book (and movie) *Hannibal*.

Pietro Pacciani, Tuscan farmer who was convicted of being the Monster, acquitted on appeal, and then ordered to restand trial. He was the alleged leader of the so-called *compagni di merende*, the "picnicking friends."

Aldo Fezzi, the last *cantastorie*, or story singer, in Tuscany, who composed a song about Pietro Pacciani.

Arturo Minoliti, carabinieri marshal, who believed that the bullet found in Pacciani's garden, used to convict Pacciani as the Monster, might have been planted by investigators.

Mario Vanni, nicknamed il Torsolo (Apple Core), the former postman of San Casciano, convicted of being Pacciani's accomplice in the

Monster killings. During Pacciani's trial, Vanni uttered the phrase that became immortalized in Italian, "We were picnicking friends."

Michele Giuttari, who took over the Monster investigation after Chief Inspector Perugini was promoted to Washington. He formed the Gruppo Investigativo Delitti Seriali, the Serial Killings Investigative Group, also known as GIDES. He engineered Spezi's arrest and Preston's interrogation.

Alpha, the first "secret witness," whose name was actually **Pucci**, a mentally retarded man who falsely confessed to having witnessed Pacciani commit one of the Monster's killings.

Beta, the second secret witness, **Giancarlo Lotti**, who was nicknamed **Katanga** (Jungle Bunny). Lotti falsely confessed having helped Pacciani with several of the Monster's killings.

Gamma, the third secret witness, named **Ghiribelli**, an aging prostitute and alcoholic who allegedly would turn a trick for a twenty-five-cent glass of wine.

Delta, the fourth secret witness, named **Galli**, a pimp by profession.

Lorenzo Nesi, the "serial witness" who suddenly and repeatedly remembered events going back decades, the star witness in the first trial against Pacciani.

Francesco Ferri, president of the Court of Appeals, who presided over Pacciani's appeals trial and declared him innocent. He later wrote a book about the case.

Prof. Francesco Introna, the forensic entomologist who examined photographs of the French tourists and stated that it was scientifically impossible for them to have been murdered Sunday night, as investigators insist.

Gabriella Carlizzi, who ran a conspiracy website that identified the Order of the Red Rose as the satanic sect behind the Monster killings (as well as the entity responsible for 9/11) and who accused Mario Spezi of being the Monster of Florence.

Francesco Narducci, the Perugian doctor whose body was

found floating in Lake Trasimeno in October 1985, subject to rumors he had been the Monster of Florence. His apparent suicide was later ruled a murder and Spezi was accused of having participated in it.

Ugo Narducci, Francesco's father, a wealthy Perugian and an important member of the Freemasons—cause for official suspicion.

Francesca Narducci, the dead doctor's wife, heir to the Luisa Spagnoli fashion house fortune.

Francesco Calamandrei, ex-pharmacist of San Casciano, accused of being the mastermind behind five of the Monster's double homicides. His trial began on September 27, 2007.

Fernando Zaccaria, ex–police detective who introduced Spezi to Luigi Ruocco and who accompanied Spezi and Preston to the Villa Bibbiani.

Luigi Ruocco, small-time crook and ex-con who told Spezi he knew Antonio Vinci and who gave Spezi directions to Vinci's alleged safe house on the grounds of the Villa Bibbiani.

Ignazio, alleged friend of Ruocco who had supposedly been to Antonio's safe house and seen six iron boxes and possibly a .22 Beretta.

Inspector Castelli, detective with GIDES who served Preston with papers and was present at his interrogation.

Captain Mora, police captain present at the interrogation of Preston.

Giuliano Mignini, the public minister of Perugia, a public prosecutor in Italy analogous to a U.S attorney or a district attorney.

Marina De Robertis, the examining magistrate in the Spezi case, who invoked the antiterrorist law against Spezi, preventing him from meeting with his lawyers following his arrest.

Alessandro Traversi, one of Mario Spezi's lawyers.

Nino Filastò, one of Mario Spezi's lawyers.

Winnie Rontini, mother of Pia Rontini, one of the Monster's victims.

Renzo Rontini, father of Pia Rontini.

INTRODUCTION

In 1969, the year men landed on the moon, I spent an unforgettable summer in Italy. I was thirteen. Our family rented a villa on the Tuscan coast, perched on a limestone promontory above the Mediterranean. My two brothers and I spent the summer hanging around an archaeological dig and swimming at a little beach in the shadow of a fifteenth-century castle called Puccini's Tower, where the composer wrote *Turandot*. We cooked octopus on the beach, snorkeled among the reefs, and collected ancient Roman tesserae from the eroding shoreline. In a nearby chicken coop I found the rim of a Roman amphora, two thousand years old, stamped with an "SES" and a picture of a trident, which the archaeologists told me had been manufactured by the Sestius family, one of the richest mercantile families of the early Roman republic. In a stinking bar, to the flickering glow of an old black-and-white television set, we watched Neil Armstrong set foot on the moon while the place erupted in pandemonium, the longshoremen and fishermen hugging and kissing each other, tears streaming down their rough faces, crying, *"Viva l'America! Viva l'America!"*

From that summer on, I knew that I wanted to live in Italy.

I grew up to become a journalist and writer of murder mysteries.

In 1999, I returned to Italy on assignment for *The New Yorker* magazine, writing an article about the mysterious artist Masaccio, who launched the Renaissance with his commanding frescoes in the Brancacci Chapel in Florence and then died at twenty-six, allegedly poisoned. One cold February night, in my hotel room in Florence overlooking the Arno River, I called my wife, Christine, and asked her what she thought of the idea of moving to Florence. She said yes. The next morning I called a real estate agency and began looking at apartments, and in two days I had rented the top floor of a fifteenth-century palazzo and put down a deposit. As a writer, I could live anywhere—why not Florence?

As I wandered around Florence that cold week in February, I started to plot the murder mystery I would write when we moved there. It would be set in Florence and involve a lost painting of Masaccio.

We moved to Italy. We arrived on August 1, 2000, Christine and I, with our two children, Isaac and Aletheia, aged five and six. We first lived in the apartment I had rented overlooking Piazza Santo Spirito and then we moved into the country, to a tiny town called Giogoli in the hills just south of Florence. There we rented a stone farmhouse tucked into the side of a hill at the end of a dirt lane, surrounded by olive groves.

I began researching my novel. Since it was to be a murder mystery, I had to learn all I could about Italian police procedure and murder investigation. An Italian friend gave me the name of a legendary Tuscan crime reporter named Mario Spezi, who for more than twenty years had worked the *cronaca nera* desk ("black story," or crime beat) at *La Nazione*, the daily paper of Tuscany and central Italy. "He knows more about the police than the police themselves," I was told.

And so it was that I found myself in the windowless back room of Caffè Ricchi, on Piazza Santo Spirito, sitting across from Mario Spezi himself.

Spezi was a journalist of the old school, dry, witty, and cynical, with a highly developed sense of the absurd. There was absolutely nothing a human being could do, no matter how depraved, that would surprise him. A shock of thick gray hair surmounted a wry, fine-looking leathery face, with a pair of canny brown eyes lurking behind gold-rimmed spectacles. He went about in a trench coat and a Bogart fedora, like a character out of Raymond Chandler, and he was a great fan of American blues, film noir, and Philip Marlowe.

The waitress brought in a tray with two black espressos and two glasses of mineral water. Spezi exhaled a stream of smoke, held his cigarette to one side, downed the espresso with one sharp movement, ordered another, and placed the cigarette back on his lip.

We began chatting, Spezi speaking slowly for the benefit of my execrable Italian. I described to him the plot of my book. One of the main characters was to be a carabinieri officer, and I asked him to tell me how the carabinieri operated. Spezi described the structure of the carabinieri, how they differed from the police, and how they conducted investigations, while I took notes. He promised to introduce me to a colonel in the carabinieri who was an old friend. Finally we fell to chatting about Italy and he asked me where I lived.

"A tiny town called Giogoli."

Spezi's eyebrows shot up. "Giogoli? I know it well. Where?"

I gave him the address.

"Giogoli . . . a lovely, historic town. It has three famous landmarks. Perhaps you already know of them?"

I did not.

With a faint smile of amusement, he began. The first was Villa Sfacciata, where one of his very own ancestors, Amerigo Vespucci, had lived. Vespucci was the Florentine navigator, mapmaker, and explorer who was the first to realize that his friend Christopher Columbus had discovered a brand-new continent, not some unknown shore of India, and who lent his name Amerigo (Americus in Latin) to this New World. The second landmark, Spezi went on, was another villa, called I Collazzi, with a façade said to be designed by Michelangelo, where Prince Charles stayed with Diana and where the prince painted many of his famous watercolors of the Tuscan landscape.

"And the third landmark?"

Spezi's smile widened. "The most interesting of all. It's just outside your door."

"There's nothing outside our door but an olive grove."

"Precisely. And in that grove one of the most horrific murders in Italian history took place. A double homicide committed by our very own Jack the Ripper."

As a writer of murder mysteries, I was more intrigued than dismayed.

"I named him," Spezi said. "I christened him *il Mostro di Firenze*, the Monster of Florence. I covered the case from the beginning. At *La Nazione* the other reporters called me the paper's 'Monstrologer.'" He laughed, a sudden irreverent cackle, hissing smoke out from between his teeth.

"Tell me about this Monster of Florence."

"You've never heard of him?"

"Never."

"Isn't the story famous in America?"

"It's completely unknown."

"That surprises me. It seems . . . an almost *American* story. And your own FBI was involved—that group Thomas Harris made so famous, the Behavioral Science Unit. I saw Thomas Harris at one of the trials, taking notes on a yellow legal pad. They say he based Hannibal Lecter on the Monster of Florence."

Now I was really interested. "Tell me the story."

Spezi downed his second espresso, lit another Gauloise, and began to talk through the smoke. As his story gathered steam, he slipped a notebook and a well-worn gold pencil from his pocket and began to diagram the narrative. The pencil cut and darted across the paper, making arrows and circles and boxes and dotted lines, illustrating the intricate connections among the suspects, the killings, the arrests, the trials, and the many failed lines of investigation. It was a long story, and he spoke quietly, the blank page of his notebook gradually filling.

I listened, amazed at first, then astonished. As a crime novelist, I fancied myself a connoisseur of dark stories. I had certainly heard a lot of them. But as the story of the Monster of Florence unfolded, I realized it was something special. A story in a category all its own. I do not exaggerate when I say the case of the Monster of Florence may be—just *may* be—the most extraordinary story of crime and investigation the world has ever heard.

Between 1974 and 1985, seven couples—fourteen people in all—were murdered while making love in parked cars in the beautiful hills surrounding Florence. The case had become the longest and most expensive criminal investigation in Italian history. Close to a hundred thousand men were investigated and more than a dozen arrested, many of whom had to be released when the Monster struck again. Scores of lives were ruined by rumor and false accusations. The generation of Florentines who came of age during the killings say that it changed the city and their lives. There have been suicides, exhumations, alleged poisonings, body parts sent by post, séances in graveyards, lawsuits, planting of false evidence, and vicious prosecutorial vendettas. The investigation has been like a malignancy, spreading backward in time and outward in space, metastasizing to different cities and swelling into new investigations, with new judges, police, and prosecutors, more suspects, more arrests, and many more lives ruined.

Despite the longest manhunt in modern Italian history, the Monster of Florence has never been found. When I arrived in Italy in the year 2000 the case was still unsolved, the Monster presumably still on the loose.

Spezi and I became fast friends after that first meeting, and I soon shared his fascination with the case. In the spring of 2001, Spezi and I set out to find the truth and track down the real killer. This book is the story of that search and our eventual meeting with the man we believe may be the Monster of Florence.

Along the way, Spezi and I fell into the story. I was accused of being an accessory to murder, planting false evidence, perjury and obstruction of justice, and threatened with arrest if I ever set foot on Italian soil again. Spezi fared worse: he was accused of being the Monster of Florence himself.

This is the story that Spezi told.

PART I

❖

The Story of Mario Spezi

CHAPTER

I

The morning of June 7, 1981, dawned brilliantly clear over Florence, Italy. It was a quiet Sunday with blue skies and a light breeze out of the hills, which carried into the city the fragrance of sun-warmed cypress trees. Mario Spezi was at his desk at *La Nazione*, where he had worked as a reporter for several years, smoking and reading the paper. He was approached by the reporter who usually handled the crime desk, a legend at the paper who had survived twenty years of covering the Mafia.

The man sat on the edge of Spezi's desk. "This morning I have a little appointment," he said. "She's not bad-looking, married . . ."

"At your age?" Spezi said. "On a Sunday morning before church? Isn't that a bit much?"

"A bit much? Mario, I'm a Sicilian!" He struck his chest. "I come from the land that gave birth to the gods. Anyway, I was hoping you could cover the crime desk for me this morning, hang around police headquarters in case something comes up. I've already made the calls, nothing's going on. And as we all know"—and then he spoke the phrase that Spezi would never forget—"nothing ever happens in Florence on a Sunday morning."

Spezi bowed and took the man's hand. "If the Godfather orders it, I shall obey. I kiss your hand, Don Rosario."

Spezi hung around the paper doing nothing until noon approached. It was the laziest, deadest day in weeks. Perhaps because of this, a feeling of misgiving that afflicts all crime reporters began to take hold— that something might be happening and he'd be scooped. So Spezi dutifully climbed into his Citroën and drove the half mile to police headquarters, an ancient, crumbling building in the old part of Florence, once an ancient monastery, where police officials had their tiny offices in the monks' former cells. He took the stairs two at a time up to the office of the chief of the mobile squad. The loud, querulous voice of the chief, Maurizio Cimmino, echoed down the hall from his open door, and Spezi was seized with dread.

Something *had* happened.

Spezi found the chief in shirtsleeves behind his desk, soaked with sweat, the telephone jammed between chin and shoulder. The police radio blared in the background and several policemen were there, talking and swearing in dialect.

Cimmino spied Spezi in the door and turned to him fiercely. "Jesus Christ, Mario, you here already? Don't go busting my balls, all I know is there's two of them."

Spezi pretended to know all about whatever it was. "Right. I won't bother you anymore. Just tell me where they are."

"Via dell'Arrigo, wherever the fuck that is . . . somewhere in Scandicci, I think."

Spezi piled down the stairs and called his editor from the pay phone on the first floor. He happened to know exactly where Via dell'Arrigo was: a friend of his owned the Villa dell'Arrigo, a spectacular estate at the top of the tiny, twisting country road of the same name.

"Get out there quick," his editor said. "We'll send a photographer."

Spezi left the police headquarters and tore through the deserted medieval streets of the city and into the Florentine hills. At one o'clock on a Sunday afternoon, the entire population was at home after church, getting ready to sit down to the most sacred meal of the week in a country where eating *in famiglia* is a hallowed activity. Via dell'Arrigo climbed up a steep hill through vineyards, cypresses, and groves of ancient olive trees. As the road mounted toward the steep, forested summits of the Valicaia hills, the views became expansive, sweeping across the city of Florence to the great Apennine Mountains beyond.

Spezi spotted the squad car of the local carabinieri marshal and pulled off next to it. All was quiet: Cimmino and his squad hadn't arrived, nor had the medical examiner or anyone else. The carabinieri officer guarding the site knew Spezi well and did not stop him as he nodded a greeting and walked past. He continued down a small dirt path through an olive grove to the foot of a lonely cypress. There, just beyond, he saw the scene of the crime, which had not been secured or sealed off.

The scene, Spezi told me, would be forever engraved in his mind. The Tuscan countryside lay under a sky of cobalt blue. A medieval castle, framed by cypress trees, crowned a nearby rise. In the vast distance, in the haze of early summer, he could spy the terra-cotta vault of the Duomo rising above the city of Florence, the physical embodiment of the Renaissance. The boy seemed to be sleeping in the driver's seat, his head leaning on the side window, eyes closed, face smooth and untroubled. Only a little black mark on his temple, which lined up with a hole in the spiderwebbed window, indicated that a crime had occurred.

On the ground, in the grass, lay a straw purse, wide open and upside down, as if someone had rummaged through it and flung it aside.

He heard the swish of feet in the grass and the carabinieri officer came up behind him.

"The woman?" Spezi asked him.

The cop gestured with his chin behind the car. The girl's body lay some distance away, at the foot of a little embankment, amid wildflowers. She had also been shot and lay on her back, naked except for a gold chain around her neck, which had fallen between her parted lips. Her blue eyes were open and seemed to be looking up at Spezi with surprise. Everything was unnaturally composed, immobile, with no signs of struggle or confusion—like a museum diorama. But there was a singular horror: the pubic area below the victim's abdomen simply wasn't there anymore.

Spezi turned back and found the cop behind him. The man seemed to understand the question in Spezi's eyes.

"During the night . . . the animals came . . . And the hot sun did the rest."

Spezi fumbled a Gauloise out of his pocket and lit it in the shade of the cypress. He smoked in silence, standing halfway between the two victims, reconstructing the crime in his head. The two people had obviously been ambushed while making love in the car; they had probably come up here after an evening dancing at Disco Anastasia, a hangout for teenagers at the bottom of the hill. (The police would later confirm this was the case.) It was the night of the new moon. The killer would have approached in the dark, silently; perhaps he watched them make love for a while, and then struck when they were at their most vulnerable. It had been a low-risk crime—a cowardly crime—to shoot two people imprisoned in the small space of a car at point-blank range, at a time when they were completely unaware of what was going on around them.

The first shot was for him, through the window of the car, and he may never have known what happened. Her end was crueler; she would have realized. After killing her, the murderer had dragged her away from the car—Spezi could see the marks in the grass—leaving her at the bottom of the embankment. The place was shockingly exposed. It lay right next to a footpath that ran parallel to the road, out in the open and visible from multiple vantage points.

Spezi's musings were interrupted by the arrival of Chief Inspector Sandro Federico and a prosecutor, Adolfo Izzo, along with the forensic squad. Federico had the easygoing manner of a Roman, affecting an air of amused nonchalance. Izzo, on the other hand, was in his first posting and he arrived wound up like a spring. He leapt out of the squad car and charged up to Spezi. "What are you doing here, sir?" he asked angrily.

"Working."

"You must leave the premises immediately. You can't remain here."

"Okay, okay . . ." Spezi had seen all he wanted to see. He shoved his pen and notebook away, got in his car, and drove back to police headquarters. In the hallway outside Cimmino's office he ran into a police sergeant he knew well; they had been able to do each other favors from time to time. The sergeant slipped a photograph out of his pocket and showed it to him. "You want it?"

It was a picture of the two victims, in life, sitting on a stone wall with their arms around each other.

Spezi took it. "I'll bring it back to you later this afternoon, after we've copied it."

Cimmino gave Spezi the names of the two victims: Carmela De Nuccio, twenty-one years old, who worked for the Gucci fashion house in Florence. The man was Giovanni Foggi, thirty, employed by the local electric utility. They were engaged to be married. A policeman on his day off, enjoying a Sunday morning walk in the country, had found the two bodies at ten-thirty. The crime had occurred a little before midnight, and there was a witness of sorts: a farmer who lived across the road. He had heard a tape of John Lennon's "Imagine" coming from a car parked in the fields. The song had been interrupted all of a sudden, in the middle. He hadn't heard any shots from what was evidently a .22 pistol, judging from the shells that were left at the scene of the crime—Winchester series "H" rounds. Cimmino said the two victims were clean, they had no enemies, excluding the man Carmela left when she began dating Giovanni.

"It's frightening," Spezi said to Cimmino. "I've never seen anything like it around here . . . And then, to think what the animals did—"

"What animals?" Cimmino interrupted.

"The animals that came during the night . . . That bloody mess . . . in between the girl's legs."

Cimmino stared at him. "Animals my ass! The killer did that."

Spezi felt his gut freeze. "The killer? What did he do, stab her?"

Inspector Cimmino answered matter-of-factly, perhaps as a way to keep the horror at bay. "No, he didn't stab her. He cut out her vagina . . . and took it away."

Spezi didn't immediately understand. "He took her vagina away? Where?" As soon as the question was out he realized how stupid it sounded.

"It's simply not there anymore. He took it away with him."

CHAPTER
2

The next day, Monday morning, at eleven o'clock, Spezi drove to the Careggi district of Florence, on the outskirts of the city. It was a hundred and five degrees in the shade, with the humidity approaching that of a hot shower. Smog lay like a pall over the city. He drove down a potholed lane toward a large yellow building, a decaying villa now part of a hospital complex, the plaster flaking off in platter-sized pieces.

The reception area of the medical examiner's office was a cavernous room dominated by a massive marble table, on which a computer sat, covered in a white sheet like a corpse. The rest of the table was empty. Behind, in a niche in the wall, a bronze bust of a bearded luminary in the field of human anatomy cast a severe gaze on Spezi.

A marble staircase went up and down. Spezi went down.

The stairway led to an underground passageway, illuminated with humming fluorescent lights and lined with doors. The walls were tiled. The last door was open and from it came the strident whine of a bone saw. A rivulet of a black liquid ran out the door and into the hall, where it disappeared down a drain.

Spezi entered.

"Look who's here!" cried Fosco, the ME's assistant. He closed his

15

eyes, stretched out his arms, and quoted Dante. *"There are not many who seek me here . . ."*

"Ciao, Fosco," Spezi said. "Who's this?" He jerked his chin at a cadaver stretched out on a zinc gurney, being worked over by a diener. The circular saw had just opened its cranium. On the gurney, next to the white face of the corpse, stood an empty coffee cup and crumbs from a recently consumed brioche.

"This one? A brilliant scholar, a distinguished professor in the Accademia della Crusca no less. But, as you can see, tonight yet another disappointment has laid me low; I have just opened the head and what do I find inside? Where is all this wisdom? Boh! Inside it looks just like the Albanian hooker I opened yesterday. Maybe the professor thinks he's better than her! But when I open them up, I find that they're equal! And they both have achieved the same destiny: my zinc gurney. Why, then, did he tire himself out poring over so many books? Boh! Take my advice, journalist: eat, drink, and enjoy yourself—"

A courteous voice sounded from the doorway, silencing Fosco. "Good afternoon, Signor Spezi." It was Mauro Maurri, the medical examiner himself, who looked more like an English country gentleman: light blue eyes, gray hair worn fashionably long, a beige cardigan, and corduroy slacks. "Shall we retire to my office upstairs? We will surely find it more congenial for conversation."

The study of Mauro Maurri consisted of a long, narrow room lined with books and magazines on criminology and forensic pathology. He had left the window shut to keep out the heat and had turned on only a single small lamp on his desk, maintaining the rest of his office in darkness.

Spezi seated himself and slid out a packet of Gauloises, offered one to Maurri, who declined with a light shake of his head, and lit one for himself.

Maurri spoke with great deliberation. "The killer used a knife or some other sharp instrument. The instrument had a notch or tooth in the middle, perhaps a defect, perhaps not. It might have been a certain type of knife that takes that form. It seems to me, although I won't swear to it, that it was a scuba knife. Three cuts were made to remove the organ. The first clockwise, from eleven o'clock to six o'clock; the second counterclockwise, again from eleven o'clock to six. The third cut was made from top to bottom to detach the organ. Three clean, decisive cuts, with an extremely sharp edge."

"Like Jack."

"I beg your pardon?"

"Jack the Ripper."

"I see, of course. Jack the Ripper. No . . . not like him. Our killer is not a surgeon. Nor a butcher. Knowledge of anatomy was not required here. The investigators have been demanding to know, 'Was the operation well done?' What does that mean, 'well done'? Who has ever done an operation of this sort? Certainly it was done by someone with no hesitation, one who perhaps uses certain tools in his professional work. Wasn't the girl a leatherworker for Gucci? Didn't she use a cobbler's knife? Wasn't her father also a leatherworker? Perhaps it was someone in her orbit . . . It had to have been someone with no mean ability with a knife—a hunter or taxidermist . . . Above all, a person with determination and nerves of steel. Although he was working on a dead body, it was, after all, only *just* dead."

"Dr. Maurri," Spezi asked, "do you have any thoughts on what he might have done with this . . . fetish?"

"I pray you, do not ask me this question."

When Monday afternoon sank into an ovenlike grayness and it seemed certain there would be no further developments in the case that day, a large staff meeting was held in the office of the managing editor of *La Nazione*. The publisher was there, the editor, the news director, several journalists, and Spezi. *La Nazione* was the only paper that had information on the mutilation of the corpse; the other dailies knew nothing. It would be a major scoop. The managing editor stated that the particulars of the crime had to be presented in the lead headline. The editor disagreed, maintaining the details were too strong. As Spezi read his notes out loud to help solve the dispute, a young journalist on the crime beat suddenly broke in.

"Excuse me for interrupting," he said, "but I just remembered something. It seems to me there was a similar killing five or six years ago."

The managing editor leapt to his feet. "Now you tell us, right before deadline! Were you waiting for the paper to be in the printing presses before you 'remembered'?"

The reporter was cowed, not realizing the man's fury was all show. "I'm sorry, sir, it just occurred to me now. Do you remember that double homicide near Borgo San Lorenzo?" He paused, waiting for an answer. Borgo San Lorenzo was a town in the mountains about thirty kilometers north of Florence.

"Go on, tell us!" the editor yelled.

"In Borgo, a young couple was murdered. They'd also been having sex in a parked car. Remember the one where the killer stuck a branch up her . . . vagina?"

"I seem to recall it now. What were you doing, sleeping? Bring me the files on it. Write a piece immediately—the similarities, the differences . . . Hurry up! Why are you still here?"

The meeting broke up, and Spezi went to his desk to write up his piece on his visit to the ME's office. Before beginning, he went over the old article that told the story of the Borgo San Lorenzo killing. The resemblances were striking. The two victims, Stefania Pettini, eighteen years old, and Pasquale Gentilcore, nineteen, were killed the night of September 14, 1974, also a Saturday night with no moon. They too were engaged to be married. The killer had taken the girl's purse and turned it upside down, scattering its contents, like the straw purse Spezi had seen in the grass. The two victims had also spent the evening in a discotheque, the Teen Club, in Borgo San Lorenzo.

Shells had been recovered from the earlier killing, and the article stated that they were Winchester series H .22 rounds, the same as used in the Arrigo murders. This detail wasn't quite as significant as it seemed, since those were the most common type of .22 bullets sold in Italy.

The Borgo San Lorenzo killer had not excised the girl's sex organs. Instead, he had dragged her away from the car and had pricked her body with his knife ninety-seven times in an elaborate design that went around her breasts and pubic area. The killing had taken place next to a vineyard, and he had penetrated her with an old, woody piece of grapevine. In neither case was there any evidence of sexual molestation of the victim.

Spezi wrote the lead while the other reporter wrote a sidebar on the 1974 killings.

Two days later, the reaction came. The police, having read the article, had done a comparison between the shells recovered from the 1974 killings and the current ones. Most handguns, aside from revolvers, eject shells after firing; if the shooter doesn't go to the trouble of retrieving them, they remain at the scene of the crime. The police lab report was definitive: the same pistol had been used in both crimes. It was a .22 caliber Beretta "Long Rifle" handgun, a model designed for target shooting. No silencer. The crucial detail was this: the firing pin had a small defect that left an unmistakable mark on the rim of the cartridge, as unique as a fingerprint.

When *La Nazione* broke the news, it caused a sensation. It meant that a serial killer was stalking the Florentine hills.

The investigation that followed lifted the lid off a bizarre underworld that few Florentines knew existed in the lovely hills surrounding their city. In Italy, most young people live at home with their parents until they marry, and most marry late. As a result, having sex in parked cars is a national pastime. It has been said that one out of every three Florentines alive today was conceived in a car. On any given weekend night the hills surrounding Florence were filled with young couples parked in shadowy lanes and dirt turnouts, in olive groves and farmers' fields.

The investigators discovered that dozens of voyeurs prowled the countryside spying on these couples. Locally, these voyeurs were known as *Indiani*, or Indians, because they crept around in the dark. Some carried sophisticated electronic equipment, including parabolic and suction-cup microphones, tape recorders, and night vision cameras. The Indiani had divided the hills into zones of operation, each managed by a group or "tribe" who controlled the best posts for vicarious sex-watching. Some posts were highly sought after, either because they allowed for very close observation or because they were where the "good cars" were most commonly found. (A "good car" is exactly what you might imagine.) A good car could also be a source of money, and sometimes good cars were bought and sold on the spot, in a kind of depraved bourse, in which one Indiano would retire with a fistful of cash, ceding his post to another to watch the finish. Wealthy Indiani often paid for a guide to take them to the best spots and minimize the risk.

Then there were the intrepid people who preyed on the Indiani themselves, a subculture within a subculture. These men crept into the hills at night not to watch lovers but to spy on Indiani, taking careful note of their cars, license plate numbers, and other telling details—and then they would blackmail the Indiani, threatening to expose their nocturnal activities to their wives, families, and employers. It sometimes happened that an Indiano would have his voyeuristic bliss interrupted by the flash of a nearby camera; the next day he would receive a call: "Remember that flash in the woods last night? The photo came out beautifully, you look simply marvelous, a likeness that even your second cousin would recognize! By the way, the negative is for sale . . ."

It didn't take long for investigators to flush out an Indiano who had been lurking about Via dell'Arrigo at the time of the double killing. His name was Enzo Spalletti, and he drove an ambulance during the day.

Spalletti lived with his wife and family in Turbone, a village outside of Florence that consisted of a cluster of stone houses arranged in a circle around a windswept piazza, looking not unlike a cowboy town in a spaghetti Western. He was not well liked by his neighbors. They said he put on airs, that he thought he was better than everyone else. His children, they said, took dancing lessons as if they were the children of a lord. The entire town knew he was a voyeur. Six days after the killing, the police came for the ambulance driver. At the time they did not believe they were dealing with the killer, but only with an important witness.

Spalletti was taken to police headquarters and questioned. He was a small man with an enormous mustache, tight little eyes, a big nose, a chin that stuck out like a knob, and a small, sphincter-like mouth. He looked like a man with something to hide. Compounding the impression, he answered the police's questions with a mixture of arrogance, evasion, and defiance. He said he had left the house that evening with the idea of finding a prostitute to his taste, whom he claimed to have picked up in Florence on the Lungarno, next to the American consulate. She was a young girl from Naples, in a short red dress. The girl had gotten into his Taurus and he had driven her to some woods near where the two young people were murdered. When they had finished, Spalletti brought the little prostitute in red back to where he'd found her and dropped her off.

The story was most improbable. For one thing, it was unthinkable that a prostitute would voluntarily get into an unknown person's car and allow herself to be driven twenty kilometers deep into the countryside to a dark wood. The questioners pointed out the many holes in his story, but Spalletti wouldn't budge. It took six hours of solid interrogation before he began to wilt. Finally the ambulance driver admitted, still as cocky and self-assured as ever, what everyone already knew, that he was in fact a Peeping Tom, that he had been out and about the evening of Saturday, June 6, and had, in fact, parked his red Taurus not far from the scene of the crime. "And so what?" he went on. "I wasn't the only one out that evening spying on couples in the area. There were a whole bunch of us." He went on to say that he knew well the copper Fiat belonging to Giovanni and Carmela: it came often and was known as a "good car." He had watched them more than once. And he knew for a fact that there were other people nosing around that field the night of the crime. He was with one of those people for quite a while, who could vouch for him. He gave the police the man's name: Fabbri.

A few hours later Fabbri was hauled downtown to police headquarters to see if he could confirm Spalletti's alibi. Instead, Fabbri stated that there was a period of an hour and a half, right around the time of the crime, when he was not with Spalletti. "Sure," Fabbri told investigators, "Spalletti and I saw each other. As usual we met at the

Taverna del Diavolo," a restaurant where the Indiani would gather to do business and swap information before going out for the evening. Fabbri added that he saw Spalletti again at the end of the evening, a little after eleven o'clock, when Spalletti stopped on his way down Via dell'Arrigo. Spalletti must have therefore passed not ten meters from the scene of the crime at around the time investigators estimated it occurred.

There was more. Spalletti insisted that he had immediately returned home after greeting Fabbri. But his wife said that when she went to bed at two o'clock in the morning her husband had still not come back.

The interrogators turned back to Spalletti: where had he been between midnight and at least 2 a.m.? Spalletti had no answer.

The police locked Spalletti up at the famous Florentine prison of Le Murate ("The Immured Ones"), accusing him of *reticenza*, reticence— a form of perjury. The authorities still did not yet believe he was the killer, but they were sure he was withholding important information. A few days in jail might just shake it out.

Forensic crime scene investigators went over Spalletti's car and house with a fine-toothed comb. They found a penknife in his car and in the glove compartment a type of gun called a *scacciacani*, a "dog flattener," a cheap pistol loaded with blanks for scaring off dogs, which Spalletti had bought through an ad on the back of a porn magazine. There were no traces of blood.

They interrogated Spalletti's wife. She was much younger than her husband, a fat, honest, simple country girl, and she admitted that she knew her husband was a Peeping Tom. "Many times," she said, weeping, "he promised me he'd stop, but then he'd get back into it. And it's true that the night of June 6 he went out to 'have a look,' as he used to call it." She had no idea when her husband had returned, except that it was after two. She went on, protesting that her husband had to be innocent, that he could never have committed such a terrible crime, since "he's got a terror of blood, so much so that at work, when there's been a highway accident, he refuses to get out of the ambulance."

In the middle of July, policed finally charged Spalletti with being the killer.

Having first broken the original story, Spezi continued to cover it for *La Nazione*. His articles for the paper were skeptical and they pointed out the many holes in the case against Spalletti, among them the fact that there was no direct evidence connecting him with the crime. Nor did Spalletti have any connection to Borgo San Lorenzo, where the first killing occurred in 1974.

On October 24, 1981, Spalletti opened the paper in his prison cell and read a headline that must have brought him great relief:

THE KILLER RETURNS
Young Couple Found Brutally Murdered in Farmer's Field

By killing again, the Monster himself had proved the innocence of the Peeping Tom ambulance driver.

CHAPTER
3

Many countries have a serial killer who defines his culture by a process of negation, who exemplifies his era not by exalting its values, but by exposing its black underbelly. England had Jack the Ripper, born in the fogs of Dickensian London, who preyed on the city's most neglected underclass, the prostitutes who scrabbled for a living in the slums of Whitechapel. Boston had the Boston Strangler, the suave, handsome killer who prowled the city's more elegant neighborhoods, raping and murdering elderly women and arranging their bodies in tableaux of unspeakable obscenity. Germany had the Monster of Düsseldorf, who seemed to foreshadow the coming of Hitler by his indiscriminate and sadistic killing of men, women, and children; his bloodlust was so great that, on the eve of his execution, he called his imminent beheading "the pleasure to end all pleasures." Each killer was, in his own way, a dark embodiment of his time and place.

Italy had the Monster of Florence.

Florence has always been a city of opposites. On a balmy spring evening, with the setting sun gilding the stately palaces lining the river, it can appear as one of the most beautiful and gracious cities in the world. But in late November, after two months of steady rain, its ancient palaces become gray and streaked with damp; the narrow cobbled streets, smelling of sewer gas and dog feces, are shut up on all sides by grim stone façades and overhanging roofs that block the already dim light. The bridges over the Arno flow with black umbrellas held up against the unceasing rain. The river, so lovely in summer, swells into a brown and oily flood, carrying broken trees and branches and sometimes dead animals, which pile up against the pylons designed by Ammanati.

In Florence the sublime and terrible go hand in hand: Savonarola's Bonfires of the Vanities and Botticelli's *Birth of Venus*, Leonardo da Vinci's notebooks and Niccolò Macchiavelli's *The Prince*, Dante's *Inferno* and Boccaccio's *Decameron*. The Piazza della Signoria, the main square, contains an open-air display of Roman and Renaissance sculpture exhibiting some of the most famous statues in Florence. It is a gallery of horrors, a public exhibition of killing, rape, and mutilation unmatched in any city in the world. Heading the show is the famous bronze sculpture by Cellini of Perseus triumphantly holding up the severed head of Medusa like a jihadist on a website video, blood pouring from her neck, her decapitated body sprawled under his feet. Behind Perseus stand other statues depicting famous legendary scenes of murder, violence, and mayhem—among them the sculpture that graces the cover of this book, *The Rape of the Sabine Women* by Giambologna. Inside Florence's encircling walls and on the gibbets outside were committed the most refined and the most savage of crimes, from delicate poisonings to brutal public dismemberments, tortures, and burnings. For centuries, Florence projected its power over the rest of Tuscany at the cost of ferocious massacres and bloody wars.

The city was founded by Julius Caesar in AD 59 as a retirement village for soldiers from his campaigns. It was named Florentia, or "Flourishing." Around AD 250 an Armenian prince named Miniato, after a pilgrimage to Rome, settled on a hill outside Florence and lived as a hermit in a cave, from which he sallied forth to preach to the pagans in town. During the Christian persecutions under the emperor Decius, Miniato was arrested and beheaded in the city square, whereupon (the legend goes) he picked up his head, placed it back on his shoulders, and walked up the hill to die with dignity in his cave. Today, one of the loveliest Romanesque churches in all of Italy stands at the spot, San Miniato al Monte, looking out across the city and the hills beyond.

In 1302, Florence expelled Dante, an act it has never lived down. In return, Dante populated hell with prominent Florentines and reserved some of the most exquisite tortures for them.

During the fourteenth century, Florence grew rich in the woolen cloth trade and banking, and by the end of the century it was one of the five largest cities in Europe. As the fifteenth century dawned, Florence hosted one of those inexplicable flowerings of genius that have occurred fewer than half a dozen times in human history. It would later be called the Renaissance, the "rebirth," following the long darkness of the Middle Ages. Between the birth of Masaccio in 1401 and the death of Galileo in 1642, Florentines largely invented the modern world. They revolutionized art, architecture, music, astronomy, mathematics, and navigation. They created the modern banking system with the invention of the letter of credit. The gold florin, with the Florentine lily on one side and John the Baptist wearing a hairshirt on the other, became the coin of Europe. This landlocked city on an unnavigable river produced brilliant navigators who explored and mapped the New World, and one even gave America its name.

More than that, Florence invented the very *idea* of the modern world. With the Renaissance, Florentines threw off the yoke of medievalism, in which God stood at the center of the universe and human existence on earth was but a dark, fleeting passage to the glorious life to come. The Renaissance placed humanity at the center of the universe and declared this life as the main event. The course of Western civilization was changed forever.

The Florentine Renaissance was largely financed by a single family, the Medicis. They first came to prominence in 1434 under the leadership of Giovanni di Bicci de' Medici, a Florentine banker of great wealth. The Medicis ruled the city from behind the scenes, with a clever system of patronage, alliances, and influence. Although a mercantile family, from the very beginning they poured money into the arts. Giovanni's great-grandson, Lorenzo the Magnificent, was the very epitome of the term "Renaissance man." As a boy, Lorenzo had been astonishingly gifted, and he was given the finest education money could buy, becoming an accomplished jouster, hawker, hunter, and racehorse breeder. Early portraits of Lorenzo il Magnifico reveal an intense young man with furrowed brows, a big, Nixonesque nose, and straight hair. He assumed leadership of the city in 1469, on the death of his father, when he was only twenty years old. He gathered around him such men as Leonardo da Vinci, Sandro Botticelli, Filippino Lippi, Michelangelo, and the philosopher Pico della Mirandola.

Lorenzo ushered Florence into a golden age. But even at the height of the Renaissance, beauty mingled with blood, civilization with savagery, in this city of paradox and contradiction. In 1478 a rival banking family, the Pazzis, attempted a coup d'état against Medici rule. The name Pazzi means, literally, "Madmen," and it was given to an ancestor to honor his insane courage in being one of the first soldiers over the walls of Jerusalem during the First Crusade. The Pazzis had the distinction of seeing two of their members cast into hell by Dante, who gave one a "doggish grin."

On a quiet Sunday in April, a gang of Pazzi murderers set upon Lorenzo the Magnificent and his brother Giuliano at their most vulnerable moment, during the Elevation of the Host at Mass in the Duomo. They killed Giuliano, but Lorenzo, stabbed several times, managed to escape and lock himself in the sacristy. Florentines were enraged at this attack on their patron family and, in a howling mob, went after the conspirators. One of the leaders, Jacopo de' Pazzi, was hanged from a window of the Palazzo Vecchio, his body then stripped, dragged through the streets, and tossed in the Arno River. Despite this setback, the Pazzi family survived, not long afterward giving the world the famed ecstatic nun Maria Maddalena de' Pazzi, who amazed witnesses with her gasping, moaning transports when seized by the love of God during prayer. A fictional Pazzi appeared in the twentieth century, when the writer Thomas Harris made one of his main characters in the novel *Hannibal* a Pazzi, a Florentine police inspector who gains fame and notoriety by solving the case of the Monster of Florence.

The death of Lorenzo the Magnificent, in 1492, at the height of the

Renaissance, ushered in one of those bloody periods that marked Florentine history. A Dominican monk by the name of Savonarola, who lived in the monastery of San Marco, consoled Lorenzo on his deathbed, only later to turn and preach against the Medici family. Savonarola was a strange-looking man, hooded in brown monk's robes, magnetic, coarse, ungainly, and muscular, with a hook nose and Rasputin-like eyes. In the San Marco church he began to preach fire and brimstone, railing against the decadence of the Renaissance, proclaiming that the Last Days had come, and recounting his visions and his direct conversations with God.

His message resonated among common Florentines, who had watched with disapproval the conspicuous consumption and great wealth of the Renaissance and its patrons, much of which seemed to have bypassed them. Their discontent was magnified by an epidemic of syphilis, carried back from the New World, which burned through the city. It was a disease Europe had never seen before, and it came in a far more virulent form than we know today, in which the victim's body became overspread with weeping pustules, the flesh sagging and falling from the face, the stricken sinking into fulminating insanity before death mercifully carried them off. The year 1500 was approaching, which seemed to some a nice round figure marking the arrival of the Last Days. In this climate Savonarola found a receptive audience.

In 1494, Charles VIII of France invaded Tuscany. Piero the Unfortunate, who had inherited the rule of Florence from his father, Lorenzo, was an arrogant and ineffective ruler. He surrendered the city to Charles on poor terms, without even putting up a decent fight, which so enraged Florentines that they drove out the Medici family and looted their palaces. Savonarola, who had accumulated a large following, stepped into the power vacuum and declared Florence a "Christian Republic," setting himself up as its leader. He immediately made sodomy, a popular and more or less socially acceptable activity among sophisticated Florentines, punishable by death. Transgressors and others were regularly burned in the central Piazza della Signoria or hanged outside the city gates.

The mad monk of San Marco had free reign to stir up religious fervor among the common people in the city. He railed against the decadence, excess, and humanistic spirit of the Renaissance. A few years into his reign, he instigated his famous Bonfires of the Vanities. He sent his minions around door to door, collecting items he thought were sinful—mirrors, pagan books, cosmetics, secular music and musical instruments, chessboards, cards, fine clothes, and secular paintings. Everything was heaped up in the Piazza della Signoria and set afire. The artist Botticelli, who fell under the sway of Savonarola, added many of his own paintings to the bonfire, and several of Michelangelo's works may also have been torched, along with other priceless Renaissance masterpieces.

Under Savonarola's rule, Florence sank into economic decline. The Last Days he kept preaching never came. Instead of blessing the city for its newfound religiosity, God seemed to have abandoned it. The common people, especially the young and shiftless, began openly defying his edicts. In 1497, a mob of young men rioted during one of Savonarola's sermons; the riots spread and became a general revolt, taverns reopened, gambling resumed, and dancing and music could once again be heard echoing down Florence's crooked streets.

Savonarola, his control slipping, preached ever more wild and condemnatory sermons, and he made the fatal mistake of turning his criticisms on the church itself. The pope excommunicated him and ordered him arrested and executed. An obliging mob attacked the San Marco monastery, broke down the doors, killed some of Savonarola's fellow monks, and dragged him out. He was charged with a slew of crimes, among them "religious error." After being tortured on the rack for several weeks, he was hung in chains from a cross in the Piazza della Signoria, at the same place where he had erected his Bonfires of the Vanities, and burned. For hours the fire was fed, and then his remains were chopped up and remixed with burning brush several times over so that no piece of him could survive to be made into a relic for veneration. His ashes were then dumped in the all-embracing, all-erasing Arno River.

The Renaissance resumed. The blood and beauty of Florence continued. But nothing lasts forever, and over the centuries Florence gradually lost its place among the leading cities of Europe. It subsided into a relative backwater, famous for its past but invisible in the present, as other cities in Italy rose to prominence, notably Rome, Naples, and Milan.

Florentines today are a famously closed people, considered by other Italians to be stiff, haughty, class-conscious, excessively formal, backward-looking, and fossilized by tradition. They are sober, punctual, and hardworking. Deep inside, Florentines know they are more civilized than other Italians. They gave the world all that is fine and beautiful and they have done enough. Now they can shut their doors and turn inward, answerable to nobody.

When the Monster of Florence arrived, Florentines faced the killings with disbelief, anguish, terror, and a kind of sick fascination. They simply could not accept that their exquisitely beautiful city, the physical expression of the Renaissance, the very cradle of Western civilization, could harbor such a monster.

Most of all, they could not accept the idea that the killer might be one of them.

CHAPTER
4

The evening of Thursday, October 22, 1981, was rainy and unseasonably cool. A general strike had been scheduled for the following day—all shops, businesses, and schools would be closed in protest of the government's economic policies. As a result it was a festive evening. Stefano Baldi had gone to the house of his girlfriend, Susanna Cambi, eaten dinner with her and her parents, and taken her out to the movies. Afterwards, they went parking in the Bartoline Fields west of Florence. It was a familiar place for Stefano, who had grown up in the area and played in the fields as a child.

By day the Bartoline Fields were visited by old pensioners who planted tiny vegetable gardens, took the air, and passed the time gossiping. By night there was a continual coming and going of cars with young couples in search of solitude and intimacy. And naturally there were Peeping Toms.

In the middle of the fields, a track dead-ended among vineyards. That is where Stefano and Susanna parked. In front of them rose the massive, dark shapes of the Calvana Mountains, and behind came the faint rumble of traffic on the autostrada. That night the stars and crescent moon were covered with clouds, casting a heavy darkness over everything.

At eleven the next morning, an elderly couple who had come to water their vegetable garden discovered the crime. The black VW Golf blocked the track, and the left-hand door was closed, the window a solid web of cracks, the right-hand door wide open—exactly the arrangement found at the previous two double homicides.

Spezi arrived at the scene of the crime shortly after the police. Again, the police and carabinieri made no effort to secure the site or seal it with crime tape. Everyone was milling around, making bad jokes—journalists, police, prosecutors, the medical examiner—jokes devoid of humor in a useless attempt to stave off the horror of the scene.

Shortly after his arrival, Spezi spotted a colonel he knew from the carabinieri, dressed in a <u>na</u>tty jacket of gray leather buttoned to his neck to keep out the autumn chill, chain-smoking American cigarettes. The colonel had in his hand a stone that he had found twenty meters from the murder scene. In the form of a truncated pyramid, it was about three inches on a side and made of granite. Spezi recognized it as a doorstop of a type often found in old Tuscan country houses, used during the hot summers to hold open the doors between rooms to aid in the circulation of air.

Turning the stone over in his hands, the colonel approached Spezi. "This doorstop is the only thing I've found at the site of any possible significance. I'm taking it back as evidence, since it's all I've got. Maybe he used it to break the car window."

Twenty years later that banal doorstop, collected by chance in a field, would become the center of a new and bizarre investigation.

"Nothing else, Colonel?" Spezi asked. "Not a trace? The ground is soaking wet and soft."

"We found the footprint of a rubber boot, of the Chantilly type, on the ground next to the row of grapevines that run perpendicularly to the dirt track, right next to the Golf. We've inventoried the print. But you know as well as I do that anyone could have left that bootprint . . . just like this rock."

Spezi, remembering his duty as a journalist to observe with his own eyes and not report secondhand, went with great reluctance to look at the female victim. Her body had been dragged more than ten meters from the car and worked on in a place that was, as in the previous homicides, surprisingly exposed. She was left in the grass, her arms crossed, with the same mutilation as before.

The victims were examined by Medical Examiner Mauro Maurri, who concluded that the cuts to the pubic region had been made with the same notched knife that resembled a scuba knife. He noted that, as in the previous killings, there was no evidence of rape, no molestation of the body or presence of semen. The mobile squad collected nine Winchester series H shells from the ground and two more inside the car. An examination proved that all had been fired by the same gun used in the previous two double homicides, with the unique mark on the rim made by the firing pin.

Spezi asked the chief of the mobile squad about the apparently anomalous fact that a Beretta .22 can only hold nine rounds in its magazine, and yet there were eleven shells at the scene. The chief explained that a knowledgeable shooter can force a tenth round into the magazine and, with another preloaded in the chamber, turn a nine-shot Beretta into an eleven.

The day after the killing, Enzo Spalletti was released.

It would not be an exaggeration to use the word "hysteria" to describe the reaction to this fresh double homicide. The police and carabinieri were swamped with letters, anonymous and signed, which had to be followed up. Doctors, surgeons, gynecologists, and even priests were among those accused, along with fathers, sons-in-law, lovers, and rivals. Up to this time Italians had considered serial killers a northern European phenomenon, something that happened in England, Germany, or Scandinavia—and, of course, in America, where everything violent seemed to be magnified tenfold. But never in Italy.

Young people were terrified. The countryside at night was utterly deserted. Instead, certain dark streets in the city, especially around the Basilica of San Miniato al Monte above Florence, were packed with cars, bumper to bumper, the windows plastered with newspapers or towels, young lovers inside.

After the killings, Spezi worked nonstop for a month, filing fifty-seven articles for *La Nazione*. He almost always had the scoop, the breaking news first, and the newspaper's circulation skyrocketed to the highest point in its history. Many journalists took to following him around, trying to discover his sources.

Over the years, Spezi had developed many devious tricks for prying information out of the police and prosecutors. Every morning he would make the rounds of the Tribunale and the prosecutor's offices, to see if anything new had turned up. He hung around the hallways, chatting to the lawyers and policemen, picking up crumbs of information. He also called Fosco, the medical examiner's technical assistant, asking if any interesting stiffs had arrived, and he put in a call to a contact in the fire department, because sometimes firemen were called to the scene of a crime to recover a body, particularly if the corpse was floating in water.

But Spezi's finest source of information was a little man who labored in the bowels of the Tribunale building, an insignificant fellow with an insignificant job, completely overlooked by the other journalists. He was charged with dusting and keeping in order the tomes into which were written, every day, the names of people who were *indagato*—that is, under investigation—and the reasons why. Spezi had arranged for this simple functionary to receive a complimentary subscription to *La Nazione*, of which he was inordinately proud, and in return he allowed Spezi to thumb through the books. To keep this mother lode of information secret from the journalists who tailed him, Spezi would wait until 1:30 p.m., when the journalists had gathered in front of the Tribunale to go home to lunch. He would duck into a side street that led by crooked and devious ways to a back entrance to the Tribunale and visit his secret friend.

When Spezi had gathered a few tantalizing pieces of a story— enough to know it was a good one—he would drop by the prosecutor's office and pretend he knew all about it. The prosecutor in charge of the case, anxious to find out just how much he did know, would engage him in conversation, and by skillful parrying, bluff, and feint, Spezi would be able to confirm what he'd been told and fill in the gaps of the rest, while the prosecutor's worst fears would be realized, that the journalist knew everything.

The young defense lawyers who came and went from the Tribunale were a final, indispensable source of information. They were desperate to get their names into the papers; it was a critical part of advancing their careers. When Spezi needed to lay his hands on an important file, such as a trial transcript or an inquest, he would ask one of the lawyers to get it for him, hinting at a favorable mention. If the man hesitated, and the file were crucial enough, Spezi would threaten him. "If you don't do me this favor, I'll see to it that your name won't appear in the newspapers for at least a year." It was a complete bluff, as Spezi had no such power, but a terrifying prospect to a naïve young lawyer. Thus intimidated, the lawyers sometimes let Spezi carry home entire sets of files from an investigation, which he would spend the night photocopying and return in the morning.

There was never a shortage of news in the Monster investigation. Even in the absence of new developments, Spezi always found something to write about in the rumors, conspiracy theories, and general hysteria surrounding the case.

The wildest rumors and unlikeliest conspiracy theories abounded, many involving the medical profession, and Spezi wrote about them all. An unfortunate headline in *La Nazione* fed the feeding frenzy: "The Surgeon of Death Is Back." The headline writer meant to throw out a sensational metaphor, but many people took it literally, and the rumors intensified that the killer must be a doctor. Many physicians suddenly found themselves the subject of vicious rumors and searches.

Some of the anonymous letters police received were specific enough that they felt obliged to investigate, raid, and search certain doctors' offices. They tried to inquire discreetly, to avoid generating more rumors, but in a small city like Florence every investigation seemed to become public, fueling the hysteria and the perception that the killer was a doctor. Public opinion began to gel around a portrait of the Monster: he was a man of culture and breeding, upper-class, and above all a surgeon. Hadn't the medical examiner stated that the operation performed on Carmela and Susanna had been done with "great ability"? Hadn't there been talk that the operation might have been done with a scalpel? And then there was the cold-blooded and highly calculated nature of the crimes themselves, which hinted at a killer of intelligence and education. Similar rumors insisted the killer must be a nobleman. Florentines have always harbored a suspicion of their own nobility—so much so that the early Florentine republic barred them from holding public office.

A week after the killing in the Bartoline Fields, a sudden flood of telephone calls came pouring in to the police, to *La Nazione*, and to the prosecutor's office. Colleagues, friends, and superiors of a prominent gynecologist named Garimeta Gentile were all demanding confirmation of something all of Florence was talking about, but that the press and police refused to admit: that he had been arrested as the killer. Gentile was one of the most prominent gynecologists in Tuscany, director of the Villa Le Rose clinic near Fiesole. His wife, rumor went, had found in his refrigerator, tucked away between the mozzarella and the rucola, the terrible trophies he had taken from his victims. The rumor had started when someone told police that Gentile had hidden the pistol in a safe-deposit box; the police searched the box in great secrecy, finding nothing, but bank employees began to gossip and the word went out. Investigators denied the rumor in the most strenuous terms, but it continued to grow. A disorderly crowd assembled in front of the doctor's house and had to be dispersed by the police. The head prosecutor finally had to go on television to scotch the rumor, threatening to lodge criminal charges against those spreading it.

Late that November, Spezi received a journalistic prize for work he had done unrelated to the case. He was invited to Urbino to collect the prize, a kilo of the finest white Umbrian truffles. His editor allowed him to go only after he promised to file a story from Urbino. Away from his sources and not having anything new to write about, he recounted the histories of some of the famous serial killers of the past, from Jack the Ripper to the Monster of Düsseldorf. He concluded that Florence now had its very own monster—and there, amid the perfume of truffles, he gave the killer a name: *il Mostro di Firenze*, the Monster of Florence.

CHAPTER
5

Spezi became *La Nazione*'s full-time Monster of Florence correspondent. The Monster case offered the young journalist a dazzling wealth of stories, and he made the most of it. As investigators pursued every lead, no matter how unlikely, they churned up dozens of odd happenings, curious characters, and bizarre incidents that Spezi, a connoisseur of human foible, seized on and wrote up—stories that other journalists passed over. The articles that fell from his pen were highly entertaining, and even though many involved wacky and improbable events, all were true. Spezi's articles became famous for their dry turns of phrase and that one wicked detail that remained with readers long after their morning espresso.

One day he learned from a beat cop that investigators had questioned and released an odd character who had been passing himself off as a medical examiner. Spezi found the story charming and pursued it for the paper. The man was "Dr." Carlo Santangelo, a thirty-six-year-old Florentine, of pleasing appearance, a lover of solitude, separated from his wife, who went about dressed in black wearing eyeglasses with smoked lenses, gripping a doctor's bag in his left hand. His card read:

PROF. DR. CARLO SANTANGELO

MEDICAL EXAMINER

INSTITUTE OF PATHOLOGY, FLORENCE

INSTITUTE OF PATHOLOGY, PISA — FORENSIC SECTION

In the ever-present doctor's bag were the tools of his profession, a number of perfectly honed and glistening scalpels. Instead of maintaining an established residence, Dr. Santangelo preferred to pass his days in various hotels or residences in small towns near Florence. And when he chose a hotel, he made sure it was near a small cemetery. If there was a room with a view of the tombstones, so much the better. Dr. Santangelo's face, eyes covered with thick dark lenses, had become familiar to the staff of OFISA, the most prominent funeral establishment in Florence, where he often passed his hours as if on important business. The doctor with the dark lenses doled out prescriptions, saw patients, and even ran a psychoanalysis business on the side.

The only problem was, Dr. Santangelo wasn't a medical examiner or pathologist. He wasn't even a physician, although he seems to have taken it upon himself to operate on live people, at least according to one witness.

Santangelo was unmasked when a serious car accident took place on the autostrada south of Florence, and somebody remembered that in a hotel nearby there lived a doctor. Dr. Santangelo was fetched to provide first aid, and all were amazed to hear that he was none other than the medical examiner who had performed the autopsies on the bodies of Susanna Cambi and Stefano Baldi, the Monster's latest victims. At least that was what several employees of the hotel said they had heard directly from Dr. Santangelo himself, when he had proudly opened his bag and showed them the tools of his profession.

Santangelo's peculiar claim got back to the carabinieri, and it didn't take them long to find out that he was no doctor. They learned of his predilection for small cemeteries and pathology rooms, and, even more alarming, his penchant for scalpels. The carabinieri promptly hauled Santangelo in for questioning.

The phony medical examiner freely admitted to being a liar and spinner of tall tales, although he wasn't able to explain his love for cemeteries at night. He hotly denied as libel, however, the story his girlfriend told of how he had broken off a night of passionate love-making by taking a dose of sleeping pills, saying this was the only way he could resist the temptation to leave his bed of love to take a turn around the tombstones.

The suspicion that Dr. Santangelo was the Monster lasted only a moment. For every night of a double homicide, he had an alibi from the employees of the hotel where he was staying. The doctor, witnesses confirmed, went to bed early, between eight-thirty and nine, in order to rise at three in the morning when the cemeteries called. "I know I do weird things," Santangelo told the magistrate who questioned him. "Sometimes it's occurred to me that I might be a little bit crazy."

The Santangelo story was just one of the many delightful pieces Spezi wrote as the paper's official "Monstrologer." He wrote about the many channelers, tarot card readers, clairvoyants, geomancers, and crystal-ball gazers who offered police their services—and some of whom were actually hired by the police and deposed, the transcripts of their "readings" duly witnessed, notarized, and filed. In middle-class living rooms across the city, an evening would sometimes end with the host and his guests seated around a three-legged table with a small glass upside down on top, questioning one of the Monster's victims and receiving his or her cryptic replies. The results were often sent to Spezi at *La Nazione*, to the police, or circulated feverishly among groups of believers. Next to the official police investigation, there developed a parallel one into the world beyond, which Spezi covered to the great amusement of his readers, as he told of attending readings and séances in graveyards with clairvoyants intent on speaking to the dead.

The case of the Monster so shook the city that it even seemed to revive the long-dead spirit of the dark monk of San Marco, Savonarola, and his thunderings against the decadence of the age. There were those who seized on the Monster as a way to once again declaim against Florence and its presumed moral and spiritual depravity, its middle-class greed and materialism. "The Monster," wrote one editorial correspondent, "is the living expression of this city of shopkeepers, sinking into an orgy of narcissistic self-indulgence perpetrated by its priests, power brokers, puffed-up professors, politicians, and various self-appointed hacks. . . . The Monster is a cheap middle-class vindicator who hides behind a façade of bourgeois respectability. He is simply a man with bad taste."

Others thought the Monster must be, literally, a monk or priest. One wrote in a letter to *La Nazione* that the shells found at the scenes of the killings were old and discolored "because in a monastery an old pistol and some bullets could have been lying around forgotten in some dark corner almost forever." The letter writer went on to point out something that had already been widely discussed among Florentines: that the murderer might be a Savonarola-like priest visiting the wrath of God upon young people for their fornication and depravity. He pointed out that the woody piece of a grapevine stuck into the first victim might be a biblical message recalling the words of Jesus that the "vines which beareth not fruit He taketh away."

Police detectives also took the Savonarola theory seriously, and quietly began looking into certain priests known to have odd or unusual habits. Several Florentine prostitutes told police that from time to time they entertained a priest with rather eccentric tastes. He paid them generously, not for normal sex, but for the privilege of shaving off their pubic hair. The police were interested, reasoning that here was a man who enjoyed working with a razor in that particular area. The girls were able to give the police his name and address.

One crisp Sunday morning, a small group of police and carabinieri in plainclothes, led by a pair of magistrates, entered an ancient country church perched among cypresses in the lovely hills southwest of Florence. The committee was received in the sacristy, where the priest was in the act of dressing in his robes, taking up the sacred vestments with which he was about to say Mass. They showed him a warrant and told him the reason for their visit, stating their intention to search the church, grounds, confessionals, altars, reliquaries, and tabernacle.

The priest staggered and almost fell to the floor in a faint. He didn't try even for a moment to deny his nocturnal avocation as a barber for ladies, but he swore in the strongest terms that he wasn't the Monster. He said he understood why they had to search the premises, but he begged them to keep the reason for their visit secret and delay the search until after he had said Mass.

The priest was allowed to celebrate Mass before his parishioners, joined by the policemen and investigators, who sat through the service looking and acting just like city folk out enjoying a country Mass. They kept a close eye on the priest so as not to run the risk that, during the service, he might make away with some vital clue.

The search took place as soon as the parishioners had filed out, but all the investigators carried away was the priest's razor, and he was soon cleared.

CHAPTER
6

Despite the huge success of his journalistic career chronicling the Monster case, all was not well for Spezi. The savagery of the crimes preyed heavily on his mind. He began to have nightmares and was fearful for the safety of his beautiful Flemish wife, Myriam, and their baby daughter, Eleonora. The Spezis lived in an old villa that had been converted into apartments high on a hill above the city, in the very heart of the countryside stalked by the Monster. Covering the case raised many unanswerable and excruciating questions in his mind about good and evil, God, and human nature.

Myriam urged her husband to seek help, and finally he agreed. Instead of going to a psychiatrist, Spezi, a practicing Catholic, turned to a monk who ran a mental health practice out of his cell in a crumbling eleventh-century Franciscan monastery. Brother Galileo Babbini was short, with Coke-bottle glasses that magnified his piercing black eyes. He was always cold, even in summer, and wore a shabby down coat beneath his brown monk's habit. He seemed to have stepped out of the Middle Ages, and yet he was a highly trained psychoanalyst with a doctorate from the University of Florence.

Brother Galileo combined psychoanalysis with mystical Christianity to counsel people recovering from devastating trauma. His methods were not gentle, and he was unyielding in the pursuit of truth. He had an almost supernatural insight into the dark side of the human soul. Spezi would see him for the duration of the case, and he told me that Brother Galileo had saved his sanity, perhaps his life.

The night of the killing in the Bartoline Fields, a couple driving through the area had passed a red Alfa Romeo at a bottleneck in one of the narrow, walled roads so common to the Florentine countryside. The two cars had to inch past each other, and the couple had gotten a clear look at the occupant of the other car. He was a man, they told police, so nervous that his face was contorted with anxiety. They furnished a description to a forensic Identi-Kit team, which used it to create a portrait of a hard-faced man with coarse features. A deeply scored forehead surmounted a strange face with large, baleful eyes, a hooked nose, and a mouth as tight and thin as a cut.

But the prosecutor's office, fearful of the climate of hysteria gripping Florence, decided to keep the portrait secret for fear it would unleash a witch hunt.

A year went by after the murder in the Bartoline Fields, and the investigation made no progress. As summer 1982 approached, anxiety gripped the city. As if on schedule, on the first Saturday of summer with no moon, June 19, 1982, the Monster struck again in the heart of the Chianti countryside south of Florence. His two victims were Antonella Migliorini and Paolo Mainardi. Both were in their early twenties and they were engaged to be married. They spent so much time together that their friends teased them with the nickname Vinavyl, a popular brand of superglue.

The couple came from Montespertoli, a town legendary for its wines and white truffles, as well as for several stupendous castles that crowned the surrounding hills. They spent the early part of the evening with a large gathering of young people in the Piazza del Popolo, drinking Cokes, eating ice cream, and listening to pop music that on warm Saturday nights blared from the ice-cream kiosk.

Afterwards, Paolo managed to persuade Antonella to take a drive in the countryside, despite her oft-stated terror of the Monster. They headed off into the velvety Tuscan night, taking a road that paralleled a rushing torrent that poured from the hills. They passed the gates of the gigantic crenellated castle of Poppiano, owned for nine hundred years by the counts of Gucciardini, and turned into a dead-end lane, the crickets shrilling in the warm night air, the stars twinkling overhead, two dark walls of fragrant vegetation on either side providing privacy.

At that moment, Antonella and Paolo were in the almost exact geographical center of what might be called the map of the Monster's crimes, past and future.

A reconstruction of the crime detailed what happened next. The couple had finished making love and Antonella had moved into the rear seat to put her clothes back on. Paolo apparently became aware of the killer lurking just outside the car, and he stamped on the accelerator and reversed the car at high speed from the dead-end track. The Monster, taken by surprise, fired into the car, striking Paolo's left shoulder. The terrified girl threw her arms around her boyfriend's head, gripping so tightly that later the clasp of her watch was found tangled in his hair. The car backed out of the lane, shot across the main road, and went into the ditch on the opposite side. Paolo threw the car into forward and tried to drive out, but the rear wheels were firmly stuck in the ditch and spun uselessly.

The Monster, standing on the opposite side of the road, was now bathed in the full glare of the car's headlights. He coolly took aim with his Beretta and shot out each headlight, one after the other, with two perfectly placed rounds. Two shells remained by the side of the road to mark the point where he had taken aim. He crossed the road, threw open the door, and fired two more rounds, one into each of the victims' heads. He yanked the boy out of the car, slipped into the driver's seat, and tried to rock the car out of the ditch. It was stuck fast. He gave up and, without committing his usual mutilation, fled up a hillside next to the road, tossing the car keys about three hundred feet from the car. Near the keys, investigators found an empty medicine bottle of Norzetam (piracetam), a dietary supplement sold over the counter, which was popularly believed to improve memory and brain function. It couldn't be traced.

The Monster took an enormous risk committing the crime next to a main road on a busy Saturday night, and he had saved himself only by acting with superhuman coolness. Investigators later determined that at least six cars had passed in the hour in which the crime had occurred. A kilometer up the road, two people were jogging, taking advantage of the cool night air, and next to the turnoff to Poppiano Castle another couple had parked by the side of the road and were chatting with the interior light on.

The next passing car stopped, thinking there had been a road accident. When medics arrived, the girl was dead. The boy was still breathing. He died in the hospital without regaining consciousness.

The next morning, a prosecutor on the case, Silvia Della Monica, called Mario Spezi and a few other journalists into her office. "You've got to give me a hand here," she said. "I'd like you all to write that the male victim was taken to the hospital alive and that he may have said something useful. It might be a waste of time, but if it frightens someone and causes him to make a false move, who knows?"

The journalists did as requested. Nothing came of it—or so it seemed at first.

That same day, after a long and contentious meeting, the magistrates in charge of the case decided to release the Identi-Kit portrait of the suspect drawn up after the previous double homicide in the Bartoline Fields. On June 30, the brutal face of the unknown suspect appeared on front pages across Italy along with a description of the red Alfa Romeo.

The reaction boggled investigators. Sacks of mail and countless phone calls flooded the offices of the police, carabinieri, prosecutors, and local newspapers. Many people saw in that crude and vicious face a rival in business or love, a neighbor, a local doctor or butcher. "The Monster is a professor of obstetrics, ex-chief of the Department of Gynecology of the Hospital of——," went one typical accusation. Another was certain it was a neighbor whose "first wife left him, then a girlfriend, and then another girlfriend, and now he lives with his mother." The police and carabinieri were paralyzed trying to follow up every lead.

Dozens of people found themselves the object of scrutiny and suspicion. The day the portrait was published, a menacing crowd formed in front of a butcher shop near the Porta Romana of Florence, many clutching newspapers with the portrait. When a new person joined the crowd, he would go into the butcher shop to see for himself, then join the crowd milling in front. The butcher shop had to close for a week.

On that same day, a pizza-maker in the Red Pony pizzeria also became the target of suspicion because he bore an uncanny resemblance to the Identi-Kit. A group of boys began making fun of him by coming into the pizzeria with the portrait, putting on a show of comparing it to him, and then rushing out as if in terror. The next day, after lunch, the man cut his own throat.

The police received thirty-two phone calls identifying a certain taxi driver from the old San Frediano quarter of Florence as the Monster. A police inspector decided to check the person out; he called the taxi company and contrived for the driver to pick him up and take him to police headquarters, where his men surrounded the cab and ordered the driver out. When the taxi driver emerged, the men were astonished: the man matched the Identi-Kit portrait so perfectly that it could have been a photograph of him. The inspector had the cabbie brought to his office, and to his surprise the man heaved a great sigh of relief. "If you hadn't brought me down here," he said, "I'd have come myself just as soon as my shift was over. Ever since that picture was published it's been total hell. I've had nothing but clients who suddenly want to get out of the cab in the middle of the ride." An investigation quickly determined that the taxi driver could not have committed the crimes—the resemblance was a coincidence.

A huge crowd attended the funeral of Paolo and Antonella, the two victims. Cardinal Benelli, the archbishop of Florence, gave the homily, turning it into an indictment of the modern world. "Much has been said," he intoned, "in these recent tragic days of monsters, of madness, of crimes of unimaginable viciousness; but we know well that madness does not arise out of nowhere; madness is the irrational and violent explosion of a world, a society, that has lost its values; that every day becomes more inimical to the human spirit. This afternoon," the cardinal concluded, "we stand here, mute witnesses to one of the worst ever defeats of all that is good in mankind."

The engaged couple were buried one next to the other, the only photograph ever taken of them together placed between their tombs.

Among the avalanche of accusations, letters, and telephone calls that arrived at carabinieri headquarters in Florence, one odd letter stood out. Inside an envelope was nothing more than a yellowed, tattered clipping from an old article published in *La Nazione*, which told of a long-forgotten murder of a couple who had been making love in a car parked in the Florentine countryside. They had been shot with a Beretta pistol firing Winchester series H rounds, the shells having been recovered at the scene. Someone had scrawled on the clipping, "Take another look at this crime." The most chilling thing about the clipping was the date it had been published: August 23, 1968.

The crime had been committed fourteen years before.

CHAPTER
7

D ue to a serendipitous bureaucratic error, the shells collected from that old crime scene, which should have been tossed out, were still sitting in a nylon pouch in the dusty case files.

Each one bore on the rim the unique signature of the Monster's gun.

Investigators reopened the old case with a vengeance. But they were immediately confounded: the 1968 double murder had been solved. It had been an open-and-shut case. A man had confessed and was convicted of the double homicide, and he could not be the Monster of Florence, as he had been in prison during the first killings and had lived since his release in a halfway house, under the watchful eye of nuns, so feeble he could barely walk. There was no possible way for him to have committed any of the Monster's crimes. Nor was his confession false—it contained specific, accurate details of the double homicide that only a person present at the scene could have known.

On the surface, the facts of the 1968 killing seemed simple, squalid, even banal. A married woman, Barbara Locci, had been having an affair with a Sicilian bricklayer. One night after going to the movies, they had parked on a quiet lane afterwards to have sex. The woman's jealous husband had ambushed them in the middle of the act and shot them to death. The husband, an immigrant from the island of Sardinia named Stefano Mele, was picked up a few hours later. When a paraffin-glove test indicated he had recently fired a handgun, he broke down and confessed to killing his wife and her lover in a fit of jealousy. He was given a reduced sentence of fourteen years due to "infirmity of mind."

Case closed.

The pistol used in the killing had never been recovered. At the time Mele claimed to have tossed it in a nearby irrigation ditch. But the ditch and the entire area had been thoroughly searched the night of the crime and no pistol had been found. At the time, nobody had paid much attention to the missing gun.

Investigators converged on the halfway house near Verona where Mele was living. They questioned him relentlessly. They wanted to know, in particular, what he had done with the gun after the killings. But nothing Mele said made any sense; his mind was half gone. He constantly contradicted himself and gave the impression he was hiding something, his demeanor watchful and tense. They could get nothing of value from him. Whatever secret he was hiding, he was hiding it so tenaciously that it looked like he would take it to the grave.

Stefano Mele was housed in an ugly white building on a flat plain near the Adige River, outside the romantic city of Verona. He lived with other ex-convicts who, having discharged their debt to society, had nowhere to go, no family, and no possibility of gainful employment. The priest running this goodly institution suddenly found himself, among his other pressing concerns, with the additional duty of protecting the diminutive Sardinian from packs of hungry journalists. Every red-blooded journalist in Italy wanted to interview Mele; the priest was equally determined to keep them away.

Spezi, the Monstrologer of *La Nazione*, was not as easily deterred as the rest. He arrived there one day with a documentary filmmaker, on the pretense of shooting a documentary on the halfway house's good work. After a flattering interview with the priest and a series of fake interviews with various inmates, they finally ended up face-to-face with Stefano Mele.

The first glimpse was discouraging: the Sardinian, although not old, paced about the room, taking tiny, nervous steps with rigid legs, almost as if he was about to topple over. To move a chair was almost a superhuman feat for him. An expressionless smile, frozen on his face, revealed a cemetery of rotten teeth. He was hardly the picture of the cold-blooded killer who, fifteen years before, had murdered two people with efficiency and sangfroid.

The interview, at the beginning, was difficult. Mele was on guard and suspicious. But little by little he relaxed, and even began to warm to the two filmmakers, glad to have finally found sympathetic listeners in whom he could confide. He finally invited them back to his room, where he showed them old photographs of his "missus" (as he called his murdered wife, Barbara) as well as pictures of their son, Natalino.

But whenever Spezi approached the old story of the crime of 1968, Mele became vague. His answers were long and rambling, and he seemed to be spouting out whatever came into his head. It seemed hopeless.

At the end, he said something odd. "They need to figure out where that pistol is, otherwise there will be more murders . . . *They* will continue to kill . . . *They* will continue . . ."

When Spezi left, Mele gave him a gift: a postcard showing the house and balcony in Verona said to have been the place where Romeo confessed his love to Juliet. "Take it," Mele said. "I'm the 'couple man' and this is the most famous couple in the world."

They will continue . . . Only after he left did the peculiar use of the plural pronoun strike Spezi. Mele had repeatedly used "they" as if referring to more than one Monster. Why would he think there were several? It seemed to imply that he had not been alone when his wife and her lover were killed. He had accomplices. Mele evidently believed that these accomplices had gone on to murder more couples.

That was when Spezi realized something that the police had also learned: the 1968 killing had not been a crime of passion. It had been a group killing, a clan killing. Mele had not been alone at the scene of the crime: he had accomplices.

Had one or more of those accomplices gone on to become the Monster of Florence?

The police began to investigate who might have been with Mele on that fateful night. This stage of the investigation delved deeply into the strange and violent Sardinian clan to which Mele belonged. It became known as the *Pista Sarda*, the Sardinian Trail.

CHAPTER
8

The Sardinian Trail investigation illuminated a curious and almost forgotten corner of Italian history, the mass emigration in the 1960s from the island of Sardinia to the Italian mainland. Many of these immigrants ended up in Tuscany, changing the character of the province forever.

To go back to Italy in the early sixties is to make a journey much longer and deeper than a mere forty-five years. Italy was another country then, a world that has utterly vanished today.

The unified country had been created in 1871, cobbled together from various grand duchies and fiefdoms, ancient lands awkwardly stitched into a new nation. The inhabitants spoke some six hundred languages and dialects. When the new Italian state chose the Florentine dialect to be official "Italian," only two percent of the population could actually speak it. (Florentine was chosen over Roman and Neapolitan because it was the language of Dante.) Even in 1960, fewer than half of the citizens could speak standard Italian. The country was poor and isolated, still recovering from the massive destruction of World War II, mired in hunger and malaria. Few Italians had running water in their homes, owned cars, or had electricity.

The great industrial and economic miracle of modern Italy was just beginning.

In 1960, the poorest, most backward area in all of Italy was the barren, sunbaked interior mountains of the island of Sardinia.

This was a Sardinia long before the Costa Smeralda, the harbors and yacht clubs, the rich Arabs and golf courses and million-dollar seaside villas. It was an isolated culture that had turned its back on the sea. Sardinians had always been afraid of the sea, because in centuries past it brought them only death, pillage, and rape. "He who comes from the sea, robs," went an ancient Sardinian expression. From the sea came ships bearing the Christian cross of the Pisans, who cut the Sardinian forests to build their navy. From the sea arrived the black feluccas of Arab pirates who carried off women and children. And many centuries ago—so the legends went—also from the sea came a giant tsunami that wiped out the seaside towns, driving the inhabitants forever into the mountains.

The police and carabinieri charged with investigating the *Pista Sarda*, the Sardinian Trail, went back into those mountains, back in time to the town of Villacidro, where many of the Sardinians connected to the Mele clan had originated.

In 1960, almost nobody in Sardinia spoke Italian, using instead a language all their own, Logudorese, considered to be the oldest and least contaminated of all the Romance languages. The Sardinians lived with indifference to whatever law happened to be imposed by *sos italianos*, as they referred to the people of the mainland. They followed their own unwritten laws, the Barbagian code, born out of the ancient region of central Sardinia called La Barbagia, one of the wildest and least populated areas in Europe.

At the heart of the Barbagian code was the man known as the *balente*, the wily outlaw, the man of cunning, skill, and courage, who takes care of his own. Stealing, particularly of livestock, was an exalted activity under the Barbagian code when it was committed against another tribe, because, aside from mere gain, it was a heroic act, an act of *balentia*. The thief, by stealing, demonstrated his cunning and his superiority to his adversary, who paid a just price for his incapacity to take care of his own property and flocks. Kidnapping and even murder were justified under similar rules. The *balente* had to be feared and respected.

Sardinians, especially shepherds who lived most of their lives in nomadic isolation, despised the Italian state as an occupying power. If a shepherd, by way of the code of *balentìa*, transgressed the laws inflicted by "foreigners" (Italians), instead of bearing the shame of prison he became an outlaw, joining groups of similar fugitives and brigands who lived in the mountains and raided other communities. Even as an outlaw, he could continue to live secretly in his community, where he was given protection, a welcome, and, beyond that, admiration. To the community, in return, the bandits distributed a share of their spoils, always keeping their depredations away from the home territory. The people of Sardinia viewed the brigand as a person who valiantly defended his rights and the honor of the community against the foreign oppressor, investing in him an almost mythic esteem, a figure of romance and courage.

It was into this clannish environment that the investigators delved as they followed the twists and turns of the Sardinian Trail, prying open an antique culture that made the Sicilian concept of *omertà* seem almost modern.

The village of Villacidro was isolated even by Sardinian standards. Lovely despite its great poverty, it sat on a high plain, divided by the river Leni, ringed by craggy peaks. Deer roamed the oak forests beyond the village and royal eagles soared above its red granite cliffs. The great waterfall of Sa Spendula outside the town, one of the natural wonders of Sardinia, was the inspiration for the poet Gabriele D'Annunzio on a visit to the island in 1882. As he gazed in wonder at the series of falls, tumbling down among boulders, he spied one of the local inhabitants:

> *In the lush valley a watchful shepherd,*
> *wrapped in animal skins,*
> *stands poised on the steep limestone cliffs,*
> *like a bronze faun, silent and still.*

The rest of Sardinia, on the other hand, considered Villacidro a cursed land, a "country of shadows and witches," as an old saying went. Everyone said that the witches up at Villacidro, *is cogas*, covered themselves with long dresses that swept the ground, to hide their tails.

Villacidro was home to a family named Vinci.

There were three Vinci brothers. The oldest, Giovanni, had raped one of his sisters and was shunned by the community. The youngest, Francesco, had a reputation for violence and was known for his ability with a knife—able to kill, skin, gut, and butcher a sheep in record time.

The middle one was named Salvatore. He had married a teenage girl, Barbarina, "Little Barbara," who had given him a baby, Antonio. One night, Barbarina was found dead in her bed, and her death was ruled a suicide by propane gas. But the rumors in Villacidro about this supposed "suicide" were ugly. There were whispers that someone had removed Antonio from his mother's bed after the gas bottle had been turned on, thus saving his life—and leaving the mother to die. Most of the townspeople believed Salvatore had murdered her.

The death of Barbarina was the final straw against the Vinci brothers. The town of Villacidro united against them, and they were compelled to leave. One fine day in 1961 they boarded a ferry for the mainland, joining the great emigration from Sardinia. They landed in Tuscany to begin a new life.

On the other side of the sea, another Barbara awaited them.

CHAPTER
9

When the three Vinci brothers arrived at the docks in Livorno, they were not typical Sardinian immigrants to Tuscany, stepping off the ferry, clutching their cardboard suitcases, with dazed looks on their faces, the first time out of their small mountain village with scarcely a lira in their pockets. The Vincis were self-assured, adaptable, and surprisingly sophisticated.

Salvatore and Francesco were the two brothers who would play a major role in the Monster of Florence story. Physically they resembled each other: short and robust, good-looking, with curly, raven-black hair, their restless eyes peering out of the deep fissures in their rough, arrogant faces. Both were blessed with an intelligence far greater than might be expected from their limited background. But despite their resemblance, the two brothers couldn't have been more different. Salvatore was quiet, reflective, introverted, given to reasoned arguments and discussions that he pursued with a mellifluous, Old World courtesy. He wore a pair of spectacles that gave him the air of a professor of Latin. Francesco, the youngest, was extroverted and cocky, the man of action with a macho swagger, the true *balente* of the two.

Naturally, they hated each other.

Once in Tuscany, Salvatore found work as a bricklayer. Francesco spent most of his time in a bar outside of Florence that was an infamous hangout for Sardinian criminals. It was the unofficial headquarters of three famous Sardinian gangsters who had exported to Tuscany a classic Sardinian business: kidnapping for ransom. These men were partly responsible for the rash of kidnappings that plagued Tuscany in the late sixties and seventies. In one instance, when a ransom was slow in coming, they killed the victim, who was a count, and disposed of the body by feeding it to man-eating pigs—a detail Thomas Harris used to great effect in his novel *Hannibal*. Francesco Vinci, as far as we know, never took part in these kidnappings. He dedicated himself to petty holdups, theft, and another venerable Sardinian tradition, rustling livestock.

Salvatore rented a room in a run-down house occupied by a Sardinian family named Mele, where Stefano Mele lived with his father, siblings, and wife, Barbara Locci. (In Italy, the wife traditionally keeps her maiden name after marriage.) Barbara Locci was slinky and sloe-eyed, with a flattened nose and thick, well-shaped lips. She favored skintight red skirts that showed off a full-bodied figure. When she was a teenager back in Sardinia, her deeply impoverished family had arranged for her to marry Stefano, who came from marginally better circumstances. He was much older than she, and on top of it *uno stupido*, a simpleton. When the Mele family had immigrated to Tuscany, she went along.

Once in Tuscany, the very lively young Barbara set about ruining the Mele family's honor. She often stole money from her in-laws and went out on the town seeking men, giving them money, and sneaking them back into the Mele home. Stefano was completely unable to control her.

In an effort to put an end to her nocturnal adventures, the patriarch of the Mele family, Stefano's father, put iron bars on the first-floor windows and tried to keep her locked in the house. It didn't work. Barbara soon took up with their lodger, Salvatore Vinci.

Barbara's husband was no obstacle to the affair. He even encouraged it. Salvatore Vinci testified later, "He wasn't jealous. He was the one who invited me to live in their house when I was looking for a place to live. 'Come live with us!' he said. 'We've got a free room.' 'What about money?' 'Give whatever you can.' So I moved into Mele's house. And right away he brought me to meet his wife in bed. Then he urged me to take her to the movies. He said that it didn't matter to him. Or he would go play cards at his social club and leave me alone with her in the house."

At one point Stefano's motorbike was hit by a car and he was laid up in the hospital for several months recuperating. The following year Barbara bore him a son, Natalino, but anyone with the ability to count to nine could see that the paternity of Natalino was in grave doubt.

Fed up with this blight on their honor, the patriarch of the family threw Stefano and his wife out of the house, along with Salvatore. Stefano and Barbara rented a hovel in a working-class suburb west of Florence, where she continued to see Salvatore, with the complete (and indeed enthusiastic) cooperation of her husband.

"What was her attraction?" Salvatore testified later about Barbara. "Well, when she made love she certainly wasn't a statue. She knew what kind of game it was, and she knew how to play it."

In the summer of 1968, Barbara left Salvatore and took up with his brother Francesco, the *balente* who played the macho man. With him, Barbara acted the part of a gangster's moll, going to the Sardinian bar, joking with the tough guys, wiggling her hips. She dressed like a femme fatale. Once she went too far, at least for Francesco's taste, and he seized her by the hair, dragged her into the street, and ripped off the offending dress, leaving her in the middle of a gaping crowd in only her slip and hosiery.

At the beginning of August 1968, a new lover appeared on the scene: Antonio Lo Bianco, a bricklayer from Sicily, tall, heavily muscled, with black hair. He too was married, but that didn't stop him from challenging Francesco: "Barbara?" he was reported to have said. "I'll fuck her in a week." Which he did.

Now both Salvatore and Francesco had reason to feel angry and humiliated. On top of that, Barbara had just stolen six hundred thousand lire from Stefano, money he had received for the motorbike accident.

The Vinci and Mele clan feared she would give it to Lo Bianco. They decided to get it back.

The story of Barbara Locci was reaching its final chapter.

The end came on August 21, 1968. A careful reconstruction of the crime, done years later, revealed what happened. Barbara went with her new lover, Antonio Lo Bianco, to the movies to see the latest Japanese horror flick. She brought along her son, Natalino, six years old. Afterwards the three of them drove off in Lo Bianco's white Alfa Romeo. The car headed out of town and turned in to a little dirt road past a cemetery. They drove a few hundred feet and stopped next to a stand of cane, a place where they often went to have sex.

The shooter and his accomplices were already hidden in the cane. They waited until Barbara and Lo Bianco began having sex—her on top, straddling him. The left rear window of the car was open—it was a warm night—and the shooter approached the car in silence, reached in the window with the .22 Beretta in hand, and took aim. The gun was poised a few feet above the head of Natalino, who was sleeping in the backseat. From almost point-blank range—there was powder tattooing—he fired seven shots: four into him and three into her. Each round was perfectly placed, penetrating vital organs, and they both died immediately. Natalino woke at the first shot and saw, in front of his eyes, the bright yellow flashes.

In the magazine of the gun remained one more shot. The shooter handed the gun to Stefano Mele, who took it, pointed it at his dead wife's body with an unsteady hand, and pulled the trigger. The shot, even from that close range, was wild and it struck the woman in the arm. No matter—she was dead and the shot had served its purpose: it had contaminated Stefano's hand with powder that the paraffin-glove test, then in use, would certainly pick up. Mele, the simpleton, would take the fall for the rest. Someone searched the glove compartment for the missing six hundred thousand lire, but it wasn't found. (Investigators would find it later, hidden elsewhere in the car.)

The remaining problem was the child, Natalino. He couldn't be left in the car with his dead mother. After the killing, he saw his father holding the gun and cried out, "That's the gun that killed Mommy!"

Mele threw the gun down and picked up his son, hoisted him to his shoulders, and set off walking. He sang a song to calm him down, "The Sunset." Two and a half kilometers down the road, Stefano dropped him at the front door of a stranger's house, rang the doorbell, and disappeared. When the homeowner leaned out the window, he saw a terrified little boy standing in the light of the front door. "Mama and Uncle are dead in the car," the little boy cried in a high, quavering voice.

CHAPTER
10

Even at the time of the 1968 double homicide, the investigation uncovered many clues that a group of men had committed the killings,
clues that were ignored or dismissed.

The police back then had questioned the six-year-old Natalino
closely, the only witness to the crime. His story was confused. His father had been there. At one point during his questioning, he said, "I
saw Salvatore in the cane." He quickly reversed that, saying it wasn't
Salvatore but Francesco, and then he admitted it was his father who
told him to say it was Francesco. He described the "shadow" of another man at the crime scene and spoke vaguely about an "Uncle
Piero" as also being present, a man who "parted his hair on the right
and worked at night"—which must have been his uncle, Piero Mucciarini, who worked as a baker. Then he said he couldn't remember
anything.

One of the carabinieri officers, frustrated by the child's incessant
contradictions, threatened him: "If you don't tell the truth, I'll take
you back to your dead mother."

The only solid piece of information the investigators felt they had
gotten from the boy was that he had seen his father at the crime scene

with a gun in hand. As the wronged husband, he was the perfect suspect. They took Stefano Mele in that very night and quickly demolished a pathetic alibi that he had been home sick. The paraffin-glove test revealed traces of nitrate powder between the thumb and index finger of his right hand, the classic pattern of someone who had recently fired a handgun. Even a simpleton like Mele realized that after the test, there was no point in further denial, and he confessed to being present at the scene of the crime. Perhaps it even dawned on him that he had been framed.

Cautiously, fearfully, Mele told the carabinieri interrogators that Salvatore Vinci was the actual killer. "One day," he said, "he told me that he had a pistol . . . It was him, he was the jealous lover of my wife. It was him, who, after she left him, threatened to kill her, he said it more than once. One day when I asked him to give me back some money, do you know what he said? 'I'll kill your wife for you,' that's what he said, 'and that'll even up the debt.' He really said that!"

But then, abruptly, Mele retracted his accusations against Salvatore Vinci and took full responsibility for the murder. As to what had happened to the gun, he never gave a satisfactory answer. "I threw it in the irrigation ditch," he claimed—but a careful search that night of the ditch and the surrounding area revealed nothing.

The carabinieri did not like his story. It seemed improbable that this man who had difficulty finding his way around a room would, by himself, have been able to find the scene of the crime, without a car, many kilometers from his house, ambush the lovers, and place seven shots into them. When they pressed him, Stefano once again turned the accusation against Salvatore. "He was the only one who had a car," he said.

The carabinieri decided to bring the two together to see what might happen. They picked up Salvatore and brought him down to the carabinieri barracks. Those present have said they never will forget that meeting.

Salvatore entered the room, suddenly the *balente* himself, full of swaggering self-assurance. He stopped and subjected Mele to a hard, wordless stare. Bursting into tears, Mele threw himself on the ground at Salvatore's feet, groveling and sobbing. "Forgive me! Please forgive me!" he cried. Vinci turned around and left, never having spoken a word. He possessed an inexplicable hold over Stefano Mele, the ability to enforce an *omertà* so powerful that Mele would risk life in prison rather than challenge it. Mele immediately retracted his accusations of Salvatore being the shooter and once again accused Salvatore's brother Francesco. But when pressed, Mele finally went back to insisting he had committed the double murder all by himself.

At this point the police and the examining magistrate (the judge who oversees the investigation) felt satisfied. Regardless of the particulars, the crime was solved in the main: they had the confession of the wronged husband, backed up by forensic evidence and the statements of his son. Mele was the only one charged with murder.

During the trial in the Court of Assizes, when Salvatore Vinci was brought in to testify, an odd scene occurred. As he was gesturing and speaking, his hand caught the attention of the judge. On one finger he wore a woman's engagement ring.

"What is that ring?" the judge asked.

"It's Barbara's engagement ring," he said, looking not at the judge but giving Mele another hard stare. "She gave it to me."

Mele was convicted as the sole perpetrator of the double homicide and sentenced to fourteen years.

In 1982, investigators began to compile a list of possible accomplices to the 1968 killing. On the list were the two Vinci brothers, Salvatore and Francesco, as well as Piero Mucciarini and the "shadow" mentioned by Natalino.

Investigators felt sure that the gun had not been thrown in the ditch, as Stefano insisted. A gun used in a homicide is almost never casually sold, given away, or tossed. One of Mele's accomplices, they felt, must have taken it home and carefully hidden it. Six years later, that gun had emerged from its hiding place, along with the same box of bullets, to become the Monster of Florence's gun.

Tracing the gun, they realized, was the key to solving the case of the Monster of Florence.

* * *

The Sardinian Trail investigation zeroed in on Francesco Vinci first, because he was the *balente*, the cocky one, the guy with a rap sheet. He was violent, he had beaten up his girlfriends, and he hung around with gangsters. Salvatore, on the other hand, seemed quieter, a man who had always worked hard and stayed out of trouble. He had a spotless record. To the Tuscan police, who had no experience with serial killers, Francesco Vinci seemed the obvious choice.

Investigators dug up bits and pieces of circumstantial evidence against Francesco. They established that he had not been far from the scenes of each crime on the dates they were committed. Between robberies, thefts of livestock, and escapades with women, he moved around a great deal. At the time of the 1974 double homicide in Borgo San Lorenzo, for example, they placed him near the scene, due to an argument between him and a jealous husband, in which his favorite nephew, Antonio, the son of Salvatore Vinci, also took part. At the time of the Montespertoli killing, Francesco had also been nearby, again visiting Antonio, who happened to live at that time in a little town six kilometers from the scene.

A prime piece of evidence against Francesco, however, took a while to surface. In the middle of July, the carabinieri in a town on the southern Tuscan coast reported to investigators in Florence that on June 21 they had discovered a car hidden in the woods, covered with branches. They had finally gotten around to running the license plate and found it belonged to Francesco Vinci.

This seemed highly significant: June 21 happened to be the day that Spezi and other journalists had published the (false) reports that one of the victims of the Montespertoli killings may have survived long enough to talk. Perhaps the news had spooked the Monster after all, prompting him to hide his car.

The carabinieri took Vinci in and asked him for an explanation. He launched into a story about a woman and a jealous husband, but it didn't make much sense and, furthermore, it didn't seem to explain why he had hidden the car.

Francesco Vinci was arrested in August of 1982, two months after the Montespertoli killings. At the time, the examining magistrate said to the press, "The danger now is that a new killing might happen, even more spectacular than before. The Monster, in fact, might be tempted to reassert his paternity claim to the killings by moving yet again into action." It was a strange thing for a judge to say on the arrest of a suspect, but it showed a high level of uncertainty among the investigators that they had the right man.

Fall and winter came, and there were no new killings. Francesco Vinci remained in custody. Florentines, however, did not rest easy: Francesco did not look like the intelligent and aristocratic Monster they had imagined; he was too much the image of a cheap hustler, ladies' man, and macho charmer.

All of Florence awaited with trepidation the arrival of the warm weather of summer, the time favored by the Monster.

CHAPTER
11

During that fall and winter of 1982–83, Mario Spezi wrote a book on the Monster of Florence case. Entitled *Il Mostro di Firenze*, it was published in May. It told the story of the case from the 1968 killings to the Montespertoli double homicide. The book was devoured by a public terrified of what the coming season might bring. But as the balmy nights of summer settled on the green hills of Florence, no new killings occurred. Florentines began to hope that perhaps the police had gotten the right man after all.

In addition to writing a book and publishing articles on the Monster case, that summer Spezi wrote a puff piece about a young filmmaker named Cinzia Torrini, who had produced a charming little documentary about the life of Berto, the last ferryman across the Arno River—an ancient, wizened man who regaled his passengers with stories, legends, and old Tuscan sayings. Torrini was pleased by Spezi's article, and she read his Monster book with interest. She called him to propose the idea of making a film on the Monster of Florence, and Spezi invited her to dinner at his apartment. It would be a late dinner, even by Italian standards, because Spezi kept journalistic hours.

And so it was that on the evening of September 10, 1983, Torrini found herself driving up the steep hill that led to Spezi's apartment. As might be expected from a cinematographer, Torrini had a vivid imagination. The trees on either side of the road, she said later, looked like the hands of skeletons twisting and clawing in the wind. She could not stop herself from questioning her wisdom at going out in the heart of the Florentine hills on a moonless Saturday night to talk to someone about hideous crimes committed in the Florentine hills on moonless Saturday nights. Around one curve of the winding road, the headlights of her old Fiat 127 spotlighted a whitish thing in the middle of the narrow road. The "thing" spread itself, becoming enormous. It detached itself from the asphalt and rose, noiselessly, like a dirty sheet carried off by the wind, revealing itself to be a great white owl. Torrini felt a tightening of her stomach, because Italians believe, as the Romans did before them, that it is an ugly omen to encounter an owl in the nighttime. She almost turned around.

She parked her car in the small parking area outside the huge iron gates of the old villa turned into an apartment building and rang the bell. As soon as Spezi opened the green door to his apartment, her sense of disquiet vanished. The place was welcoming, warm, and eccentric, with an old seventeenth-century gambling table, called a scagliola, used as a coffee table, old photographs and drawings on the walls, a fireplace in one corner. The dining table had already been set on the terrace, under a white awning, overlooking the twinkling lights sprinkling the hills. Torrini laughed at herself for the absurd uneasiness she had felt on the drive up and put it out of her mind.

They spent much of the evening talking about the possibility of making a film on the case of the Monster of Florence.

"It seems to me it would be difficult," Spezi said. "The story lacks a central character—the killer. I have my doubts the police have the right man, the man they have in prison awaiting trial, Francesco Vinci. It would be a murder mystery without an ending."

Not a problem, Torrini explained. "The main character isn't the killer: it's the city of Florence itself—the city that discovers it harbors a monster within."

Spezi explained why he thought Francesco Vinci was not the Monster. "All they have against him is that he was a lover of the first woman killed, that he beats up his girlfriends, and that he's a crook. In my view, these are elements in his favor."

"Why do you say that?" Torrini asked.

"He likes women. He's a big success with women, and that's enough to convince me he isn't the Monster. He hits them but he doesn't kill them. The Monster *destroys* women. He hates them because he wants them and can't have them. That's his frustration, the thing that damns him, and so he possesses them physically in the only way he can, which is to steal the part most indicative of their femininity."

"If you believe that," Torrini said, "then it must mean the Monster is impotent. Is that what you think?"

"More or less."

"What do you make of the ritual aspects of the killings, the careful placement of the body? The stick from a grapevine inserted in the vagina, for example, which recalls the words of Saint John that the 'vines which beareth not fruit He taketh away'? A killer who is punishing couples for having sex outside of marriage?"

Spezi blew a stream of smoke toward the ceiling and laughed. "That's a bunch of twaddle. You know why he used an old piece of grapevine? If you look at the crime scene photos, you see that they were parked right next to a vineyard! He simply grabbed the closest stick he could find. To me, his use of a stick to violate a woman seems to confirm that he is not exactly Superman. He didn't and probably can't rape his victims."

Toward the end of the evening, Spezi opened his book and read the last page out loud. "Many investigators feel the case of the Monster of Florence is solved. But if, at the end of a dinner passed in pleasant company, you were to ask me what I thought, I would tell you the truth: that it is with a strong sense of unease that I answer the first ringing of the telephone on a Sunday morning. Especially if the previous Saturday evening was the night of the new moon."

After Mario set down his book, a silence fell on the terrace that overlooked the Florentine hills.

And then the telephone rang.

It was a lieutenant of the local carabinieri, one of Spezi's contacts. "Mario, they've just found two people killed in a VW camper in Gio-goli, above Galluzzo. The Monster? I don't know. The dead are two men. But if I were you, I'd head over there for a look."

CHAPTER

12

To reach Giogoli, Spezi and Torrini took a road that climbed a steep hill behind the great monastery of La Certosa. The road is called Via Volterrana, and it is one of the most ancient in Europe, built by the Etruscans three thousand years ago. At the top of the hill, Via Volterrana makes a gentle turn and runs straight along the ridgeline. Immediately on the right lies a second road, Via di Giogoli, a narrow lane running between mossy stone walls. The wall on the right encloses the grounds of the Villa Sfacciata, which belonged to the noble family Martelli. Sfacciata means "cheeky" or "impudent" in Italian, and the mysterious appellation went back five hundred years, to at least the time when the villa was home to the man who gave America its name.

The left wall of Via di Giogoli encloses a large olive grove. About fifty meters from the beginning of the road, almost opposite the villa, stood a break in the wall, which allowed farm equipment access to the grove. The opening led to a level area that enjoyed a magical view of the southern Florentine hills, over which were sprinkled ancient castles, towers, churches, and villas. A few hundred meters away, on top of the closest hill, stood a famed Romanesque tower known as

Sant'Alessandro a Giogoli. On the next hill rose an exquisite sixteenth-century villa called I Collazzi, half hidden behind a cluster of cypress trees and umbrella pines. It belonged to the Marchi family, one of whose heirs by marriage had become the Marchesa Frescobaldi. Being a personal friend of Prince Charles and Lady Diana, she had entertained the royal pair shortly after their marriage.

Beyond this extraordinary view, the Via di Giogoli descended through torturous switchbacks through villages and small farms, ending in the monolithic working-class suburbs of Florence in the valley below. At night, those gray suburbs became a twinkling carpet of lights.

It would have been hard to find a more beautiful place in all of Tuscany.

Later—too late—the city of Florence would post a sign at this spot that said, in German, English, French, and Italian, "No parking from 7:00 p.m. to 7:00 a.m. No camping for reasons of security." On that evening, the night of September 10, 1983, there had been no sign, and someone had camped there.

When Spezi and Torrini arrived, they found the full cast of characters in the Monster investigation. There was Silvia Della Monica, a prosecutor, with the head prosecutor, Piero Luigi Vigna, his handsome face so sunken and gray it looked almost collapsed. The medical examiner, Mauro Maurri, his blue eyes glittering, was working on the two cadavers. Chief Inspector Sandro Federico was also there, pacing about in a state of high nervous tension.

A spotlight fixed to the top of a police car threw a spectral light across the scene, casting long shadows from the group of people arranged in a semicircle around the sky blue VW bus with German license plates. The stark light emphasized the ugliness of the scene, the scratches on the beaten-up old camper, the lines in the faces of the investigators, the screwlike branches of the olive trees looming against the black sky. To the left of the camper, the field sloped away into darkness toward a cluster of stone houses where, twenty years later, I would take up temporary residence with my family.

When they arrived, the left door of the camper stood open and from inside could be heard, just concluding, the music from the film *Blade Runner*. The music had been playing all day long, without ceasing, as the tape player automatically looped the tape over and over. Inspector Sandro Federico approached and opened his hand, showing two .22 caliber shells. On the base was the same unmistakable mark made by the gun of the Monster.

The Monster had struck again, and the number of his victims had now risen to ten. Francesco Vinci, still in jail, could not have committed the crime.

"Why would he strike two men this time?" Spezi asked.

"Take a look inside the camper," said Federico, with a jerk of his head.

Spezi went toward the van. Passing along its side, he noticed that in the high part of the little windows on the side, in a thin band where the glass was transparent, there were bullet holes. To look inside, he had to stand on his tiptoes. The killer, in order to aim properly, would have to have been taller than Spezi, at least five feet ten inches. He also noted bullet holes in the metal side of the van itself.

Around the van's open door stood a number of people; policemen in plainclothes, carabinieri, and crime scene investigators; their footprints lay everywhere on the dew-laden grass, obliterating any sign left by the killer. It was one more example, Spezi thought, of a botched crime scene.

But before he looked inside the van, Spezi's eye was arrested by something scattered about on the ground outside, pages ripped up from a glossy pornographic magazine entitled *Golden Gay*.

A dim light filtered into the interior. The two seats in front were empty: immediately behind was the body of a young man with a thin mustache, his eyes glazed over, lying stretched out on a double mattress, his feet toward the rear of the van. The second body was in the back of the van, in the corner. It was still crouching as if to make itself as small as possible, petrified with terror, its hands clenched, its face covered by a cascade of long blond hair. The hair was streaked with blood, black and congealed.

"Looks like a girl, don't you think?" came the voice of Sandro Federico, shaking Spezi out of his surprise.

"At first we were fooled, too. But it's a man. It seems our friend made the same mistake. Can you imagine how he felt when he discovered it?"

On Monday, September 12, the papers screamed out the news:

TERROR IN FLORENCE
The Monster Chooses His Victims at Random

The two victims, Horst Meyer and Uwe Rüsch, both twenty-four years old, had been traveling around Italy together and had parked their VW bus in this place on September 8. Their almost nude bodies had been discovered around seven o'clock the evening of September 10.

By this time, Francesco Vinci had spent thirteen months in jail, and the public had come to believe he was the Monster of Florence. It seemed that once again, as with Enzo Spalletti, the Monster himself had demonstrated the innocence of the accused.

The Monster of Florence was now international news. The *Times* of London devoted an entire Sunday section to the case. Television crews arrived from as far away as Australia.

"Even after twelve victims,[1] all we know is that the Monster is free and that his .22 caliber Beretta could kill again," wrote *La Nazione*.

Now that the Monster had killed while Francesco Vinci was in prison, his release seemed imminent. But as the days went by, Vinci remained incarcerated. Investigators suspected that the double homicide had been "made to order." Perhaps, they theorized, someone close to Vinci wished to demonstrate that he couldn't be the killer. The crime of Giogoli was anomalous, improvised, different. It seemed strange that the Monster would have made such a grave mistake, given their assumption that he took his time watching the couple having sex before killing them. And then he had killed on a Friday night, not a Saturday, as was his custom.

[1]At the time, many people considered the 1968 double homicide to have been the Monster's first murders—hence twelve victims, not ten.

A new examining magistrate had arrived in Florence shortly before the crime and was now in charge of the Monster investigation. His name was Mario Rotella. He chilled the public with one of his first public statements, in which he said, "We have never identified the so-called Monster of Florence with Francesco Vinci. For the crimes committed after the 1968 homicide he is only a suspect." And then he added, causing a furor, "He is not the only such suspect."

One of the prosecutors, Silvia Della Monica, aroused even more confusion and speculation when she said, "Vinci is not the Monster. But neither is he innocent."

CHAPTER
13

A few days following the Giogoli killings, there was a tense summit meeting in the prosecutor's offices, on the second floor of a Baroque palace in Piazza San Firenze. (The palace is one of the few seventeenth-century edifices in the city—disparaged by Florentines as "new construction.") They met in the small office of Piero Luigi Vigna, the air as thick as a Maremma fog. Vigna was in the habit of breaking his cigarettes in two and smoking both pieces, under the illusion that he was smoking less. Silvia Della Monica was there—small, blonde, herself surrounded by a self-generated cloud of smoke; also in attendance was a colonel of the carabinieri, who had brought two packs of his favorite Marlboros, and Chief Inspector Sandro Federico, who never ceased torturing a withered "toscano" cigar between his teeth. An assistant prosecutor smoked his way through pack after pack of tarry Gauloises. The only nonsmoker in the room was Adolfo Izzo, who merely had to breathe to acquire the habit.

Federico and the carabinieri colonel presented a reconstruction of the Giogoli murders. Using diagrams and flow charts, they showed the sequence of events, how the killer had shot one of the men through the little window and then had fired through the sides of the van, killing the other man where he was crouching in the corner. The Monster then entered the van, fired some more rounds into them, and discovered his mistake. In a rage, he picked up a gay magazine and ripped it up, scattering the pieces outside, and left.

The prosecutor, Vigna, expressed his view that the crime seemed anomalous, ad hoc and improvised—in short, that it had been committed not by the Monster, but by someone else trying to demonstrate the innocence of Francesco Vinci. The investigators suspected that Vinci's nephew, Antonio, had committed the killings as a way to spring his beloved uncle from prison. (Antonio, you will recall, had been the baby saved from the gas back in Sardinia.) Unlike the rest of his family, he seemed tall enough to have taken aim through the clear stripe of glass at the top of the camper's window.

A plan of brutal subtlety was secretly put in motion. Sign of it appeared ten days after the Giogoli killings, when a small and apparently unrelated news item appeared in the back pages of the newspapers, reporting that Antonio Vinci, nephew of Francesco Vinci, had been arrested for illegal possession of firearms. Antonio and Francesco were extremely close, partners in many shady activities and sketchy adventures. The arrest of Antonio was a sign that the investigators were widening their exploration of the Sardinian Trail. The examining magistrate in the Monster case, Mario Rotella, and a lead prosecutor, Silvia Della Monica, were convinced that both Francesco and Antonio knew the identity of the Monster of Florence. They were convinced, in fact, that this terrible secret was shared by the entire clan of Sardinians. The Monster was one of them, and the others knew his identity.

With both men in Florence's Le Murate prison, they could now be played against each other, and perhaps broken. The suspects were kept apart, and artfully crafted rumors were circulated through the prison, designed to arouse suspicions and pit one against the other. A program of interrogation aimed at the two prisoners was set in motion, giving each one the impression that the other had talked. It was "let slip" to each that the other had made serious accusations against him, and that he could save himself only by telling the truth about the other.

It didn't work. Neither one talked. One afternoon, in the ancient

in the end I found myself in bed with Saverio and Salvatore, who first had sex with me and then with his friend. This went on for a while. If I protested, he hit me. He forced me to have sex with Saverio while he watched, and then we made a foursome. And when it was this way, Salvatore and Saverio were touching each other, caressing each other, each taking their turn as first the man and then the woman, in front of me and Gina! And from that time on Salvatore began to bring me to the homes of his friends, even casual acquaintances, and I had to be with them. He took me to porn films, he'd have his eye on someone, and then he'd introduce me and then perhaps I'd have to have sex with them in the car, but especially at home. And it was worse for me when, in that period, his son Antonio arrived from Sardinia, who was only four years old. They called him Antonello then. I was afraid that he would witness some of these perverse doings with other couples, and our fights, and when he mistreated me."

Eventually Rosina had had enough and ran away to Trieste with another man.

"I can say to you," another of Salvatore's girlfriends told the police, "that Salvatore was the man, the *only* man, who fully satisfied me in terms of sex. He had strange ideas, but what of it? . . . He liked to make love to me while a man did it to him from behind . . ."

Salvatore Vinci picked up the players for his orgies where he could, with the help of his girlfriends, luring them from truck stops on the autostrada, in the red-light districts, and in the Cascine Park on the outskirts of Florence. His sexuality, according to those who knew him, knew no bounds. He would have sex with almost anyone, man or woman, and employed a wide range of accessories, including vibrators, zucchinis, and eggplants. If a woman was reluctant, he slapped her around a bit to get her in the mood.

When Barbara Locci arrived, everything became easier. Salvatore had finally found a woman who fully shared his appetite and tastes. She was so effective at attracting men and boys to orgies that Salvatore began calling her the "Queen Bee."

In the middle of all this, in the same small house, Salvatore's son, Antonio Vinci, was growing up. The young boy heard the rumors that his mother's death wasn't a suicide but a murder, and that his father had done it. Antonio had become deeply attached to Rosina, the second wife of Salvatore. When she fled to Trieste, for Antonio it was like losing his mother all over again. And once again it was his father's fault. He eventually left home and spent much of his free time with his uncle Francesco who became a substitute father to him. This same Antonio would later be arrested on weapons charges, in an attempt to get his uncle Francesco to talk.

The dual investigations in Villacidro and Tuscany convinced Mario Rotella and his carabinieri investigators that they had finally found their man. Salvatore Vinci had been the fourth accomplice at the killing of Barbara Locci. He probably owned a .22 Beretta. He had the only car among the conspirators. He brought the gun to the murder scene, he was the main shooter, and he took the gun home with him. The investigation confirmed he was a cold-blooded killer and sexual maniac.

Salvatore Vinci was the Monster of Florence.

CHAPTER
19

In the middle of all the sound and fury, certain facts stood above the fray, unshakably true, obtained by solid police work and expert analysis.

The first of these was the analysis of the pistol. No fewer than five ballistics analyses were done, and the answer was always the same: the Monster used one gun, a .22 Beretta that was "old and worn," with a defective firing pin that left an incontrovertible mark on the base of each shell. The bullets were the second fact. They were all Winchester series H rounds. All the bullets fired in the crimes had been taken from the same two boxes. This was demonstrated by an examination with a scanning electron microscope of the "H" stamped on the base of each shell—all had the same micro-imperfections, indicative that they were stamped by the same die. The die, which was regularly replaced when it began to wear out, also proved that both boxes were put on sale before the year 1968.

Each box contained fifty cartridges. Counting from the first crime in 1968, after the gun had shot fifty shells from one box, the killer opened a second box. The first fifty were copper-jacketed rounds, and the second were lead. Nothing was ever found that suggested a second gun had been used at the scenes of the crimes or that there was more than one killer. Indeed, the bodies of the victims had all been moved by dragging, which suggested there was no second person around to help lift.

It was the same for the knife used by the killer. Every expert analysis concluded that a single knife had been employed, extremely well honed, with a particular mark or notch in it, and three sawteeth below that of about two millimeters in depth. Some experts speculated it was a *pattada*, the typical knife used by Sardinian shepherds, but the majority of experts spoke, with some uncertainty, of a scuba knife. The experts agreed that the excisions were so nearly identical that they had been made by the same right-handed person.

Finally, the Monster avoided touching his victims, except when necessary, and stripped them by cutting their clothes off with the knife. There was never any sign of rape or sexual molestation.

The psychological experts all agreed on the Monster's psychopathology. "He always works alone," wrote one expert. "The presence of others would take away all flavor from the author of these crimes, which are fundamentally crimes of sexual sadism: the Monster is a serial killer and he only acts alone. . . . The noted absence of any sexual interest not connected to the excision, makes one think of an absolute impotence, or a marked inhibition of coitus."

In September 1984, Rotella finally freed the "Double Monsters" Piero Mucciarini and Giovanni Mele, who had been in prison during the Vicchio killings. Two months later, he released Francesco Vinci, who had also been in prison during the last Monster killings.

The pool of suspects had been reduced to one: Salvatore Vinci. They put his house under observation twenty-four hours a day, seven days a week. His telephone was tapped. When he left his front door, he was often followed.

As the winter passed and the next summer neared—the summer of 1985—a huge feeling of dread built among the investigators and the Florentine public. Everyone was certain that the Monster would strike again. The new elite unit charged with investigating the Monster, the

Squadra Anti-Mostro, worked with feverish activity but continued to make little progress.

When Francesco Vinci was released from prison, Mario Spezi, who had often maintained his innocence in his articles, was invited to the homecoming celebration at Vinci's house in Montelupo. Spezi accepted the unusual invitation, hoping to snag an interview on the side. The tables were heaped with spicy salami, strong Sardinian sheep cheese, *vermentino di Sardegna*, and *fil'e ferru*, the potent grappa of the island. At the end of the party, Vinci agreed to an interview with Spezi. He answered the questions with reserve, intelligence, and excessive caution.

"How old are you?"

"Forty-one. Or so I believe."

The interview was unenlightening, except for one answer that stayed with Spezi for many years. Spezi asked him what he imagined the real Monster to be like.

"He is very intelligent," Vinci said, "someone who knows how to move at night in the hills even with his eyes closed. One who knows how to use a knife much better than most. One," he added, fixing his glittering black eyes on Spezi, "who once upon a time experienced a very, very great disappointment."

CHAPTER
20

The summer of 1985 was one of the hottest in recent memory. A serious drought gripped Tuscany, and the hills of Florence lay stunned and prostrate under the sun, the ground cracking, the leaves turning brown and falling from the trees. The city's aqueducts began to dry up, and priests led their congregations in fervent prayer to the Lord for rain. Along with the heat, fear of the Monster hung over the city like a stifling blanket.

September 8 was another hot, cloudless day in what seemed like an endless string of them. But for Sabrina Carmignani it was a fine day, the day of her nineteenth birthday—a day she would never forget.

That Sunday, around five o'clock, Sabrina and her boyfriend pulled into a small clearing in the woods just off the main road to San Casciano, which was called the Scopeti clearing after the name of the road passing it. The dirt clearing was hidden from Via Scopeti by a curtain of oaks, cypresses, and umbrella pines, and it was well known to young people as a good place to have sex. It lay in the heart of the Chianti countryside, almost within view of the ancient stone house where Niccolò Machiavelli spent his years of exile writing *The Prince*. Today this area of villas, castles, beautifully tended vineyards, and small towns forms one of the most expensive stretches of real estate in the world.

The two young people parked their car next to another, a white VW Golf with French plates. In the center of the rear seat, attached by the seat belts, they noted a child's car seat. A few meters in front of the Volkswagen stood a small dome tent, of a metallic blue. The light struck it in such a way that it was possible to see a human outline in its interior.

"A single person," said Sabrina later, "who was stretched out and perhaps sleeping. The tent seemed shaken up, almost collapsed; the entrance was dirty and there were a lot of flies, and there was a foul dead smell."

They didn't like the look of things and turned around to leave. As they eased out of the clearing, another car was just turning in from the main road. The driver backed up to allow them to pass. Neither Sabrina nor her boyfriend noted the make of the car or saw the person inside.

They had just missed discovering the Monster's new victims.

A day later, at two o'clock in the afternoon on Monday, September 9, an avid mushroom forager drove into the Scopeti clearing. As soon as he stepped out of his car, he was assaulted by "a strange odor along with a loud buzzing of flies. I thought that around there somewhere was a dead cat. Around the tent I didn't notice anything. Then I went toward the thicket of bushes on the opposite side. And in that moment I saw them: two naked feet sticking out of the greenery . . . I didn't have the courage to go any closer."

The newly created squad, SAM, launched into action. The victims were two French tourists who had camped in the Scopeti clearing. For the first time the scene of a Monster crime was properly secured. SAM sealed off not only the Scopeti clearing, but an area one kilometer in diameter surrounding it. The discovery of a child's seat in the back of the car caused investigators great anguish for some hours, until inquiries to France established that the little daughter of the murdered woman was back in France in the care of relatives.

A helicopter landed at the sealed crime scene carrying on board a

famous criminologist who had earlier prepared a psychological and
behavioral profile of the Monster. Journalists and photographers were
grudgingly allowed in but had been corralled behind a red-and-white
plastic fence strung between trees a hundred yards away, under the watchful eyes of two policemen in a ready stance, armed with machine guns.
The journalists were angry at not having their usual access. Finally, the
assistant prosecutor allowed one, Mario Spezi, to examine the scene and
report back to all the others. Spezi climbed over the plastic barrier under
the furious gaze of his colleagues. When he saw the Monster's most
recent horror, he felt envy for those he had left behind.

The female victim was Nadine Mauriot, thirty-six years old, who
owned a shoe store in Montbéliard, France, not far from the French-
Swiss border. She had separated from her husband and for some
months had been living with Jean-Michel Kraveichvili, twenty-five
years old, an enthusiast of the hundred-meter dash, which he practiced
with the local athletic squad. They had taken a camping trip through
Italy, and on Monday would have had to be back in France for Nadine's
daughter's first day of school.

On hearing the news of the murders, Sabrina and her friend immediately went to the carabinieri to report what they had seen on Sunday
afternoon, September 8. The girl recounted exactly the same story
years later, in front of a judge of the Corte d'Assise. Twenty years
later, in an interview with Spezi, Sabrina was still certain that she had
not mistaken the date, given that that Sunday was her birthday.

Her testimony related in a critical way to the date the crime had
been committed. It had direct bearing on whether the French couple
had been murdered Saturday night, as the evidence suggested, or Sunday night, as investigators would later insist. Her testimony was incon-
venient to them, so it was completely ignored—then and now.

There was another weighty clue that the two were killed on Saturday night: if the French couple expected to be home in time to see
Nadine's daughter off to her first day of school, they would already
have to be driving back to France on Sunday.

The condition of Mauriot's cadaver on that Monday afternoon was
frightful. Her face, grotesquely swollen and black, was unrecognizable.

The heat had had devastating effects, amplified by being enclosed in a tent, and the body was covered with maggots.

SAM investigators reconstructed how the final killing took place. It was, in a word, horrifying.

The killer had crept up to the dome tent of the two French tourists, who were nude and making love. He advertised his presence by making a seven-inch cut in the fly of the tent with the tip of his knife—without, however, piercing the inner tent. The noise must have frightened the two lovers. They unzipped the door to see what it was. The Monster had already positioned himself, gun at the ready, and as soon as they peered out they were struck by a hail of bullets. Nadine was killed immediately. Four rounds struck Jean-Michel—one in a wrist, one in a finger, one in an elbow, and one grazing his lip, leaving him relatively unscathed.

The young athlete leapt up and charged out the door, perhaps bowling over the Monster in the process, and tore off running in the dark. If he had turned left, a few steps would have taken him to the main road where he might have been saved. But he ran straight ahead, toward the woods. The Monster ran after him. Jean-Michel vaulted a sort of bushy hedge that divided the clearing in two, pursued by the Monster. The Monster reached him in twelve meters, stabbed him in the back, chest, and stomach, and then cut his throat.

Observing the cadaver still under the bushes, Spezi noted that the lowest leaves of the tree above the dead body, six feet up, were splattered with blood.

Having killed Jean-Michel, the Monster returned to the tent. He pulled Nadine out by the feet and performed the two mutilations, removing her vagina and left breast. Then he dragged the body back into the tent and zipped it up. He hid the man's body under trash he collected around the clearing and put the plastic lid of a paint bucket over his head.

Despite diligent evidence collecting in the Scopeti clearing, SAM came up almost empty-handed. It appeared to have been an almost perfect crime.

On Tuesday, a letter arrived at the prosecutor's offices, addressed with letters cut from a magazine.

Inside the envelope, wrapped in tissue paper, was a piece of breast cut from the French tourist.

The letter had been mailed sometime that weekend in a little town near Vicchio, and it entered the postal system on Monday morning.

Silvia Della Monica was the only woman investigator in the Monster case. The arrival of this missive changed her life. It completely terrified her. She immediately resigned from the case and was assigned two bodyguards, who remained in her locked office even at work, for fear that the killer might be a person who could mingle with the people entering the Palazzo di Giustizia and gain access to her office. It was the end of her involvement in the case.

The letter, reproduced in the papers, caused a storm of speculation, because the killer had misspelled the Italian word "REPUBBLICA," using only one "B" instead of two. Was it merely the spelling error of an ignorant person, or did it indicate that the Monster was a foreigner? Among the Romance languages of Europe, only in Italian is the word "Republic" spelled with two "b"s.

For the first time, the Monster had made an effort to hide the two bodies. That, combined with the mailing of the note, would have forced a desperate search by the authorities for the victims, if the bodies hadn't already been found. This suggests a reason why the Monster changed his MO—it was a carefully designed plan to humiliate the police.

It almost worked.

CHAPTER
21

After the Scopeti killing, the mayors of Florence and the surrounding towns launched a campaign of prevention. Although the young people of Florence were so thoroughly traumatized that the idea of parking outside the city walls after sunset was now unthinkable, there were still millions of foreigners who poured into Tuscany every year with campers and tents who were unaware of the risk. Throughout the areas where people often camped, signs in multiple languages were posted warning of the danger of remaining there between dusk and dawn. But the mention of a serial killer was carefully avoided, so as not to scare away tourists completely.

The city of Florence printed thousands of posters, designed by the famous graphic artist Mario Lovergine, who drew a staring eye surrounded by leaves. *"Occhio ragazzi!* Watch out kids! Attention! *Jeunes gens, danger! Atención chicos y chicas! Pericolo di aggressione!* Danger of violence!" warned the poster. Using the same design, tens of thousands of postcards were printed up and passed out at tollbooths, railroad stations, campsites, youth hostels, and on public buses. Television spots reinforced the point.

Despite their most diligent efforts, SAM investigators emerged from the Scopeti clearing with few fresh leads or new evidence. The pressure on them was enormous. Thomas Harris, in his novel *Hannibal*, recounted some of the techniques SAM used to try to catch the Monster. "Some lover's lanes and cemetery trysting places had more police than lovers sitting in pairs in the cars. There were not enough women officers to go around. During hot weather male couples took turns wearing a wig and many mustaches were sacrificed."

The idea of offering a reward had earlier been rejected, but now it was resurrected by the prosecutor Vigna, who was convinced that the Monster enjoyed the protection of *omertà*, which could only be broken with a very large sum. It was a controversial idea. Rewards and bounties were never part of Italian culture, being something they knew only from American Westerns. Many feared it might incite a witch hunt or bring out a bunch of crazy bounty hunters. The decision was so controversial it had to be made by the prime minister of Italy himself, who set the reward at half a billion lire—a large sum at the time.

The reward was posted, but no one stepped forward with information to claim it.

As before, SAM was plagued with anonymous accusations and unfounded rumors that had to be followed up, no matter how unlikely. Among them was a letter the police received, dated September 11, 1985. It suggested that the police "question our fellow citizen, Pietro Pacciani, born in Vicchio." The note went on, "This individual is said by many to have been in prison for having killed his own fiancée. He has a thousand skills: a shrewd man, cunning, a farmer with big clumsy feet but a quick mind. He keeps his entire family hostage, the wife is a fool, the daughters are never allowed out, they have no friends."

Investigators looked into it. It wasn't true that Pacciani had killed his fiancée, but in 1951 he had killed a man he caught seducing his fiancée in a parked car and had served a long prison sentence for it. Pacciani lived in Mercatale, a half dozen kilometers from the Scopeti clearing. The police conducted a routine search of his house and found nothing of interest.

Still, the old farmer's name remained on the list.

A few weeks later, a rumor made the rounds, this one from Perugia, a hundred and fifty kilometers away. A young doctor, Francesco Narducci, the scion of one of the city's richest families, apparently committed suicide by drowning himself in Lake Trasimeno. Immediately rumormongers began speculating that Narducci had been the Monster, who, overcome with remorse, had done away with himself. A quick investigation showed there could be no truth to it, and investigators shelved it along with the other false leads that plagued the case.

Meanwhile, in 1985, the investigation, under relentless pressure to show results, began to crumble. A rift between the lead prosecutor, Piero Luigi Vigna, and the examining magistrate, Mario Rotella, was widening.

The disagreement centered on the Sardinian Trail investigation. Rotella was convinced that the gun used in the 1968 clan killing had never left the circle of Sardinians, and that one of them had gone on to become the Monster. His suspicions had settled on Salvatore Vinci, and he was painstakingly building the case against him with the help of the carabinieri. Vigna, on the other hand, felt the Sardinian Trail had reached a dead end. He wanted to throw everything out and start the investigation anew. The *polizia*, the police, agreed with Vigna.

The special unit known as SAM was composed of both polizia and carabinieri allegedly working together. The problem was, the carabinieri and the police rarely got along and were often antagonistic to each other. The Polizia di Stato are a civilian agency and the carabinieri are a branch of the military; both are charged with domestic law enforcement. When a major crime occurs, such as a murder, often the two agencies will rush to the scene and each try to claim the crime as their own. One story, perhaps apocryphal, tells of a bank robbery in which both carabinieri and police chased down and caught the escaping criminals. An argument broke out in front of the robbers about who should get the collar, finally settled when they divided up the spoils, the police getting the robbers and the carabinieri hauling away the getaway car, cash, and guns.

The disagreement between Vigna and Rotella, which became increasingly bitter, was kept a deep secret among the investigators for many years. Outwardly, the Sardinian Trail continued to be the major line of inquiry, but criticism of it, and of Judge Mario Rotella, began to grow.

In 1985 Rotella briefly jailed Stefano Mele on trumped-up charges in a final effort to get him to talk. The move caused a chorus of complaints that Rotella was needlessly torturing a broken-down old man whose ravings had already caused untold damage to the investigation and to the individuals he accused. Rotella found himself out on a limb, isolated and under constant attack by the press. The largest newspaper of Sardinia, the *Unione Sarda*, savaged him on a regular basis. "It's always the case," the newspaper wrote, "that whenever the investigation of the Monster of Florence becomes stuck in the mud, they always resurrect the so-called Sardinian Trail." Associations of Sardinian residents of Tuscany also took up the issue of racism, and a chorus of outrage from all sides assailed the investigation. Rotella's pontifications and circumlocutions only made matters worse.

But Rotella, who as examining magistrate in the Monster case held considerable power, plodded on. His brief arrest and interrogation of Stefano Mele, so roundly criticized, finally revealed one of the central mysteries in the case: why Stefano had protected Salvatore Vinci for so long, even at the cost of going to prison for fourteen years. Why had Mele acquiesced so meekly in being framed for the murders of Barbara Locci and Antonio Lo Bianco, when the crime had been plotted, organized, and executed by Salvatore? Why had he remained silent during the trial, when Salvatore had the impudence to wear his wife's engagement ring when taking the witness stand? Why, even after serving fourteen years in prison, did Mele refuse to tell investigators that Salvatore was one of his accomplices?

The reason, Mele finally broke down and admitted, was shame. He had participated in Salvatore Vinci's sex circus and was fond of sex with men, most especially with Salvatore himself. This was the terrible secret that Salvatore Vinci had held over Mele's head for almost twenty years, enforcing his silence. This was how Vinci, back in 1968, had been able to reduce Mele to groveling and weeping with a single hard stare. He threatened to expose him as a homosexual.

⋆   ⋆   ⋆

The double homicide of the French tourists in the Scopeti clearing would be the last known crime committed by the Monster of Florence. Although it would be a while before Florentines realized it, the string of murders that had terrorized them for so long had finally come to an end.

The investigation, however, was just getting started. As time went on, it would become a monster in its own right, consuming all in its path, engorged and distended with the many innocent lives it had ruined.

Nineteen eighty-five was only the beginning.

CHAPTER
22

By the end of 1985, Judge Mario Rotella was firmly convinced that Salvatore Vinci was the Monster of Florence. As he examined the files on Vinci, he became more and more frustrated with the many missed opportunities to nail him. For example, Vinci's house had been searched right after the 1984 killing in Vicchio, and the police had found a rag in his bedroom, stuffed in a woman's straw purse, covered with powder residues and spots of blood. Thirty-eight spots of blood. Rotella looked back through the records and saw that the rag had never been analyzed. Furious, he held it up as an egregious example of the incompetence of the investigation. The prosecutor in charge of that evidence tried to explain: it was impossible to believe a man who already knew he was on the list of suspects would keep in his room such an obvious clue.

Rotella demanded an examination of the rag. The lab it was sent to could not establish if the blood came from one or two blood groups, and the experts were unable to compare the blood on the rag to the blood of the victims of the 1984 crime because, incredibly enough, investigators had not conserved any blood from those victims. The rag was sent to the United Kingdom for further analysis, but the lab reported back that it had deteriorated beyond salvation. (Today, DNA testing might still recover important information from the rag, but so far we know of no plans to test it.)

Rotella had another reason to feel frustration. For more than a year the carabinieri had been keeping Salvatore Vinci under tight surveillance, particularly on weekends. Knowing he was being followed, Salvatore had sometimes amused himself by running red lights or pulling other tricks to lose his trackers. And yet the very weekend of the double homicide in the Scopeti clearing, the carabinieri had inexplicably suspended the surveillance. Vinci suddenly found himself free to go where he pleased, unobserved. If the surveillance had continued, Rotella felt, perhaps the double killing might never have occurred in the first place.

At the end of 1985, Rotella served Salvatore Vinci with an *avviso di garanzia*, a notification that he was the official suspect for sixteen homicides—all the killings from 1968 to 1985.

Meanwhile, the main prosecutor, Piero Luigi Vigna, was becoming fed up with the officious, methodical Rotella and his obsessive pursuit of the Sardinian Trail. Vigna and the police were itching to start afresh, and they were waiting, quietly, for Rotella to make a false move.

On June 11, 1986, Mario Rotella ordered the arrest of Salvatore Vinci for murder. To everyone's great surprise, it was not for the Monster's killings, but for the murder of his wife, Barbarina, on January 14, 1961, back in Villacidro. Rotella's strategy was to convict Vinci of murder in a case that seemed simpler and easier to prove, and then to leverage that into a conviction against him for being the Monster of Florence.

For two years, with Salvatore Vinci in prison, Rotella methodically prepared the case against him for the murder of his seventeen-year-old wife. The Monster did not kill again, which further persuaded Rotella that he had the right man.

Salvatore Vinci's trial for the murder of his wife began on April 12, 1988, in Cagliari, the capital of Sardinia. Spezi covered it for *La Nazione*.

Vinci's behavior in the dock was astonishing. Standing all the while, his tight fists wrapped around the bars of the cage in which he was locked, he responded with scrupulous care to the questions of the judges in a courteous, high, almost falsetto voice. During the breaks he conversed with Spezi and the other journalists on such themes as sexual freedom and the role of habeas corpus in a trial.

His son, Antonio, who was then about twenty-seven years old, was brought into the courtroom to testify against his father. He was serving time for an unrelated offense, and he arrived with his hands shackled, his strong, extremely tense presence noted by all. Seated to the right of the judges, on the side opposite his father, the youth never once took off the huge black sunglasses that hid his eyes. His lips remained compressed, and the nostrils of his aquiline nose were dilated with hatred. Even protected by dark lenses, his face always remained fixated on his father, never once turning elsewhere in the courtroom. Throughout this his father remained immobile as he returned his son's stare with a closed and enigmatic face. The two of them remained that way for hours, the courtroom filled with electricity from their taut and silent interaction.

Antonio Vinci refused to speak a word. He just stared. Later, he told Spezi that if there hadn't been carabinieri officers sitting between him and his father in the van as they were driven away, "I would have strangled him."

The trial came to a disastrous end. Salvatore Vinci was unexpectedly acquitted. The crime had taken place too long ago, witnesses had died and others couldn't remember, physical evidence had disappeared, and very little could actually be proved.

Vinci walked out of the courtroom a free man. He paused on the steps to speak to the press. "It was a very satisfying conclusion," he said calmly, and walked on. He went into the interior mountains to visit his birthplace of Villacidro—and then, like a Sardinian bandit of old, he disappeared forever.

The acquittal of Salvatore Vinci raised a firestorm of complaint against Rotella. It was the false move Vigna and his prosecutors had been waiting for, and they moved in like sharks, silently, with no fuss or publicity. For the next few years, a slow parrying with long knives would take place between Vigna and Rotella, the police and the carabinieri, so quietly conducted that it never came to the attention of the news media.

After the acquittal, Vigna and the police went their own way, ignoring Rotella. They decided to throw out everything and start the Monster of Florence investigation all over again, from the beginning. Meanwhile, Rotella and the carabinieri kept the Sardinian Trail investigation going. The two investigations slowly became incompatible, if not mutually exclusive.

Eventually, something would have to give.

CHAPTER
23

The Squadra Anti-Mostro was taken over by a new chief inspector of police, a man named Ruggero Perugini. A few years later, Thomas Harris would create a fictional portrait of Perugini in his novel *Hannibal*, giving him the thinly disguised fictional name of Rinaldo Pazzi. While researching the book, Harris had been a guest in Chief Inspector Perugini's home in Florence. (It was said that Perugini was not pleased with Harris's return on his hospitality, by having his alter ego gutted and hung from the Palazzo Vecchio.) The real chief inspector was more dignified than his sweaty and troubled counterpart in the film version, played by Giancarlo Giannini. The real Perugini spoke with a Roman accent, but his movements and dress, and the way he handled his briar pipe, made him seem more English than Italian.

When Chief Inspector Perugini took over SAM, he and Vigna wiped the slate clean. Perugini started with the assumption that the gun and bullets had somehow passed out of the circle of Sardinians before the Monster killings began. The Sardinian Trail was a dead end and he had no more interest in it. He also viewed the evidence collected at the crime scenes with skepticism—and perhaps rightly so. The forensic examination of the crime scenes had been, in general, incompetent. Only the last was actually secured and sealed by the police. In the others, people came and went, picking up the shells, taking pictures, smoking and throwing their butts on the ground, trampling the grass, and shedding their own hair and fibers everywhere. Much of the forensic evidence that was collected—and there was precious little—was never properly analyzed, and some, like the rag, was lost or allowed to spoil. Investigators had not generally kept samples of the victims' hair, clothing, or blood, to see if their presence might be associated with any suspects.

Instead of plodding once again through the evidence and rereading the thousands of pages of interrogations, Perugini was smitten by the idea of solving the crime in the modern way—with computers. He was in love with the scientific methods used by the FBI to hunt serial killers. He finally dusted off the IBM PC given to SAM by the Ministry of the Interior and booted it up.

He ran through it the names of every man between the ages of thirty and sixty in the province of Florence who had ever been picked up by the police, asking it to spit out all those persons convicted of sexual crimes. Then Perugini matched up their periods of incarceration with the dates of the Monster's homicides, identifying those who were in prison when the Monster didn't kill and out of prison when he did. He winnowed the list down from thousands to a few dozen people. And there, in the middle of this rarefied company, he found the name of Pietro Pacciani—the peasant farmer who had been denounced in an anonymous letter after the Monster's final killings.

Perugini then did another computer screening to see how many of these suspects had lived in or around the areas where the Monster had struck. Once again Pacciani's name surfaced, after Perugini generously expanded the definition of "in or around" to swallow most of Florence and its environs.

The appearance of Pacciani's name in this second screening again reinforced the anonymous message that had arrived on September 11, 1985, inviting the police to "question our fellow citizen Pietro Pacciani born in Vicchio." In this way, the most advanced system of criminal investigation, the computer, was married to the most ancient system, the anonymous letter—both of which fingered the same man: Pietro Pacciani.

Pietro Pacciani became Perugini's preferred suspect. All that remained was to gather the evidence against him.

Inspector Perugini ordered a search of Pacciani's house and came
up with what he considered further incriminating evidence. Prime
among this was a reproduction of Botticelli's *Primavera*, the famous
painting in the Uffizi Gallery, which depicts, in part, a pagan nymph
with flowers spilling from her mouth. The picture reminded Perugini
of the gold chain lying in the mouth of one of the Monster's first
victims. This clue so captivated him that it became the cover of the
book he would later publish about the case, which showed Botticelli's
nymph vomiting blood instead of flowers. Reinforcing this interpretation, Perugini took note of a pornographic magazine centerfold
pinned up in Pacciani's kitchen, surrounded by pictures of the Blessed
Virgin and saints, showing a topless woman with a flower clamped
provocatively between her teeth.

Right after the Monster's last double homicide, Pietro Pacciani had
been sent to prison for raping his daughters. This, for Perugini, was
another important clue. It explained why there had been no killings
for the past three years.

Most of all, it was the 1951 murder that attracted Perugini's attention. It had taken place near Vicchio, Pacciani's birthplace, where the
Monster had struck twice. On the surface it looked like a Monster
crime: two young people making love in a car in the Tassinaia woods,
ambushed by a killer hidden in the bushes nearby. She was just sixteen,
the town beauty and Pacciani's girlfriend. Her lover was a traveling
salesman who went from village to village selling sewing machines.

But on a closer look, the crime was quite different—messy, furious, and spontaneous. Pacciani had beaten the man's head in with a
stone before knifing him. He then threw his girlfriend into the grass
and raped her next to his rival's dead body. Afterwards, he slung the
salesman's corpse over his shoulders to carry it to a nearby lake. After
struggling for a while he gave up and dumped it in the middle of a
field. Criminologists would have called it a "disorganized" homicide,
as opposed to the organized ones of the Monster. So disorganized, in
fact, that Pacciani was swiftly arrested and convicted.

The murder in the Tassinaia woods had an antique flavor to it, a crime of passion from another age. It may have been the last tale of love and murder to be immortalized in song in the traditional Tuscan manner. At the time, there was one man left in Tuscany who practiced the ancient profession of *cantastorie*, or "story singer," a sort of wandering minstrel who set stories to song. Aldo Fezzi walked about Tuscany dressed in a bright red jacket, even in the heat of August, going from town to town, from country fair to country fair, singing stories in rhyme while showing drawings illustrating the action. Fezzi composed most of his own songs based on stories he collected in his travels; some were hilarious, racy, and off-color, while others were tragic tales of jealousy and murder, desperate love, and savage vendettas.

Fezzi composed a song about the murder in the Tassinaia woods that he sang across northern Tuscany:

> *I sing to you of a great and tragic tale,*
> *In the town of Vicchio in the Mugello,*
> *At the Iaccia farm of the Paterno estate,*
> *There lived a young man, brutal and cruel.*
> *Stay and hear, and your tears will flow,*
> *His name was Pier Pacciani, twenty-six years old,*
> *O, listen to the story I am about to tell,*
> *To speak of it will freeze your blood . . .*

Perugini considered it a crucial piece of evidence that Pacciani, spying on the two lovers from the bushes, told investigators he had gone into a frenzy of rage when he saw his girlfriend bare her left breast for her seducer; that was the moment when he had snapped. The story reminded Perugini of the left breast taken from the last two victims. The baring of the left breast, Perugini argued, was the event which first unleashed Pacciani's homicidal fury; it had settled in his unconscious to reappear years later, every time the same circumstances arose—when he saw two young people making love in a car.

Others pointed out that the left breast would be the one most likely seized by a right-handed killer—as the Monster was known to be. But this was far too simple an explanation for Perugini's taste.

Perugini discounted the earlier reconstructions of the Monster's crimes, which seemed to argue very much against Pacciani as the killer. For example, it was difficult to place a fat, short, alcoholic, thickset old peasant, barely five feet three inches tall, at the scene of the crime in Giogoli, in which the killer took aim through a strip of window that was five feet ten inches off the ground. It was even more difficult to put this doddering peasant at the scene of the last crime, in the Scopeti clearing, in which the killer outran a twenty-five-year-old who was an amateur champion of the hundred-meter dash. At the time of the Scopeti crime, Pacciani was sixty years old, had suffered a heart attack, and had undergone a bypass operation. His health records showed he had scoliosis, a bad knee, angina pectoris, pulmonary emphysema, chronic ear infections, multiple slipped discs, spondiloarthrosis, hypertension, diabetes, and polyps in his throat and kidney, among other ailments.

The other incriminating "evidence" Perugini and his team recovered from Pacciani's house included a round from a hunting rifle, two World War II shell casings (one of which was being used as a flower vase), a photograph of Pacciani as a young man posing with a machine pistol, five knives, a postcard sent from Calenzano, a register book that on its first page had a crude drawing of a road that could not be identified, and a package of pornographic magazines. He also interviewed a series of witnesses who described Pacciani as a violent man, a poacher, a man who at town festivals couldn't keep his hands in his pockets and annoyed all the women.

But the crown jewel of evidence found in Pacciani's house was a disturbing painting. It depicted a large, uncovered cube, inside of which was a centaur. The human half of the centaur showed a general with a skull in place of a head who brandished a saber in his right hand. The animal part was a bull whose horns became a lyre. This strange creature had both male and female sex organs and huge clown feet. There were mummies that looked like policemen, one of which was making a vulgar gesture. A hissing snake was coiled in the corner wearing a hat. And in front of all this, most significantly, were seven little crosses planted in the ground, surrounded by flowers.

Seven crosses. Seven crimes of the Monster.

The painting was signed "PaccianiPietro," and he had given it a misspelled title: "A science-fition dream." Chief Inspector Perugini submitted the painting to an expert for psychological examination. The conclusion: the painting was "compatible with the personality of the so-called Monster."

By 1989, Perugini was closing in on Pacciani. But before he could hang the sign of "Monster" around Pacciani's neck, the chief inspector had to explain how the gun used in the 1968 clan killing ended up in Pacciani's hands. He dealt with the problem in the simplest way possible: he accused Pacciani of committing the 1968 murders too.

Judge Mario Rotella, as the examining magistrate, had watched Perugini's investigation with dismay, viewing it as an effort to construct a monster out of thin air, using as a starting point the conveniently brutal person of Pietro Pacciani. But the attempt to accuse Pacciani of the 1968 double homicide, without a shred of evidence, was going too far. It was a direct challenge to the Sardinian Trail investigation. As examining magistrate, Rotella refused to sanction it.

Inspector Perugini was backed by two powerful supporters for his investigation of Pacciani: Vigna, the prosecutor, and the police. The carabinieri backed Rotella.

The struggle between Vigna and Rotella, the police and carabinieri, finally came to a head. Vigna led the charge. He argued that the Sardinian Trail investigation was nothing more than the sterile result of paying heed to the ravings of Stefano Mele. It was a red herring that had sidetracked the investigation for more than five years. Rotella and the carabinieri found themselves on the defensive, protecting the Sardinian Trail investigation, but they were on the losing side. They had allowed their primary suspect, Salvatore Vinci, to slip through their fingers after his acquittal in Sardinia. Rotella, with his condescending pontifications and lack of charisma, had become deeply unpopular with the press and the public. Vigna, on the other hand, was seen as a hero. And finally, there was Pacciani himself—brutal murderer, daughter rapist, wife-beater, alcoholic, a man who forced his family to eat

dog food—a monstrous human being in every way. To many Florentines, if he wasn't actually the Monster himself, he was close enough.

Vigna won. The carabinieri colonel in charge of the Monster investigation was transferred from Florence to another posting, and Rotella
was ordered to close his files, prepare a final report, and remove himself from the case. The report, he was instructed, must clear all the
Sardinians of any involvement in the Monster killings.

The carabinieri were furious at this turn of events. They officially
withdrew from the Monster investigation. "If one day," a colonel of
the carabinieri told Spezi, "the real Monster came to our barracks with
his pistol and perhaps even a slice of a victim, our response would be:
'Go to the police station, we've got no interest in you or your story.'"

Rotella prepared the final report. It was a curious document. In
more than a hundred pages of crisp, logical exposition, it laid out the
case against the Sardinians. It detailed the clan killing of 1968, how it
was executed, and who was involved. It traced the probable arc of the
.22 Beretta from Holland to Sardinia to Tuscany, and placed it in Salvatore Vinci's hands. It built a persuasive case that the Sardinians who
participated in the 1968 killing knew who took the gun home and,
therefore, knew the identity of the Monster of Florence. And that that
person was Salvatore Vinci.

And then, abruptly, on the last page, he wrote, "P.Q.M. [*Per questi
motivi*, For these reasons] this investigation shall proceed no further."
He dismissed all the charges and indictments against the Sardinians
and officially absolved them of any involvement in the Monster of
Florence killings and the 1968 clan killing. Mario Rotella then resigned
from the case and was posted to Rome.

"I had no other way out except for this," Rotella told Spezi in an
interview. "This ending is a source of the greatest bitterness to me and
many others."

It was clear then—as it is today—that Rotella and the carabinieri,
despite all their missteps, were in fact on the right trail. The Monster
of Florence was very likely a member of that Sardinian clan.

The official closing of the Sardinian Trail meant that the Monster
investigation could now proceed in any direction but the right one.

CHAPTER
24

The carabinieri pulled their men out of SAM, and the special anti-Monster unit was reorganized under Chief Inspector Perugini as an all-police force. Pacciani was now the only suspect, and they pursued him hammer and tongs. The chief inspector was convinced that the endgame was near, and he was determined to force it to a conclusion.

The year was 1989, and the Monster had not killed for four years. Florentines began to think that maybe, finally, the police had gotten their hands on the right man.

Perugini went on a popular television show and became an instant celebrity when, at the end, he fixed his tinted Ray-Bans on the camera and spoke directly to the Monster in firm but not unsympathetic tones: "You're not as crazy as people say. Your fantasies, your impulses, have taken your hand and govern your actions. I know that even in this moment you are trying to fight against them. We want you to know that we will help you overcome them. I know that the past taught you suspicion and silence, but in this moment I am not lying to you and never will, if you decide to free yourself from this Monster who tyrannizes you." He paused. "You know how, when, and where to find me. I will be waiting for you."

The speech, which seemed wonderfully spontaneous to millions of listeners, had actually been written in advance by a team of psychologists. Perugini had memorized it. It was specifically directed at Pacciani himself, who they knew would be at home watching the program. In the days preceding the show, the police had bugged his house in hopes of getting some incriminating reaction from him when Perugini made his carefully crafted speech.

The tape recording from the bug was collected from Pacciani's house after the program and listened to with great interest. There had been, in fact, a reaction. When Perugini concluded his statement on television, Pacciani erupted in a torrent of profanity in a Tuscan dialect so antique, so forgotten, that it would have brought joy to a linguist. He then wailed, still in dialect, "They better not name names, because I'm just a poor, innocent, unfortunate man!"

Three years passed. Between 1989 and 1992, Perugini's investigation against Pacciani made little headway. He could not find a smoking gun. The loot from the searches of his property and house had yielded just enough to satisfy the fantasies of the investigators, but not enough to actually arrest the man for murder.

When Pacciani was interrogated, he responded very differently from the cool and collected Vinci brothers. He loudly denied everything, told lies even about things of no importance, contradicted himself continually, broke down sobbing, and wailed that he was a poor innocent, unjustly persecuted.

The more Pacciani lied and bawled, the more Perugini became convinced of his guilt.

One morning in the early nineties, Mario Spezi, now a freelance writer, dropped by police headquarters and looked up an old friend from his days on the crime beat, hoping to rustle up a story. He had heard rumors that Perugini and SAM, years before, had asked the American FBI for help. The result had been a secret profile of the Monster prepared by the famed Behavioral Science Unit at Quantico. But no one had ever seen the report—if there even was one.

Spezi's contact disappeared and returned a half an hour later with a sheaf of papers. "I'm not giving you anything," he said, handing them to Spezi. "We haven't even seen each other."

Spezi took the file to a café in the loggia of Piazza Cavour. He ordered a beer and began to read. (The report had been helpfully translated into Italian; I have translated it back into English, being unable to get the original report.)

FBI Academy, Quantico, Virginia, 22135. Request for collaboration by the Polizia di Stato Italiana regarding the investigation of THE MONSTER OF FLORENCE, FPC-GCM FBIHQ 00; FBIHQ. The following investigative analysis was prepared by Special Agents John T. Dunn, Jr., John Galindo, Mary Eileen O'Toole, Fernando M. Rivera, Richard Robley and Frans B. Wagner under the direction of Special Agent in Charge Ronald Walker and other members of the National Center for the Analysis of Violent Crime (NCAVC).

It carried a date of August 2, 1989: "THE MONSTER OF FLORENCE/Our file 163A-3915.

"Please be informed," began the cautionary preface of the American experts, "that the attached analysis is based on an examination of materials furnished by your office and is not to be considered a substitute for a complete and well-conceived investigation and it should not be considered conclusive or comprehensive."

The report stated that the Monster of Florence was not unique. He was a serial killer of a type known to the FBI, on which they had a database: a lone, sexually impotent male with a pathological hatred of women, who satisfied his libidinous cravings through killing. In the dry language favored by law enforcement, the FBI report catalogued the Monster's likely characteristics, explained his probable motive, and speculated as to how and why he killed, how he chose his targets, what he did with the body parts, and even included such details as where he lived and whether or not he owned a car.

Spezi read with growing fascination. It became clear to him why the report had been suppressed: it painted a portrait of a killer very different from Pietro Pacciani.

The report stated that the Monster chose the places, not the victims, and he would kill only in places he knew well.

The aggressor in all likelihood effectuated a surveillance of the victims until they engaged in some form of sexual activity. It is at this point that the aggressor chose to strike, with the advantage of surprise, speed, and the use of a weapon able to incapacitate immediately. This particular method of approach is generally indicative of an aggressor who has doubts about his own ability to control his victims, who feels himself insufficiently prepared to interact with his victims "alive" or who feels himself incapable of confronting them directly.

The aggressor, using a sudden approach, discharged his weapon at close range, concentrating his fire first on the male victim, neutralizing in this way the greater danger to himself. Once the male victim is neutralized, the aggressor feels himself sufficiently secure to perpetrate his attack on the female victim. The use of many rounds indicates that the aggressor wanted to assure himself that both victims were deceased before initiating the mutilation post mortem on the female victim. This is the real objective of the aggressor; the man represents only an obstacle that must be removed.

According to the FBI report, the Monster acted alone. It said the killer may have a record, but only for such things as arson or petty theft. He was not a habitually violent person who would have committed serious crimes of aggression. Nor was he a rapist. "The aggressor is a person who is inadequate and immature in sexual matters, who has had little sexual contact with women in his own peer group." It said that the reason for the mysterious gap in the killings from 1974 to 1981 was probably because the killer was away from Florence during that time. "The aggressor is best described as a person of average intelligence. He would have completed his secondary studies or the equivalent in the Italian educational system. He would be experienced in work that required use of the hands."

Farther on it read, "The aggressor would have lived alone in a working-class area during the years in which the crimes occurred." And he would own his own car.

But the most interesting part, even today, is the manner in which the crimes were committed, which the FBI called his "signature." "The possession and the ritual are very important for this kind of aggressor. This would explain why the female victims were generally moved some meters from the vehicle containing their companion. The necessity of *possession*, as a ritual enacted by the aggressor, betrayed rage toward women in general. The mutilation of the sexual organs of the victims represented either the inadequateness of the aggressor or his resentment of women."

The FBI report noted that this type of serial killer often tried to control the investigation through direct or informal contact with the police, presenting himself as an informant, sending anonymous letters, or contacting the press.

One chapter of the FBI analysis discussed the so-called "souvenirs"— the body parts and perhaps trinkets and jewelry—the Monster took from the victims. "These pieces were taken as souvenirs and helped the aggressor relive the event in his fantasies for a certain period of time. These pieces are kept for a long period of time, and once they are no longer needed by the aggressor they are often left back at the scene of the crime or on the tomb of the victim. Occasionally," the report noted dryly, "the killer may, for libidinous reasons, consume the body parts of the victim to complete the act of possession."

A paragraph was dedicated to the letter that contained the piece of a victim's breast, mailed to the magistrate Silvia Della Monica. "The letter may indicate that the aggressor was attempting to mock the police, suggesting that the publicity and attention of this case were important to him, and indicating a growing sense of security on his part."

And about the pistol used by the Monster, the FBI wrote that "for him, perhaps, the pistol was a fetish." The use of the same firearm and boxes of bullets was all part of the ritualized nature of the killing, and probably included specific clothing and other accessories used only for killing, and kept well hidden at other times. "The overall behavior of the aggressor at the scene, including his use of certain accessories and instruments specific to the crime, suggests that the ritual inherent in this series of aggressions is so important to him that he must repeat the offense in the identical manner until he reaches satisfaction."

None of it sounded like Pacciani, so the FBI report was ignored and suppressed.

In the three years from 1989 to 1992, Perugini and his investigators became increasingly frustrated that they could not gather enough evidence to charge Pacciani. They finally decided to organize a massive twelve-day search of the peasant's miserable house and property.

In April of 1992 Perugini and his men launched what would become the longest and most technologically advanced property search in Italian history. From 9:50 a.m. on April 27 to noon on May 8, 1992, a well-armed squad of elite investigators searched Pacciani's hovel and garden: they examined the walls inch by inch, sounded under the paving stones, searched in every possible gap and cavity, looked in every drawer, turned over furniture, beds, chairs, sofas, closets, and bureaus, lifted the roof tiles one by one, excavated with backhoes almost three feet deep in the soil of the garden, and penetrated with ultrasound every square millimeter of the land surrounding the house.

Firemen went over the place with their special knowledge. Representatives of private firms wielded metal detectors and heat-sensing equipment. There were technicians who filmed with precision the places that were being searched. There was a doctor on hand to check on the health of Pacciani, as they feared the excitable peasant might have a heart attack during the search. They brought in an expert in "diagnostic architecture," able to pinpoint the location in a seemingly solid, load-bearing wall where, for example, one might hide a niche or cavity.

At 5:56 p.m. on April 29, when the exhausted police had already decided to abandon the search "under a sky that promised rain," a discovery was made. Ruggero Perugini would later write about this triumphant moment in his book *A Normal Enough Man* (the book that depicted the Botticelli nymph on the cover, vomiting blood). "I caught in the light of the late afternoon an almost imperceptible gleam in the earth," the chief inspector wrote.

It was a Winchester series H cartridge, completely covered with oxidation. It had not been fired, and so the base did not bear the Monster's signature firing-pin mark. It did, however, bear marks that indicated it had been inserted into a firearm. It was analyzed by ballistics experts who concluded that it was "not incompatible" with having been inserted into the Monster's gun. "Not incompatible" was as far as they would go despite (as one expert complained later) having been relentlessly pressured.

But it was enough. Pacciani was arrested on January 16, 1993, and charged with being the Monster of Florence.

CHAPTER
25

The trial of Pietro Pacciani began on April 14, 1994. The courtroom bunker was overflowing with a public divided between those who thought him guilty and those who maintained his innocence. Girls paraded around in T-shirts that read in English, "I ♥ Pacciani." There was a veritable caravansary of photographers, filmmakers, and journalists, in the middle of which, protected and led by Chief Inspector Ruggero Perugini, was the writer Thomas Harris.

A trial is perfect theater: a restricted time period, a shut room, recitations by subject, fixed roles—the prosecutor, the lawyers, the judges, the accused. There was no trial that was purer theater than Pacciani's. It was melodrama worthy of Puccini.

The peasant farmer rocked and sobbed during the proceedings, sometimes crying out in his antique Tuscan dialect, "I am a sweet little lamb! . . . I am here like Christ on the cross!" At times he would rise to his full diminutive height, pull forth from a hidden pocket a little icon of the Sacred Heart, and wave it in the judges' faces while the president of the court banged his gavel and told him to sit down. At other times he erupted in anger, face on fire, spittle flying from his lips, cursing a witness or condemning the Monster himself, invoking God with his hands joined and eyes rolled to heaven, hollering, "Burn him in hell forever!"

After only four days of the trial, Spezi broke the first big story. A central piece of evidence against Pacciani was his bizarre painting—the one with the centaur and the seven crosses—which psychologists said was "compatible" with the psychopathic personality of the Monster. The actual image had been kept under wraps, but Spezi had finally managed to extract a photograph of it from the prosecutor's office. It took him only a few days to find the actual painter—a fifty-year-old Chilean artist named Christian Olivares, exiled to Europe during the Pinochet era. Olivares was outraged when he heard that his painting was being used as evidence against a serial killer. "In this painting," he told Spezi, "I wanted to present the grotesque horror of a dictatorship. To say it is the work of a psychopath is ridiculous. It would be like saying the *Disasters of War* by Goya indicated he was a madman, a monster who needed to be locked up."

Spezi called up Perugini. "Tomorrow," he told the chief inspector, "my paper will publish an article saying that the painting that you attributed to Pacciani was not painted by him, but by a Chilean artist. Would you care to comment?"

The article was a major embarrassment. Vigna, the chief prosecutor, tried to play down the painting. "It was the mass media that exaggerated its importance," he said. Another prosecutor, Paolo Canessa, tried to minimize the damage by explaining that "Pacciani did sign the painting and told some of his friends that it was his own dream."

The trial marched on for six more months. In a corner of the courtroom, cameras with zoom lenses focused in on Pacciani and the witnesses arrayed against him. The images were projected on a screen on the left-hand side of the court, so that even those in poor seats could follow the drama. Every night the highlights of the trial were replayed on television, attracting huge audience numbers. Everyone gathered around the television at dinnertime, watching a drama in installments better than any soap opera.

The high point came when it was time for Pacciani's daughters to speak from the witness stand. All of Tuscany was glued to the television for their testimony.

Florentines have never forgotten the sight of the two daughters (one of whom had joined a convent) weeping as they told, in excruciating detail, how they had been raped by their father. In front of everyone passed a picture of Tuscan country life very different from *Under the Tuscan Sun*. Their testimony portrayed a family in which the women endured insults, drunken abuse, beatings with a stick, and sexual violence.

"He didn't want daughters," said one daughter, weeping. "Once Mamma had a miscarriage and he knew that it was a boy. He said to us, 'You both should have died and he live.' Once he gave us the meat of a groundhog to eat that he had taken for its skin. He beat us when we didn't want to go to bed with him."

None of this had anything to do with the Monster of Florence. When the questioning did turn in that direction, the two daughters weren't able to recall a single damning fact—a glimpse of the gun, a spot of blood, an incautious word dropped during his nightly drinking bouts—that could connect their father with the double homicides of the Monster of Florence.

The prosecutors lined up their meager scraps of evidence. The bullet and a rag were presented. A plastic soapdish found at Pacciani's house was put forward. (The mother of one of the victims said that she thought it looked like one belonging to her son.) A photograph of Botticelli's nymph was propped up in the courtroom, next to a blow-up of the victim with the gold chain in her mouth. A German-made block of sketching paper, also found in Pacciani's house, was advanced as evidence, with relatives saying they thought the German couple might have had one like it. Pacciani claimed he had found it in a Dumpster years before the killing, and notes Pacciani had jotted in it did clearly date to well before the murder. Prosecutors maintained that the wily peasant had added the notes later to divert suspicion. (Spezi pointed out in an article that it would have been far simpler for Pacciani to have thrown the incriminating sketchbook in the fireplace.)

Among the witnesses were Pacciani's old pals from the Casa del Popolo, the communist-built social club and meeting hall for working-class people in San Casciano. His friends were mostly country bumpkins, uneducated, ruined by bad wine and whoring. Among them was a man named Mario Vanni, a dimwitted ex-postman of San Casciano, who had been nicknamed Torsolo, "Apple Core," by his fellow citizens—in other words, the part of the apple that is no good and is thrown away.

In the courtroom Vanni was confused and terrified. In answer to the first question ("What is your current occupation?") instead of answering, he immediately launched into a quavering explanation that, yes, he knew Pacciani, but they were only "picnicking friends" and nothing more. In order to avoid making mistakes the postman had obviously memorized that phrase with which he answered almost every question, whether relevant or not. *Eravamo compagni di merende,*" he kept repeating, "We were picnicking friends."

We were picnicking friends. With those words, the unfortunate postman invented a phrase that would enter the very lexicon of the Italian language. *Compagni di merende,* "picnicking friends" is now a colloquial expression in Italian referring to friends who pretend to be doing something innocent when in fact they are bent on dark, murderous misdeeds. The phrase became so popular that it even has its own Italian Wikipedia entry.

"We were picnicking friends," Vanni continued to repeat after every question, his chin dipping, his eyes squinting about the vast courtroom.

The prosecutor became more and more irritated with Vanni and that phrase. Vanni went on to retract everything that he had said in his earlier interrogations. He denied hunting with Pacciani, denied various statements he had made, and ended up denying everything, swearing he knew nothing, protesting loudly that he and Pacciani were picnicking friends and nothing more. The president of the court finally lost his temper. "Signor Vanni, you are what we call reticent, and if you continue this way you risk being charged with false testimony."

Vanni continued to whine, "But we were just picnicking friends," while the courtroom audience laughed and the judge banged his gavel.

His behavior on the witness stand aroused the suspicions of a police officer named Michele Giuttari, who would later take over the Monster investigation from Chief Inspector Perugini. Perugini had been rewarded for capturing the Monster (i.e., Pacciani) by being given the plummiest of postings: he had been sent to Washington, D.C., to became the liaison officer between the Italian police and the American FBI.

Giuttari would take the Monster investigation to a new, spectacular, level. But for now he was waiting in the wings, watching and listening, and developing his own theories of the crimes.

The day arrived in the trial that the Italians call the "twist"—that Perry Mason moment when a key witness mounts the stand and seals the fate of the accused. This witness in the Pacciani trial was a man named Lorenzo Nesi, thin and smarmy, with slicked-back hair and Ray-Bans, shirt unbuttoned, gold chains dangling among his chest hair, a smooth talker and small-time ladies' man. Whether it was for the love of attention or the desire to be on the front page, Nesi would become a veritable serial witness, popping up when most needed and suddenly recalling events buried for years. This was his debut appearance; there would be many more.

In his first deposition, spontaneously given, Nesi said that Pacciani had boasted to him of having gone hunting at night with a pistol to shoot pheasants resting in the trees. This was taken as another damning piece of evidence against Pacciani, because it showed the peasant, who denied having a pistol, owned one after all—no doubt "that" pistol.

Twenty days later, Nesi suddenly remembered something else.

On Sunday evening, September 8, 1985, the alleged night of the murder of the two French tourists, Nesi was returning from a trip and was forced to take a detour past the Scopeti clearing because the Florence-Siena superstrada, his usual route, was blocked by construction. (It was later determined, however, that the work interrupting the superstrada occurred on the following weekend.) Between approximately nine-thirty and ten-thirty in the evening, Nesi said, he was about a kilometer from the Scopeti clearing when he stopped at an intersection to let a Ford Fiesta pass. The car was of a rosy or reddish color, and he was ninety percent certain it was driven by Pacciani. There was on board a second individual he didn't know.

Why hadn't he reported this ten years ago?

Nesi replied that at the time he was only seventy to eighty percent certain, and that you should only report things you are certain of. Now, however, he had become ninety percent certain of his identification, and that, he figured, made it certain enough to be reported. The judge praised him later for his scrupulosity.

One wouldn't normally think that Nesi, being a small dealer in sweaters, would mistake a color. But he had gotten wrong the color of Pacciani's car—it was not "rosy or reddish," it was dead white. (Perhaps Nesi was thinking back to the red Alfa Romeo reported by witnesses that led to the infamous Identi-Kit portrait.)

Nevertheless, Nesi's testimony put Pacciani within a kilometer of the Scopeti clearing on Sunday night, and that was enough to seal the peasant's fate. The judges convicted Pacciani of murder and condemned him to fourteen life sentences. In their opinion, the judges explained Nesi's mistake by the fact that the reflection of the taillights at night made the white car look red. They acquitted Pacciani of the 1968 murders, as prosecutors had presented no evidence linking him with that crime, beyond the fact that it was committed with the same gun. The judges never addressed the question of how, if Pacciani had nothing to do with that killing, he had come into possession of the gun.

At 7:02 p.m. on November 1, 1994, the president of the court began to read the verdict. All the national networks in Italy interrupted their programming to bring the news. "Guilty of the murder of Pasquale Gentilcore and Stefania Pettini," the president of the court intoned, "guilty of the murder of Giovanni Foggi and Carmela De Nuccio, guilty of the murder of Stefano Baldi and Susanna Cambi, guilty of the murder of Paolo Mainardi and Antonella Migliorini, guilty of the murder of Fredrich Wilhelm Horst Meyer and Uwe Jens Rüsch, guilty of the murder of Pia Gilda Rontini and Claudio Stefanacci, guilty of the murder of Jean-Michel Kraveichvili and Nadine Mauriot."

As the judge's stentorian voice boomed out the final "guilty," Pacciani placed his hand upon his heart, closed his eyes, and murmured, "An innocent dies."

CHAPTER
26

One chilly February in 1996, Mario Spezi crossed the little piazza toward the carabinieri barracks in the village of San Casciano. He was out of breath, and not just because of the Gauloises he smoked unceasingly; he was wearing a massive and exceedingly ugly overcoat, in garish colors, dangling with zippers, belts, and buckles that served no purpose except to obscure the real function of the garment. A small button near the collar was a microphone. Behind the silly plastic label on the breast was a video camera. Between the outer material and the lining was a recorder, a battery, and wires. The electronic apparatus hidden among the stuffing did not emit even a faint buzz. A technician from the television station had activated it inside the church of the Collegiata di San Cassiano, behind a stone column between the confessional and the baptismal font. There had been no one in the Collegiata, aside from an old lame woman kneeling on the prayer stand in front of a forest of plastic candles that spread their electric light against the darkness.

In the two years since Pacciani had been convicted, Spezi had written many articles casting doubt on the peasant's guilt. But this one promised to be the scoop to end all scoops.

The video camera would run for an hour. In those sixty minutes
Spezi had to convince Arturo Minoliti, the marshal of the carabinieri
barracks of San Casciano, to talk. He had to get the man to tell him the
truth about Perugini's discovery of the cartridge in Pacciani's vegetable garden. Minoliti, as the local carabinieri official, had been present
during the twelve-day search, the only one there not connected with
SAM or the police to witness the recovery of the infamous cartridge.

Spezi had always had deep misgivings about this type of journalism,
and he had often sworn he would never do it. It was dirty, it was shaking down someone for a scoop. But just before entering the barracks,
where Minoliti was waiting, his scruples vanished like holy water on
the tip of a finger. Taping Minoliti surreptitiously was, perhaps, the
only way to arrive at the truth, or at least a piece of it. The stakes were
high: Spezi was convinced that Pacciani was innocent, and that a huge
miscarriage of justice had taken place.

Spezi stopped in front of the entrance to the barracks and turned so
that his breast would film the sign that read "Carabinieri." He pressed
the buzzer and waited. A dog barked somewhere and an icy wind cut
his face. He didn't even think for a minute that he ran the risk of being
discovered. The desire for a scoop made him feel invincible.

The door was opened by a man in a blue uniform, his eyes wary.

"I'm Mario Spezi. I have an appointment with Marshal Minoliti."

They left him in a small room long enough to smoke another
Gauloise. From where he sat Spezi could see the empty office of the
minor functionary from whom he hoped to steal the truth. He noted
that the seat in front of the writing desk, the one that Minoliti would
occupy, was placed on the right-hand side and he calculated that the
lens of the camera, on the left side of his chest, would film only a wall.
He said to himself that as soon as he sat down, he would have to turn
the seat, with a casual gesture, in order to frame the carabinieri officer
while he spoke.

Nothing will come if it, Spezi thought, suddenly feeling insecure. *This
is like a Hollywood film, and only a bunch of overexcited television people
could possibly think that it would succeed.*

Minoliti arrived. Tall, nearly forty, off-the-rack suit, gold-rimmed shades not quite covering the face of an intelligent man. "Sorry that I kept you waiting."

Spezi had worked up a plan for bringing him around to the crucial point. He counted on chipping away at his resistance by arousing his conscience as an upholder and enforcer of the law, and to play a little on his vanity, if he had any.

Minoliti indicated a chair. Spezi took the seatback and rearranged it with a single, easy move. He seated himself facing the marshal and placed his cigarettes and lighter on the desktop. He was certain he now had Minoliti in the camera's sights.

"I'm sorry for disturbing you," he began hesitatingly, "but tomorrow I have a meeting with my editor in Milan, and I'm looking for something on the Monster of Florence. New stuff, real news. By now, you know better than me, everything and its opposite has been said and nobody gives a damn about it any longer."

Minoliti fidgeted in his seat and twisted his neck in a funny way. He moved his gaze from Spezi to the window and back. In the end he sought help in a cigarette.

"What do you want to know?" he said, blowing the smoke from his nostrils.

"Arturo," Spezi said, leaning forward confidentially. "Florence is small. You and I move in the same circles. We've both heard certain rumors, it's inevitable. Excuse me for being direct, but it seems you have doubts about the investigation against Pacciani. Grave doubts . . . ?"

The marshal took his chin between his hands and, this time, twisted his lips strangely. Then the words came like a gust of relief. "Well, yes . . . In the sense that . . . In short, if there's a strange coincidence, you let it pass. If there are two, you can still let it go. When it gets to three, well, in the end you have to say that it's no longer a coincidence. And here, with the coincidences, or more like strange happenings, there have been a few too many."

Under the lens of the microcamera Spezi's heart began to accelerate.

"What do you mean? Is there something that doesn't seem right about the investigation?"

"Well, yes. Look, I'm convinced that Pacciani is guilty. But it was up to us to prove it . . . You can't cut corners."

"Which is to say?"

"Which is to say . . . the rag, for instance. That rag just doesn't make sense to me, it just doesn't."

The rag he was alluding to was a hard piece of evidence against Pacciani. A month after the maxi-search of his property that had brought to light the cartridge, Minoliti had received an anonymous package. Inside was a spring guide rod from a gun, wrapped in a piece of rag. There was a piece of paper written in capital letters. It said:

THIS IS A PIECE OF THE PISTOL BELONGING TO THE MONSTER OF FLORENCE. IT WAS IN A GLASS JAR *REPLACED* (SOMEONE HAD FOUND IT BEFORE ME) UNDER A TREE IN LUIANO. PACCIANI USED TO WALK THERE. PACCIANI IS A DEVIL AND I KNOW HIM WELL AND YOU KNOW HIM TOO. PUNISH HIM AND GOD WILL BLESS YOU BECAUSE HE IS NOT A MAN BUT A BEAST. THANK YOU.

The business had seemed decidedly odd right away. And then, a few days after this fact, in the course of yet another search of Pacciani's garage, the agents of SAM had found a similar piece of rag that they had somehow overlooked in the twelve-day search. When the two pieces were brought together, they matched up perfectly.

Perugini theorized that the Monster himself had mailed the letter with the rag, in an unconscious wish to incriminate himself.

"This rag stinks," said Minoliti, turning toward the telecamera hidden on Spezi. "Because I wasn't called when it was found. All the operations were supposed to be conducted jointly by SAM and the carabinieri of San Casciano. But when the rag was found, I wasn't called. Strange. The rag, I say to you, is dirty. We were already in that garage and found many pieces of material, which we took and catalogued. That rag wasn't there."

Spezi lit another Gauloise to control his excitement. This was a major scoop and they had yet to arrive at the bullet found in the garden.

"In your opinion, where did the rag come from?"

The carabiniere opened his arms. "Eh, I don't know. I wasn't there. That's the trouble. And then why send a spring guide rod? Of all the parts of a pistol it's the only one that can't be matched to a specific firearm. And they just happened to mail that one!"

Spezi decided to nudge him toward the Winchester bullet. "And the cartridge. Does that also stink?"

Minoliti took a deep breath and was silent for several seconds. He turned and suddenly began, "It really burned me the way that cartridge was found. I resented how Chief Inspector Perugini put us in such a difficult situation with the truth . . ."

It was all Spezi could do to remain calm, his heart was pounding so hard.

"We were in Pacciani's garden," said the marshal, "I, Perugini, and two other agents of the squad. Those two were scraping the soles of their shoes on a cement grapevine post that lay on the ground and were joking about the fact that they both were wearing the same shoes. At a certain moment, near the shoe of one of them, the base of the cartridge just appeared."

"But," Spezi interrupted in order to make sure that the business was very clear on the tape, "Perugini described it quite differently in his book."

"Right! Right, because he says, 'The ray of light made the cartridge glisten.' What ray of light! Look, maybe he just wanted to dress up the discovery a bit."

Spezi asked, "Minoliti, did they put it there?"

The marshal's face darkened. "That's one hypothesis. More than a hypothesis even . . . I'm not saying that I'm certain . . . I have to consider this against my will. It's a quasi-certainty . . ."

"A quasi-certainty?"

"Eh, yes, because in light of the facts I can't find another explanation . . . Then, I say, when Perugini wrote about witnessing this glimmer of light, it really frosted me. I say, 'Chief Inspector, you disrespect me. If I go and contradict you, I'm fucked.' What I mean is, who're the judges going to believe? A marshal or a chief inspector? At a certain point I'm forced to back up his story."

Spezi felt like he was filming an Oscar winner, the acting was so superb, and the Neapolitan accent of Minoliti just added that much more color. The journalist saw that he had fifteen minutes of tape by the clock. He had to press him. "Arturo, did they plant it?"

Minoliti was suffering. "I just can't believe that my colleagues, my friends . . ."

Spezi couldn't lose any more time. "Okay, I understand you. But, if for a moment you were to forget they were colleagues you had known for a long time, would the facts cause you to say that this bullet had been planted?"

Minoliti became like stone. "In the light of reason, yes. I must say it was planted. I arrived at that conclusion that certain evidence is dirty: the cartridge, the spring guide rod, and the rag." Minoliti continued to speak in a low tone, almost as if to himself. "I am up against an extremely difficult situation . . . They've got my telephone tapped . . . I'm afraid . . . I am truly afraid . . ."

Spezi tried to find out if he had told anyone of this, by way of confirmation. "You never spoke to anyone?"

"I talked to Canessa." Paolo Canessa was one of the prosecutors.

"And what did he say?"

"Nothing."

A few minutes later, at the door of the barracks, Minoliti said goodbye to Spezi. "Mario," he said, "forget what I told you. It was just venting. I spoke to you because I trust you. But your colleagues, before they come in here, I order them searched!"

Feeling like a worm, Spezi crossed the piazza and walked along the sidewalk, his left shoulder almost brushing the walls of the houses, his arms rigid. He no longer felt the cold wind.

My God, he thought, *it worked!*

He went into the local Casa del Popolo where the people from the TV channel were waiting for him and drinking beer. Angling over to their table, he seated himself without saying a word. He felt their gaze on him. He continued to say nothing, and they asked him nothing. They all somehow understood it had been a success.

Later that evening, reunited at dinner after having seen the film of Minoliti, they let themselves feel euphoric. It was the scoop of the century. Spezi felt sorry to stick in the meat grinder the unwitting Marshal Minoliti. But, he told himself, even the truth must have its victims.

The next day, the Italian news agency ANSA, which had heard about the taping, ran an item on it. As soon as it was published, all three national television channels called to interview Spezi. At the news hour, Spezi parked himself on the sofa, remote in hand, to see how the news would be reported.

Not one word was aired. The following morning the newspapers did not speak of it, not even a line. Rai Tre, the national television channel that had arranged for the taping of Minoliti, canceled the segment.

Clearly, someone in a position of power had spiked it.

CHAPTER
27

In Italy, a man condemned to a life sentence is automatically granted an appeal before the Corte d'Assise d'Appello, with a new prosecutor and a fresh panel of judges. In 1996, two years after the conviction, Pacciani's case came up for appeal before the Corte d'Assise. The head prosecutor was Piero Tony, an aristocratic Venetian and lover of classical music, bald with a fringe of hair that fell below his collar. The president of the court was the aged and imposing Francesco Ferri, a jurist with a long and distinguished career.

Piero Tony had no stake in the original conviction of Pacciani, no face to save. One of the great strengths of the Italian judicial system is this appeals process, in which none of the players involved in the appeal—prosecutors or judges—have an ax to grind.

Tony, charged with upholding Pacciani's conviction, reviewed all the evidence against the peasant with dispassion and objectivity.

And he was aghast.

"This investigation," he told the court, "if it weren't so tragic, would put one in mind of the Pink Panther."

Instead of prosecuting Pacciani, Tony used his time in court to criticize the investigation and deprecate the evidence against Pacciani, taking it apart with ruthless logic, piece by piece, until not one brick of evidence was left standing on top of another. Pacciani's lawyers, seeing all their arguments usurped by the prosecution, could do little but sit in stunned silence and, when their turn came, express their amazed agreement with the prosecution.

As the trial proceeded, it generated panic and consternation among the investigators. With the prosecutor himself declaring Pacciani's innocence, the peasant would surely be acquitted, which would be an unbearable humiliation and loss of face for the police. Something had to be done—and it fell to Chief Inspector Michele Giuttari to do it.

Six months earlier, at the end of October 1995, Chief Inspector Giuttari had been installed in a sunny office high above the Arno River near the American embassy. He had taken over the Monster of Florence case after Chief Inspector Perugini left for Washington. The Squadra Anti-Mostro had been disbanded, since the case was thought to have been solved, but Giuttari would soon reconstitute a special investigative unit to take over its responsibilities. In the meantime, he had embarked on the herculean task of reading all the files on the case, tens of thousands of them, which included hundreds of interviews with witnesses, masses of expert reports and technical analyses, as well as entire trial transcripts. He also combed through the evidence lockers, examining everything that had been collected at the scenes of the crimes, no matter how irrelevant.

Chief Inspector Giuttari discovered many loose ends, unexplained evidence, and profound mysteries left to resolve. During this process, he came to a fateful conclusion: the case had not been completely solved. Nobody, not even Perugini, had understood the full and terrifying dimensions of the case.

Michele Giuttari was a Sicilian from Messina, dashing and articulate, an aspiring novelist and connoisseur of convoluted conspiracy theories. He went about with half a "toscano" cigar stuck in the corner of his mouth, coat collar flipped up, his long, thick, glistening black hair slicked back. He bore a striking resemblance to Al Pacino in the movie *Scarface*, and there was indeed something cinematic in the way he conducted himself, with style and verve, almost as if a camera were trained on him.

As Giuttari combed the files, he uncovered important but overlooked clues that, in his opinion, pointed to something far more sinister than a lone serial killer. He started with Lorenzo Nesi's claim that he saw Pacciani *with another person* in a red car (that was actually white), on Sunday night a kilometer from the last killing. Giuttari opened an investigation into this shadowy person. Who was he? What was he doing in the car? Had he participated in the murder? By uncovering the truth, the *real* truth, it went without saying that the chief inspector would be doing himself a favor. Perugini had used the Monster as a vehicle for tremendous career advancement and Vigna would soon do the same. There was plenty of mileage left in the Monster of Florence case.

Now, six months later, Pacciani's looming acquittal threatened to undo Chief Inspector Giuttari's nascent theories and carefully laid plans. The chief inspector had to do something to mitigate the damage of Pacciani's acquittal. He developed a plan.

On the morning of February 5, 1996, Chief Prosecutor Piero Tony spent four hours summing up. The case against Pacciani, he said, contained no evidence, no clues, and no proofs. There were no pieces of a pistol connecting him to the killings, there were no bullets planted in the garden capable of convicting, there wasn't a single witness in which he could believe. There was nothing. For Tony, the fundamental fact of the accusation remained unaddressed: nowhere did investigators explain how the infamous .22 Beretta used in the 1968 murder passed from the Sardinian clan into Pacciani's hands.

"Half a clue plus half a clue," Tony thundered, "does not make a whole clue: it makes zero!"

On February 12, Pacciani's lawyers, robbed of their arguments, said little in summation. The following day, Ferri and his associate justices shut themselves up in their chambers to deliberate.

On that same afternoon, Chief Inspector Giuttari slipped on his black coat, raised his collar, stuck the half "toscano" in his mouth, and gathered together his men. Their unmarked cars blasted out of police headquarters and headed to San Casciano, where they surrounded the house of Mario Vanni—the ex-postman who, at Pacciani's first trial, had mumbled over and over that he and Pacciani were just "picnicking friends."

Giuttari and his men seized Vanni and bundled him into a squad car, not even giving the poor fellow time to put in his false teeth. Vanni, they said, was the "other man" Lorenzo Nesi had seen in the car. They charged him with being Pacciani's accomplice in murder.

The timing was exquisite. On the morning of February 13, the very day the appeals court judges were to announce their verdict, the newspapers were trumpeting the news of Vanni's arrest as Pacciani's co-Monster.

As a result, the great bunkerlike courtroom was like a volcano waiting to explode. The arrest of Vanni was a direct challenge to the judges, should they dare acquit Pacciani.

As the proceedings began, a policeman sent by Chief Inspector Giuttari arrived breathlessly in court, carrying a bundle of papers. He demanded the right to speak. Ferri, the president of the court, was annoyed by this last-minute move. Nevertheless, he coolly invited the emissary from police headquarters to say his piece.

The man announced that four new witnesses in the Monster case had surfaced. He presented them as Greek letters: Alpha, Beta, Gamma, and Delta. For reasons of security, he said, the Tribunale could not render the names. Their testimony was absolutely crucial to the case—because two of these witnesses, the emissary told the stunned court, were *actually present* at the double homicide of 1985 when the French tourists were killed. They had witnessed Pacciani at the very scene of the crime, committing the murders, and one had actually confessed to helping him. The others could corroborate their testimony. These four witnesses, after more than a decade of silence, had suddenly been moved to speak out just twenty-four hours before the final judgment that would decide Pacciani's fate.

A frozen silence fell over the courtroom. Even the Bics of the journalists remained stuck in their notebooks. This was an incredible revelation, the kind of thing you saw in the movies—never in real life.

If Ferri had been annoyed, now he was incensed. But he maintained an icy calm, his voice dripping with sarcasm. "We cannot hear Alpha and Beta. We are not here for a lesson in algebra. We cannot wait for the Procura [the prosecutor's office] to lift the veil of secrecy from the names. Either they tell us immediately who this Alpha, Beta, Gamma, and Delta are and we will invite them into the courtroom to take their testimony, or else we will ignore this and take no action whatsoever."

The policeman refused to name the names. Ferri was livid at what he considered an offense to the court, and he dismissed the emissary and his news of witnesses. Then he and the other judges rose and retired to their chambers to decide their verdict.

Later, it was suggested that Ferri had fallen into a clever trap. By presenting the witnesses in a deliberately offensive manner, Giuttari had provoked Ferri into refusing to hear them—thus creating grounds to appeal Ferri's verdict to the Italian Supreme Court.

It was eleven in the morning. By four in the afternoon, the rumors began to circulate that the appeals court was about to issue its verdict. In all the bars in Italy, the televisions were tuned to the same channel, while pro-Pacciani and anti-Pacciani factions faced off, arguing and laying bets. Many "I ♥ Pacciani" T-shirts were dusted off and donned for the occasion.

Standing, his voice marked with age, President of the Court Ferri announced the absolute and unconditional acquittal of Pacciani for being the Monster of Florence.

The shaky old peasant was freed. He later greeted well-wishers from the shabby window of his house, flanked by his lawyers, weeping and spreading his hands to bless the crowd, as if he were the pope.

The public trial was finished, but the trial of public opinion continued. Giuttari's timely arrest of Vanni and his courtroom gambit had done the trick. Pacciani had been acquitted of a crime that two people had *seen* him commit—his accomplices. There was a public uproar. Pacciani was guilty—he had to be. And yet the court had acquitted him. Ferri came under public criticism. Surely, many said, there must be some way to undo this travesty of justice.

There was: Ferri's refusal to hear the four witnesses. The Italian Court of Cassation (equivalent to the Supreme Court) took up the matter, vacated the acquittal, and opened the door for a new trial.

Giuttari swung into action, marshaling the evidence, preparing for fresh indictments and a trial. Only this time, Pacciani was not a lone serial killer. He had accomplices: his picnicking friends.

CHAPTER
28

Spezi and other journalists immediately rose to the challenge of identifying the four "algebraic" witnesses. The veil of secrecy was easily rent. They turned out to be quite a collection of half-wits and lowlifes. Alpha was a mentally retarded man named Pucci. Gamma was a prostitute named Ghiribelli, in the final stages of alcoholism, known to turn a trick for a twenty-five-cent glass of wine. Delta was a pimp named Galli.

Of them all, Beta would be the most important, as he had confessed to helping Pacciani murder the French tourists. His name was Giancarlo Lotti, and he came from the same town as Vanni, San Casciano. Everyone in San Casciano knew Lotti. They had given him the racist nickname Katanga, an Italian slang term that might be loosely translated as "Jungle Bunny," even though he was white. Lotti was a sort of village idiot of the classic kind that have largely disappeared from the modern world, a man who subsisted on the charity of the village, who was fed, clothed, and housed by his fellow citizens, and who entertained all with his unwitting antics. Lotti hung about the town square, grinning and hailing people. He was often subjected to pranks and taunts by schoolboys. They used to chase him around: "Katanga!

Katanga! Run! Run! Martians have landed on the soccer field!" And Lotti would happily start running. He maintained himself in a felicitous state of inebriation, consuming two liters of wine a day, more on holidays.

Spezi, in search of information on Lotti, spent a long evening with the owner of the trattoria where Lotti got a free meal every evening. The owner regaled him with amusing stories. He told of the time that one of his waiters—the same fellow who every evening laid a free bowl of *ribollita* under the hangdog jowls and bloodshot eyes of the poor unfortunate—dressed up as a woman, with a pair of napkins for a hat and rags stuffed in his shirt for breasts. The waiter, thus decked out, strutted and sashayed in front of Lotti, winking at him lasciviously. Lotti was immediately smitten. "She" pretended to accept an appointment with him in the bushes the following night. The next evening Lotti returned to the trattoria, boasting loudly of his imminent conquest, and he ate and drank with gusto. Then the owner arrived, saying Lotti was wanted on the telephone. Lotti was astonished and pleased to receive a telephone call in a restaurant like a man of affairs. He swaggered to the phone, which in reality was manned by another waiter in the kitchen, who pretended to be the young lady's father.

"If you lay a finger on my daughter," the alleged father roared, "I'll smash your ugly mug!"

"What daughter?" Lotti babbled, terrified, his knees shaking. "I swear I don't know any daughter, you've got to believe me!"

Everyone had a good laugh over that one.

What was not so amusing was the story Lotti and the other algebraic witnesses had told Giuttari, which was soon leaked to the press.

Pucci said that ten years ago, he and Lotti were returning to Florence on Sunday evening, September 8, 1985. This was the night investigators had decided the French tourists were killed, the night that Lorenzo Nesi claimed to have seen Pacciani with another man. They stopped at the Scopeti clearing to relieve themselves.

"I remember well," said Pucci, "that we saw a car of a light color stopped a few meters from a tent, and, to our view, two men who were inside that car got out of it and started to shout at us with menacing gestures, so much so that we went away. The two threatened to kill us if we didn't go away immediately. 'Why did you come here busting our balls, get the hell out or we'll kill both of you!' We were frightened and got out of there."

Pucci claimed that he and Lotti had stumbled across the scene of the Monster's last crime at the very moment when it was being committed. Lotti corroborated the story and added that he clearly recognized both men. They were Pacciani and Vanni—Pacciani waving a pistol and Vanni clutching a knife.

Lotti also implicated Pacciani and Vanni in the 1984 double murder in Vicchio. And then Lotti explained that it was no coincidence they had stopped in the Scopeti clearing that night to take a piss. He knew the crime was scheduled to take place, and he had stopped to assist in the killings. Yes, Lotti said, he had to confess it, he could hold back no longer—he was one of the murderers himself! Along with Vanni, he was one of the accomplices of the Monster of Florence.

Lotti's confession was of enormous importance to the police. As their star witness, he was well taken care of. They moved him into a secret place that much later was revealed to be police headquarters in Arezzo, a beautiful medieval town south of Florence. After living in the police barracks for many months, Lotti's story, which had begun with many contradictions, began to line up with the facts already ascertained by the police. But Lotti was unable to give the investigators a single objective, verifiable piece of evidence that they didn't already have. The first iteration of Lotti's story, before he had spent months in Arezzo, didn't match the evidence gathered at the crime scene. For example, he swore to having seen Vanni make the cut in the tent. Then he said Pacciani entered the tent through the cut. Kraveichvili jumped out in a flash past Pacciani, and the fat sixty-year-old man pursued him into the woods firing his gun, killing him with the pistol.

None of this agreed with the evidence. The cut in the tent was only seven inches long, and it was made in the rain fly of the tent, not in the tent itself. Nobody could have entered through the cut. The shells had all been found at the front door of the tent. If it had happened as Lotti claimed, the shells would have been scattered along the path of pursuit. Lotti's initial descriptions of the crime not only contradicted the evidence gathered in the Scopeti clearing, but also contradicted the psychiatric and behavioral analyses, the results of the autopsies, and the reconstructions of the crime.

Even shakier was Lotti's "confession" regarding the killing in Vicchio. Lotti said that the girl was only wounded by the first shots and that Vanni, so as not to dirty himself, had donned a long duster coat. Then, while she screamed, he pulled her out of the car, dragged her into the field of flowers and herbs, and finished her off with a knife. Again, none of this matched the evidence: the girl had been killed by the first shot, a bullet into the brain, and did not have the time even to cry out. The medical examiner had established that all the knife marks had been made post mortem. And there was no evidence at either crime of more than one killer at the scene.

Finally, there was the fundamental question of *when* the killing of the French tourists had taken place. Investigators had settled on Sunday night as the night of the crime. Naturally, Lotti claimed it was Sunday, and Nesi's testimony also involved Sunday night. But there was a great deal of evidence, including the testimony of Sabrina Carmignani, that suggested they had been killed Saturday night.

Why would Lotti make a false confession? The answer isn't hard to see. Lotti had gone from village idiot to star witness and co–Monster of Florence. He was the center of attention of the entire country, his picture on the front page of the newspapers, investigators hanging on his every word. On top of that, he had free room and board in Arezzo and perhaps even a liberal supply of wine.

In addition to the central story, Giuttari and his interrogators took down testimony from the algebraic witnesses of Vanni's sexual depravity. Some of this evidence was inadvertently hilarious. In one such story, the ex-postman had taken the bus to visit a whore in Florence. The bus driver took a curve a little fast, which caused a vibrator to fall out of Vanni's pocket. It rolled and bounced around the bus as Vanni, scrabbling about on his hands and knees, tried to scoop it up.

"The second investigation of the Monster of Florence has passed from an inquiry into serial killings committed by a single individual to a series of killings committed by more than one person," the prosecutor Vigna told the press. Instead of a lone psychopathic killer, a band of Monsters had roamed the Tuscan countryside—the picnicking friends.

Ghiribelli, the alcoholic prostitute, told investigators another story that would eventually loom large in the investigation. She claimed that Pacciani and his picnicking friends frequented the house of a self-styled druid or wizard (whose day job was that of pimp) where they held black masses and worshiped the devil. "In the room just as you entered," said Ghiribelli, "there were old wax candles, a five-pointed star drawn on the floor with carbon, an unspeakable dirtiness and messiness everywhere, condoms, liquor bottles. On the sheets of the big bed there were traces of blood. There were spots as large as a piece of letter paper. These traces I saw every Sunday morning in 1984 and 1985."

The wizard-pimp she named had died ten years before, and it proved impossible to check Ghiribelli's assertions. Nevertheless, Giuttari took it all down and pushed the case forward, convinced he was finally on the right track.

The president of the appeals court, Francesco Ferri, the man who had acquitted Pacciani, watched the new investigation proceed with growing dismay and anger. He resigned his judgeship to write a book, entitled *The Pacciani Case*, which was rushed into print in late 1996.

In his book, Ferri denounced the new investigation into the picnicking friends. "The worst thing," Ferri wrote about Giuttari's new witnesses, "is not the improbability of their accounts, their lack of believability, but the clear falsity of the accounts. These two individuals [Pucci and Lotti] . . . have described particulars of the homicides, of which they claim to be eyewitnesses, that do not in fact conform to the evidence revealed at the time. . . . It is certain that Pucci and Lotti are coarse and habitual liars. . . . It is very difficult to believe that their stories contain even the minimum basis of truth."

The judge continued, "It smells to high heaven. . . . It is stupefying, however, that no one has up to this time exposed the grave deficiencies of the stories of Pucci and Lotti, neither investigators, defense attorneys, or journalists. . . . The most extraordinary thing, however, and more extraordinary still that nobody has noted it, is that for months Lotti has been kept in custody in an undisclosed location, where he has slept, eaten and perhaps above all drunken, and possibly even received compensation, in a place beyond the reach of the press, like a golden hen from which they ask, from time to time, a golden egg. In this way the revelations dribble out, bit by bit, more or less contradictory."

The judge advanced an explanation. "The mental flexibility of the subjects, their complete absence of morality and the hope of gaining impunity or other advantage is enough to explain their contorted testimony." Ferri concluded, "I could not remain quiet in the face of an investigation so far outside logic and justice, conducted with prejudice and equipped with confessions that are maintained at all cost."

Ferri, unfortunately, was not a compelling wordsmith, and he was innocent in the ways of publishing. He placed his book with a tiny publisher that had little distribution and which printed very few copies. *The Pacciani Case* sank like a stone, virtually unnoticed by the press or the public. The new investigation of the Monster of Florence, under the doughty captainship of Chief Inspector Michele Giuttari, sailed on, untroubled by Ferri's accusations.

In October of 1996, Vigna, the lead prosecutor in the Monster case, was appointed director of the Antimafia Investigation Department in Italy, the most powerful and prestigious law enforcement position in the country. (Perugini, you may recall, had earlier leveraged the Monster case into an appointment in Washington, D.C.) Others responsible for putting Pacciani on trial had also used the case as a springboard to greater things. Regarding the Monster investigation, a highly placed carabinieri officer entertained a unique theory of criminal justice that he shared with Spezi.

"Have you ever considered," he said, "that Pacciani's trial might be nothing more than a case of the acquisition and management of power?"

CHAPTER
29

Pacciani remained free and technically innocent while Giuttari mustered up a new case against him. But the excitement was too much for the Tuscan peasant, and on February 22, 1998, the "sweet little lamb" dropped dead of a heart attack.

It took no time at all for the rumor mill to declare that Pacciani had not died of a heart attack, but had in fact been murdered. Giuttari sprang into action and directed an exhumation of the peasant's body. The remains were tested for poisoning. The results? His death was "compatible" with having been poisoned—by an excess of his own heart medicine. Doctors pointed out that patients, in the throes of a heart attack, often overconsume their heart medicine. But that was far too prosaic an explanation for Chief Inspector Giuttari, who theorized that Pacciani may have been murdered by a person or persons unknown, to keep him from telling what he knew.

The trial of Pacciani's picnicking friends, Vanni and Lotti, began in June of 1997. The evidence against them consisted of Lotti's word, backed up by the feeble-minded Pucci, against Vanni's ineffective and disorganized protestations of innocence. It was a sad spectacle. Vanni and Lotti were convicted of all fourteen Monster killings; Vanni was sentenced to life in prison and Lotti to twenty-six years. Neither the press nor Italian public opinion seemed skeptical of the idea that three quasi-illiterate inebriates of marginal intelligence could have successfully killed fourteen people over a period of eleven years with the goal of stealing the women's sex organs.

The trial, furthermore, never addressed the central motive: why had Pacciani and his picnicking friends stolen those sex organs? Chief Inspector Giuttari, however, had already embarked on an investigation of this very question. And he had an answer: behind the Monster killings lay a satanic cult. This shadowy cabal of wealthy and powerful people, seemingly beyond reproach, who occupied the highest positions in society, business, law, and medicine, had hired Pacciani, Vanni, and Lotti to kill couples in order to obtain the sex organs of girls for use as the obscene, blasphemous "wafer" in their Black Masses.

To investigate this new theory, Chief Inspector Giuttari formed an elite police unit, which he called the Gruppo Investigativo Delitti Seriali, the Serial Killings Investigative Group, or GIDES. They set up shop on the top floor of a monstrous, modern cement structure called Il Magnifico, after Lorenzo il Magnifico, erected near the Florence airport. He assembled a crack team of detectives. Their sole mission: to identify and arrest the *mandanti*, the "masterminds" or instigators behind the killings of the so-called Monster of Florence.

Out of the Everest of evidence in the Monster case, Giuttari had pried out a few pebbles that he felt supported his new theory. First, Lotti had made an offhand statement, ignored at the time, that "a doctor asked Pacciani to do a few little jobs for him." For Giuttari, this revived the old suspicion that a doctor was responsible for the killings— this time not as the killer himself, but as a mastermind. And then there was Pacciani's money. After the old peasant died, it turned out he was rich. He owned two houses and had post office bonds worth more than the equivalent of a hundred thousand dollars. Giuttari was unable to track the source of this wealth. This should not have been all that surprising—a large percentage of the Italian economy at the time was underground and many people had unexplained riches. But Giuttari ascribed a more sinister reason to Pacciani's affluence: the peasant farmer had gotten rich from selling the body parts he and his picnicking friends had collected in their years of labor.

In a later book on the case, Chief Inspector Giuttari explained his satanic sect thesis more particularly. "The best sacrifices for evoking demons are human sacrifices, and *the death most favorable* [emphasis his] for such sacrifices are those that occur during orgasm and are called *mors iusti*. A similar motive led to the killings of the 'monster,' who struck his victims while they were making love. . . . In that precise moment [of orgasm] powerful energies are released, indispensable for the person acting out satanic rituals, which bring power to himself and to the ritual he is celebrating."

Digging deep into medieval lore and legend, the chief inspector found a possible name for this sect: the School of the Red Rose, an ancient, almost forgotten diabolical order that had left its mark across centuries of Florentine history, a perverse Priory of Sion in reverse, all pentacles, black masses, ritual killings, and demonic altars. The school, some said, was a deviant offshoot of an ancient order, Ordo Rosae Rubae et Aurae Crucis, an esoteric Masonic sect connected to the English Golden Dawn, and, therefore, with Aleister Crowley, the most famous satanist of the last century, who called himself "the Great Beast 666" and who in the 1920s founded a church in Cefalù, Sicily, called the Abbey of Thelema. There, it was said, Crowley practiced perverted magical and sexual rituals involving men and women.

There were several other elements that guided Giuttari in the formation of his theory. The most important of them was Gabriella Carlizzi, an energetic little Roman lady with a big smile who ran a conspiracy theory Internet site and had self-published a string of books. Carlizzi claimed to know a great deal of hidden information about many infamous European crimes of the past decades—including the kidnapping and murder of the former Italian prime minister Aldo Moro and the Belgian pedophile ring. Behind them all, she said, was the School of the Red Rose. On the day of the September 11, 2001, terrorist attacks, Carlizzi shot a fax out to Italian newspapers: "It was them, the members of the Red Rose. Now they want to strike Bush!" The Red Rose was also behind the Monster killings. Carlizzi had earlier been convicted of defamation for claiming the well-known Italian writer Alberto Bevilacqua was the Monster of Florence, but since that time her theories on the Monster had apparently evolved. Her site was also filled with religious and inspirational stories and a section in which she detailed her conversations with the Madonna of Fatima.

Carlizzi became an expert witness for the investigation. Giuttari and his GIDES detectives called her in and listened to her for hours—perhaps even days—as she recounted her knowledge of the activities of the satanic sect hidden in the green hills of Tuscany. The police had to give her a protective escort, she would later claim, because of the grave danger she faced from members of the sect intent on silencing her.

In rummaging through old evidence lockers, Giuttari found physical evidence to back up his theories that a satanic sect was behind the killings. The first was the doorstop that had been collected a few dozen meters from the place where the Monster had killed a couple in the Bartoline Fields in October 1981. For the chief inspector, that stone was something far more sinister than a doorstop. He described its significance to a reporter for the *Corriere della Sera*, one of Italy's major daily newspapers: it was, he claimed, a "truncated pyramid with an hexagonal base that served as a bridge between this world and Hell." He dug out of an old file some photographs taken by police of some suspicious circles of stones with some berries and a cross where an old gamekeeper claimed the French tourists had camped four days preceding their murder. (Many other witnesses said they had been camping in the Scopeti clearing for at least a week.) Investigators later concluded that the stone circles had no connection with the case. Giuttari did not agree. He turned the photographs over to an "expert" in the occult. The chief inspector reported the expert's conclusions in his book: "When the circle of stones is closed it represents the union of two people, that is to say a pair of lovers, while when it is open it signifies that the couple has been selected. The photograph of the berries and the cross show the murder of the two people; the people are the berries, while their death is represented by the cross. The photograph of the scattered stones shows the destruction of the circle after the execution of the two lovers."

Seeing that Pacciani & Co. were all from San Casciano, Giuttari figured that the satanic sect must be headquartered in or around that idyllic little Tuscan village, set like a jewel in the rolling hills of Chianti. Once again he delved deeply into fusty Monster files and found a startling clue. In the spring of 1997, a mother and a daughter had gone to the police with a strange story. They managed a rest home for old people in a place called Villa Verde, a beautiful old country house surrounded by gardens and a park situated a few kilometers outside San Casciano. The two women complained that a guest of the villa, a half-Swiss, half-Belgian painter named Claude Falbriard, had disappeared, leaving behind a huge mess in his room and a pile of suspicious things—things that might have something to do with the Monster of Florence, including an unregistered pistol and hideous drawings of women with their arms, legs, and heads cut off. The two women had piled all of Falbriard's belongings in a box and delivered them to the police.

At the time, the police had dismissed it as irrelevant. Giuttari saw the situation in a different light and launched an investigation of the two women and their villa. Right away he struck pay dirt: he discovered that Pacciani had actually worked for a while as a gardener at Villa Verde during the time of the killings!

Giuttari and his investigators now believed that the villa might have served as the headquarters of the Order of the Red Rose, whose members commissioned the gardener, Pacciani, and his friends to collect female body parts for use in satanic rituals at the villa. In Giuttari's scenario, the mother and daughter were actually part of the satanic cult. (Why they would have brought attention to themselves by going to the police was left unexplained.)

Between the time of the murders and Giuttari's investigation, Villa Verde had become a super-luxury hotel with a swimming pool and restaurant, renamed Poggio ai Grilli, Hill of the Crickets. (The sign, almost as soon as it went up, was altered by some Tuscan wag to read

"Poggio ai Grulli," Hill of the Morons.) The new owners were not at all pleased by the attention.

The press, with *La Nazione* leading the way, picked up the story with ferocious glee.

OWNERS OF NURSING HOME UNDER SUSPICION
THE VILLA OF HORRORS
ALLEGED TO HAVE HOSTED SECRETS OF
MONSTER OF FLORENCE

"After ten o'clock, the villa was sealed up against outsiders. Various people arrived and performed magical and satanic rites." So claimed one of the ex-nurses of Poggio ai Grilli, the villa between San Casciano and Mercatale where Pietro Pacciani, once accused of committing the Monster of Florence killings, had worked as a gardener. During the period of the Tuscan murders, the "Villa of the Horrors" hosted a rest home for old people where for several months the painter Claude Falbriard lived, first investigated for illegal possession of a firearm, who then became a key witness in the investigation into the possible instigators behind the Monster's serial killings.

Falbriard at this time was still blithely floating around Europe, completely unaware he was a "key witness" and possibly even a mastermind behind the Monster killings. GIDES enlisted the help of Interpol and they tracked him down in a village on the Côte d'Azur near Cannes. They were disappointed to learn the painter had arrived in Tuscany for the first time in 1996, eleven years after the Monster's final double homicide. Nevertheless, Falbriard was brought to Florence for questioning. He was a disappointing witness—an angry, unhinged, decrepit old man who harangued the police with wild accusations of his own.

"At Villa Verde," he testified, "I was drugged and locked up in a room. They robbed me of billions of lire. Strange things happened, especially at night." The mother and daughter were behind it all, he claimed.

Based on Falbriard's statement, the two women were charged with kidnapping and fraud. *La Nazione* wrote a series of lurid articles on the villa. "From the depositions of the former personnel of the rest home," ran one article, "there came many important clues. In fifty pages of testimony were hidden evidence of disturbing secrets. The old people held at Poggio ai Grilli were left abandoned among their own feces and urine without assistance. At night the aides were absolutely forbidden to set foot in the villa, which was transformed into a place where Black Masses were performed. Giuttari suspects that the genital organs and the parts of the breasts amputated from the victims of the Monster were used to conduct these satanic rituals."

Despite the renovation of the villa, Giuttari hoped that some trace of the Order of the Red Rose might remain, or that the sect might still be active in the villa. Old Tuscan villas have huge basements and underground areas for making and storing wine and aging prosciutto, cheese, and salami, and this is where Giuttari believed the actual room used as the temple of sacrifice might be found—and perhaps still in use.

One fine fall day, GIDES raided Poggio ai Grilli. After searching the enormous villa, the men of GIDES entered the room that their information indicated had been the sanctum sanctorum of the cult, the temple of Satan. In the room they found some cardboard human skeletons, plastic bats hung on strings, and other decorations. The search had come a few days before Halloween and a party had been planned—or so they claimed at the villa.

"Without doubt an attempt to sidetrack the investigation," Giuttari fumed to *La Nazione.*

Giuttari and GIDES made little progress into the satanic sect investigation, and by the year 2000 it seemed to be sputtering out.

Then, in August 2000, I arrived in Italy with my family.

PART II

❖

The Story of Douglas Preston

CHAPTER
30

On November 4, 1966, after forty days of rain, the Arno River burst its banks and laid waste to Florence, one of the most extraordinary cities in the world.

This was no gentle rise of water. The river flash-flooded; it boiled over the Lungarni embankments and tore through the streets of Florence at thirty miles an hour, carrying along tree trunks, smashed cars, and dead cattle. Ghiberti's great bronze doors to the Baptistery were bashed down and knocked to pieces; the Cimabue Crucifix, possibly the greatest example of medieval art in Italy, was reduced to a mound of sodden plaster; Michelangelo's David was fouled to his buttocks with fuel oil. Tens of thousands of illuminated manuscripts and incunabula in the Biblioteca Nazionale were buried under muck. Hundreds of old master paintings stored in the basement of the Uffizi Gallery flaked apart, leaving layers of paint chips in the mud.

The world watched with horror as the waters receded, leaving the birthplace of the Renaissance a wasteland of ooze and debris, its art treasures devastated. Thousands of volunteers—students, professors, artists, and art historians—converged from all over the world to undertake an emergency salvage effort. They lived and worked in a city without heat, water, electricity, food, or services. After a week some rescuers had to don gas masks to protect themselves from the toxic fumes being released by rotting books and paintings.

They called the volunteers the Angeli del Fango, the "Mud Angels."

I had long wanted to write a murder mystery set at the time of the Florentine flood. The novel, entitled *The Christmas Madonna*, involved an art historian who rushes to Florence to volunteer as a Mud Angel. He is an authority on the mysterious artist Masaccio, the young genius who single-handedly launched the Italian Renaissance with his extraordinary frescoes in the Brancacci Chapel, and who then died abruptly, at twenty-six, amid rumors that he had been poisoned. My character goes to work as a volunteer in the basement of the Biblioteca Nazionale, pulling books and manuscripts out of the mire. One day he discovers an extraordinary document, which contains a clue to the whereabouts of a famous lost painting by Masaccio. Called *The Christmas Madonna*, the painting was the central panel in a triptych described vividly by Vasari in the 1600s, which had subsequently disappeared. It is considered to be one of the most important lost paintings of the Renaissance.

My art historian abandons his volunteer work and sets off on a mad search for the painting. He vanishes. A few days later they find his body high in the Pratomagno Mountains, dumped by the side of the road. His eyes have been gouged out.

The murder is never solved and the painting is never found. Now, thirty-five years later, we fast-forward to the present day. His son, a successful artist in New York, hits a midlife crisis. He realizes there is something he must do: solve the murder of his father. The way to do it is to find the lost painting. So he flies to Florence and begins his search—a journey that will take him from crumbling archives to Etruscan tombs and finally to a ruined village high into the Pratomagno Mountains, where a horrifying secret lies buried, and where an even more terrifying destiny awaits him . . .

This was the novel I came to Italy to write. I never did. Instead, I got sidetracked by the Monster of Florence.

★   ★   ★

Living in Italy was going to be the adventure of a lifetime, for which we were singularly unprepared. None of us spoke Italian. I had spent a few days in Florence the previous year, but my wife, Christine, had never been to Italy in her life. Our children, on the other hand, were at that age of delightful flexibility in which they seemed to meet even the most extraordinary life challenges with a cheerful nonchalance. Nothing in life was out of the ordinary to them, since they hadn't learned what was ordinary to begin with. When the time came, they boarded the plane with complete insouciance. We were a nervous wreck.

We arrived in Florence in August 2000: myself, Christine, and our two children, Aletheia and Isaac, who were six and five. We enrolled our children in local Italian schools, Aletheia in first grade and Isaac in kindergarten, and we ourselves began taking language classes.

Our transition to Italy was not without its challenges. Aletheia's teacher reported that it was a joy to have such a happy child in class who sang all day long, and she wondered just what it was she was singing. We soon learned:

> *I don't understand anything she's saying,*
> *She talks and talks all day long,*
> *But I can't understand a word . . .*

Cultural differences quickly reared up. A few days after Isaac went off to kindergarten, he came back, wide-eyed, and told how the teacher smoked cigarettes during recess and tossed the butts on the playground—and then she spanked (spanked!) a four-year-old who tried to smoke one of them. Isaac called her "the Yelling Lizard." We quickly transferred him and his sister to a private school run by nuns on the other side of town. Nuns, we hoped, wouldn't smoke or spank. We were correct, at least on the former assumption, and came to accept the occasional spanking as a cultural difference we had to live with, along with smokers in restaurants, death-defying drivers, and waiting in line at the post office to pay bills. The school was located in a magnificent eighteenth-century villa hidden behind massive stone walls, which the sisters of the order of San Giovanni Battista had turned into a convent. The schoolchildren took recess in a two-acre formal Italian garden, with cypress trees, clipped hedges, flowerbeds, fountains, and marble statues of naked women. The gardener and the children were constantly at war. Nobody at the school, not even the English teacher, spoke English.

The *direttrice* of the school was a stern, beady-eyed nun who needed only to fix her withering glare on someone, student or parent, to reduce the person to abject terror. She took us aside one day to advise us that our son was *un monello*. We thanked her for the compliment and rushed home to look up the word. It meant "rascal." After that we brought a pocket dictionary to parent-teacher meetings.

As we hoped, our kids began to learn Italian. One day Isaac sat down to dinner, looked at the plate of pasta we'd prepared, made a face, and said, *"Che schifo!"* a vulgar expression meaning "Gross!" We were so proud. By Christmas they were speaking in full sentences, and by the end of the school year their Italian was so good they began making fun of our own. When we had Italian guests for dinner, Aletheia would sometimes march around the room, swinging her arms and bawling an imitation of our atrocious American accent, "How do you do, Mr. and Mrs. Coccolini! What a pleasure it is to meet you! Won't you please come in, accommodate yourselves, and enjoy a glass of wine with us!" Our Italian guests would be helpless with laughter.

And so we adjusted to our new life in Italy. Florence and its surrounding villages turned out to be a delightfully small place, where everyone seemed to know everyone else. Life was more about the process of living than reaching some end result. Instead of a once-a-week, efficient trip to the supermarket, shopping became a shockingly inefficient but charming routine of visiting a dozen or more shops and vendors, each of which sold a single product. This meant exchanging news, discussing the quality of the various choices, and listening to how the shopkeeper's grandmother prepared and served the item under discussion, which was the only way to do it despite what anyone might say to the contrary. Never were you allowed to touch the food being purchased;

it was a breach of etiquette to test the ripeness of a plum or place an onion yourself in your shopping bag. For us, shopping was an excellent Italian lesson, but one fraught with danger. Christine made an indelible impression on the handsome *fruttivendolo* (fruit seller) when she asked for ripe *pesce* and *fighe* instead of *pesche* and *fichi* (fish and pussy instead of peaches and figs). It took many months before we felt even a little bit Florentine, although we quickly learned, like all good Florentines, to look with scorn on the tourists who wandered about the city, gaping and slack-jawed, in floppy hats, khaki shorts, and marshmallow athletic shoes, with giant water bottles strapped around their waists as if they were crossing the Sahara Desert.

Life in Italy was a strange mixture of the quotidian and the sublime. Driving the children to school in the morning in the dead of winter, bleary-eyed, I would come over the hill of Giogoli—and there, rising magically from the dawn mists, would be the cloisters and towers of the great medieval monastery of La Certosa. Sometimes, wandering about the cobbled streets of Florence, on a whim I would duck into the Brancacci Chapel and spend five minutes looking at the frescoes that launched the Renaissance, or I would take a turn through the Badia Fiorentina at Vespers to listen to Gregorian chants in the same church where young Dante gazed on his love, Beatrice.

We soon learned about the Italian concept of the *fregatura*, indispensable for anyone living in Italy. A fregatura is doing something in a way that is not exactly legal, not exactly honest, but just this side of egregious. It is a way of life in Italy. We had our first lesson in the fine art of the fregatura when we reserved tickets to see Verdi's *Il Trovatore* at the local opera house. When we got there, the box office informed us they could find no record of our tickets, despite our presentation of the reservation number. There was nothing they could do—the opera was completely and totally sold out. The large crowd seething in front of the box office attested to the truth of that.

As we were leaving, we ran into a shopkeeper from our neighborhood decked out in a mink coat and diamonds, looking more like a countess than the owner of Il Cantuccio, the tiny shop where we bought biscotti.

"What? Sold out?" she cried.

We told her what had happened.

"Bah," she said, "they gave your tickets to someone else, someone important. We'll fix them."

"Do you know somebody?"

"I know nobody. But I *do* know how things work in this town. Wait here, I'll be back in a moment." She marched off while we waited. Five minutes later, she reappeared with a flustered man in tow, the manager of the opera house himself. He rushed over and took my hand. "I am so, *so* sorry, Mr. Harris!" he cried out. "We didn't know you were in the house! No one told us! Please accept my apologies for the mix-up with the tickets!"

Mr. Harris?

"Mr. Harris," said the shopkeeper grandly, "prefers to travel quietly, without a large entourage."

"Naturally!" the manager cried. "Of course!"

I stared dumbfounded. The shopkeeper shot me a warning glance that said, *I got you this far, don't blow it.*

"We had a few tickets in reserve," the manager went on, "and I do hope that you will accept them as compensation, compliments of the Maggio Musicale Fiorentino!" He produced a pair of tickets.

Christine recovered her presence of mind before I did. "How very kind of you." She swiped the tickets from the man's hand, hooked her arm firmly into mine, and said, "Come on, *Tom.*"

"Yes, of course," I mumbled, mortified at the deception. "Most kind. And the cost . . . ?"

"*Niente, niente!* The pleasure is ours, Mr. Harris! And may I just say that *The Silence of the Lambs* was one of the finest—one of *the finest*—movies I have ever seen. All of Florence is awaiting the release of *Hannibal.*"

Front-center box seats, the finest in the house.

It was a short trip by bicycle or car from our Giogoli farmhouse into Florence through the Porta Romana, the southern entrance to the old city. The Porta Romana opened into a warren of crooked streets and medieval houses that make up the Oltrarno, the most unspoiled part of the old city. As I explored, I often saw a curious figure taking her afternoon *passeggiata* through the narrow medieval streets. She was a tiny ancient woman, sticklike, dressed to the hilt in furs and diamonds, her face rouged, lips coral red, an old-fashioned little hat with netted pearls perched on her diminutive head, walking with assurance in high-heeled shoes over the treacherous cobblestones, looking neither to the right nor left, and acknowledging acquaintances with an almost imperceptible movement of her eyes. I learned she was the Marchesa Frescobaldi, from an ancient Florentine family that owned half the Oltrarno and much of Tuscany besides, a family that had financed the Crusades and given the world a great composer.

Christine often jogged though the city's crooked medieval streets, and one day she stopped to admire one of the grandest palaces in Florence, the Palazzo Capponi, owned by the other great family of the Oltrarno district—and indeed one of the leading noble families of Italy. The palace's rust-red neoclassical façade stretches for hundreds of feet along the banks of the Arno, while its grim, stone-faced, medieval backside runs along the sunken Via de' Bardi, the Street of the Poets. As she was gawking at the grand *portone* of the palazzo, a British woman came out and struck up a conversation with her. The woman worked for the Capponi family, she said, and after hearing about the book I was trying to write about Masaccio, she gave Christine her card and said we should call upon Count Niccolò Capponi, who was an expert in Florentine history. "He's quite approachable, you know," she said.

Christine brought back the card and gave it to me. I put it away, thinking there was no chance I would make a cold call on Florence's most famous and intimidating noble family, no matter how approachable.

The rambling farmhouse we occupied in Giogoli stood high on the side of a hill, shaded by cypresses and umbrella pines. I turned a back bedroom into a writing studio, where I intended to write my novel. A single window looked past three cypress trees and over the red-tiled roofs of a neighbor's house to the green hills of Tuscany beyond.

The heart of Monster country.

*   *   *

For weeks after hearing the story of the Monster of Florence from Spezi, I found myself wondering about the murder scene so close to our house. One fall day, after a frustrating struggle with the Masaccio novel, I left the house and climbed up through the grove to the grassy meadow to see the spot for myself. It was a lovely little meadow with a sweeping view of the Florentine hills running southward toward some low mountains. The crisp fall air smelled of crushed mint and burning grass. Some claim that evil lingers in such places as a kind of malevolent infection, but I could feel nothing. It was a place outside good and evil. I loitered about, hoping in vain to extract some glimmer of understanding, and almost against my will I found myself reconstructing the crime scene, positioning the VW bus, imagining the tinny sound of the *Blade Runner* score playing endlessly over the scene of horror.

I took a deep breath. Below, in our neighbor's vineyard, the *vendemmia* was in progress, and I could see people moving up and down the rows of vines, heaping clusters of grapes into the back of a three-wheeled motorized cart. I closed my eyes and listened to the sounds of the place—a cock crowing, distant church bells, a barking dog, an unseen woman's voice calling out for her children.

The story of the Monster of Florence was taking hold.

CHAPTER
31

Spezi and I became friends. About three months after we met, unable to shake myself loose from the Monster story, I suggested to him that we collaborate on an article about the Monster of Florence for an American magazine. As a sometime contributor to *The New Yorker*, I called up my editor there and pitched the idea. We got the assignment.

But before putting pen to paper, I needed a crash course from the "Monstrologer." A couple of days a week I shoved my laptop into a backpack, hauled my bike out, and pedaled the ten kilometers to Spezi's apartment. The last kilometer was a murderous ride uphill through groves of knotted olive trees. The apartment he shared with his Belgian wife, Myriam, and their daughter occupied the top floor of the old villa, with a living room, dining room, and a terrace overlooking Florence. Spezi worked in an upstairs garret, crammed with books, papers, drawings, and photographs.

When I arrived, I would find Spezi in the dining room, a Gauloise invariably hanging from his lip, layers of smoke drifting in the air, papers and photographs spread out on the table. While we worked, Myriam would bring us a steady stream of espresso in tiny cups.

Spezi would always put away the crime scene photographs before she came in.

Mario Spezi's first job was to educate me about the case. He went through the history chronologically, in minute detail, from time to time plucking a document or a photograph from the heap by way of illustration. All our work was conducted in Italian, as Spezi's English was rudimentary and I was determined to use the opportunity to learn the language better. I took notes furiously on my laptop while he spoke.

"Nice, eh?" he often said when he had finished recounting some particularly egregious example of investigative incompetence.

"*Si, professore,*" I would answer.

His view of the case was not complicated. He had nothing but contempt for the conspiracy theories, alleged satanic rituals, hidden masterminds, and medieval cults. The simplest and most obvious explanation, he felt, was the correct one: that the Monster of Florence was a lone psychopath who murdered couples for his own sick, libidinous reasons.

"The key to identifying him," Spezi said repeatedly, "is the gun used in the 1968 clan killing. Trace the gun and you find the Monster."

In April, when the vineyards were beginning to stripe the hills in fresh green, Spezi took me to see the scene of the 1984 killing of Pia Rontini and Claudio Stefanacci, outside Vicchio. Vicchio lies north of Florence in a region known as the Mugello, where the hills grow steep and wild as they pile up toward the great chain of the Apennines. Sardinian shepherds settled in this area in the early sixties, after the migration to Tuscany, to raise sheep in the mountain meadows. Their pecorino cheese was highly prized, so much so that it became a signature cheese of Tuscany.

We drove along a country road, following a rushing stream. It had been years since Spezi had last been there, and we had to stop several times before we found the place. A turnoff from the road led to a grassy track at a place known locally as La Boschetta, the Little Wood. We parked and walked in. The track dead-ended at the base of a hill covered with oak trees, opening on one side to a field of medicinal herbs. An ancient stone farmhouse with terra-cotta roofs stood a few hundred yards off. A rushing stream, hidden by poplars, ran through the valley below. Beyond the farmhouse the land mounted up, hills upon hills, receding into blue mountains. Emerald-green pastures had been cut into the shoulders and lower slopes of the hills, pastures that the artist Giotto had wandered through as a boy in the late 1200s, tending sheep, daydreaming, and drawing pictures in the dirt.

The track ended at a shrine to the victims. Two white crosses stood in a grassy plot. Plastic flowers, faded by the sun, had been arranged in two glass jars. Coins had been placed on the arms of the crosses; the site had become a place of pilgrimage for young couples from the area, who left the coins as a way to pledge their love for each other. The sun poured in across the valley, bringing with it the scent of flowers and freshly mown fields. Butterflies fumbled about, birds twittered in the woods, and puffy white clouds scudded across a sky of blue.

Gauloise in his hand, Mario sketched out the scene of the crime for me while I took notes. He showed me where the light blue Panda of the two lovers had been parked and where the killer must have been hiding in the dense vegetation. He pointed out where the shells had lain, ejected after each shot, which told the pattern and order of shooting. The boy's body had been found trapped in the rear seat, almost in a fetal position, curled up as if to defend himself. The killer had shot him dead and then, later, stabbed the body several times in the ribs, either to make sure he was dead or as a sign of contempt.

"It happened at about nine-forty," Spezi said. He pointed to a field across the river. "We know that because a farmer, plowing that field at night to escape the heat, heard the shots. He thought it was the backfiring of a *motorino*."

I followed Mario into the open field. "He dragged the body and laid it down here—within full view of the house. An absurdly exposed place." He gestured toward the farmhouse with his cigarette hand, tufts of smoke drifting off. "It was a terrible scene. I'll never forget it. Pia lay on her back, arms thrown wide as if crucified. Her bright blue eyes were open and staring into sky. It's awful to say this, but I couldn't help noticing how beautiful she was."

We stood in the field, drowsy bees visiting the flowers around us. I had finished taking notes. The whisper of the river came up through the trees. Again, no evil lingered. On the contrary, the place felt peaceful, even holy.

Afterwards we drove into Vicchio. It was a small town set amid lush fields alongside the river Sieve. A ten-foot-tall bronze statue of Giotto, holding his palette and brushes, stood in the center of the cobbled piazza. The shops nearby included a small household appliance store still owned by the Stefanacci family, where Claudio Stefanacci had worked.

We ate lunch in a modest trattoria off the piazza and then walked down a side street to pay a visit to Winnie Rontini, the mother of the murdered girl. We came to a high stone wall with iron gates surrounding a grand in-town villa, one of the most imposing in Vicchio. Through the gates I could see a formal Italian garden gone to seed. Beyond rose the three-story façade of the house, badly run-down, the pale yellow stucco cracked and peeling off. The villa's windows were shuttered. It looked abandoned.

We pressed the buzzer on the iron gate, and a voice quavered out of the tinny speaker. Mario gave his name and the gate clicked open. Winnie Rontini met us at the door and invited us into the darkened house. She moved slowly and heavily, as if under water.

We followed her into a dark sitting room, almost devoid of furniture. One window shutter was partway open, admitting a bar of light like a white wall dividing the darkness, through which drifted dust motes that blazed for a moment and vanished. The air smelled of old fabric and wax polish. The house was almost empty, only a few shabby pieces of furniture left, as all the antiques and silver had been sold long ago to finance the search for her daughter's killer. Signora Rontini was so impoverished she could no longer afford a telephone.

We seated ourselves on the faded furniture, raising a storm of motes, and Signora Rontini seated herself opposite us, settling into a lumpy chair with slow dignity. Her fair skin, fine hair, and sky blue eyes revealed her Danish heritage. Around her neck she wore a gold necklace with the initials of P and C on it, for Pia and Claudio.

She talked slowly, the words spoken as if weights were attached to them. Mario told her about our writing project and our continuing search for the truth. She stated her opinion, almost as if she no longer cared, that it was Pacciani. She told us that her husband, Renzo, a highly paid marine engineer who traveled all over the world, had quit his job to pursue justice for his daughter full-time. Every week he visited police headquarters in Florence, asking for fresh news and consulting with investigators, and on his own he had offered large monetary rewards for information. He had frequently appeared on television or radio, appealing for help. He had been scammed more than once. The effort eventually ruined his health and drained their finances. Renzo died of a heart attack on the street outside the police station after a visit. Signora Rontini remained in the big villa all alone, selling off the furniture piece by piece, and sinking ever deeper into debt.

Mario asked about the necklace.

"For me," she said, touching the necklace, "life ended on that day."

CHAPTER
32

If you believe you are beyond harm, will you go inside? Will you enter this palace so prominent in blood and glory, follow your face through the web-spanned dark . . . ? Inside the foyer the darkness is almost absolute. A long stone staircase, the stair rail cold beneath our sliding hand, the steps scooped by the hundreds of years of footfalls . . .

So it was on a cold January morning that Christine and I found ourselves climbing the stairs so vividly described by Thomas Harris in *Hannibal*. We had an appointment in the Palazzo Capponi to meet Count Niccolò Piero Uberto Ferrante Galgano Gaspare Calcedonio Capponi, and his wife, the Contessa Ross. I had finally made that cold call. *Hannibal* the film, directed by Ridley Scott, had recently been shot in the Palazzo Capponi, where Hannibal Lecter, alias "Dr. Fell," was fictionally employed as the curator of the Capponi library and archives. I thought it would be interesting to interview the real curator of the Capponi archives, Count Niccolò himself, and write a "Talk of the Town" piece about it for *The New Yorker*, to coincide with the release of the film.

The count met us at the top of the stairs and guided us into the library, where the countess was waiting. He was a man of about forty, tall and solid, with curly brown hair, a Vandyke beard, keen blue eyes, and a pair of schoolboy ears. He looked strikingly like a grown-up version of the 1550 portrait of his ancestor Lodovico Capponi by the artist Bronzino, which hangs in the Frick Museum in New York. When the count greeted my wife, he kissed her hand in a most peculiar way, which I later learned was an ancient gesture in which the nobleman takes the lady's hand and with a rapid, elegant twist raises it to within six inches of his lips, while making a crisp half-bow—never, of course, allowing his lips to actually brush the skin. Only titled Florentines greet ladies in this manner. Everyone else shakes hands.

The Capponi library lay at the end of a dim, ice-cold hall decorated with coats of arms. The count settled us in a brace of giant oaken chairs, then perched himself on a metal stepstool behind an old refectory table and fiddled with his pipe. The wall at his back consisted of hundreds of pigeonholes containing family papers, manuscripts, account books, and rent rolls going back eight hundred years.

The count wore a brown jacket, a wine-colored sweater, slacks, and—rather eccentric for a Florentine—beaten-up ugly old shoes. He held a doctorate in military history and taught at the Florentine campus of New York University. He spoke perfect Edwardian English that seemed a relic from an earlier age. I asked him where he had acquired it. English, he explained, had entered his family when his grandfather married an Englishwoman and they raised their children speaking English at home. His father, Neri, in turn, had passed his English on to his children like a family heirloom—and in this way the language of the Edwardian age had been fossilized inside the Capponi family, unchanged for almost a century.

The Countess Ross was American, very pretty, guarded and formal, with a dry sense of humor.

"We had Ridley Scott in here with his cigar," said the count, referring to the director of the movie.

"The group would arrive," the countess said, "led by the cigar, followed by Ridley, followed by an attentive crowd."

"It created quite a bit of smoke."

"There was a lot of fake smoke, actually. Ridley seems to be obsessed with smoke. And busts. He was always needing marble busts."

The count glanced at his watch, then apologized. "I'm not being discourteous. I myself smoke only twice a day, after twelve and after seven."

It was three minutes to twelve.

The count continued: "He wanted more busts in the *Gran Salone* during the shooting. He ordered up papier-mâché busts that were made to look old. But they wouldn't do. So I said that I had a few of my ancestors down in the basement, shall we bring them up? He said marvelous. They were quite dirty, so I asked him, shall we dust them? Oh *no*, he said, please *don't*! One of them was my *quadrisnonna*, my great-great-great-grandmother, born Luisa Velluti Zati of the Dukes of San Clemente, who was a very proper woman. She refused to attend the theater. She thought it was immoral. Now she is appearing as a prop in a movie. And what a movie! Violence, disembowelments, cannibalism."

"You never know, she might be pleased," the countess said.

"The movie crew behaved very well. On the other hand, the Florentines were really bloody-minded while they were filming. Naturally, now that it's over, these same shopkeepers have put up signs in their windows: 'Hannibal was filmed here.'"

He checked his watch, found it had attained *mezzogiorno*, and lit his pipe. A cloud of fragrant smoke rose up toward the distant ceiling.

"Aside from smoke and busts, Ridley was fascinated with Henry the Eighth." The count rose and rummaged through the archives, finally extracting a letter on heavy parchment. It was a letter from Henry VIII to a Capponi ancestor, requesting two thousand soldiers and as many harquebusiers as possible for Henry's army. The letter was signed by Henry himself and from the document dangled something brown and waxy, the size of a squashed fig.

"What is that?" I asked.

"That is Henry the Eighth's broad seal. Ridley quipped that it looked rather more like Henry's left testicle. I made a photocopy for him. Of the document, I mean."

We moved from the library into the Gran Salone, the palace's main reception room, where Hannibal Lecter plays the clavier while Inspector Pazzi, hiding in the Via de' Bardi below, listens. The Salone contained a piano, not a clavier, which Anthony Hopkins played in the film. The room was decorated with dark portraits, fantastical landscapes, marble busts, armor, and weapons. Due to the expense of heating such a vast space, the air temperature hovered just above that of a Siberian torture chamber.

"Most of that armor is fake," said the count, with a dismissive wave. "But this suit over here, this is a good suit of armor. It dates from the 1580s. It probably belonged to Niccola Capponi, who was a knight in the Order of Saint Stephen. It once fit me well. It's quite light. I could do push-ups in it."

There was a lusty wail from a hidden room in the palace and the countess bustled off.

"These are mostly Medici portraits. We have five Medici marriages in our family. A Capponi was exiled from Florence with Dante. But in those days Dante was probably looking down his long nose at us. We were among, as Dante wrote, *la gente nova e i subiti guadagni*—'the new people and the suddenly rich.' Neri Capponi helped bring Cosimo de' Medici back to Florence in 1434 after his exile. It was an enormously profitable alliance for the family. We were successful in Florence because we were never the first family. We were always second or third. There is a Florentine saying: 'The nail that sticks out gets hammered back in.'"

The countess reappeared with a baby, Francesca, named after Francesca Capponi, a great beauty who married Vieri di Cambio de' Medici, and who died in childbirth at the age of eighteen. Her rosy-cheeked portrait, attributed to Pontormo, hung in the next room.

I asked the count who his most famous ancestor was.

"That would be Piero Capponi. All Italian schoolchildren know his story. It's like Washington crossing the Delaware, oft repeated and much embellished."

"He's downplaying the story, as usual," said the countess.

"I am not, my dear. The story *is* largely exaggerated."

"It's largely true."

"Be that as it may. In 1494, Charles the Eighth of France, on his way with his army to claim Naples, passed Florence and, seeing a way to make some fast money, demanded a huge payment from the city. 'We shall blow our trumpets' and attack, he declared, if the ransom were not paid. Piero Capponi's answer was, 'We shall then ring our bells,' meaning they would call up the citizens to fight. Charles backed down. He is reputed to have said, *Capon, Capon, vous êtes un mauvais chapon.* 'Capon, Capon, you are one evil chicken.'"

"Chicken jokes are quite prevalent in the family," the countess said.

The count said, "We eat capons at Christmas. It's a little cannibalistic. On that subject, let me show you where Hannibal Lecter took his meals."

We followed him into the *Sala Rossa*, an elegant drawing room with draped chairs, a scattering of tables, and a mirrored sideboard. The walls were covered in red silk that was woven from cocoons produced on the family's silkworm estates two hundred and fifty years ago.

"There was a poor woman in the film crew," said the countess. "I had to keep saying to her, 'Don't move anything without permission.' She kept moving everything around. Every day while they were filming, Niccolò's little brother Sebastiano, who runs Villa Calcinaia, the family estate in Chianti, brought up a bottle of their wine, and he would place it in a strategic location in this room. But it never managed to get into the picture. This woman kept moving it out. The producers had an arrangement with Seagram's to use only their brands."

The count smiled. "Nevertheless, by the end of the day the bottle had always managed to get itself uncorked and was empty. It was always the best *riserva*."

Many years ago, when Thomas Harris was researching the Monster of Florence case for his novel *Hannibal*, and attending Pacciani's trial, he met Count Capponi and was invited to the palazzo. Much later Harris called the count and said he would like to make Hannibal Lecter curator of the Capponi archive—would that be all right?

"We had a family meeting," the count said. "I told him that we agreed, on one condition—that the family would not be the main course."

Niccolò and I became friends. We met for lunch every so often at Il Bordino, a tiny trattoria behind the church of Santa Felicità, where his family's chapel and crypt were located, a short walk from his palazzo. Il Bordino was one of the last old-time trattorias in Florence; small, crowded, with a glass counter displaying the dishes available that day. Its dim interior was more like a dungeon, with blackened stone and plaster walls, scarred wooden tables, and ancient terra-cotta floors. The fare was quintessentially Florentine, simple dishes of meat and pasta accompanied by slabs of coarse bread, served at working-class prices, with tumblers of rough red wine.

One day over lunch, I mentioned to Niccolò that Mario Spezi and I were researching the case of the Monster of Florence.

"Ah," he said, keenly interested. "The Monster of Florence. Are you sure you want to get involved in that business?"

"It's a fascinating story."

"A fascinating story indeed. I should be careful if I were you."

"Why, what could happen? It's an old story. The last killing was twenty years ago."

Niccolò slowly shook his head. "To a Florentine, twenty years is the day before yesterday. And they are still investigating. Satanic sects, black masses, a villa of horrors . . . Italians take these things very seriously. Careers have been made—and ruined—over this case. Take care that you and Mario do not poke too vigorously with your sticks into that nest of vipers."

"We'll be careful."

He smiled. "If I were you, I should get back to that delightful novel you described to me about Masaccio—and leave the Monster of Florence well enough alone."

CHAPTER
33

One fine spring day, Monster 101 neared its end. I knew all the facts that were known, an expert on the case second only to Spezi and the Monster himself. But there was one point on which Spezi had been resolutely coy, and that was his opinion as to who the Monster of Florence might be.

"*Eccoci qua,*" said Spezi. "And so here we are: satanic sects, blasphemous hosts, and hidden masterminds. What next?" He leaned back in the chair with a crooked smile and spread his hands. "Coffee?"

"Please."

Spezi shot back his demitasse of espresso, an Italian habit I could never quite acquire. I sipped mine.

"Any questions?" His eyes twinkled.

"Yes," I said. "Who do you think is the Monster?"

Spezi flicked the ash off his cigarette. "It's all there." He gestured at the heap of papers. "Who do you think?"

"Salvatore Vinci."

Spezi shook his head. "Let's look at it as Philip Marlowe might. It's all about the Beretta. Who brought the gun to the 1968 crime? Who used it? Who carried it home? And, most important, what happened to it later? It's all there in the story, if you care to look for it."

"The gun belonged to Salvatore Vinci," I said. "He brought it with him from Sardinia, he planned the 1968 killing, he had the car, and he was the shooter."

"Bravo."

"So he must have carried the gun home."

"Exactly. He handed the gun to Stefano Mele to take the last shot, so that Mele would contaminate his hands with powder residue. Afterwards, Mele threw the gun down. Vinci picked it up and took it home. He was no fool. He wasn't about to leave the murder weapon at the scene. A gun used in a murder is dangerous, because ballistics can connect it to bullets recovered from the victims. A gun like this would never be sold or given away. It would either be destroyed or carefully hidden. Since we know the gun wasn't destroyed, Salvatore Vinci must have hidden it. Along with the boxes of bullets. Six years later it emerged to kill again—in the hands of the Monster of Florence."

I nodded. "So you think Salvatore Vinci is the Monster—just as Rotella did."

Spezi smiled. "Really?" He reached into the pile of papers, withdrew the FBI report. "You've read it. Does it sound like Salvatore Vinci?"

"Not really."

"Not at all! The profile is insistent on one crucial point: the Monster of Florence is impotent, or nearly so. He suffers from sexual dysfunction and would have little or no sexual contact with women his own age. He kills to satisfy his libidinous desires, which can't be satisfied in the normal way. Strong evidence of this is that none of the crime scenes showed any evidence of rape, molestation, or sexual activity. But Salvatore was the opposite of impotent—he was a veritable Priapus. Salvatore doesn't match the rest of the FBI report either, particularly in the psychological details."

"If Salvatore Vinci isn't the Monster," I asked, "then you still have the problem of how the Beretta passed from him to the Monster."

The question hung in the air. Spezi's eyes twinkled.

"Was it stolen from him?" I said.

"Exactly! And who was in the best position to take the gun?"

Although all the clues were there, I could not see them.

Spezi tapped his finger on the table. "I don't have the most important document in the case. I know it exists, because I spoke to someone who'd seen it. I tried *everything* to get it. Can you guess what document that might be?"

"The complaint of the theft?"

"*Appunto!* In the spring of 1974, four months before the Monster's first killing in Borgo San Lorenzo, Salvatore Vinci went to the carabinieri to file a complaint. 'The door of my house was forced and my house was entered.' When the carabinieri asked him what was stolen, he said, 'I don't know.'"

Spezi rose and opened the window. The stream of fresh air eddied the blue layers of smoke in the room. He shook another Gauloise out of a pack lying on the table, stuck it in his mouth and lit it, then turned from the window. "Think about it, Doug. This fine fellow, a Sardinian with a deep and ancient suspicion of authority, probably a murderer, goes to the carabinieri to report a breaking and entering when nothing was stolen. Why? And why would anyone rob his house in the first place? It's a sorry house, poor, there's nothing in there of value. Except . . . perhaps . . . a .22 Beretta and two boxes of bullets?"

He tapped the ash off the cigarette. I was on the edge of my seat.

"I haven't told you the most extraordinary thing of all. Vinci *named* the person responsible for the breaking and entering. The person he denounced was just a boy. A member of his Sardinian clan, a close relation. The last person he would have thrown to the carabinieri. Why file charges against him if he took nothing? *Because he was afraid of what the thief might do with the gun.* Salvatore Vinci wanted the breaking and entering to be on record, to protect himself. In case the boy did something with the gun that might be . . . *terrible.*"

Spezi pushed his finger a few inches closer to me, as if sliding the nonexistent document forward. "Right there, on that document, we would find the name that Salvatore Vinci gave the carabinieri. The name of the thief. That person, my dear Douglas, is the Monster of Florence."

"And who is it?"

Spezi smiled teasingly. "*Pazienza!* Back in 1988, after the rift between Rotella and Vigna, the carabinieri officially withdrew from the investigation. But they couldn't leave it well enough alone. They kept it going in secret. And the missing document is one of the things they dug out of God knows what dusty file in the basement of some dingy barracks."

"A secret investigation? Did they find out anything else?"

Mario smiled. "Many things. For example, after the first Monster killing, Salvatore Vinci checked himself into the psychiatric department at Santa Maria Nuova hospital. Why? We don't know—the medical records seem to have disappeared. Perhaps the boy who had stolen his gun had gone and done something terrible with it."

He reached out and shuffled through a pile, extracting the FBI report. "Your FBI, in this report, lists a number of characteristics the Monster is likely to have. Let's apply it to our suspect.

"The report says that the Monster is likely to have a record of petty crimes such as arson and theft, but not crimes such as rape and violence. Our man has a rap sheet of auto theft, illegal possession of weapons, breaking and entering, and an arson.

"The report says that during the seven years between the crime of 1974 and the next one in 1981, the Monster was not in Florence. Our man left Florence in January of 1975. He returned to Florence at the end of 1980. In several months, the killings started again.

"The report says that the Monster probably lived alone during the period of the crimes. When not living alone, he would probably be found living with an older woman such as an aunt or grandmother. During much of the seven-year period he was away from Florence, our suspect lived with an aunt. Several months after the last killing, in 1985, our man met an older woman and moved in with her. The killings stopped. True, from 1982 to 1985 he was married, but according to a carabinieri officer who was part of the secret investigation into the Monster case, the marriage was annulled for *impotentia coeundi*—nonconsummation. To be fair, *impotentia coeundi* was sometimes invoked as a way to obtain a divorce in Italy at that time, even when it wasn't necessarily true.

"The FBI report says that this type of killer will often contact the police and try to mislead the investigation, or at least collect news about the crime. Our man offered himself as an informant to the carabinieri.

"Finally, studies of sexual serial killers often turn up a history of maternal abandonment and sexual abuse within the family unit. Our man's mother was murdered when he was one year old. He suffered a second traumatic separation from a mother figure when his father's longtime girlfriend left. And he may have been exposed to his father's bizarre sexual activities. He was living with his father in a small house while his father presided over sex parties involving men, women, and perhaps even children. Did his father force him to participate? There's no evidence that he did . . . or didn't."

I was beginning to see where he was going.

Spezi took a long drag of smoke and exhaled. "The report says the killer probably began in his twenties. However, at the time of the first killing, our man was only fifteen years old."

"Wouldn't that rule him out?"

Spezi shook his head. "The fact is, many serial killers begin at a surprisingly young age." He reeled off the names of famous American serial killers and their ages of debut—sixteen, fifteen, fourteen, seventeen. "He almost botched the first crime in 1974. It was the work of a panicky and impulsive beginner. He managed to pull it off only because the man had been killed by the first shot, but only by accident. The bullet struck his arm and then, deflected by the bone, entered the chest and stopped his heart. The girl had enough time to get out of the car and run. The killer fired after her, but only hit her in the legs. He had to kill her with the knife. Then he lifted her cadaver and moved it behind the car. He tried to possess her, but couldn't do it. 'Sexual inadequacy.' *Impotentia coeundi.* He took a woody vine instead and pushed it into her vagina. He remained with the body and caressed it with the only instrument that gave him a thrill, his knife. He made ninety-seven cuts in her flesh. He may have wanted to sexually molest the corpse but he couldn't. He made the cuts around the breasts and around the pubic area, as if to underline that she was now his."

A long silence in the small dining room. The window at the far end of the table looked out on the very hills the Monster had stalked.

"It says the Monster owned his own car. Our man had a car. The murders were committed in places well known to the killer, near his house or place of work. When you map our man's life and movements, he had either lived near or was familiar with every single place."

Mario's finger touched the table again. "If only I could find that document of the breaking and entering."

"Is he still alive?" I asked.

Spezi nodded. "And I know where he lives."

"Have you ever spoken to him?"

"I tried. Once."

"Well?" I finally asked. *"Who is it?"*

"Are you sure you want to know?" Mario winked.

"Damn it, Mario!"

Spezi took a long drag on his Gauloise and let the smoke trickle out. "The person Salvatore Vinci denounced for breaking and entering in 1974, according to my informant, was his son, *his own son*. Antonio Vinci. The little baby who was rescued from the gas back in Sardinia in 1961."

Of course, I thought. I said, "Mario, you know what we have to do, don't you?"

"What?"

"Interview him."

CHAPTER
34

Mother than three decades after the murder of Barbara Locci and her lover in 1968, only two people involved in the Sardinian Trail investigation remained alive: Antonio Vinci and Natalino Mele. The rest had died or disappeared. Francesco Vinci's body had been found hogtied and locked in the trunk of a burned car, after he had apparently gotten on the wrong side of the Mafia. Salvatore had disappeared after his acquittal. Stefano Mele, Piero Mucciarini, and Giovanni Mele were long dead.

Before interviewing Antonio Vinci, we decided to speak with Natalino Mele, the six-year-old boy who was in the back of the car in 1968 and witnessed his mother's murder. Natalino agreed to speak to us and chose as a meeting place a duck pond in the Cascine Park in Florence, next to a shabby Ferris wheel and merry-go-round.

The day was overcast and dull, the air smelling of wet leaves and popcorn. Mele arrived, hands shoved in his pockets, a heavy, sad man in his early forties, with black hair and a haunted look in his eyes. He spoke in the excitable, querulous voice of a boy relating an injustice. After his mother was killed and his father imprisoned, his relatives had packed him off to an orphanage, a particularly cruel fate in a country where family means everything. He was alone in the world.

We sat on a bench with the disco beat of the merry-go-round thumping in the background. We asked if he could remember any details of the night of August 21, 1968, the night his mother was murdered. The question set him off.

"I was six years old!" he cried in a high-pitched voice. "What do you want me to say? After all this time, how could I remember anything new? This is what they all keep asking me: What do you remember? *What do you remember?*"

The night of the crime, Natalino said, he was so terrified he couldn't speak at all, until the carabinieri threatened to take him back to his dead mother. Fourteen years later, when the investigators established the connection between the 1968 killing and the Monster's killings, the police took him in for questioning again. They hammered him relentlessly. He had witnessed the 1968 double murder and they seemed to feel he was holding back vital information. The questioning lasted over the course of a year. He told them, over and over, that he couldn't remember anything of that night. The interrogators showed him graphic photographs of the Monster's mutilated victims, yelling at him, "Look at these people. This is your fault! It's your fault, because you can't remember!"

As Natalino spoke of the merciless questioning, his voice filled with anguish, rising in volume. "I *told* them I couldn't remember anything. *Anything*. Except one thing. There is one thing I remembered!" He paused, drawing in breath. "All I remember now is that I opened my eyes in that car and I saw in front of me my mamma, *dead*. That's the only thing I remember of that night. And," he said, his voice quavering, "that's the *only* memory I have of her."

CHAPTER
35

Years earlier, Spezi had called Antonio Vinci on the telephone and tried to arrange an interview. He had been categorically rebuffed. In light of that rejection, we discussed how we should best approach the man. We decided not to call ahead and give him another chance to say no. Instead, we would show up at his door and use false names, to avoid a second refusal and to protect ourselves from possible retaliation after the article was published. I would be an American journalist writing a piece on the Monster of Florence, and Spezi would be a friend giving me a hand as a translator.

We arrived at Antonio's apartment building at 9:40 p.m., late enough to be sure of finding him at home. Antonio lived in a tidy, working-class area west of Florence. His apartment building stood on a side street, a modest structure of stucco with a small flower garden and bicycle rack in front. At the end of the street, beyond a row of umbrella pines, rose the skeletons of abandoned factories.

Spezi buzzed the intercom and a woman answered. "Who is it?"

"Marco Tiezzi," said Spezi.

We were buzzed in with no further questions.

Antonio met us at the door dressed only in a pair of shorts. He stared at Mario. "Ah, Spezi, it's you!" he said, recognizing him instantly. "I didn't hear the name well. I've wanted to meet you for a long time!"

He seated us at the kitchen table with the air of an affable host and offered us a glass of a special Sardinian spirit called *mirto*. His companion, a silent and invisible older woman, finished washing spinach in the sink and left the room.

Antonio was a handsome man with a dimpled smile; his curly black hair was peppered with gray and his body was tanned and heavily muscled. He projected a cocky air of self-confidence and working-class charm. While we chatted about the case, he casually rippled the muscles of his upper arms or slid his hands over them in what seemed an unconscious gesture of self-admiration. He had a tattoo of a four-leaf clover on his left arm and twinned hearts on his right; there was a large scar in the middle of his chest. He spoke in a low, husky, and compelling voice reminiscent of the young De Niro in the movie *Taxi Driver*. His black eyes were animated and at ease, and he seemed amused at our unexpected arrival.

Spezi began the conversation, speaking casually and slipping a tape recorder out of his pocket. "May I use it?" he asked.

Antonio flexed his muscles and smiled. "No," he said, "I am jealous of my voice. It is too velvety, too rich in tone, to be put in that box."

Spezi put the recorder back in his pocket and explained: I was a journalist from *The New Yorker* magazine writing an article on the Monster case. The interview was part of a series, all routine, of those still alive with a connection with the case. Antonio seemed satisfied with the explanation and very much at ease.

Spezi began asking questions of a general nature, and established a friendly, conversational atmosphere, jotting notes in longhand. Antonio had followed the Monster of Florence case closely and had an astonishing command of the facts. After a series of general questions, Spezi began to close in.

"What kind of relationship did you have with your uncle, Francesco Vinci?"

"We were very close. It was a friendship with a bond of iron." He paused for a moment and then said something incredible. "Spezi, I'd like to give you a scoop. Do you know when Francesco was arrested for having hid his car? Well, I was with him that night! Nobody knew that, until now."

Antonio was referring to the night of the double murder in Montespertoli, near Poppiano Castle, in June of 1982. At the time Antonio was living six kilometers away. It was this crime that led to the arrest of Francesco Vinci for being the Monster of Florence, and an important piece of evidence against Vinci was that he had inexplicably hidden his car in the brush around the time of the killing. This was indeed a major scoop: if Antonio had been with Francesco that night, it meant Francesco had had an alibi that he never used—and as a result spent two years in jail needlessly.

"But that means your friend Francesco had a witness in his favor!" Spezi said. "You could have helped Francesco avoid being accused of being the Monster and of spending years in jail! Why didn't you say anything?"

"Because I didn't want to get mixed up in his affairs."

"And for that you let him serve two years in prison?"

"He wanted to protect me. And I had faith in the system."

Faith in the system. A totally incredible statement coming from him. Spezi moved on.

"And what was your relationship like with your father, Salvatore?"

The faint smile on Antonio's face seemed to freeze a little, but only momentarily. "We never saw eye-to-eye. Incompatibility of character, you might say."

"But were there specific reasons why you didn't get along? Perhaps you held Salvatore Vinci responsible for the death of your mother?"

"Not really. I heard something said about it."

"Your father had strange sexual habits. Perhaps that was a reason you hated him?"

"Back then I knew nothing about that. Only later did I learn about his . . ." He paused. "*Tics.*"

"But you and he had some serious fights. Even when you were young. In the spring of 1974, for example, your father filed a complaint against you for robbing his house . . ." Spezi paused nonchalantly. This was a crucial question: it would confirm if the missing document actually existed—if Salvatore Vinci had indeed filed charges against Antonio just before the Monster killings began.

"That's not quite right," Antonio said. "Since he couldn't say if I'd taken anything, I was charged only for violation of domicile. Another time we had a fight and I pinned him, planting my scuba knife at his throat, but he managed to get away and I locked myself in the bathroom."

We had confirmed a crucial detail: the breaking and entering of 1974. But Antonio had, all of his own accord—almost like a challenge—added a critical fact of his own: that he had threatened Vinci with his "scuba knife." The medical examiner in the Monster case, Mauro Maurri, had written years before that the instrument used by the Monster may have been a scuba knife.

Spezi continued his questions, spiraling in toward our goal.

"Who do you think committed the double murders of 1968?"

"Stefano Mele."

"But the pistol was never found."

"Mele might have sold it or given it to someone else when he left prison."

"That's impossible. The pistol was used again in 1974, when Mele was still in prison."

"Are you sure? I never thought of that."

"They say your father was the shooter in 1968," Spezi went on.

"He was way too much of a coward to do that."

Spezi asked, "When did you leave Florence?"

"In '74. First I went to Sardinia and after to Lake Como."

"Then you returned and got married."

"Right. I married a childhood sweetheart, but it didn't work. We married in 1982 and separated in 1985."

"What didn't work?"

"She couldn't have children."

This was the marriage that had been annulled for nonconsummation: *impotentia coeundi*.

"And then you remarried?"

"I live with a woman."

Spezi assumed an easy tone of voice, as if he were concluding the interview. "Can I ask you a rather provocative question?"

"Sure. I may not answer."

"The question is this: if your father owned the .22 caliber Beretta, you were the person in the best position to take it. Perhaps during the violation of domicile in the spring of 1974."

Antonio didn't answer immediately. He seemed to reflect. "I have proof I didn't take it."

"Which is?"

"If I had taken it"—he smiled—"I would have fired it into my father's forehead."

"Following this line of reasoning," Spezi continued, "you were away from Florence from 1975 to 1980, precisely during the time when there were no killings. When you returned, they began again."

Antonio didn't respond directly to the statement. He leaned back in the chair, and his smile spread. "Those were the best years of my life. I had a house, I ate well, and all those girls . . ." He whistled and made an Italian gesture signifying fucking.

"And so . . ." Spezi said nonchalantly, "you're not . . . the Monster of Florence?"

There was only a brief hesitation. Antonio never stopped smiling for a moment. "No," he said. "I like my pussy alive."

We got up to leave. Antonio followed us to the door. While he opened it, he leaned toward Spezi. He spoke in a low voice, his tone remaining cordial, and he switched into the informal, "*tu*" form. "Ah, Spezi, I was almost forgetting something." His voice took on a hoarse, threatening tone. "Listen carefully: I don't play games."

CHAPTER
36

Spezi and I submitted the article on the Monster of Florence to *The New Yorker* in the summer of 2001. My family and I went back to the States for the summer, to an old family farm on the Maine coast. I spent much of the summer working with our editor at *The New Yorker*, revising and fact-checking the piece. It was tentatively scheduled for publication the third week of September 2001.

Spezi and I both anticipated a huge reaction in Italy to the publication of the article. Italian public opinion had long ago settled on the guilt of Pacciani and his picnicking friends. Most Italians had also swallowed Giuttari's theory, that Pacciani & Co. had been working for a shadowy, powerful cult. While Americans might scoff at the very idea that a satanic sect was behind the killings, Italians did not find it unusual or unbelievable. From the very beginning, there had been rumors that a powerful and important person must be behind the killings, a doctor or nobleman. The satanic sect investigation seemed a logical extension of this idea, and most Italians believed it was justified.

We hoped to overthrow that complacency.

The New Yorker piece laid out a very strong case that Pacciani was not the Monster. If not, then his self-confessed "picnicking friends" were liars and Giuttari's satanic sect theory, built on their testimony, collapsed. Which would leave only one avenue of investigation left: the Sardinian Trail.

The carabinieri, Mario knew, had continued a secret investigation into the Sardinian Trail. A secret informant in the carabinieri, someone whose identity even I don't know, had told Mario they were awaiting the right moment to unveil the results of their investigation. *"Il tempo è un galantuomo,"* the informant had told Spezi, "Time is a gentleman." Spezi hoped that publication of the *New Yorker* article would spur the carabinieri into action, set the investigation back on the right track— and lead to the unmasking of the Monster.

"Italians," Mario said to me, "are sensitive to American public opinion. If an American magazine of the stature of *The New Yorker* proclaims Pacciani innocent, that will cause a furor, and I mean a *furor.*"

As the summer of 2001 drew to a close, our family made preparations to fly from Boston to Florence on September 14 so the children could make the start of school on the seventeenth.

On September 11, 2001, everything changed.

Around two o'clock on that long and terrible day, I turned off the television in the kitchen of our old farmhouse in Maine. I had to get out of the house. Taking my six-year-old son, Isaac, with me, I went out for a walk. The day glowed with autumnal glory, the last hurrah of life before winter, the air snappish and smelling of wood smoke, the sky a vibrant blue. We crossed the freshly mown fields behind the farmhouse, past the apple orchard, and headed down an abandoned logging road into the woods. A mile in we left the road and plunged into the trees, looking for a beaver pond hidden in the deepest part of the forest, where the moose live. I wanted to get away from any trace of human existence, to escape, to lose myself, to find a place untainted by the horror of the day. We forced our way through stands of spruce and fir and slogged across bogs and carpets of sphagnum moss. Half a mile in, sunlight loomed through the tree trunks and we came to the beaver pond. The surface of the pond was utterly still and black, mirroring the forest leaning over it, here and there splashed with red from the leaves of an autumnal maple crowding the pond's edge. The air smelled of green moss and damp pine needles. It was a primeval place, this nameless pond on an unknown brook, beyond good and evil.

While my son gathered beaver-gnawed sticks, I had a moment to collect my thoughts. I wondered if it was right to leave the country when it was under attack. I considered whether it was safe to fly with my children. And I wondered how this day would affect our lives in Italy if we did return. It occurred to me then, as an afterthought, that the *New Yorker* article on the Monster of Florence was not likely to be published.

Like most Americans, we decided to continue our lives as before. We flew back to Italy on September 18, soon after flights resumed. Our Italian friends held a dinner for us at an apartment on Piazza Santo Spirito, overlooking the great Renaissance church built by Brunelleschi. When we walked into the apartment, it was like arriving at a funeral; our Italian friends came forward and embraced us, one by one, some with tears in their eyes, offering their condolences. The evening was somber, and at the end, a friend who taught Greek at the University of Florence recited Constantine Cavafy's poem "Waiting for the Barbarians." She read it first in the original Greek and then in Italian. The poem describes the Romans of the late empire waiting for the barbarians to come, and I have never forgotten the last lines she read that evening:

> . . . *night is here but the barbarians have not come.*
> *And some people arrived from the borders,*
> *and said that there are no longer any barbarians.*
>
> *And now what shall become of us without any barbarians?*
> *Those people were some kind of solution.*[1]

As I expected, *The New Yorker* killed the Monster piece, generously paying us in full and releasing the rights back to us so we could publish it elsewhere. I made a few halfhearted attempts to place it with an-

---

[1]Translation from the Greek by George Barbanis.

other magazine, but after 9/11 no one was interested in the story of a long-ago serial killer in another country.

In the days following 9/11, many commentators on television and in the newspapers pontificated on the nature of evil. Literary and cultural lions were called upon to express their grave and considered opinions. Politicians, religious leaders, and psychological experts all waxed eloquent on the subject. I was struck by their perfect failure to explain this most mysterious of phenomena, and I began to feel that the very incomprehensibility of evil might be, in fact, one of its fundamental characteristics. You cannot stare evil in the face; it has no face. It has no body, no bones, no blood. Any attempt to describe it ends in glibness and self-delusion. Maybe, I thought, this is why Christians invented the devil and Monster investigators invented a satanic sect. They both were, as the poem goes, "some kind of solution."

During that time I began to understand my own obsession with the Monster case. In twenty years of writing thrillers involving murder and violence, I had tried and largely failed to understand evil at its core. The Monster of Florence attracted me because it was a road into the wilderness. The case was the purest distillation of evil I had ever encountered, on many levels. It was, first of all, the evil of the depraved killings of a highly disturbed human being. But the case was about other kinds of evil as well. Some of the top investigators, prosecutors, and judges in the case, charged with the sacred responsibility of finding the truth, appeared to be more interested in using the case to leverage their power to greater personal glory. Having committed themselves to a defective theory, they refused to reconsider their beliefs when faced with overwhelming contradictory evidence. They cared more about saving face than saving lives, more about pushing their careers than putting the Monster behind bars. Around the Monster's incomprehensible evil had accreted layer upon layer of additional falsehood, vanity, ambition, arrogance, incompetence, and fecklessness. The Monster's acts were like a metastasized cancer cell, tumbling through the blood to lodge in some soft, dark corner, dividing, multiplying, building its own network of blood vessels and capillaries to feed itself, swelling, expanding, and finally killing.

I knew that Mario Spezi had already struggled with the evil expressed by the Monster case. One day I asked him how he had dealt with the horrors of the case—the evil—which I felt was starting to affect me.

"Nobody understood evil better than Brother Galileo," he told me, referring to the Franciscan monk turned psychoanalyst he had turned to for help when the horrors of the Monster case began to drag him under. Brother Galileo had since died, but Mario credited him with saving his life during the time of the Monster's killings. "He helped me understand what is beyond understanding."

"Do you remember what he said?"

"I can tell you exactly, Doug. I wrote it down."

He dug out his notes of the session where Brother Galileo spoke about evil and read them to me. The old monk began by making a powerful play on words of the fact that the Italian word for "evil" and "sickness" is the same, *male*, and that the word for "speech" and "study" is also the same, *discorso*.

"'Pathology' can be defined as *discorso sul male* [study of sickness (or evil)]," Brother Galileo said. "I prefer to define it as *male che parla* [evil (or sickness) that speaks]. Just so with psychology, which is defined as the 'study of the psyche.' But I prefer 'the study of the psyche struggling to speak through its neurotic disturbances.'

"There is no longer true communication among us, because our very language is sick, and the sickness of our discourse carries us inevitably to sickness in our bodies, to neurosis, if not finally to mental illness.

"When I can no longer communicate with speech, I will speak with sickness. My symptoms are given life. These symptoms express the need for my soul to make itself heard but cannot, because I don't have the words, and because those who should listen cannot get beyond the sound of their own voices. The language of sickness is the most difficult to interpret. It is an extreme form of blackmail which defies all our efforts to pay it off and send it away. It is a final attempt at communication.

"Mental illness lies at the very end of this struggle to be heard. It is the last refuge of a desperate soul who has finally understood that no one is listening or ever will listen. Madness is the renunciation of all efforts to be understood. It is one unending scream of pain and need into the absolute silence and indifference of society. It is a cry without an echo.

"This is the nature of the evil of the Monster of Florence. And this is the nature of the evil in each and every one of us. We all have a Monster within; the difference is in degree, not in kind."

Spezi was crushed by the failure of our article to see print. It was a great blow in his lifelong effort to unmask the Monster. With his disappointment and frustration, his obsession with the case, if anything, deepened. I moved on to other things. That year I began work on a new thriller, *Brimstone*, with my writing partner, Lincoln Child, with whom I had created a series of best-selling novels featuring an investigator named Pendergast. *Brimstone* was set partly in Tuscany and it involved a serial killer, satanic rituals, and a lost Stradivarius violin. The Monster of Florence was dead and I began dissecting the corpse for my fiction.

One day, as I was strolling through Florence, I passed a tiny shop that made hand-bound books. It gave me an idea. I went home and printed out our Monster article in octavo book format and carried it into the shop for binding. The shopkeeper created two handmade volumes, covered in full Florentine leather, with marbled endpapers. Each cover was stamped in gold leaf with the title, our names, and the Florentine lily.

THE MONSTER

SPEZI
&
PRESTON

It was a signed, numbered edition of two. During our next dinner at Spezi's house, sitting at the table on his terrazzo overlooking the hills of Florence, I presented him with copy number one. He was impressed. He turned it over in his hands, admiring the gold tooling and fine leather. After a while, he looked up at me, his brown eyes twinkling. "You know, Doug, with all this work we've already done . . . we *should* write a book about the Monster."

I was immediately smitten with the idea. We talked about it and decided that we would first publish the book in Italy, in Italian. Then we would rework it for an American readership and try to get it published in the United States.

For years my novels had been published in Italian by Sonzogno, a division of RCS Libri, part of a large publishing conglomerate that included Rizzoli and the *Corriere della Sera* newspaper. I called my editor at Sonzogno and she was intrigued, especially after we sent her the ex–*New Yorker* article we had written. She invited Mario and me to Milan to discuss the idea. One day, we took the train to Milan, pitched the idea, and walked away with a handsome contract.

RCS Libri was particularly interested in the idea because they had recently published another book about the Monster case, which had been a major best-seller. The author of the book? Chief Inspector Michele Giuttari.

CHAPTER
37

Meanwhile, Giuttari's investigation, which had stalled badly after the business of the "Villa of Horrors," had began to revive. In 2002, a new line of investigation erupted in the neighboring province of Umbria—in the ancient and beautiful hill town of Perugia, one hundred and fifty kilometers from Florence. The first sign of it was an odd telephone call that Spezi got early that year from Gabriella Carlizzi. Carlizzi, you may recall, was the crank who claimed the cult of the Red Rose had not only ordered the Monster killings but was also behind 9/11.

Carlizzi had quite a story to tell Spezi, the Monstrologer. One day, while providing assistance to the inmates of Rebibbia prison near Rome, she had received an alarming confidence from an inmate who had been a member of the infamous Italian Gang of Magliana. The man had said that a Perugian doctor who drowned in 1985 in Lake Trasimeno had not met his end through accident or suicide, as the inquest had concluded at the time, but had been murdered. He had been killed by the Order of the Red Rose, which the doctor himself belonged to. The other members of the order had eliminated him because he had become unreliable and was about to expose their nefarious activities to the police. To hide the evidence of crime, his body had been substituted for another before dumping it in the lake. Therefore, buried in the doctor's grave wasn't his body, but that of the other person.

Spezi, who had a great deal of experience dealing with conspiracy theorists, had thanked Carlizzi very much and explained that, most regrettably, he was not interested in pursuing the story. He got her off the phone as quickly and politely as possible.

Nevertheless, Spezi vaguely remembered the story of the drowned doctor. One month after the last Monster killing in 1985, a handsome young man from a wealthy Perugian family, Francesco Narducci, had drowned in Lake Trasimeno. Rumors circulated at the time that he had killed himself because he was the Monster, rumors which were routinely investigated and dismissed.

In early 2002 the indefatigable Carlizzi, turned down by Spezi in her quest for publicity, brought her story to the public minister of Perugia, a man named Giuliano Mignini, whose jurisdiction covered the province of Perugia. (The public minister is the public prosecutor of a region, a position similar to a U.S. attorney or a district attorney. The public minister represents the interests of the state and argues the case in court, as the advocate for the state.) Judge Mignini *was* interested. The story seemed to mesh with another case he was pursuing involving a group of loan sharks who lent money to shopkeepers and professionals at stratospheric interest rates and who, if they didn't get repaid, exacted a brutal revenge. A small shopkeeper who was behind in her payments decided to expose them. She recorded one of their threatening telephone calls and sent the tape to the public minister's office.

One morning, while working in my farmhouse office in Giogoli, I got a call from Spezi. "The Monster's in the news again," he said. "I'm coming up to your house. Put the coffee on."

He arrived clutching a stack of that morning's newspapers. I began to read.

"Be careful or we'll do to you the same as that dead doctor in Lake Trasimeno," the papers quoted the loan shark as saying in the tape recording of the threatening call. That was it: no names or facts. But Public Minister Giuliano Mignini read a great deal into those words. He concluded,

apparently based on information given him by Carlizzi, that Francesco Narducci had been murdered by the loan sharks, some of whom might be in contact with the Red Rose or another diabolical sect. Therefore, the loan sharks and the Narducci killing might be connected in some way with the Monster of Florence murders.

Judge Mignini, the public minister, informed Chief Inspector Giuttari of the connection to the Monster case, and Giuttari and his GIDES squad embarked on a determined effort to prove that Narducci hadn't committed suicide. He had been murdered, to silence him and the terrible secrets he knew. Mignini had ordered the reopening of the Narducci case as a murder investigation.

"I can't follow this at all," I said, trying to read the paper. "It makes no sense."

Spezi nodded, smiling cynically. "In my day they never would have printed this *merda*. Italian journalism is going downhill."

"At least," I said, "it's more fodder for our book."

A while later, more news about the story broke in the papers. This time, still quoting unnamed sources, the papers printed a new version of the so-called tape recording. Now the loan shark was reported to have said, *"Be careful or we'll do to you the same as we did to Narducci and Pacciani!"* This version of the recording directly connected the dead doctor Narducci with the so-called murder of Pacciani—and thus with the Monster case.

Later, Spezi would learn from a source that what was said on the tape was much less specific: *We'll do to you like the dead doctor at the lake.* No mention was made of Narducci or Pacciani. A little digging uncovered the existence of another doctor, a man who had lost more than two billion lire gambling, whose body had been found on the shore of Lake Trasimeno with a bullet in the brain not long before the threatening telephone call. The phrase *"at* the lake" as opposed to the earlier *"in* the lake" seemed to point to this doctor, and not to Narducci, who, after all, had died fifteen years before the call was made.

But by the time this new information came out, the investigation into the dead Dr. Narducci had become a juggernaut, unstoppable. Giuttari and his elite squad, GIDES, looked for—and found!—many links between Narducci's death and the Monster of Florence killings. The new investigative theories offered up succulent gothic scenarios that were leaked to the press. Dr. Narducci, the press reported, had been the guardian of the fetishes cut from the women. He had been killed to keep from spilling the beans. Some of the richest families in Perugia were involved in sinister cults, perhaps under the cover of Freemasonry, a brotherhood to which both Narducci's father and father-in-law belonged.

Giuttari and his investigators from GIDES painstakingly pieced together the final day of Narducci's life, looking for clues.

Dr. Francesco Narducci came from a rich Perugian family, a young man blessed with brains and talent who at age thirty-six was the youngest medical professor in the field of gastroenterology in Italy. In photographs, he is strikingly handsome in a boyish way, tanned and smiling, fit and elegant. Narducci had married Francesca Spagnoli, the beautiful heiress to the fortune of Luisa Spagnoli, the maker of high-fashion clothing for women.

Despite, or perhaps because of, its power and wealth, the Narducci family was not well liked in Perugia. Behind that façade of wealth and privilege there was, as is not unusual, unhappiness. For some time, and in ever-increasing doses, Francesco Narducci had been taking meperidine (Demerol). According to a medical report, by the time of his death he was taking it every day.

The morning of October 8, 1985, was hot and sunny. The doctor made his rounds at the Policlinico di Monteluce in Perugia until about 12:30, when a nurse called him to the telephone. After that, the facts become confused. One witness said that after the call, Narducci cut short his rounds and seemed nervous and preoccupied. Another claimed he finished his rounds in regular order and left the hospital uneventfully, asking a colleague if he wanted to take a spin on Lake Trasimeno in his boat.

At one-thirty he arrived home and ate lunch with his wife. At two o'clock, the owner of the marina where Narducci had a villa received a phone call from the doctor, asking him if his motorboat was ready to go out on the lake. The man answered it was. But as Narducci left his house, he lied to his wife, saying he was going back to the hospital and would be home early.

Narducci took his Honda 400 motocross bike and set off for the lake, but not directly to the marina. First he went into his family's house in San Feliciano. There were rumors, which investigators could not substantiate, that he wrote a letter there and left it on a window-sill, sealed in an envelope. The letter, if it ever existed, never came to light.

At three-thirty the doctor finally arrived at the marina. He jumped in his motorboat, a sleek red Grifo, and fired up the seventy-horsepower engine. The owner of the marina advised him not to go too far, since the gas tank was half empty. Francesco told him not to worry and pointed the boat toward Polvese Island, a kilometer and a half offshore.

He never returned.

At around five-thirty, when it began to grow dark, the marina owner became alarmed and called Francesco's brother. At seven-thirty the carabinieri launched a boat to help with the search. But Lake Tra-simeno is one of the largest in Italy, and it wasn't until the next evening that they found the red Grifo empty and adrift. On board were a pair of sunglasses, a wallet, and a packet of Merit cigarettes, Narducci's brand.

Five days later, they found the body. A single black-and-white pho-tograph was taken of the scene when the body was brought to shore, showing the corpse stretched lengthwise on a dock, surrounded by a group of people.

Carlizzi had told the public minister that the body of Narducci had been substituted for another, which had been tossed in the lake as a decoy. To investigate that statement, Giuttari commissioned an expert analysis of the photograph. Taking as a standard unit of measurement the width of a plank on the dock, the experts concluded that the ca-daver in the photograph belonged to a man four inches shorter than Narducci. They also calculated that the dead man's waist was far too large to be that of the trim Narducci.

Other experts disagreed. Some pointed out that a body floating in water for five days does tend to swell. Planks of a dock are not all equal in width, and the dock in question had been replaced. Who knew the width of the planks seventeen years ago? All those in the crowd who were actually standing around the body, including the medical examiner himself, swore the body was Narducci's. At the time, the medical examiner listed the cause of death as drowning, which he estimated had occurred about a hundred and ten hours previously.

Contrary to Italian law, no autopsy had been performed. Narducci's family, led by his father, had managed to bypass the legal requirement. At the time, people in Perugia quietly understood that it was because the family feared that an autopsy would have shown that Narducci was up to his gills in Demerol. But to Giuttari and GIDES, the lack of an autopsy was most significant. They said the family had finagled their way out of an autopsy because it would have shown the body was not that of Narducci at all. The family was somehow complicit, not only in his murder, but in the substitution of his body with another to cover up the crime.

Francesco Narducci—or so Giuttari theorized—had been murdered because he was a member of the satanic sect behind the Monster of Florence killings, to which his father had introduced him. He had been named custodian of the grisly fetishes taken by Pacciani and his picnicking friends. Shaken by the reality into which he had fallen, the young doctor became indecisive, unreliable, prey to depression, and difficult to trust. The leaders of the sect decided he had to be eliminated.

The satanic cult investigation, led by Chief Inspector Giuttari, once moribund, was revived. Giuttari had now identified at least one member of the invidious sect behind the Monster killings—Narducci. All that remained was to find his killer and bring the other members of the sect to justice.

CHAPTER
38

As the Monster investigation heated up, the phone calls from Mario became a regular occurrence. "Did you read the papers this morning?" he would ask me. "Stranger and stranger!" And we would enjoy another coffee up at my place, poring over the news, shaking our heads. At the time, I found it all amusing, even charming.

Spezi was not so charmed. He wanted, more than anything, for the truth in the Monster case to come out. His dedication to unmasking the Monster was a passion. He had seen the dead victims; I had not. He had met most of the families and seen the damage to them. I had wiped away a few tears on leaving Winnie Rontini's dark house, but Spezi had been wiping away tears for more than twenty years. He had seen the lives of innocents ruined by false accusations. What I found deliciously peculiar and even quaint, he found deadly serious. To see the investigators wandering ever deeper into a wilderness of absurdity pained him greatly.

On April 6, 2002, with the press standing by, the coffin of Francesco Narducci was exhumed and opened. His body was inside, instantly recognizable even after seventeen years. A DNA test confirmed it.

This blow to their theories did not stop GIDES, Giuttari, and the public minister of Perugia. Even in the lack of a substituted corpse they found evidence. The body was *too* recognizable for someone who had spent five days in the water and then another seventeen in a coffin. Giuttari and Mignini promptly concluded that the body had been substituted *again*. That's right—Narducci's real body, hidden for seventeen years, had been put back in the coffin and the other body removed, because the conspirators knew ahead of time that the exhumation was coming.

The body of Narducci was shipped off to the medical examiner's office in Pavia to see if it showed signs of murder. That September, the results came in. The medical examiner reported that the left horn of the laryngeal cartilage had been fractured, which made it "more or less probable" that death resulted from a "violent mechanical asphyxiation produced from the constriction of the neck (either from manual strangulation or from strangulation by other homicidal means)."

In other words, Narducci had been murdered.

Once again the newspapers had a field day. *La Nazione* trumpeted:

MURDER IS THEORIZED
BURNING SECRETS

Was Narducci murdered because he knew something or had seen something that he must not see? Almost all the current investigators are by now convinced of the story of secret sects and masterminds behind the double homicides executed by Pacciani and his picnicking friends. . . . A group of persons, around ten, ordered the killings by henchmen composed of Pacciani and his picnicking friends. . . . The search into secret, deviant, and esoteric groups dedicated to horrendous "sacrifices" has even drawn in investigators from Perugia.

Once again, Spezi and I marveled at the banquet of half-baked and ill-formed speculations that constituted press coverage of the case, printed as the wide-eyed truth by journalists who knew absolutely nothing of the history of the Monster of Florence, who had never heard of the Sardinian Trail, and who merely parroted whatever investigators or the prosecutor's office leaked. The conditional tense was hardly ever used, as were qualifiers such as "alleged" and "according to." Question marks were thrown in only for sensationalistic effect. Spezi once again bemoaned the sorry state of Italian journalism.

"Why," he said, "would Narducci's killers concoct such an elaborate scheme of murder? Haven't these journalists asked themselves that obvious question? Why not just drown him and make it look like suicide? Why substitute bodies once, and then yet again? And where on earth did the second body come from? The original ME who examined Narducci's cadaver, along with his family, friends, and all the people in that photograph who saw the dead body insist it was Narducci. They *still* insist it was Narducci! Were *all* these people in on the conspiracy?" He shook his head sadly.

I read the rest of the article with growing disbelief. The credulous reporter at *La Nazione* never explored any of the obvious discrepancies with the story. He went on to write that the "saponification of the cadaver (internal organs, skin, and hair were in a good state of preservation) was not compatible with immersion in water for five days." More support for the substitution theory.

"What does this mean, 'not compatible'?" I asked Spezi, putting aside the paper. It was a phrase I had seen again and again in the Monster investigation.

Spezi laughed. "Compatible, not compatible, and incompatible are the baroque inventions of Italian experts who don't want to take responsibility. Using 'compatible' is a way to avoid admitting they haven't understood anything. Was the bullet in Pacciani's garden inserted into the Monster's pistol? 'It is compatible.' Was that laryngeal break inflicted by someone who intended to kill? 'It is compatible.' Was the painting done by a monstrous psychopath? 'It is compatible.' Perhaps yes, perhaps no—in short, we don't know! If the experts are chosen by the investigators, they say their results are 'compatible' with the theories of the prosecution; if they are chosen by the defendants they say that their results are 'compatible' with the theories of the defense. That adjective should be outlawed!"

"So where's this going?" I asked. "Where will it end up?"

Spezi shook his head. "The very thought scares me."

CHAPTER
39

Meanwhile, in the picturesque little town of San Casciano, Giuttari opened up yet a new front in the search for the masterminds behind the Monster killings. San Casciano seemed to lie at the very heart of the satanic sect; it was only a few kilometers from Villa Verde, the Villa of Horrors; it had been home to the hapless postman, Vanni, and the village idiot, Lotti, convicted as Pacciani's accomplices.

Spezi called me one morning. "Have you seen the paper? Don't bother buying it, I'm coming over. You won't believe this."

He entered the house, visibly upset, the paper clutched in his hand, Gauloise dangling from his lip. "This is a bit too close to home." He slapped the paper on the table. "Read this."

The article announced that the home of a man named Francesco Calamandrei, the ex-pharmacist of San Casciano, had been searched by GIDES. Calamandrei was suspected of being one of the masterminds behind the Monster killings.

"Calamandrei is an old friend of mine." Spezi said. "He's the man who introduced me to my wife! This is utterly absurd, patently ridiculous. The man wouldn't hurt a fly."

Spezi told me the man's story. He had met Calamandrei back in the mid-sixties, when both were students, Spezi studying law and Cala-mandrei studying pharmacology and architecture. A brilliant student, Calamandrei was the son of San Casciano's only pharmacist, which in Italy is a well-paid and high-status profession, all the more so for the Calamandrei family, because San Casciano was a wealthy town with only one pharmacy. Calamandrei cut quite a figure in those days, tool-ing around Florence in a sleek Lancia Fulvia Coupé, tall, elegant, and handsome, impeccably dressed in the Florentine style. He had a dry, cutting Tuscan sense of humor and always seemed to have a new girl-friend more beautiful than the last. Calamandrei introduced Mario to his future wife, Myriam ("I've got a nice Belgian girl for you, Mario"), at a famous restaurant; afterwards they all piled into Calamandrei's car and set off on a crazy trip to Venice to play baccarat in the casino. Calamandrei was an expression of that brief period in Italian history known as *La Dolce Vita*, captured so memorably on film by Fellini.

At the close of the sixties Calamandrei married the daughter of a wealthy industrialist. She was a small, high-strung woman with red hair. They had a grand wedding in San Casciano, which Mario and Myriam attended. A few days later the newlyweds stopped by Spezi's house while heading off on their honeymoon. Calamandrei was driv-ing a brand-new cream-colored Mercedes 300L convertible.

That was the last Spezi saw of him for several decades.

He ran into him by chance twenty-five years later and was shocked by the change in his friend. Calamandrei had become morbidly obese and suffered from a deep depression and declining health. He had sold the pharmacy and taken up painting—tragic, anguished pictures, not created with paintbrushes and canvas, but with objects such as rubber hoses, sheet metal, and tar, sometimes putting real syringes and tour-niquets in his paintings, and often signing them with his social security number, because, he said, that's all people were in modern Italian so-ciety. His son had become a drug addict and then a thief to support his habit. Desperate and not knowing what else to do, Calamandrei had gone to the police and denounced his own son, hoping a stint in prison might shake him up and lead to a turnaround. But the boy continued to take drugs after his release, and then disappeared completely.

What had happened to his wife was equally tragic. She had succumbed to schizophrenia. Once, at a dinner party at a friend's house, she began screaming and breaking objects, stripped off all her clothes, and ran naked into the street. She was hospitalized after that, the first of many such hospitalizations. She was finally declared mentally incompetent and committed to a sanatorium, where she remains to this day.

In 1991, Calamandrei divorced her. She then wrote a letter to the police accusing her husband of being the Monster of Florence. She claimed to have found pieces of the victims hidden in the refrigerator. Her letter—which was completely mad—was duly checked out by investigators at the time and dismissed as absurd.

But Chief Inspector Giuttari, sorting through old police files, came across the wife's handwritten statement, in a strange orthography that sloped ever upward toward the top of the page. To Giuttari, "pharmacist" was close enough to "doctor." The fact that Calamandrei had once been a wealthy and prominent resident of San Casciano, the presumed center of the satanic cult, only whetted Giuttari's interest. The chief inspector opened an investigation of him and several other leading citizens of the town. On January 16, 2004, Giuttari asked for a warrant to search the pharmacist's house; he received it on the seventeenth; on the eighteenth at dawn Giuttari and his men rang the buzzer of the door on Piazza Pierozzi in San Casciano.

On the nineteenth the story of the Monster of Florence was once again all over the news.

Spezi could only shake his head in wonder. "I don't like the way this is moving at all. *Mi fa paura*. It makes me afraid."

Back in Perugia, the inquiry into Narducci's death moved along at a brisk pace. The investigators realized that in order for the bodies to have been switched twice, a large and powerful conspiracy among influential people must have taken place. The public minister of Perugia, Judge Mignini, was determined to unmask it. And in short order he did. Once again, the newspapers, including even the sober *Corriere della Sera*, dedicated entire pages to it. The news was sensational: the ex–chief of police of Perugia at the time of Narducci's death had, it was alleged, conspired with a colonel in the carabinieri and with the family's lawyer to prevent the truth of Narducci's death from coming out, all working in concert with the father of the dead doctor, his brother, and the doctor who had signed the death certificate. Among their crimes were conspiracy, racketeering, and destruction and hiding of a human corpse.

Beyond the conspiracy to cover up the Narducci murder, the investigators also had to show that Narducci had a connection to Pacciani, his picnicking friends, and the village of San Casciano, where the satanic cult seemed to be centered.

They succeeded in this as well. Gabriella Carlizzi made a statement to the police asserting that Francesco Narducci had been initiated into the Order of the Red Rose by his father, who was trying to resolve certain sexual problems in his son—the same diabolical sect, Carlizzi claimed, active for centuries in Florence and its environs. Police and prosecutors seemed to accept Carlizzi's statements as solid, actionable evidence.

As if on cue, Giuttari and his GIDES squad produced witnesses swearing to have seen Francesco Narducci hanging around San Casciano and meeting with Calamandrei. It took a while for the identity of these new witnesses to come out. When Spezi first heard the names, he thought it was a bad joke: they were the same algebraic witnesses, Alpha and Gamma, who had been the surprise witnesses at Pacciani's appeal trial many years before—Pucci, the mentally retarded man who claimed to have witnessed Pacciani killing the French couple, and Ghiribelli, the alcoholic prostitute who would turn a trick for a glass of wine. And then a third witness popped out of the woodwork—none other than Lorenzo Nesi! This was the same fine fellow who had so conveniently remembered Pacciani and a companion in a "reddish" car a kilometer from the Scopeti clearing on Sunday night, the alleged night of the murder of the French tourists.

These three witnesses had earth-shaking new information to impart, which all of them had forgotten to mention eight years earlier when they had first stunned Italy with their extraordinary testimony.

Ghiribelli claimed that the "doctor from Perugia," whose name she did not know, but whose face she recognized as Narducci's from a photograph, came to San Casciano almost every weekend. How could she forget it? She proudly told investigators she had had sex with him four or five times in a hotel and "for each trick he gave me three hundred thousand lire."

In the offices of GIDES, they showed the mentally retarded Pucci photographs of various people and asked him if he had ever seen them before and where. Pucci's recall was phenomenal, crystal clear even when reaching back twenty years, even if he didn't know their names. He recognized Franceso Narducci, "tall and thin, kind of faggoty." He recognized Gianni Spagnoli, brother-in-law of the drowned doctor. He recognized one of the most notable physicians of Florence arrested for child molestation, who had been included in the photo lineup because investigators believed the satanic sect was into pedophilia. He recognized a respected dermatologist and a distinguished gynecologist of San Casciano, both of whom had also fallen under suspicion for being members of the cult. He recognized Carlo Santangelo, the phony ME who liked to wander around cemeteries at night. He recognized a young African-American hairstylist who had died several years before in Florence from AIDS.

But most crucially to the investigation, he recognized the pharmacist of San Casciano, Francesco Calamandrei.

Pucci wasn't stingy with the particulars. "I saw all these people together in San Casciano, in the Bar Centrale under the clock. I can't say if on every occasion I saw them together because it happened that I would see them separately, but anyway these were people who saw each other a lot."

Lorenzo Nesi, the serial witness, also recognized these people and added another. He had seen, palling around with this motley crowd, none other than Prince Roberto Corsini, the nobleman killed by a poacher, who, like Narducci, had been the subject of rumors that he was the Monster.

Gamma, the prostitute Ghiribelli, told another story, one that involved the Villa Sfacciata, near where I lived in Giogoli, across the lane from where the two German tourists had been killed. "In 1981," she said, as recorded in an official statement taken by the police, "there was a doctor who was doing experiments in mummification in the villa . . . Lotti also talked about this place on many occasions and always in the eighties, when we went there. He told me that inside, without saying where, there were murals covering entire walls with paintings just like those done by Pacciani. Lotti always told me that this villa had a laboratory underground, where the Swiss doctor did his mummification experiments. I'll explain it better: Lotti said that this Swiss doctor, following his travels in Egypt, got hold of an old papyrus that explained how to mummify bodies. He said the papyrus was missing a piece relating to the mummification of the soft parts and, I mean, among them the sex organs and the breasts. He told me this was why the girls were mutilated in the murders of the Monster of Florence. He explained to me that in 1981 the daughter of this doctor was killed and the death was not reported, so much so that the father had said that he had to go back to Switzerland to explain her absence. The mummification process required that he keep the body of his daughter in that underground laboratory."

Perhaps remembering the embarrassment of the plastic bats and cardboard skeletons, investigators decided not to search the Villa Sfacciata for the Pacciani frescoes, underground laboratory, and mummified daughter.

CHAPTER
40

*D*ietrologia," said Count Niccolò. "That is the only Italian word you need to know to understand the Monster of Florence investigation."

We were having our usual lunch at Il Bordino. I was eating *baccalà*, salt cod, while the Count enjoyed stuffed *arista*.

"Dietrologia?" I asked.

"*Dietro*—behind. *Logia*—the study of." The count spoke grandly, as if still in the lecture hall, his plummy English accent echoing in the cavelike interior of the restaurant. "Dietrologia is the idea that the obvious thing cannot be the truth. There is always something hidden behind, *dietro*. It isn't quite what you Americans call conspiracy theory. Conspiracy theory implies *theory*, something uncertain, a possibility. The dietrologist deals only in fact. This is how it *really* is. Aside from football, dietrologia is the national sport in Italy. Everyone is an expert at what's really going on, even . . . how do you Americans say it? . . . even if they don't know jack shit."

"Why?" I asked.

"Because it gives them a feeling of importance! This importance may only be confined to a small circle of idiotic friends, but at least they are *in the know*. *Potere*, power, is that *I* know what *you* do not

221

know. Dietrologia is tied to the Italian mentality of power. You *must* appear to be in the know about all things."

"How does this apply to the Monster investigation?"

"My dear Douglas, it is the very heart of the matter! At all costs, they have to find something behind the apparent reality. There cannot *not* be something. Why? Because it is not possible that the thing you see is the truth. Nothing is simple, nothing is at it seems. Does it look like a suicide? Yes? Well then it must be murder. Somebody went out for coffee? Aha! *He went out for coffee* . . . But what was he *really* doing?"

He laughed.

"In Italy," he continued, "there is a permanent climate of witch-hunting. You see, Italians are fundamentally envious. If somebody makes money, there must be a fiddle there somewhere. *Of course* he was in cahoots with someone else. Because of the cult of materialism here, Italians envy the rich and powerful. They're suspicious of them and at the same time want to be them. They have a love-hate relationship with them. Berlusconi is a classic example."

"And that's why the investigators are looking for a satanic sect of the rich and powerful?"

"Precisely. And at all costs they have to find something. Once they've started, to save face they have to go on. For the sake of this idea, they will do anything. They cannot give it up. You *anglosassoni* do not understand the Mediterranean concept of *face*. I was doing historical research in an ancient family archive and I came across some interesting little thing that a distant ancestor had done three hundred years ago. Nothing very bad, just a naughty thing that was already largely known. The head of the family was aghast. He said, 'You can't publish this! *Che figura ci facciamo*! What shame it would cast upon our family!"

We finished and rose to pay at the counter. The count as usual insisted on picking up the tab ("They know me," he explained, "and give me *lo sconto*, the discount").

As we stood on the cobbled street outside the restaurant, Niccolò gazed at me gravely. "In Italy, the hatred of your enemy is such that he has to be built up, made into the ultimate adversary, responsible for all evil. The investigators in the Monster case know that behind the simple facts hides a satanic cult, its tentacles reaching into the highest levels of society. This is what they will prove, no matter what. Woe to the person"—he eyed me significantly—"who disputes their theory because that makes him an accomplice. The more vehemently he denies being involved, the stronger is the proof."

He laid a large hand on my shoulder. "Then again, perhaps there is some truth to their theories. Perhaps there *is* a satanic sect. After all, this is Italy . . ."

CHAPTER
41

During 2004, our last year in Italy, the Monster investigation picked up a major head of steam. It seemed that almost every month another wildly improbable story would break in the papers. Mario and I continued to work on our book, outlining and gathering information and accumulating a file of newspaper clippings on the latest developments. Mario also continued his own freelance investigative journalism, regularly plying his contacts in the carabinieri for fresh information, poking around, always looking for a new scoop.

Mario called me one day. "Doug, meet me in Bar Ricchi. I've got some splendid news!"

We met once again in our old haunt. My family and I had now been living in Italy for four years, and I was well enough known in Bar Ricchi not only to greet the owner and his family by name, but sometimes to get *lo sconto* myself.

Spezi was late. He had, as usual, parked his car illegally in the piazza, putting in the window his "JOURNALIST" sign, next to the special journalist permit that allowed him to drive into the old city.

He strode in, trailing smoke, and ordered an espresso *"stretto stretto"* and a glass of mineral water. A heavy object weighed down his trench coat.

He tossed his Bogart fedora on the banquette, slid in, and removed an object wrapped in newspaper, which he placed on the table.

"What is it?"

"You shall see." He paused to shoot down his coffee. "Ever seen the television program *Chi L'ha Visto?* [Who Has Seen Him?]."

"No."

"It's one of the highest-rated programs on Italian television—a rip-off of your show *America's Most Wanted*. They've asked me to collaborate on a series of programs that would reconstruct the entire history of the Monster of Florence case, from the beginning to today."

Spezi wreathed himself in a triumphant cloud of blue smoke.

"*Fantastico!*" I said.

"And," he added, his eyes twinkling, "I've got a scoop for the show that nobody knows about, not even you!"

I sipped my coffee and waited.

"You remember when I spoke to you of the detective who told me the French tourists must have been killed on Saturday night, because they had larvae on them as big as cigarette butts? Well, I managed to get my hands on the photographs taken by the forensic team that Monday afternoon. Printed in the corner was the actual time the photographs were taken, around five o'clock, three hours after the bodies were discovered. Blowing them up you can see the larvae very well, and they are truly big. I did some research and discovered the top Italian expert on forensic entomology, internationally known, who with an American colleague ten years ago developed a technique for establishing the time of death based on the development of larvae. His name is Francesco Introna, director of the Istituto di Medicina Legale in Padova, director of the Laboratorio di Entomologia Forense at the Istituto di Medicina Legale of Bari, where he teaches; he's got three hundred scientific publications in medical journals and he's an expert consultant for the FBI! So I called him, sent him the photographs, and he gave me the results. Beautiful results. Here's the definitive proof we've always sought, Doug, that Pacciani was innocent, that Lotti and Pucci were liars, and that his picnicking friends had nothing to do with the killings!"

"Fabulous," I said. "But how does it work? What's the science behind it?"

"The professor explained it to me. The larvae are fundamentally important for arriving at the time of death. The *calliforidi*, the so-called blue flies, deposit on the cadaver a large number of eggs in a cluster. They lay eggs only during the day, because the flies don't fly at night. The eggs require between eighteen and twenty-four hours to hatch. And then they develop on a rigid schedule."

He pulled out the report. "Read it for yourself."

It was short and to the point. I parsed my way through the dense, scientific Italian. The larvae in the photographs of the French victim, the report stated, "had already passed the first phase of development and were in the second. . . . They could not have been deposited on the remains less than thirty-six hours previously. As a result, the theory that the homicide could have been committed the night of September 8 [Sunday night] and that the deposition of the eggs could have taken place at dawn on the ninth, with the photographs taken twelve hours later—at five o'clock in the afternoon—finds no support in the entomological data. The data places the time of death in the preceding day, at the minimum."

In other words, the French tourists *must* have been killed Saturday night.

"You understand what this means?" Spezi asked.

"It means the self-confessing eyewitnesses are damned liars—because they all claimed to have witnessed the killings on Sunday night!"

"And Lorenzo Nesi's testimony putting Pacciani near the scene of the crime Sunday night is irrelevant! If that's not enough, Pacciani had an alibi for his whereabouts Saturday night—the actual night of the murder. He had been at a country fair!"

This was absolutely decisive. The entomological evidence proved (as if more proof were needed) that Pacciani and his alleged accomplices had nothing to do with the Monster of Florence killings. It also, therefore, demolished the satanic sect theory—which had been built entirely on the guilt of Pacciani, the false confession of Lotti, and the testimony of the other algebraic witnesses. They were exactly what Judge Ferri had called them in his book: "coarse and habitual liars."

This new evidence, Spezi said, would force investigators to reopen the Sardinian Trail. Somewhere in the murky depths of the Sardinian clan, the truth would be found and the Monster unmasked.

"This is incredible," I said. "When this is broadcast, it'll cause one big beautiful uproar."

Spezi nodded silently. "And that's not all." He unwrapped the object on the table, to reveal a peculiar stone, carved in the shape of a truncated pyramid with polished sides, old and chipped, weighing perhaps five pounds.

"What is it?"

"According to Chief Inspector Giuttari, this is an esoteric object used to communicate between this world and the infernal regions. To everyone else it is a doorstop. I saw this one behind a door at the Villa Romana in Florence, now the German Cultural Institute. The director, Joachim Burmeister, is a friend of mine and he lent it to me. It looks almost identical to the stone collected in the Bartoline Fields near the scene of a Monster killing in 1981.

"*Chi L'ha Visto?*" Spezi went on, "will be shooting a segment in the Bartoline Fields, at the scene of the crime. I'll be standing at the very spot where the earlier doorstop was found, holding this one—proof that Giuttari's 'esoteric object' was merely a doorstop."

"Giuttari won't like it."

Spezi cracked a small, wicked smile. "I can't help that."

The program aired on May 14, 2004. Professor Introna appeared, presented his data, and explained the science of forensic entomology. Spezi appeared with his doorstop in the Bartoline Fields.

Instead of one fine, big, beautiful uproar, absolutely nothing happened. Neither the prosecutor's office nor the police showed a crumb of interest. Chief Inspector Giuttari dismissed out of hand Professor Introna's results. Police and prosecutors had no comment on the doorstop. As for the murder convictions of Lotti and Vanni, Pacciani's so-called picnicking friends, officials issued a bland statement that the

Italian judicial system had reached verdicts in those cases and saw no need to revisit them. In general, officialdom carefully avoided commenting on the program. The press let them get away with it. The great majority of Italian newspapers ignored it completely. This was science—not another sexy story on satanic sects—and it wouldn't sell papers. The investigation into satanic sects, hidden masterminds, bodies exchanged in tombs, conspiracies among powerful people, and doorstops mistaken for esoteric objects continued unabated.

Spezi's appearance on television did have one definitive effect. It seemed to inspire Chief Inspector Giuttari's undying hatred.

On our last night in Florence before moving back to America, we joined Mario and Myriam with other friends for a farewell dinner in their apartment, on the terrazzo overlooking the Florentine hills. The date was June 24, 2004. Myriam had prepared an extraordinary dinner, starting with crostini with sweet peppers and anchovies served with a spumante from the Alto Adige; wild pheasant and partridge, shot by a friend the day before, wrapped in grape leaves; a Chianti classico from the Viticchio estate; wild field greens served with the spicy local olive oil and an intense twelve-year-old balsamico; fresh pecorino cheese from Mario's village of Sant'Angelo; and zuppa inglese.

The morning before, on June 23, Spezi had published an article in *La Nazione*, in which he had interviewed Vanni, the ex-postman of San Casciano, convicted of being Pacciani's accomplice. Spezi regaled us with the story of how he had encountered Vanni, by sheer chance, at a nursing home while pursuing an unrelated story. Nobody knew Vanni had been released from prison, for reasons of ill-health and advanced age. Spezi recognized him and seized the opportunity to interview him on the spot.

"I Will Die as the Monster But I Am Innocent," ran the headline. Spezi got the interview because, he said, he reminded Vanni of the "good old days" in San Casciano, when he and Vanni had briefly encountered each other during a festival, long before the poor postman became one of Pacciani's infamous picnicking friends. They had ridden around together in a car full of people, Vanni waving the Italian flag. Vanni remembered Spezi and waxed nostalgic—and that was how Spezi got him to talk.

The sun set over the Florentine hills as we ate dinner, filling the landscape with a golden light. The bells of the nearby medieval church of Santa Margherita a Montici tolled out the hour, answered by the bells of other churches hidden in the hills around us. The air, warmed by the sinking rays of the sun, carried up the scent of honeysuckle. In the valley below, the crenellated towers of a large castle cast long shadows across its surrounding vineyards. As we watched, the hills sank from gold to purple and finally disappeared into the evening twilight.

The contrast between this magical landscape and the Monster that once stalked it struck me particularly hard at that moment.

Mario took the occasion to bring out a present for me. I unwrapped it to find a plastic Oscar statue, with a base that read, "The Monster of Florence."

"For when the film is made from our book," Mario said.

He also gave me a pencil drawing he had made many years earlier of Pietro Pacciani, sitting in the dock during his trial, on which he had written, "For Doug, in memory of a vile Florentine and our glorious labor together."

When we returned to the house we had built in Maine, I hung the drawing on the wall of my writing hut in the woods behind our house, along with a photograph of Spezi in his trench coat and fedora, Gauloise stuck in his mouth, standing in a butcher shop under a rack of hog jowls.

Spezi and I spoke frequently as we continued to work on the Monster book. I missed my life in Italy, but Maine was quiet, and with the frequent foul weather, fog, and cold, I found it a marvelous place to work. (I began to understand why Italy produced painters while England produced writers.) Our little town of Round Pond has five hundred and fifty residents and looks like something out of a Currier and Ives lithograph, with a white steepled church, a cluster of clapboard houses, a general store, and a harbor filled with lobster boats, surrounded by forests of oak and white pine. In the winter, the town is buried under a thick blanket of glittering snow and sea smoke rises from the ocean. The crime rate is almost nonexistent and few bother to lock their homes even when they go away on vacation. The annual bean supper at the local Grange is the front-page news in the paper. The "big town," twelve miles away, is Damariscotta, population 2,000.

The culture shock was considerable.

We continued to work on the book by e-mail and telephone. Spezi did most of the actual writing, while I read and commented on his work, adding some chapters in my miserable Italian, which Spezi had to rewrite. (I write Italian at what might generously be called a fifth grade level.) I wrote additional material in English, which was kindly translated by Andrea Carlo Cappi, the translator of my novels, who had become a good friend during our years in Italy. Spezi and I spoke on a regular basis and made excellent progress with the book.

On the morning of November 19, 2004, I went into my writing shack and checked my voice mail, to find an urgent message from Mario. Something shocking had happened.

CHAPTER
42

"*Polizia! Perquisizione!* Police! This is a search!"

At 6:15 on the morning of November 18, 2004, Mario Spezi woke to the sound of his door buzzer and the raucous voice of a police detective demanding entrance.

Spezi's first clear thought, on rousing himself from bed, was to hide the floppy disk that contained the book we were writing together. He leapt out of bed and ran up the narrow staircase to his garret office, where he yanked open the plastic box containing the diskettes for his ancient computer, took the one with "Monster" written in English on the label, and shoved it down into his underwear.

He reached the front door just as the police came pouring in. There seemed to be no end to them, three . . . four . . . five. In the end Spezi counted seven. Most of them were fat and their big jackets of gray and brown leather bulked them up even more.

The oldest one was a commander from Giuttari's GIDES squad. The others were carabinieri and policemen. "Graybeard," the commander, wished Spezi a dry "*buongiorno*" and shoved a piece of paper at him.

"*Procura della Repubblica presso il Tribunale di Perugia,*" read the letterhead—Office of the Public Prosecutor in the Tribunal of Perugia—and below that, "Search Warrant, Information and Guarantee to the Accused on the Right of Defense."

It had come straight out of the office of the public minister of Perugia, Giuliano Mignini.

"The person named above," the document read, "is hereby under official investigation for having committed the following crimes: A), B), C), D) . . ." They were listed up to the letter R. Nineteen crimes, none of them specified.

"What are these crimes, A, B, C, etcetera?" Spezi asked Graybeard.

"It would take volumes to explain them" was the man's response. Spezi could not know what the crimes were—they were under a judicial order of secrecy.

Spezi read with incredulity the reason for the search. It said he had "evinced a peculiar and suspicious interest toward the Perugian branch of the investigation" and that Spezi "demonstrated a zealous effort in attempting to undermine the investigation through the medium of television." This, he figured, must refer to the *Chi L'ha Visto?* program of May 14, in which Professor Introna had completely cut the legs off the satanic sect investigation and Spezi had waved around the doorstop, making Chief Inspector Giuttari look like a fool.

The warrant authorized the search of the house but also of the "persons present or who may arrive" in search of any object that might have something to do with the Monster case, even peripherally. "There is sufficient reason to believe that such objects may be present in the premises of the person above indicated and on his own person."

Spezi went cold when he read this. It meant they could search his body. He could feel the angular plastic case of the diskette digging into his flesh.

Meanwhile, Spezi's wife, Myriam, and twenty-year-old daughter, Eleonora, stood in the living room in their bathrobes, alarmed and confused.

"Tell me what you're interested in," Spezi said, "and I'll show you, so you won't trash my house."

"We want everything you have on the Monster," said Graybeard.

Which meant not only the entire archive Spezi had accumulated over a quarter of a century of researching and reporting on the case, but all the material that we were using to write the Monster book. Spezi was custodian of all the research; I had only copies of the most recent documents.

It suddenly occurred to him what this was about. They wanted to prevent publication of the book.

"Shit! When will you give it back to me?"

"As soon as we have checked through it," said Graybeard.

Spezi brought him up to his garret and showed him the masses of files that constituted his archive: packages of yellowed newspaper cuttings, mountains of photocopies of legal documents, ballistic analyses, ME reports, entire trial transcripts, interrogations, verdicts, photographs, books.

They began to load it all into big cardboard boxes.

Spezi called a friend of his at the news agency ANSA, the Italian equivalent to the Associated Press, and had the luck to catch him. "They're searching my house," he said. "They're taking away everything that I need to write my book with Douglas Preston on the Monster. I won't be able to write another word."

Fifteen minutes later the first story about the search broke on the computer screens of every newspaper and television station in Italy.

Meanwhile Spezi called the president of the Order of Journalists, the president of the Press Association, and the director of *La Nazione*. They were more scandalized than surprised. They told him they would raise hell with the story.

Spezi's cell phone began to ring like mad. One after another his colleagues called, even as the search plodded on. They all wanted to interview him. Spezi assured them that as soon as the search was over, he would meet with them.

The journalists began arriving under the house even while the search was still in progress.

The police didn't content themselves to taking only documents that Spezi had showed them. They began to rummage through drawers, pull books off the shelves, and open up CD holders. They went into his daughter's room and searched her closet, her files, her books, letters, diaries, scrapbooks, and photographs, scattering stuff on the floor and making a mess.

Spezi put his arm around Myriam. His wife was trembling. "Don't worry, this is just routine." Myriam was wearing a jacket and at the opportune moment he dove for the diskette, extracted it, and slid it into one of her pockets. He then gave her a kiss on the cheek as if to console her. "Hide it," he whispered.

Several minutes later, pretending to be upset, she sagged into a low ottoman that was coming apart at one of the seams. When the police had their backs turned she quickly slid the floppy disk into the ottoman.

After three hours of searching, they seemed to be finished. They strapped the loaded cartons onto luggage carriers and asked Spezi to follow them to the carabinieri barracks, where they would make an inventory, which he would be required to sign.

In the barracks, while he was seated on a brown Naugahyde chair waiting for the list to be ready, he received a telephone call on his cell phone. It was from Myriam, who was trying to put the house back in order, and who unwisely spoke to her husband in French. Spezi and his wife habitually spoke French in their home, as she was Belgian and they were a bilingual family. Their daughter had gone to French schools in Florence.

"Mario," she said in French, "don't worry, they didn't find what really interests you. But I can't find the documents about the scagliola." A scagliola is a type of antique table, and Spezi owned an extremely valuable one dating back to the seventeenth century, which they had just had restored and were thinking of selling.

It wasn't the most felicitous thing to say at that moment, in French, when it was obvious their cell phone was being tapped. He cut her off. "Myriam, this really isn't the time . . . not now . . . ." Spezi flushed as he closed the phone. He knew his wife's comment was completely innocent, but that it could be interpreted in a sinister light, particularly since it had been spoken in French.

Not long after, Graybeard came in. "Spezi, we need you in here for a moment."

The journalist rose from the chair and followed them into the next room. Graybeard turned and stared at him, his face hostile. "Spezi, you're not cooperating. This isn't working at all."

"Not cooperating? What's that supposed to mean, cooperate? I left my entire house at your disposal so you could put your grubby hands wherever you pleased, what the hell more do you want?"

He stared at Spezi with his hard, marblelike eyes. "That's not what I'm talking about. Don't feign ignorance. It would be much better for you if you would only cooperate."

"Ah, now I understand . . . It's about what my wife said in French. You think she was trying to tell me something in code. But you see, that's my wife's language, and it's normal for her to speak French, we often speak French at home. As for the contents of what she said"— Spezi figured that Graybeard wasn't bilingual—"if you didn't understand it, she was referring to a document that you didn't see, which was my contract with the publishing house for my book on the Monster. She wanted to tell me that you hadn't taken it. That's all."

Graybeard continued to fix him with narrowed eyes, his expression unchanging. Spezi began to think that the problem might be with the word "scagliola." Not many Italians outside the antiquarian field knew what it meant.

"Is it the scagliola?" he asked. "Do you know what a scagliola is? Is that the problem?"

The policeman didn't respond, but it was clear that this was, in fact, the problem. Spezi tried to explain, to no avail. Graybeard was not interested in explanations.

"I regret to say, Spezi, that we're going to have to start all over again."

They turned around. The policemen and carabinieri got back into their vehicles, and they all drove back to the apartment with Spezi. For four more hours they turned the place upside down—and this time they trashed it for real.

They didn't miss anything, not even the space behind the books in the library. They took the computer, all the floppy disks (except the one still hidden in the ottoman), and even the menu of a Rotary Club dinner where Spezi had attended a conference on the Monster. They took his telephone book and all his letters.

They were not in a good humor.

Spezi was also beginning to lose his temper. When he passed through the door to the library, he gestured to the stone doorstop that he had borrowed from his German friend, the one he had waved about on the television show. It was sitting behind the door, doing what it was supposed to do—being a doorstop. "You see that?" he said sarcastically to the detective. "It's like the truncated pyramid found at the scene of one of the crimes which you insist on claiming is an 'esoteric object.' There it is, take a good look: can't you see it's only a doorstop?" He gave a mocking laugh. "You find them everywhere in Tuscan country houses."

It was an extremely serious mistake. The detective seized the doorstop and packed it away. And thus was added to the evidence against Spezi an object identical to the one that GIDES and Giuttari believed to be of prime importance to their investigation, something the *Corriere della Sera* had written about in a front-page story, calling it, without a trace of irony, "an object that served to put the earthly world in contact with the infernal regions."

In the report prepared by the police of the items taken from Spezi's house, the doorstop was described as a "truncated pyramid with a hexagonal base concealed behind a door," the wording implying that Spezi had made a special effort to hide it. The public minister of Perugia, Giuliano Mignini, justified the retention of the doorstop in a report that stated the object "connected the person under investigation [i.e., Spezi] directly with the series of double homicides."

In other words, because of that doorstop, Spezi was no longer suspected of merely obstructing or interfering with the Monster of Florence investigation. Now they believed that an object discovered in his house tied him directly with one of the crimes.

The *Chi L'ha Visto?* program and the June 23 article had fixed Giuttari's hatred and suspicion of Spezi. In a book Giuttari published about the case, *The Monster: Anatomy of an Investigation*, the chief inspector explained how his suspicions developed. It is an interesting look into the way his mind worked.

"On June 23," Giuttari wrote, "one of [Spezi's] articles came out in *La Nazione*, an 'exclusive' interview with the lifer Mario Vanni, entitled *I Will Die as the Monster but I Am Innocent*."

In the story, Spezi mentioned that he had encountered Vanni once, many years before the Monster killings, in San Casciano. This struck Giuttari as an important clue. "I was mildly surprised that the two had known each other since the days of their youth," he wrote. "But I was struck even more by the curious coincidence that the bitter public foe of the official investigation into the Monster case and the strenuous defender of the 'Sardinian Trail' had not only revealed himself as having excellent rapport with the indicted ex-pharmacist [Calamandrei] . . . but now stood revealed as a longtime friend of Mario Vanni."

Giuttari went on to say that Spezi had "participated in a television series" that attempted to focus attention back on the Sardinian Trail, "recycling the same old tired and unverified theories" that had been discredited long ago.

"Now," Giuttari wrote, Spezi's "interfering presence was beginning to look suspicious."

With the doorstop in hand, Giuttari and Mignini had the physical evidence they needed to connect Spezi to one of the actual crime scenes of the Monster.

When the policemen had left, Spezi slowly walked up the staircase to his garret, afraid of what he might find. It was even worse than he'd feared. He fell into the chair that I had given him upon my departure from Florence, in front of the empty space where his computer had been, and stared for a long time at the wreck all around him. In that moment, he thought back to that crystal-clear morning of Sunday, June 7, 1981—twenty-three years earlier—when his colleague had asked him to take the crime desk, assuring him that "nothing ever happens on a Sunday."

Never in a million years could he have imagined where it would end up.

He wanted to call me, he told me later, but by that time it was late at night in America. He couldn't write an e-mail—he didn't have a computer. He decided to leave the house, walk around the streets of Florence, and look for an Internet café where he could e-mail me.

Outside the apartment, a crowd of journalists and television cameras awaited. He said a few words, answered questions, and then got into his car and drove into town. In Via de' Benci, a few steps from Santa Croce, he went into an Internet café, full of pimply American students talking to their parents through VOIP. He seated himself in front of a machine. From somewhere, a little muted, came the sad trombone of Marc Johnson playing "Goodbye Pork Pie Hat" by Charlie Mingus. Spezi connected to his mail server, entered the information for his mailbox, and saw that there was already a message from me, with an attachment.

While writing the Monster book, we had been exchanging e-mails on what we had corrected of each other's chapters. What he found was the last chapter of the book, which I had written, about the interview with Antonio. He sent me an e-mail telling me of the search of his home.

The next morning, after receiving the e-mail, I called and he related to me the story of the search. He asked for my help in publicizing the seizure of our research materials.

Among the documents taken by police were all the notes and drafts of the article we had written for *The New Yorker*, which had never been published. I called Dorothy Wickenden, the managing editor of the magazine, and she gave me a list of people who could help, while at the same time explaining that, since they hadn't actually published the article, the magazine did not feel it appropriate to intervene directly.

For days I called and wrote letters, but the response was minimal. The sad truth was that few in North America could get excited about an Italian journalist who had irritated the police and gotten his files taken away, at a time when journalists were being blown up in Iraq and murdered in Russia. "Now, if Spezi had been *imprisoned* . . ." I heard many times, "well, then we could do something."

Finally, PEN intervened. On January 11, 2005, the Writers in Prison

Committee of PEN International, in London, sent Giuttari a letter criticizing the search of Spezi's home and seizure of our papers. The letter stated that "International PEN is concerned that there has been a violation of Article 6.3 of the European Convention on Human Rights that guarantees the right of everyone charged with a criminal offence to be informed promptly 'and in detail of the nature and cause of the accusation against him.' "

Giuttari responded by ordering another search of Spezi's house, which took place on January 24. This time they took a broken computer and a walking stick that they suspected might contain a concealed electronic device.

But they never did get the diskette Spezi had stuffed down his undershorts, and we were able to resume working on the book. In succeeding months, the police eventually returned, in bits and pieces, most of Spezi's files, his archives, our notes, and his computer—but not the infamous doorstop. Giuttari and Mignini now knew exactly what was in the book, since they had captured all the drafts from Spezi's computer. And it seemed they did not like what they read.

One fine morning, Spezi opened his newspaper to read a headline that almost knocked him out of his chair.

NARDUCCI MURDER:
JOURNALIST INVESTIGATED

Giuttari's suspicions had matured, like wine turning to vinegar in a poorly sealed cask. Spezi had gone from interfering journalist to murder suspect.

"When I read that," Spezi told me on the telephone, "I felt like I was inside a film of Kafka's *The Trial*, remade by Jerry Lewis and Dean Martin."

CHAPTER
43

For a year, from January 2005 to January 2006, Spezi's two lawyers tried and failed to learn what the specific charges were against him. The public minister of Perugia had sealed the accusations under an order of *segreto istruttorio*, a judicial secrecy order that makes it illegal to reveal anything about the charges. In Italy, an order of *segreto istruttorio* is often followed by selected leaks by prosecutors to their chosen reporters, who publish without fear of being charged. In this way, prosecutors allow their side of the story to be told while journalists are barred from publishing anything else. This is what seemed to happen now. Spezi was suspected of obstructing the inquiry into the Narducci murder, the newspapers claimed, which had aroused suspicions that he might be an accessory to the murder and the instigator of a cover-up. The implications of this were unclear.

In January of 2006, our book was finished and sent to the publishing house. The title was *Dolci Colline di Sangue*. A literal translation would be *Sweet Hills of Blood*, a play on the Italian phrase *dolci colline di Firenze*, the sweet hills of Florence. It was scheduled for publication in April 2006.

In early 2006, Spezi called me from a pay phone in Florence. He said that while working on a completely different story, unconnected with the Monster of Florence, he had met an ex-con named Luigi Ruocco, a petty criminal who, it turned out, was an old acquaintance of Antonio Vinci. This Ruocco told Spezi an extraordinary story—a story that would blow the case wide open. "This is the breakthrough I've been searching for for twenty years," Mario told me. "Doug, it's absolutely incredible. With this new information, the case will finally be solved. They're tapping my telephone and the e-mail is unsafe. So you have to come to Italy—and then I'll tell you all about it. You'll be part of it, Doug. *Together we'll expose the Monster!*"

I flew to Italy with my family on February 13, 2006. Leaving them in a spectacular apartment on Via Ghibellina we had borrowed from a friend, owned by one of the Ferragamo heirs, I went up to Spezi's house to hear the incredible news.

Over dinner, Mario told me the story.

A few months back, he said, he had been researching an article about a woman who had been victimized by a doctor working for a pharmaceutical company. The doctor had used her, without her permission, as a test subject for a new psychopharmatropic drug. The case had been brought to his attention by Fernando Zaccaria, an ex–police detective who had once specialized in infiltrating drug trafficking rings, and who was now president of a private security firm in Florence. A crusader against injustice, Zaccaria had collected, pro bono, the evidence that helped convict the doctor for injuring the woman with his illegal experiments. He wanted Spezi to write the story.

One evening, when Spezi was at the injured woman's house with her mother and Zaccaria, he casually mentioned his work on the Monster of Florence case and took out a photograph he happened to be carrying of Antonio Vinci. The mother, who was pouring coffee, peered over at the photograph and suddenly exclaimed, "Why, Luigi knows that man there! And I knew him and all of them too, when I was a little girl. I remember they used to take me to their festivals in the country." The Luigi she referred to was Luigi Ruocco, her ex-husband.

"I've got to meet your husband," Spezi said.

They gathered the next evening around the same table: Zaccaria, Spezi, the woman, and Luigi Ruocco. Ruocco was the quintessential specimen of a small-time hood, taciturn, with a neck like a bull, a huge square face, and curly brown hair. He was dressed in gym clothes. There was, however, a cautious but open look in his blue eyes that Spezi liked. Ruocco looked at the photograph and confirmed that he knew Antonio and the other Sardinians very well.

Spezi quickly gave Ruocco a summary of the Monster of Florence case and his belief that Antonio might be the Monster. Ruocco listened with interest. In a few minutes Spezi got to the point: did Ruocco know of a secret house that Antonio may have used during the period of the killings? Spezi had often said to me that the Monster had probably used an abandoned house in the country, perhaps a ruin, as a place of retreat to use before and after a killing, where he hid his gun, knife, and other items. At the time of the killings the Tuscan countryside was dotted with such abandoned houses.

"I heard talk about it," Ruocco said. "I don't know where it is. But I know someone who does. 'Gnazio."

"Of course, Ignazio!" Zaccaria exclaimed. "He knows a whole bunch of Sardinians!"

Ruocco called Spezi a few days later. He had spoken to Ignazio and had the information on Antonio's safe house. Spezi and Ruocco met in front of a supermarket outside Florence. They retired to a café where Mario downed an espresso and Ruocco drank a Campari with a splash of Martini & Rossi. What Ruocco had to say was electrifying. Ignazio not only knew the safe house, but had actually been there only a month before with Antonio. He had observed an old armoire with a glass front in which he could see six locked metal boxes, lined up in a row. His eye fell on a drawer not fully closed below, in which he glimpsed two, possibly three pistols, one of which might have been a .22 Beretta. Ignazio asked the Sardinian what was in those metal boxes and the man had responded brusquely, "That's *my* stuff," slapping his chest.

Six metal boxes. Six female victims.

Spezi could hardly contain his excitement. "That's the detail that convinced me," he said over dinner. "Six. How could Ruocco know? Everyone talks about the seven or eight double killings of the Monster. But Ruocco said six boxes. Six: the number of female victims killed by the Monster, if you eliminate the 1968 killing, which he didn't do, and the time he mistakenly killed a gay couple."

"But he didn't mutilate all the victims."

"Yes, but the psychological experts said he would have taken souvenirs from each one. In almost every crime scene, the girl's purse was found lying on the ground, wide open."

I listened with fascination. If the Monster's Beretta, the most sought-after gun in Italian history, were in that armoire, along with items from the victims, it would be the scoop of a lifetime.

Spezi went on. "I asked Ruocco to go to the house, in order to tell me exactly where it was and describe it to me. He said he would. We met again a few days later. Ruocco told me that he had gone and looked inside, and could see the armoire through a window with the six metal boxes. He gave me directions to the house."

"Did you go?"

"I certainly did! Nando and I went together." The ruined house, Spezi said, was on the grounds of an enormous, thousand-acre estate west of Florence, called Villa Bibbiani, near the town of Capraia. "It's a spectacular villa," Spezi said, "with gardens, fountains, statues, and a stupendous park planted with rare trees."

He took out his cell phone and showed me a couple of pictures he had snapped of the villa. I gaped at the magnificence of it.

"How did you get in?"

"No problem! It's open to the public for sales of olive oil and wine, and they rent it out for weddings and such. The gates are wide open and there's even a public parking area. Nando and I walked around. Several hundred meters beyond the villa, a dirt road leads to two decrepit stone houses, one of which fit Ruocco's description. The houses can be reached by a separate road through the forest, very private."

"You didn't break in, did you?"

"No, no! I sure did think about it! Just to see if the armoire was really there. But that would be an insane thing to do. Not only would it be trespassing, but what would I do with the boxes and gun once I found them? No, Doug, we have to call the police and let them handle it—and hope to get the scoop afterwards."

"Have you called the police then?"

"Not yet. I was waiting for you." He leaned forward. "Think of it, Doug. In the next two weeks, the case of the Monster of Florence may be solved."

I then made a fateful request. "If the villa's open to the public, can I go see it?"

"Of course," said Spezi. "We'll go tomorrow."

CHAPTER
44

What the hell happened to your car?" It was the following morning, and we were standing in the parking area next to Spezi's apartment building. The door of his Renault Twingo had been ineptly forced open with what looked like a wrecking bar, ruining the door and much of the right side of the car.

"They stole my radio," Spezi said. "Can you believe it? With all these Mercedes, Porsches, and Alfa Romeos parked along here, they picked my Twingo!"

We drove to the security firm run by Zaccaria, a nondescript building in an industrial area on the outskirts of Florence. The ex-cop received us in his office. He looked every inch a movie detective, dressed in a pinstriped blue suit of the sharpest Florentine cut, his long gray hair almost to his shoulders, strikingly handsome, dashing, and animated. He spoke with a raffish Neapolitan accent, tossing in a bit of gangsterish slang every once in a while to great effect, and speaking with his hands as only a Neapolitan can do.

Before going to the villa, we went to lunch. Zaccaria treated us to a repast at a local dive, and there, over a plate of *maltagliata al cinghiale*, he regaled us with stories of his undercover work infiltrating drug smuggling rings, some involving the American Mafia. I marveled that he had survived.

"Nando," Spezi said. "Tell Doug the story of Catapano."

"Ah, Catapano! Now there was a real Neapolitan!" He turned to me. "There was once a boss of the Neapolitan Camorra named Catapano. He was locked up in Poggioreale prison for murder. It just so happened that the murderer of his brother was in the same prison. Catapano vowed revenge. He said, *I will eat his heart.*"

Zaccaria took a moment to dig into his *maltagliata* and take a swig of wine.

"Slow down," said Spezi, "and stop using so much dialect. Doug doesn't understand dialect."

"My apologies." He went on with the story. The prison authorities segregated the two men at opposite ends of the prison and made sure they would never encounter each other. But one day, Catapano heard that his nemesis was in the infirmary. He took two guards hostage with a spoon sharpened into a knife, used them to force his way to the infirmary, got the key, and entered, surprising three nurses and a doctor. He immediately set upon his enemy, cutting his throat and stabbing him to death while the doctor and nurses looked on in horror. Then he cried out, in a strangled voice, "Where's the heart? Where's the liver?" The doctor, under threat, gave Catapano a quick lesson in anatomy. With one enormous swipe of the knife Catapano opened the man up and ripped out the heart and liver, one in each hand, and then took a bite out of each in turn.

"Catapano," Zaccaria said, "became a legend among his people. In Naples, the heart is everything—courage, happiness, love. To rip it out of your enemy and bite it is to reduce your enemy to the level of meat, animal meat. It deprives him of what makes him human. And all the television coverage of it afterwards was useful in sending a signal to Catapano's enemies that he could administer justice with the most refined methods, even in prison. Catapano had proved his courage, his capacity for organization, his exquisite sense of theater, and he did it inside one of the highest-security prisons in Italy, under the horrified gaze of five witnesses!"

Lunch over, we set off for the Villa Bibbiani in an icy winter drizzle under skies the color of dead flesh. It was still raining when we arrived, entering the grounds through a pair of iron gates and up a long, curving driveway lined with massive umbrella pines. We parked in the parking area, got our umbrellas out, and walked to the salesroom. The wooden door was locked and barred. A woman leaned out the window and said the salesroom was closed for lunch. Zaccaria charmed her, asking where the gardener was, and she said we might find him around the back. We walked through an archway and entered a stupendous formal garden behind the villa, with sweeping marble steps, fountains, reflecting pools, statues, and hedges. The villa was originally built in the 1500s by the Frescobaldi family of Florence. The gardens were created a hundred years later by Count Cosimo Ridolfi; in the 1800s, thousands of rare botanical specimens and trees were added to the gardens and park by an Italian explorer and botanist who collected plants from the far ends of the earth. Even in the gray winter rain, the gardens and massive dripping trees retained a cold magnificence.

We moved past the villa to the far end of the park. A dirt road ran along the edge of the arboretum into a thick wood, where, in a clearing beyond, we could see a cluster of crumbling stone houses.

"That's it," murmured Spezi, pointing to one of the houses.

I gazed down the muddy road to the house that held the ultimate secret of the Monster of Florence. A chill mist drifted through the trees and the rain drummed on our umbrellas.

"Maybe we could just walk down there and take a look," I said.

Spezi shook his head. "Not a chance."

We returned to the car, shook out our umbrellas, and got in. It was a disappointing visit, at least to me. Ruocco's story seemed too perfect, and the setting struck me as an unlikely one for the secret hideout of the Monster of Florence.

As we drove back to Zaccaria's firm, Spezi explained the plan he and Zaccaria had worked out for communicating this information to the police. If they merely gave it to the police, and the police found the Monster's gun, the news would be all over Italy and Mario and I would lose the scoop. We also had to consider the physical danger to ourselves if Antonio knew we were the ones who had turned him in. Instead, Spezi and Zaccaria would approach a certain chief inspector of their acquaintance with what they claimed was an anonymous letter, which they were duly passing along as good citizens. That way, they would have the scoop but not the blame.

"If we pull this off," Zaccaria said, slapping Mario's knee, "they'll make me minister of justice!" We all laughed.

A few days after our visit to Villa Bibbiani, Spezi called me on my cell phone. "We did it," he said. "We did it all." He didn't go into details, but I knew what he meant: he had given the anonymous letter to the police. As I began to ask too many questions, Spezi cut me off, saying *"Il telefonino è brutto,"* literally, "The cell phone is ugly," meaning he believed it was being tapped. We arranged to meet in town, so he could tell me the full story.

We met at Caffè Cibreo. A strange thing happened, Spezi said, when they had approached the chief inspector. The inspector inexplicably refused to accept the letter, and brusquely told them to take it and their story to the head of the mobile squad instead, a special police unit that investigates homicides. He appeared anxious to have nothing to do with the whole affair and was decidedly unfriendly.

Why, Spezi asked me, would a chief inspector turn down out of hand what could be the most important coup in his career?

Zaccaria, a former inspector himself, had no answer.

CHAPTER
45

The morning of February 22, I headed out of the apartment into the streets of Florence to fetch espressos and pastries to carry back for breakfast. As I was crossing the street to a little café, my cell phone rang. A man speaking Italian informed me he was a police detective and wanted to see me—immediately.

"Come on," I said, laughing. "Who is this really?" I was impressed by the flawless, officious-sounding Italian, and I racked my brains as to who it might be.

"This is not a joke, Mr. Preston."

There was a long silence as it sank in that this was real.

"Excuse me—what's this about?"

"I cannot tell you. You must see us. It is *obbligatorio*."

"I'm very busy," I said, in a rising panic. "I don't have time. So sorry."

"You must *make* time, Mr. Preston," came the reply. "Where are you right now?"

"Florence."

"*Where?*"

Should I refuse to tell him or lie? That didn't seem a wise thing to do. "Via Ghibellina."

"Don't go anywhere—we're coming to you."

I looked around. It was a part of town I didn't know well, with narrow side streets and few tourists. This would not do. I wanted witnesses—American witnesses.

"Let's meet in the Piazza della Signoria," I countered, naming the most public square in Florence.

"Where? It's a big place."

"At the spot where Savonarola was burned. There's a plaque."

A silence. "I'm not familiar with that place. Let's meet instead at the entrance to the Palazzo Vecchio."

I called Christine. "I'm afraid I can't bring you coffee this morning."

I arrived early and walked around the piazza, thinking furiously. As an American, an author and journalist, I had always enjoyed a smug feeling of invulnerability. What could they possibly do to me? Now I wasn't feeling so untouchable.

At the appointed time I saw two men wending their way through the tourist masses, dressed casually in jeans, black shoes, and blue jackets, shades pushed up on their crew-cut heads. They were *in borghese*, in plainclothes, but even from a hundred yards away I could tell they were cops.

I went over. "I am Douglas Preston."

"Come this way."

The two detectives took me into the Palazzo Vecchio, where, in the magnificent Renaissance courtyard surrounded by Vasari's frescoes, they presented me with a legal summons to appear for an interrogation before the public minister of Perugia, Judge Giuliano Mignini. The detective politely explained that a no-show would be a serious crime; it would put them in the regrettable position of having to come and get me.

"Sign here to indicate you have received this piece of paper and understood what it says and what you must do."

"You still haven't told me what it's about."

"You'll find out in Perugia tomorrow."

"At least tell me this: is it about the Monster of Florence?" I asked.

"Bravo," said the detective. "Now sign."

I signed.

I called Spezi, and he was deeply shocked and concerned. "I never thought they'd act against you," he said. "Go to Perugia and answer the questions. Tell them just what they ask and no more—and for God's sake, don't lie."

CHAPTER
46

The next day I drove to Perugia with Christine and our two children, passing the shores of Lake Trasimeno on the way. Perugia, a beautiful and ancient city, occupies an irregular rocky hill in the upper Tiber valley, surrounded by a defensive wall that is still largely intact. Perugia has long been a center of learning in Italy, graced by a number of universities and schools, some of which date back five hundred years. Christine planned to sightsee with the kids and have lunch while I was interrogated. I had decided the whole interrogation was a bluff, a crude attempt at intimidation. I'd done nothing wrong and broken no law. I was a journalist and writer. Italy was a civilized country. Or so I kept repeating to myself on the drive down.

The offices of the Procura, where the public minister worked, were in a modern travertine building just outside the ancient city walls. I was ushered into a pleasant room on a high floor. A couple of windows looked down to the beautiful Umbrian countryside, misty and green, wreathed in drizzle. I had dressed smartly and I carried a folded copy of the *International Herald Tribune* under my arm as a prop.

Present in the room were five people. I asked their names and wrote them down. One of the detectives who had summoned me was there, an Inspector Castelli, fashionably dressed for the important occasion in a black sports jacket and black shirt buttoned at the collar, wearing lots of hair gel. There was a small, extremely tense police captain named Mora with orange hair implants, who seemed determined to put on a good show for the public minister. There was a blonde female detective, who, at my request, wrote her name in my notebook in a scribble I have yet to decipher. A stenographer sat at a computer.

Behind a desk sat the public minister of Perugia himself, Judge Giuliano Mignini. He was a short man of indeterminate middle age, well groomed, his fleshy face carefully shaved and patted. He wore a blue suit and carried himself like a well-bred Italian, with a large sense of personal dignity, his movements smooth and precise, his voice calm and pleasant. Bestowing upon me the honorific of *dottore*, which in Italy denotes the highest respect, he addressed me with elaborate courtesy using the *"lei"* form. I had the right to an interpreter, he explained, but that finding one might take many hours, during which I would be inconveniently detained. In his opinion I spoke Italian fluently. I asked if I needed a lawyer and he said that, although it was of course my right, it wasn't necessary, as they merely wanted to ask a few questions of a routine nature.

I had already decided not to assert journalistic privilege. It's one thing to fight for your rights in your own country, but I had no intention of going to prison on principle in a foreign land.

His questions were gentle, and posed almost diffidently. The secretary typed the questions and my answers into the computer. Sometimes Mignini rephrased my answers in better Italian, checking solicitously if that was what I really meant to say. At first he rarely, if ever, looked at me, keeping his eyes down to his notes and his papers, occasionally looking over the shoulder of the stenographer to see what she was typing on the screen.

At the end of the interrogation, I would be refused both a transcript of the interrogation and a copy of the "statement" I was required to sign. My account of the interrogation appearing here is taken from notes I jotted down immediately after the interrogation and a much fuller account I wrote up two days later from memory.

Mignini asked many questions about Spezi, always listening with respectful interest to the answers. He wanted to know what our theories were involving the Monster case. He questioned me closely about one of Spezi's two lawyers, Alessandro Traversi. Did I know who he was? Had I met him? Had Spezi ever discussed with me Traversi's legal strategies? If so, what were those legal strategies? On this latter point he was particularly insistent, probing deeply for what I might know of Spezi's legal defense. I truthfully claimed ignorance. He reeled off lists of names and asked if I had ever heard them. Most of the names were unfamiliar. Others, such as Calamandrei, Pacciani, and Zaccaria, I knew.

The questions went on like this for an hour, and I was starting to feel reassured. I even had a glimmer of hope that I might get out of there in time to join my wife and children for lunch.

Mignini then asked me if I had ever heard the name Antonio Vinci. I felt a faint chill. Yes, I said, I knew that name. How did I know it and what did I know of him? I said we had interviewed him, and under further questioning described the circumstances. The questioning turned to the Monster's gun. Had Spezi mentioned the gun? What were his theories? I told him our belief that the gun had always remained within the circle of Sardinians, and that one of them had gone on to become the Monster.

At this, Mignini dropped the genteel tone and his voice became edged with anger. "You say that you and Spezi persist in this belief, even though the Sardinian Trail was closed in 1988 by Judge Rotella, and the Sardinians were officially absolved of any connection in the case?"

I said yes, that we both persisted in this belief.

Mignini steered the questions toward our visit to the villa. Now the tone of his voice became darker, accusatory. What did we do there? Where did we walk? What did we talk about? Were Spezi and Zaccaria always within sight of me? Was there any moment, even briefly, when they were out of my sight? Was there talk of a gun? Of boxes of iron? Was my back ever to Spezi? When we spoke, how far were we from one another? Did we see anyone there? Who? What was said? What was Zaccaria doing there? What was his role? Did he speak about his desire to be appointed minister of justice?

I answered as truthfully as I could, trying to suppress a damnable habit of overexplanation.

Why did we go there? Mignini finally asked.

I said that it was a public place and we went there in our capacity as journalists—

At the mention of the world "journalist" Mignini interrupted me in a loud voice, overriding me before I had finished. He made an angry speech that this had nothing to do with freedom of the press, that we were free to report on whatever we wanted, and that he didn't care a whit what we wrote. This, he said, was a *criminal* matter.

I said it did matter, because we were journalists—

Again he interrupted me, drowning me out with a lecture that freedom of the press was irrelevant to this inquiry and that I should not bring up the subject again. He asked me in a sarcastic tone if I thought that, just because Spezi and I were journalists, did that mean we could not *also* be criminals? I had the distinct feeling he was trying to prevent anything I might say about press freedom or journalistic privilege from reaching the tape recording that was surely being made of the interrogation.

I began to sweat. The public minister began repeating the same questions over and over again, phrased in different ways and in different forms. His face flushed as his frustration mounted. He frequently instructed his secretary to read back my earlier answers. "You said *that*, and now you say *this*? Which is true, Dr. Preston? *Which is true?*"

I began to stumble over my words. If the truth be known, I am far from fluent in Italian, especially with legal and criminological terms. With a growing sense of dismay, I could hear from my own stammering, hesitant voice that I was sounding like a liar.

Mignini asked, sarcastically, if I at least remembered speaking by telephone to Spezi on February 18. Flustered, I said I couldn't remember a particular conversation on that exact date, but that I had talked to him almost every day.

Mignini said, "Listen to this." He nodded to the stenographer, who pressed a button on the computer. Through the set of speakers attached to the computer, I could hear the ringing of a phone, and then my voice answering:

"*Pronto.*"

"*Ciao, sono Mario.*"

They had wiretapped our phone calls.

Mario and I chatted for a moment while I listened in amazement to my own voice, clearer on the intercept than in the original call on my lousy cell phone. Mignini played it once, then again, and yet again. He stopped at the point where Mario said, "We did it all." He fixed his glittering eyes on me: "What exactly did you do, Dr. Preston?"

I explained Spezi was referring to delivering the information to the police.

"No, Dr. Preston." He played the recording again and again, asking over and over, "What is this thing you did? *What did you do?*" He seized on Spezi's other comment, in which he had said, "The cell phone is ugly."

"What does this mean, 'The cell phone is ugly'?"

"It meant he thought the phone was tapped."

Mignini sat back and swelled with triumph. "And why is it, Dr. Preston, that you were concerned about the telephone being tapped *if you weren't engaged in illegal activity?*"

"Because it isn't nice to have your phone tapped," I answered feebly. "We're journalists. We keep our work secret."

"That is *not* an answer, Dr. Preston."

Mignini played the recording again, and again. He kept stopping at several other words, repeatedly demanding to know what I or Spezi meant, as if we were speaking in code, a common Mafia ploy. He asked me if Spezi had a gun in the car with us. He asked me if Spezi had carried a gun during our visit to the villa. He wanted to know exactly what we had done there and where we had walked, minute by minute. Mignini brushed all my answers aside. "There is so much more behind this conversation than you are telling us, Dr. Preston. You know much more than you are letting on." He demanded to know what kind of evidence the Sardinians might have hidden in the villa, in

the boxes, and I said I didn't know. Take a guess, he said. I replied perhaps arms or other evidence—jewelry from the victims, maybe pieces
of the corpses.

"Pieces from the *corpses*?" the judge exclaimed incredulously, looking at me as if I were a lunatic for even thinking of such a vile thing.
"But the killings took place twenty years ago!"

"But the FBI report said—"

"Listen again, Dr. Preston!" And he pressed the button to play the
call again.

This time the police captain jumped in, speaking for the first time,
his voice as tense and shrill as a cat's.

"I find it very strange that Spezi laughs at that point. Why does he
laugh? The Monster of Florence case is one of the most tragic in the
history of the Italian republic, and it is no laughing matter. So why
does Spezi laugh? *What is so funny?*"

I refrained from answering the question, since it hadn't been addressed to me. But the indefatigable man wanted an answer, and he
turned and repeated the question to me directly.

"I am not a psychologist," I answered as coldly as I could, the desired effect ruined when I mispronounced the word *psicologo* and had
to be corrected.

The captain stared at me, his eyes narrowing, then turned to Mignini and with the expression on his face of a man who refuses to
allow himself to be fooled. "This is something I note for the record,"
he shrilled. "It is *very* strange that he laughs at that point. It is not psy-
chologically normal, no, *not normal at all.*"

I remember at this point looking at Mignini, and finding his gaze
on me. His face was flushed with a look of contempt—and triumph. I
suddenly knew why: he had expected me to lie, and now I had met his
expectation. I was proving to his satisfaction that I was guilty.

But of what?

I stammered out a question: did they think we had committed a
crime at the villa?

Mignini straightened up in his chair and with a note of triumph in
his voice said, "Yes."

"What?"

He thundered out, "You and Spezi either planted, or were planning to plant, a gun or other false evidence at that villa in an attempt to frame an innocent man for being the Monster of Florence, to derail this investigation, and to deflect suspicion from Spezi himself. *That* is what you were doing. This comment: 'We did it all'—that's what he meant. And then you tried to call the police. But we had warned them ahead of time—and they would have nothing to do with the deception!"

I was floored. I stammered that this was just a theory, but Mignini interrupted me and said, "These are not theories! These are facts! And you, Dr. Preston, you know a great deal more about this business than you are letting on. Do you realize the utmost seriousness, the enormous gravity, of these crimes? You well know that Spezi is being investigated for the murder of Narducci, and I think you know a great deal about it. That makes you an accessory. Yes, Dr. Preston, I can hear it in your voice on that telephone call, I can hear the tone of knowledge, of deep familiarity with these events. Just listen again." His voice rose with restrained exultation. "Listen to yourself!"

And for maybe the tenth time he replayed the conversation.

"Perhaps you have been duped," he went on, "but I don't think so. *You know.* And now, Dr. Preston you have one last chance—*one last chance*—to tell us what you know—or I will charge you with perjury. I don't care, I will do it, even if the news goes around the world tomorrow."

I felt sick and I had the sudden urge to relieve myself. I asked for the way to the bathroom. I returned a few minutes later, having failed to muster much composure. I was terrified. As soon as the interrogation ended, I would be arrested and taken off to jail, never to see my wife and children again. Planting false evidence, perjury, accessory to murder . . . Not just any murder, but one connected to the Monster of Florence . . . I could easily spend the rest of my life in an Italian prison.

"I've told you the truth," I managed to croak. "What more can I say?"

Mignini waved his hand and was handed a legal tome that he placed on his desk with the utmost delicacy, then opened to the requisite page. In a voice worthy of a funeral oration, he began to read the text of the law. I heard that I was now *indagato* (indicted) for the crime of reticence and making false statements.[1] He announced that the investigation would be suspended to allow me to leave Italy, but that it would be reinstated when the investigation of Spezi had concluded.

In other words, I was to get out of Italy and not come back.

The secretary printed out a transcript. The two-and-a-half-hour interrogation had been boiled down to two pages of questions and answers, which I corrected and signed.

"May I keep this?"

"No. It is under *segreto istruttorio*."

Very stiffly, I picked up my *International Herald Tribune*, folded it under my arm, and turned to leave.

"If you ever decide to talk, Dr. Preston, we are here."

On rubbery legs I descended to the street and into a wintry drizzle.

---

[1] Here and elsewhere I have translated the word *indagato* as "charged" or "indicted." To be more precise, to be *indagato* is to be formally named as the official suspect of a crime, your name recorded in a book along with the reasons why. It is one step short of an actual indictment in the American sense, although in Italy it amounts to much the same thing, especially in terms of public opinion and the effect it has on the person's reputation.

CHAPTER
47

We drove back to Florence in the pouring rain. Along the way, I called the American embassy in Rome on my cell phone. An official in the legal department explained they could do nothing for me since I had not been arrested. "Americans who get into trouble in Italy," he said, "need to hire a lawyer. The American embassy can't intervene in a local criminal investigation."

"I'm not some American who did something stupid and got involved in a local criminal investigation!" I cried. "They're harassing me because I'm a journalist. This is a freedom-of-press issue!"

That did not impress the embassy official. "Regardless of what you think, this is a local criminal matter. You're in Italy," he said, "not America. We can't intervene in criminal investigations."

"Can you at least recommend a lawyer?"

"We're not in the business of rating Italian lawyers. We'll send you a list of the lawyers known to the embassy."

"Thanks."

Above all, I had to speak to Mario. Something big was coming—my interrogation was only a shot across the bow. Even for a man as powerful as the public minister of Perugia, it was a brazen step to take into custody an American journalist and subject him to the third degree. If they were willing to do that to me, at the risk of bad publicity (which I fully intended to bring down upon their heads like a ton of bricks), what would they do to Spezi? He was the man they were really after.

I couldn't call Spezi on my cell phone. When I got back to Florence, I arranged a meeting through borrowed cell phones and calls from phone booths. At close to midnight, Spezi, Zaccaria, and Myriam showed up at our apartment in Via Ghibellina.

Spezi, Gauloise stuck in his mouth, paced the elegant living room, trailing clouds of smoke. "I never would have thought they would take this step. Are you *sure* they charged you with perjury?"

"I'm sure. I'm a *persona indagata.*"

"Did they serve you with an *avviso di garanzia?*"

"They said they would mail it to my address in Maine."

I related to them as much as I could remember of the interrogation. When I got to the point where Mignini accused us of planting a gun at the villa to incriminate an innocent man and to deflect suspicion from Spezi himself, Spezi stopped me.

"He said that? 'To deflect suspicion' from me?"

"That's what he said."

Spezi shook his head. "*Porca miseria!* Those two, Giuttari and Mignini, don't just think me guilty of some journalistic shenanigans, planting a gun for a scoop. They think I was directly involved in the Monster's murders—or at least in the murder of Narducci!"

"In a crazy way," I said, "their fantasy fits the facts. Look at it from their point of view. For years we've been insisting Antonio is the Monster. Nobody's paid any attention. So we go to the villa, we walk around, then a few days later we call the police and say Antonio hid evidence at the villa, come and get it. I hate to say it, Mario, but it's a believable theory that we might have planted something."

"Come now!" Spezi cried. "It's a theory not only lacking all investigative logic, but all logic entirely! A moment's thought would discredit it. If I was behind the murder of Narducci, to 'deflect suspicion' from myself, would I really enlist in my plot an ex-con I didn't know, a policeman who had been one of the finest detectives in the Florentine mobile squad, and a famous American writer? Who could possibly think that you, Doug, would come to Italy and sneak around like a crook planting evidence for the police to find? You're a best-selling author here already! You don't need a scoop! And Nando, he's president of an important security company. Why would he risk everything for a sordid scoop? It doesn't make any sense at all!"

He paced, scattering ashes.

"Doug, you have to ask yourself: why are Giuttari and Mignini working so hard to attack us now? Is it perhaps because in just two months we'll publish a book on this same subject, questioning their investigation? Might this be an effort to discredit our book before publication? They know what's in the book already—they've read it."

He took a turn around the room.

"The worst thing for me, Doug, is the accusation that I did this to *deflect suspicion from myself.* Suspicion of what? That I'm one of the instigators of the Narducci killing! The newspapers have all been writing the same thing, a strong indication that they have been using the same source, well informed, and certainly official. What does that make me?"

Pace, turn.

"Doug, do you realize what they really think? I'm not just an accessory or someone involved in the Narducci killing. I'm one of the *masterminds* behind the Monster killings. *They think I'm the Monster!*"

"Give me a cigarette," I said. I didn't normally smoke but now I needed it.

Spezi gave me a cigarette and lit another one for himself.

Myriam began to cry. Zaccaria sat on the edge of the sofa, his long hair disheveled, his once crisp suit limp and wrinkled.

"Consider this," Spezi said. "I'm supposed to have planted the Monster's gun at the villa to incriminate an innocent man. Where did I get the Monster's gun, if I'm not the Monster myself?"

The ash hung in a curl from the end of his cigarette.

"Where's the damn ashtray?"

I fetched Spezi and myself a plate from the kitchen. Spezi stubbed out his half-smoked cigarette with violence and lit another. "I'll tell you where Mignini gets these ideas. It's that woman from Rome, Gabriella Carlizzi, the one who said the cult of the Red Rose was behind the 9/11 attacks. Have you read her website? This is the woman the public minister of Perugia listens to!"

Spezi had gone full circle, from Monstrologer to Monster.

I left Italy the next morning. When I returned to my house in Maine, which stands on a bluff overlooking the gray Atlantic, and I listened to the rhythmic breakers on the rocks below and the seagulls wheeling above, I was so glad to be free, so happy not to be rotting in some Italian jail, that I felt the tears trickling down my face.

Count Niccolò called me the day after my return. "So, Douglas! I see you have been making trouble in Italy! Good show!"

"How did you know?"

"They say in the papers this morning that you're now an official suspect in the Monster of Florence case."

"It's in the papers?"

"Everywhere." He laughed quietly. "Don't be concerned."

"Niccolò, for God's sake, they accused me of being an accessory to murder, they said I planted a gun at that villa, they've indicted me for making false statements and obstruction of justice! They threatened me if I ever return to Italy. And you tell me I shouldn't be concerned?"

"My dear Douglas, anyone who is anybody in Italy is *indagato*. I offer you my congratulations on becoming a genuine Italian." His voice lost its cynical drawl and became serious. "It is our mutual friend Spezi who should be concerned. *Very* concerned."

CHAPTER
48

I began to make calls to the press as soon as I got home. I was terrified for Mario; he was obviously their real target. I hoped that if I could make a big enough stink in America, it might provide Spezi with some protection against an arbitrary and capricious arrest.

When Spezi had had his house searched, the American press could not have cared less about an Italian journalist who had his papers taken away. But now, because an American was the target, the press picked it up. "Trapped in His Own Thriller" ran the front-page headline in the *Boston Globe*. "Life was fine for Douglas Preston as he worked on his latest book. Then he became part of the story." The *Washington Post* ran a piece: "Best-selling thriller author Douglas Preston entangled in probe of Tuscan serial killings." Stories went out on the AP wire, and news items appeared on CNN and ABC News.

Back in Italy, the papers were also full of my interrogation. A headline in the *Corriere della Sera* read:

MONSTER CASE:
DUEL BETWEEN PUBLIC MINISTER AND
AMERICAN WRITER

Serial killings of Florence. Thriller writer indicted for
perjury. His colleagues mobilize.

A report went out over ANSA, the Italian news agency: "The prosecutor's office of Perugia interrogated the American writer Douglas Preston as a material witness, and then indicted him for perjury.
Preston and Mario Spezi have written a book on the case, which will
be published in April, entitled *Dolci Colline di Sangue*, which Spezi has
called a kind of counterinvestigation to the official one. Two years
ago, Spezi was investigated for being an accessory to the murder of
Narducci, and subsequently he was accused of participating in the
murder." Other articles contained information that appeared to have
been leaked from Mignini's office, claiming that Spezi and I had tried
to plant the infamous .22 Beretta—the Monster's pistol—at the villa,
in order to frame an innocent man.

But the bright light of press scrutiny and publicity, if anything,
seemed to make Giuttari and Mignini more aggressive. On February 25, two days after I left Italy, the police raided Spezi's apartment
yet again. He was placed under intense police surveillance, followed
whenever he left his house and secretly videotaped. His phones were
tapped and he assumed his apartment had also been bugged and his
e-mail was being intercepted.

In order to communicate, Spezi and I arranged for the use of various e-mail addresses and borrowed phones. Spezi managed to send
an e-mail to me from an Internet café after losing his police tail. In
it he proposed a system: when he sent me an e-mail from his regular
account saying *"salutami a Christine"* ("say hi to Christine for me"), it
meant he wanted me to call him on a borrowed telephone number the
following day at a certain time.

Niccolò regularly sent me news stories about the case, and we spoke
often by telephone.

On March 1, Spezi finally took his car to a neighborhood mechanic
to fix the broken door and put in a new radio. The mechanic emerged
from the car holding a fistful of sophisticated electronic equipment
from which dangled red and black wires. It consisted of a black box

the size of a cigarette package, with a piece of tape covering the LCDs indicating "On" and "Off," wired to a second mysterious device, two inches by five, which had been connected to the old radio's power supply wires.

"I don't know a lot," said the mechanic, "but this looks like a microphone and recorder to me."

He went around and opened the hood. "And that," he said, pointing to another black cigarette pack tucked in a corner, "must be the GPS."

Spezi called *La Nazione*, and they sent a photographer to take pictures of the journalist holding up the electronic equipment in both hands, like a pair of prize fish.

That very day Spezi went to the prosecutor's office in Florence and filed a legal complaint against persons unknown, seeking damages for the wrecking of his car. He presented himself to a prosecutor in Florence, a man he knew, with the complaint in hand. The man didn't want to touch it. "This business, Dr. Spezi, is far too delicate," he said. "Present your complaint in person to the head prosecutor." So Spezi carried it into the office of the head prosecutor, where, after having to wait, a policeman came and took the complaint, saying the prosecutor would accept it. Spezi heard nothing more about it.

On March 15, 2006, Spezi received a call from his local carabinieri post, inviting him down to the barracks. He was received in a tiny room by an officer who seemed strangely embarrassed. "We're giving you back your car radio," the man explained.

Spezi was flabbergasted. "You're . . . *admitting* you took it and wrecked my car doing it?"

"No, not us!" He fiddled nervously with his papers. "We were given the job of returning it by the prosecutor's office of Perugia, by Judge Mignini, who gave the orders to Chief Inspector Giuttari of GIDES to return your radio."

Spezi with difficulty tried to stifle a laugh. "That's incredible! You mean they actually put it in an official document that they wrecked my car to steal my radio?"

The carabinieri officer shifted uncomfortably. "Sign here, please."

"Well," Spezi said triumphantly, "what if they broke it? I can't possibly take it back without knowing!"

"Spezi, will you just sign, please?"

Spezi quickly filed a second complaint for damages, this time against Mignini and Giuttari, now that they had (unaccountably) provided him with the very proof he needed.

In that same month, March 2006, Giuttari's new book on the Monster of Florence was published by RCS Libri, *The Monster: Anatomy of an Investigation*, and it became a huge best-seller. In the book, Giuttari took several shots at Spezi, accusing him of being an accessory to Narducci's murder and darkly hinting that he was involved in some way in the Monster killings.

Spezi promptly filed a civil lawsuit against the chief inspector for libeling him in the book and for violating the laws of judicial secrecy relating to the Monster case. The lawsuit was filed in Milan, where Giuttari's book was published by Rizzoli, another imprint of our publisher, RCS Libri. (In Italy libel suits must be filed in the place of publication.) It asked for the seizure and destruction of all copies of Giuttari's book. "It is no pleasure for a writer to call for the seizure of a book," Spezi wrote, "but this is the only remedy that will limit the damage to my reputation."

Spezi wrote most of the lawsuit himself, every word perfectly pitched to infuriate his foe:

> For more than a year, I have been the victim not just of half-baked police work, but of what could be said to be authentic violations of civil rights. This phenomenon—which pertains not just to me, but to many others—brings to mind the most dysfunctional societies, such as one might expect to find in Asia or Africa.
>
> Mr. Michele Giuttari, a functionary of the State Police, is the inventor and indefatigable promoter of a theory, according to which the crimes of the so-called Monster of Florence are the work of a mysterious satanic, esoteric, and magical sect, an organized "group" of upper-middle-class professionals (bureaucrats,

police and carabinieri, magistrates—and in their service, writers and journalists) who commissioned individuals from the very poorest levels of society to commit serial killings of pairs of lovers, paying handsomely to gain possession of female anatomical parts with the goal of using them in certain inscrutable, undetermined, and otherwise improbable "rites."

According to the fantastic conjectures of this self-described brilliant and diligent investigator, this criminal assembly of seemingly upstanding persons dedicated itself to orgies, sadomasochism, pedophilia, and other vile abominations.

Spezi then proceeded to deliver an uppercut to Giuttari's soft underbelly—his literary talent. In the lawsuit, Spezi quoted extract after extract from Giuttari's book, savaging his logic, ridiculing his theories, and mocking his writing ability.

The suit was dated March 23 and filed a week later, on March 30, 2006.

CHAPTER
49

Back in America, I watched the gathering storm from afar. Spezi and I had received a curt e-mail from our editor at RCS Libri, who was seriously alarmed at what was happening. She was terrified that the publishing house would be dragged into a legal mess, and she was particularly incensed that I had given her telephone number to the reporter for the *Boston Globe*, who had called and asked her to comment. "I must tell you," she wrote me and Mario, "that this call seriously annoyed me. . . . Right or wrong, personal disputes have nothing to do with me nor do they interest me. . . . I pray both of you to keep RCS out of any eventual legal disputes connected to your personal business."

Meanwhile, curious to find out more about this Gabriella Carlizzi and her website, on a whim I went online and checked it out. What I read infuriated me. Carlizzi had posted pages of personal information on me. With the diligence of a rat collecting its winter store of seeds, she had gathered bits and pieces of information about me from all over the Web, managed to find someone to translate it all into Italian (she herself was monolingual), and had mixed it all together with out-of-context excerpts from my novels—usually descriptions of people being murdered. She managed to dig up public remarks I had made in

Italy that I had no idea were even being taped, and she made particular use of a lame joke I had told at a book presentation, that had Mario Spezi decided not to write about crime, he would have made a marvelous criminal himself. To this brew she added her own sinister insinuations, creepy asides, and animadversions. The end result was a toxic portrait of me as a mentally disturbed person who wrote novels full of gratuitous violence that toadied to the basest human instincts.

That was bad enough. But what really enraged me the most was to see my wife's and children's names, taken from my biography, posted next to pictures of the serial killer Jeffrey Dahmer and the burning Twin Towers.

I fired off an outraged e-mail to Carlizzi, demanding that my wife's and children's names be removed from her website.

Her response to my e-mail was unexpectedly mild, even ingratiating. She apologized and promised to take down the names, which she promptly did.

My e-mail had achieved the results I'd hoped, but now Carlizzi had my e-mail address. She wrote me back: "Even if brief, our little exchange of ideas, touching as they do upon spheres both delicate and in a certain sense intimate, it seems silly to address each other formally using '*lei*.' Souls, when they speak from the heart, speak to each other using '*tu*.' Would it displease you, Douglas, if we used the '*tu*' form with each other?"

I should have known better than to reply to that one. But I did.

A flood of e-mails from Carlizzi followed, each one running to many pages, written in an Italian so contorted, so full of smarmy confidences and loopy conspiracy logic that they were almost impossible to decipher. Decipher them I did.

Gabriella Carlizzi knew the truth about the Monster of Florence, and she desperately wanted to share it with me.

Hi Douglas, did you get my long e-mail? Are you perhaps frightened of the fact that I asked you to reserve the front page of *The New Yorker* to reveal the name and the face of the Monster of Florence? . . . I will write on my website a piece, declaring my invitation to you to reserve this prestigious page, and I will notify *The New Yorker* as well . . .

Re: I PRAY YOU . . . YOU MUST BELIEVE ME . . . IF ONLY YOU AND YOUR WIFE COULD LOOK INTO MY EYES . . .

Dearest Douglas,

. . . Know that even while I write you, I am thinking that I am speaking not just to you, but also to your wife, and to those you love and that I know well how much they mean to your life as a man, beyond that of a journalist and a writer, but simply a man, a friend, a father. . . . I have embarked on this battle, this search for the truth, I do it only to maintain a promise I made to the Good Lord and to my Spiritual Father, a famous Exorcist, Father Gabriele . . . I made this promise, Douglas, as a way of thanking the Lord for the miracle of my own son Fulvio, who after only a quarter of a day of life died, and while in the hospital, when they were dressing him for his coffin, I telephoned to Father Gabriele for a blessing, and the Father answered me, "Don't pay it any mind my daughter, your son will live longer than Methuselah." After a few instants, a hundred doctors in the hospital of San Giovanni in Rome cried out, "But it is a miracle, the baby is revived." Back then I didn't have the Faith I have now, but with regard to the gift God gave to me, in some way, sooner or later, I would have to pay him back. . . . Dear Douglas, I have the photographs of every crime, when the victims became aware of the Monster, and screamed, their scream was photographed by a minicamera given by the secret service. . . .

. . . And I found, dear Douglas, in Japan, a document that I think is useful, which would prevent the Monster from killing someone close to you. I am undertaking investigations of this document. . . .

Look at the article I have published on my site, where I have written that truly I invite you to come to see me, and to prepare the first page of *The New Yorker* . . . I wrote that only to convince you that I am not joking.

Alarmed by these references to *The New Yorker* and this business of the Monster killing "someone close" to me, which would appear from the creepy references to be my wife, I went back to Carlizzi's site and discovered she had added a page, in which she reproduced the cover of my novel *Brimstone* next to the cover of a novel Spezi had written, *Il Passo Dell'Orco*.

Gabriella [read the website] *has not wasted any time and has invited Preston to come visit her and gaze with his own eyes on the Monster and his victims. She puts it in black and white and responds to the e-mail of Preston:* "Save the front page of The New Yorker *and come to me, I will give you the scoop that you've been waiting for for a long time." How will Douglas react? Will he accept the invitation or suffer the prohibition of an Italian friend? Certainly* The New Yorker *will not let this scoop slip away. . . .*

And above all—she continues—I want to serenely ask Douglas Preston: "You, what would happen to you if one day proof comes in that 'your' Monster is a blunder, while the real Monster is another. . . . You would discover that he is very close to you, that you worked with him, you became friends with him, you held him in esteem as a professional, and that never did you perceive that inside such a person so cultivated, so sensitive, so full of goodwill, there was a labyrinth in which the Beast had hidden itself since completing its Great Work of Death . . . a Monster who is respected, who knows how to fool everyone. . . . Wouldn't that be for you, dear Preston, the most upsetting experience of your life? Then you surely could write the most unique thriller in the world, and perhaps, with the royalties you receive, even buy The New Yorker.

So that was it. Spezi was the Monster. The flood of crazy e-mails came in like the tide at full moon, hitting my inbox multiple times during the course of each day. In them Carlizzi elaborated on her theories and urged and begged me to come to Florence. She hinted that she had a special relationship with the public minister, and that if I came to Italy she could guarantee I would not be arrested. She would, in fact, see to it that the charges against me were dropped.

. . . Florence has always been under orders to protect the true Monster, and these orders come from on high, because the Monster could at any time reveal horrible things regarding the pedophilia of illustrious magistrates, who because of this threat of blackmail will never capture him. Dear Douglas, you, unknowingly, are being used, in Italy, by the Monster, who uses as a cover illustrious names. . . . I pray you, Douglas, come to me immediately even with your wife, or give

me your telephone number, I have sent you mine, we will consult with each other . . . don't say anything to Spezi. . . . I will explain all. . . . I pray to God that you and your wife will believe me . . . I can show you everything. . . .

●

One day, if you would care to write my biography, you will realize that you can leap beyond fantasy and fiction, with a true story.

●

You can well imagine that the investigation marches along even at night and on holidays. For this I pray you CONTACT ME WITH THE GREATEST URGENCY! . . . Remember: this is to be treated with the maximum secrecy.

●

Dear Douglas, I still haven't received a response to my e-mails: is there a problem? I pray you, let me know, I am worried and I want to understand what to do to bring clarity.

I soon stopped reading all but the subject lines:

Re: WHERE ARE YOU?

Re: LET US PRAY FOR MARIO SPEZI.

Re: NOW DO YOU BELIEVE ME?

Re: URGENTISSIMO URGENTISSIMO

And finally, forty-one e-mails later:

Re: BUT WHAT IN THE WORLD HAS HAPPENED TO YOU?

The e-mail barrage left me reeling, not from the sheer madness of it, but from the fact that the public minister of Perugia and a chief inspector of police took a person like this seriously. And yet, as Carlizzi herself claimed, and as Spezi's later investigative work would show, this woman was the key witness who had convinced Judge Mignini and Chief Inspector Giuttari that the death of Narducci was connected—through a satanic sect—to the crimes of the Monster of Florence. It was Carlizzi who directed the public minister's suspicions to Spezi and who first claimed he was involved in the so-called murder of Narducci. (Spezi was later able to show that entire paragraphs in legal documents produced by the public minister's office closely paralleled the paranoid ramblings that Carlizzi had earlier posted at her website. Carlizzi, it might seem, had a Rasputin-like influence over Mignini.)

Even more incredibly, Gabriella Carlizzi had somehow managed to become an "expert" in the Monster case. Around the same time she was filling my inbox with e-mails, she was much sought after by magazines and newspapers in Italy to comment on the Monster investigation, and quoted at length as a reliable expert. She appeared on some of the most noted talk shows in Italy, where she was treated as a serious and thoughtful person.

In the middle of this bombardment, I mentioned to Mario that I'd been exchanging e-mails with Carlizzi. He chided me. "Doug, you may find it amusing, but you're playing with fire. She can do great harm. For God's sake, stay away from her."

Carlizzi, for all her craziness, seemed to have excellent sources of information. I had been shocked at what she'd managed to dig up on me. Sometimes, she seemed almost prescient in her predications about the case, so much so that Spezi and I wondered if she might not have an inside source in the public minister's office.

At the end of March, Carlizzi had some special news to announce on her site: the arrest of Mario Spezi was imminent.

CHAPTER
50

The call came on Friday, April 7, 2006. Count Niccolò's voice boomed over the transatlantic line. "They've just arrested Spezi," he said. "Giuttari's men came to his house, lured him outside, and bundled him in a car. I don't know any more than that. The news is just breaking."

I could hardly speak. I never really believed it would go this far. I croaked out a stupid question. "Arrested? What for?"

"You know very well what for. For several years now, he has made Giuttari, a Sicilian, look like an arrant fool in front of the entire nation. No Italian could tolerate that! And I have to say, dear Douglas, that Mario has a wickedly sharp pen. It's all about *face*, something you Anglo-Saxons will never understand."

"What's going to happen?"

Niccolò drew a long breath. "This time they have gone too far. Giuttari and Mignini have stepped over the line. This is too much. Italy will be embarrassed before the world, and that cannot be allowed to happen. Giuttari will take the fall. As for Mignini, the judiciary will close ranks and wash their dirty linen behind closed doors. Giuttari's comeuppance may very well come at him from an entirely different direction, but he is going down—mark my words."

"But what will happen to Mario?"

"He will, unfortunately, spend some time in prison."

"I hope to God it won't be long."

"I will find out all I can and call you back."

I had a sudden thought. "Niccolò, you should be careful. You're the perfect candidate for this satanic sect yourself . . . a count from one of the oldest families of Florence."

Niccolò laughed heartily. "The idea has already crossed my mind." He broke out in a singsong Italian, as if reciting a nursery rhyme, speaking not to me, but to a hypothetical person wiretapping our telephone conversation.

> *Brigadiere Cuccurullo,*
> *Mi raccomando, segni tutto!*

> Brigadier Cuccurullo,
> Be sure to record everything!

"I always feel so dreadfully sorry for the poor fellow who has to listen to these calls. *Mi sente, Brigadiere Gennaro Cuccurullo? Mi dispiace per lei! Segni tutto!*" ("Are you listening, Brigadier Gennaro Cuccurullo? I am sorry for you! Record everything!")

"Do you really think your phone is being tapped?" I asked.

"Bah! This is Italy. They're probably tapping the pope's telephones."

There was no answer at Spezi's house. I went online to look for news. The story was just breaking on ANSA, the Italian news agency, and Reuters:

MONSTER OF FLORENCE:
JOURNALIST SPEZI ARRESTED
FOR OBSTRUCTION OF JUSTICE

Our book was to be published in twelve days. I was seized with fear that this was a prelude to stopping publication of the book, or that our publisher would get cold feet and withdraw it. I called our editor at

Sonzogno. She was already in a meeting about the situation and un-available, but I spoke to her later. She was rattled by Spezi's arrest—it isn't often that one of your best-selling authors orders the arrest of another one—and she was angry at me and Spezi. Her view was that Spezi, in pursuing a "personal" vendetta against Giuttari, had unnecessarily provoked the chief inspector, possibly dragging RCS Libri into an ugly legal mess. I rather hotly pointed out that Spezi and I were pursuing our legitimate rights as journalists seeking the truth, and that we had broken no laws nor done anything unethical. She seemed, to my surprise, to be somewhat skeptical of that last assertion. It was an attitude I would find all too prevalent among Italians.

News from the meeting, at least, was encouraging. RCS Libri had made a decision to forge ahead with publication of our book. More than that, the house would push the book's distribution up by a week to get it into the bookstores quickly. As part of this effort, RCS had ordered the release of the book from their warehouses as soon as possible. Once out of the warehouse, it would be far more difficult for the police to seize the print run, since the books would be scattered across Italy in thousands of bookstores.

I finally got hold of Myriam Spezi. She was holding up, but barely. "They tricked him into coming down to the gate," she said. "He was in slippers, he had nothing with him, not even his wallet. They refused to show a warrant. They threatened him and forced him in a car and took him away." They drove him first to GIDES's headquarters in the Il Magnifico building for an interrogation and then spirited him away, sirens blaring, to the grim Capanne prison in Perugia.

The evening news in Italy carried the story. Flashing pictures of Spezi, the Monster's murder scenes, the victims, and pictures of Giuttari and Mignini, the announcer intoned, "Mario Spezi, the writer and longtime chronicler of the Monster of Florence case, was arrested with the ex-convict Luigi Ruocco, accused of having obstructed the investigation into the murder of Francesco Narducci . . . in order to cover up the doctor's role in the Monster of Florence murders. The public minister of Perugia . . . hypothesizes that the two tried to plant false evidence at Villa Bibbiani in Capraia, including objects and documents, as a way to force the reopening of the Sardinian investigation, closed in the nineties. Their motive was to divert attention from the investigations linking Mario Spezi and the pharmacist of San Casciano, Francesco Calamandrei, with the murder of Francesco Narducci . . ."

And then a video of me appeared on the television, taken as I walked out of Mignini's office after the interrogation.

"For the same alleged crime," the announcer said, "two other people are under investigation, an ex–inspector of police and the American writer Douglas Preston, who with Mario Spezi has just written a book on the Monster of Florence."

Among the many calls I received, one came from the State Department. A pleasant woman informed me that the American embassy in Rome had made inquiries about my status to the public minister of Perugia. The embassy could confirm that I was indeed *indagato*—that is, a person officially suspected of committing a crime.

"Did you ask what the *evidence* was against me?"

"We don't get into the details of cases. All we can do is clarify your status."

"My status was already clear to me, thank you very much, it's in every paper in Italy!"

The woman cleared her throat and asked if I had engaged a lawyer in Italy.

"Lawyers cost money," I muttered.

"Mr. Preston," she said, in a not unkindly tone of voice, "this is a very serious matter. It isn't going to go away. It's only going to get worse, and even with a lawyer it could drag on for years. You can't let it fester. You've got to spend the money and hire a lawyer. I'll have our embassy in Rome e-mail you their list. We can't recommend any particular one, unfortunately, because—"

"I know," I said. "You're not in the business of rating Italian lawyers."

At the end of the conversation, she asked, tentatively, "You aren't, by any chance, planning a return to Italy in the near future?"

"Are you kidding?"

"I'm *so* glad to hear that." The relief in her voice was palpable.

"We certainly wouldn't want the, ah, problem of dealing with your arrest."

The list arrived. It was mostly lawyers who dealt in child custody cases, real estate transactions, and contract law. Only a handful dealt in criminal matters.

I called a lawyer on the list at random and spoke to him in Rome. He'd been reading the papers and already knew of the case. He was very glad to hear from me. I had reached the right person. He would interrupt his important work to take the case, and enlist as a partner one of the preeminent lawyers in Italy, whose name would be well known and respected by the public minister of Perugia. The very hiring of such an important man would go halfway toward settling my case—that was how things worked in Italy. By hiring him, I would show the public minister that I was a *uomo serio*, a man not to be trifled with. When I timidly inquired about the fee, he said it would take a mere twenty-five thousand euros, as a retainer, to get the ball rolling—and that low, *low* fee (practically pro bono) was only possible because of the high profile of the case and its implications for freedom of the press. He would be glad to e-mail me the fund-wiring instructions, but I had to act *that very day* because this most-important-lawyer-in-Italy's schedule was filling up . . .

I went to the next lawyer on the list, and then the next. I finally found one who would take my case for about six thousand euros and who actually sounded like a lawyer, not a used-car salesman.

Before Mario's arrest, we would later learn, Villa Bibbiani in Capraia and its grounds were searched by the men of GIDES, looking for the gun, objects, boxes, or documents we were supposed to have planted. Nothing was found. To the ever resourceful Giuttari, this was not at all a problem. He had acted so promptly, he said, that we hadn't time to carry out our nefarious plot—he had stopped it dead in its tracks.

CHAPTER
51

On April 7, the day of his arrest, Spezi finally arrived at Capanne prison, twenty kilometers outside Perugia. He was hustled into the prison grounds and brought to a room with nothing but a blanket spread on the cement floor, a table, a chair, and a cardboard box.

His guards told him to empty his pockets. Spezi did so. They told him to take off his watch and the crucifix he wore around his neck. Then one of them yelled at him to strip.

Spezi took off his sweater, shirt, and undershirt, and shoes. And waited.

"Everything. If your feet are cold, stand on the blanket."

Spezi stripped until he was completely naked.

"Bend over three times," the head guard ordered him.

Spezi wasn't sure what he meant.

"Do like this," said another, demonstrating a crouch. "All the way to the ground. Three times. And push."

After a degrading search, he was told to dress himself in the prison garb he would find in the cardboard box. The guards allowed him a single pack of cigarettes. They filled out some forms and ushered him to a cold cell. One of the guards opened the door and Spezi went in.

Behind him, he heard the four loud clashings of steel as the cell door was slammed shut and barred, and the lock turned.

His dinner that night was bread and water.

The next morning, April 8, Spezi was allowed to meet with one of his lawyers, who had arrived at the prison early. Later, he would supposedly be allowed a short visit with his wife. The guards escorted him into a room where he found his lawyer seated at a table, a stack of files in front of him. They had barely exchanged greetings when a new guard rushed in with a big smile on his pockmarked face.

"This meeting is canceled. Orders of the prosecutor's office. Counsel, if you don't mind—?"

Spezi barely had the time to tell his lawyer to reassure his wife that he was well, before he was hauled back and locked up in isolation.

For five days, Spezi wouldn't know why he had been suddenly denied a lawyer and placed in isolation. The rest of Italy learned the next morning. The day of Spezi's arrest, Public Minister Mignini had asked the examining magistrate in Spezi's case, Judge Marina De Robertis, to invoke a law normally used only against dangerous terrorists and Mafia kingpins who pose an imminent threat to the state. Spezi would be denied access to his lawyers and kept in isolation. The purpose of the law was to prevent a violent criminal from ordering the killing or intimidation of witnesses through his lawyers or visitors. Now it was applied against the extremely dangerous journalist Mario Spezi. The press noted that Spezi's treatment in prison was even harsher than that meted out to Bernardo Provenzano, the Mafia boss of bosses, captured near Corleone, Sicily, four days after Spezi was arrested.

For five days, nobody had any idea of what had happened to Spezi, where he was, or what they might be doing to him. His judicial disappearance caused exquisite psychological anguish to all of his friends and family. The authorities refused to release any information about him, his state of health, or the conditions of his imprisonment. Spezi simply vanished into the black maw of Capanne prison.

CHAPTER
52

Back in America, I recalled Niccolò's words—that Italy would be ashamed before the world. I was determined to make that happen. I hoped to cause an uproar in America that would embarrass the Italian state and force it to remedy this miscarriage of justice.

I called every organization I knew that was concerned with freedom of the press. I wrote an appeal and broadcast it on the Web. It concluded, "I ask all of you, please, for the love of truth and freedom of the press, come to Spezi's aid. This should not be happening in the beautiful and civilized country that I love, the country that gave the world the Renaissance." The appeal included the names, addresses, and e-mail addresses of the prime minister of Italy, Silvio Berlusconi, the minister of the interior, and the minister of justice. The appeal was picked up and published at many websites, translated into Italian and Japanese, and written about by various bloggers.

The Boston branch of PEN organized an effective letter-writing campaign. A novelist friend of mine, David Morrell (the creator of Rambo), wrote a letter of protest to the Italian government, as did many other well-known writers who belonged to International Thriller Writers (ITW), an organization I helped found. Many of these writers were best-selling authors in Italy, too, and their names carried weight. I received an assignment from the *Atlantic Monthly* to write a story about the Monster case and Spezi's arrest.

The worst was not knowing. Spezi's disappearance created a void filled with grim speculations and terrible rumors. Spezi was at the mercy of the public minister of Perugia, a man of great power, and Chief Inspector Giuttari, whom the newspapers had dubbed *il super-poliziotto*, the supercop, because he operated with an apparent lack of oversight. For those five silent days I woke up thinking of Spezi in prison, not knowing what they might be doing to him, and it drove me crazy. We all have a psychological breaking point and I wondered whether they would find Spezi's—because breaking him was surely their plan.

Every morning I would sit in my hut in the Maine woods, having made every call I could think of, shaking with frustration, feeling powerless while waiting for return phone calls, waiting for the organizations I had contacted to take some kind of action.

The managing editor of *The New Yorker* had put me in touch with Ann Cooper, executive director of the Committee to Protect Journalists (CPJ), a New York–based organization. This organization, above all others, understood the urgency of the situation and leapt into action. CPJ immediately launched an independent investigation of the Spezi case in Italy, directed by Nina Ognianova, program coordinator for Europe, interviewing journalists, police, judges, and colleagues of Spezi.

In the early days following Spezi's arrest, most of the major daily newspapers in Italy—especially in Tuscany and Umbria, and particularly Mario's home paper, *La Nazione*—shied away from covering the full story. They reported Spezi's arrest and the charges against him, but they treated it as a simple crime story. Most remained silent on the larger questions of freedom of the press raised by the arrest. There were almost no protests. Few journalists commented on one of the most insidious charges against Spezi, that of "obstructing an official investigation by means of the press." (Inside *La Nazione*, we would learn later, a number of Spezi colleagues were fighting with the paper's management over the newspaper's lily-livered coverage.)

In my conversations with Italian friends and journalists, I was surprised to discover that quite a few suspected that at least some of the accusations were true. Perhaps, some of my Italian colleagues demurred, I didn't understand Italy well after all, as this was the sort of thing Italian journalists did all the time. They viewed my outrage as naïve and a bit gauche. To be outraged is to be earnest, to be sincere—and to be a dupe. Some Italians were quick to strike the pose of the world-weary cynic who takes nothing at face value and who is far too clever to be taken in by Spezi's and my protestations of innocence.

"Ah!" said Count Niccolò in one of our frequent conversations. "*Of course* Spezi and you were up to no good at that villa! *Dietrologia* insists that it be so. Only a naïf would believe that you two journalists went to the villa 'just to have a look.' The police wouldn't have arrested Spezi for no reason! You see, Douglas, an Italian must always appear to be *furbo*. You don't have an English equivalent for that marvelous word. It means a person who is wily and cunning, who knows which way the wind is blowing, who can fool you but never be fooled himself. Everyone in Italy wants to believe the worst of others so they don't end up looking gullible. Above all, they want to be seen as *furbo*."

I had trouble, as an American, appreciating the climate of fear and intimidation in Italy surrounding the issue. True freedom of the press does not exist in Italy, especially since any public official can ask that criminal charges be lodged against a journalist for "*diffamazione a mezzo stampa*"—defamation by means of the press.

The intimidation of the press was particularly evident in the refusal of our book publisher, RCS Libri, part of one of the largest publishing conglomerates in the world, to make a statement of support for Spezi. Indeed, our editor assiduously avoided the press except when tracked down by a reporter from the *Boston Globe*. "Journalist Spezi and the main police investigator hate each other," she told the *Globe*. "Why? I don't know. . . . If they [Preston and Spezi] think they have discovered something useful to police and law, they should say something without insulting police and judges."

Meanwhile, from the Capanne prison near Perugia, there was no word on the fate of Mario Spezi.

CHAPTER
53

On April 12, the five-day blackout was lifted, and Spezi was finally allowed to meet with his lawyers. On that day, his case would be reviewed by the examining magistrate, Marina De Robertis, in the Italian equivalent of a habeas corpus hearing. Its purpose was to determine if Spezi's arrest and incarceration were justified.

On that day, for the hearing, Spezi was for the first time given a change of clothes, a bar of soap, and a chance to shave and take a bath. The public minister, Guiliano Mignini, appeared before Judge De Robertis to argue why Spezi was a danger to society.

"The journalist," Mignini wrote in his brief, "accused of obstructing the investigation of the Monster of Florence is at the center of a genuine disinformation campaign, not unlike that which might be undertaken by a deviant secret service." This disinformation operation, Mignini explained, was an attempt to derail the investigation into the "group of notable people" who had been the masterminds behind the killings of the Monster of Florence. Among these notables was Narducci, who had hired and directed Pacciani and his picnicking friends to kill young lovers and take their body parts. Spezi and his fellow criminal masterminds had a strategy: to keep the blame for the

Monster of Florence murders restricted to Pacciani and his picnicking friends. When that strategy failed, and the investigation began to
strike closer to home—with the reopening of Narducci's death—Spezi
had desperately tried to redirect the investigation back to the Sardinian Trail, because "in that case there wouldn't be even the minimum
danger that the investigation might touch the world of the notables
and the masterminds."

The statement included not a shred of solid forensic evidence—just
a cockamamie conspiracy theory spun out to fantastic lengths.

Dietrologia at its purest.

At the hearing, Spezi protested the conditions in which he was
being held. He insisted he was merely conducting legitimate research
as a journalist, not running a "disinformation campaign of a deviant
secret service."

Judge Marina De Robertis looked at Spezi and asked a single question: the only question she would ask during the entire hearing.

"Have you ever belonged to a satanic sect?"

At first Spezi wasn't sure he had heard correctly. His lawyer nudged
him in the side and hissed, "Don't laugh!"

A simple no to the question seemed insufficient. Dryly, Spezi said,
"The only order I'm a member of is the Order of Journalists."

With that, the hearing was over.

The judge took four leisurely days making up her mind. On Saturday, Spezi met with his lawyer to hear the verdict.

"I have good news and bad news," said Traversi. "Which do you
want to hear first?"

"The bad news."

Judge De Robertis had ruled he must remain in preventive detention, because of the danger he posed to society.

"And the good news?"

Traversi had seen, in the window of a bookstore in Florence, a
bunch of copies of *Dolci Colline di Sangue* for sale. The book was finally out.

CHAPTER
54

Meanwhile, Chief Inspector Giuttari forged ahead with the investigation, "toscano" cigar clamped between his determined teeth. For some time, the lack of a second body in the so-called Narducci murder had been an embarrassment, two corpses being necessary to make the double switch with Narducci's. Giuttari finally found a suitable body in that of a South American, bashed on the head, which had been left unclaimed in the morgue of Perugia since 1982, kept under refrigeration. The man seemed, at least to some, to resemble the dead body of Narducci in the photograph taken on the dock after he had been fished out of the water. After Narducci had been murdered, the body of this previously dead South American had been stolen from the morgue and dumped in the lake in its stead, Narducci's body had been hidden, perhaps in the morgue, perhaps somewhere else. Then, many years later, when the exhumation of Narducci looked imminent, the bodies were switched again, Narducci's being put back in his coffin and the South American's spirited away and parked back in the refrigerator.

With Spezi in prison, Giuttari spoke to *La Nazione* about the excellent progress he was making in the Narducci case: "Yes, we're working on the death of this man which occurred in '82, and there are elements that are quite interesting and which may lead us to something concrete. . . . I believe that it is now beyond doubt that the body recovered from Lake Trasimeno was not Narducci's. . . . And now, in light of these new facts, the situation may become clearer." But something must have gone wrong with this particular theory, since the dead South American was never mentioned by Giuttari again and the facts surrounding the alleged double body switch remained—and still remain—as murky as ever.

Spezi's lawyers began working to obtain a hearing before the Tribunal of Reexamination, an appeals court for those ordered imprisoned before trial, similar to a bail hearing in the United States, to determine whether there were grounds to hold Spezi in "preventive detention" until the time of his trial, or to release him under house arrest or other conditions. Italian law has no provisions for monetary bail, and the judgment is made on the basis of how dangerous the accused is and whether there is a likelihood he will flee the country.

A date was set for Spezi's hearing: April 28. The review would take place before three other judges from Perugia, close colleagues of the public minister and of the examining magistrate. The Tribunal of Reexamination was not known for reversing its colleagues, especially in a highly visible case like this one, on which the public minister had placed all his credibility as a prosecutor.

On April 18, twelve days after Spezi's arrest, the Committee to Protect Journalists had finished its investigation into Spezi's case. The next day, Ann Cooper, the executive director, faxed a letter to the prime minister of Italy. It said, in part:

> Journalists should not be fearful to conduct their own investigations into sensitive matters or to speak openly and criticize officials. In a democratic country such as your own, one that is an integral part of the European Union, such fear is unacceptable. We call on you to make sure that Italian authorities clarify the serious charges against our colleague Mario Spezi and make public all available evidence supporting those charges, or release him immediately.

The persecution of Mario Spezi and his U.S. colleague Douglas

Preston, who is afraid to travel to Italy for fear of prosecution, sends a dangerous message to Italian journalists that sensitive stories such as the Tuscany killings should be avoided. Government efforts to promote this climate of self-censorship are anathema to democracy.

Copies of the letter went to Public Minister Mignini, the U.S. ambassador to Italy, the Italian ambassador to the United States, Amnesty International, Freedom Forum, Human Rights Watch, and a dozen other international organizations.

This letter, along with protests from other international organizations, including Reporters sans Frontières in Paris, seemed to turn the tide in Italy. The Italian press found its courage—with a vengeance.

"The Jailing of Spezi Is an Infamy," cried an editorial in *Libero*, written by the vice director of the magazine. *Corriere della Sera* ran a major editorial on the front page entitled "Justice without Evidence," calling Spezi's arrest a "monstrosity." The Italian press finally took up the question of what Spezi's arrest meant for freedom of the press and Italy's international image. A flood of articles followed. Spezi's colleagues at *La Nazione* signed an appeal, and the paper issued a statement. Many journalists began to recognize that Spezi's arrest was an attack on a journalist for the "crime" of disagreeing with an official investigation—in other words, the criminalization of journalism itself. Protests mounted in Italy from press organizations and newspapers. A group of eminent journalists and writers signed an appeal, which said in part, "Frankly, we did not think that in Italy the strenuous search for the truth could be misunderstood as illegally favoring and assisting the guilty."

"The case of Spezi and Preston casts a heavy weight on the international image of our country," the president of Italy's Information Safety and Freedom organization told the *Guardian* newspaper of London, "and risks relegating us to the bottom of any list defining press freedom and democracy."

I was besieged with calls from the Italian press and I gave a number of interviews. My lawyer in Italy was not pleased to see me quoted so liberally. She had had a meeting with the public minister of Perugia,

Giuliano Mignini, to discuss my case and to try to find out what the charges were against me, which had been sealed, naturally, in *segreto istruttorio*. She wrote me a letter saying that she sensed a "certain disapproval" from the public minister of statements I had made to the press after my interrogation. She added, dryly, "The Public Minister must not have welcomed the raising of the issue to the international diplomatic level. . . . It is not helpful to your case to make personal statements against the Public Minister . . . and it would be opportune that, after having reexamined some of the statements made by you at that time (which must have had a negative impact on Dr. Mignini), you would mitigate their effects by distancing yourself from them."

She confirmed that the charges against me were for making false statements to the public minister, for the crime of "calumny" in attempting to frame an innocent person for a crime, defamation by means of the press, and interference with an essential public service. I was not being charged, as I had feared, with being an accessory to the murder of Narducci.

I wrote back, saying that I was sorry that I could not distance myself from the statements I had made, and that there was nothing I could do to mitigate the discomfort Mignini might be feeling about the case being raised to the "international diplomatic level."

In the midst of this, I received another long e-mail from Gabriella Carlizzi, who had, it seemed, been one of the very first purchasers of our book, *Dolci Colline di Sangue*.

Here I am, dear Douglas. . . . Yesterday evening I came back from Perugia very late, in this last week I have been to the magistrate's office three times, because you know, since Mario Spezi has been imprisoned, many people who were living for years in terror have contacted me, and each one has wanted to tell of his experiences with Mario's actions. . . .

You might ask: why did these people not speak before?

For fear of Mario Spezi and those they suspect, very strongly, of having an interest in "covering up for him."

And so we turn to you.

As I have been deposed in these recent days, it has given me the opportunity to make it understood to Dr. Mignini how you couldn't possibly be involved, and I repeat to you Douglas, as far as you are concerned the magistrate is convinced and serene. . . .

Meanwhile I renew my invitation for you to come to Italy, and you will see that all will become cleared up with the magistrate, who if you wish you can meet even in Perugia, you and your lawyer, I hope different from Spezi's lawyers, and you will be completely absolved of any accusations.

I read the book, *Dolci Colline di Sangue*: I say to you right away that it would have been much better had your name not been on that book. The book has been obtained by the prosecutor's office and I think there will be judicial consequences. . . . Unfortunately, Douglas, you signed the contents of this book. This is a very serious business, that has nothing to do with the work of Mignini, but is by now under the eye of the Criminal Justice System, and it risks blemishing your career as a writer. . . . Spezi, leaning on the prestige of your name, has involved you in a situation that if you come to Italy, I will help you mitigate your responsibility, and I repeat, it is urgent that we see each other, believe me. . . . On this book, *porca miseria*, there is your name! Excuse me but it makes me furious when I think of the diabolicalness of this Spezi. . . .

I await your news and I warmly embrace you and your family.

Gabriella

One other thing: Since I think it is right that *The New Yorker* should also "dissociate" itself from Spezi and his actions, if you wish, I can explain certain things in an interview, getting you out of the situation into which Spezi has pulled you, that is to say I can demonstrate to the American press your lack of involvement in the "fraud."

I read the e-mail with disbelief, and finally, for the first time in weeks, I found myself laughing at the absurdity of it all. Could any novelist, even a writer with the *coglioni* of, say, Norman Mailer, have dared invent a character like this woman? I think not.

★　　★　　★

April 28, the day of Spezi's appearance before the Tribunal of Re-examination, approached. I spoke to Myriam on April 27. She was extremely fearful of what might happen at the hearing, and she told me Spezi's lawyers shared her pessimism. If the judges kept Spezi in preventive detention, he would remain in prison for at least another three months before the next judicial review could take place, and a reversal of his imprisonment would be even more unlikely. The Italian judicial system moves at a glacial pace; the ugly truth was that Spezi could remain in prison for years before his case finally came to trial.

Spezi's lawyers had learned that Mignini was preparing a full-court press at the hearing to make absolutely sure Spezi wasn't released. This had become the most visible case the public minister had undertaken in his career. The criticism of him in the national and worldwide press had been scorching and was rising daily. His reputation depended on winning this hearing.

I called Niccolò and asked if he had any predictions on what Mario's fate would be. He was guarded and pessimistic. "Judges in Italy protect their own" was all he would say.

CHAPTER
55

On the appointed day, April 28, 2006, a van arrived at Capanne prison to take Spezi and the other prisoners with hearings that day to the Tribunale of Perugia. Spezi's guards brought him out and he was herded into a cage in the back of the van with the others.

The Tribunale, one of the famous edifices in the medieval heart of Perugia, rises from Piazza Matteotti like an airy Gothic castle of white marble. It is listed in the guidebooks and admired by thousands of tourists every year. Designed by two famous Renaissance architects, it was built on the foundations of a twelfth-century wall that once surrounded Perugia, itself laid upon a three-thousand-year-old Etruscan foundation of massive stone blocks that had once been part of the wall enclosing the ancient city of Perusia. Above the building's grand entrance stands a statue of a woman in robes, sword clasped in her hands, beaming an enigmatic smile at all who enter; the inscription below identifies her as IUSTITIAE VIRTUTUM DOMINA, Ruler of the Virtue of Justice. She is flanked by two griffins, symbols of Perugia, grasping in their claws a calf and a sheep.

The van parked in the piazza outside the Tribunale, where a crowd of journalists and television reporters awaited Spezi's arrival. Because of them, tourists began to gather, curious to see the infamous criminal who merited such attention.

The other prisoners were taken out, one by one, for their hearings. The hearing for each prisoner lasted twenty to forty minutes. They were closed to everyone: journalists, the public, even spouses. Myriam had arrived in Perugia by car and had seated herself on a wooden bench in the corridor outside the courtroom, awaiting news.

At ten-thirty, Spezi's turn came. He was taken out of the cage and brought up to the courtroom. He had a chance to smile at Myriam from a distance as he was led in, giving her a thumbs-up for courage.

The three judges sat behind the long table. They were three women, wearing traditional robes. Spezi was seated in the middle of the room, before the judges, in a hard wooden chair with no arms or table in front. At a table to his right sat the public minister, Mignini, and his assistants; to the left, Spezi's lawyers, of which he now had four.

Instead of taking twenty to forty minutes, the hearing would last seven and a half hours.

Later, Spezi would write about the hearing, "I don't have a complete memory of all seven and a half hours, only snippets. . . . I remember the passionate words of my lawyer, Nino Filastò, one who knew like no one else the entire history of the Monster of Florence case and the monstrousness of the investigations, a man who possessed a fiery sense of righteousness. I remember the red face of Mignini, bending over his papers, while the voice of Nino thundered. I remember the wide eyes of the young court reporter, perhaps stunned by the ardor of a lawyer who did not care to bandy about euphemisms. I heard Filastò mention the name of Carlizzi. . . . I heard Mignini say that I denied being involved in the murder of Narducci and in the Monster of Florence case, but little did I know that he, Mignini, had in his possession 'extremely delicate and sensitive material' that proved my guilt. I heard Mignini shouting . . . that in my house they had found 'hidden behind a door, a satanic stone that the accused persists in calling a doorstop.'"

Spezi remembered Mignini pointing a shaking finger at him and railing about "the inexplicable rancor that Spezi has demonstrated toward the investigation." But most of all he remembered Mignini speaking of the "extremely dangerous manipulation of information and the mass-media chorus that the subject succeeded in raising" against his arrest. He remembered Mignini shouting, "The accusations brought before this Tribunal today are only the tip of an iceberg of horrifying dimensions."

What surprised Spezi most of all was the many parallels between Mignini's arguments before the Tribunal and the accusations made by Gabriella Carlizzi on her conspiracy website months before. Sometimes even the wordings were similar, if not identical.

The three judges in robes listened impassively, taking notes.

After a break for lunch, the hearing resumed. At one point Mignini rose and went into the corridor. And there, outside the courtroom, Myriam had been waiting. When she saw the public minister walking alone in the corridor, she rose in a fury and, like an avenging angel, pointed an accusing finger at the man. "I know you are a believer," she cried out in a voice full of fire. "God will punish you for what you have done. *God will punish you!*"

Mignini's face flushed a deep red, and without saying a word he walked stiffly down the corridor and disappeared around a corner.

Later, Myriam said to her husband that she couldn't be silent when "I heard Mignini shouting inside the courtroom, saying terrible things about you, that you were a criminal."

When Mignini returned to the courtroom, he resumed his brief, and it began to sound more like an inquisition than a judicial proceeding. He spoke of Spezi's "high intelligence, which renders even more dangerous his great criminal capacity." He concluded his speech with "The reasons for Spezi to remain in prison have become even more urgent. Because he has now demonstrated his enormous dangerousness by succeeding, even when locked up in a prison cell, in organizing a mass-media campaign in his favor!"

Spezi remembered that moment. "A pen fell from the hand of the president of the Tribunal and made a little *click* on the table . . . from that moment on, she took no more notes." She had clearly come to some kind of conclusion.

At the end, after everyone else had spoken, it was Spezi's turn.

I had long admired Spezi's abilities as a public speaker—his witty turn of phrase, his light and impromptu delivery, the logical organization of his information, the facts presented one after another like the paragraphs of a perfectly written news story, neat, concise, and clear. Now he turned those considerable gifts on the court. Facing Mignini directly, Spezi began to speak. Mignini refused to meet his eyes. Those who were there said he demolished Mignini's accusations, one after another, with an edge of quiet contempt in his voice, bulldozing his rickety conspiracy logic and pointing out that Mignini lacked any physical evidence at all to back up his theories.

As he spoke, Spezi told me later, he could see his words were having a visible effect on the judges.

Spezi thanked the public minister for praising his intelligence and memory, and he pointed out, word for word, the phrases in Mignini's brief that were identical to those posted, months before, by Gabriella Carlizzi on her website. He asked if Mignini could explain this singular coincidence between his words now and her words then. He asked if it was not a fact that Carlizzi had already been convicted of defamation, having written ten years before that the writer Alberto Bevilacqua was the Monster of Florence? And was it not also a fact that this same Carlizzi was currently on trial for fraud against incapacitated persons?

Then Spezi turned to the president of the Tribunal. "I am only a journalist who tries his best to do what is right in his work, and I am a good person."

He was finished.

The hearing was over. Two guards in the courtroom escorted Spezi down the elevators, into the ancient basements of the medieval palace, where they locked him in a tiny, barren cell that had probably been holding prisoners for centuries. He leaned his back against the stone wall and slid to the ground, utterly exhausted, his mind empty.

After a while, he heard a sound and opened his eyes. It was one of his guards, standing with a cup of hot espresso that he had purchased with his own money. "Spezi, take it. You look like you need it."

CHAPTER
56

That night they loaded Mario Spezi into the van and carried him back to his cell in Capanne prison. The next day was Saturday, and the Tribunal closed at one o'clock. The judges would issue their decision before that time.

That Saturday, as one o'clock neared, Spezi waited in his cell. His fellow prisoners in his cellblock—who had come to know him even if they couldn't see him—were also waiting to hear the verdict. One o'clock passed, and then one-thirty. As two o'clock neared, Spezi began to resign himself to the fact that the verdict had gone against him. And then a cheer went up among his fellow prisoners at the far end of the row of cells. Someone had heard something on an unseen television blaring somewhere. "Uncle! You're free! Uncle! You can go! Uncle, they've let you go without conditions!"

Myriam, waiting in a café for the news, received a call from a colleague of Mario's at the paper. "Fantastic news! Congratulations! We won! Won! On every single point!"

"After twenty-three days in prison," RAI, the national television station of Italy reported, "journalist Mario Spezi, accused of obstruction of justice in the serial killings of Florence, has been set free. Such is the decision of the Tribunal of Reexamination." The three judges hadn't even attached conditions to his release, as was normal—no house arrest, no passport confiscation. He was absolutely and unconditionally freed.

It was an enormous rebuke to the public minister of Perugia.

A guard came to Spezi's cell holding a big black garbage bag. "Hurry up. Put all your stuff in here. Let's go."

Spezi threw it all in and turned to leave, to find the door blocked by the guard. One more indignity remained. "Before you leave," the guard said, "you have to clean your cell."

Spezi thought he must be kidding. "I never asked to come here," he said, "and I was put here illegally. If you want it clean, clean it yourself."

The guard narrowed his eyes, yanked the metal door from Spezi's hands, and slammed it shut. He turned the key and said, "If you like it so much, go ahead and stay!" He began to walk off.

Spezi could hardly believe it. He seized the bars. "Listen, you cretin. I know your name, and if you don't let me out immediately, I'll denounce you for false imprisonment. You understand? I'll report you."

The guard paused, took a few more steps toward his post, then turned slowly and came back, as if graciously conceding the point, and unlocked the door. Spezi was passed off to another stone-faced guard, who escorted him to a waiting room.

"Why aren't you letting me out?" Spezi asked.

"There's some paperwork. And . . ." The guard hesitated. "Then there's the problem of keeping public order outside."

Spezi finally emerged from Capanne prison, holding the big black garbage bag, and was greeted by a roar from the waiting crowd of journalists and onlookers.

Niccolò was the first to call me. "Extraordinary news!" he cried. "Spezi is free!"

CHAPTER
57

Spezi and I had a long conversation that day, and he said he was going off with Myriam to the sea, just the two of them. But only for a few days. "Mignini," he said, "is hauling me back to Perugia for another interrogation. On May 4."

"About what?" I asked, aghast.

"He's preparing new charges against me."

Mignini had not even waited for the written opinion of the Tribunal of Reexamination to be issued. He had appealed Spezi's release to the Supreme Court.

I asked a question I had been wanting to ask for weeks. "Why did Ruocco do it? Why did he make up that story about the iron boxes?"

"Ruocco really knew Antonio Vinci," he said. "He said it was Ignazio who told him about the iron boxes. Ignazio is a kind of *padrino* to the Sardinians . . . I haven't spoken to Ruocco since our arrest, so I don't know if it was Ruocco who made up the story, or if Ignazio was involved in some way. Ruocco might have done it for money—from time to time I gave him a few euros to cover his expenses, buy gas for his car. But it never amounted to much. And he paid a heavy price—he was jailed too as my 'accomplice.' Who knows? Maybe the story is true."

"Why the Villa Bibbiani?"

"Sheer chance, perhaps. Or perhaps the Sardinians really did use the old farmhouses at some time."

Spezi called me on May 4, immediately after the interrogation. To my great surprise, he was in an expansive mood. "Doug," he said, cackling with laughter, "the interrogation was beautiful, just beautiful. It was one of the finest little moments of my life."

"Tell me."

"That morning," Spezi said, "my lawyer picked me up in his car and we stopped by the newsstand for the paper. I could hardly believe my eyes when I saw the headline. I have it here. I'll read it to you."

There was a dramatic pause.

" 'Chief of GIDES Giuttari Indicted for Falsifying Evidence.' *Bello*, eh?"

I laughed gleefully. "*Fantastico*! What did he do?"

"It had nothing to do with me. They say he doctored a tape recording of a conversation with some other person in the Monster case—an important person, a judge. But that's not even the best part. I folded the newspaper so that the headline was displayed and carried it into Mignini's office for the interrogation. When I sat down, I placed the paper on my knees, so that the headline was turned toward Mignini."

"What did he do when he saw it?"

"He never saw it! Mignini never once looked at me, he kept his eyes averted the whole time. The interrogation didn't last long—I invoked my right not to answer questions and that was it. Five minutes. The funny thing was, the *stenographer* did see the headline. I watched the man as he arched his neck like a turtle to read it, and then the poor fellow tried frantically to signal Mignini's attention! No luck. Not a second after I left the office, when I was still in the hall, the door to Mignini's office flew open and a carabinieri officer went hurtling down the stairs toward the door, without a doubt heading to the nearest newsstand." He laughed wickedly. "Apparently, Mignini hadn't read the papers that morning! He knew nothing about it!"

Back outside the public minister's office, following the brief interrogation, a crowd of journalists awaited. While the cameras whirred and clicked, Spezi held up the paper and opened it to the headline. "This is all the comment I need to make today."

"Is it not as I said?" Count Niccolò told me the next day. "Giuttari is taking the fall. With your campaign, you have *sputtanato* [cast aspersions on] the Italian judiciary in front of the whole world, with the risk of making them an international laughingstock. They don't give a damn about Spezi and his rights. They just wanted to get it over with as quickly as possible. All they care about is preserving face. *La faccia, la faccia*! The only surprise to me is that it happened a great deal sooner than I expected. My dear Douglas, this is the beginning of the end for Giuttari. How swiftly does the pendulum swing!"

That very same day, our book, *Dolci Colline di Sangue*, hit best-seller lists in Italy.

The pendulum indeed had swung in our direction, and it swung hard. The Supreme Court of Italy summarily rejected Mignini's appeal with a curt opinion that it was "inadmissible," and dismissed all the proceedings against Spezi. There would be no trial and no more investigations of him. "An enormous load has been lifted," Spezi said. "I am a free man."

A few months later, Giuttari's and Mignini's offices were raided by the police, who carried away boxes of files. They discovered that Mignini had been invoking a special antiterrorist law to order wiretaps of journalists who had written critically about his Monster of Florence investigation—wiretaps carried out by Giuttari and GIDES. In addition to wiretapping journalists, Giuttari had also been taping telephone calls and conversations with a number of Florentine judges and investigators, including his counterpart in Florence, the public minister Paolo Canessa. It seemed that Mignini suspected them of being part of a vast Florentine conspiracy working against his investigation into the masterminds behind the Monster killings.

In the summer of 2006, both Giuttari and Mignini were indicted for abuse of office. GIDES was disbanded, and questions were immediately raised that indicated it had never been officially authorized in the first place. Giuttari lost his staff and the Monster of Florence case was taken away from him. He became a chief inspector *a dispozione*, that is, with no portfolio and no permanent assignment.

Mignini so far has retained his position of public minister of Perugia, but two more prosecutors were added to his staff, allegedly to help him with his workload; their real assignment, everyone knew, was to keep him out of trouble. Both Mignini and Giuttari will have to stand trial for abuse of office and other crimes.

On November 3, 2006, Spezi was awarded the most coveted journalistic prize in Italy for *Dolci Colline di Sangue* and named Writer of the Year for Freedom of the Press.

CHAPTER
58

The article in the *Atlantic Monthly* was published in July. A few weeks later the magazine received a letter on old-fashioned stationery, hand-typed on a manual typewriter. It was an extraordinary letter, written by Niccolò's father, Count Neri Capponi, the head of one of Italy's most ancient and illustrious noble families.

When I first met Niccolò, he had mentioned the reason for his family's long success in Florence: they had never thrust themselves into controversy, remained discreet and circumspect in all their dealings, and never tried to be first. For eight hundred years the Capponi family had prospered by avoiding being "the nail that sticks out," as Niccolò had put it in his drafty palace seven years earlier.

But now, Count Neri had broken with family tradition. He had written a letter to the editor. This was no ordinary letter, but a ripping indictment of the Italian criminal justice system from a man who was himself a judge and a lawyer. Count Neri knew whereof he spoke, and he spoke plainly.

THE
COUNT CAPPONI

Sir

The travesty of justice undergone by Douglas Preston and Mario Spezi is the tip of the iceberg. The Italian judiciary (which includes the public prosecutors) is a branch of the civil service. This particular branch chooses its members, is self ruling and is accountable to no one: a state within a state! This body of bureaucrats can be roughly divided into three sections: a large minority, corrupt and affiliated with the former communist party, a large section of honest people who are too frightened to stand up to the political minority (who controls the office of the judiciary), and a minority of brave and honest men with little influence. Political and dishonest judges have an infallible method of silencing or discrediting opponents, political or otherwise. A bogus, secret indictment, the tapping of telephones, the conversations (often doctored) fed to the press who starts a smear campaign which raises the sales, a spectacular arrest, prolonged preventive detention under the worst possible conditions, third degree interrogations, and finally a trial that lasts many years ending in the acquittal of a ruined man. Spezi was lucky because the powerful Florentine public prosecutor is no friend of the Perugia one and, I am told, "suggested" that Spezi be freed: the Perugia court, I am told, accepted the "suggestion".

It may be of interest to know that miscarriages of justice in Italy (excluding acquittals with a ruined defendant) amount to four million and a half in fifty years.

Yours sincerely,
Neri Capponi

P.S. If possible I would ask you to withhold my signature or reduce it to initials because I fear reprisals on myself and my family. If withholding my signature is not possible, then go ahead, God will look after me! The truth must out.

The *Atlantic* printed the letter, with his name.

The British newspaper the *Guardian* also ran an article on the case and interviewed Chief Inspector Giuttari. He said I had lied when I claimed to have been threatened with arrest if I returned to Italy, and he insisted that Spezi and I were still guilty of planting false evidence at the villa. "Preston did not tell the truth," he said. "Our recordings will prove this. Spezi," he insisted, "will be prosecuted."

The *Atlantic* article attracted the attention of a producer at *Dateline NBC*, who asked Mario and me to participate in a program on the Monster of Florence. I returned to Italy in September 2006 with some trepidation, traveling with the *Dateline NBC* film crew. My Italian lawyer had informed me that given Giuttari's and Mignini's legal troubles, it was probably safe to return, and NBC promised to raise hell if I were arrested at the airport. Just in case, an NBC television crew met me at the airport ready to capture my arrest on tape. I was glad to deprive them of that scoop.

Spezi and I took Stone Phillips, the show's anchor, to the scenes of the crimes, where we were filmed discussing the murders and our own brush with Italian law. Stone Phillips interviewed Giuttari, who continued to insist that Spezi and I had planted evidence at the villa. He also criticized our book. "Evidently, Mr. Preston did not do the least bit of fact-checking . . . In 1983, when the two young Germans were killed, this person [Antonio Vinci] was in prison for another crime unrelated to the monster crimes." Phillips managed a brief interview with Antonio Vinci, off camera. Vinci confirmed what Giuttari said, that he had been in prison during one of the Monster's killings. Perhaps Giuttari and Vinci didn't expect NBC to check the facts. In the show, Stone Phillips said, "We later checked his record and found that [Antonio] had never been in jail during any of the Monster killings. He and Giuttari were either mistaken or lying about that."

Vinci was far more incensed about being accused of impotence than of being the Monster of Florence. "If Spezi's wife were younger and prettier," he told Phillips, "I'd show them who isn't impotent—I'd show you right here, right now, on this table."

At the very end of the program, Phillips asked Antonio Vinci a question: "Are you the Monster of Florence?"

"He locked eyes," said Phillips, "gripped my hand, and said one word. *Innocente.*"

CHAPTER
59

W hile filming with *Dateline NBC*, Spezi and I had one experience in Italy that never made it on camera. Stone Phillips wanted to interview Winnie Rontini, the mother of Pia Rontini, one of the Monster's victims, murdered at La Boschetta near Vicchio on June 29, 1984. While the crew waited by the parked vans in the town square, in the shadow of the statue of Giotto, Spezi and I walked down the street to the old Rontini villa to see if she was willing to be interviewed.

We gazed at the house in silent dismay. The rusty iron gate hung from a single hinge. Skeletonized shrubbery in the garden rattled in the wind, and dead leaves had piled up in the corners. The shutters were closed, the slats broken and hanging. A half dozen crows lined the roof peak, like so many black rags.

Mario punched the gate buzzer but no sound came. It was dead. We looked at each other.

"It doesn't look like anyone lives here," Mario said.

"Let's knock on the door."

We pushed open the broken gate with a groan of rust and stepped into the dead garden, our footfalls crunching dried leaves and twigs. The door to the villa was locked tight, its green paint cracked and peeling up in tiny rolls, the wood underneath splitting. The house buzzer was gone, leaving a hole with a frayed wire sticking out.

"Signora Rontini?" Mario called out. "Is anybody home?"

The wind whispered and chuckled about the deserted house. Mario pounded on the door, the sound of his blows echoing, in a muffled way, through the empty rooms within. With a flapping of wings, the birds took off, rising into the sky, their irritated cries like fingernails on a blackboard.

We stood in the garden, looking up at the abandoned house. The crows circled above, cawing and cawing. Mario shook his head. "In town they'll know what happened to her."

In the piazza, a man told us the bank had finally foreclosed on the house and Signora Rontini now lived on public assistance in housing for indigents near the lake. He gave us the address.

With a feeling of dread we searched for the housing project, finding it tucked behind the local Casa del Popolo. It was unlike anything an American might imagine as public housing, a cheerful building, stuccoed a pale cream, neat as a pin, with flowers on the windowsills and pretty views of the lake. We walked around to the back and knocked on the door to her apartment. She met us and showed us in, offering us seats in a tiny kitchen-dining area. Her apartment was the reverse of the dark, cadaverous house; bright and cheerful, it was filled with plants, knickknacks, and photographs. The sun streamed in the windows and warblers chirped and flitted about in the sycamore trees outside. The room smelled of fresh laundry and soap.

"No," she said with a sad smile in response to our question, "I won't be interviewed again. Never again." She was dressed in a sparkling yellow dress, her dyed red hair carefully coiffed, her voice mild.

"We still hope to find the truth," said Mario. "One never knows . . . this could help."

"I know it might help. But I'm not interested in the truth anymore. What difference will it make? It won't bring Pia or Claudio back. For a long time I thought knowing the truth would somehow make everything better. My husband died searching for the truth. But now I know it doesn't matter and that it won't help me. I had to let it go."

She fell silent, her small, plump hands folded in her lap, her ankles crossed, a faint smile hovering about her face.

We chatted some more and she told us matter-of-factly how she had lost the house and all she owned to bankruptcy. Mario asked her about some of the photographs on the walls. She rose and plucked one off, passing it to Mario, who then passed it to me. "That was the last photograph taken of Pia," she said. "It was for her driver's license a few months before." She moved on to the next one. "This is Pia with Claudio." It was a black-and-white photo of them smiling, arms about each other's neck, utterly innocent and happy, she giving a thumbs-up to the camera.

She moved to the far wall. "This is Pia at fifteen. She was a pretty girl, wasn't she?" The hand moved along the wall. "My late husband, Renzo." She unhooked a black-and-white photograph, gazed at it awhile, and handed it to us. We passed it around. It was a portrait of a vigorous, happy man, in the prime of life.

She lifted a hand and gestured toward the photographs, turning her blue eyes on me. "Just the other day," she said, "I walked in here and realized that I was surrounded by the dead." She smiled sadly. "I'm going to take these photographs down and put them away. I don't want to be surrounded by death anymore. I'd forgotten something—that I'm still alive."

We rose. At the door she took Mario's hand. "You're welcome to keep searching for the truth, Mario. I hope you find it. But please don't ask me to help you. I'm going to try to live my last years without that burden—I hope you understand."

"I understand," said Mario.

We walked out into the sunlight, the bees droning in the flowers, the bright sun throwing a shimmering trail on the surface of the lake, the light spilling over the red-tiled roofs of Vicchio and flinging streamers of gold through the vineyards and olive groves beyond the town. The *vendemmia*, the grape harvest, was in progress, the fields full of people and carts. The air carried up from the vineyards the perfume of bruised grapes and fermenting must.

Another flawless afternoon in the immortal hills of Tuscany.

CHAPTER
60

The trial of Francesco Calamandrei, for being one of the instigators behind the Monster killings, began on September 27, 2007.

Mario Spezi attended the first day of the trial, and he sent me a report by e-mail a few days later. This is what he wrote:

The morning of September 27 dawned unexpectedly cold after a month of dry heat. The real news that morning was the absence of spectators at the trial of a man alleged to be a mastermind behind the Monster. In the courtroom, where more than ten years before Pacciani had first been convicted and then acquitted, nobody was seated in the space reserved for the public. Only the benches reserved for journalists were occupied. I had trouble understanding the indifference of Florentines toward a person who, according to the accusation, was almost the very incarnation of Evil. Skepticism, incredulity, or disbelief of the official version must have kept spectators away.

The accused entered the courtroom taking hesitant little steps. He looked meek, even resigned, his dark eyes lost in unknowable thoughts, carrying with him the air of a retired gentleman, wearing an elegant blue overcoat and gray fedora, his obese body swelled with unhappiness and psychopharmacological drugs. He was half-supported by his lawyer, Gabriele Zanobini, and his daughter Francesca. The pharmacist of San Casciano, Francesco Calamandrei, seated himself on the front bench, indifferent to the flashes of the news photographers and the television cameras that swung his way.

A journalist asked him how he felt. He answered: "Like someone who has fallen into a film, knowing nothing of the plot or characters."

The prosecutor's office of Florence had accused Calamandrei of masterminding five of the Monster's killings. They claim he paid Pacciani, Lotti, and Vanni to commit the crimes and take away the sex organs of the female victims so that he could use them for horrendous, but unspecified, esoteric rites. He stands accused of actually participating in the killings of the two French tourists at the Scopeti clearing in 1985. He is also charged with having ordered the killings in Vicchio in 1984, those of September 1983 in which the two Germans were killed, and those of June 1982 in Montespertoli. The prosecution is silent on the vexing question of who might have committed the other Monster killings.

The evidence against Calamandrei is risible. It consists of the delirious ravings of his schizophrenic wife, so desperately ill that her doctors have forbidden her to give testimony in the courtroom, and the same "coarse and habitual liars" known as Alpha, Beta, Gamma, and Delta, who testified against Pacciani and his picnicking friends ten years before. Notably, all four of these algebraic witnesses are now dead. Only the serial witness Lorenzo Nesi remains alive, ready to remember whatever might be required.

Also arrayed against Calamandrei is a mountain of paper: twenty-eight thousand pages of the trial against Pacciani; nineteen thousand pages of the investigation of his picnicking friends; and nine thousand pages collected on Calamandrei himself: fifty-five thousand pages in all, more than the Bible, *Das Kapital* of Marx, Kant's *Critique of Pure Reason*, the *Iliad*, the *Odyssey*, and *Don Quixote* all put together.

In front of the accused, mounted high behind an imposing bar, was seated Judge De Luca in the place of the usual two magistrates and the nine members of the popular jury who comprise the Court of

Assizes, the Tribunal reserved for judging the most serious crimes. In a surprise move, Calamandrei's lawyer had asked for a so-called abbreviated trial, usually only requested by those who have admitted guilt in order to obtain a reduced sentence. Zanobini and Calamandrei asked for it for another reason entirely: "In order that the trial be conducted as rapidly as possible," Zanobini said, "seeing that we have nothing to fear from the result."

To the left of the pharmacist, on another bench in the front row, sat the public minister of Florence, Paolo Canessa, with another prosecutor. The two smiled and joked in low voices, perhaps to give an outward show of confidence, or perhaps to needle the defense.

Before the end of the day, Zanobini would wipe the smiles off their faces.

Zanobini launched into his case with fire, pointing out a technical but very embarrassing legal oversight by Canessa. He then attacked the Perugian branch of the Monster investigation, conducted by Public Minister Mignini, which had linked Calamandrei to the death of Narducci. "Almost all the results of the Perugian investigation are like so much wastepaper," he said. "Allow me to give you an example." He raised a sheaf of papers, which he said constituted a statement taken by Public Minister Mignini and kept under seal until now. "How is it possible that a magistrate would take seriously and believe a document like the one I will read to you now?"

As Zanobini began to read, the cameras swung from Calamandrei to . . . me. I couldn't believe it, Doug, but I was the star of the document! This document was the so-called spontaneous statement of a woman who had been in contact with Gabriella Carlizzi. She repeated many of Carlizzi's theories to Judge Mignini, claiming she had heard them years ago from a long-deceased Sardinian aunt who knew all the people involved. Mignini had it all written down, recorded, sworn, and signed. Despite the clear absurdity and lack of proof of the woman's allegations, Judge Mignini had then slapped a seal of secrecy on the document, "given the gravity and sensitivity" of the accusations.

As Zanobini read the document in the gray courtroom of the Tribunale, I heard, along with everyone else, that I wasn't really the son of my father. My real father—or so this woman claimed in her statement—was a famous musician of sick and perverse habits who had committed the first two killings of 1968; I heard that my mother had conceived me on a Sardinian farm in Tuscany; I heard that upon discovering the truth about my real father, I had carried on his diabolical work as a family tradition, becoming the "real Monster of Florence." This crazy aunt claimed we were all conspiring together: me, the Vinci brothers, Pacciani and his picnicking friends, Narducci, and Calamandrei. From our diabolical association, she told Mignini, "each derives his own benefit: the voyeurs enjoyed their particular activities, the cultists used the anatomical parts taken from the victims for their rites, the fetishists conserved the pieces taken from the victims, and SPEZI, my aunt always told me, mutilated the victims with a tool known as a cobbler's knife. . . . Certain fellow citizens of Villacidro told me, recently, that the writer Douglas Preston, Spezi's friend, is connected to the American Secret Service."

She explained to Mignini, "I hadn't spoken of this up until now because I am afraid of Mario SPEZI and his friends. . . . When Spezi was arrested by you I gathered up my courage and decided to speak about it with Carlizzi, because I trusted her and I knew she sought the truth. . . ."

It was absurd stuff and I had to smile as Zanobini read the statement. But I felt no mirth; I couldn't forget that I had ended up in prison partly because of Carlizzi's black-hearted accusations.

The first day of Calamandrei's trial ended with a clear win for the defense. Judge De Luca fixed the next three trial days for November 27, 28, and 29. Breaks of this length in trials are, unfortunately, the norm in Italy.

That was the end of the e-mail.

I called up Mario. "So I'm in the American Secret Service? Damn."

"It was all reported in the press the next day."

"What are you going to do about these absurd accusations?"

"I've already brought suit against the woman for defamation."

"Mario," I said, "the world is full of crazy people. How is it that in

Italy, the statements of such people are taken down by a public minister as serious evidence?"

"Because Mignini and Giuttari will never give up. This is clear evidence they're still out to get me, one way or another."

As of this writing, Calamandrei's trial continues, with an acquittal nearly certain, leaving the old pharmacist to live out what is left of his ruined life—one more victim of the Monster of Florence.

The Monster investigation grinds on with no end in sight. Spezi's complaint against Giuttari for defamation was rejected by the Tribunal. He has heard nothing about his suit against Giuttari and Mignini for damages relating to the wrecking of his car. The Supreme Court ruling in Spezi's favor allowed him to ask for damages for his illegal detention. Spezi asked for compensation in the amount of three hundred thousand euros; the lawyers for the state countered with forty-five hundred euros. Mignini is dragging his heels officially closing the investigation against Spezi, while at the same time claiming that Spezi cannot ask for any damages at all because the investigation is still open.

In November 2007, Mignini became involved in another sensational case, that of the brutal murder of a British student, Meredith Kercher, in Perugia. Mignini quickly ordered the arrest of an American student, Amanda Knox, whom he suspected of involvement in the murder. As of this writing, Knox is in Capanne prison, awaiting the outcome of Mignini's investigation. It appears from press leaks that Mignini is spinning an improbable theory about Knox and two alleged co-conspirators in a dark plan of extreme sex, violence, and rape.

As if on cue, Perugian prosecutors were reported to be looking into a potential satanic sect angle, because the crime had occurred the day before the traditional Italian Day of the Dead. "I will give you ten to one odds," said Niccolò, "that they will eventually drag the Monster of Florence into this." I declined the wager.

Within a week of the murder, Gabriella Carlizzi had weighed in at her website:

Meredith Kercher: a brutal murder . . . Perhaps connected to the Narducci case and the Monster of Florence, to ask Satan for protection in exchange for a human sacrifice? For what purpose? In the end to save those under investigation in the Narducci case who are responsible for his homicide.

Giuttari was acquitted for falsifying evidence in the Monster case, but is now serving a suspended sentence after he was convicted of making false statements in an unrelated case.

On January 16, 2008, the first pretrial hearing took place for Giuttari and Mignini, accused of abuse of office and, in Mignini's case, conflict of interest in favor of Giuttari. The public minister of Florence, Luca Turco, shocked the court with his blunt language. The two accused, he said, were "two diametrically different people." Mignini was "on a crusade in thrall to a sort of delirium," a person "ready to go to any extreme defending himself against anyone who criticized his investigation." Giuttari exploited this form of delirium, Turco said, "for his own personal, vindictive interests beyond the bounds of his professional responsibilities."

As Mignini left the courtroom after the hearing, he cried out to the waiting press, "I contest this!"

I remain a *persona indagata* in Italy for a series of crimes that are still, more or less, under judicial seal and secret. Not long ago I received a registered letter from Italy to my little post office in Round Pond, informing me that I had been denounced before the Tribunal of Lecco, a city in the north of Italy, for *diffamazione a mezzo stampa*, defamation through means of the press, a criminal offense. Curiously, the person or persons asking for the state to bring charges against me, and for what article or interview, were omitted from the document. To even know the name of my accuser and the crime I am supposed to have committed, I will have to pay thousands more euros to my Italian lawyer.

The question I am most often asked is this: Will the Monster of Florence ever be found? I once believed fervently that Spezi and I would unmask him. Now I'm not so sure. It may be that truth can disappear from the world completely, forever unrecoverable. History is replete with questions that will never be answered—among them, perhaps, the identity of the Monster of Florence.

As a thriller writer, I know that a crime novel, to be successful, must contain certain elements. There must be a killer who has a comprehensible motive. There must be evidence. There must be a process of discovery that leads, one way or another, to the truth. And all novels, even *Crime and Punishment*, must have an ending.

The fatal mistake that Spezi and I made was in assuming that the Monster of Florence case would follow this pattern. Instead, these were murders without motive, theories without evidence, and a story with no end. The process of discovery has led investigators so far into a wilderness of conspiracy theory that I doubt they will ever find their way out. Without solid physical evidence and reliable witnesses, any hypothesis about the Monster case will remain like a speech by Hercule Poirot at the end of an Agatha Christie novel, a beautiful story awaiting a confession. Only this is not a novel, and there won't be a confession. Without one, the Monster will never be found.

Perhaps it was inevitable that the investigation would end up in a bizarre and futile search for a satanic sect dating back to the Middle Ages. The Monster's crimes were so horrific that a mere man could not possibly have committed them. Satan, in the end, had to be invoked.

After all, this is Italy.

INDEX

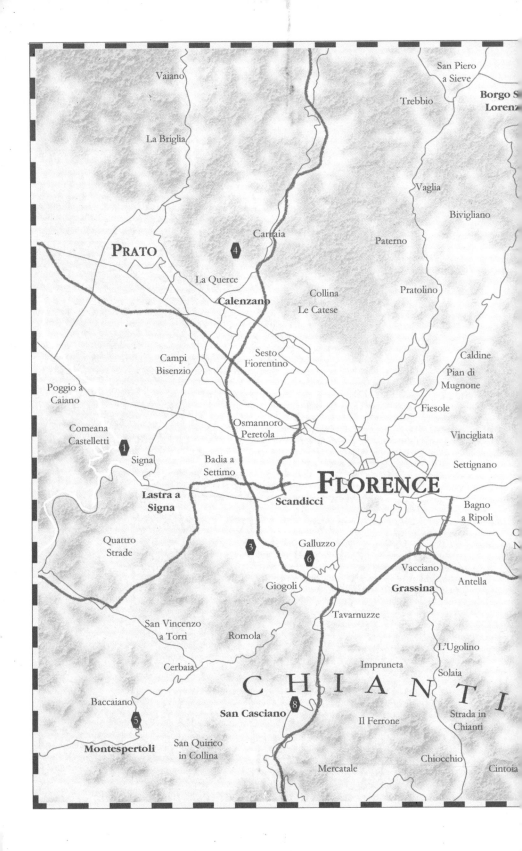